THE ORIGINS OF THE ENGLISH
PARLIAMENT, 924–1327

THE ORIGINS
OF THE
ENGLISH
PARLIAMENT,
924–1327

J. R. MADDICOTT

The Ford Lectures
delivered in the University of Oxford
in Hilary Term 2004

OXFORD
UNIVERSITY PRESS

OXFORD

UNIVERSITY PRESS

Great Clarendon Street, Oxford OX2 6DP

Oxford University Press is a department of the University of Oxford.
It furthers the University's objective of excellence in research, scholarship,
and education by publishing worldwide in

Oxford New York

Auckland Cape Town Dar es Salaam Hong Kong Karachi
Kuala Lumpur Madrid Melbourne Mexico City Nairobi
New Delhi Shanghai Taipei Toronto

With offices in

Argentina Austria Brazil Chile Czech Republic France Greece
Guatemala Hungary Italy Japan Poland Portugal Singapore
South Korea Switzerland Thailand Turkey Ukraine Vietnam

Oxford is a registered trade mark of Oxford University Press
in the UK and in certain other countries

Published in the United States
by Oxford University Press Inc., New York

British Library Cataloguing in Publication Data
Data available

Library of Congress Cataloging in Publication Data
Data available

Typeset by Laserwords Private Limited, Chennai, India
Printed in Great Britain
on acid-free paper by
CPI Antony Rowe, Chippenham, Wiltshire

ISBN 978–0–19–958550–2

3 5 7 9 10 8 6 4

To the undergraduate historians
of Exeter College, Oxford, 1969–2006,
who made me take the long view

Preface

It is a surprising fact that no general account of the English parliament's origins has appeared in the last hundred years. There is, of course, a profusion of modern writing on the supposed beginnings of parliament, but mainly in the form of specialized studies and mainly focused on the thirteenth and early fourteenth centuries, by which time the word 'parliament' has become an everyday item in the vocabulary of politics. To claim that the start of the story comes much earlier, a claim followed through here, is to revive what may seem to be an archaic and outdated orthodoxy. We have to go back to Stubbs's *Constitutional History* to find work of any magnitude that makes a case for the antiquity of parliament's roots and attempts to trace its more distant antecedents. But even Stubbs treated the subject only as part, though a central one, of a much broader canvas, and not in any continuous way.

There is an evident gap here, and one which this book attempts to fill by the presentation of an argument. Its subject is bounded by the accession of King Æthelstan in 924 and the deposition of King Edward II just over 400 years later in 1327. Both dates marked significant points in the history of the conciliar assemblies which came to be known as 'parliaments'. Æthelstan's reign saw the first appearance of truly national assemblies, drawing in men from a more or less unified kingdom which was in process of expanding far beyond its original West Saxon base to comprehend something like modern England. From this time onwards these meetings, large in size and heterogeneous in function, played an essential role in the kingdom's government. At the other end of the period, Edward II's deposition saw the parliamentary commons, the knights from the shires and the burgesses from the towns, fully engaged for the first time in a great national act of state. The lengthy parliamentary session which spanned the early months of 1327 marked a sort of coming-of-age for the fully formed medieval parliament. The long period between these two boundary points saw some dramatic changes in the organization of assemblies, but they were subsumed within an essential continuity of composition, work, and purpose. What William of Malmesbury called 'vital business affecting the realm' was as much their main concern 200 years before William's time, in the days of Æthelstan, as it was to be 200 years later, in the reign of Edward II.

If what follows has any claim to originality, it lies in its charting this combination of change and continuity, and in its identifying particular periods of mutation: Æthelstan's reign itself, which saw the novel elevation of charismatic kingship within assemblies through the probable introduction of crown-wearing; the Norman Conquest, when attendance at assemblies became linked to the tenure of land; the years around 1200, when taxation first became tied to corporate consent; the middle years of Henry III, when opposition to the king's personal rule created a new parliamentary politics; and the middle years of his grandson Edward II, when the commons began to emerge as a political force separate from the magnates. Most recent commentators on the origins of parliament have concentrated on the later part of this sequence, in the second half of the thirteenth century and the early years of the fourteenth century, when comparable representative institutions were developing throughout western Europe. This book takes a different view, arguing that the most important of these various transformative phases lay further back, in the seventy years between 1188 and 1258, when the crown's fiscal demands changed both the modes and mechanisms of representation, and also, and more significantly, the whole status of central assemblies. But this transformation was only possible because the conciliar stock from which parliament was to spring was so deeply and strongly grounded in the Anglo-Saxon and Anglo-Norman past.

Despite its exploration of these more distant origins, the book's centre of gravity inevitably lies in the period between 1215 and 1327. This is partly because the sources for this period are much fuller than for any earlier one, but more particularly because some distinctive and familiar features of parliament then took shape and became manifest. Taxation by consent, legislation by statute, county and borough representation, relations between lords and commons, the identity of assembly and nation, and new forms of two-way contact between royal government and provincial England, all move to the centre of the stage, giving the English parliament a general character which it would retain for many hundreds of years. In setting out the various episodes in this story there is an obvious danger of falling into an antiquated and Whiggish teleology of necessary progress. The argument seeks to avoid this trap by emphasizing the countervailing elements of the contingent and the unexpected which went to parliament's making. Succession disputes in the eleventh and twelfth centuries, the unpredictable effects of the Norman Conquest, the long crusading absence of Richard I, the early death of King John, the consequentially long minority of his son, and the personal devotion of the adult Henry III to Westminster: all these twists and turns, among others, meant that the course of parliamentary history was far from steady or predetermined or purely evolutionary, but was affected at every stage by chance and accident. As the book's final chapter shows, these were also among the many factors, some of them dating from as early as Æthelstan's reign, which set the English parliament on its own peculiar course, divergent from that of continental assemblies. A study of parliamentary origins provides the notion of English exceptionalism with an essential component.

'The History of Institutions', Stubbs famously (and forbiddingly) wrote, 'cannot be mastered—can scarcely be approached—without an effort.' It is to be hoped that what follows may not prove too effortful; or, if it does, that the effort may be thought worthwhile.

This book began life as the Ford Lectures on British History given at Oxford in Hilary Term 2004. With one small change, its title, chapter numbers, and chapter headings are those of the original seven lectures. Although the substance of the lectures has been greatly expanded, the main lines of the argument remain the same, as I hope those in the original audience who go on to read the book may recognize. I am grateful indeed to the Electors for honouring me with the invitation to give the lectures. I am also grateful to those in the audience who offered advice, comment, and encouragement, among them Rowena Archer, Tom Bisson, John Blair, Paul Brand, James Campbell, Michael Clanchy, Peter Coss, the late Rees Davies, Jean Dunbabin, Malcolm Godden, Barbara Harvey, Margaret Howell, Henrietta Leyser, Paul Slack, Christopher Tyerman, and the late Patrick Wormald. I owe a special debt to David Carpenter who read Chapters 4 and 5 and made many helpful suggestions. At a late stage I profited very greatly from the informative and encouraging comments of the publisher's two readers, subsequently revealed as John Hudson and Mark Ormrod. They will recognize my debt to them in the amendments made to the draft which they saw. If I have sometimes disregarded or overlooked what all these friendly critics told me, the blame is mine—and so, of course, is full responsibility for what follows.

A special and final word of thanks should go to the staff at Oxford University Press: to Christopher Wheeler, Matthew Cotton, and Kate Hind on the editorial side, to Jackie Pritchard, an eagle-eyed copy editor, and to Andrew Hawkey, an equally observant proofreader. All have been models of helpfulness and efficiency, and I can only hope that the book will be thought to have deserved the care which they have given to it.

J.M.

July 2009

Contents

Abbreviations

Ann. Burton	*Annales Monasterii de Burton, 1004–1263, Ann. Mon.* i
Ann. Dunstable	*Annales Prioratus de Dunstaplia,* A.D.1–1297, *Ann. Mon.* iii
Ann. London	*Annales Londonienses, Chronicles of the Reigns of Edward I and Edward II,* ed. W. Stubbs, 2 vols., RS (London, 1882)
Ann. Mon.	*Annales Monastici,* ed. H. R. Luard, 5 vols., RS (London, 1864–9)
Ann. Oseney	*Annales Monasterii de Oseneia, 1016–1347, Ann. Mon.* iv
Ann. Tewkesbury	*Annales Monasterii de Theokesberia, Ann. Mon.* i
Ann. Waverley	*Annales Monasterii de Waverleia,* A.D. 1–1291, *Ann. Mon.* ii
Ann. Winchester	*Annales Monasterii de Wintonia, 519–1277, Ann. Mon.* ii
ANS	*Anglo-Norman Studies*
ASC, ed. Whitelock	*The Anglo-Saxon Chronicle,* ed. and trans. D. Whitelock (London, 1961)
ASCh.	Anglo-Saxon Charters
ASE	*Anglo-Saxon England*
B	W. de Gray Birch, *Cartularium Saxonicum,* 3 vols. (London, 1885–93)
BAR	British Archaeological Reports
BIHR	*Bulletin of the Institute of Historical Research*
Blackwell Enc.	M. Lapidge (ed.), *The Blackwell Encyclopaedia of Anglo-Saxon England* (Oxford, 1999)
C. and S.	*Councils and Synods*
Chrons. Stephen . . . Richard I	*Chronicles of the Reigns of Stephen, Henry II and Richard I,* ed. R. Howlett, 4 vols., RS (London, 1884–9)
CPR	*Calendar of Patent Rolls*
CR	*Close Rolls*

CRR	*Curia Regis Rolls*
Davies and Denton (eds.), *Eng. Parl.*	R. G. Davies and J. H. Denton (eds.), *The English Parliament in the Middle Ages* (Manchester, 1981)
DBM	*Documents of the Period of Baronial Reform and Rebellion, 1258–1267*, ed. R. E. Treharne and I. J. Sanders, OMT (Oxford, 1973)
EETS	Early English Text Society
EHD	*English Historical Documents*
EHR	*English Historical Review*
EME	*Early Medieval Europe*
EPMA	H. G. Richardson and G. O. Sayles, *The English Parliament in the Middle Ages* (London, 1981)
Foedera	*Foedera, Conventiones, Litterae et Acta Publica*, ed. T. Rymer, new edn., ed. A. Clark and F. Holbrooke, Record Comm. (London, 1816)
Harper-Bill and Vincent (eds.), *Henry II*	C. Harper-Bill and N. Vincent (eds.), *Henry II: New Interpretations* (Woodbridge, 2007)
HBC	E. B. Fryde et al., *Handbook of British Chronology*, 3rd edn. (Cambridge, 1986)
Historical Studies	E. B. Fryde and E. Miller, *Historical Studies of the English Parliament*, i: *Origins to 1399* (Cambridge, 1970)
Ideal and Reality	P. Wormald (ed.), *Ideal and Reality in Frankish and Anglo-Saxon Society: Studies Presented to J. M. Wallace-Hadrill* (Oxford, 1983)
K	*Codex Diplomaticus Aevi Saxonici*, ed. J. M. Kemble, 6 vols. (London, 1839–48)
ODNB	*Oxford Dictionary of National Biography*
OMT	Oxford Medieval Texts
Paris	*Matthaei Parisiensis, Monachi Sancti Albani, Chronica Majora*, ed. H. R. Luard, 7 vols., RS (London, 1872–83)
Parl. Writs	*Parliamentary Writs and Writs of Military Summons* [Edward I–Edward II], ed. F. Palgrave, 2 vols. in 4, Record Comm., London, 1827–34)
PR	*Patent Rolls of the Reign of Henry III*, HMSO (London, 1901–3)

PR (regnal year)	*Pipe Roll*
PROME	*Parliament Rolls of Medieval England*
PRS	Pipe Roll Society
RRAN	*Regesta Regum Anglo-Normannorum*
RS	Rolls Series
S	P. H. Sawyer, *Anglo-Saxon Charters: An Annotated List and Bibliography*, Royal Historical Soc. (London, 1968)
Sayles, *Functions*	G. O. Sayles, *The Functions of the Medieval Parliament of England* (London, 1988)
Stat. Realm	*Statutes of the Realm*, ed. A. Luders et al., vol. i, Record Comm. (London, 1810)
TCE	*Thirteenth Century England*
TNA	The National Archives
TRHS	*Transactions of the Royal Historical Society*
VCH	*Victoria County History*
Wykes	*Chronicon vulgo dictum Chronicon Thomae Wykes, 1066–1288, Ann. Mon.* iv

I

Genesis

'The Witan of the English People', 924–1066

1. Introduction

The origins of the English parliament lie in a simple and primitive practice: a leader, usually a king, taking counsel with his great men. This interchange defined both Henry III's parliaments in the thirteenth century and the tribal assemblies of a much more distant past. Regional and regal in their focus, the primordial assemblies of early Europe were parliament's ancestors. In the three or four centuries following the fall of Rome they were common to most of the successor states that filled Rome's former empire, coming to form a characteristic feature of Germanic political organization. They were used to confirm the accession of kings, to resolve legal cases, and, above all, to promote royal ends and policies through cooperative discussion. Occasionally crowds of ordinary freemen might swell the numbers of those attending beyond the ranks of the nobility who had a natural interest in such things. This was especially true of the great army assemblies, part musters, part councils, which, in the Frankish kingdoms and, as we shall see, sometimes in late Anglo-Saxon England, preceded spring campaigns. In the Frankish kingdom too, whether under the Merovingians or their Carolingian successors, these central assemblies were complemented by the *mallus*, the local court-cum-convention, where freemen played a much more prominent part as suitors and judges under the supervision of the king's representative, the count. Both sorts of gathering rested on a broad social span of political participation which made them to a degree representative of peoples and places long before the days of elections and constituencies.[1]

Kings taking counsel are thus such a commonplace feature of early Germanic societies that it may seem difficult to find an appropriate starting point for an investigation of the English parliament's origins. We could equally well lead off with the assembled peoples and leaders of first-century Germany described by Tacitus, who were the ancestors of the English, or with Bede's Edwin of Northumbria changing his religion after discussion with his *sapientes*, his wise men, in the late 620s, or with Ine of Wessex making laws in consultation with his bishops and ealdormen in the early 690s.[2] Given our broad counsel-giving and counsel-taking definition of assembly functions, all could reasonably be seen as augmenting the tributary streams of a much larger and longer river.

While we should recognize the contribution of these early assemblies to later developments, there are two good reasons for passing over them in any account of parliament's origins.[3] First, the assemblies of the seventh and eighth centuries were in no sense national, as parliament most certainly was, but rather particular to the often contending kingdoms which had yet to become England. For the middle Saxon period, from about 670 to about 850, the only assemblies which transcended the boundaries of individual kingdoms were the councils and synods of the church, such as that convened by Archbishop Theodore at Hertford in 672.[4] And secondly, so far as we can see, these royal assemblies lacked the institutional qualities of regularity, formality of structure, and a distinctive agenda which gave definition to their successors, both pre- and post-Conquest. To all appearances they were more ad hoc and more inchoate than what came later.

Change came in the tenth century. From this point onwards royal assemblies developed rapidly, and in ways which made them the direct

---

[1] P. S. Barnwell, 'Political Assemblies: Introduction', and 'Kings, Nobles, and Assemblies in the Barbarian Kingdoms', in P. S. Barnwell and M. Mostert (eds.), *Political Assemblies in the Earlier Middle Ages* (Turnhout, 2003), 1–28; id., 'The Early Frankish *mallus*: Its Nature, Participants and Practices', in A. Pantos and S. Semple (eds.), *Assembly Places and Practices in Medieval Europe* (Dublin, 2004), 233–44; C. Wickham, *The Inheritance of Rome: A History of Europe from 400 to 1100* (London, 2009), 101–2, 122–3, 385–7, 446, 451, 552, 562–3.
[2] Tacitus, *Germania*, trans. J. B. Rives (Oxford, 1999), 80–2; *Bede's Ecclesiastical History of the English People*, ed. B. Colgrave and R. A. B. Mynors, OMT (Oxford, 1969), ii. 13, 183–7; *The Laws of the Earliest English Kings*, ed. and trans. F. L. Attenborough (Cambridge, 1922), 36–7.
[3] The fullest account of early assemblies, prior to 900, will be found in F. Liebermann, *The National Assembly in the Anglo-Saxon Period* (Halle, 1913).
[4] *Bede's Ecclesiastical History*, ed. Colgrave and Mynors, iv. 5, pp. 348–55.

forebears of the councils of post-Conquest England and the parliaments which were the councils' descendants. In terms of frequency, attendance, and business, they became for the first time truly national assemblies, with a central role in politics and government. The cause, and in part the consequence, of this change was the emergence of a newly unified English state. It was grounded on the effective resistance to the Danes by King Alfred's Wessex in the late ninth century, on the conquest of the eastern Danelaw by his son Edward the Elder between 917 and 920, and on Æthelstan's more tentative successes in the north, culminating in the submission of British and Scottish rulers in 927 and the subsequent capture of York. Eadred's later expulsion of the restored Norse king Eric Bloodaxe from York in 954 set the seal on the territorial expansion of what had been merely the kingdom of Wessex. Within the boundaries of the new kingdom, though more so to the south of the Humber than to the north, royal control was imposed through a common pattern of institutions: shires and hundreds, boroughs and mints, ealdormen and (by Æthelred's day in the 990s) sheriffs. Beyond its borders lay British and Viking kingdoms in the north and west over which English kings from Æthelstan to Edgar intermittently claimed lordship. Here the instruments of power were not administrative units, their courts, and officials, but armies, fleets—especially fleets—periodic submissions, and tribute, such as the twenty pounds of gold and 300 pounds of silver that, according to William of Malmesbury, Æthelstan was able to exact annually from the Welsh princes.[5] The quarter-century on either side of the year 950 saw the kingdom of England at its pre-Conquest apogee.

Its size presented new problems of government: of exerting royal control at a distance, of maintaining the allegiance of peripheral magnates, of making the king's power felt through lordship and patronage in regions where its wielder was invariably and inevitably absent. From Æthelstan's reign onwards assemblies helped to provide a solution to these problems, and it is with Æthelstan that any discussion of the origins of parliament must begin. This is for reasons both substantive and evidential. The first king to rule something like a united England, Æthelstan was also the first to use a new kind of assembly to facilitate his rule. Our main source for this development

---

[5] William of Malmesbury, *Gesta Regum Anglorum*, ed. and trans. R. A. B. Mynors, R. M. Thomson, and M. Winterbottom, 2 vols., OMT (Oxford, 1998–9), i. 214–17. For a good account of the tenth-century conquests and their consequences, see P. Stafford, *Unification and Conquest: A Political and Social History of England in the Tenth and Eleventh Centuries* (London, 1989), 24–68, 134–49.

is the charters which were issued in these assemblies. Many of these charters are unusually informative, thanks largely to their writer, the scribe known as 'Æthelstan A', who worked between 928 and 935, the central period of the reign.[6] For these years 'Æthelstan A' provided his charters with exceptionally long witness lists and specific place-dates, so revealing with uncommon precision both the location of the assemblies at which they were drafted and the identity of those attending. But although these particular charters shed an especially bright light on some of Æthelstan's assemblies, there is much else to suggest that their qualities and functions were perpetuated beyond his reign. From then on central assemblies with a defined role in the country's government had a continuous history to the Conquest and beyond. Since many of their features were also those of the parliaments which were their lineal descendants, Æthelstan might be thought to have a better claim than the popularly recognized Simon de Montfort to be the true if unwitting founder of the English parliament.

There is one particular issue of terminology which needs a word of explanation before any general account of the assembly's work. It is common to use the vernacular 'witan', literally 'wise men', for late Anglo-Saxon assemblies, since this word is frequently used for such gatherings in the Anglo-Saxon Chronicle and other vernacular sources. But the word carries with it, however unjustifiably, a fustian air of decayed scholarship, and, in addition, its use may seem to prejudge the answer to an important question: do we have here an institution, a capitalized 'Witan', as it were, or merely a lower-case ad hoc gathering of the wise men who were the king's councillors?[7] For these reasons, and in order to avoid any such prejudgement, the more neutral word 'assembly' will be used in most of what follows, and discussion of the witan, word and thing, reserved for the Conclusion.[8]

2. Assemblies: Size and Composition

Æthelstan's assemblies were often large in size, geographically and socially diverse in composition, and frequent and regular in occurrence. Here, as in

---

[6] For 'Æthelstan A', see S. Keynes, *The Diplomas of King Æthelred 'the Unready', 978–1016* (Cambridge, 1980), 15–17, 24–5, 42–4; P. Wormald, *The Making of English Law: King Alfred to the Twelfth Century*, i: *Legislation and its Limits* (Oxford, 1999), 434–5; *Charters of St Paul's, London*, ed. S. E. Kelly, ASCh. X (Oxford, 2004), 158–9; S. Keynes, 'England, *c.900–1016*', in T. Reuter (ed.), *The New Cambridge Medieval History*, iii: *c.900–c.1024* (Cambridge, 1999), 470.

[7] Cf. Wormald, *Making*, 94 and n. 326.   [8] Below, 49–56.

other ways, they initiated a broad trend which would persist through the reigns of his successors. The witness lists to the king's charters suggest that those attending might number at least a hundred. Æthelstan's grant to his thegn Wulfgar, made at Lifton in Devon in 931, has 101 witnesses; that to his thegn Ælfwald, made at Winchester in 934, has 92; while the well-known grant of Amounderness to the church of York, made at Nottingham in 934, has 59.[9] Although 'Æthelstan A' had a special predilection for long witness lists,[10] the numbers which he recorded were not entirely exceptional, for later charters sometimes had similarly lengthy lists. Edgar's 959 charter for Abingdon has 80 witnesses, and Æthelred's 1005 foundation charter for Eynsham has 87.[11] Of course, such large numbers are by no means the rule, and for most of the charters made between the 920s and the end of Æthelred's reign in 1016 twenty-five to forty witnesses was nearer the norm. On the other hand, the witness lists themselves occasionally make it clear that other unnamed men were present at the assembly, so that, for example, the list appended to Æthelstan's Amounderness charter ends with the words 'and many other thegns (*et plures alii milites*)'. In some cases the number of names on the list might be determined by nothing more significant than the size of the parchment available for the charter.[12] We should assume, therefore, that the witness list is a minimum statement of those attending the assembly.

By comparison with what we know of later assemblies, the largest of these gatherings were large indeed. Even the longest post-Conquest witness lists point to meetings which were no larger: 57 witnesses to a charter of Henry I made *in concilio* in 1131, 52 to the Constitutions of Clarendon in 1164, 65 for the confirmation of the Charters in 1225.[13] Most thirteenth-century parliaments are unlikely to have numbered more than a hundred or so bishops, abbots, and nobles.[14] These comparisons and contrasts might lead us to wonder whether all the many names on the witness lists for tenth-century assemblies represent men actually present: might they merely

[9] S 416 (B 677); S 425 (B 702); S 407 (B 703); *EHD* i: *c.500–1042*, ed. and trans. D. Whitelock, 2nd edn. (London, 1979), no. 104.
[10] Wormald, *Making*, 438.
[11] S 658, 911; *Charters of Abingdon Abbey*, part 2, ed. S. E. Kelly, ASCh. VIII (Oxford, 2001), no. 84; *Eynsham Cartulary*, ed. H. E. Salter, 2 vols., Oxford Historical Soc. (Oxford, 1907–8), i. 27–8.
[12] Keynes, *Diplomas*, 154–6.
[13] *RRAN 1066–1154*, ii: *Regesta Henrici Primi, 1100–1135*, ed. C. Johnson and H. A. Cronne (Oxford, 1956), no. 1715; *Select Charters and Other Illustrations of English Constitutional History from the Earliest Times to the Reign of Edward the First*, ed. W. Stubbs, 9th edn. (Oxford, 1913), 164; *Stat. Realm*, i. 25.
[14] Below, 190–4.

reflect scribal notions about those who ought to have been present? But Professor Simon Keynes has shown that any such scepticism is misplaced. At least for Æthelred's reign, and by implication for earlier reigns too, the ordering of the witnesses on the lists, generally consistent from one charter to another, can be explained only by assuming that the scribes who produced the lists regularly came to meetings and wrote down what they observed.[15] They have left us a true record of those who attended.

As far as we can see, these intermittently very large assemblies were a novelty, which began in Æthelstan's time but soon came to be a regular feature of royal government. The total absence of charters for Edward the Elder between 909 and 924 precludes direct comparisons with the years preceding Æthelstan's accession.[16] Yet if we go back to the relatively few genuine charters from Alfred's reign we find that the longest witness list runs to a mere nineteen names and that the average is many fewer.[17] With one or two exceptions,[18] the early charters of Edward the Elder do not look very different. Æthelstan's reign appears to have marked a real change of direction, of which the peculiar interests of the 'Æthelstan A' scribe were a mere symptom.

This view is confirmed when we turn to the composition of assemblies revealed by the charters. In terms of categories of attenders, if not of numbers, tenth-century assemblies largely resembled those of earlier periods. Those present almost always included the archbishop of Canterbury; quite often York; always many bishops; a few abbots; half a dozen to a dozen ealdormen; and a large number of thegns. Because there were no separate church councils at this time, as there had been before about 850 and would be again after 1066, the whole weight of the ecclesiastical and lay nobility was brought to bear in a single assembly. Its unitary nature was one reason for the assembly's political significance. *Mutatis mutandis*, and substituting 'earls' for 'ealdormen' and 'barons' for 'thegns', we are not so very far from the general look of an early parliament.

---

[15] Keynes, *Diplomas*, 37, 130–2.

[16] For this see D. N. Dumville, *Wessex and England from Alfred to Edgar* (Woodbridge, 1992), 151; P. Wormald, '*On þa wæpnedhealfe*: Kingship and Royal Property from Æthelwulf to Edward the Elder', in N. J. Higham and D. H. Hill (eds.), *Edward the Elder, 899–924* (London, 2001), 264–77.

[17] S 348 (B 567); D. Whitelock, 'Some Charters in the Name of King Alfred', in M. H. King and W. M. Stevens (eds.), *Saints, Scholars and Heroes: Studies in Medieval Culture in Honor of Charles W. Jones*, 2 vols. (Collegeville, Minn., 1979), i. 78–83; R. Abels, *Alfred the Great* (Harlow, 1998), 263.

[18] e.g. S 368 (B 600)—14 witnesses. S 362 (B 595) has an exceptional list of 35 witnesses.

There were, however, some notable newcomers. It has long been known that Æthelstan's assemblies, and to some extent those of his successors, drew in men both from the territories recently taken over by the West Saxon monarchy and from other regions beyond the borders of the realm, where West Saxon authority was more an assertion of lordship than direct rule.[19] The most permanent group would prove to be those from the kingdom's peripheries in the east, the north, and, to a lesser extent, the midlands. Among the first of these to appear were representatives of the newly conquered. The early 'Æthelstan A' charter drafted at Lifton in 931 had seven men with Scandinavian names among its witnesses; six Scandinavians were present at the Nottingham assembly of 934; and Danes continued to appear occasionally under Eadred and Æthelred.[20] Edgar's charters frequently show the attendance at assemblies of the greatest men from Mercia and Northumbria: Ealdorman Ælfhere, *princeps Merciorum*, who was almost invariably the first witness to virtually all Edgar's charters from 959 to 975, or Earl Oslac of Northumbria, a regular witness from 970 to 975, and the first such Northumbrian to witness with any frequency.[21] Sometimes the assembly attendances signified by these witnessings represented a specific royal reaction to some urgent necessity. The rise in the number of northern and eastern thegns witnessing Æthelred's charters after 1002, for example, is likely to have been a response to the renewed Viking threat to those regions.[22] But in general the enlargement of the assembly's catchment area was part of a policy of governance, intended to assimilate new subjects, to tie the periphery more closely to the royal court, and to maintain links with ministers whose high status and distant locations gave them a degree of independence from royal control.

From Æthelstan to Edgar assemblies were also to a degree supranational, embodying the hegemonic and imperial ambitions of a monarchy whose claims stretched beyond England. One mark of this was their attendance by 'outsiders', the rulers of the statelets of Wales and the far north and

[19] See, e.g. F. M. Stenton, *Anglo-Saxon England*, 3rd edn. (Oxford, 1971), 351–2.

[20] Ibid.; S 416 (B 677); S 407 (B 703); H. Loyn, *Society and Peoples: Studies in the History of England and Wales, c.600–1200* (London, 1992), 189; *The Will of Æthelgifu*, trans. D. Whitelock, Roxburghe Club (Oxford, 1968), 40–4; Keynes, *Diplomas*, 161–2. For Danish nobles from East Anglia at Æthelstan's assemblies, see C. Hart, *The Danelaw* (London, 1992), 577.

[21] S. Keynes, *An Atlas of Attestations in Anglo-Saxon Charters, c.670–1066* (Cambridge, 1998), table LVI; N. Banton, 'Monastic Reform and the Unification of Tenth-Century England', in S. Mews (ed.), *Religion and National Identity* (Oxford, 1982), 78–9.

[22] P. Stafford, 'The Reign of Æthelred II: A Study in the Limitations of Royal Policy and Actions', in D. Hill (ed.), *Ethelred the Unready*, BAR British ser. 59 (Oxford, 1978), 33.

west, who in most cases had acknowledged the superiority of the English ruler. The most frequent of these attenders was Hywel Dda of Deheubarth, in south-west Wales, who witnessed eleven of the 'Æthelstan A' charters and another five of Eadred's. Others of the same group included Morgan ap Owain of Morgannwy and Gwent (seven 'Æthelstan A', six Eadred), Owen Mac Domnaill, sub-king of Strathclyde (three 'Æthelstan A'), and Constantine, king of Scots (two 'Æthelstan A'). Of these, Hywel, Owen, and Constantine had submitted to Æthelstan at Eamont in Cumbria in 927.[23] An outlying member of the group, Malcolm, king of Strathclyde, may also have appeared at one of Edgar's assemblies in 970—a hint perhaps that Edgar's charters, bare though they are of other 'outsider' witnesses, do not necessarily indicate the absence of westerners and northerners from his assemblies.[24]

Although these exotic visitors were only a temporary phenomenon, concentrated in the period when the imperial claims of the English monarchy were at their zenith, their appearance bears witness both to the power of that monarchy and to the importance which its holders attached to assemblies. The presence of sub-kings from Wales and Scotland, at assemblies which met mainly in distant southern England, was a double demonstration of royal might. It not only showed the king's authority in securing a positive response to what must have been a royal summons, but it enhanced that authority with the king's more local subjects by displaying these men as in some ways his subjects too. Their honourable but public subordination, made visible in assemblies, was from the king's point of view perhaps a more genteel species of Roman triumph. Not until Llywelyn ap Gruffudd and then John Balliol were summoned to attend at Westminster by Edward I (with not dissimilar aims in mind) would the arm of an English king stretch so far.

More routine, and for that reason more regularly supportive of kingship, was the attendance of the *ministri*, the thegns. At almost every assembly thegns were in the majority. Edgar's Abingdon charter had 60 out of 79

---

[23] Keynes, *Atlas of Attestations*, table XXXVI; William of Malmesbury, *Gesta Regum*, i. 213–15; Loyn, *Society and Peoples*, 179–80.

[24] S 779 (B 1266); Keynes, *Atlas of Attestations*, table LVI; Banton, 'Monastic Reform', 79 n. 1, 80 n. 51; A. Macquarrie, 'The Kings of Strathclyde, *c.*400–1018', in A. Grant and K. J. Stringer (eds.), *Medieval Scotland: Crown, Lordship and Community: Essays Presented to G. W. S. Barrow* (Edinburgh, 1993), 16; D. E. Thornton, 'Edgar and the Eight Kings, AD 973: *Textus et Dramatis Personae*', *EME* 10 (2001), 66–7; S. Keynes, 'Edgar, *Rex Admirabilis*', in D. Scragg (ed.), *Edgar, King of the English, 959–975* (Woodbridge, 2008), 27.

thegnly witnesses, Æthelred's Eynsham charter 44 out of 85. Most of these witnesses were king's thegns—big men, barons rather than gentry, subject to the king's immediate lordship and jurisdiction, and sometimes holding office in his household.[25] On at least one occasion, under Edgar, a meeting of the king's thegns is described as though it were the assembly itself.[26] That they were big men too in their own districts made them important local allies of the king who had often put them there. One example is the thegn Eanulf: a fairly regular attender at Edgar's assemblies, where he twice witnessed charters as Edgar's *discthegn* or steward. He was almost certainly the same Eanulf to whom, in 958, Edgar granted what would become the Oxfordshire village of Ducklington, carved out of the great royal manor of Bampton which lay just north of the Thames. Since Edgar ruled only Mercia at this time, leaving his brother Eadwig as king in Wessex, it was doubtless useful for him to have a loyal and well-endowed supporter strategically placed near the border of the two kingdoms.[27] The assembly's purpose was not only to bring in the distantly powerful but also to maintain regular links with equally essential subordinates closer to home.

But by no means all the thegns attending assemblies were great nobles. Some were more like gentry than barons, members of that emerging class of small landowners who—like Eanulf but at a different level in the hierarchy—profited from the fragmentation of old royal estates to set themselves up as manorial lords and founders and patrons of villages and village churches.[28] These lesser men from the localities were to be the forerunners of a group with a persisting presence at royal councils from this point onwards, as we shall see. *Mutatis mutandis*, they were the ancestors of the knights of the shire. That such men may have been especially prominent at assemblies which met in their own districts is implied by a

---

[25] *Charters of Abingdon Abbey*, ed. Kelly, no. 84; *Eynsham Cartulary*, ed. Salter, i. 27–8. For thegns and king's thegns, see H. M. Chadwick, *Studies on Anglo-Saxon Institutions* (Cambridge, 1905), 308–15; A. Williams, 'Some Notes and Considerations on Problems Connected with the English Royal Succession, 860–1066', *Proceedings of the Battle Conference, 1978/ANS*, i (1979), 154; ead., *The English and the Norman Conquest* (Woodbridge, 1995), 109–12; S. Keynes, 'Thegns', in *Blackwell Enc.*, 443–4.

[26] *Anglo-Saxon Charters*, ed. and trans. A. J. Robertson (Cambridge, 1939), 122–3.

[27] *Charters of Abingdon*, ed. Kelly, no. 82 (the best commentary on Eanulf and the grant); A. Crossley (ed.), *VCH Oxford*, vol. xiii (Oxford, 1996), 111; J. Blair, *Anglo-Saxon Oxfordshire* (Far Thrupp, 1994), 133.

[28] For the emergence of the Anglo-Saxon gentry, see P. Stafford, *The East Midlands in the Early Middle Ages* (Leicester, 1985), 33–6; Blair, *Anglo-Saxon Oxfordshire*, 133–4; J. Gillingham, 'Thegns and Knights in Eleventh-Century England. Who was then the Gentleman?', in his *The English in the Twelfth Century* (Woodbridge, 2000), 164–8; J. Campbell, 'England, c.991', in his *The Anglo-Saxon State* (London, 2000), 168.

group of charters drafted in Kent between 995 and 1005 and witnessed by a number of minor Kentish thegns.[29] Another charter drafted at Cookham in Berkshire between 995 and 999 points to a much wider world, beyond the locality, by concluding with a flourish of suggestively anonymous witnesses: '. . . and Wulfric, Wulfrun's son, and all the thegns who were gathered there from far and wide, both West Saxons and Mercians, Danes and English.'[30] Not all these 'far and wide' thegns are likely to have been members of the higher nobility. One final source leaves us following a thegnly trail in an unexpected and seemingly different direction, towards the towns. If we can trust Byrhtferth of Ramsey, one of Edgar's Easter assemblies, probably that of 965, brought together 'all the important leading men, and the outstanding ealdormen, and powerful thegns from all the boroughs and towns and cities and territories (. . . *prepotentes milites ex omnibus castellis et oppidis atque civitatibus* . . .)'.[31] It is impossible to know to what these urban- and military-sounding words can refer if not to the fortified burhs, the new towns of tenth-century England. Unreliable historian though Byrhtferth generally is, his statement is not out of keeping with what Dr Robin Fleming tells us about the thorough involvement of the thegns in towns, town property, and town commerce.[32] If we can take him at face value, he may be recording not so much the first known appearance of townsmen at a central council, but rather the fusion of rural and urban interests which the thegns represented and the incorporation of those interests, on at least one occasion, within an increasingly comprehensive assembly.

The witness lists to the charters provide us with our best guide to the social, geographical, and even ethnic range of these assemblies. They were closely related to the government of a new kingdom of unprecedented size, and one where royal power, in terms of lands and historical authority, was unevenly distributed: strongest in Wessex, strong in Mercia, weaker

---

[29] Keynes, *Diplomas*, 132–4.

[30] S 939; *Diplomatarium Anglicum Aevi Saxonici*, ed. B. Thorpe (London, 1865), 539–41; *EHD*, ed. Whitelock, no. 121; Keynes, *Diplomas*, 161–2.

[31] Byrhtferth of Ramsey, *The Lives of St Oswald and St Ecgwine*, ed. and trans. M. Lapidge, OMT (Oxford, 2009), 72–3.

[32] M. Lapidge, 'Byrhtferth and Oswald', in N. Brooks and C. Cubitt (eds.), *St Oswald of Worcester* (London, 1996), 64–83 *passim*; R. Fleming, 'Rural Elites and Urban Communities in Late-Saxon England', *Past and Present*, 141 (1993), 3–37 *passim*. But note Byrhtferth's use of a similar phrase for a town-and-country gathering on a much less appropriate occasion: Byrhtferth, *Lives*, ed. Lapidge, 224–5.

in the eastern Danelaw, weakest north of the Humber. The size and diversity of the kingdom was now matched by the size and diversity of the assemblies which played a part in its government. Though earlier kings, ruling smaller kingdoms, had certainly convened assemblies, they had generally maintained contacts with their subjects by other means. Asser tells us that Alfred's thegns had served at his court in three shifts, each group coming into the king's presence for a month before returning home.[33] But with the kingdom's expansion, distance would have made such a system (if it had ever been usual) quite impracticable. Increasingly impracticable too was the more ancient method of provincial control via royal itineration, the regular travelling of the king and his entourage around his kingdom.[34] Suitable for small and medium-sized territories, this could not be maintained throughout a kingdom perhaps three times the size of Alfred's West Saxon and Mercian dominions, and one largely lacking the royal vills, royal estates, and obligatory food rents which provided the essential support system for itinerant kingship.[35] Of the kings from Æthelstan onwards, only Æthelstan himself appears to have travelled much north of the Thames; and after Edward the Elder's conquests, and with the exception of occasional visits to Ely by Æthelred and Cnut, no pre-Conquest king appears to have set foot in East Anglia.[36] This was the new world in which royal assemblies had an enlarged and more creative part to play. To an extent they were the novel alternative to royal itineration: when the king could no longer meet his great men on tour, they had to come to him. In this momentous change lay one of the roots of parliament.

[33] *Asser's Life of King Alfred*, ed. W. H. Stevenson, 2nd edn., with introduction by D. Whitelock (Oxford, 1959), 86–7, 337. Cf. Keynes, *Diplomas*, 160 n. 27.

[34] Cf. T. Charles-Edwards, 'Early Medieval Kingships in the British Isles', in S. Bassett (ed.), *The Origins of Anglo-Saxon Kingdoms* (London, 1989), 29–33.

[35] See the map of royal lands as they were under Edward the Confessor in 1066, in D. Hill, *An Atlas of Anglo-Saxon England* (Oxford, 1981), 101. The tenth-century pattern would not have been so very different, though some allowance has to be made for Edward's grants to the Godwinesons in eastern England, e.g. to Harold in Essex: R. Fleming, *Kings and Lords in Conquest England* (Cambridge, 1991), 96–7. Cf. Stafford, 'The Reign of Æthelred II', 19–21.

[36] See the itineraries in Hill, *Atlas*, 91, 94. To a degree these itineraries may be deceptive in that they are largely derived from place-dates recorded in charters made at assemblies meeting, conventionally, in southern England. They may do more to record where assemblies met than where the king travelled. The possibility of different pattern is tantalizingly suggested by Æthelred's Christmas visit to Shropshire in 1006 to receive his food rents, recorded not in a charter but in the Chronicle: *ASC*, ed. Whitelock, 88. For visits to Ely, see S. Keynes, 'Ely Abbey, 672–1109', in P. Meadows and N. Ramsey (eds.), *A History of Ely Cathedral* (Woodbridge, 2003), 30, 36.

3. Assemblies: Times, Proceedings, Places

From Æthelstan's reign onwards assemblies had not only a frequent but also a regular place in the royal calendar. They came to be particularly associated with the great feasts of the church, in a sequence that was not wholly new but drew on past precedent. In Mercia there appear to have been regular festal assemblies at Easter and Christmas from the reign of Coenwulf (796–821) and in Wessex from that of Ecgberht (802–39); though, as with so many features of English government, their ultimate origins were probably Carolingian.[37] By Æthelstan's time (quite possibly *in* Æthelstan's time) a further assembly at Whitsun had been intercalated, so that Byrhtferth can describe churchmen and magnates coming together at Whitsun 973 *solito more*, 'in accordance with custom', for Edgar's coronation.[38] In the contemporary Germany of the Ottonians—to which in some ways England was closely comparable in matters of curial ceremony—the Whitsun court was also a late and poor relation of the other two.[39] This triadic pattern, once established, was to persist into the twelfth century and to be revived, in slightly different terms, during the thirteenth.[40]

It can first be seen in the 'Æthelstan A' charters, whose meticulous dating reveals assemblies at Easter 928, Christmas 932, Easter and Whitsun 934, and probably Christmas 935.[41] Not all these occasions had equal weight. Throughout the tenth and eleventh centuries the parvenu Whitsun assemblies appear to have been less regular and may have been those most often omitted from the cycle—perhaps because they followed so closely after those at Easter. Between Edgar's accession and Æthelred's death (959–1016), for instance, we know of seven Easter assemblies but of only one at Whitsun.[42] If the charter evidence is too haphazard in its

---

[37] M. Hare, 'Kings, Crowns and Festivals: The Origins of Gloucester as a Royal Ceremonial Centre', *Trans. Bristol and Gloucestershire Archaeological Soc.* 115 (1997), 46–7. For other Carolingian features of Æthelstan's assemblies, see below, 31–2.

[38] Byrhtferth, *Lives*, ed. Lapidge, 104–5; H. G. Richardson and G. O. Sayles, *The Governance of Medieval England* (Edinburgh, 1963), 406. Lapidge has shown that Byrhtferth's account of Edgar's coronation is fabricated from a pontifical and is not the work of an eyewitness: Lapidge, 'Byrhtferth and Oswald', 70–2. But there is no reason to think that he was wrong about what he clearly regarded as a matter of routine.

[39] K. J. Leyser, *Rule and Conflict in an Early Medieval Society: Ottonian Saxony* (London, 1979), 99–100.

[40] Below, 31–2.   [41] Wormald, *Making*, 431–2.

[42] Ibid. 431, 433; Liebermann, *National Assembly*, 48–50.

survival and incidence for much weight to be placed on these figures, the prominence of the Easter assembly nevertheless stands out. This may have been in part because it sometimes served a dual function, marking not only a council but the gathering of an army in advance of a spring campaign. When Æthelstan held an Easter assembly at Exeter in 928, untypically far west in his kingdom, it is not unlikely that he was about to campaign against the west-country Britons, as William of Malmesbury says he did about this time.[43] John of Worcester similarly tells us that Edgar's great naval expeditions around the coasts of Britain followed after the Easter feast: an unsupported statement which gains some credence from a law of Æthelred, made in 1008 in anticipation of the return of the Vikings, and stipulating that ships should be made ready after Easter if it was so decreed.[44] More telling still is the evidence of one of Æthelred's earlier charters, issued in two stages. At the Easter assembly of 997, which met at the royal vill of Calne in Wiltshire, the king restored land to the Old Minster at Winchester; and this decision was corroborated a few days later at a meeting of 'the whole army' (*omni exercitus*) and a throng (*caterva*) of bishops, abbots, ealdormen and nobles, which came together at another royal vill, Wantage in Berkshire.[45] This second, post-Easter, assembly, both military and conciliar, may have been the prelude to a new campaign against the Danes, who launched a damaging raid on the south-western counties at some point in the same year.[46]

Scrappy though this evidence is, it has a certain persuasive consistency. It suggests that during English kingship's 'imperial' phase from about 925 to 975, and again during Æthelred's Danish wars, the Easter assembly may have been something like the Mayfield, the great spring army assembly of the Carolingians. At this particular assembly (and perhaps at others), the army was the council in another form, and the nobility comprised the core of each. This quasi-identity of the two institutions was to persist over the

---

[43] S 399, 400 (B 664, 663); Wormald, *Making*, 432; William of Malmesbury, *Gesta Regum*, i. 216–17. William assigns no date to Æthelstan's western campaign, but in his account it follows after the northern submission, dated by the Chronicle to July 927 (*ASC*, ed. Whitelock, 68–9), and the subsequent submission of the Welsh at Hereford.

[44] *The Chronicle of John of Worcester*, ed. and trans. R. A. Darlington, P. McGurk, and J. Bray, 2 vols., OMT (Oxford, 1995–8), ii. 424–7; V. Atr. 27—*The Laws of the Kings of England from Edmund to Henry I*, ed. and trans. A. J. Robertson (Cambridge, 1925), 86–7; Wormald, *Making*, 332–3.

[45] S 891 (K 698); P. Stafford, 'Political Ideas in Late Tenth-Century England: Charters as Evidence', in P. Stafford, J. L. Nelson, and J. Martindale (eds.), *Law, Laity and Solidarities: Essays in Honour of Susan Reynolds* (Manchester, 2001), 74; Keynes, *Diplomas*, 101–2, 255; Wormald, *Making*, 329, 443.

[46] *ASC*, ed. Whitelock, 84.

centuries. After the Conquest, and to the end of our period, conciliar and parliamentary summonses had a military basis, with the use of the same list of tenants-in-chief owing military service for both musters and consultative assemblies.[47]

That these three festal assemblies dominated the political year is suggested by their probable monopoly of law-making and by the association of our few examples of crown-wearing with these three occasions alone. Both activities are discussed below.[48] But if these were the greatest and busiest assemblies, they were by no means the only ones. In 931 there were at least five meetings, none of which coincided with a church festival; in 956—a year particularly well covered because of the sixty or so charters issued during its course—there were almost certainly four meetings; and John of Worcester and the Chronicle record between them three meetings in 977, only one of which appears to have been a festal gathering.[49] It says much for the power of these kings that they could convene assemblies so frequently.

Their meetings were already characterized by a degree of formalism and routine which marked another stage in the assembly's emergence as a regular instrument of government. We can show, what we might expect, that those attending were selected by the king. Æthelstan's fourth law code, for example, was made 'in the presence of the archbishops and all the bishops and members of the royal council nominated by the king himself'.[50] When the Chronicle tells us that in 1010 'all the councillors were summoned to the king (*Ðonne bead man ealle witan to cynge*)', it hints at a formal practice, though one whose mechanisms are obscure.[51] Even in the case of the three great feasts, when the presence of at least the higher nobility may have been assumed, it must have been necessary to notify those

[47] T. N. Bisson, 'The Military Origins of Medieval Representation', *American Historical Review*, 71 (1966), 1199–218, esp. 1200–1; T. Reuter, 'Assembly Politics in Western Europe from the Eighth Century to the Twelfth', in his *Medieval Polities and Modern Mentalities*, ed. J. L. Nelson (Cambridge, 2006), 197–8; J. R. Maddicott, ' "An Infinite Multitude of Nobles": Quality, Quantity and Politics in the Pre-Reform Parliaments of Henry III', *TCE* 7 (1999), 20–1. In the areas of Danish settlement the identity of assembly and army was sometimes replicated at a local level: see *Charters of Peterborough Abbey*, ed. S. E. Kelly, ASCh. XIV (Oxford, 2009), 24, 339, for a late tenth-century reference to 'the whole army (*here*)' as constituting the Northampton shire court.

[48] Wormald, *Making*, 431, 446; below, 18–22, 28–30.

[49] Wormald, *Making*, 432–3; Keynes, *Diplomas*, 49, 62; *John of Worcester*, ii. 428–9; *ASC*, ed. Whitelock, 79.

[50] *Laws of the Earliest English Kings*, ed. and trans. Attenborough, 146–7, 167.

[51] *ASC*, ed. Whitelock, 90; *Two of the Saxon Chronicles Parallel*, ed. C. Plummer, 2 vols. (Oxford, 1892), i. 140.

coming of the assembly's meeting place. In the case of borough assemblies (*gemot*), another of Æthelstan's laws lays down that seven days' notice is to be given before the meeting and that fines are to be imposed on those failing to attend on three occasions.[52] Superior meetings of the national assembly may have been no less tightly regulated. When summonses were issued it is entirely possible that they already took the form of writs, in the way first made known by the Chronicle's account of Henry I's assembly of 1123.[53]

Once gathered, those attending are likely to have been ranked in the strict order of precedence visible in the charter witness lists, where, for example, ealdormen appear in order of seniority of appointment. It would be surprising if such a hierarchy was not also reflected in the seating plan. Precedence, strictly observed at feasts, is unlikely to have been abandoned at the assemblies to which feasting was integral.[54] Under Æthelred, and possibly also under Edgar, there is some evidence that the bishops met separately and that the assembly opened and concluded with a sermon.[55] If these assemblies were at all like those of Charles the Bald (which they may well have been) their discussions may have involved formal and quite complicated procedures, entailing the backwards-and-forwards transmission of written business drafts between king and counsellors.[56] It was a final mark of order and system that a royal scribe was in attendance at the assembly, certainly to draft the king's charters and quite possibly to write out any administrative orders which came from the session. The uniformity of the charters written by 'Æthelstan A' can be

---

[52] II Æthelstan 20: *Laws of the Earliest English Kings*, ed. and trans. Attenborough, 136–7.

[53] 'Then, soon after, the king sent his writs over all England, and ordered his bishops and abbots and thegns to come and meet him for his council meeting on Candlemas Day at Gloucester': *ASC*, ed. Whitelock, 188. Cf. Keynes, *Diplomas*, 136–8, for the comparable use of writs in the late Anglo-Saxon period.

[54] Keynes, *Diplomas*, 154–62; M. K. Lawson, *Cnut: The Danes in England in the Early Eleventh Century* (London, 1993), 241–2. Cf. *Charters of Peterborough*, ed. Kelly, 243.

[55] M. K. Lawson, 'Archbishop Wulfstan and the Homiletic Element in the Laws of Æthelred II and Cnut', in A. R. Rumble (ed.), *The Reign of Cnut* (London, 1994), 146, 150–2; F. Barlow, *The English Church, 1000–1066* (London, 1963), 139; *The Homilies of Wulfstan*, ed. D. Bethurum (Oxford, 1957), 39–41, 339; D. A. Bullough, *Friends, Neighbours and Fellow-Drinkers: Aspects of Community and Conflict in the Early Medieval West*, H. M. Chadwick Memorial Lecture (Cambridge, 1991), 13–14; below, 34, 36.

[56] Hincmar, *De Ordine Palatii*, ed. T. Gross and R. Schieffer, Monumenta Germaniae Historica (Hanover, 1980), 90, 92, trans. in *The History of Feudalism*, ed. D. Herlihy (London, 1970), 225; J. L. Nelson, 'Legislation and Consensus in the Reign of Charles the Bald', in her *Politics and Ritual in Early Medieval Europe* (London, 1986), 104–6; J. Campbell, 'Stubbs and the English State', in his *Anglo-Saxon State*, 262–3. For the possibility of similar procedures in England, in oral if not written form, see C. Insley, 'Assemblies and Charters in Late Anglo-Saxon England', in Barnwell and Mostert (eds.), *Political Assemblies*, 52–4.

explained only on the assumption that their scribe travelled with the king from meeting to meeting.[57] Here again, Æthelstan seems to have established something novel. Large and regular assemblies, royal clerks, and consistency of charter production, all suggest that there was nothing ad hoc and formless about the assemblies on which his government partly rested.

In only one way was irregularity conspicuous in the ordering of assemblies. In the places where they met assemblies were both regionally circumscribed and geographically heterogeneous. They almost always came together at a medley of places in southern England, sometimes in towns like Winchester (934, 993) or Dorchester (933/934), but more often at royal vills in the countryside: Cheddar (941, 956, 968) and Somerton (949) in Somerset, Calne (978, 997) and Amesbury (932, 977) in Wiltshire, and so on.[58] These were often the assembly places of the old West Saxon kingdom: Amesbury, for instance, had seen an earlier assembly in 858 and Somerton in 860.[59] In one respect alone was there something of a change in the tenth century, as places along the middle Thames, often just to its north, moved into prominence. Kirtlington in Oxfordshire hosted assemblies in the 940s and again in 977, Woodstock in Oxfordshire and Cookham in Berkshire about 997, Headington in Oxfordshire in 1004. This northward shift marked the amalgamation of Wessex and Mercia under a single ruler, and must have catered for the convenience of ealdormen and thegns who now came as much from the midlands, the east, and the north as from the heartlands of historic Wessex.[60]

The reasons for this general conservatism were surely practical. As well as being royal vills, most assembly places were or would soon become important hundredal manors, presumably with facilities as markets and as collection points for the king's food rents, his farm, which made them particularly suitable for provisioning large gatherings. Further north and east such places were much rarer, and it is noticeable that the few recorded assemblies outside Wessex, south-west Mercia, and the Thames valley

[57] Keynes, *Diplomas*, 39–83; id., 'Royal Government and the Written Word in Late Anglo-Saxon England', in R. McKitterick (ed.), *The Uses of Literacy in Early Medieval Europe* (Cambridge, 1990), 247, 256–7.
[58] Tenth- and eleventh-century assembly places are listed in Wormald, *Making*, 431–4, and in Keynes, *Diplomas*, 269–73.
[59] P. Sawyer, 'The Royal *Tun* in Pre-Conquest England', in *Ideal and Reality*, 290, 296.
[60] Wormald, *Making*, 433; Keynes, *Diplomas*, 270–3. Cf. Blair, *Anglo-Saxon Oxfordshire*, 108, 159; Reuter, 'Assembly Politics', 436.

were almost always in towns: in Colchester in 931 and 940, Nottingham and Buckingham in 934, York in 936 and 966.[61] The lack of royal lands in the new territories, and the other factors which restricted the king's travels and made assemblies a more expedient instrument of government than itineration, also worked to determine their location. One further peculiarity of this pattern is striking: with the exception of Winchester, the great monastic centres of the tenth century almost never served as assembly places.[62]

About the more intimate setting of assemblies we are badly informed. Though we know of two meetings in buildings at Calne in 971 and 978, one of them (and probably the other) in the hall of the royal vill,[63] it seems unlikely that most royal vills would have possessed similar halls of the size needed to accommodate the numbers present, and it is perhaps more likely that they often met in the open air. Hincmar tells us that the Frankish general assembly met outdoors when the weather was fine, and this was often the practice of English shire and hundred courts.[64] It may have been with just such a contingency in mind that in 970 Bishop Ælfsige of Chester-le-Street brought his tent to what was probably an assembly at the royal vill of Woodyates in Dorset.[65] The setting for a rural assembly may have resembled a rather grand campsite. That the bishop should have travelled more than 300 miles, almost from the far north to the far south of England, in order to be present illuminates a factor not often considered in relation to assemblies: that is, the state of the roads. The great gatherings of the tenth century were made possible only by circumstances which favoured relatively speedy and direct travel, deriving in part perhaps from the keen interest which Anglo-Saxon kings traditionally took in the maintenance of roads and bridges. Æthelstan's ten-day journey of about 200 miles from Winchester to Nottingham in 934, from one assembly to another, and the two-day journey of Bishop Æthelwold's body and

[61] Wormald, *Making*, 432–4; Keynes, *Diplomas*, 270, 272–3.

[62] Though for assemblies at Abingdon, in *c*.926 and 930 respectively, see William of Malmesbury, *Gesta Regum*, i. 218–19, and *Anglo-Saxon Charters*, ed. and trans. Robertson, 44–5.

[63] *ASC*, ed. Whitelock, 79; S 891 (K 698).

[64] Hincmar, *De Ordine Palatii*, ed. Gross and Schieffer, 92, 94, trans. in *History of Feudalism*, ed. Herlihy, 226. Cf. J. Blair, *The Church in Anglo-Saxon Society* (Oxford, 2004), 279; Sawyer, 'Royal *Tun*', 286.

[65] Wormald, *Making*, 437; Keynes, 'Edgar, *Rex Admirabilis*', 51 n. 238. For this and other instances of the use of tents, see C. Cubitt, *Anglo-Saxon Church Councils, c.650–c.850* (London, 1995), 35 and n. 71; and J. L. Nelson, 'Kingship and Royal Government', in Reuter (ed.), *New Cambridge Medieval History*, iii. 470.

its escort from Beddington in Surrey to Winchester in 984, a distance of about sixty miles, give us an idea of what might be done.[66] English rulers may have convened their assemblies in plain and rural locations which could not rival the splendid settings for the great festal courts of their Ottonian contemporaries at such palatial and monastic sites as Magdeburg and Quedlinburg.[67] But that they could bring men together from so far away was a tribute not only to their political enterprise and authority but also to English travelling conditions, for which they too may have been partly responsible.

4. Functions: Charisma

It would be easy enough to enumerate the many functions which tenth- and early eleventh-century assemblies performed, but we may get a clearer view of their work if we classify those functions rather than merely list them. The simplest taxonomy has two broad divisions which between them define the assembly's role in the relationship between king and subjects: 'charisma' and 'consensus'. The first embodied the ideological and representational side of kingship, and the second the practical, though this is a modern distinction which neither the king nor those attending assemblies would have recognized. Manifested on the same occasions, both also shared the same characteristic of being strongly conducive to royal authority.

What Weber meant by 'charisma' will do for us: the exceptional, often superhuman, quality which sets one man, usually the leader, apart from other men.[68] In tenth-century England this quality came to be expressed most powerfully through festal crown-wearing. Until quite recently the practice of crown-wearing in pre-Conquest England has been doubted, but Mr Michael Hare has now convincingly argued its case, if only by laying out a trail which is inevitably thin and episodic. Lacking the rich narrative sources which reveal so much about royal ceremony in tenth-century Germany, we are dependent on scraps. The first comes from the dating clause of a charter of King Eadred, drawn up at Somerton on Easter Day

---

[66] Sawyer, 'Royal *Tun*', 286–7; Wulfstan of Winchester, *Life of St Æthelwold*, ed. M. Lapidge and M. Winterbottom, OMT (Oxford, 1991), 62–3; Hill, *Atlas*, 115; J. Campbell, 'Was it Infancy in England? Some Questions of Comparison', in his *Anglo-Saxon State*, 183–4.

[67] Leyser, *Rule and Conflict*, 90–1.

[68] An abbreviated paraphrase of Weber's definition: see M. Weber, *The Theory of Social and Economic Organization*, trans. A. M. Henderson and T. Parsons (London, 1947), 329.

949, when we are told that the king 'was exalted with royal crowns (*regalia sublimavit diademata paschali sollempnitate)*'.[69] Next comes a more informative account relating to an even more special occasion, the coronation feast of King Eadwig in 956. A famous story in the *Life of Dunstan* relates how Eadwig left the feast abruptly; Dunstan and another cleric went in search of him; the king was found roistering with two loose women, the glittering crown abandoned on the floor; but the outraged Dunstan replaced it on the king's head and marched him back to the feast. Though this anecdote throws no light on the more routine festal crown-wearings, it remains good evidence for the king's wearing of the crown, all the more credible because it was almost certainly written by an eyewitness.[70] A third and last vignette takes us back to a festal occasion. Byrhtferth of Ramsey describes an Easter assembly when Edgar was present 'mighty in arms, exulting in sceptres and diadems'. The same as that attended by 'urban' thegns, and probably datable to 965, the assembly witnessed a meeting between the king and Oswald, bishop of Worcester, which led eventually to the foundation of the monastery of Ramsey. Byrhtferth is, as usual, unspecific, and his special interest in royal ceremony, especially coronations, provides another reason for treating his words with caution.[71] But he is unlikely simply to have invented the plausible detail of Edgar's crown-wearing, which tallies with what we already know.

With two partial exceptions, the crown-wearing trail, spasmodic at best, then goes cold until we pick it up again in Edward the Confessor's time.[72] Yet if these three references seem insubstantial, they gain greatly in weight from their political and international context. The origins of crown-wearing were Carolingian, but the more immediate precedents were German,[73] and

---

[69] *Charters of Burton Abbey*, ed. P. H. Sawyer, ASCh. II (Oxford, 1979), no. 8; Hare, 'Kings, Crowns and Festivals', 45. The crown-wearing was recognized in C. R. Hart, *The Early Charters of Northern England and the North Midlands* (Leicester, 1975), 105. 'Diadema' and 'corona' are used interchangeably in pre-Conquest sources; and Ælfric's Glossary equates 'diadema' with 'kynehelm' or crown: *Aelfrics Grammatik und Glossar*, ed. J. Zupita (Berlin, 1880), repr. with preface by H. Gneuss (Hildesheim, 2003), 303.

[70] *Memorials of St Dunstan*, ed. W. Stubbs, RS (London, 1874), 32–3; *EHD*, ed. Whitelock, no. 234; M. Lapidge, 'B. and the *Vita S. Dunstani*', in his *Anglo-Latin Literature, 900–1066* (London, 1993), 280.

[71] Byrhtferth, *Lives*, ed. Lapidge, pp. xvii–xviii, 72–81; Hare, 'Kings, Crowns and Festivals', 45; M. Lapidge, 'Byrhtferth and the Early Sections of the *Historia Regum* Attributed to Symeon of Durham', in his *Anglo-Latin Literature*, 328. For 'urban' thegns, above, 10.

[72] Below, 43–4.

[73] Hare, 'Kings, Crowns and Festivals', 44; K. Leyser, 'Ritual, Ceremony and Gesture: Ottonian Germany', in his *Communications and Power in Medieval Europe: The Carolingian and Ottonian Centuries*, ed. T. Reuter (London, 1994), 190, 192–4.

the conduit for their transmission to England almost certainly Æthelstan
and his continental connections. Beginning in his reign, there was a novel
interest in the crown as an object both physical and symbolic: the sort of
object described in the story of Eadwig's coronation feast, 'bound with
wondrous metal, gold and silver and gems', that 'shone with many-coloured
lustre'.[74] By this time it had replaced the helmet as the 'chief royal headgear'
and symbol of kingship.[75] The second English coronation *ordo*, probably
used for the first time at Æthelstan's coronation in 925, was the first to
prescribe the king's actual crowning,[76] and it cannot be any coincidence
that Æthelstan was also the first king to appear crowned on coins (the
BC type introduced in the 930s), or that he should be shown wearing a
three-pointed crown similar to that on his coins in a contemporary copy
of the *Life of Cuthbert* given by him to Chester-le-Street.[77] He was a king
to whom his crown was clearly of high significance.

　　Two further considerations point to Æthelstan as innovator here. First,
his putative crown-wearing chimes resonantly with the whole elevated
style of his kingship. His conquests, and in particular his subordination
of the Welsh and Scottish rulers, were reflected in the grandeur of his
titles. He was the first to claim to be 'king of the English' ('Rex Anglorum'), in two charters of 928,[78] and his more bombastic and imperial charter-styles are well known—'king of the English, raised by the
Almighty to the throne of Britain', 'king of the whole of Britain', and so
on.[79] The latter title, usually abbreviated to 'rex tot. Brit.', also appears
on Æthelstan's later coins.[80] Since both the minting of coins and also
the making of charters were at this time under royal control, we can

[74] *EHD*, ed. Whitelock, no. 234.

[75] J. L. Nelson, 'The Earliest Royal *Ordo*: Some Liturgical and Historical Aspects', in her *Politics and Ritual*, 356–8.

[76] Nelson, 'The Second English *Ordo*', in her *Politics and Ritual*, 365–9, argues for the *ordo*'s first use at Edward the Elder's coronation in 900. But Wormald, *Making*, 447 n. 114, and G. Garnett, 'Coronation', in *Blackwell Enc.* 123, put a more persuasive case for Æthelstan.

[77] C. E. Blunt, B. H. I. H. Stewart, and C. S. S. Lyon, *Coinage in Tenth-Century England* (Oxford, 1989), 11; Nelson, 'The Earliest Royal *Ordo*', 357 and n. 83; M. Wood, 'The Making of King Aethelstan's Empire: An English Charlemagne ?', in Wormald (ed.), *Ideal and Reality*, 254, 268 and plate VI.

[78] S 399, 400 (B 664, 663); P. Wormald, '*Engla Lond*: The Making of an Allegiance', in his *Legal Culture in the Early Medieval West* (London, 1999), 364.

[79] S 416, 421 (B 677, 694); Wormald, *Making*, 444–5; E. John, *Orbis Britanniae* (Leicester, 1966), 50–1.

[80] C. E. Blunt, 'The Coinage of Athelstan, King of England, 924–939', *British Numismatic Journal*, 42 (1974), 55–6.

assume that these grand titles represent Æthelstan's own view of his new position. Secondly, Æthelstan had particularly close ties with Germany, where crown-wearing came into special prominence in the tenth century as part of a general resurgence of royal ceremonial. In 929 the young Otto, son of Henry I and future emperor, had married Edith, Æthelstan's half-sister, after an exchange of embassies between England and the Reich, and a strong contingent of Germans subsequently became established in the English church.[81] Though Æthelstan's coronation, with its novel use of the crown, pre-dated these contacts, it is highly likely that festal crown-wearings began under German influence in Æthelstan's later years.

Its purpose, as in Germany, was to show kingship, in Karl Leyser's words, 'as something God-given, sacrosanct and awe-demanding':[82] a demonstration which gained in theocratic force from the great feasts of the church which provided its temporal setting. Its locative setting, however, was the assembly, a religious as well as a political occasion, and its function there to impress the king's majesty on the many who were present, particularly perhaps the exotic visitors from the far north and west who resided at or beyond the limits of regularly deployable English power. In a society where visual culture counted for more than literacy, such a public act of display was a more instant and powerful medium of royal communication than writs or charters whose readership or audience was inevitably more limited. It was all the more powerful because the kingship which it represented was underlain by a strong institutional structure of pervasive government, operating through laws, courts, and officials, to which charisma added what Patrick Wormald has aptly termed a 'gloss'. In the less governed Ottonian kingdom crown-wearing was in part a substitute for institutional strength, but in England its complement.[83]

We can judge the importance which at least one king attached to this aspect of festal activity by looking at the deal struck by Edgar with Kenneth II of Scotland about 975. It centred on the cession of Lothian, in south-east

[81] Leyser, 'Ritual, Ceremony and Gesture', 192–4; id., 'The Ottonians and Wessex', in his *Communications and Power*, 76–83; Wood, 'Making of King Aethelstan's Empire', 259–62.
[82] Leyser, *Rule and Conflict*, 90.
[83] P. Wormald, 'Germanic Power Structures: The Early English Experience', in L. Scales and O. Zimmer (eds.), *Power and the Nation in European History* (Cambridge, 2005), 106–8.

Scotland. In exchange for the return of Lothian, the Scottish ruler was to come to the English court 'every year at the principal festivals, when the king and his successors wore their crowns (*diadema*) . . . and joyfully celebrate the feast with the rest of the nobles of the kingdom'.[84] This neglected supplement to the history of tenth-century crown-wearing is preserved only in the thirteenth-century chronicle of Roger of Wendover. But Wendover was drawing on a set of lost northern annals containing original material otherwise unavailable and partly supported by another early northern source. His account gains further weight, if only inferentially, from the likely presence of another northerner, Malcolm, probably the king of Strathclyde, at Edgar's great Easter court of 970.[85] Crown-wearing was clearly an imperial exercise as well as a domestic one, and attendance at the festal assemblies which were its occasion a habit worth seeking to impose.

How the exercise struck spectators at Æthelstan's or Edgar's court we have no means of telling. But after the Conquest, in another famous episode, William the Conqueror's jester, confronted by the king at table 'crowned and resplendent in gold and robes' on one of the three great feast days, could exclaim 'Behold I see God!' The jester's reaction may have been sceptical, even sarcastic, and was certainly extreme; Archbishop Lanfranc evidently thought so, for he ordered him to be flogged for blasphemy.[86] But for a crown-wearing king it was probably gratifyingly close to what was intended. Pre-Conquest reaction to similar spectacles may have been little different.

The assembly was therefore a kind of theatre, a forum where the king's charisma was made manifest and his semi-divine character exemplified through crown-wearing. Stemming ultimately from continental precedents and from the triumphs of contemporary English kingship, this was a new

[84] Roger of Wendover, *Chronica sive Flores Historiarum*, ed. H. O. Coxe, 4 vols. (London, 1842), i. 416; *EHD*, ed. Whitelock, 255, 258 (Whitelock gives further reasons for trusting Wendover's account); Symeon of Durham, *Opera Omnia: Historia Regum*, ed. T. Arnold, 2 vols., RS (1882–5), ii. 382. The passage was noted and accepted by Richardson and Sayles, *Governance*, 406. It was dismissed by M. O. Anderson, 'Lothian and the Early Scottish Kings', *Scottish Historical Review*, 39 (1960), 107–8, but only on the grounds that Wendover's reference to crown-wearing was anachronistic, which we now know not to be the case.

[85] Above, 8.

[86] 'Vita Lanfranci', ed. M. Gibson, in G. Onofrio (ed.), *Lanfranco di Pavia e l'Europa del secolo XI, nel IX centenario della morte (1089–1989)* (Rome, 1993), 708–9. Cf. J. L. Nelson, 'The Rites of the Conqueror', in her *Politics and Ritual*, 400–1.

development which elevated the status not only of the king but of the assembly too.

5. Functions: Consensus

The affirmation of royal charisma was not always easily separable from the second and more latent purpose of assemblies, the promotion of consensus between the king and his great men. A central part of any such promotion lay in entertainment: the eating, drinking, and general socializing which were as much assembly business, and as important for the king's authority, as any items on the more formal political agenda. Only infrequently do the sources hint at this side of the assembly's work—when, for example, Byrhtferth of Ramsey tells us that the great crowd of bishops, thegns, and ealdormen brought together for Edgar's Easter assembly of c.965 were 'royally received (*suscepit regaliter*)' by the king, who 'bestowed on them the warmth of his welcome'.[87] The records of some associated occasions may be more revealing. One such took place in 980. In that year, following an assembly at the royal vill of Andover, the whole company, including King Æthelred, moved on to Winchester for the dedication of the Old Minster. This was celebrated with a feast, lovingly described in Wulfstan of Winchester's *Narratio Metrica de Sancto Swithuno*: the tables piled high with food, the multiple courses, the great drinking bowls filled with spiced wine, the frequent trips of the stewards to the cellars.[88] If such feasts broke down the boundaries between the secular and ecclesiastical worlds, as Professor James Campbell has noted,[89] they also united king and nobles in inebriant conviviality. Drink was the bond of the ruling classes (though it could lead as easily to fighting as to fellowship).[90] At the same time the feasts themselves were very probably the occasions for crown-wearing. It is striking that the stories of Eadwig's scandalous behaviour at his coronation banquet, and of the jester who saw God in William the Conqueror's crowned majesty, both show or imply that the king actually wore his crown while he sat feasting.

---

[87] Byrhtferth, *Lives*, ed. Lapidge, 72–3.
[88] M. Lapidge, *The Cult of St Swithun*, Winchester Studies 4, ii (Oxford, 2003), 376–9.
[89] J. Campbell, 'England, c.991', in his *Anglo-Saxon State*, 162–3 (where other examples of great feasts are given).
[90] Bullough, *Friends, Neighbours and Fellow-Drinkers*, 11–18.

(If the crown had a chinstrap, as Henry I's did, this may not have been so difficult as it sounds.[91]) At such great assemblies charisma and consensus lived in easy harmony, and the charismatic demonstration of royal might gained rather than lost from its setting at a feast which was as much culinary as religious.

The other informal aspects of consensual practice at assemblies are no more frequently evident than feasting, but they are unlikely to have been very different from the Carolingian model set out in Hincmar's *De Ordine Palatii*. Probably describing Charles the Bald's assemblies of the 880s, Hincmar writes:

> [The king] himself was occupied with the rest of the assembled people, receiving presents, greeting important persons, chatting with those rarely seen, sympathizing with the aged, rejoicing with the young and involving himself in spiritual as well as secular affairs. Nevertheless, as often as those withdrawn in council wished it, the king would go to them and remain with them as long as they desired. They then in all friendliness told him how they had found individual matters; they frankly related what they had discussed on one side or the other, in disagreement or argument or friendly rivalry.[92]

What Hincmar calls *familiaritas*, combining good fellowship and patrimonial authority,[93] was probably as characteristic of English as of Frankish assemblies. Though English sources have nothing to rival his description in vividness or particularity, we do know, for example, that Alfred distributed gifts of money at Easter, presumably at a festal assembly, to those who served him, and that Æthelstan, speaking of disorders in the preface to his fifth law code, could remark that 'my councillors (*witan*) say that I have suffered this too long'.[94] The king's words hint at an informal dialogue of complaint and response which is likely to have been commonplace. Such an exchange, redolent of an easygoing relationship between the king and those around him, and one in which both sides could speak their minds, does not seem so far from the social world of the assembly revealed by

[91] William of Malmesbury, *Gesta Pontificum Anglorum*, ed. and trans. M. Winterbottom and R. M. Thomson, 2 vols., OMT (2007–8), i. 212–13.

[92] The translation is mainly that of *History of Feudalism*, ed. Herlihy, 225–6, supplemented by that of J. L. Nelson, 'Legislation and Consensus in the Reign of Charles the Bald', in her *Ritual and Politics*, 108–9.

[93] J. L. Nelson, 'The Lord's Anointed and the People's Choice: Carolingian Royal Ritual', in D. Cannadine and S. Price (eds.), *Rituals of Royalty: Power and Ceremonial in Traditional Societies* (Cambridge, 1987), 165.

[94] *Select English Historical Documents of the Ninth and Tenth Centuries*, ed. F. E. Harmer (Cambridge, 1914), 18, 51; *Laws of the Earliest English Kings*, ed. and trans. Attenborough, 152–3.

Hincmar; nor indeed from the consensual milieu of the later great councils of Anglo-Norman and Angevin England.

Through feasting and conversation, gift-giving and petitioning, the assembly thus became a forum for the resolution of social tensions. But a stronger cement for consensus was patronage, for which these meetings were the chief focus and dispersal point to a degree unparalleled after the Conquest. The pre-eminent form of patronage lay in grants of bookland, land granted by charter, by long tradition made in assemblies because they alone could provide the quality and quantity of witnesses needed to validate the grant;[95] hence the value of the charters as our chief source. In the mid tenth century such grants were made with unprecedented liberality. Though the number fluctuated greatly from year to year, the period from 940 to 975 saw more grants of bookland than any comparable period before 1066, and between 939 and 959 a much larger number of these went, quite unprecedentedly, to laymen rather than ecclesiastics.[96] As we have already noted in another context, charters rose to a maximum of some sixty in 956.[97] The reasons for this development are not clear, but they must be related to political tensions and the need for kings to buy support, particularly perhaps in 956, when King Eadwig faced a possible rival in his younger brother Edgar. The result was in part the fragmentation of former royal estates, their dispersal into lay hands, and the promotion to manorial lordship of men such as Edgar's thegn Eanulf who were to form the core of the lesser nobility and local gentry.[98]

The scale of royal grants, and the subsequent multiplication of charters, was one factor which kept assemblies vigorously in business. In 956 as many as twenty grants, twelve of them for laymen, might be made in a single session: an alienation of royal property which saw assemblies contributing to the weakening of royal power rather than, more characteristically, to its confirmation.[99] Those attending were drawn into charter-making not merely as passive witnesses to the charter but as active consenters to the grant. 'I Bishop Cenwald have consented to the aforesaid grant', typically says one witness to a charter of c.950.[100] The role of such men as more than witnesses is occasionally confirmed by evidence which allows us to go

[95] Wormald, *Making*, 435.
[96] Hill, *Atlas*, 26; Keynes, *Diplomas*, 47; Stafford, *Unification and Conquest*, 37–9.
[97] Keynes, *Diplomas*, 49; above, 14.
[98] Williams, 'Some Notes and Considerations', 155–6; above, 9.
[99] Keynes, *Diplomas*, 54–6, 62.   [100] S 578 (B 888).

behind the scenes. When the charters of Ealdorman Æthelfrith were burnt sometime before 903, it was not just Edward the Elder and his Mercian deputies, Ealdorman Æthelred and his wife Æthelfleda, whom Æthelfrith petitioned for replacements, but also all the *senatores Merciorum*; and all consented to the drafting of new charters.[101] So in the making of charters, king, donees, and witnesses were sharers in a royal *actum* which was also a kind of consensual compact.

In providing a stage for the distribution of patronage, the assembly had taken over another of the functions of royal itineration; for in the earliest days of Anglo-Saxon kingship it was through the royal circuit that men were most often enabled to approach the king for favour and reward.[102] But patronage lay almost as much in office as in land, and here again the assembly's role was crucial to a central act of governance: appointing. When we are told about appointments to bishoprics, the consent of assemblies seems always to be invoked. Dunstan's first appointment to Worcester about 957 was made in 'a great assembly of councillors (*magnus sapientium conventus*) . . . in the place which is called *Brandanford* . . . by the choice of all', while Oscetel's appointment to York in 956 was made 'by the consent of King Eadred and of all his councillors'.[103] We know less about secular appointments. But it was probably in an assembly at York in 966, on one of King Edgar's rare visits to the north, that the decision was taken to divided the Northumbrian ealdormanry and to appoint Oslac as earl for the southern half;[104] and the likelihood is that other ealdormen were appointed in the same way.

With regard to patronage, therefore, tenth-century assemblies were very much a part of the consensual apparatus of English government. At least in relation to land grants and appointments, they had a more pronounced role than later parliaments. Although these provided high points for the

---

[101] S 367 (B 603). Cf. S 361 (B 607) for another example. For comment on these 'replacement' charters characteristic of Edward the Elder's early years, see S. Keynes, 'A Charter of Edward the Elder for Islington', *Historical Research*, 66 (1993), 312–13; id., 'England, *c*.900–1016', 463.

[102] Charles-Edwards, 'Early Medieval Kingship', 29.

[103] *Memorials of St Dunstan*, ed. Stubbs, 36; *EHD*, ed. Whitelock, no. 234; *ASC*, ed. Whitelock, 76; Keynes, 'Edgar, *Rex Admirabilis*', 8.

[104] 'The Chronicle Attributed to John of Wallingford', ed. R. Vaughan, *Camden Miscellany* xxi (1958), 54; D. Whitelock, 'The Dealings of the Kings of England with Northumbria in the Tenth and Eleventh Centuries', in P. Clemoes (ed.), *The Anglo-Saxons: Studies in Some Aspects of their History and Culture Presented to Bruce Dickins* (London, 1959), 71, 77. The date of Oslac's appointment is disputed: see S. Keynes, 'The Additions in Old English', in *The York Gospels*, ed. N. Barker, Roxburghe Club (London, 1986), 87 and n. 35; and Wormald, *Making*, 441–2 and n. 90.

dispersal of patronage, in general its granting stretched more evenly across the year and was less intensively concentrated in parliamentary bursts. The greater need for witnesses to validate pre-Conquest grants, in an age when memory as well as written record contributed to title, helps to explain the contrast. And if assemblies were well attended, as they seem to have been, it was perhaps because the participants saw benefits in coming, not just to participate in government, but also to catch the king's eye and to put themselves in the way of royal favour. If magnates and bishops were less scrupulous about attending parliaments in the later middle ages,[105] it may have been partly because their meetings were less exclusively the occasions for royal generosity.

Other functions these assemblies did share with later parliaments, most clearly those of political decision-making, legislation, and justice. These again were consensual activities, carried through by collaboration between the king and his great men. At mid tenth-century assemblies the first of these activities may seem to have been not much in evidence. But this apparent hiatus is almost certainly deceptive: the narrative sources for this period, which might have recorded political discussion, are desperately thin, and the charters, which otherwise tell us so much, are usually uninformative on politics *per se*. Perhaps paradoxically, we have to wait until the later period of the uncounselled Æthelred before we find much consistent evidence for the consultative role of assemblies in national business. It is supplied *inter alia* by the detailed 'E' version of the Chronicle, by Æthelred's numerous law codes, and by a few diplomatic texts. So, for example, we learn from a papal letter that Æthelred's treaty with Duke Richard of Normandy in 991 was made after the king had summoned for consultation 'his faithful subjects both religious and secular who were particularly wise';[106] from the Chronicle and from the law-code-cum-treaty known as II Æthelred, that both the decision to assemble ships in London in 992, prior to an expedition against the Danes, and the subsequent treaty of 994, were made by 'the king and all his councillors (*witan*)';[107] from a charter, that the decree for the extermination of the Danes in 1002, in what became known as the St Brice's Day massacre, was issued by the king 'with the counsel

---

[105] Cf. J. S. Roskell, 'The Problem of the Attendance of the Lords in Medieval Parliaments', in his *Parliaments and Politics in Late Medieval England*, 3 vols. (London, 1981), i, ch. 2.

[106] William of Malmesbury, *Gesta Regum*, i. 278–9; *EHD*, ed. Whitelock, no. 230.

[107] *ASC*, ed. Whitelock, 82; *Laws of the Kings of England*, ed. and trans. Robertson, 56–7, on which see Wormald, *Making*, 321–2.

of my leading men and magnates';[108] and from the Chronicle, that general defence measures were discussed in 1010, after 'all the councillors (*witan*) were summoned to the king'.[109] Part of the usefulness of such meetings must have lain in the ability of those present to provide the king and his closest advisers with information on provincial conditions and popular opinion. The allusion in both 991 and 1010 to the *summoning* of the councillors suggests that these were special advisory assemblies and not merely ad hoc gatherings of courtiers and king's friends. No doubt the prolonged crisis of Æthelred's reign compelled more frequent consultation and thrust assemblies into greater prominence. But we have no reason to think that the mechanisms of decision-making were in any way out of the ordinary at this time, and we have already noted the probability that Easter assemblies preceded earlier campaigns.[110] Under Æthelred, as earlier and later, affairs of state were at the heart of the assembly's business.

Equally consensual was legislation: one of the oldest functions of Anglo-Saxon assemblies and a main part of their legacy to post-Conquest councils. By the tenth century those attending were working actively with the king to make new law. Their partnership is almost invariably mentioned in the legal texts themselves, and perhaps nowhere more explicitly than in the epilogue to II Æthelstan, 'the major "official" statement of the reign': 'All this was established at the great assembly at Grately, at which Archbishop Wulfhelm was present, with all the nobles and councillors whom King Æthelstan had assembled.'[111] Twenty-two law codes are extant for the period from 899 to 1022, from Edward to Elder to Cnut, and nineteen of these show similar conciliar participation.[112] The apparent care taken to demonstrate this in the wording of the codes themselves suggests that they were thought to derive their authority, not simply from their status as royal decrees, but from the joint responsibility of king and assembled councillors for their making. That those at the centre drew

---

[108] S 909 (K 709); *EHD*, ed. Whitelock, no. 127.

[109] *ASC*, ed. Whitelock, 90; *Two of the Saxon Chronicles*, ed. Plummer, i. 140.   [110] Above, 13.

[111] *Laws of the Earliest English Kings*, ed. and trans. Attenborough, 142–3; Wormald, *Making*, 300. For other examples, see J. M. Kemble, *The Saxons in England*, 2 vols., new edn. (London, 1876), ii. 209–13.

[112] Wormald, *Making*, 431, 446. *Laws of the Earliest English Kings*, ed. and trans. Attenborough, 118–19, 122–3, 126–7, 142–3, 146–7, 152–3, 168–9; *Laws of the Kings of England*, ed. and trans. Robertson, 6–7, 8–9, 12–13, 20–1, 28–9, 52–3, 56–7, 64–5, 78–9, 90–1, 108–9, 116–17, 130–1, 154–5, 174–5.

on the advice and experience of the leading men of the localities—from whom they themselves of course were partly drawn—seems very likely.[113]

In other parts of the West, the Germanic and Carolingian legislative tradition died out in the tenth century.[114] Its energetic preservation and promotion in England was quite exceptional. Like the great tide of tenth-century charter-making, this strong legislative current helped to maintain assemblies in one of their essential functions. Its volume and pattern have been tentatively explained by Patrick Wormald, who argued that since law-making tended to coincide with festal crown-wearing, and sometimes to embody imperial ideas, it reflected the ebb and flow of attempts to project the king's majesty and hegemonic status.[115] But the profusion of new laws reflected the peculiarities of English conditions in another and broader way by contributing powerfully to the expanding role of government in a new kingdom. It was an aspect of that general intensity of regulation and—since the laws were in part a formulation of Christian ideology—moral direction through which royal government attempted to impose itself on the lives of its now more numerous subjects.

To this end, the job of attenders at assemblies may have been not just to authorize the laws by sharing in their making, but also to disseminate, publicize, and quite possibly enforce them. Only one text says almost as much. The penultimate clause of IV Edgar, dating probably from the 970s, lays down that 'many documents are to be written concerning this, and sent both to Ealdorman Ælfhere and Ealdorman Æthelwine, and they are to send them in all directions, so that this measure may be known to both the poor and the rich'.[116] The uniqueness of this clause prevents us from assuming that the arrangements which it prescribes were typical. Yet Æthelstan's extensive legislation assumes the similar use of written texts at many different points, if not so directly;[117] and if IV Edgar was directed towards the Danelaw, as seems most likely,[118] the clause would fit well enough with the general assumption that the assembly's work had much

---

[113] Insley, 'Assemblies and Charters in Late Anglo-Saxon England', 50–1.

[114] Wormald, *Making*, 431, 481, 483; T. Reuter, 'The Making of England and Germany, 850–1050: Points of Comparison and Difference', in his *Medieval Polities*, 293; id., 'Assembly Politics', 205.

[115] Wormald, *Making*, 444–9.

[116] *Laws of the Kings of England*, ed. and trans. Robertson, 38–9. The translation is that of Keynes, 'Royal Government', 242. Cf. Wormald, *Making*, 317, and for the date, ibid. 441–2.

[117] Keynes, 'Royal Government', 235–41.

[118] So Wormald, *Making*, 317; but contrast Keynes, 'Royal Government', 242 n. 62.

to do with the government of 'colonial' territory. What was new may
not have been the provision for making legislation known in the localities
but rather the setting down of the king's instructions in writing. We are
reminded both of post-Conquest arrangements for the local proclamation
of new law, such as Henry I's coronation charter, and of the new statutes
which the knights of the shire sometimes took back to their constituencies
from fourteenth-century parliaments.[119] In law-making, as in much else and
as in later days, Anglo-Saxon assemblies were a point of contact between
crown and provinces.

The final consensual function of assemblies, the doing of justice, was,
like law-making, already well established by the tenth century. Like law-
making too, it had a long future before it. Although most judicial business,
including even some disputes about bookland, was now dealt with in
the local courts of shire and hundred,[120] the central assembly remained
the court for special cases and its suitors the doomsmen or judges. Its
business included difficult property suits, but more particularly 'state trials':
pleas involving the king or some overmighty subject or some especially
heinous case of treachery or disobedience. In the late tenth century both
the king's novel obligation to do justice, an item in the coronation oath
from Edgar's time onwards,[121] and a series of high-profile trials in the
disturbed circumstances of Æthelred's reign, may have given this aspect of
the assembly's work a special prominence. Typical was the condemnation
of Ealdorman Ælfric in 985 for a crime so serious (though unspecified) that
it was even mentioned in the Chronicle as well as in the charter of Æthelred
which is our main source. The culprit was condemned in 'a synodal council
at Cirencester . . . when all my leading men assembled together . . . and
expelled the same Ælfric, guilty of high treason, as a fugitive from this
country'.[122] Already we can see the same sort of judicial procedures later
directed in councils and parliaments against William of St Calais in 1088

---

[119] R. L. Poole, 'The Publication of Great Charters by the English Kings', *EHR* 28 (1913), 414;
J. R. Maddicott, 'Parliament and the Constituencies, 1272–1377', in Davies and Denton (eds.), *Eng.
Parl.* 81; below, 284, 336–7, 364.
[120] A. Kennedy, 'Law and Legislation in the *Libellus Æthelwoldi episcopi*', *ASE* 24 (1995), 136–44.
[121] *Memorials of St Dunstan*, ed. Stubbs, 355–6; Wormald, *Making*, 447–8; below, 34.
[122] S 937 (K 1312); *EHD*, ed. Whitelock, no. 123; *ASC*, ed. Whitelock, 81; P. Wormald, 'A
Handlist of Anglo-Saxon Lawsuits', in his *Legal Culture*, 268, no. 63. For other examples, see *Select
English Historical Documents*, ed. Harmer, no. 23, *c*.904 (Wormald, 'Handlist', no. 32); *Anglo-Saxon
Charters*, ed. Robertson, nos. 44, 63, 962, and *c*.996 (Wormald, 'Handlist', nos. 40, 57). For comment,
see P. Wormald, 'Giving God and the King their Due: Conflict and its Resolution in the Early English
State', in his *Legal Culture*, 349–50.

or Thomas Becket in 1164 or Simon de Montfort in 1252.[123] By doing
justice in partnership king and council were coming together to promote
one of the state's central functions and to prosecute those who jeopardized
political security and social cohesion.

As the regular occasions for social exchanges, patronage, and a wide range
of consensual business, assemblies thus helped to stabilize and harmonize
the relationship between the king and his great men on which the peace
ultimately depended. In their general features—large size, regularity, consensual functions—they resembled Carolingian assemblies,[124] and so they
did too, as we have seen, in some of their more particular ones. The coincidence of assemblies with the great feasts of the church, the crown-wearing
associated with feast and assembly, the intermittent use of assemblies as
army muster-points, and the legislation often promulgated there, were
all features of tenth-century English gatherings that replicated those of
the Carolingian world. The legislation of Æthelstan and his successors is
particularly suggestive. Carrying forward a Carolingian tradition that had
been lost in continental Europe, it resembled the Carolingian capitularies
both in its general form and in some of its specific provisions: for example,
Æthelstan's laws relating to false coining and the ordeal appear to have had
Carolingian antecedents.[125] His assemblies clearly had some of their roots
in those of the preceding heptarchic kingdoms. But the closeness of these
resemblances might lead us to wonder whether the meetings convened by
Æthelstan, the first of a new kind, did not have those of Charlemagne and
his successors as their direct inspiration and model.[126] Much has rightly been
made of the extent to which the late Anglo-Saxon state apparently took
over and adapted many of the local features of Carolingian rule: the county
and the hundred, the general oath, the earl's third penny, estate surveys,
and danegeld, most of them first becoming visible on this side of the Channel in the tenth century.[127] These local borrowings (if that is what they

---

[123] For these later cases, see below, 66, 88, 116, 185.

[124] For Carolingian assemblies, see esp. Nelson, 'Legislation and Consensus in the Reign of Charles
the Bald'. Assemblies under Æthelstan appear to have been both larger and more frequent than those
of Charles the Bald: compare ibid. 100–2, with above, 4–6, 12–14.

[125] J. Campbell, 'Observations on English Government from the Tenth to the Twelfth Century', in
his *Essays in Anglo-Saxon History* (London, 1986), 159–61; Wormald, *Making*, 306; Reuter, 'Making of
England and Germany', 292.

[126] Cf. Wickham, *Inheritance of Rome*, 462.

[127] See Stubbs, *Constit. Hist.* i. 223–7, but more esp. Campbell, 'Observations on English Government', 159–70; id., 'The Significance of the Anglo-Norman State in the Administrative History of

were) strengthen the case for a comparable process of appropriation and adaptation at the centre. Æthelstan himself, the possessor of some important Carolingian relics and host to the exiled last descendant of the Carolingians, was almost self-consciously the heir of Charlemagne in his cultural interests, military prowess, and notions of empire.[128] His need for assemblies of a new scope and magnitude to share in the government of a 'new English king-dom, in so many ways the avatar of the Carolingians',[129] and one larger and less traversable than its more limited predecessors, may have been met by drawing on Carolingian prototypes. If we range rather more widely we can see too that the whole moralizing thrust of legislation, from Alfred's code onwards and including Æthelstan's laws, followed closely on from Carolin-gian example. Exhortatory and admonitory in their pronouncements, these kings, like Charlemagne and his successors, saw the enforcement of God's laws via their own as very much their business. Assemblies, the occasions for the promulgation of new law, had a central part to play in this process.[130]

Since most of the evidence for these continental connections surfaces late, after the final demise of the Carolingians and their empire, it is not easy to be sure about the channels of transmission. It would be carrying speculation to extremes to see Charlemagne (or even Charles the Bald) as much as part founders of the English parliament. Yet it was their style of government, including large-scale legislative assemblies, that in the tenth century was rebuilt on English soil.

It remains to be seen how far English assemblies also had an independent role in politics and government, and one which might even impose restraints on the king.

6. Kingship and the Constitution

The kingdom's great men played their most decisive political role during the usually brief interregnum separating one king's death from another's

Western Europe', in his *Essays in Anglo-Saxon History*, 182–4; id., 'The Late Anglo-Saxon State: A Maximum View', in his *Anglo-Saxon State*, 7. Cf. S. Reynolds, *Kingdoms and Communities in Western Europe, 900–1300*, 2nd edn. (Oxford, 1997), 224–5.

[128] Stenton, *Anglo-Saxon England*, 345; Wood, 'Making of King Aethelstan's Empire', *passim*, esp. 266–7; Wormald, *Making*, 445.

[129] Wormald, *Making*, 431.

[130] Ibid. 143, 223–4, 306–8, 345, 363, 417–29, 462–4. For the 'moralized political practice' of the Carolingians, see Wickham, *Inheritance of Rome*, 382–4, 555.

accession. That role was magnified when the succession was disputed and the strong elective element which always contributed to the accession of a new king correspondingly enhanced.[131] It may seem less immediately obvious that election was the work of a formally constituted assembly. When we read in Æthelweard's chronicle that Edward, Alfred's son, was chosen king by the chief men (*a primatis electus*), we might perhaps envisage an ad hoc gathering put together in a hurry.[132] But almost always the opposite seems to be true. Succeeding his brother Edmund in 946, Eadred became king 'by the election of the nobles (*electione optimatum*)'; and since the electing assembly comprised magnates from all parts of the kingdom, including Welsh princes and Scandinavian earls, it was clearly no last-minute expedient.[133] These two sources indicate that election preceded consecration; and in the pre-Conquest period election rather than consecration—which might take place some considerable time after the king's accession—was both the first and most essential act in king-making. The power thus vested in assemblies was another way in which their standing outstripped that of their successors after 1066, when coronation and consecration replaced election as the constitutive act.[134] Sometimes the assembly's authority, going beyond the right to elect, proceeded to sanction other contingent arrangements. On Edgar's death in 975 the assembly which chose Edward as his successor included, according to a later statement by King Æthelred, 'all the leading men of both orders', who made over to Æthelred, Edward's unchosen younger brother, the lands reserved for the king's sons, evidently a special holding set apart for the ætheling.[135] The statement is doubly suggestive of formal procedures and powers. In all these cases assemblies conducted themselves as politically responsible bodies, concerned to preserve order and continuity and to use their own authority to enhance that of the incoming king.

Could the assembly act independently to restrain the king? From the mid tenth century onwards kings were certainly subject to new constraints, first

---

[131] For the elective element in early kingship, see Liebermann, *National Assembly*, 54–7; Chadwick, *Anglo-Saxon Institutions*, 357–66; and J. L. Nelson, 'Inauguration Rituals', in her *Politics and Ritual*, 287, 289–91, 330–1.

[132] *The Chronicle of Æthelweard*, ed. and trans. A. Campbell (London, 1962), 51.

[133] S 520 (B 815); *EHD*, ed. Whitelock, no. 105; J. L. Nelson, 'Ritual and Reality in the Early Medieval *Ordines*', in her *Politics and Ritual*, 330 and n. 6.

[134] G. Garnett, 'Coronation and Propaganda: Some Implications of the Norman Claim to the Throne of England in 1066', *TRHS* 5th ser. 36 (1986), 92–3; id., 'Coronation', in *Blackwell Enc.* 123.

[135] S 937 (K 1312); *EHD*, ed. Whitelock, no. 123; D. N. Dumville, 'The Ætheling: A Study in Anglo-Saxon Constitutional History', *ASE* 8 (1979), 5–6.

moral, then political, and sometimes (to answer our question) collectively applied. Those constraints sprang from several sources: from the growing political influence of churchmen seeking to create a disciplined Christian society; from the exceptional powers which English kings were in the process of accruing—to judge, to punish, to tax, to coerce, and to abuse; and from the warfare of Æthelred's reign, when these powers were brought to bear on the king's subjects with little compensation in the way of national victories or even successful defence. Initially, before 973, the limitations on kingship, often Irish and Carolingian in their immediate origins, were no more than moral and admonitory in substance. Their written formulation derived in part from the 'vastly influential' early Irish tract 'On the Twelve Abuses of the World', usually known as 'Pseudo-Cyprian', which, among much else, laid down the norms for righteous kingship: the king should avoid oppression, judge justly, feed the poor, defend both the church and his country, and so on.[136] Much of this found its way into one of the earliest English homiletic works, the 'Constitutions of Archbishop Oda', a general statement of Christian principles for king, clergy, and people, written about 945 and evidently recited before King Edmund.[137] But it was only with Edgar's coronation at Bath in 973 that mere admonition began to acquire both prescriptive force and a premonitory and latent undertone of institutional restraint. The catalyst was the first appearance of the coronation oath, very probably drawn up for this occasion, and the root of much constitutional thinking for the rest of the middle ages. It bound the king by a threefold oath to defend the church, to root out wickedness, and to judge with justice and mercy: the core requirements of Pseudo-Cyprian made newly obligatory. From the time of Æthelred's coronation in 979, and probably from that of Edgar six years earlier, these injunctions were also incorporated into a vernacular homily preached to the new king by the archbishop. Since the oath-taking was a precondition of the public consecration which followed, a great assembly had witnessed the king's acceptance of formal limitations on his

---

[136] *Pseudo-Cyprianus, De XII Abusivi Saeculi*, ed. S. Hellmann (Leipzig, 1909), 51–3; R. Meens, 'Politics, Mirrors of Princes, and the Bible: Sins, Kings and the Well-Being of the Realm', *EME* 7 (1998), 349–52; Wormald, *Making*, 123, 448.

[137] *C. and S.* I: *AD. 871–1204*, ed. D. Whitelock, M. Brett, and C. N. L. Brooke, 2 vols. (Oxford, 1981), i. 67–74; Lawson, 'Archbishop Wulfstan and the Homiletic Element', 145. Cf. Wormald, *Making*, 306, 310, for other sources of Oda's 'Constitutions'.

powers.[138] In his acceptance and his magnates' approval an assembly-based consensus was established at the reign's outset.[139]

Through all this material ran the theme of good counsel, the king's need for it and his duty to take it, though admittedly only as one among many of the royal duties. The injunctions of Pseudo-Cyprian that the king should retain old, wise, and sober counsellors were complemented in Oda's 'Constitutions' (the king should have prudent counsellors, fearing God in their conduct of the kingdom's business) and repeated more or less verbatim in the coronation homily.[140] Archbishop Wulfstan of York, the inheritor and re-invigorator of this homiletic tradition, expanded on the theme and gave it a slightly more institutional twist in his *Institutes of Polity*, the first version of which was written between 1008 and 1014. The king must frequently seek out wisdom with his council (*witan*) and take counsel against violators of the law; for counsel was one of the eight columns supporting lawful kingship.[141] It is no surprise to find that Oda's 'Constitutions' survive in a manuscript compiled for Wulfstan.[142] Ælfric, the other great homilist of the period, writes similarly that the king would do well to call upon his counsellors and to follow their advice.[143] If the king's need for good counsel had thus become almost a cliché of homiletic discourse, it was none the less normative for that. Both the frequency and centrality of assemblies in the late Anglo-Saxon polity may in part have reflected the weight of moral exhortation now directed towards counsel-taking as a duty of kingship.

That there was some such connection between exhortation and practice is suggested by a development identified by Professor Pauline Stafford: the

---

[138] *Memorials of St Dunstan*, ed. Stubbs, 355–7; Byrhtferth, *Lives*, ed. Lapidge, 108–9; Nelson, 'The Second English Ordo', 369–73; P. Stafford, 'The Laws of Cnut and the History of Anglo-Saxon Royal Promises', *ASE* 10 (1982), 185–6; Wormald, *Making*, 447–8.

[139] J. L. Nelson, 'Liturgy or Law: Misconceived Alternatives?', in S. Baxter, C. E. Karkov, J. L. Nelson, and D. Pelteret (eds.), *Early Medieval Studies in Memory of Patrick Wormald* (Farnham, 2009), 445.

[140] Meens, 'Politics, Mirrors of Princes', 350; *C. and S.* I. i. 70; *Memorials of St Dunstan*, ed. Stubbs, 356–7.

[141] *Die 'Institutes of Polity, Civil and Ecclesiastical': Ein Werk Erzbischof Wulfstans von York*, ed. K. Jost (Bern, 1959), 48, 52–4; *Anglo-Saxon Prose*, ed. and trans. M. Swanton (London, 1975), 126–7. For the date, see Wormald, *Making*, 458 n. 153.

[142] *C. and S.* I. i. 67.

[143] M. Clayton, 'Ælfric and Æthelred', in J. Roberts and J. Nelson (eds.), *Essays on Anglo-Saxon and Related Themes in Memory of Lynne Grundy* (London, 2000), 81.

invoking of the counsel of the great men in many of Æthelred's early- and middle-period charters in order to justify or explain the acts which the charter recounts or validates. This goes well beyond the usual recording of the witnesses' consent. In confirming the privileges of Abingdon in 993, for example, the king acts 'inspired by grace and at the request of his great men, lay and ecclesiastic, and taking counsel with them', and, later in the charter, 'taking the advice of the great men'.[144] In sixteen charters issued between 990 and 1005 Æthelred states that he is acting with counsel. Typical is another charter recording a grant to Bishop Wulfsige of Sherborne, which begins 'I Æthelred . . . with the counsel of my bishops and great men and nobles . . .'.[145] No doubt one reason for this insistence on counsel was to put as much moral authority as possible behind some dubious transactions.[146] But the charters are also imbued with a new awareness on the king's part of the value of counsel as an essential constituent of his kingship; and this cannot but have owed something to the teaching of the reforming churchmen who, from Oda to Wulfstan, stood close to the throne and were regular attenders at the king's assemblies.

One effect of this new stress on the king's need for counsel, whether urged homiletically by high-minded churchmen seeking a truly Christian society or acknowledged by the king himself in his charters, was a concomitant if oblique emphasis on the need for assemblies. The coronation oath was taken, and the coronation homily preached, before a gathering of the kingdom's great men. Since both oath and homily were in the vernacular, and not in the Latin of the remainder of the coronation ritual,[147] they may have been intended to be immediately intelligible not only to the king but to the assembled congregation. The ideal of counsel subsequently articulated in the charters witnessed by the great made the association between counsel and assemblies still more explicit. If these developments created a growing awareness among those attending of the king's dependence on them, and hence of their own powers, it would hardly have been surprising.

By the end of Æthelred's reign that awareness had become powerfully evident. From being an advisory body, to which the king should look for good counsel, the assembly showed itself as one which—at least in

---

[144] Stafford, 'Political Ideas in Late Tenth-Century England', 73–6; S 876; *Charters of Abingdon*, ed. Kelly, no. 124.

[145] S 895; *Charters of Sherborne*, ed. M. A. O'Donovan, ASCh. III (Oxford, 1988), no. 11.

[146] Stafford, 'Political Ideas in Late Tenth-Century England', 73–4; Keynes, *Diplomas*, 200–2.

[147] Stafford, 'Laws of Cnut', 186.

special circumstances—might seek to impose its own terms on its ruler. The turning point came in 1014: a year of disasters in which the victories of the Danish king Swein, culminating in his capture of London, had forced Æthelred to take refuge overseas. What followed set a precedent for future bargaining between kings and councils. Æthelred was recalled from a brief exile in Normandy by 'all the councillors (*þa witan ealle*) who were in England'. In advance of his return he promised to be a gracious lord to his people and to reform what they all hated, on condition that they gave him their unqualified allegiance. John of Worcester adds that he also undertook to fall in with their advice.[148] These terms were clearly imposed by the councillors as the price of Æthelred's restoration. As Sir Frank Stenton long ago pointed out, they are 'of great constitutional interest as the first recorded pact between an English king and his subjects'.[149]

Such a pact was conceivable only *in extremis*; it was hardly a matter of routine, nor would it become so. Made possible only by Æthelred's desire to regain his throne, the price demanded was a reaction to royal rule judged to have been both unsuccessful in war and unjust in government. Æthelred's oppressive measures for his kingdom's defence, such as the levying of geld and the demand for more military gear as heriot (or death duty),[150] lay close to the heart of his problems and of his subjects' grievances. Yet the pact did not stand alone, for Cnut very probably, and remarkably, was made to accept the same conditions. Stafford has plausibly suggested that the precise terms for Æthelred's return, unstated in the Chronicle, are to be found in chapters 69 to 83 (the so-called 'alleviatory clauses') of Cnut's second law code of 1020 × 21.[151] These clauses offered relief from some of the abuses of royal government—the exaction of excessive heriots, the misbehaviour of the king's reeves, and other wrongs—which had certainly characterized Æthelred's later years. These terms, once accepted by Cnut and given a new sacrosanctity by their incorporation in a law code, may be regarded, Stafford argues, as a sort of 'coronation charter',[152] presumably designed to legitimize Cnut's kingship by showing that he was prepared to rule under the same restraints as his predecessor. If Henry I's coronation charter was

---

[148] *ASC*, ed. Whitelock, 93; *Two of the Saxon Chronicles*, ed. Plummer, i. 145; *John of Worcester*, ii. 478–9.

[149] Stenton, *Anglo-Saxon England*, 386.

[150] N. Brooks, 'Arms, Status and Warfare in Late Saxon England', in *Ethelred the Unready*, ed. Hill, 89–90; Wormald, *Making*, 362 and n. 441.

[151] *Laws*, ed. and trans. Robertson, 208–17; Stafford, 'Laws of Cnut', 176–82.

[152] Stafford, 'Laws of Cnut', 179–82.

'a political gesture', so was this.[153] Although the whole code was the work of Wulfstan, it was formally made 'with the advice of [Cnut's] councillors' in a Christmas gathering at Winchester.[154] The homiletic, legislative, and conciliar elements in English government had moved into alignment in order to establish a royal rule that was intended to be both morally just and politically acceptable.

The striking of an earlier bargain between Cnut and the great men of the kingdom is implied in the account of events following Æthelred's death in April 1016. The Chronicle tells us that his son Edmund Ironside was then chosen as king by the councillors (*witan*) in London and by the London garrison (*burhwaru*).[155] But John of Worcester adds that what was obviously a much larger body of bishops, abbots, ealdormen, and other magnates elected Cnut as king, came to him at Southampton, renounced Æthelred's descendants, and swore fealty to Cnut, after which he swore to be a faithful lord to them.[156] This looks like a contractual arrangement parallel to, and perhaps based upon, Æthelred's agreement with 'all the councillors' on his return to England in 1014. In both cases the incomer promised to be a gracious or loyal lord (*hold hlaford*—Chronicle, 1014; *fidelis dominus*—John of Worcester, 1016); a reciprocal undertaking was made by the council; and the agreement was sealed with mutual oaths. Following Edmund's death later in 1016, those present at a further assembly in London attested, at Cnut's prompting, that Edmund had wished Cnut to be regent for his two sons, and then swore that they were willing to have Cnut as their king.[157]

This whole sequence of events, from Æthelred's conditional return to the election of Cnut and the subsequent issuing of his law code, with its 'alleviatory' clauses, suggests that a peculiar *conjoncture* of invasion, oppressive government, political crises, and succession disputes had given the crown's greatest subjects a good deal of bargaining power. This they exercised collectively, through assemblies which were able to name their terms and to demand guarantees of good government as the price of their recognition. Under the pressure of circumstance, and fortified by the moral weight of Wulfstan's authority, which was in part the product of the same

[153] Wormald, *Making*, 400–1.
[154] *Laws of the Kings of England*, ed. and trans. Robertson, 154–5; Wormald, *Making*, 349–55.
[155] *ASC*, ed. Whitelock, 95; *Two of the Saxon Chronicles*, ed. Plummer, i. 148–9; Chadwick, *Anglo-Saxon Institutions*, 359 and n. 1.
[156] *John of Worcester*, ii. 484–5.   [157] Ibid. 494–5.

pressure, the traditional elective element in kingship had hardened into a notion of formal and external restraints which went beyond the internal and weaker bonds of the coronation oath.

The elements of formal conciliar procedures, though not of restraints, were seen again in the events which followed Cnut's death in 1035. Once again, the background was a disputed succession. An assembly of 'all the councillors (*ealra witena gemot*)', meeting at Oxford, divided over the succession; Earl Leofric and the thegns of Mercia chose Harold, Cnut's son by Ælfgifu of Northampton (though as regent rather than king); Earl Godwine and the 'chief men' of Wessex chose Harthacnut, his son by Emma, his queen; the difference of opinion was prolonged; the Mercian championship of Harold eventually carried the day; but it was agreed that Wessex should remain to Harthacnut, then absent in Denmark, under his mother's guardianship. As Dr Ann Williams has pointed out, 'the language of the Chronicle implies a formal assembly, a debate and a corporate decision':[158] a rare insight into how assemblies worked, and the circumstances of evacuated royal power in which, as in 1014–16, their initiative was at its strongest. In such situations the assembly held the ring. It was equally remarkable that what was evidently a large number of thegns shared in that initiative. In a matter as momentous as the succession to the throne it was not only the very great who had a voice.

One final episode provides a tailpiece to the series of 'constitutional occasions' which had begun with Æthelred's return in 1014. The Anglo-Norman author of the legal collection known as 'Quadripartitus', written by about 1109 but probably begun before 1100, tells us that when Edward the Confessor was recalled to England in 1041 through the good offices of Bishop Ælfwine of Winchester and Earl Godwine, after his long exile in Normandy, he was met at a place called 'Hursteshevet'—almost certainly Hurst Head on the Hampshire coast—by 'the thegns of all England (*totius Angliae baronibus*)'. There he was told that he would be accepted as king only if he guaranteed on oath to maintain the laws of Cnut; and it is strongly implied, though not directly stated, that he did so. There is good reason to think that this terse account is broadly

---

[158] *ASC*, ed. Whitelock, 102–3; *Two of the Saxon Chronicles*, ed. Plummer, i. 159–60; Williams, 'Some Notes and Considerations', 161–2. Cf. *John of Worcester*, ii. 520–2, who omits the Oxford council, but reports a decision to divide the kingdom by lot (which is not incompatible with the report in the Chronicle).

reliable.[159] It shows us an assembly, probably more of a deputation than a full-blown council, meeting unconventionally on what was a sand spit jutting into the Solent in order to impose on a returning exile terms intended to govern his future role as king. The situation was clearly parallel to Æthelred's return, also from Normandy, some twenty-seven years earlier, which indeed the initiators of the Hurst Head meeting may well have had in mind. That the terms took the form of sworn adherence to the laws of Cnut is especially striking; for Cnut's laws were not only in the process of acquiring the status of 'the good old law', the totemic if undefined standard of good government, but they also embodied the specific 'alleviatory' clauses which, if Stafford is right, had probably been imposed on Æthelred in 1014 and were certainly accepted by Cnut in 1020 or 1021. Here again we can see restraints which went beyond the merely moral imperatives of the coronation oath and of homiletic exhortation, to take on an institutional shape via an assembly.

Between Edgar's coronation in 973, when the coronation oath was first sworn, and Edward the Confessor's return to England in 1041, when 'the thegns of all England' demanded the maintenance of Cnut's laws as the price of Edward's future kingship, there had been a critical shift in both political thinking and political practice. It is this period, rather than any later one, which sees 'the origins of the constitutional tradition in England': the emergence of that nexus of limitations and restraints on royal authority which Sir James Holt has dated to the Norman Conquest and the subsequent coronation charters of the twelfth century.[160] The degree to which those coronation charters had been anticipated, possibly in form and certainly in substance, by Cnut's laws has already been pointed out. But Cnut's laws were tributary to a larger stream which flowed from the traditional elective and consultative role of the king's great men, as well as from coronation promises, the moral teaching of churchmen who sought to shape both kingship and society to Christian ends, and the political opportunities offered to the king's subjects by his need for support when his throne was subject to threats or competition. What

[159] J. R. Maddicott, 'Edward the Confessor's Return to England in 1041', *EHR* 119 (2004), 650–66. For the date of 'Quadripartitus' see R. Sharpe, 'The Prefaces of "Quadripartitus" ', in G. Garnett and J. Hudson (eds.), *Law and Government in Medieval England and Normandy: Essays in Honour of Sir James Holt* (Cambridge, 1994), 150–1.
[160] J. C. Holt, 'The Origins of the Constitutional Tradition in England', in his *Magna Carta and Medieval Government* (London, 1985), 1–22, esp. 13–18.

materialized was a collective process in which those assembled, the king's councillors, moved from being a passive audience, as they probably were at coronations, towards a more active bargaining role. In time the procedures thus haltingly established would re-emerge in the parliamentary relations of king and nobility.

In all this there was no radical undermining of the generally consensual role of assemblies. They could strike bargains and impose terms only in exceptional circumstances. The acceptance of those terms, whether by Æthelred, Cnut, or Edward, was in itself a mark of consensus and a means to establishing a new *modus vivendi* between the king and his much governed subjects. Even in kingship's vacuum, as in the period following Cnut's death, an assembly divided by faction could be brought to a united decision. Debate was the substitute for what might have been civil war in societies where councils and consensus counted for less. The old ideal of political harmony was not incompatible with the new move towards constitutional restraints.

7. The Eve of the Conquest

Between Edward the Confessor's conditional return from Normandy in 1041 and the Norman Conquest changes in the working of assemblies were mainly a matter of development rather than of anything more fundamental or innovatory. Our sources are more exiguous than hitherto, largely because we have fewer charters and no law codes to offer guidance on participants, places, and policies.[161] But within these limitations the solid shape of large assemblies combining ceremonial, social, and judicial functions with 'parliamentary' type involvement in national affairs continues to be clearly discernible. The number of those attending, when the existence of charters allows them to be assessed, remains high. The most fully attested surviving charter of the period was Edward's 1044 grant of Dawlish in Devon to Leofric, the future bishop of Exeter, witnessed by the king himself, the two archbishops, five bishops, five abbots, four earls, nine *nobiles* (including Harold and Tostig), and twenty-six thegns: fifty-one in

---

[161] Keynes, *Atlas of Attestations*, table XXVI (3); id., *Diplomas*, 140–4. For possible explanations for the absence of law codes, see Campbell, 'Late Anglo-Saxon State', 23, and Maddicott, 'Edward the Confessor's Return', 666.

all.[162] The second surviving charter of the reign, a grant to Abingdon in 1043, had a witness list numbering forty-nine men, including seventeen thegns.[163] The murder of one of the leading figures of the north, the thegn Cospatric, at the Christmas court of 1064 suggests that the great festal assemblies were still used to draw in important men from the kingdom's periphery, just as they had been under Æthelstan and Edgar.[164] Although the numbers do not match the exceptional tallies of charter witnesses listed by the 'Æthelstan A' scribe, or of those appearing on some of Edgar's and Æthelred's diplomas, the Confessor's assemblies were nonetheless well-attended occasions. In other ways too they continued to resemble their predecessors. The condemnation of Earl Swein, Godwine's son, as *nithing*, a scoundrel disgraced, by the king and 'all the host' in 1051, possibly at Winchester, showed that armies and assemblies might still merge, in this case not as the prelude to a campaign but to do justice.[165]

Some evolutionary change is perhaps perceptible in the regularity of assembly meetings and in their ceremonial side. Festal assemblies are now sometimes more routinely visible, though probably not more routine, than they had been in the past. In 1062 the ecclesiastical business of the papal legates then visiting England, including the securing of Wulfstan's consent to his election as bishop of Worcester, was deferred 'until the royal court of the approaching Easter': clearly a fixed point in the political calendar.[166] When, in 1065, Robert fitz Wimarc wrongfully alienated to his son-in-law land belonging to the canons of Bromfield, Edward ordered the restoration of the land to the church, waiting 'until, at the imminent Christmas court', he could order Robert to provide other land for the deprived man.[167] Predictable and established, the Christmas court would be the occasion for the transaction of a minor piece of business combining politics and justice. Both these cases anticipate the common thirteenth-century practice

---

[162] S 1003; J. B. Davidson, 'On Some Anglo-Saxon Charters at Exeter', *Jnl. of the British Archaeological Assoc.* 39 (1883), 292–5.

[163] S 999; *Charters of Abingdon*, ed. Kelly, no. 142.

[164] *John of Worcester*, ii. 596–9; F. Barlow, *Edward the Confessor* (London, 1970), 235. For Cospatric, see also W. E. Kapelle, *The Norman Conquest of the North* (London, 1979), 43, 94–5. For northerners at earlier assemblies, above, 7–8, 26.

[165] *ASC*, ed. Whitelock, 114 (C); *Two of the Saxon Chronicles*, ed. Plummer, i. 171; Barlow, *Edward the Confessor*, 235.

[166] *John of Worcester*, ii. 590–1; William of Malmesbury, *Saints' Lives*, ed. M. Winterbottom and R. M. Thomson, OMT (Oxford, 2002), 42–5.

[167] R. Fleming, *Domesday Book and the Law: Society and Legal Custom in Early Medieval England* (Cambridge, 1998), 224–5, no. 1319; Wormald, 'Handlist', 270, no. 98.

of deferring contentious or difficult matters to a forthcoming session of parliament.[168]

The predictability of festal assemblies was thrown into sharper relief by their role as a setting for ceremonies which may have become more elaborate under Edward. Crown-wearing becomes visible once more as an assembly practice. The gap in its history since the mid tenth century is partly bridged by the story, recorded by Goscelin of Canterbury, of how Cnut once came to Winchester for the Easter festivities, but instead of wearing his crown, as would have been appropriate, he renounced it and placed it on a crucifixion head of Christ. If our source can be trusted—and Goscelin's writing c.1090 should not put him out of court—this little vignette not only shows Cnut's adoption of an English royal custom but also provides the earliest evidence for Winchester's association with the king's Easter crown-wearing, otherwise vouched for only from the reign of William I.[169] But it is not until the reign of the Confessor that we once again come across a small clutch of references to crown-wearing. The author of the *Carmen de Hastingae Proelio*, now rehabilitated as an early and trustworthy source written only about two years after Hastings, could speak of the Conqueror's being attracted to Westminster as a place where 'kings were accustomed to wear their crown'.[170] William of Malmesbury tells us that Edward wore his crown in London, presumably at Westminster, on Christmas Day 1066, shortly before his death.[171] Another late writer, from Bury St Edmunds, interpolating material after 1131 into a copy of John of Worcester, introduces a miracle story by relating how Edward wore his crown during the Easter Day service at Westminster and continued to wear it at the feast which followed.[172] Though all three of these authors wrote after 1066, they clearly believed that crown-wearing had been a conventional and customary part of festal celebrations in the Confessor's reign. Given that the practice was already well established in the tenth century and attested with reasonable certainty under Cnut, it is hard to

---

[168] Below, 184–6.

[169] D. W. Rollason, 'Goscelin of Canterbury's Account of the Translation and Miracles of St Mildrith (BHL 5961/4): An Edition with Notes', *Mediaeval Studies*, 48 (1986), 140, 163; Lawson, *Cnut*, 134. For post-Conquest crown-wearings at Winchester, see below, 57–9.

[170] *The Carmen de Hastingae Proelio of Guy, Bishop of Amiens*, ed. and trans. F. Barlow, OMT (Oxford, 1999), 40–1. For authorship and date, see ibid., pp. xxiv–xlii.

[171] William of Malmesbury, *Gesta Regum*, i. 418–19.

[172] *The Life of King Edward*, ed. and trans. F. Barlow, 2nd edn., OMT (Oxford, 1992), pp. xli, 102–3; *John of Worcester*, ii. 648.

think that such an effective demonstration of royal charisma would have been later abandoned.

Edward's own style and image appear to have been more self-consciously regal, even imperial, than those of any other late Anglo-Saxon king except perhaps Æthelstan. The author of the *Vita Ædwardi* tells us that his clothes were of unparalleled splendour and his throne covered with cloth of gold.[173] He commissioned Spearhavoc, abbot of Abingdon and a famous craftsman, to make him a new 'imperial' crown, fashioned out of 'plenty of gold and chosen gems', probably about 1050.[174] His pendant seal, almost certainly the first of its kind in England, showed the king enthroned with orb and sceptre, an image repeated, again uniquely, on Edward's 'Sovereign/Martlets' coinage of the late 1050s.[175] His crown, sceptre, and 'royal ring' were among the regalia found when his tomb was opened in 1102.[176] Both on his seal and on some of his charters he is styled 'basileus', the revival of an imperial title much more frequently used by his tenth-century predecessors. Less frequently his title embodied the old claim to rule all Britain: 'rex totius Brittanniae'.[177] There is enough here to suggest that he took a particularly elevated view of his royal office, perhaps, like the Ottonians (but unlike Æthelstan), in reaction to the practical weaknesses of his situation;[178] and that he would not have neglected the potentialities of crown-wearing.

That Edward almost certainly went further to enhance the ceremony we now know, thanks to the pioneering work of Professor Michael Lapidge and Mr Michael Hare. The latter has persuasively argued that in Edward's middle and later years crown-wearing may have been accompanied by the singing of the *laudes regiae*, the great acclamations of divine and earthly kingship used by the Carolingians and thence by the Ottonians, and formerly thought to have been introduced into England only after the

---

[173] *Life of King Edward*, ed. and trans. Barlow, 24–5.

[174] *Historia Ecclesie Abbendonensis, The History of the Church of Abingdon*, ed. and trans. J. Hudson, 2 vols., OMT (Oxford, 2002–7), i. 196–9; Barlow, *Edward the Confessor*, 106; C. R. Dodwell, *Anglo-Saxon Art: A New Perspective* (Manchester, 1982), 46–7, 257 n. 26.

[175] B. B. Rezak, 'The King Enthroned: A New Theme in Anglo-Saxon Royal Iconography: The Seal of Edward the Confessor and its Political Implications', in J. Rosenthal (ed.), *Acta*, xi: *Kings and Kingship* (New York, 1986), 60–2.

[176] 'La Vie de S. Édouard le Confesseur par Osbert de Clare', ed. M. Bloch, *Analecta Bollandiana*, 41 (1923), 121–2; J. A. Robinson, *Gilbert Crispin, Abbot of Westminster* (Cambridge, 1911), 24–5.

[177] Rezak, 'The King Enthroned', 65; Barlow, *Edward the Confessor*, 135–7.

[178] Leyser, 'Ritual, Ceremony and Gesture', 192–5; Wormald, 'Germanic Power Structures', 108; above, 21.

Conquest. Their importer was very probably Ealdred, bishop of Worcester from 1046 to 1060 and then archbishop of York, and in 1054 Edward's envoy on a visit to Cologne which may have familiarized him with German royal ritual. A man with a perceptible interest in royal ceremonial, Ealdred possessed a manuscript containing the first surviving English text of the *laudes*, as Lapidge has shown; and he may even have remodelled the crown-wearing ceremony to take account of this new means of elevating his master's theocratic authority.[179]

There is much here to suggest that Edward may have had a special interest in crown-wearing, and nothing which goes against the grain of his known inclinations. Any multiplication of the elements of royal display, such as the singing of the *laudes*, would have enhanced the importance of the assemblies which provided display with its necessary setting and audience. As in the tenth century, however, high ceremony at assemblies continued to be combined with socializing, eating, and drinking. The Bury writer's story shows how the king might wear his crown while actually feasting, just as Eadwig had done at his coronation in 956, and it was during an Easter feast at Winchester in 1053 that Godwine died, seated at table with the king and the earl's three sons, Harold, Tostig, and Gyrth.[180] The sort of entertainment which may have been provided on these occasions, unknown for the tenth century, is illuminated by the curious but highly circumstantial story in the much later *Longer Saga of King Olaf Tryggvason* of how Edward 'made it a custom to relate the Saga of Olaf Tryggvason to his great men and his bodyguard on the first day of Easter': a story important because it shows the attendance at festal assemblies of a hitherto unseen group, the housecarles who lived at the king's court.[181]

But the assembly also continued to provide a more formal stage for political manoeuvre and decision-making, in ways which were certainly not new but which are more difficult to perceive for earlier reigns. This was most clearly shown during the reign's great crisis of 1051–2, when Earl Godwine and his sons were first exiled and then restored. At every stage in the crisis, assembly decisions moved the action forward. During

[179] M. Lapidge, 'Ealdred of York and MS. Cotton Vitellius E. XII', in his *Anglo-Latin Literature*, 453–66; Hare, 'Kings, Crowns and Festivals', 49–52. For the view that the *laudes* was a post-Conquest importation, see H. E. J. Cowdrey, 'The Anglo-Norman *Laudes Regiae*', in his *Popes, Monks and Crusaders* (London, 1984), viii, esp. 48–52.
[180] Above, 23–5; *ASC*, ed. Whitelock, 127; *John of Worcester*, ii. 572–3.
[181] C. E. Wright, *The Cultivation of Saga in Anglo-Saxon England* (Edinburgh, 1939), 66–7; *Life of King Edward*, ed. and trans. Barlow, 102 n. 156.

the first confrontation between Edward and Godwine in Gloucestershire in September 1051 it was 'the councillors' (*witan*) who advised the king to make peace and who, in conjunction with Edward, issued summonses for a later meeting in London.[182] But before the meeting could convene Godwine and his sons fled overseas, having been refused the hostages which he needed to guarantee his safe conduct to the meeting.[183] At the council meeting (*witena gemot*) the king and 'all the army' declared Godwine an outlaw.[184] Next year, however, he returned and at a 'big council'—*mycel gemot* in the 'E' version of the Chronicle, *witena gemot* in 'C' and 'D'—held outside London (at Westminster, according to the *Vita Ædwardi*) and attended by 'all the earls and the chief men who were in the country', Godwine expounded his case, cleared himself of the charges against him, and was readmitted to royal favour on the advice of the council.[185]

Throughout this dramatic period events turned on the decisions of councils. The initial peace with Godwine, the summoning of a further meeting in London, the outlawry of Godwine, and his subsequent restoration, all rested on conciliar advice. In some instances the will of the council appears to have counted for more than the king's. The restoration of Godwine seems to have been contrary to the king's wishes, at least initially,[186] and the subsequent decision to outlaw Edward's Norman friends, but to allow him to retain those who were loyal, was wholly conciliar.[187] It was not only during an interregnum that the political initiative might lie with an assembly.

Behind this conciliar façade, however, we should probably see the manoeuvrings of faction. Both in Gloucestershire and later in London Earls Leofric and Siward and their forces appear to have guided decisions; hence the revealing equation of the council with the army at the time of Godwine's expulsion. Yet those attending were not only from the midland and northern earldoms of these two great men but from 'elsewhere' as well.[188] As with the council meeting and debate following Cnut's death in 1035, and as also with Edward the Confessor's seashore meeting with

---

[182] *ASC*, ed. Whitelock, 118-20 (D, E); *Two of the Saxon Chronicles*, ed. Plummer, i. 174 (E).

[183] *ASC*, ed. Whitelock, 119-21 (D, E).

[184] Ibid. 119 (D); *Two of the Saxon Chronicles*, ed. Plummer, i. 175.

[185] *ASC*, ed. Whitelock, 124, 126; *Two of the Saxon Chronicles*, ed. Plummer, i. 180, 183; *Life of King Edward*, ed. and trans. Barlow, 44-5.

[186] *ASC*, ed. Whitelock, 125 (E).   [187] Ibid. 124 (C, D).

[188] Ibid. 118-19 (D); Campbell, 'Late Anglo-Saxon State', 19-21: S. Baxter, *The Earls of Mercia: Lordship and Power in Late Anglo-Saxon England* (Oxford, 2007), 41-2.

'the thegns of all England' in 1041, participation in these great events
seems to have been broadly based. That was perhaps what helped to make
conciliar decisions both authoritative and conducive to peace. The council's
activities were marked too by a high degree of procedural formality: the
issuing of summonses, the handing over of Godwine's thegns to the king
at his request,[189] the apparent willingness of the king to offer safe-conducts
but not hostages to ensure Godwine's appearance before the council, the
outlawry of Godwine by the council, and then, in the 1052 assembly, the
formal response of Godwine to the charges against him. To a marked degree
the council combined factional conflict with constitutional propriety; and
it is not too far-fetched to see propriety keeping conflict within bounds.
The later Chronicle accounts of Earl Ælfgar's expulsion in 1055, for reasons
probably connected with his family's rivalry with the house of Godwine,
again show the council pronouncing a formal verdict of outlawry and
exile.[190] Had these accounts been less terse and gnomic, we might have
been able to see the same processes at work.

The council's role in 1051–2 was a sort of coda to the increasingly
large and independent part which assemblies had played in politics since
Æthelred's return in 1014. In John of Worcester's remark that when
peace had been made between king and earl in 1052 'they promised
a just law to the whole people', there is even a hint of the sort of
general concessions that Æthelred had made in 1014, that Cnut had
confirmed in his law code, and that Edward himself had reiterated on
his return to England in 1041.[191] But in one respect there was material
change rather than insensible development in the history of Edward's
assemblies. In a transition which had begun before his accession, they
now almost always met in towns rather than in rural vills. From Cnut's
reign onwards, and to some extent as far back as Æthelred's, the rural
assembly places in western and southern England favoured by Æthelstan
and his successors drop out of the picture, to be replaced by London and
a variety of other towns, especially perhaps Gloucester and Oxford. Of the
twenty-two places where assemblies and festal courts are known, or can
reasonably be supposed, to have convened during Edward's reign, London
or Westminster saw seven meetings, Gloucester five, Winchester two,
Windsor two, and Canterbury, Lincoln, Northampton, and Oxford one

[189] *ASC*, ed. Whitelock, 121 (E); Campbell, 'Late Anglo-Saxon State', 20.
[190] *ASC*, ed. Whitelock, 130 (C, D, E); Baxter, *Earls of Mercia*, 45–6.
[191] 'Omni populo rectam legem promiserunt': *John of Worcester*, ii. 570–1.

each.[192] Between 1015 and 1035 we could add another two meetings at Oxford.[193] Edward's kingship in general was by no means exclusively town-based. The functioning food-rent system in some of the counties of historic Wessex implies that he still travelled extensively, especially perhaps to hunt.[194] One of his very few known rural assemblies, at the royal manor of Britford in Wiltshire, came in the aftermath of a hunting expedition and in the emergency circumstances of the 1065 rebellion by the northerners.[195] But when he wanted to gather his great men around him he more usually chose towns.

There were some obvious reasons for his choice. In general, towns were now a more prominent feature of the landscape than had been the case a hundred years earlier. Growing in size, they were probably better placed to accommodate the very large numbers likely to have attended assemblies—and here we should think of servants and retainers as well as active participants. In particular, Edward's own religious and regal interests drew him towards towns. At Westminster the rebuilding of the abbey and the building of the palace—scene of the 1052 council where Godwine was restored[196]—provided his court with a central place which now rivalled, if not outstripped, Winchester in importance. It is striking that the three crown-wearing episodes associated with Edward are all located at Westminster. Towns as assembly places were more consonant with the dignity of Edward's kingship, and with the crown-wearing ceremonies which he and Ealdred may have amplified, than were the rural estate centres utilized by his predecessors. More specifically, the minster at Gloucester, rebuilt by Eadred, may have been intended to provide a grand setting for crown-wearing and the new *laudes regiae*.[197] Gloucester was possibly, and Westminster more certainly, being transformed into the sort of monastery-palace complex which the Ottonians had possessed at Quedlinburg and Magdeburg but which had been unknown to the kings of

---

[192] Based on the list of royal councils and their meeting places in Wormald, *Making*, 434; the list of festal assembly places in M. Biddle, 'Seasonal Festivals and Residence: Winchester, Westminster and Gloucester in the Tenth to Twelfth Centuries', *ANS* 8 (1986), 69; and the possible additional Christmas court at Gloucester in 1059 noted by Hare, 'Kings, Crowns and Festivals', 52. Only Wormald's list (15 places) can be regarded as definitive; place-dates noted for assemblies by the other two authorities cannot always be regarded as certain.

[193] *ASC*, ed. Whitelock, 102; Wormald, *Making*, 433.

[194] P. A. Stafford, 'The "Farm of One Night" and the Organisation of King Edward's Estates in Domesday', *Economic History Review*, 33 (1980), 491–502.

[195] *Life of King Edward*, ed. and trans. Barlow, 78–9.

[196] Ibid. 44.   [197] Hare, 'Kings, Crowns and Festivals', 51–2.

tenth-century England.[198] Gloucester, Westminster, and Winchester were already beginning to be associated with the special festal assemblies; though only with the two certain and three possible Christmas visits of the king and court to Gloucester can we begin to see the association of particular places with particular feasts which was to become slightly more obvious after the Conquest.[199] Yet in these general circumscriptions, from rural to urban and from a miscellany of towns to a few, post-Conquest developments are already foreshadowed.

There was, therefore, nothing that was precisely new about Edward's assemblies. The probable enlargement of their ceremonial role, their more frequent location in towns, and their place at the heart of political relationships were all evolutionary changes, growing from past practice. Even so, their effect was to set the assembly still more firmly within the matrix of English government and to provide a model for Edward's successors.

8. 'The Witan of the English People'

For a period of nearly 150 years, from Æthelstan's accession in 924 to Edward the Confessor's death in 1066, central assemblies summoned by the king played a crucial part in the management of the English polity. Drawing the king's great men and others less great into the government of the realm, they both overtopped and complemented the local assemblies of shire and hundred which drew the freemen of the shires into its government at a subordinate level. Both exemplified a society where participation in the processes of the state was, by comparison with any other European country, uniquely widespread. It was one where the early Germanic tradition of large assemblies in which non-noble freemen had some part to play not only survived but flourished, while elsewhere in Europe during the late tenth and eleventh centuries that tradition failed, as 'assembly politics slowly turned into the politics of royal and princely courts'.[200] From the start of the period the regularity and frequency of the meetings of central assemblies, and the broad but consistent range of their business, gave them

---

[198] Leyser, *Rule and Conflict*, 90–1; above, 18. For the palace and monastic church at Gloucester, see N. Baker and R. Holt, *Urban Growth and the Medieval Church: Gloucester and Worcester* (Aldershot, 2004), 20–1, 24.

[199] Hare, 'Kings, Crowns and Festivals', 52; below, 58–9, 71.

[200] Campbell, 'Late Anglo-Saxon State', 12–13; Wormald, 'Germanic Power Structures', 116–19; Wickham, *Inheritance of Rome*, 451–2, 522.

the character of an institution. These features should in themselves inhibit us from regarding assemblies as no more than gatherings of the king's 'wise men': the literal translation of the word 'witan' almost always used in laws, charters, and the narratives of the Chronicle, and often too in poetry and homiletic prose, to describe this body. Its members were not merely 'witan'; they comprised 'the witan'.

A minor development in linguistic usage in the three extant versions of the Chronicle may suggest a hardening of that institutional sense towards the end of the period. Between 1035 and 1055 the Chronicle uses the relatively new term 'witena gemot', 'witan meeting', on nine occasions to describe central assemblies. That four of these fell within the critical years 1051–2, and that three are used for the great Oxford meeting following Cnut's death and for the 1055 meeting which saw the condemnation and exiling of Ælfgar, hints that the perceptions of an institution implicit in this consistent pattern were shaped and intensified by political crisis.[201] The only two earlier uses of the term support these institutional connotations. In the Epilogue to his Old English translation of the Book of Judges, written between 1001 and 1005, Ælfric uses 'witena gemot' to denote the Roman senate;[202] while in his *Grammar* he employs the same term again for 'sinodus', a word often used in Latin sources for a national assembly.[203] By contrast, the Alfredian translation of Orosius, written probably in the 890s, had left the senate as 'senatus' in the English version.[204] With only nine pre-Conquest examples, the term 'witena gemot', if not the thing, remains a rarity, contrary to the popular misapprehension that it was a standard usage. But it is employed in a sufficiently uniform way, and in sufficiently similar contexts, to suggest that contemporaries had a clear sense of the 'witena gemot' as a body with a defined identity and role.

Contributing to the witan's institutional quality was an emerging view of its status as a national assembly, a body which in several senses stood for England. This view crystallized in the tenth century as the range and scope of royal government extended beyond its original West Saxon and

---

[201] *Two of the Saxon Chronicles*, ed. Plummer, i. 159 (1035, E), 171 (1050, C), 174–5 (1051, D, E), 180–1 (1052, C, D), 184–5 (1055, C, E); Wormald, *Making*, 94 and n. 326.

[202] *The Old English Version of the Heptateuch*, ed. S. J. Crawford, EETS 160 (London, 1922), 415; Wormald, *Making*, 94 n. 326. For the date, see Dumville, *Wessex and England*, 141.

[203] *Aelfrics Grammatik und Glossar*, ed. J. Zupita (Berlin, 1880), 30. For the use of 'sinodus', see Barlow, *English Church, 1000–1066*, 137 and n. 2.

[204] *The Old English Orosius*, ed. J. Bately, EETS, Supplementary ser. 6 (Oxford, 1980), pp. xcii, 388–9; Abels, *Alfred the Great*, 261 and n. 8.

Mercian heartland. The notion of *Angelcynn*, 'the English people', was already becoming established under Alfred, and beginning to take on a strongly political and national colouring, before 'the making of England' which justified it but which followed only with the conquests of the next generation.[205] A cognate usage quickly attached itself to the witan. As early as the 880s, the body assenting to Alfred and Guthrum's peace could be described as *ealles Angelcynnes witan*, 'the witan of all the English people'.[206] Within a hundred years, as 'the English people' moved from aspiration towards reality, this phrase had become almost a commonplace. The 'Ordinance concerning the Dunsæte', a treaty between the English and Welsh of south-west Herefordshire made about 930 but set down in a text dating from Æthelred's reign, records its making by *Angelcynnes witan*, 'the witan of the English people'.[207] It was *yldestan Angel cynnes witan* 'the senior witan of the English people', who, according to the Chronicle, fell through the floor of their upper-room meeting place at Calne in 978; and it is the Chronicle too which tells us that Æthelred was consecrated in the following year with much rejoicing by *Angel cynnes witon*.[208] According to a letter written by Dunstan to Æthelred in the 980s, it was *eall Anglecynnes witena* which had formerly agreed to the division of the West Saxon sees under Edward the Elder.[209] The law code V Æthelred, issued in 1008, is headed in one version *Be Angolwitena gerednesse*, 'On the decrees of the English witan'.[210] Finally, we have already seen that it was *totius Angliae baronibus*, 'the thegns of all England', described in what seems to be the Latin equivalent of the vernacular phrase, who were deemed to have come together to impose terms on Edward the Confessor when he returned to England in 1041.[211]

After a possible early appearance under Æthelstan, 'the witan of the English people' thus moves into common usage from the 970s, and in a wide range of contexts, official and unofficial: legal texts, the Chronicle,

[205] S. Foot, 'The Making of *Angelcynn*: English Identity before the Norman Conquest', *TRHS* 6th ser. vi (1996), 25–49; ead., 'English People', in *Blackwell Enc.* 170–1.
[206] *Die Gesetze der Angelsachsen*, ed. F. Liebermann, 3 vols. (Halle, 1903–16), i. 126; *EHD*, ed. Whitelock, no. 34.
[207] *Gesetze*, ed. Liebermann, i. 374, trans. in F. Noble, *Offa's Dyke Reviewed*, ed. M. Gelling, BAR, British ser. 114 (Oxford, 1983), 104–9. For the Ordinance's date and purpose, see Wormald, *Making*, 381–2, and A. Williams, *Kingship and Government in Pre-Conquest England, c.500–1066* (Basingstoke, 1999), 94.
[208] *Two of the Saxon Chronicles*, ed. Plummer, i. 123; *ASC*, ed. Whitelock, 79–80.
[209] S 1296; *C. and S.* i. i. 170.   [210] *Gesetze*, ed. Liebermann, i. 236; Wormald, *Making*, 431.
[211] Above, 39–40.

the letter of an archbishop. Its emergence reflects in the first place a growing sense of national identity, of the English as one nation, which was mainly a result of political and cultural circumstance: the conquest of the Danelaw, the spread of common administrative institutions, the existence of a common language, religion, and currency. More particularly, it also reflected the real nature of these assemblies, drawing in as they did magnates and churchmen from all parts of the kingdom, and superseding other rival groupings with earlier claims to speak for England's constituent parts. The Mercian witan, for example, makes its last appearance in 957, during the brief period of Edgar's semi-autonomous rule in Mercia.[212] Geographically comprehensive and socially diverse, the witan could be regarded as 'of the English people' without too much in the way of hyperbole or wishful thinking. But more remarkable is the development in political notions which the phrase implies. The witan is seen as a representative body—not, of course, in any elective way, but in the sense that those attending were seen to stand for a whole people, the English. That great men in their assemblies spoke for all was becoming a commonplace in the medieval West,[213] but in no other country was their spokesmanship linked so clearly to a single people with a distinctive identity—in effect, a nation.

The idea of representation, however, was more than merely notional. In the reigns of both Æthelred and Cnut the action of the witan in negotiating with the king appears to have elicited a royal response directed to a much wider audience than that body alone. The witan spoke, but the king responded to its constituency, the nation. In Æthelred's reign this can be dimly surmised from the circumstances of the king's return in 1014. When 'all the witan (*þa witan ealle*)' sent for Æthelred, saying that they would accept him as their lord 'if he would govern them more justly than he did before', it is a reasonable assumption that the witan had named its terms for Æthelred's restoration. As we have seen, those terms were probably embodied in the 'alleviatory' clauses of Cnut's second law code. Sending back his reply via his son Edmund and other messengers, Æthelred 'bade them greet all his people', saying that he would be a gracious lord to them and promising reforms.[214] The Chronicle's wording

[212] A. Williams, '*Princeps Merciorum Gentis*: The Family, Career and Connections of Ælfhere, Ealdorman of Mercia, 956–83', *ASE* 10 (1982), 162–3.

[213] Reynolds, *Kingdoms and Communities*, 250–1.

[214] *ASC*, ed. Whitelock, 93; *Two of the Saxon Chronicles*, ed. Plummer, i. 145.

here suggests a quotation from a writ, presumably one circulated widely.[215] The king's response showed that 'all the witan' could be seen as having been negotiating for 'all his people'.

The second case is more clear cut. The 'C' version of the Chronicle tells us that in 1018 the Danes and the English reached an agreement at Oxford, 'according to Edgar's law', in the additional words of the 'D' version, or 'about keeping' that law (*de lege regis Eadgari tenenda*) in those of John of Worcester.[216] A record of at least part of what was agreed is preserved in Cnut's law code of 1018, 'determined and devised', according to its preamble, by the witan and resulting from the full establishment of 'peace and friendship between the Danes and the English'. In the code's first clause the witan undertook 'to love King Cnut with due loyalty and zealously observe the laws of Edgar'. Subsequent clauses, almost all headed 'and the decree of the witan is (*and witena gerædnes is*)', mainly embodied the usual moral and homiletic preoccupations of Archbishop Wulfstan, who was the code's author.[217] In effect, the Oxford agreement and the subsequent legislation marked the final stage in Cnut's recognition as king, following his coronation in 1017, and the formal acceptance by the witan of Wulfstan's prescriptions for the nation's well-being.[218] Equally important, it saw the adoption of 'the laws of Edgar' as the standard of good government—not in any specific way, but rather as the 'good old law', conceived and enforced during a past age of divinely blessed national prosperity.[219] Cnut's laws themselves were soon to acquire the same mythical aura and reputation.[220]

The Oxford agreement was complemented by a 'letter-proclamation' issued by Cnut from Denmark in 1019 or 1020. It was written in English, and addressed to 'his archbishops and his diocesan bishops and Earl Thorkel and all his earls, and all his people, whether men of a twelve-hundred wergild or of a two-hundred, ecclesiastic and lay, in England, with friendship'; and in both style and language it follows the form of a writ with much

[215] The suggestion of Harmer, *Anglo-Saxon Writs*, ed. F. Harmer (Manchester, 1952), 541–2, expanded on by Campbell, 'Late Anglo-Saxon State', 22.
[216] *ASC*, ed. Whitelock, 97; *John of Worcester*, ii. 504–5.
[217] A. G. Kennedy, 'Cnut's Law Code of 1018', *ASE* 11 (1983), 57–83, esp. 72–3; *EHD*, ed. Whitelock, no. 47; Wormald, *Making*, 129–33.
[218] Lawson, *Cnut*, 82–3.   [219] Wormald, *Making*, 346–7.
[220] J. Hudson, 'Administration, Family and Perceptions of the Past in Late Twelfth-Century England: Richard FitzNigel and the Dialogue of the Exchequer', in P. Magdalino (ed.), *The Perception of the Past in Twelfth-Century Europe* (London, 1992), 94–8.

more precision than the Chronicle's paraphrase of Æthelred's earlier letter. A writ directed to such a wide audience, including even the 200-shilling ceorls, may well have been intended, so Campbell has convincingly argued, for publication in the shire courts, perhaps even in the hundred courts. The letter incorporates Cnut's promise to be a 'gracious lord', enjoins just government on the king's reeves, and again follows Wulfstan's prescriptions on moral and ecclesiastical matters. But it also includes a direct reference back to the Oxford meeting: 'all the nation' was 'to observe Edgar's law, which all men have chosen and sworn to at Oxford'.[221] A second similar letter to 'all the people of England' followed in 1027, though with no obvious connection to a meeting of the witan.[222]

The relationship between the Oxford meeting and Cnut's letter is of some constitutional significance. First, we notice how the undertaking of the witan at Oxford to observe the laws of Edgar is transformed in Cnut's letter into that of 'all men (*ealle men*)', while the laws themselves are to be observed by 'all the nation (*eal þeodscype*)'. Clearly the witan is regarded as representing the nation and its consent as binding on all men. Second, and more interesting still, comes the linkage between a central meeting and a probable circulation to the local courts of the outcome of that meeting, with royal directions for the observance of its decisions. Through those courts the obligations entered into by the witan can be made known to, and binding on, those whom the witan represents. Only in England, where the realm was divided into shires and hundreds, and where shire and hundred courts met regularly,[223] would this have been possible. Communication between the centre and the localities, the way in which the decisions of the witan can be passed back to the local courts via a royal writ, moves representation away from a mere idea towards a direct and practical reality.

Those addressed in Cnut's letter, for whom the witan had spoken at Oxford, were not unlike the national groupings represented by magnate assemblies whom Richard I later addressed in seeking the payment of his ransom in 1193 or whom Henry III recognized as having conceded an aid to him in 1225.[224] Virtual representation, with assembly standing for

---

[221] *C. and S.* I. i. 435–41; Wormald, *Making*, 347–8; Campbell, 'Late Anglo-Saxon State', 22–3.

[222] *C. and S.* I. i. 506–13.

[223] According to Edgar's laws, the hundred court meets every four weeks and the shire twice a year: I and III Edgar, in *Laws of the English Kings*, ed. and trans. Robertson, 16–17, 26–7.

[224] Below, 141, 206.

nation, was a concept and practice as fully formed in the early eleventh century as in the late twelfth and early thirteenth. (As we shall see, there would be a hiatus in between.[225]) But this was only one of the ways in which central assemblies already possessed some of the characteristics of proto-parliaments. They drew in great men from all parts of the realm; they met regularly at the great feasts of the church and often at other times as well; they participated in legislation and in state trials; they discussed the affairs of the realm; and they had begun to negotiate with kings and would-be kings over the terms for their recognition. The parliamentary tradition owed its inception to the nation created by Æthelstan and his successors, and its preservation and enlargement to the Danish conquest by Swein and Cnut.

Assemblies had another and more oblique role in preserving that tradition. They helped to maintain social harmony and political stability. If England managed to avoid 'the feudal revolution'—that disintegration of royal authority and that privatization of royal power which elsewhere in western Europe delivered royal prerogatives into magnate hands—it was partly because regular and frequent assemblies kept potentially disruptive magnates in close and mutually profitable contact with kings.[226] Assemblies were so much the dispersal point for royal patronage and favour, and so much the locus for political manoeuvring, the exercise of political influence, and what would nowadays be called 'networking', that even the greatest nobles could hardly afford to stay away. That was why such a man as Ælfhere, the most powerful of Edgar's ealdormen, is found witnessing 103 out of 107 of Edgar's charters between 959 and 975, and why Godwine witnessed all but one of the Confessor's thirty-one charters between 1042 and 1053.[227] Because the assembly incorporated the nation's great men and provided a central arena for politics, its existence could defuse political tension by argument, debate, and formal procedures. This happened most conspicuously in 1035, following the death of Cnut, and in 1051–2, during

---

[225] Below, 140, 443–4.

[226] For a related explanation, which emphasizes the absence of seigneurial justice in England, and the dominance of the public courts, see S. Baxter, 'Lordship and Justice in Late Anglo-Saxon England: The Judicial Functions of Soke and Commendation Revisited', in Baxter et al. (eds.), *Early Medieval Studies in Memory of Patrick Wormald*, 418–19, and below, 383–433. For a view which places more stress on the disruption brought by magnate violence, and the comparisons, rather than the contrasts, between English and French conditions, see D. Bates, 'England and the "Feudal Revolution"', in *Il feudalesimo nell'alto medioevo*, Settimane di Studio, 2 vols. (Spoleto, 2000), 611–45 *passim*, but esp. 621–5.

[227] Keynes, *Atlas of Attestations*, tables LVI, LXXIV; Williams, '*Princeps Merciorum Gentis*', 157–8.

the confrontation between Edward and the Godwines: both occasions when intense factional rivalries could have resulted in civil war but were instead resolved peacefully.

The assembly, therefore, was not just a proto-parliamentary institution. It also helped to create the conditions of peace and order necessary for its own survival and for its forward transmission into the post-Conquest world.

2

Confluence

English Council, Feudal Counsel, 1066–1189

1. The Councils of the Conquest

The great assemblies which had shared in the government of late Anglo-Saxon England underwent few obvious changes in the immediate aftermath of 1066. William I followed his English predecessors in continuing to summon them, and for similar purposes: to demonstrate his charismatic authority, to discuss national business, to legislate and to do justice, and to maintain those social and convivial ties with his great men on which political harmony partly rested. Nor did assemblies differ much in numbers and composition from what had gone before, to judge, for example, from a charter drafted at the Whitsun assembly of 1081 whose forty witnesses included two archbishops, thirteen bishops, six abbots, the king's three sons, and thirteen magnates.[1] The appropriation of an already strong conciliar tradition was, like the maintenance of the local courts or the geld, another instance of William's use of English institutions in the interests both of efficient government and of his own legitimate standing as Edward's rightful heir. In retrospect it also proved to be a means of perpetuating that tradition towards a future age of parliaments.

Yet it would be a mistake to regard William's assemblies as merely another example of continuity *tout court*. Like the castle and the mounted knight, if less obtrusively, they were also an instrument of conquest. So

---

[1] *RRAN: The Acts of William I (1066–1087)*, ed. D. Bates (Oxford, 1998), no. 39.

much at least can be deduced from the two best-known passages in the
sources which relate to these gatherings. In his obituary of William I the
Peterborough chronicler writes:

> Also, he was very dignified. Three times every year he wore his crown, as
> often as he was in England. At Easter he wore it at Winchester, at Whitsuntide
> at Westminster, and at Christmas at Gloucester; and then there were with
> him all the powerful men over all England, archbishops and bishops, abbots
> and earls, thegns and knights.[2]

In his *Life of Wulfstan* William of Malmesbury says something similar:

> King William had introduced a custom that his successors for some time
> complied with but afterwards allowed to lapse. Three times a year the great
> men would all come to court, to deal with vital business affecting the realm,
> and at the same time to see the king in his pomp, how he went crowned with
> a bejewelled diadem.[3]

Although both these authors bring out well the combination of ceremony
and business which marked these councils, not all that they tell us can be
accepted. This is especially true of their remarks on festal assemblies and
crown-wearings. Despite following a pattern already beginning to emerge
under Edward the Confessor,[4] the Peterborough chronicler's association
of assemblies with particular feasts and particular places was in reality
never more than approximate. Of William's known Easter locations, five,
possibly six, were at Winchester, and at least eleven in Normandy. Of
his Whitsuns, two were spent at Westminster, two at Windsor, one at
Winchester, and at least ten in Normandy. Of his Christmases, two were
spent at Gloucester, one each at London, York, and Winchester, and at
least twelve in Normandy.[5] This certainly suggests a festal concentration on
important places, throwing assemblies into high relief and tending to bear
out the chronicler's statement. Yet even allowing for the writer's implicit
recognition of William's Norman sojourns as exceptions to his rule, the
king's festal locations when in England were too varied to permit more
than a very general sense of regularity.

　　Nor was it true that the Conqueror introduced the custom of crown-
wearing, as William of Malmesbury states. His words are contradicted by
his own notice of Edward the Confessor's crown-wearing at Westminster
on Christmas Day 1065 and by the other evidence for pre-Conquest

---

[2] *ASC*, ed. Whitelock, 164.　　[3] William of Malmesbury, *Saints' Lives*, 82–3.
[4] Above, 43, 48–9.　　[5] *RRAN*, ed. Bates, 76–8, 84.

crown-wearings, going back to the tenth century, which has already been cited.[6] William's mistake may have been a false conclusion drawn from his knowledge of the Peterborough chronicler's passage[7] or perhaps from an uncritical adherence to what may have been said in Colman's *Life of Wulfstan*, the old English source, now lost, which William was translating. Besides his words, there is nothing to suggest that the Conqueror innovated here and much to suggest that he did not.

But despite their errors these two sources tell us something important. Through their specific comments they imply that crown-wearing at festal assemblies, though it may not have been new, nevertheless became newly prominent after the Conquest. The evidence for pre-Conquest crown-wearings is mostly incidental, allusive, and fragmentary; yet here we have two direct statements about the practice. To these we could perhaps add a third in the story of William's jester who saw God in the crowned and feasting king, and a possible fourth in a passage found in one of the forged royal charters drafted for Westminster by Osbert of Clare about 1140. In it William is made to confirm various offerings to the three churches of Westminster, Winchester, and Gloucester, where he wore his crown—offerings long the custom, according to the affirmation of English nobles and wise men.[8] Forged though the charter may have been, it hints again at a heightened awareness of the crown-wearing ceremony and its particular locations, and it points to the key role of English testimony in transmitting knowledge of English practices to the new regime.

If crown-wearing was thus more prominent, it was surely because it was more necessary. These displays were central to the definition of William's new royal status and to impressing it upon his magnates. He who had been their duke was now their king, blessed by God and transcendent in his authority. The lesson had initially been taught through William's coronation on Christmas Day 1066 and it was pushed home by the singing of the *laudes regiae*, probably another inheritance from the pre-Conquest past and first known to have been used by William at Queen Matilda's coronation during the Whitsun assembly of 1068.[9] All these elements in William's

---

[6] William of Malmesbury, *Gesta Regum*, i. 418–19; above, 18–22, 43–5.

[7] Wormald, *Making*, 446 n. 110. For William's use of the Chronicle, see William of Malmesbury, *Gesta Regum*, ii. 12–13.

[8] Above, 22; *RRAN*, ed. Bates, no. 290; G. Garnett, 'The Origins of the Crown', in J. Hudson (ed.), *The History of English Law: Centenary Essays on 'Pollock and Maitland'* (Oxford, 1996), 202–4.

[9] Cowdrey, 'The Anglo-Norman *Laudes Regiae*', 50–3; above, 44–5.

charismatic transformation linked him to the English past, emphasizing his claims to legitimacy as the true heir of Edward the Confessor which was one of the leitmotifs of his rule. Nor was it only the Normans whom festal ceremonies were intended to impress. It is William of Malmesbury again who tells us that one of their purposes was to draw in 'all great men of whatever walk of life . . . summoned to them by royal edict, so that envoys from other nations (*exterarum gentium legati*) might admire the large and brilliant company and the splendid luxury of the feast'. These were also occasions when lavish gift-giving to such foreign visitors could be turned to subsequent advantage as they reported home on William's wealth and generosity.[10] They were a means of buying a reputation and a name.

An *arriviste* king could thus mark out his glory and emphasize the establishment of his rule. But for William's English subjects in particular his crown-wearing may have had another significance as an imperious exhibition of rightful power, the power of the conqueror over the conquered. This was best shown in December 1069, when William was in Yorkshire, bloodily putting down the third northern rebellion against his rule. 'In the midst of the fighting', Orderic Vitalis tells us, 'he sent to Winchester for his crown and other royal insignia and plate, left his army in camp, and came to York to celebrate Christmas.'[11] His sending south for the crown, entailing as it did a midwinter round-trip of some 500 miles, demonstrated the weight which he attached to the ceremony, perhaps conducted in the presence of English prisoners of war and certainly in hostile territory. In William's dangerous last years, when invasion threatened and crown-wearings may have been staged more regularly in response, similar needs may have asserted themselves.[12] But it was perhaps at the start of the reign, and on more ordinary occasions than that at York, that crown-wearing was most necessarily deployed in support of conquest. William's early festal courts, such as the Whitsun assembly for the queen's coronation at Westminster in 1068, were often attended both by Edwin, Morcar, and other leading members of the previous regime, as well as by numbers of English abbots:[13] men often rooted in their localities, instinctively loyal to the old order, and less malleable in their sympathies than the more adept and adaptable

---

[10] William of Malmesbury, *Gesta Regum*, i. 508–9.
[11] *The Ecclesiastical History of Orderic Vitalis*, ed. and trans. M. Chibnall, 6 vols., OMT (Oxford, 1969–80), ii. 232–3.
[12] Nelson, 'The Rites of the Conqueror', 400.
[13] *RRAN*, ed. Bates, no. 181. For English abbots at other festal assemblies, see e.g. ibid., nos. 68 (Whitsun 1072), 39 (Whitsun 1081).

bishops.[14] For both categories of survivors William's crown-wearings may have been not only an assertion of his legitimacy but also an implied demand for continuing submission from men who may not always have been minded to give it.

Just as crown-wearing came from the English past but gained a new significance after the Conquest, so also did the more mundane business agenda of legislation, policy-making, and justice. Summed up as what William of Malmesbury calls the 'vital business affecting the realm', it again points us forward to the parliaments of the thirteenth century, whose work could be described in near identical terms.[15] In all these areas consensus ruled, perhaps even more markedly than had been the case before 1066. It was most visible with regard to legislation. The English tradition of legislative codes, vigorously maintained through the tenth and early eleventh centuries but ceasing after Cnut's second code of 1020 × 21, was not revived. This was another way in which William fell into line with Edwardian precedent, no doubt fortuitously in this case. But legislation there was, if not by code then by writ. The famous ordinance on the church courts, drawn up between 1072 and 1085 as a writ for distribution to the shire courts, was made 'in common council and with the counsel of the archbishops and bishops and abbots and all the magnates (*principes*) of my kingdom'. It clearly came out of an assembly; and since its purpose was to remove ecclesiastical pleas from the hundred courts, the rights to the profits from which were sometimes in private hands, consultation in its making must have seemed prudent for reasons other than those deriving from ecclesiastical reform. Fewer pleas, less profit.[16]

The murdrum legislation has the same context. Recorded as one of a number of enactments in the so-called Ten Articles of William I (a title with no contemporary warrant), it too bore on the interests of the magnates. The new law laid down that if the killer of a murdered Norman could not be apprehended, a heavy financial penalty should fall in the first instance on the lord of the dead man. Along with its companion enactments, this ruling was said to have been made by William and his magnates and to have

---

[14] D. Knowles, *The Monastic Order in England*, 2nd edn. (Cambridge, 1963), 103–6; Keynes, 'Ely Abbey, 672–1109', 42–4.

[15] Compare William of Malmesbury's 'de necessariis regni tractaturi' with the description of parliament's work in the 1258 Provisions of Oxford, 'pur treter de bosoingnes le rei et del reaume': William of Malmesbury, *Saints' Lives*, 82; *DBM* 110.

[16] *C. and S.* I. ii, no. 94; Wormald, *Making*, 399. For the lord's role in hundred courts, see id., *Legal Culture*, 317–18, 325–6, 331.

been drawn up at Gloucester: a pointer perhaps to a Christmas assembly. This little group of ordinances is the nearest we come in the Conqueror's reign to a law code, though Wormald has pointed out that the Gloucester legislation could equally well have been issued in writ form.[17] As with the withdrawal of pleas from the hundred courts, the magnates were consulted when their financial interests were at stake, and legislation came before councils as it had always done.

Discussion of other public business besides legislation might also affect the fortunes of the nobility. It did so most conspicuously at the two assemblies of 1085 summoned to deal with a threatened invasion from Denmark. The greatest potential challenge to Norman control of England during the entire reign, the threat was met in the first instance by William's bringing a mercenary army to England in the autumn of 1085, and then by a council meeting of king and magnates where the magnates agreed to Lanfranc's proposal that the mercenaries should be quartered on their households for their maintenance.[18] At the second (and much more famous) meeting which convened shortly afterwards at Gloucester at Christmas 1085, the king had 'very deep discussion with his council about this country, how it was occupied and with what sort of people'. The outcome of the meeting was the Domesday survey, whose purpose in part was almost certainly fiscal: it was intended to tap the country's resources in order to make renewed provision for the mercenary army needed to hold off the Danes (who in the event never came).[19] In the case of both these meetings consultation was politic, and a united decision in the interests of all. Failure to counter the expected invasion would jeopardize the whole achievement of the conquest; the billeting of mercenaries meant expense and disturbance for the magnates; the Domesday survey depended on their cooperation for its execution;[20] and its fiscal consequences were likely to cut into the resources of their peasant tenants. In these circumstances it was prudence as well as precedent which led the Conqueror to bring before two successive magnate assemblies 'the vital business of the realm'.

---

[17] *Laws of the Kings of England*, ed. and trans. Robertson, 238–9; G. Garnett, ' "Franci et Angli": The Legal Distinction between Peoples after the Norman Conquest', *ANS* 8 (1985), 116–17 and n. 57; Wormald, *Making*, 402–3.

[18] William of Malmesbury, *Saints' Lives*, 130–1; J. R. Maddicott, 'Responses to the Threat of Invasion, 1085', *EHR* 122 (2007), 986–97.

[19] *ASC*, ed. Whitelock, 161; *John of Worcester*, iii. 42–3; Maddicott, 'Responses to the Threat of Invasion', 986–91. For the fiscal purpose of the Domesday survey, see below, 102.

[20] J. C. Holt, '1086', in J. C. Holt (ed.), *Domesday Studies* (Woodbridge, 1987), 46–7, 55–6.

In the case of our third category of conciliar business, the doing of justice and in particular the conduct of state trials, magnate involvement was prudential in another way, as a means to afforce royal authority. When the rebel earls of 1075 were tried before the subsequent Christmas court at Westminster, and Odo of Bayeux before a comparable magnate assembly in 1082 or 1083, there were precedents no further back than the proceedings against Earl Godwine in 1051 and Earl Ælfgar in 1055.[21] The crown's position was secured through the English practice of using assemblies to mobilize magnate support against public enemies. In fact, this whole conciliar agenda of legislation, national affairs, and justice was carried forward from the Anglo-Saxon past. Consensual discussion was the rule after 1066, as it had been before, and if the terms on which the magnates offered their counsel now reflected the new vassalic obligations of man to lord, as we shall see that they did,[22] this made little difference either to the substance or to the mechanism of consultation. Not for nothing did the Peterborough chronicler refer to the meeting of the king and his witan at Gloucester in 1085.[23]

The means by which the conciliar practices of the English state were passed on to the incoming Normans cannot have differed from those by which knowledge of a much wider range of English governmental procedures was transmitted. We have already noticed the possible role of English nobles in testifying to earlier crown-wearing customs. If we had to guess at William's other possible informants we might identify some less shadowy survivors from Edwardian England, notably perhaps the king's priest Regenbald, and Stigand, archbishop of Canterbury from 1052. Regenbald appears to have been the royal chancellor, in charge of the central writing office both before and after 1066. As such, he was the king's leading minister, and even after his retirement, probably early in 1068, he remained in royal favour. Stigand, a prominent counsellor at Edward's court, retained his position until 1070 before falling from grace much more precipitately. Both men must have been intimately familiar with the mechanisms of English government and administration—the geld, the writ system, the local courts, and the shrievalties, as well as councils. In the crucial few years after Hastings they were well placed to educate their new masters, and the promise of survival gave them every incentive

---

[21] *ASC*, ed. Whitelock, 158; *John of Worcester*, iii. 26–7; *Orderic*, ii. 318–21, iv. 40–3; above, 45–7.
[22] Below, 76–9.   [23] *Two of the Saxon Chronicles*, ed. Plummer, i. 216.

to do so.[24] Other English survivors, men such as Earls Edwin and Morcar, and Bishop Wulfstan of Worcester, may have been equally important as sources of information. The continuity of English government, including the summoning and agenda of councils, can only be explained on the assumption that, at the centre as in the localities, some key figures among the conquered were prepared to collaborate with their conquerors and to show them how things worked.

Was there then no contribution from Normandy to the councils of the Conquest? 'Very little indeed' would seem to be the answer. Though the Carolingian legacy to ducal Normandy was a generous one in matters such as taxation, control of fortifications, and regalian rights over coinage,[25] it did not extend to the earlier tradition of well-attended and regular assemblies. There were occasional large gatherings. In the duchy's early days the ceremonies accompanying the designation of the ruler's heir, involving oaths of fealty and performance of homage, must have drawn in many magnates.[26] The witness list to Duke Richard II's charter of 1025 in favour of the abbey of Bernay runs to 135 names, suggesting greater numbers than at any meeting known from English charters.[27] Special circumstances might call for other great assemblies, such as those preceding Duke Robert's departure for Jerusalem in 1035 or the invasion of England in 1066.[28] There was even a tendency, evident from the 1030s and continuing beyond 1066, for an Easter festal court to meet with some regularity in the same place, Fécamp.[29] Yet even at festal courts there could, of course, be no crown-wearing, and although a case has been made for the singing of the *laudes regiae*, it is perhaps more likely that this was introduced into the duchy from

[24] S. Keynes, 'Regenbald the Chancellor (*sic*)', *ANS* 10 (1987), 195–222; H. E. J. Cowdrey, 'Stigand', *ODNB*; J. Campbell, 'Some Agents and Agencies of the Late Anglo-Saxon State', in his *Anglo-Saxon State*, 225 (where it is suggested that Stigand may have been 'Edward the Confessor's Roger of Salisbury').

[25] D. Bates, *Normandy before 1066* (Harlow, 1982), 153, 155, 162–3; L. Musset, 'Gouvernés et gouvernants dans le monde scandinave et dans le monde Normand (XIᵉ–XIIᵉ siècles)', in *Gouvernés et gouvernants: recueils de la société Jean Bodin*, 17 (1968), 459–60.

[26] G. Garnett, ' "Ducal" Succession in Early Normandy', in *Law and Government in Medieval England and Normandy: Essays in Honour of Sir James Holt* (Cambridge, 1994), 89, 106.

[27] *Recueil des actes des ducs de Normandie de 911 à 1066*, ed. M. Fauroux (Caen, 1961), no. 35; Bates, *Normandy before 1066*, 158.

[28] *The Gesta Normannorum Ducum of William of Jumièges*, ed. and trans. E. M. C. van Houts, 2 vols., OMT (Oxford, 1992–5), ii. 80–1; *The Gesta Guillelmi of William of Poitiers*, ed. and trans. R. H. C. Davis and M. Chibnall, OMT (Oxford, 1998), 100–3; *Orderic*, ii. 140–3.

[29] See C. H. Haskins, *Norman Institutions* (New York, 1918), 55 n. 262, for a list of Easter courts at Fécamp. Cf. *RRAN*, ed. Bates, 76–7; Musset, 'Gouvernés et gouvernants', 463; J. Le Patourel, *The Norman Empire* (Oxford, 1976), 126.

England after the Conquest.[30] Altogether absent were the large, regular, multi-purpose assemblies of late Anglo-Saxon England which were the occasions for these displays and for much else.[31]

An explanation is to be found in the alternative ways by which Normandy was governed: by ducal itineration, more possible within the duchy's constricted boundaries than in the much larger kingdom of England; by the frequent attendance on the duke, at least in the generation before 1066, of a group of powerful nobles, making for curial rather than conciliar government;[32] and, above all perhaps, by ecclesiastical councils in which the duke exerted a powerful influence and the boundaries between secular and ecclesiastical business were blurred. It was in an ecclesiastical council near Caen, and in William's presence, that the Truce of God was first proclaimed in 1047.[33] It was at another council at Lisieux in 1054 that Archbishop Mauger of Rouen was deposed by William's sentence, with the bishops merely consenting, and for offences which were ostensibly moral and ecclesiastical but tacitly secular and political as well.[34] Legislation was another feature of Carolingian government which had failed to come through to ducal Normandy, and there were no Norman equivalents of the Anglo-Saxon law codes or of Anglo-Norman legislation by writ. But ecclesiastical legislation such as the Truce of God, which held out the prospect of more effective government, provided a partial substitute.[35] In England king and witan made law, at least until Cnut's reign. In Normandy such law-making as there was, and with it the responsibility for order, lay with ecclesiastical councils operating under ducal supervision.

For all these reasons Norman modes of government contributed little to post-Conquest assemblies in England, whose pedigree was almost wholly indigenous. It was through Lanfranc's church councils, which brought into England both the framework and the substance of the ecclesiastical reforms

[30] For contrasting views, see Cowdrey, 'The Anglo-Norman *Laudes Regiae*', 48, and Nelson, 'Rites of the Conqueror', 396–7.

[31] The point was first made by Stenton, *Anglo-Saxon England*, 555–6.

[32] Bates, *Normandy before 1066*, 152, 159–61; G. Davy, *Le Duc et la loi: héritages, images et expressions du pouvoir normatif dans le duché de Normandie, des origines à la mort du Conquérant (fin du IXe siècle–1087)* (Paris, 2004), 314, 324–30.

[33] D. C. Douglas, *William the Conqueror* (London, 1964), 51–2.

[34] *William of Poitiers*, 87–9; R. Foreville, 'The Synod of the Province of Rouen in the Eleventh and Twelfth Centuries', in C. N. L. Brooke, D. E. Luscombe, G. H. Martin, and D. Owen (eds.), *Church and Government in the Middle Ages: Essays Presented to C. R. Cheney* (Cambridge, 1976), 23–4.

[35] Bates, *Normandy before 1066*, 163–4; Musset, 'Gouvernés et gouvernants', 163–4; Wormald, *Making*, 483; Davy, *Le Duc et la loi*, 359–69.

already implemented in Normandy, that Norman conciliar traditions made most impact;[36] and the frequent coincidence or merging of these councils with festal assemblies was perhaps the main structural innovation which affected ancient conciliar practice. The Easter court at Winchester in 1072, for example, saw the temporary settlement of the dispute between Canterbury and York over the primacy, and the subsequent church council allowed Lanfranc to set about his reform of the English church.[37] Their more conspicuous ecclesiastical element must have added to the weight which councils had already possessed in the English polity. But even without this particular augmentation of their work, the purposes of William's assemblies went beyond those of the English predecessors which they otherwise so closely resembled. Their role in displaying the king's majesty, whether to a conquered people, to magnates unused to royal rule, or to foreign visitors, in disciplining rebels, whether English in 1069 or Normans and English in 1075, and in forging consensus and unity in the face of internal revolt and external attack, made them an essential part of the armoury of conquest. The twin assemblies of 1085, summoned by William to counter the threat of an impending Danish invasion, showed how they might be used to consolidate the common interests of king and magnates in circumstances which remained precarious. If central assemblies were a valuable instrument of government to the pre-Conquest English monarchy, they were still more so to its usurping Norman successor. It was hardly surprising that they survived and flourished, to form an essential link between witan and parliament.

One seemingly anomalous assembly should be placed in the same context. The great gathering of the ecclesiastical and lay nobility and their knights that took place at Salisbury on 1 August 1086 is now generally seen as one in which William confirmed his magnates and their tenants in the lands assigned to them by the returns to the Domesday survey, first made available at Salisbury, and received their homage and fealty in exchange.[38] The oath of Salisbury sealed a compact. But it also marked a conciliar occasion, whose exceptional nature was more apparent than real. Identifying those present, the Peterborough chronicler gives priority to the king's councillors, his 'witan' as he calls them, above the landholding barons and their tenants; though no doubt there was much overlap between the

---

[36] H. E. J. Cowdrey, *Lanfranc: Scholar, Monk and Archbishop* (Oxford, 2003), 121–9.
[37] *C. and S.* I. ii, no. 91; Cowdrey, *Lanfranc*, 124
[38] *ASC*, ed. Whitelock, 162; *John of Worcester*, iii. 44–5; Holt, '1086', 42–4, 56, 62.

two groups.[39] In addition, the Salisbury assembly was as much muster as council, an unseasonal throwback to the Carolingian Mayfield and to the spring military assemblies which had sometimes preceded the campaigns of Athelstan, Edgar, and Æthelred. It came in advance of William's departure to wage war in France—though probably not far in advance, since the chronicler speaks of his going directly from Salisbury to the Isle of Wight, en route for Normandy, and he may have had a French expedition in mind for some months before the Salisbury meeting. One purpose of the oath which he exacted there was probably to guarantee loyalty and service on his forthcoming expedition, from the knights as much as from the magnates.[40] But if the knights were present for this special reason, we know, again from the Peterborough chronicler, that they were also regularly in attendance at William's festal courts. Their appearance at Salisbury provides another link in the catena of instances which could be cited to show the presence of small landholders at central assemblies.

None of this is incompatible with the stress traditionally laid on homage and fealty in the events at Salisbury. It is simply to suggest that these recognitions of William's lordship constituted part of the 'vital business affecting the realm' which was seen as the staple fare of royal councils, and one entirely consistent with their customary agenda. It was, for example, by another oath of allegiance taken at a meeting of the witan that Æthelred had been re-accepted as king in 1014.[41] Whatever else they may have been, the Salisbury proceedings were conciliar in form. If they were the complement of the earlier proceedings at Gloucester in December 1085, with homage for Domesday lands envisaged from the start as the final outcome of the survey initiated there (as has been argued),[42] then the two councils at Gloucester and Salisbury encompassed and linked the most important political *acta* of William's final years.

2. Functions, Times, Places, 1087–1189

From the Conqueror's death in 1087 to that of his great-grandson Henry II in 1189, the outward history of assemblies is relatively easy to chart.

---

[39] *ASC*, ed. Whitelock, 162; *Two of the Saxon Chronicles*, ed. Plummer, i. 217.
[40] Above, 13–14; *ASC*, ed. Whitelock, 162–3; Holt, '1086', 43, 62–3. For William's movements in 1086–7, see also Douglas, *William the Conqueror*, 354–7; *RRAN*, ed. Bates, 82.
[41] *ASC*, ed. Whitelock, 93; *John of Worcester*, ii. 478–9; above, 37.   [42] Holt, '1086', 43, 62–3.

It combines continuity in the assembly's central role as an instrument of government (broken inevitably under Stephen) with a general loosening of its temporal and spatial setting. Throughout the period, Stephen's reign again excepted, it was business as usual, with the usual conciliar programme of public discussion, legislation, appointments, and state trials as prominent as it had always been. Taking a leading example from each of these four categories, we could cite, for political discussion, the debate on the succession, and Matilda's recognition as Henry I's heir, at the Christmas court of 1126;[43] for legislation, the making of the Assize of Northampton at the council held there in January 1176;[44] for appointments, the filling of numerous bishoprics and abbacies at the Westminster council of August 1107;[45] and for state trials, the appearance of William of St Calais, bishop of Durham, before the king's court at Salisbury in November 1088, charged with deserting the king during the revolt of that year.[46] None of this would have looked out of place at a meeting of the witan under Edgar or Æthelred, and in continuing to bring 'vital business affecting the realm' before such great gatherings Norman and Angevin kings, like their Anglo-Saxon predecessors, had no choice but to disown autocracy.

But in other ways assemblies shifted ground. Most significant over the long term was their decline as a forum for festal crown-wearing. The practice was maintained by William Rufus—in conditions of particular splendour at the Westminster court of Whitsun 1099[47]—and maintained too in the early years of his successor. But the Peterborough chronicler noted with surprise that neither at Christmas 1110 nor at Easter or Whitsun 1111 did Henry I wear his crown,[48] and from then on the ceremony was rarely more than intermittent. Revived by Henry for special occasions, such as his second marriage in 1121,[49] it probably became a regular custom once again in Stephen's early years, only to be abandoned in the ensuing

[43] ASC, ed. Whitelock, 192–3; John of Worcester, iii. 166–7; William of Malmesbury, Historia Novella, ed. E. King, trans. K. R. Potter, OMT (Oxford, 1998), 6–9.
[44] Gesta Regis Henrici Secundi Benedicti Abbatis, ed. W. Stubbs, 2 vols., RS (London, 1867), i. 291. This work, formerly ascribed to Benedict of Peterborough, is now known to have been written by Roger of Howden and will henceforward be cited under his name.
[45] ASC, ed. Whitelock, 180; John of Worcester, iii. 110–13.
[46] English Lawsuits from William I to Richard I, ed. R. C. van Caenegem, 2 vols., Selden Soc. 106–7 (1990–1), i. 90–106.
[47] William of Malmesbury, Gesta Regum, i. 508–9; F. Barlow, William Rufus (London, 1983), 399–401.
[48] ASC, ed. Whitelock, 182.
[49] Eadmer, Historia Novorum in Anglia, ed. M. Rule, RS (London, 1884), 292–3; J. A. Green, The Government of England under Henry I (Cambridge, 1986), 21.

civil war. After 1140 there were just two occasions when Stephen is known to have worn his crown: at Canterbury in 1142, in a 're-coronation' after his release from captivity, and at Lincoln in 1146;[50] though Stephen's general liking for pomp and circumstance makes it possible that there were others. In his early years Henry II resurrected what was by now a decaying tradition, sometimes using it as the Conqueror had done to intimidate his opponents. It was presumably to this end that he wore his crown at Bury St Edmunds at Whitsun 1157, when rebellion threatened in East Anglia.[51] Yet in 1158, according to both Roger of Howden and Ralph Diceto, he explicitly renounced the practice, and the assertion that it was maintained thereafter rests only on one record of the singing of the *laudes regiae* at Whitsun 1188.[52] If crown-wearings continued to be staged, they certainly failed to attract the public attention which was in part their purpose.

The reasons for the decline of crown-wearing can only be surmised. Clearly the special needs which had existed immediately after the Conquest, to cow the English and to impress William's novel regality on the Normans, were no longer present.[53] Henry I may have found crown-wearing, and the entertainment that went with it, too expensive, and its abandonment to fit well with his other economical reforms. It was the feasting, rather than the crown-wearing itself, whose abandonment William of Malmesbury stresses.[54] Perhaps the theocratic kingship which crown-wearing implied became harder to justify in the face of the post-Gregorian papacy's claim to spiritual supremacy and of Henry's parallel abandonment of lay investiture in 1106. Perhaps the elaboration of bureaucratic routine and the widening range of government made charisma less necessary. In an age of pipe rolls, and when royal rule could be enforced by eyre and exchequer, the king's transcendent status may have mattered less. Perhaps the debates and contentions attendant on crown-wearings, particularly those between rival

---

[50] Henry of Huntingdon, *Historia Anglorum*, ed. D. Greenway, OMT (Oxford, 1996), 706–7, 724–5, 748–9; *John of Worcester*, iii. 278–9; *The Historical Works of Gervase of Canterbury*, ed. W. Stubbs, 2 vols., RS (London, 1868–71), i. 123.

[51] *The Chronicle of Battle Abbey*, ed. E. Searle, OMT (Oxford, 1980), 175–7; W. L. Warren, *Henry II* (London, 1973), 66–8.

[52] *Chronica Rogeri de Houedene*, ed. W. Stubbs, 4 vols., RS (London, 1868–71), i. 216; *Radulfi de Diceto Decani Lundoniensis, Opera Historica*, ed. W. Stubbs, 2 vols., RS (London, 1876), i. 302; *PR 34 Henry II*, 19; N. Vincent, 'The Court of Henry II', in Harper-Bill and Vincent (eds.), *Henry II*, 326; H. G. Richardson, 'The Coronation in Medieval England', *Traditio*, 16 (1960), 127–8, denies that Henry II discontinued crown-wearings. Cf. M. Strickland, 'On the Instruction of a Prince: The Upbringing of Henry, the Young King', in Harper-Bill and Vincent (eds.), *Henry II*, 197.

[53] Above, 58–60; M. Aurell, *The Plantagenet Empire, 1154–1224* (Harlow, 2007), 121.

[54] William of Malmesbury, *Gesta Regum*, i. 509–10; Green, *Government of England*, 21.

churchmen, made them seem too troublesome to be worthwhile.[55] Perhaps the practice simply began to seem old-fashioned. But whatever may have lain behind this change it is hard to doubt that the ceremony meant less to Henry II than it had to William I.

A related change may be seen in the growing separation of festal courts from councils dedicated to business in the narrow sense. Under Henry I important business could, as always, be carried through by councils meeting at any time. But the most important matters were still reserved for festal assemblies, probably because they attracted the largest attendance. The arrangements for Matilda's marriage to the emperor were discussed at the Christmas court of 1109, just as her succession was later settled at the Christmas court of 1126.[56] Stephen followed suit, exploiting the grandeur of his first Easter court of 1136 in order to affirm his kingship, and using the occasion to issue a new charter of liberties for the church.[57] But under Henry II the greatest affairs of state were no longer reserved for festal courts. None of the three councils associated with the Becket dispute—Westminster in October 1163, Clarendon in January 1164, Northampton in October 1164—coincided with one of the three great feasts: matters were dealt with as they arose. The councils associated with dated legal reforms similarly disregarded the church calendar: the Assize of Clarendon was made in council in February 1166, and the Assize of Northampton in late January 1176.[58] Henry's arbitration between the kings of Navarre and Castile took place at a council meeting in early March 1177.[59] Festal courts remained great social occasions, to which men might be summoned from far and wide, as they were to Henry's particularly splendid Christmas court at Caen in 1182.[60] Their splendour should warn us against assuming that expense alone explains the discontinuance of crown-wearing. No doubt too they continued to provide plenty of opportunities for informal consultation between the king and his great men, as they had always done. But they were rarely any longer the setting

[55] G. Koziol, 'England, France and the Problem of Sacrality in Twelfth-Century Ritual', in T. N. Bisson (ed.), *Cultures of Power: Lordship, Status and Process in Twelfth-Century Europe* (Philadelphia, 1995), 137–9.

[56] *ASC*, ed. Whitelock, 181; above, 68.

[57] D. Crouch, *The Reign of King Stephen, 1135–54* (Harlow, 2000), 42–9.

[58] R. W. Eyton, *Court, Household and Itinerary of Henry II* (London, 1878), 64–5, 67–8, 74, 89, 198.

[59] Ibid. 211.

[60] Howden, *Gesta Regis Henrici*, i. 291; Walter Map, *De Nugis Curialium*, ed. and trans. M. R. James, rev. C. N. L. Brooke and R. A. B. Mynors, OMT (Oxford, 1983), 488–93; D. Power, 'Henry, Duke of the Normans (1149/50–1189)', in Harper-Bill and Vincent (eds.), *Henry II*, 121–2.

for legislation, state trials, formal display, or other defined components of high politics.

There was a similar disjunction with regard to place. Under Rufus the seasonal prescriptions of the Peterborough chronicler were still partly observed, with festal courts meeting at least twice at Winchester for Easter, twice at Westminster for Whitsun, and twice at Gloucester for Christmas. But under Henry I there were, so far as we can see, no Gloucester Christmases, and the Winchester/Easter, Westminster/Whitsun rotation was largely abandoned after 1108.[61] It looks as if festal crown-wearings and the cycle of itineration associated with them had both gone down together, the result of a conscious royal decision rather than mere inadvertence or insensible change.

From then on assembly meeting-places conformed to no particular pattern. Two trends, however, became conspicuous. First, councils met with increasing frequency at London or Westminster. These place-names were sometimes used interchangeably by the chroniclers, but by no means always. Henry of Huntingdon's careful distinction between a royal council in London and an ecclesiastical council meeting simultaneously at Westminster in 1127, and Henry II's council of 1185 at Clerkenwell, just outside the city, showed that 'London' might not always mean 'Westminster'.[62] The rise of London as a meeting place was particularly marked under Henry II and its role particularly noted by contemporaries. Writing to Gilbert Foliot in 1163, Thomas Becket could speak of 'the city of London where the public affairs (*publica negocia*) of the whole kingdom require both the presence of the lord king and the very frequent assembly of the great men of the realm . . . more famous and celebrated than any other city in the land'; and William fitz Stephen's description of London, written about 1173, mentioned the great London houses maintained by prelates and magnates for use when they attended councils and assemblies.[63] This was not, of course, an entirely new development, but one which had

---

[61] Biddle, 'Seasonal Festivals', 65, 67.

[62] Henry of Huntingdon, *Historia Anglorum*, 476–7; Eyton, *Itinerary*, 261. Cf. S. M. Christelow, 'A Moveable Feast? Itineration and the Centralization of Government under Henry I', *Albion*, 28 (1996), 203.

[63] *The Correspondence of Thomas Becket, Archbishop of Canterbury, 1162–70*, ed. and trans. A. Duggan, 2 vols., OMT (Oxford, 2000), i. 20–1; *Norman London, by William Fitz Stephen*, introd. F. D. Logan (New York, 1990), 55. For the date, see F. Barlow, *Thomas Becket* (London, 1986), 6. The abbots of Abingdon had possessed a London house since 1085: *Historia Ecclesie Abbendonensis*, ed. Hudson, ii. 18–19, 274–5.

emerged in the first half of the eleventh century and had been maintained into the twelfth by occasional crown-wearings at Westminster. Nor was London overwhelmingly dominant among English assembly places. Of the forty-four recorded councils under Henry II, only nine met at London or Westminster, though this was more than at any other place. Windsor with five, and Northampton with four, were the runners-up.[64] But contemporary writers now recognized London's special quality as a place where councils met, and that recognition was new.

A second trend lay in an opposite direction, towards the holding of assemblies in the countryside, often at hunting lodges on the edge of royal forests. From Henry I's reign Woodstock became a favourite resort. The three Easter courts which met at Woodstock in 1127, 1130, and 1132 were the first recorded assemblies to do so since Æthelred's witan had twice gathered there to legislate.[65] Another royal hunting lodge, Clarendon, may have provided the setting for an assembly in April 1121 and was to be the scene of two famous councils under Henry II.[66] At a third hunting lodge, Brampton in Huntingdonshire, Henry I wore his crown three times and set aside land for the lodgings of his barons when they came there to meet him. We know this from an entry in a much later plea roll, but contemporary chronicle and record evidence shows that a festal court did indeed meet there at least once, at Christmas 1120.[67] Under Henry II Brampton was visited, but not (so far as we know) for conciliar purposes. Geddington, in neighbouring Northamptonshire and on the edge of Rockingham forest, was more favoured: an assembly may have met there in 1176 and others certainly did so in 1177 and 1188.[68] Meetings at these rural locations marked something like a reversion to the 'royal vill' tradition of meeting places which had been so evident in the tenth century;[69] but one now governed less by the ancient habits of itinerant kings and by the need to provision large gatherings from adjacent royal estates than by the simple proximity of hunting.

[64] Above, 47–9. The figures are derived from an analysis of the councils listed in Eyton, *Itinerary*, *passim*.

[65] Biddle, 'Seasonal Festivals', 67; *Laws of the Kings of England*, ed. and trans. Robertson, 52–3, 130–1.

[66] *RRAN* ii, nos. 1270–5.

[67] *CRR*, 1213–15, 349–50; Henry of Huntingdon, *Historia Anglorum*, 466–7; *RRAN* ii, nos. 1239–40; Richardson, 'Coronation in Medieval England', 127–9.

[68] Howden, *Gesta Regis Henrici*, i. 160; Eyton, *Itinerary*, 199–200, 213, 285; R. A. Brown, H. M. Colvin, and A. J. Taylor (eds.), *The History of the King's Works*, i–ii: *The Middle Ages*, HMSO (London, 1963), ii. 901, 943.

[69] Above, p. 16.

There is no overarching explanation for these various twelfth-century perturbations of established practice and custom in the holding of assemblies. One factor which clearly inhibited any regular pattern in their convening lay in the king's foreign commitments. Under both Henries these could dictate the timing of assemblies, which often met just prior to the king's departure abroad and again just after his return. So, for example, Henry I summoned a council at Salisbury in March 1116, before going abroad in April, while his return in November 1120 was shortly followed by the holding of the Christmas court at Brampton.[70] In a similar way Henry II held a Christmas court at Westminster in 1155 to dispose of business before his crossing to Normandy in January 1156. Returning in early April 1157, he held a Whitsun court at Bury St Edmunds, attended by a great crowd of prelates and magnates, in May.[71] During the king's absence there was a moratorium on assemblies in England and a corresponding transference of their functions to others abroad. When Henry I was in Normandy in 1106–7 Orderic records councils at Lisieux in October 1106 and March 1107 and at Falaise in January 1107, mainly for Norman magnates and for Norman affairs.[72] The great feasts were often celebrated abroad, particularly under Henry II, of whose thirty-five Christmases only thirteen were spent in England and the rest mainly in Normandy and Anjou.[73]

Much about the holding of assemblies has also to be explained in terms of the king's own policies, habits, and preferences. If the decline of crown-wearing represented a series of conscious royal choices, other variations on the assembly theme owed more to quirks of character and personality. Henry II's temperamental restlessness, his need to be always on the move, his almost literal inability to sit down, even when ill, were none of them traits conducive to a regular rhythm for conciliar meetings.[74] And when the author of the *Gesta Stephani* describes Woodstock as 'the favourite seat of [Henry I's] retirement and privacy (*regis Henrici familiarem priuati secreti recessum*)',[75] and the Battle chronicler has Henry II speak about Clarendon

<hr/>

[70] *John of Worcester*, iii. 138–41; Henry of Huntingdon, *Historia Anglorum*, 466–7.

[71] *Chronicle of Battle*, ed. Searle, 160–1, 174–7.   [72] *Orderic*, vi. 92–3, 136–7, 138–9.

[73] Warren, *Henry II*, 302 and n. 2. For Henry II's assemblies in Normandy, see esp. Power, 'Henry, Duke of the Normans', 118–23.

[74] Map, *De Nugis Curialium*, 476–7; Howden, *Gesta Regis Henrici*, ii, p. xxxii; *History of William Marshal*, ed. A. J. Holden, 3 vols., Anglo-Norman Text Soc. (London, 2002–6), i. 459, ll. 9014–28. Cf. Aurell, *The Plantagenet Empire*, 25–6.

[75] *Gesta Stephani*, ed. and trans. K. R. Potter, rev. R. H. C. Davis, OMT (Oxford, 1976), 138–9 (the translation is that of Colvin, Brown, and Taylor (eds.), *King's Works*, ii. 1009). For Henry I's

'which I dearly love',[76] we can see how personal preferences may well have affected the location as well as the timing of assemblies.

These stops and starts in the institutional history of twelfth-century assemblies suggest that the period saw no steady evolution, no teleological progression, up the smooth slope from witan to parliament. There are dominant continuities in the fact and frequency of royal assemblies (though interrupted by royal sojourns overseas), and continuities too in the work that they do. But outside that central thrust we can see the waning of some early traditions, such as crown-wearing, the revival of others, such as assemblies in the countryside, and, in general, conciliar processes which are less predictable and less determined by the past. Yet a time-travelling ealdorman, magically given the gift of tongues and transported, say, from one of Æthelred's legislative assemblies at Woodstock to his great-great-great-great-grandson's council meeting at the same place in 1175, would not have felt entirely out of place. He might not have observed the king wearing his crown, but he would otherwise have recognized a familiar scene: a great gathering of bishops, abbots, and magnates in the king's presence, political discussion, the granting of charters, the filling of vacant sees and abbacies.[77] Through all the changing scenes of conciliar life there persisted some essential similarities.

3. Council, Counsel, and Counsellors

Some of the haphazardness which characterized conciliar developments in the twelfth century was initially reflected in conciliar terminology. If there was an emerging consistency in what contemporary chroniclers chose to call central assemblies, it hardly amounted to uniformity. In the early part of the century plain 'concilium', sometimes amplified by 'universale', 'generale', or 'maximum', was the most usual word, found too in the official language of royal charters.[78] But it vied with 'conventus', 'conventio', and 'magnum placitum' (a phrase emphasizing the council's judicial side), while 'curia'

---

special interest in Woodstock, see also William of Malmesbury, *Gesta Regum*, i. 740–1, and Henry of Huntingdon, *Historia Anglorum*, 470–1, 486–7 (an apparent state trial takes place there).

[76] *Chronicle of Battle*, ed. Searle, 216–17.

[77] Howden, *Gesta Regis Henrici*, i. 92–3; *Diceto*, i. 401; Eyton, *Itinerary*, 192–3.

[78] e.g. Henry of Huntingdon, *Historia Anglorum*, 476–7, 482–3; *RRAN* ii, nos. 918, 919, 1091.

remained the normal term for a festal court with its assembled barons.[79] In the English vernacular 'witan', formerly a more standard word than any other for these gatherings, survived the Conquest in the work of the Peterborough chronicler. He used it not only for the Domesday assembly of Christmas 1085, but also for the great meeting of 1123, a 'ge witene mot', where William of Corbeil was chosen as archbishop—showing that at least one English observer saw continuity of a sort between pre- and post-Conquest assemblies.[80] By Henry II's day, however, such variations were less in evidence. 'Concilium' was now overwhelmingly dominant, used almost always, for example, by that inveterate recorder of councils, Roger of Howden.[81] But it was frequently inflated as 'generale concilium' or 'magnum concilium';[82] and the latter phrase in particular was already beginning to move away from being a mere indicator of size towards becoming that term of art for an especially important central assembly which modern historians have used to identify such pre-parliamentary councils.

But more significant is the first appearance under Henry II of the French word 'parlement' to denote a council of king and magnates. Three vernacular sources, all dating from the 1170s, are the first to use it. Becket's biographer Guernes de Pont-Sainte-Maxence speaks of the meeting between Henry and Becket at the council of Northampton in 1164 as a 'parlement'.[83] The word here is used somewhat equivocally, since it may stand for the conversation between the two men, a relatively common usage, rather than the council itself. Less equivocal are Jordan Fantosme's account of William the Lion's holding 'sun plenier parlement', 'a full meeting of his *parlement*', in order to obtain the advice of his wise men in 1173,[84] and Wace's retrospective reference to Duke William of Normandy's assembling 'un parlement' at Bayeux to witness Harold Godwineson's oath-taking in 1064.[85] 'Concile' remains the commonest French word for an assembly,[86] but this little cluster of references from

[79] Henry of Huntingdon, *Historia Anglorum*, 454–5, 486–7, 488–9; *John of Worcester*, iii. 138–9.
[80] *Two of the Saxon Chronicles*, ed. Plummer, i. 216, 251; above, 63.
[81] e.g. Howden, *Gesta Regis Henrici*, i. 118–19, 124, 133, etc.   [82] e.g. ibid. 93, 107, etc.
[83] Guernes de Pont-Sainte-Maxence, *La Vie de Saint Thomas Becket*, ed. E. Walberg (Paris, 1936), 50, l. 1525. For the date, see ibid., p. v.
[84] *Jordan Fantosme's Chronicle*, ed. R. C. Johnston (Oxford, 1981), 22–3. For the date, see ibid., p. xxiii.
[85] Wace, *The Roman de Rou*, trans. G. S. Burgess with the text of A. J. Holden, Société Jersiaise (St Helier, 2002), 222–3, l. 5682. For the date, see ibid., pp. xxvi–xxvii.
[86] e.g. Guernes de Pont-Saint-Maxence, 43, l. 1583.

the 1170s suggests that 'parlement' was becoming an alternative: perhaps already moving into use in the everyday French speech of the magnates as a term for the councils that they attended. So in a literal sense, if in no other, the history of parliament may be said to begin in the middle years of Henry II.

But the most pregnant change which affected post-Conquest councils was not directly institutional and still less merely semantic. It lay instead in the feudal concepts, drawn from the continental world of lordship and vassalage, which were now grafted onto a pre-existing English stem. They embodied a view of the obligations of men to their lords which was new to England and which would eventually do much to shape the transition from council to parliament.

The most significant of those obligations was the vassal's duty to render his lord 'council and aid', *consilium et auxilium*. The first was a primarily verbal quality, while the second entailed service, usually military service; and both were closely related.[87] The collocation had its origins in classical and patristic literature, but it was developed and popularized only with the writings of Archbishop Hincmar of Rheims in the late ninth century.[88] It was thence passed down to the intellectuals and courts of the post-Carolingian world. Commenting about 1021 on the oath of fealty for the benefit of Duke William V of Aquitaine, in what came to be seen as a classic statement of feudal obligation, Fulbert of Chartres wrote that the vassal's duty was to give his lord 'faithful counsel and aid'.[89] In the twelfth century John of Salisbury spoke in precisely similar terms, and Ivo of Chartres too saw the duty to give counsel, if not aid, as a direct consequence of fealty.[90] By then the phrase and the concept had already broken surface in England, first appearing in Eadmer's account of Archbishop Anselm's trial at the Rockingham council of 1095. There, Eadmer recalled, writing later between 1109 and 1115, the archbishop had promised to God what was God's and to William

---

[87] See the discussion in Bisson, 'Military Origins of Medieval Representation', 1202–5. At a later stage *auxilium* would come to mean pecuniary aid, first in the form of the three feudal aids, and then in the form of tax: see A. Chauou, *L'Idéologie Plantagenêt: royauté arthurienne et monarchie politique dans l'espace Plantagenêt (XIIᵉ–XIII ᵉ siècles)* (Rennes, 2004), 131.

[88] T. D. Hill, '*Consilium et auxilium* and the Lament for Æschere: A Lordship Formula in *Beowulf*', *Haskins Soc. Jnl.* 12 (2002), 76 n. 9, 81–2; J. Devisse, 'Essai sur l'histoire d'une expression qui a fait fortune: *consilium et auxilium* au IXᵉ siècle', *Le Moyen Âge*, 74 (1968), esp. 183–7.

[89] *The Letters and Poems of Fulbert of Chartres*, ed. and trans. F. Behrends, OMT (Oxford, 1976), 92–3.

[90] *Ioannis Saresberiensis Policratici*, ed. C. C. J. Webb, 2 vols. (Oxford, 1909), ii. 76; E. Bournazel, *Le Gouvernement Capétien au XIIᵉ siècle, 1108–1180* (Limoges, 1975), 139.

Rufus' Caesar 'faithful counsel and aid', *fidele consilium et auxilium*.[91] Anselm evidently regarded this, as Fulbert of Chartres had done, as the defining principle of the vassal's obligation.

No comparable principle had existed in pre-Conquest England. Although attempts have been made to detect the *consilium et auxilium* formula in *Beowulf*,[92] they offer no precise parallel to the feudal ideal and were certainly never developed. Such information as we have on Anglo-Saxon obligations of fealty, in the tract *Swerian* and in the law codes II Edward and III Edmund, does not suggest that 'counsel and aid' played any part in the quite intensive contemporary thinking about lordship.[93] In the slightly later homiletic tradition the stress is all on the king's duty to seek good counsel and not at all on the subject's duty to give it.[94] So what appears in post-Conquest England is essentially a Carolingian principle transmitted, not internally, but from abroad. Its immediate source must have been Normandy. Although the phrase itself seems to be unknown to Norman records before 1066, there are enough close parallels to it, both from Normandy and from the adjacent kingdom of France, for us to think that the obligation which it embodied was generally recognized throughout the northern French lands,[95] and that we should therefore view both phrase and obligation as a unitary Norman import.

The vassal's duty to give counsel, transmuted as it later came to be into the vassal's *right* to give counsel, was one of the building blocks of parliament. The connection was forged through a second change, again unparalleled before the Conquest: those attending royal councils came to do so, not simply through royal choice (as appears to have been the case in Anglo-Saxon England), but as an obligation of the tenure which normally went with their vassalage. The king's tenants-in-chief are obliged to attend councils because it is there that their primary and precedent obligation to

[91] Eadmer, *Historia Novorum*, 57. For the date, see R. W. Southern, *St Anselm and his Biographer* (Cambridge, 1963), 298–300.

[92] Hill, '*Consilium et auxilium*', 72–6.

[93] *Gesetze*, ed. Liebermann, i. 397; *Laws of the Earliest English Kings*, ed. and trans. Attenborough, 118–19; *Laws of the Kings of England*, ed. and trans. Robertson, 12–13; Wormald, *Making*, 383–4.

[94] Above, 35–6.

[95] Davy, *Le Duc et la loi*, 257–60. The Norman document which comes closest to embodying the 'consilium et auxilium' obligation is perhaps an agreement between Viscount Rannulf of Bayeux and the bishop of Bayeux, dated 1087 × 1106, in which each party promises to aid the other in war and to help him in court 'by prayers and counsel': E. Z. Tabuteau, *Transfers of Property in Eleventh-Century Norman Law* (Chapel Hill, NC, 1988), 52–3, 59, 298–9.

give counsel can best be fulfilled. 'Counsel' and 'council', *consilium* and *concilium*, go intimately together.

Our first indication of this new linkage comes with Orderic's account of the council at Winchester preceding William II's invasion of Normandy in 1090. Those summoned, according to the speech which Orderic puts into William's mouth, are 'my father's vassals', *patris mei homines*, holding from the king their fees in England and Normandy. They were urged by William not only to back his invasion of Normandy, thus giving him *auxilium*, but also to advise him: 'I ask you to meet together in a council (*concilium*), discuss measures wisely among yourselves (*prudenter inite consilium*), and tell me what you decide should be done in this crisis.'[96] The neat connection made here between feudal tenure and the obligation to render counsel, seemingly all the more convincing for being casually assumed rather than directly stated, cannot necessarily be taken at face value: Orderic was writing some forty years after the event and provides our only record of the Winchester council. But that he was right to imply that a summons to the king's council was now determined by tenure is shown by a second source. The Peterborough chronicler tells us that in 1095 Rufus summoned to his Christmas court 'all who held land of him', intending that they should give judgement against the rebel Robert de Mowbray.[97] We can deduce that, in feudal language, councils sometimes act as judicial courts, tenants-in-chief owe suit (that is, the duty of attendance), and that counsel may take the form of a judgement. The point was made later, but more explicitly, in the 1164 Constitutions of Clarendon: all clergy holding of the king in chief, like other barons, 'ought to be present with the barons at judgements of the king's court'.[98]

In the beginning, in the generation after 1066, tenure cannot have always, or perhaps even regularly, determined attendance at councils, for the obvious reason that Norman magnates acquired land in England piecemeal and over a period of years.[99] They must often have come to councils before they had land. Even at a later date tenure did not invariably govern attendance. The bishops of Rochester, for example, technically

[96] *Orderic*, iv. 178–81. Cf. Barlow, *William Rufus*, 211, 273. For further discussion of the obligations following from tenure, see below, 84, 90–1, 120.

[97] *ASC*, ed. Whitelock, 173; Barlow, *William Rufus*, 355–6.

[98] Cap. xi: Stubbs, *Select Charters*, 166.

[99] Cf. J. C. Holt, 'The Introduction of Knight-Service in England', in his *Colonial England, 1066–1215* (London, 1997), 96.

held their lands from the archbishop of Canterbury, yet they still attended councils.[100] It is likely to have been only under Rufus that the obligation to give counsel at councils was first clarified, defined, and enforced, along with other feudal obligations. Domesday Book, which listed the names and holdings of all tenants-in-chief, made this possible for the first time, just as it made possible the more rigorous exaction of feudal dues.[101] If the reign provides us with our earliest examples of the summoning of tenants-in-chief to give counsel, it also demonstrates perhaps the origins, and certainly a new severity in the enforcement, of the king's right to reliefs, wardships, and marriages.[102] His particular enforcement of the feudal summons to give counsel made William Rufus one of the distant and unwitting architects of parliament.

If a summons to the king's council was generally determined by status as a tenant-in-chief, how was the principle applied in practice? The answer to this question may be significant, for on it depended in all probability the eventual summoning to parliament of the knights of the shire. The imposition of universal dependent tenure by the Conqueror, with all land held ultimately from the king, meant that there was from the start a very large number of tenants-in-chief, by no means all of them great magnates. Precise numbers are hard to come by, and historians' figures have differed widely. Professor J. J. N. Palmer reckons that 846 secular tenants-in-chief are recorded in Great Domesday (so excluding the landholders of Essex, Norfolk, and Suffolk recorded in Little Domesday); Professor Keefe calculated that 273 lay tenants of the crown were recorded in the Cartae Baronum of 1166 (but the returns to the Cartae are unlikely to have been comprehensive); while Professor Painter believed that there were about 500 of these men under John, excluding those holding by peripheral tenures such as serjeanty.[103] We would expect tenancies to have multiplied after the initial Norman land settlement as estates were broken up by sub-division

---

[100] Reynolds, *Kingdoms and Communities*, 307. For a full discussion of the position of the bishop of Rochester, see G. Garnett, *Conquered England: Kingship, Succession and Tenure, 1066–1215* (Oxford, 2007), 58–60.

[101] Cf. S. P. J. Harvey, 'Domesday Book and Anglo-Norman Governance', *TRHS* 5th ser. 25 (1975), 189–93.

[102] W. Stubbs, *The Constitutional History of England*, 5th edn., 3 vols. (Oxford, 1891), i. 325–6; Barlow, *William Rufus*, 253–7; Garnett, *Conquered England*, 52–6.

[103] J. J. N. Palmer, 'The Wealth of the Secular Aristocracy in 1086', *ANS* 22 (2000), 279; T. K. Keefe, *Feudal Assessments and the Political Community under Henry II and his Sons* (Berkeley, Calif., 1983), 42, 157–88; S. Painter, *Studies in the History of the English Feudal Barony* (Baltimore, 1943), 48.

and as undertenancies were converted into tenancies-in-chief;[104] though this process may have been offset by the consolidation of multiple tenancies in fewer hands. It is probably safe to reckon that throughout the twelfth century tenants-in-chief numbered several hundreds and perhaps many hundreds of men.

Were they all summoned to councils? It seems almost certain that they were, at least for special occasions and from time to time. We may work back towards this conclusion from a starting point in the fairly distant future. In 1215 Magna Carta discloses the operation of a 'two-tier' system of summoning. Clauses 12 and 14 of the Charter laid down that 'common counsel' was necessary for the levying of aids (that is, general taxes). To obtain this 'common counsel' individual summonses were to go to 'archbishops, bishops, abbots, earls and greater barons', while all (others) holding in chief (that is, the lesser tenants) were to be summoned 'generally (in generali) through our sheriffs and bailiffs'.[105] Summons by individual writ for the greater tenants, summons through the sheriffs for the lesser: this system went far back into the past, and certainly to the reign of Henry I if we can believe a letter of Gilbert Foliot. Writing circa 1143, but referring back to the Christmas court of 1126 which had settled the succession on Matilda, Foliot stated that all those accustomed to be summoned in their own names (consueuerant appellari nominibus) had sworn to assist Matilda to obtain the kingdom after her father's death. It is clearly implied that others were present who were not summoned by name and who were outside the circle of oath-takers.[106] We catch another glimpse of the same practice when William fitz Stephen tells us that Becket was gratuitously insulted in 1164 by being summoned to the council of Northampton, not 'by letters which were addressed to him, as was the ancient custom', but by others delivered via the sheriff of Kent.[107]

One further piece of evidence takes us back to the immediate post-Conquest period. In the famous writ of about 1070 sent by William I to Æthelwig, abbot of Evesham, Æthelwig is summoned to Clarendon

---

[104] Holt, 'Introduction of Knight-Service', 84. For an example of the latter process, see J. F. A. Mason, William the First and the Sussex Rapes, Historical Assoc. (London, 1966), 21, which shows how, after Roger of Montgomery's rebellion in 1075, his former undertenants in the Isle of Wight were all made direct vassals of the king.

[105] J. C. Holt, Magna Carta, 2nd edn. (Cambridge, 1992), 454–5.

[106] The Letters and Charters of Gilbert Foliot, ed. A. Morey and C. N. L. Brooke (Cambridge, 1967), 63; Stubbs, Constit. Hist. ii. 608; Maddicott, ' "An Infinite Multitude of Nobles" ', 23.

[107] English Lawsuits, ed. van Caenegem, ii. 425.

with his knights; and he is also told to summon for the same gathering all those under his jurisdiction (*sub ballia et iustitia tua*), with their knights.[108] Now we know that Æthelwig had authority over seven midland shires and their shire courts, working alongside, and probably as the superior of, the local sheriff.[109] It looks very much, therefore, as if the abbot receives a personal summons as a royal tenant-in-chief, but that he also acts as a sheriff, summoning the lesser tenants-in-chief beneath him.

The possibility that the lesser tenants were summoned to councils by similar means may be assessed in another way, via the evidence for the king's communicating on other occasions with the tenants-in-chief, whether lesser or greater, through the sheriffs. Henry II's enquiries of 1166 into the knights' fees and feudal quotas of his tenants, which resulted in the Cartae Baronum, provide some guidance here. The king's requests to these men for a return of knights enfeoffed and other information were in some cases delivered through the sheriffs in the form of an oral announcement almost certainly made in the shire courts. This is the firm implication of Badern of Monmouth's return to the enquiry, which begins 'Lord, I have heard your precept in Hereford (*audivi praeceptum vestrum in Herefordia*)'. William fitz Siward's return is equally informative: 'Your precept, promulgated throughout England, came to me, as to others, through (*per*) your sheriff of Northumberland.'[110] That a similar system was used for conciliar summonses is suggested by Rufus' action against Robert de Mowbray in 1095, already noticed. Then, the king had ordered it 'to be announced (*beodan*) very peremptorily all over this country that all those who held land of the king must be at court in season'.[111] This procedure must have entailed the same sort of proclamation referred to

[108] *RRAN*, ed. Bates, no. 131, where the date and authenticity of the writ are also discussed. As to its authenticity, Bates is agnostic, but Garnett, 'Origins of the Crown', 178 n. 29, more firmly favourable.
[109] Thomas of Marlborough, *History of the Abbey of Evesham*, ed. and trans. J. Sayers and L. Watkiss, OMT (Oxford, 2003), 162–3; R. R. Darlington, 'Æthelwig, Abbot of Evesham', *EHR* 48 (1933), 10–14.
[110] *The Red Book of the Exchequer*, ed. H. Hall, 3 vols., RS (London, 1896), i. 280, 440. The Liber Niger version of the first of these returns reads 'in consulate Herefordiae', meaning 'in the shire court', but this is deleted: ibid. i. 280 n. 16. Badern of Monmouth had a feudal quota of fifteen, so he was not among the smallest tenants-in-chief; but William fitz Siward owed only one knight: Keefe, *Feudal Assessments*, 172, 178. '*Per*' may indicate that the sheriff acted as messenger in delivering the writ: see the discussion in R. C. van Caenegem, *Royal Writs in England from the Conquest to Glanvill*, Selden Soc. 77 (London, 1959), 149–51, 159.
[111] *ASC*, ed. Whitelock, 173; *Two of the Saxon Chronicles*, ed. Plummer, i. 231. Cf. Crouch, *Reign of King Stephen*, 39 n. 28.

more explicitly in 1166, presumably—for it is hard to see how else it could be done—made by the sheriff in the shire court.

The likelihood of the lesser tenants' summoning is similarly suggested by a comparison between the forms of the military and of the conciliar summons. When feudal military service was demanded the tenants-in-chief would be expected to turn out *en masse*; though from the late twelfth century service was increasingly commuted and quotas reduced. For the campaigns of Henry III and Edward I, when information first becomes available, the list of those summoned for military service and for its conciliar counterpart are approximately the same—as we would expect, since tenure determined both sorts of obligation. It is also clear that in raising a feudal army the greater tenants-in-chief were summoned individually and the lesser through the sheriffs; and it is likely that this 'two-tier' system of conciliar summoning first made explicit in Magna Carta was modelled on the types of summons used for both earlier councils and earlier feudal armies.[112] The writ directed to Æthelwig takes the double summons for military service back to the Conqueror's day; for the instruction that Æthelwig should come with his knights, and that they should appear before the king armed and ready to go (*parati*), indicates a summons to a muster rather than to a council.[113] The parallelism perhaps follows from the underlying 'consilium et auxilium' formula itself. If the two most important feudal obligations were to render council and (military) aid, it is hardly surprising that a single mechanism should have served for exacting both.

To show that there were mechanisms which allowed the king to contact the lesser tenants-in-chief and to summon them to councils is not to show that they attended. Yet there is good evidence that they did. In a general way the sources show that there were often men present at councils who were neither churchmen nor magnates. The Peterborough chronicler included 'thegns and knights' among the 'powerful men over all England' who attended the Conqueror's crown-wearings; and among those sitting in judgement on William of St Calais in 1088—and so participating in the feudal procedures of the king's court—were sheriffs, reeves, and huntsmen.[114] The sort of men mentioned by the Peterborough chronicler

---

[112] Maddicott, ' "An Infinite Multitude of Nobles" ', 28–9; Bisson, 'Military Origins of Medieval Representation', 1212–15.

[113] *RRAN*, ed. Bates, no. 131.

[114] *ASC*, ed. Whitelock, 164; *English Lawsuits*, ed. van Caenegem, i. 98; Gillingham, 'Thegns and Knights in Eleventh-Century England', 166–7.

may not always have been lesser tenants-in-chief, for knightly sub-tenants and household knights might be expected by the king to accompany their lords to court, especially perhaps to the festal courts. Their presence added to the splendour of these great gatherings.[115] But on other occasions we can be certain that such men came in their own right and even had a part to play in the proceedings. That lesser tenants might be described merely as 'knights' is more an indication of the lack of an appropriate vocabulary to identify them than a denial of their status as tenants of the crown. Roger of Howden provides the clearest instance of this equation when he recounts how Henry II, preparing to campaign in Normandy in 1177, assembled 'all the earls and barons and almost all the knights of the kingdom who held anything from him in chief (*et fere omnes milites regni, qui de rege aliquid in capite tenuerunt*)'.[116] Holding fees from the king which might comprise no more than a manor or two, these men were clearly not among the *barones*, and there was no other word which could adequately describe their position. 'Knight' was the best available.

An early indication of their conciliar role comes from the various accounts of the Christmas court of 1126, where Matilda was recognized as Henry's heir. William of Malmesbury tells us that the oath to Matilda was taken by 'all in that council . . . who were regarded as carrying any weight (*quicumque in eodem concilio alicuius viderentur esse momenti*)'. This tallies with Foliot's remark, already discussed, that the oath was sworn by all those customarily summoned in their own names.[117] John of Worcester provides corroboration, writing that the oath was taken by the earls, barons, sheriffs 'and the more noble knights (*nobiliores milites*)', showing once again that tenants-in-chief might be described as 'knights', implicitly distinguishing between their two categories, and hinting that the less noble knights, though present, were at best no more than witnesses.[118] When we come to Henry II's reign we can identify one occasion when this group takes on a more active role. At the council of Northampton in 1176, according to Howden, it was 'by the counsel (*per consilium*) of Henry, the king's son, and of earls and barons and knights and of their men' that the Assize of Northampton was made. Diceto independently states that the counsel was

---

[115] For an example, see *Cartularium Monasterii de Rameseia*, ed. W. H. Hart and P. A. Lyons, 3 vols., RS (London, 1884–94), i. 235; Richardson and Sayles, *Governance*, 68.

[116] Howden, *Gesta Regis Henrici*, i. 167.

[117] William of Malmesbury, *Historia Novella*, 8–9; above, 80.

[118] *John of Worcester*, iii. 178–81.

that of the Young King, but that earls, barons, knights, and other men
were present and consenting.[119] Whichever of these reports we take to be
true, both suggest that the knights at Northampton were more than mere
passive observers. Literary sources sometimes share some of the chroniclers'
assumptions about those present at such meetings. The Anglo-Norman
Life of St Edmund, for example, written in Henry II's reign, has Edmund's
father summoning to his royal council not just earls and barons but also
vavassors and knights.[120] Scanty though the evidence is, it is consistent; and
enough to suggest that men below baronial rank were at least sometimes
summoned to councils. For settling the succession or for the making of
new law, if not for more mundane conciliar occasions, their presence was
thought necessary.

If we are correct in assuming that the knights who appear in these
passages are the lesser tenants-in-chief, for whom contemporaries had no
proper term, we must next ask why the king thought it worthwhile to
summon them. In part their summoning was simply the enforcement of
an obligation. Just as they were obliged, along with all tenants-in-chief,
to give the *auxilium* of feudal military service, so they were also obliged
to provide *consilium*. For the king not to have summoned them would
have been to forgo an important right. Their appearance at councils may
also have allowed him to name and identify men on whom he could
fasten the profitable feudal incidents of reliefs, wardships, and marriages
owed by all military tenants to their lords.[121] Left at home in provincial
obscurity, they might otherwise have escaped. There were other equally
practical considerations. The king had an exigent desire for counsel, as
we shall see, and the lesser tenants were surely summoned because the
counsel which they could give on matters such as the making of the Assize
of Northampton was valued. In rather different circumstances Orderic
records Henry I taking advice from 'country knights', rather than the earls
and magnates, when suppressing the rebellion of Robert de Bellême in

[119] Howden, *Gesta Regis Henrici*, i. 107; *Diceto*, i. 404. Cf. A. B. White, 'Some Early Instances of the
Concentration of Representatives in England', *American Historical Review*, 19 (1914), 747 n. 26.

[120] *Memorials of St Edmund's Abbey*, ed. T. Arnold, 3 vols., RS (London, 1890–6), ii. 164–5. For
the date, M. D. Legge, *Anglo-Norman Literature and its Background* (Oxford, 1963), 81–5.

[121] A suggestion supported by the crown's concern to identify the minor tenants-in-chief at a slightly
later date, and for this reason—as can be deduced from John's feudal enquiry of 1212 and those of
Henry III in 1236 and 1242–3: *The Book of Fees, Commonly Called Testa de Nevill*, ed. H. Maxwell-
Lyte, 3 vols., HMSO (London, 1920–31), i. 52–228; Maddicott, ' "An Infinite Multitude of
Nobles" ', 31.

1102; while the Battle chronicler has the abbot of Battle taking counsel with Roger of Pont l'Evêque, archbishop of York, Thomas Becket, the chancellor, and 'a whole flock of knights (*militum multitudinem non modicam*)' in the abbot's lawsuit over the immunity of his house.[122] In neither case are the parallels with the attendance of the lesser tenants at royal councils at all exact, but they nevertheless suggest that these minor figures were not a negligible quantity.

This was partly because of their collective social weight. From at least the time of Domesday landed society embodied a very broad spectrum, with no gulf at any point between the leading tenants-in-chief and their inferiors; landed wealth tapered downwards rather than descending in steps.[123] The proceedings at Salisbury in 1086, when knights and undertenants were among those swearing loyalty to the king, were in part a testimony to that broad spread and to the collective standing of the not so very great.[124] So too were the tax concessions made by Henry I in his coronation charter to the knights holding by military service, the *milites qui per loricas terras suas deserviunt*, a phrase probably intended to denote the lesser tenants-in-chief as well as the knightly sub-tenants.[125] Some confirmation of the importance of this *petite noblesse* in the twelfth-century polity comes from the stress occasionally laid by contemporary literature, notably the prose *Lancelot*, on the need for kings to take account of their interests.[126] If this was a group worth conciliating, it was also one whose advice was worth having. That advice may have been especially sought on a subject on which no sources are likely to throw light: the local conditions and opinions with which men rooted in their fees are likely to have been more conversant than the itinerant and cosmopolitan magnates.

At the end of what may seem in part to have been a long excursus we have established that the obligation to render counsel and aid lay on all crown tenants; that procedures existed for distinguishing between the greater and the lesser tenants-in-chief and for summoning each group to councils; that the lesser tenants were sometimes so summoned, though we cannot say how frequently; and that their presence was a mark of the

---

[122] *Orderic*, vi. 26–7; *Chronicle of Battle*, ed. Searle, 196–7.

[123] Palmer, 'Wealth of the Secular Aristocracy', 286–9.

[124] *John of Worcester*, iii. 44–5; J. O. Prestwich, 'Mistranslations and Misinterpretations in Medieval English History', *Peritia*, 10 (1996), 333–5; above, 66–7.

[125] Stubbs, *Select Charters*, 119; J. A. Green, 'The Last Century of Danegeld', *EHR* 96 (1981), 246; Gillingham, 'Thegns and Knights in Eleventh-Century England', 167.

[126] Chauou, *L'Idéologie Plantagenêt*, 162–3.

importance collectively attached to them. By the early twelfth century
one distinguishing feature of the later English parliament had thus already
emerged: the occasional participation of small landholders, below the level
of the higher nobility, in the proceedings of central assemblies.

4. The Value of Councils and Assemblies

The counsel given to kings in their councils was not the only sort available
to them. Every king could also call on what J.E.A. Jolliffe termed 'familiar
counsel',[127] the advice of his intimates, the congenial and trusted men who
enjoyed the everyday access to the king which distinguished their regular
counselling from the more occasional advice given by bishops and barons,
and sometimes by knights, in assemblies. Ranulf Flambard under William
Rufus, Robert of Meulan and Roger of Salisbury under Henry I, Robert
de Beaumont, earl of Leicester, Richard of Ilchester, and Ranulf Glanvill
under Henry II: every king had such *familiares* as these, though they were
less the isolated figures that this list suggests than the leading members
of small groups of dependable magnates and ministers perpetually about
the court. Their advice, readily available and unconstricted by the formal
structure of assembly counselling, was particularly valued by their royal
masters.

The proper emphasis given to familiar counsel has sometimes led to a
more questionable depreciation of the role of *concilia* in advising the king
and in providing a stable basis for royal government. When councils met,
we are told, 'recognition or assent rather than debate was required of the
great men'. They were 'more concerned with ratification and publicity than
with debate'. 'Their formal proceedings often had more to do with royal
display, and perhaps with the spreading of information, than with the taking
of advice. In general they ratified decisions made beforehand by the king,
perhaps in consultation with his closest advisers.'[128] There is something of a
consensus here that royal councils, the *witan* of the Peterborough chronicler
or the *magna concilia* of Howden, were largely a front, a means to secure
formal public confirmation of decisions taken elsewhere.

---

[127] J. E. A. Jolliffe, *Angevin Kingship*, 2nd edn. (London, 1963), ch. VIII, 'Familiar Counsel'.
[128] T. N. Bisson, 'Celebration and Persuasion: Reflections on the Cultural Evolution of Medieval
Consultation', *Legislative Studies Quarterly*, 7 (1962), 184; Green, *Government of England*, 23; J. Hudson,
'Henry I and Counsel', in J. R. Maddicott and D. M. Palliser (eds.), *The Medieval State: Essays Presented
to James Campbell* (London, 2000), 112.

But this imbalance is hardly reflected in the sources, where familiar counsel and feudal counsel appear as complementary rather than hierarchical in their relationship. For the king 'good counsel', given in assemblies, was a desideratum, greatly valued and often carefully considered, and his need for it almost a craving, sometimes expressed in imperative terms. Its taking was no mere exercise in public relations. ' "Give me good counsel" (*salubre consilium michi queso tribuite*)', Orderic has the Conqueror say to his assembled magnates at the opening of the trial of Odo of Bayeux. ' "Tell me what you decide should be done in this crisis" ', Orderic again reports as Rufus' words to his barons before his invasion of Normandy in 1090.[129] ' "My lords" ', says Henry II to his magnates in the midst of the Young King's rebellion of 1173, according to Jordan Fantosme, ' "give me your counsel" (*Seignurs kar me cunseilliez!*)'.[130] Later, faced with a particularly tricky challenge from King Philip II of France, Henry makes a similar appeal to his great men. ' "Give me your advice" ', the author of the *History of William Marshal* has him saying, ' "What is your opinion?" ' When silence ensues and no one speaks, Henry lets fly: ' "God's eyes, I never saw anything like it . . . You who are my counsellors have no wish to counsel me." '[131] Coming from writers who cannot in most cases have been present at the scenes which they describe, these snatches of direct speech may be imaginative reconstructions. But the authors are at least consistent in seeing nothing implausible in couching the king's demand for counsel in such peremptory terms. That they are supported by similar scenes from the romances, in which kings again positively demand counsel from their barons, tends to confirm their general thrust. Tristan's King Mark, for example, offered the possibility of Iseut's return to his side and Tristan's to his service, assembles his barons and asks them to consider the offer: ' "I beg you to give me your counsel. You must advise me well." '[132] Here and elsewhere the language of literature appears to have mirrored the language of real life.

We can approach the king's need for public counsel from another direction; for the same need was reflected in the frequency of conciliar

[129] *Orderic*, iv. 40–1, 180–1.   [130] *Jordan Fantosme's Chronicle*, ed. Johnston, 16–17.
[131] *History of William Marshal*, ed. Holden, i. 382–5, ll. 7529–58.
[132] Béroul, *Roman de Tristan*, ed. E. Muret, 4th edn., rev. L. M. Defourques (Paris, 1957), 78, ll. 2524–30. For other examples, see ibid. 20, ll. 627–34; Chrétien de Troyes, *Erec et Enide*, ed. M. Roques (Paris, 1952), 10, ll. 307–12. Translations: Beroul, *The Romance of Tristan*, trans. A. S. Fedrick (London, 1970), 104, 61; *Erec and Enide*, trans. D. Gilbert (Berkeley, Calif., 1992), 50.

assemblies, especially in difficult circumstances or in others where important decisions had to be taken. Some twenty-three are known to have met during the period of just over eighteen years which Henry I spent in England, and Professor Robert Bartlett reckons that there may have been more—as many as two or three a year.[133] Under Henry II the tempo may have quickened further in response to circumstance. In Henry's first thirteen months, an uncertain and dangerous time, five councils met to discuss such matters as the state of the peace, the restoration of the law, the destruction of adulterine castles, and the future conquest of Ireland.[134] In the year before Henry's departure to France in August 1177 there were a further six councils dealing with foreign relations, the keeping of the peace, the government of Ireland, and much else.[135] We do not know, of course, how often Henry consulted his *familiares* in private or what advice they gave him,[136] but we can be certain that he saw frequent public consultation with his assembled magnates as an essential part of political decision-making and almost as certain that his grandfather had taken the same view.

Why was the king's desire for counsel so intense and relentless? Counsel delivered at councils suited his purposes in a variety of ways. At state trials, for example, when the giving of counsel merged with the giving of judgement, it might be a means of uniting the whole political community against the king's enemy. So it was at the trial of Odo of Bayeux and later at that of Becket at Northampton in 1164. 'Give me a speedy judgement on him', Henry II is reported by Howden as saying to his barons, 'who is my liege man and refuses to stand trial in my court.'[137] A feudal summons to give counsel at court might also function as a sort of loyalty test. Failure to appear was the mark of a rebel, as Robert de Mowbray found in 1095,

---

[133] G. B. Adams, *Councils and Courts in Anglo-Norman England* (New Haven, 1926), 112; Green, *Government of England*, 22; R. Bartlett, *England under the Norman and Angevin Kings, 1075–1225* (Oxford, 2000), 143.

[134] *Gervase of Canterbury*, i. 160, 162; *Chronicle of Battle*, ed. Searle, 154–5, 160–1; *The Chronicle of Robert of Torigni*, in *Chrons. Stephen . . . Richard I*, iv. 184; Eyton, *Itinerary*, 2, 6–12, 14; Warren, *Henry II*, 194. S. Duffy, 'Henry II and England's Insular Neighbours', in Harper-Bill and Vincent (eds.), *Henry II*, 132–3, shows that, *pace* Warren, the council to consider the conquest of Ireland did in fact take place.

[135] Howden, *Gesta Regis Henrici*, i. 124, 133–4, 144–51, 160, 177–8; Eyton, *Itinerary*, 206, 209–14, 216.

[136] For Henry's use of familiar counsel, see e.g. Giraldus Cambrensis, *Opera*, ed. J. S. Brewer, J. F. Dimock, and G. F. Warner, 8 vols., RS (London, 1861–91), i. 43; Jolliffe, *Angevin Kingship*, 175; and Vincent, 'Court of Henry II', 312–13.

[137] *English Lawsuits*, ed. van Caenegem, ii. 435.

when he ignored Rufus' summons.[138] Or again the need to take counsel might provide the king with a useful pretext for declining to do what he had no intention of doing. Asked by Pope Calixtus II to receive Thurstan as archbishop of York in 1120, 'the king said that he would reply after first taking counsel with his men'—which he then failed to do.[139] Henry II exploited the need for counsel in a similar way in 1185. After the patriarch of Jerusalem had appealed to him for crusading help, Henry responded by seeking counsel from a great magnate assembly at Clerkenwell. It gave him the answer that he almost certainly wanted: it would be better for the country if he stayed at home. 'Kings of England', J. O. Prestwich once wrote, 'were never more "constitutional" than when confronted with demands from the church as unwelcome to their leading subjects as to themselves.'[140]

But royal demands for counsel were by no means merely a matter of subterfuge and ulterior motive. More often than not, counsel was genuinely what was wanted, and the response appears to have been spontaneous and unforced. It often took the form, not of mere ratification of what had already been decided behind the scenes, but of real debate and of a decision which emerged from the meeting. The proceedings of the first council summoned by William I in 1085 to deal with a threatened Danish invasion offer a case in point, and one already mentioned in another context. 'The king was very scared,' William of Malmesbury tells us in his *Life of Wulfstan*. 'He summoned a council and threw open discussion on what should be done', and at Lanfranc's suggestion it was agreed that the magnates' households should maintain contingents of William's mercenary troops in order to defend 'public weal and private fortunes'.[141] This piece of reportage, all the more valuable because it probably rests on the recollections of Wulfstan himself, shows us the summoning of a council to deal with an emergency, the proposal made by a named speaker, and the subsequent adoption of that proposal by king and council. There was probably some real debate too at

[138] *ASC*, ed. Whitelock, 172. Cf. *Orderic*, vi. 20–1, for the similar case of Robert de Bellême in 1102.
[139] Hugh the Chanter, *The History of the Church of York, 1066–1327*, ed. and trans. C. Johnson, rev. M. Brett, C. N. L. Brooke, and M. Winterbottom, OMT (Oxford, 1990), 156–7; Hudson, 'Henry I and Counsel', 123.
[140] *Diceto*, ii, pp. xlviii–xlix, 33–4; C. Tyerman, *England and the Crusades, 1095–1588* (Chicago, 1988), 50–3; J. O. Prestwich, 'Anglo-Norman Feudalism and the Problem of Continuity', *Past and Present*, 26 (1963), 49–50.
[141] William of Malmesbury, *Saints' Lives*, 130–1; Maddicott, 'Responses to the Threat of Invasion', 986–8; above, 62.

the Christmas court of 1126, when Matilda was recognized as Henry I's heir. Though the king got his way here, and the assembly endorsed what was clearly a prior decision, Roger of Salisbury's later statement that he had taken the oath to Matilda only on condition that she should not be married outside the kingdom without his counsel carries with it a suggestion of discussion and dissent.[142] If a royal decision was ratified, it was probably not rubber-stamped.

Henry II's reign in particular shows us a king who wanted counsel, facilitated its giving, and took note of its direction. When, in 1176, William II of Sicily sent ambassadors to ask for the hand of Henry's daughter Joanna, Henry's reaction was to convene a council in London and to ask the assembled prelates, earls, and 'wiser men of his kingdom' how he should respond. Having taken their advice, which must have been positive, he sent the ambassadors to Winchester to view the girl.[143] In March of the following year, when Henry undertook to arbitrate in the dispute between the kings of Castile and Navarre, he again summoned prelates and magnates to London, 'for he would need their advice concerning what judgement to give'. Because the earls and barons could not understand the speeches of the rival envoys, Henry ordered that their claims and demands should be put in writing. Evidently the magnates were expected to be able to follow the arguments, without knowledge of which proper counsel would have been impossible. This provision must have been effective, for the final judgement, though issued by the king, was that of the prelates, earls, and barons.[144] Later in that year another council met at Winchester, prior to Henry's projected campaign in France. But on the advice of the council Henry's crossing was postponed until his envoys had returned from the French court.[145] In none of these cases was a request for counsel merely formal and in each case the counsel given influenced the decision taken.

Consilium would hardly have evolved as a feudal obligation had it not been valued by the ruler. The need for it provides us with a rare insight into the mental state of kings. The doubts and uncertainties of a William I when threatened with a Danish invasion, or of a Henry II when considering a daughter's marriage, were deep and genuine. The taking of counsel was a

---

[142] William of Malmesbury, *Historia Novella*, 7–11; E. King, 'Stephen of Blois, Count of Mortain and Boulogne', *EHR* 115 (2000), 288–9.

[143] Howden, *Gesta Regis Henrici*, i. 115–16.

[144] Ibid. i. 144–51; *English Lawsuits*, ed. van Caenegem, ii. 538–47, esp. 542.

[145] Howden, *Gesta Regis Henrici*, i. 177–8.

means both to their resolution and to the creation of a common platform of responsibility for decisions taken. If the course of action which resulted proved to be mistaken or ineffective, the blame could not be laid on the king alone. The result was to bind the king and his great men together in a common purpose and to identify the counsel which was sought and given in assemblies as the basis for consensus. The strongly autocratic elements in Anglo-Norman and Angevin kingship, the elements of *vis et voluntas*, 'force and will', were modified and balanced by *consilium* in a way which made possible political harmony in the face of an often oppressive government.[146] Counsel privately given by *familiares*, on the other hand, though it might be better informed, technically more proficient, and more to be trusted, could not be invoked to justify royal action in the same way. If relied on too frequently it might even undermine the political stability which more public forms of consultation could produce.

If counsel-taking was an essential buttress for kingship, assemblies in general, and councils in particular, also had much to offer the king's magnates. Some of their chief amenities were divorced from counsel-giving itself. The festal courts, for example, linked to councils at the start of the period but less so thereafter,[147] were great social events, parties on a grand scale, just as the festal meetings of the witan are likely to have been before the Conquest. Writing about 1138, Geoffrey of Monmouth, a more accurate guide to the social and political conventions of his own day than to past history, describes the attractions of King Arthur's festal crown-wearings to those who attended: the eating and drinking, the competitive games, the distribution of rewards for good service. He also casually mentions—what no chronicle tells us—that the wives and daughters of the nobility were present to join in the festivities. Arthur's purpose, so Geoffrey says, was not only to celebrate the feasts of the church, but also 'to renew the closest possible pacts of peace with his magnates (*proceres*)'.[148] Though cast in a legendary context, this account is likely to have reflected political reality in the stress which it laid both on the pleasures offered by festal assemblies and on the creation of political harmony which was a part of their purpose.

[146] Cf. Green, *Government of England*, 23–4; Chauou, *L'Idéologie Plantagenêt*, 127–30.
[147] Above, 57–8, 70–1.
[148] *The Historia Regum Britannie of Geoffrey of Monmouth*, ed. N. Wright (Cambridge, 1985), 96, 109–12. Translation: Geoffrey of Monmouth, *The History of the Kings of Britain*, trans. L. Thorpe (London, 1966), 204–5, 226–31. For Geoffrey of Monmouth's value as a guide to contemporary conditions, see esp. J. O. Prestwich, 'The Military Household of the Norman Kings', *EHR* 96 (1981), 30–3.

The other material advantages of attendance at assemblies of all kinds were manifold. These gatherings provided opportunities for access to the king, private speech, and the pressing of personal interests. The Battle chronicler paints a memorable picture of petitioners crowding the court, the abbot of Marmoutier among them, at one of Henry I's Easter crown-wearings,[149] while Henry II's councils were often marked by grants and charters, just as Arthur's festal courts saw the comparable distribution of land and office.[150] Here again the function of assemblies as dispersal points for patronage differed little from that of the earlier meetings of the witan.

But the main benefits brought by assemblies to those who attended them lay perhaps in a congeries of prospects less tangible than the material patronage which can never have been available to more than a few: the enhancement of honour, the magnification of prestige, and the confirmation of rank. To receive a personal summons to a council, and not a mere summons through the sheriff, in itself conferred honour and rank, as was shown by Becket's chagrin at being denied the privilege in 1164. The division at the Christmas council of 1126 between those personally summoned, who took the oath to Matilda, and the rest, presumably summoned through the sheriffs, who did not, suggests that rank might be reflected in the procedures of the assembly.[151] Seating arrangements, often highly contentious, mirrored similar divisions and a political world in which royal favour was made manifest through visible precedence. To sit by the king, Stephen Langton was later to write, is indeed a mark of a greater position than to sit far from him.[152] This was borne out when councils met. During Anselm's trial at Rockingham in 1095 the bishops who supported the king were given 'seats of honour (*honorifice sederi*)' near to him, while Anselmian dissenters were banished to distant corners.[153] At the Christmas court of 1126 Stephen of Blois, the king's nephew, had what was clearly the most honourable seat on the king's right hand, while Robert of Gloucester, his illegitimate son, sat on his left.[154] At Stephen's

[149] *Chronicle of Battle*, ed. Searle, 112–15.
[150] e.g. Eyton, *Itinerary*, 192 (Woodstock council, 1175), 214 (Oxford council, 1177), 271–2 (Marlborough council, 1186); *Geoffrey of Monmouth*, ed. Wright, 112; trans. Thorpe, 230.
[151] Above, 80.
[152] J. W. Baldwin, *Masters, Princes and Merchants: The Social Views of Peter the Chanter and his Circle*, 2 vols. (Princeton, 1970), i. 177, ii. 117–18. Seating arrangements by rank at councils probably mirrored those at feasts, which are much better evidenced: see J. Kerr, 'Food, Drink and Lodging: Hospitality in Twelfth-Century England', *Haskins Soc. Jnl.* 18 (2006), 80–2.
[153] Eadmer, *Historia Novorum*, 65.
[154] *John of Worcester*, iii. 178–81; King, 'Stephen of Blois', 289.

own great Easter court of 1136 seating arrangements caused a scene when the king gave Henry of Scotland, son of King David, the seat of honour on his right-hand side, provoking a walk-out by the archbishop of Canterbury and an indignant response from the nobles.[155] Precedence was to be gauged by physical proximity to one who was the fount of honour. If we can believe Richard of Devizes, reporting on a council meeting of 1192, the order of speaking, as well as that of seating, may also have been determined by rank.[156]

For a few of the very great, honour at assemblies was bestowed by what came to be known as the coronation services: ceremonial attendance on the king by particular nobles, usually bearing symbols of office and usually at festal courts as well as coronations. So, according to Gaimar (whose account may derive from an eyewitness), at Rufus' magnificent Whitsun court of 1099 four earls, each bearing a sword, processed before the king, while the earl of Chester bore a golden wand.[157] Something similar took place at Henry II's Christmas court of 1186, when the earls of Leicester, Arundel, and Norfolk served the king at table, performing 'the service which pertains to them at coronations and at the king's solemn feasts'.[158] Such services, sometimes menial, conferred status and respect and, like seating arrangements, they gave a strongly visual element to royal assemblies. If the king derived honour from the charismatic display inherent in crown-wearing, so those whom he summoned benefited in a comparable though inferior way from the visibility of their rank.

Assemblies had another beneficial role to play—this time more ritualistic than ceremonial[159]—in resolving conflicts peacefully, so again promoting social and political harmony. Professor Timothy Reuter, guru among medieval political anthropologists, has told us that twelfth-century polities 'lacked a language in which conflict or opposition could be expressed in a controllable form'.[160] One remedy for this lack was the use of ritual at assemblies in order to publicize grievances in an unthreatening way and so to defuse their potentially disruptive power. Gaimar's account of Rufus'

---

[155] *The Chronicle of Richard, Prior of Hexham*, in *Chrons. Stephen . . . Richard I*, iii. 146; Crouch, *Reign of King Stephen*, 42.

[156] *The Chronicle of Richard of Devizes*, ed. J. T. Appleby (London, 1963), 61–2.

[157] Geffrei Gaimar, *L'Estoire des Engleis*, ed. A. Bell, Anglo-Norman Text Soc. (Oxford, 1960), pp. lxxii–lxxiii, 190–1, ll. 6001–36; Barlow, *William Rufus*, 400–1.

[158] Howden, *Gesta Regis Henrici*, ii. 3.

[159] For the distinction, see Leyser, 'Ritual, Ceremony and Gesture', 190–1.

[160] Reuter, 'Assembly Politics', 203.

Whitsun court of 1099 again provides an example. Giffard the Poitevin, Rufus' kinsman, had brought thirty young men to court for the king to knight, but the king had kept them waiting for a month. Giffard was angry. By way of a protest he had his own and his companions' hair cut short and presented his party to the king, cocking a public snook at Rufus' fashionably long-haired entourage. This distinctly risky tactic paid off. The king took the slight with surprising good humour, followed suit by ordering his own men to be shorn, and knighted the shaven thirty.[161] The story shows how tension could be relaxed through ritual and gesture flaunted in the public milieu of a festal court; Giffard's demonstration would hardly have been effective if made to the king in private. But it also shows another possible advantage to be derived from assembly attendance: Giffard used the court as the instrument through which royal patronage, in the form of knighting, could be directed towards his followers.

A second and later example has a rather darker background. Henry II suspected the loyalties of his chamberlain, the great Norman magnate William de Tancarville, and set out to ruin him, depriving him of office, destroying his castles, and denying him justice. William retaliated with a dramatic performance. At the Christmas court held at Caen in 1182 he strode into the king's presence, seized the silver water bowls which traditionally belonged to the chamberlain and which were now being used by the king's attendants, and ostentatiously set about washing the hands of the king and his party before taking his seat. This ritualistic reassertion of his rights as chamberlain proved effective, and William was restored to office.[162] Here again a symbolic gesture of grievance and protest, carried through in the setting of a festal court, had brought about the restoration of royal favour and the settlement of political differences. That the gesture entailed a menial service peculiar to the chamberlain's office showed how such services had an honorific content for their performer which was out of all proportion to their practical utility for their recipient.

In the particular type of assembly which was the *concilium* one acquirement above all others could gain a man honour and reputation: the quality of his advice. Evoked by the king's need for counsel, and recognized by him, it could bring promotion, favour, and reward. The give and take of

---

[161] Gaimar, *L'Estoire des Engleis*, 192–3, ll. 6076–103; Barlow, *William Rufus*, 105–6.
[162] Map, *De Nugis Curialium*, 488–95; J. H. Round, *The King's Serjeants and Officers of State* (London, 1911), 115–17; Koziol, 'England, France and the Problem of Sacrality', 138–9. For a general discussion of this council, see Power, 'Henry, Duke of the Normans', 120–1.

counselling, barely revealed in our chronicle sources, is particularly well brought out in the *History of William Marshal*. The Marshal's biography, written in the 1220s, makes it clear that his growing reputation under Henry II owed much, not only to his knightly prowess, but to his ability to provide good counsel, both to Henry himself and to his son, the Young King. In the section of text ending with Henry II's death in 1189 there are some seven points at which the Marshal is singled out, or more frequently praised, for his counsel, given both in private and in public, and almost always in relation to the conduct of the war with France.[163] Often his accomplishments here are seen as chivalric ones, an aspect of the *cortoisie*, 'courtesy', which was one of the classic knightly virtues. ' "Marshal, you are very courteous (*molt estes corteis*) and have advised me very well" ', says Henry II at one point, and at another, ' "By God, Marshal", said the king, "you speak well and like a courtly man (*e que corteis*)." '[164] The *sens*, 'wisdom', for which the Marshal was well known was placed alongside his prowess, nobility of heart, and generosity (*proëce e . . . bonté e . . . largesse*) as an integral part of his constellation of chivalric virtues.[165] When manifested in public this quality elevated the Marshal above his fellow counsellors. At the council described earlier, when Henry, facing a challenge from the king of France, had appealed to his mute counsellors for advice and been disappointed, it was the Marshal who broke the silence, though with preliminary words of deference to the earls and barons who had failed to speak up. His imaginative and carefully thought-out answer to the problems posed by the French challenge was applauded by the king: ' "Marshal, you have spoken very well and your advice will not be gainsaid." '[166] At least in the eyes of his biographer, and apparently in those of the king, wisdom had trumped rank to win royal favour. We do not perhaps think of the Marshal as a natural committee-man, with the powers of exposition needed to persuade the chairman of the value of his clever ideas. But that, among much else, is what he was.

The assembly, whether festal court or feudal council or both, was thus a public arena, highly structured and with a strong element of theatre. For the king, it provided access to wider counsels than he could obtain from his *familiares*. By comparison with 'familiar counsel', assembly counsel carried

---

[163] *History of William Marshal*, ed. Holden, ii. 326–7, ll. 6420–5, 330–3, ll. 6517–26, 372–3, ll. 7308–11, 386–7, ll. 7617–19, 396–7, ll. 7799–802, 398–9, ll. 7849–52, 454–5, ll. 8947–52.
[164] Ibid. 396–7, ll. 7800–1, 432–3, ll. 8509–10.   [165] Ibid. i. 260–1, ll. 5105–7.
[166] Ibid. 382–7, ll. 7531–618.

fewer political risks, allowed responsibility to be more broadly shared, and drew a larger body of prelates and magnates into the making of decisions. So far as can be seen, the discussions which formed its fabric were 'free and unfettered', in Stubbs's words, and not the contrived formalities which some have supposed. The debates in the *parlement*, a word coming into limited use in the 1170s and combining notions of 'assembly' and 'conversation', were the true forerunners of the later 'assembly conversations' located in parliament.[167]

In these ways assemblies promoted social harmony and political consensus, just as they had done under earlier English kings. All that had changed (though the change was momentous) were the feudal terms which now governed the conciliar summons, and the larger body of landholders which those terms sometimes drew in to the court. For the lay magnates the assembly provided a stage on which a man's place could be publicly established, elevated, and measured against the places held by others in this hierarchical and competitive society. Assembly procedures and conventions, in the form of summonses, seating arrangements, coronation services, and the skills shown in giving counsel, might make or mar honour and reputation. Occasionally too they might provide the means to resolve quarrels and restore peace between king and dissident. The assembly had a special value because it was virtually the only occasion which gathered the nobility together around the king for their mutual benefit and made all this possible.

For all these reasons the role of the assembly cannot be exclusively defined in the formal terms of items on an agenda. As well as the public role it played in such business proceedings as legislation and state trials, its function was the more insensible one of accommodation between the king and his magnates. If the king was entitled to counsel, he also bought it through the conferment of patronage, favour, and place. Honour, represented in early days by crown-wearing, and throughout by the magnificence of court ceremony and hospitality and by the assembly's hierarchical arrangements, was a commodity which moved in both directions. In order to understand how twelfth-century councils came to be so deeply entrenched in the English polity, bridging the gap between witan and parliament, we need to appreciate that the benefits which they brought to all who attended them went beyond the mere giving and receiving of counsel.

---

[167] *Diceto*, ii, p. xlix; H. G. Richardson, 'The Origins of Parliament', in *EPMA* i. 146–51; above, 75–6.

5. Councils, Consent, and the Constitution

Could assemblies impose any constitutional restraints on kings, in the manner of later parliaments? Were kings in any way bound to consult them for reasons other than prudential ones? Were they the settings for debates between king and magnates which arose, not from their sense of common purpose, but from divisions between them? To all these questions we can hardly give positive answers. It is a negative confirmation of the consensus which generally seems to have prevailed at councils and assemblies that although there was discussion about royal policies there was almost never opposition to them; or if there was it has gone unreported by some unusually well-informed chroniclers.[168] Henry I's intention, successfully realized, to have Matilda acknowledged as his heir at the Christmas court of 1126 made for one of the rare occasions when dissent emerged.[169] Courts and councils were open to the protests of individuals with grievances, as we have seen in the cases of Giffard the Poitevin and William de Tancarville, but these were peacefully resolved. Collective opposition was another matter and one seemingly not contemplated—perhaps partly because it was not yet distinguishable from disloyalty, a breach of the feudal *fides* which tenants-in-chief, meeting in council, owed to their royal lord.[170]

This does not, of course, mean that the king could rule without restraint. In the last resort he had to reckon on the possibility of rebellion, feudally sanctioned by the *diffidatio*, the formal renunciation of fealty, if he failed to rule well. But in general the restraints on his position were moral rather than constitutional or ones of applied violence, and so found no expression through institutions. The ancient distinction between rightful government and tyranny, government according to law and government by will, first worked out by classical writers, was forcefully restated in the twelfth century by a contemporary who had much first-hand knowledge of the ways of kings. The tyrant oppresses his people, wrote John of Salisbury; but the prince rules by law and should act upon the counsel of the wise. He is the head of the republic; the heart is the senate, 'from which

---

[168] This was also the conclusion of Stubbs, *Constitutional History*, i. 611–13.

[169] C. W. Hollister, 'The Anglo-Norman Succession Debate of 1126', in his *Monarchy, Magnates and Institutions in the Anglo-Norman World* (London, 1986), 152–60; King, 'Stephen of Blois', 288–90.

[170] Reuter, 'Assembly Politics', 203.

proceeds the beginning of good and bad works'.[171] It might be possible to deduce from this that the king is morally obliged to act on the collective advice of his barons; but this hardly follows from so vague a prescription, and in any case the argument is hardly original. The king's duty to seek good counsel had been one of Wulfstan's preoccupations in his *Institutes*, written in Æthelred's day. Nor was John of Salisbury intending to provide a blueprint for political action. More a writer in the 'Mirror for Princes' tradition than a forerunner of the thirteenth-century lawyer who was to speak of the barons' right to 'bridle' a king who acted outside the law,[172] he provides a guide to the thinking of contemporary intellectuals but not to the practices of contemporary politicians.

If John of Salisbury's views on just rule drew heavily on the past, so too did the more substantial set of restraints embodied in the coronation oath. The king's threefold coronation promise, to protect the church, to do justice to the people, and to suppress evil laws and customs, was in essentials that administered by Dunstan at Edgar's coronation in 973.[173] At particular points in the twelfth century it was certainly called to mind by barons, and perhaps by lesser landholders too, as a prescription for good government. Diceto tells us that when the magnates in council at Clerkenwell in 1185 advised Henry II not to crusade but to stay at home, it was the king's coronation oath that influenced their thinking. It would be more profitable for the king's soul to protect and govern his own kingdom—duties which could be inferred from the oath—than to go east.[174] On occasion, the oath could be invoked more aggressively to remind the king of his obligations. Gerald of Wales tells the story of Roger of Asterby, a Lincolnshire knight known to have lived late in Henry II's reign, who was instructed by heavenly visitors to lay before Henry seven divine commandments, the first of which was that he should abide by the three articles of his coronation oath and maintain the just laws of his realm.[175] Since the other six commandments mainly concerned abuses of royal government, we can assume that the oath was seen as

---

[171] *Policratici*, ed. Webb, ii. 345–6, i. 300, 282–3; John of Salisbury, *Policraticus*, trans. C. J. Nederman (Cambridge, 1990), 190, 70, 67.

[172] Bracton, *De Legibus et Consuetudinibus Anglie*, ed. G. E. Woodbine, trans. and rev. S. E. Thorne, 4 vols. (Cambridge, Mass., 1968–77), ii. 110.

[173] Richardson, 'Coronation in Medieval England', 189, 165–7; Richardson and Sayles, *Governance*, 138; above, 34.

[174] *Diceto*, ii. 33–4; above, 89.

[175] Giraldus Cambrensis, *Opera*, viii. 183–6; Holt, *Magna Carta*, 72–3.

the subject's safeguard against such abuses. Both these episodes testify to laymen's knowledge of the coronation oath and to the appeals which could be made to it as a yardstick of good government. But in the first case it was used by a magnate council to determine the most virtuous course of action for the king, and in the second to enjoin just rule on the same king. Important though the coronation oath was in establishing the norms of good kingship, its usefulness did not go beyond that of moral suasion. It was in no way what Magna Carta became later, a rod to be applied by assemblies to the king's back.

Coronation charters, which were in a sense outgrowths of the coronation oath,[176] created a closer link between assemblies and restraints on kingship. Made during the magnate gatherings attendant on coronations, they represented a practical amplification of the oath's moral undertakings. Their post-Conquest exemplar, Henry I's charter, was more clearly a response to magnate grievances than were those of the two succeeding kings, and it invoked baronial counsel at several points. It was 'by the common counsel of the barons of the whole kingdom of England' that the king had been crowned; he would take the counsel of his barons before disposing of the marriages and lands of the daughters of his tenants-in-chief; by the common counsel of the barons the king had retained the royal forest in his hand; and he restored 'the laws of King Edward', which his father had amended with the counsel of his barons. The coronation charters of Stephen and Henry II both referred back to Henry I's concessions and were presumably intended as confirmations of what he had granted.[177] All three charters, especially that of Henry I, gave formal and public recognition to the linkage made by intellectuals, whether the earlier Wulfstan or the later John of Salisbury, between good government and the king's moral duty to take counsel. All three can also be seen as part of a 'constitutional tradition', embodying the notion of limitations on the crown and the defence of its subjects against oppressive royal lordship, which had probably begun with the concessions made by Æthelred on his return to England in 1014, continued with Cnut's peacetime confirmation of those concessions, and culminated in Edward the Confessor's confirmation of Cnut's laws as the price of his future kingship in 1041.[178] Edward's own mythical laws had

---

[176] Richardson, 'Coronation in Medieval England', 163; C. W. Hollister, *Henry I* (New Haven, 2001), 108–9; J. A. Green, *Henry I: King of England and Duke of Normandy* (Cambridge, 2006), 44–5.
[177] Stubbs, *Select Charters*, 117–19, 142, 158.   [178] Above, 36–40.

been promised to the Conqueror's new subjects after 1066 and re-promised by Henry I in his coronation charter.[179] Later, in King John's day, about the time of the drafting of Magna Carta, the three twelfth-century coronation charters were collected up and translated into French,[180] and it was then too that the confirmation of Henry I's coronation charter was demanded from the king, in what came to be seen as a prelude to the Great Charter itself.

There were continuities and consistencies here: in the subject matter of the pre-Conquest laws and agreements and of the later charters, in their general circumscription of royal power, and in the circumstances of their making. Cnut's laws, their confirmation by Edward, and the three coronation charters, were all associated with the start of new reigns. They can be seen as attempts by incoming kings to win support and so to shore up what was in all these cases a questionable claim to the throne. This was most true in the case of Henry I's coronation charter: a blatant 'election manifesto', launched in the face of a potential challenge from Henry's brother Robert of Normandy and designed to placate all who had suffered from Rufus' oppressive regime. The appeal of such a programme extended well beyond the higher nobility. The extensive circulation of Henry's charter, in the first place to the shire courts, and its possible translation into English, bear witness to the social breadth of the English political nation at an early date.[181] So, in another way, does the intrusion of the coronation oath into the dreams of a Lincolnshire knight. We can see again why kings may have thought it useful, as well as feudally correct, to summon the lesser tenants-in-chief to councils. Well informed and politically aware, they were men qualified to provide both counsel at the centre and support in the localities.

That there was a tradition here cannot be doubted, for almost every one of these texts looked back to, and often cited, its predecessor. Yet it was a tradition which hardened and contributed to political action only when invoked from the retrospective vantage point of John's reign. No more than coronation oaths were coronation charters drawn on by assemblies to

---

[179] *Laws of the Kings of England*, ed. and trans. Robertson, 230–1; Wormald, *Making*, 398–9; Stubbs, *Select Charters*, 119 (c. 13).

[180] Holt, 'Origins of the Constitutional Tradition', 15.

[181] *RRAN* ii, n. 488; Wormald, *Making*, 400; Campbell, 'Late Anglo-Saxon State', 23; J. A. Green, ' "A Lasting Memorial": The Charter of Liberties of Henry I', in M. T. Flanagan and J. A. Green (eds.), *Charters and Charter Scholarship in Britain and Ireland* (Basingstoke, 2005), 53–69, esp. 63–6.

limit royal power. Made as they were in situations of emergency, by kings of doubtful legitimacy, their importance was temporary until they were rediscovered and consolidated on the eve of Magna Carta. Once the king was established, electoral promises could be ignored.[182]

Were there then no circumstances in which kings were obliged to consult councils and so perhaps to risk the threat of restraint? The summoning of councils was itself a prudential recognition of the need to consult, one which took account of what barons wanted as well as of the practical value of their advice. Once summoned, those present may sometimes have used their obligation to give counsel to impose a brake on royal policy through their criticisms of it. ' "Because you are my lord, I owe and I offer you my counsel and service," ' Becket wrote to Henry II in 1166—before following up these dutiful feudal words with a blasting denunciation of Henry's interference in ecclesiastical liberties.[183] One area of royal activity, law-making, already appears to have been subject to more formal restraints. In the course of a lawsuit dating from about 1140 the abbot of Battle alleged that 'although the king could at will change the ancient rights of the country for his own time', he could not do so for posterity 'except with the common consent of the barons of the realm'.[184] This is an ex parte statement and therefore suspect. But it reflects both pre- and post-Conquest practice, and it is buttressed fore and aft by the claim in Henry I's coronation charter that the king's father had amended the laws of King Edward 'by counsel of his barons', and by Glanvill's later statement that laws were rulings 'promulgated about problems settled in council on the advice of the magnates and with the supporting authority of the prince'. 'The advice of the magnates' was no mere formality, as was shown in the conciliar discussions which contributed to the making of the grand assize.[185] Though the abbot of Battle's assertion may seem to give too hard a constitutional edge to what was a matter of custom rather than principle, long-standing practice may by this time have acquired a prescriptive force. That permanent changes in the law required the collective consent of the

---

[182] As, especially, under Henry I: J. A. Green, ' "Praeclarum et Magnificum Antiquitatis Monumentum": The Earliest Surviving Pipe Roll', *BIHR* 55 (1982), 6–7, 10–11; Hollister, *Henry I*, 109–12.

[183] *Correspondence of Thomas Becket*, ed. Duggan, i. 292–9.

[184] *Chronicle of Battle*, ed. Searle, 144–5; Hudson, 'Henry I and Counsel', 120–2.

[185] Stubbs, *Select Charters*, 119 (c. 13); *Glanvill*, ed. G. D. G. Hall (London, 1965), 2, 28; P. Brand, 'Henry II and the Creation of the English Common Law', in Harper-Bill and Vincent (eds.), *Henry II*, 230–1.

baronage, given in council, is the nearest we come to a constitutional rule in the twelfth century.

As central as law-making to the agenda of later parliaments, and as subject to constitutional rules, was taxation. If this eventually proved to be the issue which changed the whole nature of royal councils, doing much to turn them into parliaments, the transformation was by no means predictable. Initially, assemblies had little to do with taxation, and until the last years of Henry II taxation and consent were only very rarely part of their business. Under Æthelred tribute payments to the Danes had often been sanctioned at meetings of the witan,[186] but with no constitutional implications. After the Conquest the occasional hints of change which we find usually result from emergencies. The decision at the autumn council of 1085 to billet the king's mercenaries on magnate households, taken in the face of a threatened invasion, was in effect an act of conciliar consent to the exploitation of magnate resources; one from which all might be expected to benefit.[187] Faced with the same threat, the council at Gloucester which followed shortly afterwards initiated the Domesday survey. This almost certainly had a related fiscal purpose: either singly or in combination, to reassess the geld (levied in 1086 at the exceptional rate of 6s. per hide), to identify those responsible for paying it, and to facilitate the king's feudal access to the wealth of his tenants-in-chief.[188] Both these councils could be viewed as 'tax parliaments' *avant la lettre*, the remote precursors of the tax-granting assemblies of the thirteenth century. Eleven years later William II's heavy geld of 4s. per hide, taken to restore his control over Normandy, was conceded (says the not entirely reliable *Leges Edwardi Confessoris* of the mid twelfth century) by the king's barons, from whom he had sought *auxilium*: the first occasion on which this word was used with fiscal rather than military implications.[189] The further aid of 3s. per hide given for the marriage of Henry I's daughter in 1110 may also have received some form of baronial consent.[190] But these levies were all unusual, both in their occasions and in their high rates. Even if they were linked to collective

---

[186] e.g. *ASC*, ed. Whitelock, 83 (994), 86 (1002), 91 (1011).

[187] Maddicott, 'Responses to the Threat of Invasion', 986–91; above, 62, 89.

[188] See e.g. Harvey, 'Domesday Book and Anglo-Norman Governance', 186–91; Prestwich, 'Mistranslations and Misinterpretations', 327–32.

[189] *Gesetze*, ed. Liebermann, i. 636; B. R. O'Brien, *God's Peace and King's Peace: The Laws of Edward the Confessor* (Philadelphia, 1999), 45, 168–9; Barlow, *William Rufus*, 211, 246–7.

[190] *Historia Ecclesie Abbendonensis*, ed. Hudson, ii. 166; Henry of Huntingdon, *Historia Anglorum*, 456–7; Hudson, 'Henry I and Counsel', 119.

consent (and the evidence is not beyond doubt), they do not suggest that the more routine operations of the royal fisc were in any way subject to baronial or conciliar intervention. General taxes were at most only rarely and barely linked with consent.

The reasons for this contrast with later parliamentary practice are fairly clear. Until its probable abandonment after 1161–2,[191] the only direct tax was the geld. This fell largely on the peasantry. Domesday suggests that the demesne manors of the tenants-in-chief were either heavily marked down or altogether exempt;[192] and although this privilege was later abrogated, perhaps under Rufus, individual exemptions, granted by way of patronage, remained numerous. We shall return to this subject in our final chapter.[193] Geld remained an important royal resource. It produced about 10 per cent of the total revenue paid in at the exchequer in 1129–30,[194] and it was onerous enough for a seven-year remission by Henry I in 1131 and a permanent remission by Stephen in 1136 (probably later rescinded) to be presented as political concessions.[195] But so far as we can tell it was never so burdensome to the whole magnate class as to generate a collective protest, and it had behind it the sanction of custom and antiquity. Most of the crown's other revenues from 1066 onwards came from land, regalian rights over vacant churches, and—increasingly from the 1090s—from the feudal incidents and the profits of justice.[196] The prerogative and feudal impositions among these resources were often oppressive and resented, as Henry I's coronation charter suggests, but they were difficult to challenge. Nowhere was there much scope for consultation on fiscal matters.

It was only in Henry II's reign that consent to taxation first appeared on the conciliar agenda in any way which was to prove decisive. But it did so obliquely, with taxes levied for ecclesiastical rather than secular purposes. The stimulus for change lay in the east, in the needs of the crusader states, and then in the crusade itself. In 1166, at Le Mans, Henry imposed a tax on revenues and moveables for the relief of the Holy Land. He did so in an assembly of the archbishops, bishops, and magnates of his

---

[191] Green, 'Last Century', 241–58, esp. 242.
[192] S. P. J. Harvey, 'Taxation and the Economy', in Holt (ed.), *Domesday Studies*, 258–64. Contrast Green, 'Last Century', 245–6, where it is argued that only the demesne sections of demesne manors were exempt.
[193] Below, 418–19.   [194] Green, 'Last Century', 246–52, 254.
[195] *John of Worcester*, iii. 202–3; Henry of Huntingdon, *Historia Anglorum*, 704–5 and n. 19; Green, 'Last Century', 242.
[196] Green, ' "Praeclarum et Magnificum Antiquitatis Monumentum" ', 3–17, esp. 7–9, 11.

continental fiefs, 'with the counsel and assent of all', each of those present
swearing to levy the tax from his subjects. Though granted in France, the
tax was also collected in England on a parish basis, at a rate of 6d. in the
pound (or a fortieth), and via the oaths of the taxpayers. Consent was here
given abroad, and seemingly by individuals rather than collectively; but for
the first time it was linked with a general levy which all were expected
to pay.[197]

Less is known about a further and related levy, put in hand by Henry
II and Philip Augustus in 1184–5, again imposed for the relief of the
Holy Land, approved 'by the common counsel of bishops and earls and
barons', and levied in England as well as in the continental lands.[198] But
much more portentous was the famous Saladin Tithe of 1188, levied to
support Henry's projected crusade. First authorized 'by common counsel
(de communi consilio)' at an assembly at Gisors, on the borders of France and
Normandy,[199] the tax received a more local sanction from a council which
Henry convened at Geddington in Northamptonshire in February 1188.
It was again levied on revenues and moveables, but at the extremely high
rate of a tenth. For three reasons the Saladin Tithe was momentous. First,
in the manner of its making it prefigured with precision the tax grants
made in later parliaments: the consent of the magnates was given at a royal
assembly to the levying of a general tax. Second, its universal incidence
produced a massive yield. Unknown in total, but certainly running into tens
of thousands of pounds, the yield showed the very considerable potential
of this form of taxation. And, third, its severity provoked widespread
opposition—not, so far as we can tell, among the conciliar magnates
present at Geddington, but certainly in the country at large.[200]

Here was both a tempting resource for future kings and an impending
threat to the consensus which had generally governed the conciliar relationships between past kings and their magnates. Here too was a means
by which the merely moral restraints on kingship, set out implicitly in the
writings of those who distinguished between princely government by will

[197] Gervase of Canterbury, i. 198–9; S. K. Mitchell, Taxation in Medieval England (New Haven, 1951),
114–15, 168–9; Tyerman, England and the Crusades, 45.

[198] W. E. Lunt, 'The Text of the Ordinance of 1184 Concerning an Aid for the Holy Land', EHR
37 (1922), 240–2; Mitchell, Taxation, 169; C. and S. II. ii. 1023–4.

[199] William of Newburgh, Historia Rerum Anglicarum, in Chrons. Stephen . . . Richard I, i. 273.

[200] Howden, Gesta Regis Henrici, ii. 30–3; Mitchell, Taxation, 169–71; C. and S. II. ii. 1024–9;
Tyerman, England and the Crusades, 76–80.

and by law, and explicitly in the coronation oath, might in future become both political and constitutional. The *concilium* of prelates and magnates inherited from the pre-Conquest English past, and since reinforced by feudal notions of the king's right to counsel, would soon become the instrument of change.

3

Transformation

The Making of the Community of the Realm, 1189–1227

1. The Great Council of 1225

The English parliament descended directly from the great assemblies of the pre-Conquest past, their role strengthened in the post-Conquest world by the novel tenurial obligation to attend and, much later, by the beginnings of their association with tax grants. Yet parliament's most formative antecedents lay in the period between Richard I's accession in 1189 and the end of Henry III's minority in 1227. During the first part of that period the oppressiveness of royal government, the result of the interaction between the fiscal pressures brought by warfare and the rule of kings determined to exploit their political freedom from legal restraints, destroyed the consensus which had marked the relationship between king and magnates for much of the twelfth century. In the resulting confrontations counsel and consent became contentious issues, as they had rarely been in the past. The regulation of these issues in Magna Carta was adventitiously to shape the way in which parliament evolved for much of Henry III's reign; and by the end of that reign it had assumed the approximate form and functions which it was to maintain for the rest of the middle ages.

These changes were by no means exclusively insular. In other European kingdoms too, the late twelfth and early thirteenth centuries proved to be an era of particular political unrest, whose causes—war, royal taxation, demands for military service, disputes over rights of consultation—were similar to those which shaped the pattern of English politics.[1] The search for liberties provoked by harsh royal government resulted in other national charters besides Magna Carta, and what has been called 'the shift from assemblies to proto-parliaments' which was a related development that occurred in other countries besides England.[2] Yet if change followed a common pattern, it was in England that its institutional consequences were most sharply felt, for reasons which have as much to do with chance and contingency, notably King John's premature death and his son's long minority, as with any planned or directed transformation. Though the rise of the English parliament can be placed in a pan-European 'age of estates' context, it nevertheless followed an almost wholly individual course.[3]

We will begin at the end of this short period in order to show the new forces which had by then emerged to shape political life. On 2 February 1225 an assembly termed by one chronicler a 'general colloquium' (*generale colloquium*) and by another a 'great council' (*magnum concilium*) met in London to confront a crisis. Poitou had been lost to the French in the previous year, Gascony was now under threat, and an invasion of England seemed probable.[4] Before a large audience—the archbishop of Canterbury, 11 other bishops, 20 abbots, 9 earls, and at least 23 barons—the justiciar, Hubert de Burgh, spelt out the king's need for money for the kingdom's defence. After a long debate, lasting at least a week, agreement was finally reached by 11 February: the magnates would grant a general tax of a fifteenth on moveable goods if the king would confirm and reissue Magna Carta and the Charter of the Forest. The tax grant was formally said by the king to have been conceded by the 'archbishops, bishops, abbots, priors, earls, barons, knights, free tenants and everyone in our kingdom', and the king's reciprocal grant was made to the same group without express mention of the knights and free tenants.[5] In 1264 Simon de Montfort's reforming barons would refer back to the assembly's grant as one made by 'the community of the realm' and the king's grant as made to the

---

[1] Cf. Bisson, 'Celebration and Persuasion', esp. 189–91; id., 'The Politicising of West European Societies (*c*.1175–*c*.1225)', in C. Duhamel-Amado and G. Lobrichon (eds.), *George Duby: l'écriture de l'histoire* (Brussels, 1996), esp. 247–50.

[2] Reuter, 'Assembly Politics', 194; Holt, *Magna Carta*, 24–7, 76–81.

[3] Cf. A. R. Myers, *Parliaments and Estates in Europe to 1789* (London, 1975), part 1, 'Obligation and Privilege: The Age of Estates'. For further comparisons, see below, 377–80.

[4] *Ann. Dunstable*, 93; *Ann. Tewkesbury*, 68; *The Historical Collections of Walter of Coventry*, ed. W. Stubbs, 2 vols., RS (1872–3), ii. 256; *Pat. Rolls, 1216–25*, 503.

[5] Wendover, *Chronica*, iv. 99–100; *Stat. Realm*, i. 22–5; Stubbs, *Select Charters*, 350.

synonymous 'community of the land'.[6] Those who were absent from the
assembly, such as the bishop of Durham, were regarded as being bound by
the terms of the grant and later paid their share.[7] A few days later royal
orders went out to the counties for the assessment and collection of the tax
and simultaneously for the proclamation and observance of the Charters.[8]
Wiltshire's copy of the Great Charter was laid up by the county's knights
in the local nunnery at Lacock. At the council's insistence the money raised
was kept apart in two separate castle treasuries and in the custody of two
bishops, presumably to ensure that it was spent exclusively on the war.
From there it was disbursed to Richard of Cornwall, the king's brother
and leader of his forces in France, enabling him to secure Gascony and save
the day.[9]

In many respects the great council of 1225 provides a paradigm for the
later parliaments of the thirteenth and fourteenth centuries. It is summoned
in advance of a foreign campaign and in order to finance that campaign,
as well as to provide more generally for the kingdom's defence. A leading
minister puts the case for a money grant, and a grant is conceded. But
at the same time a bargain is struck: redress of grievances, meaning in
this case the confirmation and reissue of the Charters, is traded against
supply. Those making the grant, a restricted number of churchmen and
magnates, are considered to stand for the whole kingdom: notionally the
great council is a representative body. Its members' gains are announced to
their 'constituents' in the shires, just as Edward III's concessionary statutes
would sometimes be announced at the conclusion of his parliaments.
Finally, the proceeds of the tax are appropriated to the purpose for which
it was granted.

In essentials, and allowing for the absence of an elected commons, we
seem to be no distance from the parliaments of the Hundred Years War.
But we are a long distance, in development if not in time, from the great
councils of Henry II's reign. Only Henry's council at Geddington which
granted the Saladin Tithe in 1188 bore any resemblance, and that a remote
one, to the London council of 1225. What follows will attempt to identify
the forces and circumstances which gave rise to this second council—a

---

[6] *DBM* 268–9.

[7] S. K. Mitchell, *Studies in Taxation under John and Henry III* (New Haven, 1914), 161–2.

[8] D. A. Carpenter, *The Minority of Henry III* (London, 1990), 383.

[9] *Stat. Realm*, 'Table of the Charters', no. XI; Mitchell, *Studies in Taxation*, 167–8; Carpenter, *Minority of Henry III*, 376–9.

'model parliament' *avant la lettre*—and to trace the evolution of Henry III's proto-parliament from the conciliar assemblies of his grandfather's day.

2. Council and Counsel

We start with council and counsel, the institution and its function, because they provide the main link between Henry II's assemblies and the tax-granting council of 1225. That progression was divided into three distinct phases: the early years of Richard I, when the great council attained an unprecedented prominence; the reign of John when, by contrast, its role contracted; and the minority of Henry III, when the council once again exercised a semi-independent authority comparable to, but more prolonged and wide-ranging than, that of the councils of the early 1190s. The first two phases will be discussed here, leaving the minority councils for treatment later.

Henry II's death brought an important break in regnal continuity, marked by his successor's absence, first on crusade and then in captivity, from 1189 to 1194. The prominence of the great council in Richard I's early years owed almost everything to this.[10] From the time of Richard's accession the intricate texture of events rapidly transformed the council's role, making it more difficult for us to depict its evolution with the broad brush-strokes adequate enough for the previous century, and more necessary to look closely at the politics of the period. The primary reason for the rapidity of change lay here, in politics, and especially in the 'shambolic'[11] arrangements made for the kingdom's government while Richard was away. The lack of a single regent-justiciar, in disregard of the precedents set by previous royal absences; the division of authority between shifting combinations of ministers; the resulting feuds, both between ministers and between ministers and magnates; the need for ministers to reinforce themselves with magnate backing; and the disloyalty of Richard's brother John, against whom united action proved in the end to be necessary: these circumstances conferred a novel authority, if only intermittently and episodically, on the great council of magnates. At times it held the ring, at others it initiated policy.

---

[10] See especially B. Wilkinson, 'The Government of England during the Absence of Richard I on the Third Crusade', *Bulletin of the John Rylands Library*, 28 (1944), offprint, 3–27.

[11] Carpenter's word: D. Carpenter, *The Struggle for Mastery: Britain, 1066–1284* (Oxford, 2003), 246.

Even before Richard's departure the council may already have had a hand in business traditionally reserved for the king. Richard's initial appointment of William de Mandeville, earl of Essex, and Hugh de Puiset, bishop of Durham, as joint justiciars, at a meeting of the great council at Pipewell in Nottinghamshire in September 1189, presumably involved no more than conciliar ratification of a royal decision.[12] Yet this in itself may be significant; at any rate there seem to be no other twelfth-century examples of major secular appointments made in assemblies. More conclusively significant was the reaction to Richard's subsequent committing of his kingdom to his unpopular chancellor William Longchamp, undertaken, according to William of Newburgh, 'without the counsel and consent of the nobility'.[13] The eventual deposition of Longchamp in 1191 and his replacement by Walter of Coutances, archbishop of Rouen, as the king's justiciar and chief minister, was carried through with the assent of bishops, earls, and barons at meeting at St Paul's: a procedure which combined the council's traditional role as the locus for state trials with a more novel intrusion of conciliar initiative into ministerial appointments.[14] Rapidly emerging here were magnate claims for corporate consultation in matters of appointments, at the latent expense of a royal prerogative whose exercise was prevented by the king's absence. Under Henry III the issue would come to the fore again as one of the central points of contention between king and magnates.

Confirmed in office by a magnate council, Walter of Coutances himself relied consistently on the great council's continuing support. He summoned a *magnum concilium* when Longchamp tried to return to England in 1192; he convened another when news of Richard's capture came through in 1193; and it was Walter, the other justices, and the magnates who refused John's subsequent request for his brother's kingdom.[15] The effect of this regular recourse to magnate councils, for appointments, for the afforcement of the justiciar's authority, and for much else, seems to have been to increase the sense among magnates and ministers of their corporate standing and of their ability to speak for a constituency beyond their own ranks. The proceedings of 1191 by 'the common council of the kingdom' against Longchamp were reported to Richard in a letter from the justiciars, bishops, earls, and barons

---

[12] Howden, *Gesta Regis Henrici*, ii. 85–7; Wilkinson, 'Government of England', 4.

[13] William of Newburgh, 306–7; Wilkinson, 'Government of England', 5.

[14] Howden, *Gesta Regis Henrici*, ii. 213–14; Howden, *Chronica*, iii. 140–1; Giraldus Cambrensis, *Opera*, iv. 407–8; Wilkinson, 'Government of England', 25–6.

[15] Giraldus Cambrensis, *Opera*, iv. 414; William of Newburgh, 345; Howden, *Chronica*, iii. 197, 204. For these examples and others, see Wilkinson, 'Government of England', 26.

'written in common (*in communi scripto*)'; while after John's rebellion and alliance with Philip Augustus of France in 1193 the decision to dispossess him and to besiege his castles was taken at a further meeting in February 1194 'by the common counsel of the kingdom (*per commune consilium regni*)'.[16] So Howden, our reporter, certainly saw those present as standing for the kingdom; as they probably did themselves.

During Richard's absence meetings of the great council thus provided points of stability in a rapidly shifting political environment, the necessary sanction for ministerial initiatives, and a growing claim to represent the real interests of the king and kingdom. The product of peculiar circumstances, this phase did not last beyond Richard's return in March 1194. When he left England again in the following May, this time permanently, his new justiciar, Hubert Walter, had the energy, acumen, and political weight to govern effectively for the king and to do so without the dependence on magnate councils which had characterized the justiciarship of his predecessor.[17] Yet the part played by the great council in the early 1190s was no mere episode. Its memory survived, if only passively, to help to shape future views on what the collective body of the magnates might do and represent.

It was perhaps that not-so-distant memory, in combination with the king's own practices, which underlay the emergence of counsel as a political issue in the next reign. Almost from the time of King John's accession in 1199 there was a widespread perception that he was the willing recipient of 'evil counsel'. It was evil counsel, according to Howden, which led him to keep back rents from the York archiepiscopal manors when he restored his brother Geoffrey to the see and its estates in 1199;[18] that, according to Diceto, led him to divorce his wife in the same year;[19] that, again according to Howden, led him to demand that the earls who refused to come to France with him in 1201 should surrender their castles;[20] that, according to Gervase of Canterbury, led him to refuse to meet Archbishop Langton when Langton tried to return to England in 1209;[21] and that, according to Roger of Wendover, led him towards the cruelties

[16] Howden, *Chronica*, iii. 155, 236–7.
[17] Cf. R. V. Turner and R. R. Heiser, *The Reign of Richard Lionheart* (Harlow, 2000), 149–50.
[18] Howden, *Chronica*, iv. 92; J. Gillingham, 'Historians without Hindsight: Coggeshall, Diceto and Howden on the Early Years of John's Reign', in S. D. Church (ed.), *King John: New Interpretations* (Woodbridge, 1999), 13.
[19] *Diceto*, ii. 167; Gillingham, 'Historians without Hindsight', 9.
[20] Howden, *Chronica*, iv. 161; Gillingham, 'Historians without Hindsight', 14.
[21] *Gervase of Canterbury*, ii. 104; C. R. Cheney, *Pope Innocent III and England* (Stuttgart, 1976), 319.

advocated by Master Alexander the Mason, who taught that a king should rule his people with a rod of iron.[22] Of these writers, both Diceto and Howden had ceased writing by the end of 1201, and Gervase by the end of 1210. Only Wendover wrote after John's defeat and death in 1215–16.[23] So all but one of these accusations are either early or contemporary. With the partial exception of Gervase's claim, they are not the product of the dark view of John which grew from the loss of Normandy in 1204, the interdict of 1208, John's excommunication in 1209, and Magna Carta; nor was 'evil counsel' yet the 'ubiquitous trope' that it was to become.[24]

None of this necessarily makes it any easier to assess the tradition which these accusations embody. If Howden could criticize John for following evil counsel, there were other occasions for which he noted John's acceptance of 'the counsel of good men', even 'the counsel of the kingdom'.[25] The rolls of the chancery and the king's court seem to bear this out, recording as they do numerous *acta* carried through 'by the common counsel of our realm' or by some similar warrant. The assize of bread in 1204, the assize of money in 1205, the defence plans of the same year against a French invasion, and a variety of legal cases were all made or settled in these terms.[26] Yet all may not be as it seems here. Holt has written that 'it is now impossible to define the reality which lay behind these phrases',[27] and they may have testified, not so much to consultative practice, as to the ability of John's clerks to apply an acceptable constitutional gloss to more narrowly based decisions. John may have consulted magnate councils on uncontentious matters or when, like his father, he genuinely wanted advice, as, for example, when a French invasion threatened in 1212.[28] But when opposition seemed likely he could be disingenuous in the support which he claimed, and when magnate interests were at stake, altogether more evasive.

Two examples illustrate John's attitude to counsel in matters of business. In 1201 an exchequer ordinance was published at Windsor. In effect it constituted a little set of rules which tightened up procedures for collecting

---

[22] Wendover, *Chronica*, iii. 229–30; Holt, *Magna Carta*, 88.

[23] For the dates when each chronicler finished writing, see Gillingham, 'Historians without Hindsight', 8, 12; A. Gransden, *Historical Writing in England, c.550–c.1307* (London, 1974), 254.

[24] The phrase of L. Ashe, *Fiction and History in England, 1066–2000* (Cambridge, 2007), 178.

[25] Howden, *Chronica*, iv. 118–19, 140; D. A. Carpenter, 'Abbot Ralph of Coggeshall's Account of the Last Years of King Richard and the First Years of King John', *EHR* 113 (1998), 1223–4.

[26] For these examples, see H. G. Richardson, 'The Commons and Medieval Politics', in *EPMA* xxiv. 24 n. 1; J. C. Holt, *The Northerners* (Oxford, 1961), 191–2; id., *Magna Carta*, 97.

[27] Holt, *Magna Carta*, 97.   [28] *History of William Marshal*, i. 227, ll. 14499–527.

debts owed to the crown. Mostly concerned with ensuring that stewards were able to pay their lords' debts at the exchequer, and with the lord's liability if the steward failed to pay, it also stipulated that when a debt had been incurred as a fine for land and the lord lacked the chattels to pay the debt, then the land for which the fine was made could also be seized. If, hypothetically, the fine was levied for a relief (and about this the ordinance says nothing specific), then all the lord's lands might be liable for seizure. To whatever degree, the ordinance certainly affected magnate interests. Yet it was published before a small gathering 'in the presence of the king and . . . of certain magnates', and confirmed 'by the king's precept'.[29] Unlike, say, the new rules set out in Henry II's assizes, it received no general conciliar assent. When John surrendered his kingdom to the pope in 1213—our second and more momentous example—such assent was certainly claimed: John said that he had acted 'with the common counsel of our barons (*communi consilio baronum nostrorum*)'.[30] Yet the charter of surrender was witnessed by only thirteen men, five of whom appear later on Wendover's list of John's 'most wicked counsellors';[31] and it seems clear that the kingdom's humiliation, as some saw it, was widely resented.[32] We shall see later that there are similar grounds for wariness in accepting that the 'common counsel' also claimed to justify the collection of the thirteenth in 1207 is to be taken literally.[33] Slippery at the best of times, such phrases may have acquired under John an extra patina of deliberate deceptiveness.

One reason for such suspicions lies in what contemporaries saw as John's predilection for 'familiar counsel': the counsel of intimates and confidants, usually given in private, often on a daily basis, by men mostly drawn from outside the baronage. As we have seen, the possible tensions between the private counsel of the king's *familiares* and the public counsel of his great men was always a potential source of political conflict.[34] But under John such tensions became more marked and palpable. This was

---

[29] Howden, *Chronica*, iv. 152; *PR 13 John*, p. xxxii (the best account). For a maximal interpretation of this text, see Jolliffe, *Angevin Kingship*, 81–2; and for a minimal, Holt, *Magna Carta*, 109–10 (cf. id., *The Northerners*, 186, 192). I am very grateful to Dr Paul Brand for his guidance here.

[30] Stubbs, *Select Charters*, 279.

[31] Wendover, *Chronica*, iii. 237–8, 252–5. The five names common to both lists are those of John de Gray, bishop of Norwich, William, earl of Salisbury, Geoffrey fitz Peter, Peter fitz Herbert, and William Brewer.

[32] Cheney, *Pope Innocent III and England*, 332–4; R. V. Turner, *King John* (Harlow, 1994), 199.

[33] Below, 125–6.   [34] Above, 86, 95–6.

partly because many of John's *familiares* were aliens, partly because familiar counsel was seemingly used to subvert individual magnates, and partly because it could be made to share the blame for the whole disastrous course of events, combining oppressive government with military failure, which lay between the loss of Normandy in 1204 and the defeat of John's allies at Bouvines in 1214. 'Evil counsel' often meant familiar counsel, and the specific examples of the former given by the chroniclers were symptomatic of broader, vaguer, and less clearly defined perceptions and suspicions.

John's alien friends and counsellors formed a distinct group. Mainly military captains from Touraine, and men of no great social standing, they had arrived in England after the defeat of 1204. Their initial landlessness and consequent dependence on John's generosity, as well as their parvenu status, prevented any easy assimilation with the English-born magnates and gentry.[35] Their leading figure, Peter des Roches, became bishop of Winchester in 1205 and justiciar in 1214,[36] but the prominence achieved by most—men such as Gerard d'Athée and Philip Mark—owed more to their forceful roles as sheriffs, castellans, and general royal agents in the localities than to their position at the centre. John's undertaking in Magna Carta to dismiss nine of them, including Mark and the relations of d'Athée, together with their followers, showed their unpopularity.[37] But although it was their government of the counties that caused most resentment, they were also seen to be among John's closest counsellors, and so resented for that reason too. The concessions which John made to his opponents in 1213 apparently included a promise to remove aliens from his 'familarity' (*a familiaritate sua*) and to rely on the counsels of the native nobility;[38] while six of the aliens, including des Roches, d'Athée, and Mark, appear on Wendover's list of John's evil counsellors.[39] A little vignette from the *History of William Marshal* shows how such 'familiarity' might be turned against magnate interests. According to the *History*'s author, John's plot against the Marshal's position in Ireland in 1208 was hatched one day after dinner, when the king had retired to his chamber with Gerard d'Athée, Meilyr fitz Henry, justiciar of Ireland and John's retainer, 'and all his chief counsellors who liked to

---

[35] N. Vincent, *Peter des Roches: An Alien in English Politics, 1205–1238* (Cambridge, 1996), 26, 31, 37–8.

[36] Ibid. 47–55, 89.   [37] Cap. 50: Holt, *Magna Carta*, 464–5.

[38] *Memorials of St Edmund's Abbey*, ed. Arnold, ii. 24–5; Holt, *The Northerners*, 85; id., *Magna Carta*, 215; Vincent, *Peter des Roches*, 112.

[39] Wendover, *Chronica*, iii. 237.

advise him'.[40] What made alien counsels objectionable was not only their source and their private setting, but their use to perverted ends.

That familiar counsel might be an alternative to magnate counsel is suggested by two other episodes. The first centres on a plea of 1204 in the royal court by which William Marshal claimed seisin of the Dorset manor of Sturminster against both William de Redvers, earl of Devon, and his wife, the countess of Meulan. After the failure of the two latter parties to appear had caused the case to be successively postponed from day to day, the Marshal finally came forward once again to demand seisin. The king then took counsel with those who were present with him (*consuluit super hoc illos qui tunc cum illo erant*). But there were few of them, and because they were inexperienced in such matters they advised a further delay 'until the archbishop and the other great and wise men of the land could be present'.[41] The second episode, also involving the Marshal, occurred in 1205, by which time the Marshal had performed homage to Philip Augustus, after John's loss of Normandy, and, on the grounds of his homage, had refused to join John's projected campaign in Poitou. John, at Portsmouth and preparing to cross the Channel, asked his barons for a judgement on the Marshal's contumacy. Because they declined to give this, John turned to his *bachilers*, his household knights, a section of his *familia* which included many aliens. Although some were prepared to speak out against the Marshal, no one was prepared to take up his offer of trial by battle, and so no judgement was reached.[42]

In the first of these cases John's initial reaction to an importunate litigant, who was also one of his most senior magnates, had been to turn to his immediate entourage for a judgement. Only when those around him advised it did he consider convening a larger assembly of barons. It was surprising that a plea involving such great persons had not been taken before a magnate council in the first place. In the second case, a customary resort to the judgement of the barons present with John could hardly be avoided when the accused was a man of the Marshal's standing. But when the barons declined to act John clearly thought that he would

---

[40] *History of William Marshal*, ii. 181, ll. 13587–614, iii. 152.

[41] *CRR* iii: 1203–5, 124; R. V. Turner, *The King and his Courts: The Role of John and Henry III in the Administration of Justice, 1199–1240* (Ithaca, NY, 1968), 170–1; Holt, *Magna Carta*, 174–6.

[42] *History of William Marshal*, i. 157–65, ll. 13107–262; S. Painter, *William Marshal* (Baltimore, 1933), 140–3; Holt, *Magna Carta*, 108; S. D. Church, *The Household Knights of King John* (Cambridge, 1999), 5, 34–5.

get more satisfaction from his bachelors. Both cases show John inclining towards a preference for familiar counsel rather than that of the magnates; and the same tendency to rely on those who lacked aristocratic weight and independence, and who could be trusted to respond more readily to the king's wishes, showed itself more broadly in judicial matters. 'State trials', the conciliar trials of recalcitrant or seemingly disloyal magnates and ministers, of the sort to which Becket had been subjected in 1164 and Longchamp in 1191, were conspicuous by their absence under John. Only three cases involving great men are known to have been taken before baronial councils. One of these was the plea over Sturminster which John had at first wanted to settle with his close companions, and two came from the summer of 1204, the time of the loss of Normandy, when he may have been particularly anxious to conciliate his magnates. After 1204 there are no similar cases on the plea rolls.[43]

From this time onwards John's judicial relations with his barons, which was often to say his fiscal relations, were increasingly regulated by the exchequer court: a body usefully 'subservient to the king's interests within the broad limits of its own routine'.[44] At the exchequer, the king's leading alien *familiaris*, Peter des Roches, probably played a leading role.[45] It was 'according to the custom of the realm and by the law of the exchequer' that John proceeded against William de Briouze in 1209, in what was to be the prelude to Briouze's destruction.[46] His ostensible offence, the failure to pay monies owing to the king, was not so very different from the fiscal offences, also involving debts to the crown, with which Becket had been charged at the council of Northampton in 1164. But in Becket's case the king had sought a conciliar judgement against his enemy.[47] In Briouze's, the king's invocation of 'the custom of the realm' involved no magnate judgement but instead a superior appeal to a bureaucratic ruling essentially determined by the king himself. Other magnates too, men such as Nicholas de Stuteville and John de Lacy, found themselves similarly disciplined by debt and at the mercy of an exchequer which existed to do the king's will.[48] John's need for money, his distrust of his magnates, and his fear of their opposition took these cases out of the public domain and into the arcana of a private and ministerial tribunal.

---

[43] Turner, *The King and his Courts*, 169–72; id., *King John*, 200.
[44] Holt, *Magna Carta*, 109.   [45] Vincent, *Peter des Roches*, 56–61.
[46] S. Painter, *The Reign of King John* (Baltimore, 1949), 238–49; Holt, *The Northerners*, 184–6.
[47] Barlow, *Thomas Becket*, 110–11.   [48] Holt, *The Northerners*, 181–2.

One riposte to these procedures came in cap. 39 of Magna Carta, which stipulated that no legal or extra-legal action should be taken against any free man 'except by the lawful judgement of his peers or by the law of the land'.[49] Despite its breadth, applying as it did to all free men and posing 'the law of the land' as an alternative to 'judgement by peers', this clause was the particular product of magnate interests. For the magnates, 'judgement by peers' meant a conciliar judgement, given in a court composed of their fellows. With just such a meaning the phrase had been used previously in Roger Bigod's quest of 1189–90 for the earldom of Norfolk, during which he had sought assurance that his half-brother Hugh should not be given seisin of the Bigod lands 'except by judgement of the king's court made by his peers (*nisi per judicium curie domini Regis factum per pares suos*)'.[50] That this was seen as the antithesis of an exchequer ruling is suggested by the Charter's complementary cap. 21, which forbade the amercement of earls and barons except by their peers: a prohibition directed at the arbitrary and excessive amercements imposed on magnates by the exchequer, and a tacit demand, not this time for conciliar judgement, but for conciliar penalties.[51] These were powerful pragmatic criticisms of John's circumvention of one of the customary activities of magnate councils.

Among the baronial grievances of 1215 the king's counsel-taking habits hardly loomed as large as some of his other practices. His fiscal exploitation of his feudal rights, his denial and sale of justice, and his intensive fiscal racking of the counties, for example, were all seemingly more offensive. Nor was there ever a clear-cut distinction between magnate counsel, regularly avoided, and familiar counsel, regularly sought. Great councils met, and some magnates were among John's *familiares*: two earls, three bishops, and some leading barons appear on Wendover's list of evil counsellors.[52] Yet counsel remained a pervasive issue, affecting much else. The enforcement of the king's feudal rights necessitated resort, not to a man's peers, but to a complicit and compliant exchequer; the sale and denial of justice meant an evasion of the more independent justice dispensed by magnate councils. Tied into these issues was the role of aliens and the perception

[49] Cap. 39: Holt, *Magna Carta*, 460–1. For discussion, see ibid. 327–31.

[50] *PR 2 Richard I*, 101; Holt, *Magna Carta*, 331.

[51] Cap. 21: Holt, *Magna Carta*, 456–7. For discussion, see ibid. 332–4. Note that the council at Northampton in 1164 had discussed the financial penalties to be imposed on Becket: Barlow, *Thomas Becket*, 111.

[52] Wendover, *Chronica*, iii. 237–8. For an antiquated list of great councils under John, much in need of revision, see C. H. Parry, *The Parliaments and Councils of England* (London, 1839), 20–3.

that John was too dependent on the advice of men who had no native or baronial roots, no inherited wisdom, no stake in the country, and therefore no compunction about its exploitation. The giving of counsel would have been less controversial had not those giving it seemed to lack most qualifications for doing so.

If 'evil counsel', or the lack of any counsel at all, made a significant contribution to the tally of baronial objections to John's government, it may still seem surprising that these things surfaced only obliquely in Magna Carta: in demands for the dismissal of the aliens, for judgement and amercement by peers, and, most crucially, for conciliar consent to taxation (to which we shall return). Yet the truth was that notions of proper counsel were a matter of unstated conventions, as yet too shapeless and amorphous to be easily codified. The occasions and personnel appropriate for counsel-taking could hardly be precisely defined, and it was not until the Provisions of Oxford in 1258 that this was attempted.[53] But that these notions, vague though they may have been, were currently in the air, and in the minds of those who made the Charter, seems certain. Opinion gives us a better guide to their content than any principles set down in legislation. Stephen Langton, in his days as a theologian in the Paris schools, had strongly emphasized the need for royal actions to rest on legal judgements and had even justified political resistance in the absence of judicial process; just as, in another set of theoretical curbs on royal power, he had set limits to the king's right to tax.[54] Closer perhaps to the contemporary political world, though similar in tone to Langton's views, were those of the author of the famous London recension of the Laws of Edward the Confessor, who wrote in the first decade of the thirteenth century. The king should act rightly in his kingdom, he says, and by the judgement of the magnates of the realm (*et per iudicium procerum regni*). He should hold to justice by the counsel of his magnates (*per consilium procerum*) and rule through regular annual meetings of magnates and people.[55] Part restatement of custom, part visionary aspiration, the London text here to some extent anticipated the Charter's demand for judgement by peers. But we can also detect a silent

---

[53] Below, 237–9.

[54] Baldwin, *Masters, Princes and Merchants*, i. 170; id., 'Master Stephen Langton, Future Archbishop of Canterbury: The Paris Schools and Magna Carta', *EHR* 123 (2008), 817–20, 829–30, 833; D. L. d'Avray, ' "Magna Carta": Its Background in Stephen Langton's Academic Biblical Exegesis and its Episcopal Reception', *Studi Medievali*, 3rd ser. 38 (1997), 424–32.

[55] *Gesetze*, ed. Liebermann, i. 635–6, 655–7; Holt, *Magna Carta*, 93–5.

move away from the old feudal rule that the magnates have a duty to advise the king and towards a new ideal: that they are entitled to give counsel, which the king has at least a moral obligation to follow. That this was not mere theory but a live principle in political bargaining is suggested by Gervase of Canterbury's brief account of a great council at Oxford in 1205, when the magnates compelled the king to swear that he would preserve the rights (*iura*) of the kingdom by their counsel in return for their due service.[56]

Those new claims may have rested in part on the memory of the leading role played by magnate counsel in the kingdom during Richard's absence, but their more immediate roots lay in the government of John, his wariness of magnate counsel, particularly in judicial matters, his preference for that of his *familiares*, and his connected reputation for taking bad advice, a reputation seemingly vindicated by the disasters of his reign. Some of these failings may have been more matters of perception than of political reality; but, whether real or merely perceived, their effect was to give counsel and its circumstances an unprecedentedly high place in the political thinking of John's opponents and to some extent on their political agenda too. That place can be assessed most fully and precisely in relation to taxation.

3. Taxation and Consent

By the time of the great council of 1225 with which this chapter opened direct taxation had come to depend irrevocably on conciliar consent. As we have seen, the process had begun with the Saladin Tithe of 1188, first authorized 'by common counsel' at an overseas assembly at Gisors and then put in hand at a further meeting of the great council at Geddington.[57] Thirty-six years later, and ten years before the council of 1225, Magna Carta had formalized the linkage by declaring that no general aid (meaning tax) was to be levied except by common counsel. The progression from origins to codified principle to binding practice seems clear enough.

Yet much remains uncertain about the mechanisms for seeking consent, the reasons for doing so, and the need for the Charter's regulatory intervention in procedures which by 1215 had behind them the weight of

---

[56] *Gervase of Canterbury*, ii. 97–8; Holt, *Magna Carta*, 121; id., 'Rights and Liberties in Magna Carta', in his *Magna Carta and Medieval Government*, 206, 208–9.
[57] Above, 104.

both precedent and royal recognition. After 1188 it had become established quite rapidly, though as yet only as a matter of convention, that consent should be sought for national taxes. The next after the Saladin Tithe was the huge levy of a quarter imposed in 1193–4 to raise the £100,000 required for Richard's ransom.[58] The levy seems to have been formally authorized by the queen mother, Eleanor of Aquitaine, the justices, and the small ministerial council which governed the kingdom.[59] In law and in custom it needed no wider consent, since the ransoming of the lord's body—in this case the king's body—was one of the three gracious aids to which all the lord's tenants, and by extension his tenants' tenants, were expected to contribute.[60] But a king's ransom was quite exceptional, and the sum demanded for Richard's so large, that the securing of some form of consent must have seemed only prudent. The chronicles hint at this, though they say nothing specific. When news of Richard's captivity reached England in February 1193 the justiciar immediately convened a council at Oxford to take stock.[61] During the levying of the ransom money there were repeated meetings of the clergy and laity in London to consider what remained to be paid.[62] Going beyond this mere conciliar bracketing of a putative conciliar grant, Diceto tells us that payment was agreed by common assent (*statutum est assensu communi persolvere*).[63] It is highly probable, therefore, that the association between national taxation and general consent established in the granting of the Saladin Tithe was confirmed by the levy for Richard's ransom.

The scope of consent widened in 1197 when this same principle was extended towards a new form of tax. In December of that year a great council met at Oxford to consider Richard's urgent financial and military needs in his war against Philip Augustus. The case for an aid was put to the meeting by Hubert Walter: one of the earliest instances of what was to become a standard practice in later parliaments, a plea for taxation laid before an assembly by a leading royal minister. The only known precedent is Lanfranc's proposal, made and accepted at the autumn council of 1085,

[58] For this tax see esp. Mitchell, *Taxation*, 171–5, and M. Jurkowski, C. L. Smith, and D. Crook, *Lay Taxes in England and Wales, 1188–1688*, Public Record Office Handbooks 31 (Kew, 1998), 3–4.

[59] Howden, *Chronica*, iii. 210, 225; Wilkinson, 'Government of England', 18–20.

[60] F. M. Stenton, *The First Century of English Feudalism, 1066–1166*, 2nd edn (Oxford, 1961), 173–5; Holt, *Magna Carta*, 317–18.

[61] Howden, *Chronica*, iii. 196–7; Wilkinson, 'Government of England', 26.

[62] *Gervase of Canterbury*, i. 519; Mitchell, *Taxation*, 174.

[63] *Diceto*, ii. 110. Cf. Wilkinson, 'Government of England', 27: 'There can be little doubt that the details of the excessive taxation necessary for raising the ransom were settled in a general assembly.'

that the magnates should bear the expense of billeting the king's mercenaries in their households as a safeguard against invasion.[64] The justiciar's request was for 300 knights to serve for a year in the king's service or, alternatively, for the money to support the same number at a wage rate of 3*s*. per day (£16,425 in total). But the bishops of Lincoln and Salisbury refused to consent, and the council was dissolved without a grant.[65] In the first instance this was to be a levy on tenants-in-chief, yet it was clearly regarded as a supplement to normal feudal obligations, for which consent, for whatever reason, was thought necessary. Stubbs saw its rejection as 'the first clear case of the refusal of a money grant demanded directly by the crown', and so 'a landmark in English constitutional history'.[66] Though his language is of its day, his judgement has much to be said for it.

Three further levies, the carucages of 1198 and 1200 and the seventh on moveables of 1203, lack evidence for consultation and consent in their making.[67] But about one other tax, generally overlooked, we are better informed. In 1201 King John and King Philip Augustus of France jointly agreed to the levying of a fortieth on ecclesiastical and lay property in their respective kingdoms for the relief of the Holy Land. In John's case this was conceded, as the writs for the tax's collection said, 'by the counsel of his magnates overseas'.[68] The precedent here lay in Henry II's levy of 1166 for the relief of the Holy Land, also initiated overseas and with the counsel of the magnates present with the king.[69] Both were direct and national taxes, and although not levied for 'national' purposes, they point to another strand in the web of connections which was coming to link taxation and consent: that is, the needs of the Holy Land, recognized most fully in the Saladin Tithe of 1188. But the most momentous of all these taxes for the future history of parliament was the thirteenth on moveables taken by John in 1207. The significance of this tax lay in its large yield, its apparent concession by a great council of magnates, and its position as the last such tax before direct taxation was regulated in Magna Carta. To all these points we shall return.

[64] Above, 62, 102.
[65] Howden, *Chronica*, iv. 40; *Magna Vita Sancti Hugonis*, ed. D. L. Douie and H. Farmer, 2 vols. (London, 1961), ii. 98–100. There are some differences between these two accounts, which I have elided. Cf. Mitchell, *Taxation*, 175–6; *PR 10 Richard I*, pp. xix–xx.
[66] In his preface to Howden, *Chronica*, iv, p. xcii.   [67] Mitchell, *Taxation*, 177.
[68] Howden, *Chronica*, iv. 187–9; W. E. Lunt, *Financial Relations of the Papacy with England to 1327* (Cambridge, Mass., 1939), 190, 240–2; Mitchell, *Studies in Taxation*, 45–6.
[69] Above, 103–4.

Why was consent now judged necessary for taxation? It had after all not been necessary for geld, the earlier direct tax: a precedent which may explain the absence of any evident consent to the carucages of 1198 and 1200, both of them land taxes comparable to the geld. To this question two alternative answers have usually been given.[70] The first, a feudal answer, derives from a statement of Glanvill that a lord cannot take an aid from his tenants against their wishes in order to support his wars.[71] The need for consent is clearly implied. But there is a large conceptual gulf between what a lord may take from his tenants by way of a feudal aid and what a king may take from his subjects by way of national taxation. There is no sign that the case for taxation was presented in these feudal terms; nor were all the taxes of the period taken in support of the king's wars. A second answer may therefore seem more plausible and has indeed won more acceptance. According to Roman law, a ruler could appeal to the necessity to defend the common good, which was often a military necessity, in order to justify exceptional demands on his subjects. Provided that they acknowledged the necessity, his subjects could not deny his claim; but the need for them to make that acknowledgement opened the way for debate and for a sort of consent. They had the right to question the ruler's plea of necessity, but once it had been recognized they had no right to deny him the consequent tax.

This may seem a more promising lead to follow. Certainly 'necessity' sometimes appears as a justification for royal demands. It was used in 1197, when Hubert Walter put before the Oxford council 'the king's necessities (*regias proposuit necessitates*)';[72] and the plea of necessity had a long parliamentary future before it. Certainly, too, knowledge of Roman law was quite widespread, both among the king's clerks and more particularly, and in this case more significantly, among the clerks in Hubert's household.[73] Yet it is unlikely that the debate of 1197 was wholly conducted along these lines. There seems little doubt that the justiciar would have been capable of couching his plea in Roman law terms and he may well have

---

[70] The rest of this paragraph draws on the discussion in G. L. Harriss, *King, Parliament and Public Finance in Medieval England to 1369* (Oxford, 1975), 18–26.

[71] *Glanvill: The Treatise on the Laws and Customs of the Realm of England*, ed. G. D. G. Hall (London, 1965), 112.

[72] *Magna Vita Sancti Hugonis*, ii. 98; Harriss, *King, Parliament and Public Finance*, 23 n.1.

[73] R. V. Turner, 'Roman Law in England before the Time of Bracton', in his *Judges, Administrators and the Common Law in Angevin England* (London, 1994), 53–4, 56–8; C. R. Cheney, *Hubert Walter* (London, 1967), 164–6. Hubert himself does not seem to have been especially learned in the law.

been briefed to do so. But would his audience of magnates and prelates have known how they were entitled to respond, with the right to question the necessity but the duty to pay up once it was acknowledged? This seems much less likely. When taxation was refused by Bishop Hugh of Lincoln in 1197, after the justiciar's plea of necessity which has just been mentioned, it was not because he denied the necessity but because his church had no customary obligation to provide knight service overseas.[74]

The need for consent was surely less a question of legal justification, whether from feudal or from Roman law, than of practicality. In matters of direct taxation the need for consent was dictated by political prudence. Because these taxes were national in their incidence, the sums which they raised were unprecedentedly large. The £5,000 or so brought in by the final geld of 1161–2[75] was trivial compared with the yield of the Saladin Tithe, possibly as much as £70,000,[76] with the £100,000 demanded for Richard's ransom, and with the £60,000 or more (the most reliable of these figures) produced by the thirteenth of 1207.[77] All three of these taxes were regarded as exceptionally oppressive by contemporaries.[78] The burden of taxation on the magnates, the proportionately heavier burden on their tenants, at the indirect expense of the magnates again, via a decline in the tenants' rent-paying capacities, and the probable expectation of resistance, all underlay the need for consent. For none of these taxes was there any discernible pattern of magnate pardons and exemptions, as there had been for the earlier geld. To trench heavily on the property rights of all his subjects in this way no king could simply rely on the force of his will. He had to carry his great men with him, not only to win their own cooperation in payment, but also to use their consent as a lever to induce payment and cooperation in the localities. This was why the writs directed to the counties for the assessment and collection of both the fortieth of 1201 and the thirteenth of 1207 stressed the elements of counsel and consent which had gone to their granting.[79] Roman law and the doctrine

[74] *Magna Vita Sancti Hugonis*, ii. 99.
[75] J. H. Ramsay, *A History of the Revenues of the Kings of England, 1066–1399*, 2 vols. (Oxford, 1925), i. 78; Green, 'Last Century', 254.
[76] The figure comes from *Gervase of Canterbury*, i. 422, and is not reliable. But it does not seem out of line with the comparable figures for the yield of other taxes. Cf. Tyerman, *England and the Crusades*, 98–9.
[77] Mitchell, *Studies in Taxation*, 91; Holt, *The Northerners*, 147.
[78] For reaction to the Saladin Tithe and to Richard's ransom tax, see Tyerman, *England and the Crusades*, 78–9, and Mitchell, *Taxation*, 87; and to the thirteenth of 1207, below, 125.
[79] Howden, *Chronica*, iv. 188; Stubbs, *Select Charters*, 278.

of necessity may have reinforced royal pleas for consent to taxation, but it was caution and calculation which gave rise to those pleas in the first place.

If the need for consent to taxation was pragmatically recognized by 1207, why was it necessary to prescribe for it in Magna Carta? The Charter's prescriptions, set out in two famous clauses, are detailed and specific, and have already been discussed in another context.[80] Here we partly recapitulate. With the exception of the three gracious aids for the ransoming of the king, the knighting of his eldest son, and the marriage of his eldest daughter, the Charter states that no scutage or aid (that is, tax) is to be levied 'except by the common counsel of our realm (*nisi per commune consilium regni nostri*)'. To obtain this 'common counsel' the greater magnates are to be summoned individually by letter and all (others) holding of the king in chief (meaning the lesser tenants-in-chief) are to be summoned through the sheriffs. The summons is to give at least forty days' notice, for a meeting at a stated date and place, and must provide the reason for the summons. At the meeting the business is to go forward, even if not all those summoned are present.[81]

To two connected questions raised by these clauses, scutage and the role of the lesser tenants-in-chief, we shall return later. The more central issue is that of consent. The need for 'the common counsel of the realm' before the levying of general aids (or taxes) is difficult to interpret as anything but a demand for conciliar and magnate consent. Professor Gavin Langmuir has put forward the alternative view that 'common counsel' need have involved no more than the king's need to consult and to take note of (but not necessarily be bound by) any resulting collective will.[82] But this would provide no adequate safeguard against the king's own will, whose room for manoeuvre the Charter everywhere sets out to restrict. It is more plausible to see these clauses as rules intended to make taxation dependent on the consent of a properly constituted assembly; and although they were omitted from the Charter's reissues of 1216, 1217, and 1225, this was in fact to be their future effect.[83] By bringing together taxation and consent

---

[80] Above, 80.   [81] Caps. 12, 14: Holt, *Magna Carta*, 454–5.

[82] G. L. Langmuir, '*Per Commune Consilium Regni* in Magna Carta', *Studia Gratiana*, 15 (1972), esp. 479–85. Cf. Holt, *Magna Carta*, 317 n. 103, for a criticism, and, more generally, Maddicott, ' "An Infinite Multitude of Nobles" ', 22–5.

[83] Below, 172, 198–9. T. N. Bisson, *The Crisis of the Twelfth Century: Power, Lordship and the Origins of European Government* (Princeton, 2009), 552–3, accepts the equation between the Charter's 'common counsel' and consent to taxation.

within a conciliar context the Charter had provided a baseline for the future development of parliament.

The immediate stimulus for these restraints, in an era when the need for consent to taxation was already tacitly acknowledged, has never been identified. But in 1215 the most recent aid had been the thirteenth of 1207, and it is almost certainly to the circumstances of its granting that we should look for a solution to our problem. Symptomatic of the enormous pressure which John's military needs and foreign aspirations placed on his resources, the tax had been levied for the future recovery of his lost French lands.[84] He had faced great difficulty in securing it. A levy had first been debated at a meeting of ecclesiastical and lay magnates which convened in London on 8 January 1207—probably at short notice, since John had returned to England from Poitou only on 12 December, and the writs of summons for the council are unlikely to have been issued before his arrival.[85] The Charter's demand for a forty-day period of notice in advance of any council called to discuss taxation may be a riposte to this deficiency. At the London council the prelates had refused to grant a tax on the revenues of the beneficed clergy and the meeting had been adjourned to 9 February at Oxford. That we hear nothing of any demand put to the laity at this meeting, and that the subsequent Oxford meeting was attended by an 'infinite multitude of prelates and magnates', may indicate that few lay magnates had been present at the first session.[86] The intervention of the Christmas season between the December summons and the January meeting perhaps helps to account for any shortfall. At Oxford the clergy again refused a tax on their revenues, but eventually, and apparently after some considerable delay, John was granted a thirteenth to fall on the property of both clergy and laity. According to Wendover, all grudged this but did not dare to gainsay it (*cunctis murmurantibus sed contradicere non audentibus*).[87] The draconian penalties laid down for evasion of the tax, entailing the confiscation of all the offender's goods and his imprisonment at the king's pleasure, may be an indication of the local resistance which conciliar protests had led John to expect. In the event both resistance and evasion were widespread, and heavily punished.[88]

---

[84] Mitchell, *Studies in Taxation*, 85 and n. 1.
[85] *Ann. Waverley*, 258; Wendover, *Chronica*, iii. 209–10.   [86] *Ann. Waverley*, 258.
[87] Wendover, *Chronica*, iii. 210; Mitchell, *Studies in Taxation*, 86–7.
[88] Stubbs, *Select Charters*, 278; *PR 9 John*, pp. xix–xxi; Holt, *The Northerners*, 207.

In the writ for the assessment of the thirteenth John spoke of its having been granted 'by common counsel and by the assent of our council'.[89] Yet the history of the tax suggests that these words cannot necessarily be taken at face value. Here, as on other occasions when he sought to justify his actions by appealing to a broad consensus, John may have employed a creative vocabulary. The short period of notice for the first council, the refusal of the clergy to make any grant by themselves both at Oxford and in London, and the signs of a more general reluctance to give the king his money, all suggest that the granting of the tax was in some measure irregular and may have come about only after the application of pressure by the king. 'The assent of our council' may have been neither unanimous nor freely given. If we possessed writs of summons for these councils, we might be able to detect other ways in which the two meetings fell short of the desiderata set out in the Charter. Were they called, for example, with no stated purpose, so that the demand for a tax was sprung on those present as a surprise? It was perhaps one mark of the opposition which all this raised that after 1207, despite the very high yield of the thirteenth, John never sought another general aid, preferring to rely mainly on customary revenues from the counties which needed no consent.

The questionable circumstances of the tax grant of 1207 almost certainly provided the background to the rules laid down in 1215. Rooted in a specific set of events, the Charter's regulations provided in response a code for the levying of direct taxes which was to affect the whole future development of parliament.

4. Lesser Landholders and the Community of the Shire

In some particular ways Magna Carta identified and sought to protect the interests of the lesser landholders of the shires whose descendants would later be prominent in parliament. In doing so it helped to form them as a political class, with a stake in politics comparable to but partly separate from that of the baronage, and so to enlarge their role at the centre and ultimately in central assemblies. Defined by their grievances in the years leading up to the Charter and by the remedies for those grievances set

---

[89] Stubbs, *Select Charters*, 278.

out in the Charter itself, these men fell into two overlapping groups: the lesser tenants-in-chief, and the knights who were the leaders of their local societies. The discontents of both groups are implicit in the Charter's two clauses relating to taxation, in the demand set out there for conciliar consent to scutages as well as to general aids, and in the assumption that the lesser tenants-in-chief will be present when either of these two levies appears on the conciliar agenda. Some account of the relationship of the lesser landholders to these two issues should give us a clearer idea of how the middling men of the shires came to gain a voice at the centre and ultimately in the parliaments of the next reign.

We will look first at scutage, the money payment due to the king from the tenants-in-chief, and thence transmissible to their knightly sub-tenants, in commutation of feudal military service. Under John this became a major grievance among the class of knightly sub-tenants, as it had not been in any earlier reign. There was no doubt about the king's entitlement to scutage: since his tenants owed him military service, they owed him scutage if they failed to serve. But in three ways John expanded this entitlement beyond custom and to his own fiscal advantage. First, he levied scutage with increasing frequency. Henry II had taken 8 in 35 years and Richard 4 in 10 years, but John took 11 in 16 years. Secondly, he increased the rate sharply. Formerly the usual figure had been one mark or £1 per fee, but John generally took two marks and once took £2.[90] Thirdly, he extended its occasions. Scutage was twice collected in years which saw no campaigns (1205 and 1209),[91] and in 1214 John tried to collect it for a campaign in Poitou, provoking the refusal of the northern magnates to pay on the grounds that no service was owed there.[92] Suspicions that scutage was becoming something like a regular levy are likely to have been heightened by the 1204 grant of an aid for the defence of Normandy in the form of a scutage at $2\frac{1}{2}$ marks per fee: an imposition that confounded the distinction between a set of fee-based commutation payments and a general tax.[93]

By this time a second levy had been introduced as a supplement to scutage: the fine paid by the tenant-in-chief, sometimes in addition to

[90] Keefe, *Feudal Assessments*, 30; Turner, *King John*, 101.

[91] Mitchell, *Studies in Taxation*, 94, 315; Holt, *Magna Carta*, 319; Turner, *King John*, 102; B. Feeney, 'The Effects of King John's Scutages on his East Anglian Subjects', *Reading Medieval Studies*, 11 (1985), 60.

[92] Mitchell, *Studies in Taxation*, 112–13.

[93] Wendover, *Chronica*, iii. 174–5; Holt, *Magna Carta*, 319.

scutage and sometimes as a composition payment in its place, when he and his men were permitted by the king to escape personal service.[94] Fines *ne transfretet* ('that he should not cross the sea'), as they were usually known, had developed from the mid 1190s as part of a royal attempt to reshape the whole system of feudal military service so as to provide smaller forces serving for the longer periods which were necessary for continental campaigns. They were introduced at the same time as the crown began to reduce the quotas of knight service owed by tenants-in-chief, and their purpose, in conjunction with scutage, was 'to charge an amount commensurate with the amount of service which the king had lost'.[95] The money thus raised would allow the king to hire substitute knights. Though they were occasionally levied at a fixed rate per fee, fines were more often negotiated individually between the tenant-in-chief and the king's justices or the justiciar, and bore no obvious relationship to the amount of service owed.[96]

John's exploitation of both scutage and the fines which were now often imposed alongside it stirred up resentments which have perhaps been underplayed in recent discussions.[97] There were particular objections to the increase in scutage rates. Coggeshall spoke of John's first scutage of 1199, taken at two marks per fee, as a 'severe exaction' compared with the usual £1 levy, and the 'Unknown' Charter preceding Magna Carta sought to fix the rate at one mark per fee: a demand which was to give way in the Charter itself to the much more radical call for consent to scutage.[98] Fines elicited no similarly direct comments. But few fines accompanied the scutages for the Welsh campaign of 1211 and none the Poitou campaign of 1214, at times when John was having to make concessions to his opponents, nor were any levied in parallel with the three scutages of Henry III's minority.[99] John's tactical retreat, and the regency government's unwillingness to recover the ground lost in abandoning fines, both hint strongly at their unpopularity.

It was the particular social incidence of these levies rather than their generalized burden which contributed most to the emergence of the smaller landholders as a group whose grievances were to bring them to central

---

[94] The best account of fines is Mitchell, *Studies in Taxation*, 322–7. See also A. L. Poole, *Obligations of Society in the XII and XIII Centuries* (Oxford, 1946), 41–5.

[95] Mitchell, *Studies in Taxation*, 324 n. 104.

[96] Ibid. 44, 53, 61, 323–6; Poole, *Obligations of Society*, 43.   [97] Cf. Holt, *Magna Carta*, 318–19.

[98] *Radulphi de Coggeshall, Chronicon Anglicanum*, ed. J. Stevenson, RS (London, 1875), 101–2; Mitchell, *Studies in Taxation*, 316–17; Holt, *Magna Carta*, 318–19, 428.

[99] Mitchell, *Studies in Taxation*, 101, 112, 323, 327.

assemblies. Scutages and fines collectively bore down much more heavily on the knightly class and the lesser tenants-in-chief than on the magnates. In the case of scutage the actual payers were the lord's sub-tenants, men owing knight service, whose payments were simply collected by the tenant-in-chief for dispatch directly to the exchequer or to the sheriff.[100] If the tenant-in-chief possessed fees beyond the number for which he owed service to the crown, he could even make a profit by keeping for himself the scutage from the excess; though the payment of an additional fine might negate this advantage.[101] If the sub-tenant failed to pay, his lord could invoke the help of the sheriff and the royal courts in order to enforce payment, sometimes via distraint.[102] It is true that the sub-tenants could sometimes pass on the burden to their own peasant tenants,[103] but they probably lacked the coercive means available to their own lords to exact payment; and the general weight of taxation under John, falling directly as much of it did on the villeins and freeholders of the localities, is likely to have set limits to what could be transmitted downwards.

Fines were also socially discriminating, though in different ways. Here the main sufferers were not the knightly sub-tenants but the lesser tenants-in-chief. The reduction in quotas which was part and parcel of the justification for the fine was carried much further for the greater tenants than for the lesser. On the Poitou campaign of 1214, for example, the earl of Devon served with only twenty of the eighty-nine knights he owed, while Geoffrey de Pavilly, a minor Northamptonshire tenant-in-chief, owed four knights and served with two: a 79 per cent reduction for the big man, a 50 per cent reduction for the small.[104] Such differences must reflect not only the greater scope for reducing large quotas, as against the near impossibility of making already small quotas smaller still, but also the lesser tenants' lack of political weight when it came to bargaining with the crown and its agents. Since the reduced quotas seem to have been fixed, not systematically, but by individual negotiation, the minor tenants were badly placed to strike political bargains. The arbitrary

---

[100] Ibid. 335–8.
[101] Ibid. 330–1; Poole, *Obligations of Society*, 41; Painter, *Studies in the English Feudal Barony*, 126; Feeney, 'The Effects of King John's Scutages', 53.
[102] Mitchell, *Studies in Taxation*, 31, 76, 140, 152, 188, 330.
[103] Ibid. 333; Poole, *Obligations of Society*, 47.
[104] Mitchell, *Studies in Taxation*, 110. For other examples, see M. Prestwich, *Armies and Warfare in the Middle Ages: The English Experience* (New Haven, 1996), 68. For Geoffrey de Pavilly, see *Book of Fees*, i. 18.

nature of the deals thus struck may help to explain the draft concession in the 'Unknown' Charter by which John supposedly undertook to alleviate quotas of ten knights for service in Normandy and Brittany 'with the counsel of my barons'.[105] Nothing came of this. It nevertheless suggests not only the expanding range of political matters for which baronial counsel was thought appropriate—part of the drive for greater conciliar authority already discussed—but also the probable unwillingness of individual tenants-in-chief to face the king alone when quota reduction was under discussion.

The lesser tenants-in-chief found themselves at a similar disadvantage in relation to fines. When they failed to serve they paid proportionately much heavier fines than their greater cousins. For the 1204 campaign, for example, the greater tenants possessing more than five fees paid fines averaging four marks per fee, while the lesser tenants with fewer than five fees averaged nearly seven marks. The same disproportion in payment was evident in other campaigns.[106] As with the lesser tenants' quota reductions, it is likely to have been their relative lack of bargaining power in confronting the king and his officials that underlay their plight. They suffered too from other disabilities. They served less frequently and so fined more often, and, like knightly scutage payers, they were less able to pass on the burden of payment to their own tenants.[107] Keefe has written that 'feudal assessments [meaning primarily scutages] were a minor factor in the taxation of lay tenants-in-chief and . . . their incidence tended to be inversely proportional to the tenants' wealth'.[108] The fines which supplemented those assessments were similarly inequitable.

Other burdens laid on the lesser tenants-in-chief were common to all who held directly from the king. The payment of relief was a case in point. Magna Carta fixed the relief due from the heirs of an earl or baron at £100 and that from the heir of a knight holding from the king at a maximum of £5 per fee. As well as showing once again that knights and lesser tenants might be identical, the Charter implies that this group had been as open to exploitation in the matter of the feudal incidents as their superiors (but tenurial equals) among the magnates. Evidence from the counties in the thirty years prior to 1215 suggests that this had indeed been so, with holders

---

[105] Holt, *Magna Carta*, 315, 427; Prestwich, *Armies and Warfare*, 68.

[106] Mitchell, *Studies in Taxation*, 66. Cf. ibid. 57, 73, 79, 326; and Feeney, 'The Effects of King John's Scutages', 62–4.

[107] Cf. Holt, *The Northerners*, 90 n. 6.   [108] Keefe, *Feudal Assessments*, 134.

of single fees occasionally being charged as much as £100 in relief by the exchequer.[109]

One other 'feudal' group among the lesser landholders was particularly hard hit by John's exactions: the tenants of escheated manors which were temporarily in the king's hands. When an honor escheated to the crown, usually through confiscation or through failure of heirs, John's policy was to regard all its former sub-tenants as temporary tenants-in-chief, holding directly from him. The consequence was that many small landholders now found themselves owing the crown both the feudal incidents of relief, wardship, and marriage, and also a much more frequent duty of military service. They were probably more likely than others to be called on to serve in person and they were certainly loaded with excessively heavy fines if they failed to do so.[110] In 1212, for example, John compelled the non-serving tenants of the honors formerly held by Robert fitz Walter and Eustace de Vesci, then in his hands, to fine at the rate of ten marks per fee for overseas service—some five times more than the usual scutage rate and an exaction so exorbitant as to be remarked on by a chronicler.[111] In 1215 there were about 400 of these tenants *de honore*, many of them later prominent among the rebels.[112] That such men, once private lordship over them had been restored, would revert to being scutage payers at campaign times, with all the burdens that scutage entailed, points to one way in which these groups of put-upon lesser landholders interlocked and overlapped.

We should now be better placed to appreciate the significance of Magna Carta's demand for conciliar consent, including the consent of the lesser tenants-in-chief, to the levying of scutage. A step in this direction had already been taken in the 'Unknown' Charter which, in laying down that scutage should be levied at one mark per fee, had permitted more 'by the counsel of the barons if the burden of an army occurred'. Since scutage was the commutation of an acknowledged obligation to perform military service, taken at a rate customarily determined by the king, there was no

[109] Cap. 2: Holt, *Magna Carta*, 150–1. For some examples, see I. J. Sanders, *Feudal Military Service in England* (Oxford, 1956), 100–1 (with useful discussion), and H. M. Thomas, *Vassals, Heiresses, Crusaders and Thugs: The Gentry of Angevin Yorkshire* (Philadelphia, 1993), 176.

[110] Mitchell, *Studies in Taxation*, 39–43; Holt, *Magna Carta*, 316–17; Turner, *King John*, 90; Thomas, *Vassals, Heiresses*, 183, 191.

[111] *Ann. Dunstable*, 35; Mitchell, *Studies in Taxation*, 363.

[112] Painter, *Studies in the English Feudal Barony*, 48; Holt, *The Northerners*, 47–8; Feeney, 'The Effects of King John's Scutages', 62–3.

legal basis for this rather ambiguous proposal, and still less for the more direct demand in Magna Carta itself for conciliar consent to the actual levying of scutage.[113] But John's exploitation and expansion of his rights here, with regard to scutage's weight, frequency, and occasion, provided a tacit justification for the extension to scutage of the consent now needed for general aids. It seems highly likely that conciliar restraints were also intended to apply to fines,[114] for until the recent campaigns in Wales and Poitou scutage and fines had been regularly levied on the same occasions and for the same purposes, and if the one was denied the other would fall too: no scutage, no fines. It seems equally likely that the pressure for these restraints came from the knightly sub-tenants and the lesser tenants-in-chief, for whom the king's frequent monetary commutation of military service was a larger issue than his less frequent demands for general aids. Magnates had less to complain about. They were often made to serve in person, so avoiding altogether the fiscal alternatives to service. When they failed to serve they merely collected scutage for the king, and in some cases for themselves, which the sub-tenants paid; and they were burdened less frequently and proportionately less heavily by fines than were the lesser tenants. Grievances arising from the fiscality now attached to military service are thus likely to have been more loudly voiced by the lesser landholders than by the greater. That this was indeed the social group which both stood in need of relief and pressed for it is suggested by the comparable remedy offered to the exploited tenants of escheated honors. By the Charter's terms these men were to owe only such services as they had owed to their previous lords; so they were no longer to be regarded as crown tenants, with all the ensuing obligations.[115] Here, indubitably, the lesser landholders had made their voices heard.

As we have seen, the lesser tenants-in-chief had long been attenders at central assemblies, though perhaps only occasionally, when especially important business was to be discussed, or at the king's discretion.[116] In 1215 that discretion was removed. Whenever else the lesser tenants might be present at councils, it was expected that they would be there when general aids or scutages were on the agenda. Scutages and fines, the peculiar grievances of a knightly class which comprehended but was more extensive than that of the lesser tenants alone, were probably crucial in

[113] Holt, *Magna Carta*, 318–19, 428.   [114] Holt, *Magna Carta*, 319–20, disagrees.
[115] Ibid. 316–17, 462–3.   [116] Above, 80–6.

giving the lesser tenants their place on these special conciliar occasions.[117] That place was their remedy. But in the Charter's reissues the two clauses were dropped, and thereafter scutage was normally levied with the consent only of those present on campaign, not with that of the whole council.[118] Conciliar consent to scutage was thus a dead letter from the start. Consent to general aids, however, remained a principle of political action, in practice if not in the law gradually defined in the Charter's successive reissues; and that consent equally called for the presence of the lesser tenants-in-chief. The lesser landholders were given a definitive place at some sorts of council meeting in 1215 because of the grievances arising from the fiscal exploitation of their military service; they stayed there to participate in discussion of the general aids which, under John, had almost certainly mattered less to them. This was to some extent a paradox. But it was also a factor which was to give the lesser landholders, first as tenants-in-chief, then as knights of the shire, an established place in parliament.

There was, however, one other probable reason for the Charter's assumption that the lesser tenants-in-chief would be present at councils meeting to discuss taxation—one determined by the king's interest rather than by that of the lesser tenants themselves. It hinged on the relationship between taxation and the feudal and tenurial structure of the realm. The terms for the grant of the thirteenth in 1207 had made it clear that the tenants-in-chief attending the council were making a grant on behalf of all the king's subjects. It had there been provided, John had stated in his writ for the collection of the tax, that the thirteenth was to be paid 'by every layman of all England from the fee of whomsoever he may be': that is, no matter whose tenant he is. John's intention in part was surely to block any claim that because particular magnates had not agreed to the tax, whether by reason of their absence from the council or, once there, by outright refusal to consent, their tenants and those below them in the tenurial hierarchy were thereby exempted from payment.[119] In 1215 the king's interest was the same: the effectiveness of future tax grants might be impeded if conciliar absentees could claim that their absence exonerated

---

[117] Langmuir, 'Per Commune Consilium Regni in Magna Carta', 478, also stresses the centrality of scutage to the Charter's two clauses on taxation.

[118] Mitchell, Studies in Taxation, 144–5, 151, 186; id., Taxation, 193.

[119] Stubbs, Select Charters, 278. For a variant on the argument put forward above, see D. A. Carpenter, 'The Second Century of English Feudalism', Past and Present, 168 (2000), 63. I have followed Carpenter's translation of the writ.

their men from payment. Hence the stipulation in the Charter's cap. 14 that conciliar business could go forward even in the absence of some of those summoned—and hence too, we may well think, the need for the presence of the lesser tenants. Though absence was not to be allowed to hold up business, as full a complement as possible of tenants-in-chief, both greater and lesser, was still necessary in order to bind their own tenants to payment and to give the tax full legitimacy. The need for the presence of the lesser tenants-in-chief at future 'tax councils' may reflect their past fiscal grievances, but it was also to the king's advantage that they should be there.

The grievances of the lesser landholders which brought them to political prominence did not arise solely from their position as tenants, either as the mesne tenants of other lords or as the tenants-in-chief of the crown. If they had a place on the vertical ladder of lordship, with all the burdens which that entailed, they were also members of the horizontal societies of their counties. It was their local interests, those of men who were the leading figures in their local communities, as well as their interests as tenants, which were recognized in the Great Charter.

Under Richard and John the county moved beyond its ancient function as the basic unit of English local government to take on a new and more proactive role. No longer simply responding to direction from above, it became a more overtly political community, with a corporate will and a voice through which grievances could be expressed, and with the capacity to be represented at the centre of government. The transforming agent here, as in so much else which is the subject of this chapter, was the fiscal pressure brought by war. The demands of war bore down especially heavily on the counties. From 1194 onwards most of Richard's revenues were derived from this source, mainly in the form of the county farms, demesne income, scutage, tallage, forest penalties, and the judicial profits of the eyre.[120] In the next reign county revenues were 'the backbone of John's resources', never producing much less than 85 per cent of revenues recorded in the pipe rolls between 1199 and 1210.[121] Central to local grievances were the sums extracted via the sheriffs. Both Richard (from 1194) and John (from 1204) demanded additional sums from the sheriffs,

---

[120] N. Barratt, 'The English Revenues of Richard I', *EHR* 116 (2001), 642; id., 'The Revenue of King John', *EHR* 111 (1996), 845–9.
[121] Barratt, 'Revenue of King John', 845.

over and above the traditional county farms. The result was a sharp rise in fiscal pressure as the sheriffs sought both to satisfy a rapacious exchequer while also making a profit for themselves.[122] The point made to Louis IX by the baronial reformers of 1264, in reaction to the comparable increments above the farm imposed by Henry III, would have been as true under Richard and John as it came to be under Henry: 'the sheriffs and bailiffs . . . not being able to pay otherwise the payments thus imposed and so frequently increased, of necessity had recourse to illicit extortions.'[123] Intermittently as burdensome were the penalties imposed by the general eyre, which at its peak in 1211 was producing some 11 per cent of royal revenues, and by the forest eyre, at its most oppressive in 1212 hardly lower at 9 per cent.[124]

There was an everyday persistence about some of these pressures, especially the sheriff's exactions, which made them even less tolerable than the frequent but intermittent scutages and the heavier but infrequent direct taxes. Their effect was to politicize local society, to promote spontaneous local organization at a county level, and to stimulate the search for relief through the purchase of exemptions from burdens. The wave of sales which had preceded Richard I's departure on crusade in 1190, mainly of offices but including some county privileges, had already shown that the crown was prepared to part with its rights in return for cash.[125] Under John county purchases became more marked. The counties' desiderata were disafforestation (reflecting both the great extension of the forest under Henry II and the contemporary oppressiveness of the forest eyre), curbs on the sheriffs' powers, and—more desirable still—the right to choose their own sheriffs. In 1199 the men of Lancashire gave 100 marks to have Richard de Vernon as their sheriff for five years. That Geoffrey fitz Peter, the justiciar, was told by the king to try to raise this to £100 shows how the process of purchase might promote bargaining and negotiation between centre and locality.[126] In 1204 the men of Devon and Cornwall bought the disafforestation of their counties, while the Devonians also secured restrictions on the sheriff's tourn, his profitable twice-yearly itineration

---

[122] D. A. Carpenter, 'The Decline of the Curial Sheriff in England, 1194–1258', in his *The Reign of Henry III* (London, 1996), 156–9; Turner, *King John*, 109–11.

[123] *DBM* 274–5.   [124] Barratt, 'Revenue of King John', 846.

[125] *PR 2 Richard I*, pp. xxi–xxii; Holt, *Magna Carta*, 50–1, 183; Turner and Heiser, *Reign of Richard Lionheart*, 105–6.

[126] *Rotuli de Oblatis et Finibus Tempore Regis Johannis*, ed. T. D. Hardy, Record Comm. (London, 1835), 38; *PR 6 John*, 6; Holt, *Magna Carta*, 62.

round the hundred courts.[127] In 1210 the men of Somerset and Dorset proffered 1,200 marks to be quit of the 100-mark increment on the shire farm and to have a resident sheriff appointed from among themselves.[128] As Holt has noted, some of these concessions looked forward to the Charter, which provided freely and for the whole kingdom privileges and liberties comparable to those earlier sold to the counties.[129]

Central to these arrangements were the knights of the shire. The term is used advisedly, since in status, county affiliations, and political aspirations the local knights who became politically conspicuous under John were the true forerunners of the knights of the shire who were to form the commons in parliament: just as the county proffers of John's reign on matters such as the need for local and resident sheriffs were the ancestors of the later common petitions directed towards the same end.[130] By 1200 the knights had emerged as a discrete social group, members of the lowest rank of the nobility, and also the political core of a broad band of minor local landholders ranging from minor barons to prosperous freeholders.[131] Their discreteness was recognized in 1194, when Richard I's new tourneying regulations established a descending tariff of payments for participation in tournaments by earls, barons, and knights with and without land.[132] Their rise owed something to the growing body of civil and judicial duties laid on them by Henry II's legal and administrative reforms: both a recognition and an enhancement of their status. As grand assize jurors, judging rival claims to the ownership of land; as investigators of the essoin of bed-sickness, deciding whether a litigant pleading sickness was in fact too ill to appear in court; as bearers of the record of the county court to the king's court at Westminster when cases were transferred there; and as participants in a mass of other administrative business, the knights were the indispensable workhorses of local government and local justice.[133] Under the justiciarship of Hubert Walter from 1194 to 1198 their duties multiplied. For the eyre of 1194 twelve knights were to be elected in each county to answer the

---

[127] Foedera, I. i. 89; Rotuli Chartarum, ed. T. D. Hardy, Record Comm. (London, 1837), 122b; Holt, Magna Carta, 63.

[128] PR 12 John, 75.   [129] Holt, Magna Carta, 62–3.

[130] Cf. J. R. Maddicott, 'Magna Carta and the Local Community, 1215–1259', Past and Present, 102 (1984), 61–2.

[131] The best brief account of the rise of the knights is D. Crouch, The Birth of Nobility: Constructing Aristocracy in England and France, 900–1300 (Harlow, 2005), 243–8.

[132] Foedera, I. i. 65; Crouch, Birth of Nobility, 246–7.

[133] For knightly duties, see Poole, Obligations of Society, 53–6, and P. Coss, The Knight in Medieval England, 1000–1400 (Far Thrupp, 1993), 31–9.

articles of the eyre, one of which demanded the election of three knights and a clerk in each county to keep the pleas of the crown; and in 1195 they were appointed to supervise the oath for the keeping of the peace in each county.[134] As grand jurors, coroners, and peace keepers they had a long future before them.

The framework for all these duties was the county, and their effect was to establish the county's leading knights more formally at the head of their communities. It was thus not surprising that they should often have acted for their counties when privileges were to be purchased and royal oppressions bought off. It was the knights of Surrey who in 1190 secured the disafforestation of parts of the county;[135] the knights of Staffordshire who in 1200 paid to have the forest liberties which they held under Henry I;[136] the knights of Somerset, Devon, and Cornwall, twelve from each county, who in 1214 were summoned to speak with the king about the proffer which they had made for having forest liberties at the previous forest eyre;[137] and the knights of Devon who in 1214 defended the county's chartered privileges when these were under attack from the sheriff.[138] Sometimes we can glimpse the wider community which must have lain behind these activities. It was, for example, the barons, knights, free tenants, and all the men of the rape of Hastings who made a proffer to be free of various forest impositions in 1207.[139] But the knights are always likely to have been at the centre of these provincial groupings. More local in their interests and more heavily burdened with local duties than the barons, and a wealthier elite than the freeholders, they were both the representatives and the leaders of their counties.

By the time of Magna Carta they had also begun to be drawn into affairs at the centre. Though this reflected their local importance, the agent here was the king and not the locality. On two famous occasions John summoned the knights to appear at central assemblies. In August 1212 the sheriffs were told to appear before the king bringing with them 'six of the

[134] Stubbs, *Select Charters*, 252, 254, 257; Howden, *Chronica*, iii. 299–300. The best account of the changes of the 1190s is Stubbs's introduction to Howden, iv, at pp. xcvi–cii.

[135] *PR 2 Richard I*, 155; Holt, *Magna Carta*, 60.   [136] *PR 2 John*, 253; Holt, *Magna Carta*, 61.

[137] *Rotuli Litterarum Clausarum*, ed. T. D. Hardy, 2 vols., Record Comm. (London, 1833–44), i. 181.

[138] *CRR* vii: *1213–15*, 158–9; J. C. Holt, 'The Prehistory of Parliament', in Davies and Denton (eds.), *English Parl.* 23; K. Faulkner, 'The Knights in the Magna Carta Civil War', *TCE* 8 (2001), 7.

[139] *PR 9 John*, xxvi. 41. For other similar examples of group actions, see Maddicott, 'Magna Carta and the Local Community', 48–9.

more lawful and discreet knights of your bailiwick who are to do what we shall tell them'. In November 1213 they were told to send up four knights from each county to a general assembly at Oxford 'to speak with us concerning the affairs of our realm'.[140] In neither case are John's intentions entirely clear, though the first order, issued just after John's discovery of a baronial plot against his life, may have reflected his wish to discover from the knights the identities of his enemies in the counties.[141] Both writs suggest that the knights might now represent their counties, not only in negotiating with the king and his agents for relief from burdens, but at the king's own bidding and for his purposes. The second episode has a further and fortuitous importance as the first known summons of the knights of the shire to a national assembly.[142]

The grievances of the knights and of county society in general were well represented in Magna Carta: in undertakings to prohibit increments on the farms of counties and hundreds, to appoint sheriffs and other local officials who 'know the law of the land and mean to observe it well', and to establish panels of knights to investigate 'evil customs' in each county, especially those laid at the door of forest officials and sheriffs.[143] Few concessions were offered on the forest, but an elaborate Forest Charter was to be issued separately in 1217.[144] Other clauses benefited the knights in particular rather than their societies: for example, those limiting castleguard obligations and fixing the figure for the relief from a knight's fee held in chief at £5.[145] Both grievances and remedies can have been fed into the Charter only by the magnates, who may well have been under pressure from their own men to provide the means of redress.[146] They supplied the link, though one invisible in the records, between aggrieved knights and those they represented in the counties, and the crown and chancery which alone could provide remedies.

The probable medium of magnate transmission for knightly grievances should remind us that the knights were not only representative figures from their localities. They were also tenants, overlapping and often coinciding

---

[140] *Rot. Litt. Claus.* i. 132; Stubbs, *Select Charters*, 282.

[141] Holt, 'Prehistory of Parliament', 5–9.

[142] Ibid. 6; F. M. Powicke, 'England: Richard I and John', in *The Cambridge Medieval History*, vol. vi, ed. J. R. Tanner, C. W. Previté-Orton, and Z. N. Brooke (Cambridge, 1929), 230.

[143] Caps. 25, 45, 48: Holt, *Magna Carta*, 456–7; Faulkner, 'Knights in the Magna Carta Civil War', 8–9; P. Coss, *The Origins of the English Gentry* (Cambridge, 2003), 120.

[144] Caps. 44, 47, 48: Holt, *Magna Carta*, 338–40, 462–5; Stubbs, *Select Charters*, 344–8.

[145] Caps. 2, 29: Holt, *Magna Carta*, 450–1, 458–9; Coss, *Origins of the English Gentry*, 120.

[146] Coss, *Origins of the English Gentry*, 120.

with all those other 'feudal' groups of lesser landholders—scutage payers, minor tenants-in-chief, tenants of escheated honors—whose grievances we have already discussed. When in 1194 the knights of the Isle of Wight paid £10 'that scutage may not be demanded from them contrary to their customs', they stood for their own group interests as feudal tenants rather than the wider interests of the locality by which they were identified.[147] When in 1245 Henry III ordered all those non-knights holding from the crown who possessed either a knight's fee or £20 worth of land to come to receive knighthood from the king in person, he gave proof of the potential common identity of knights and lesser tenants-in-chief, which had been no less a feature of the social scene in his father's reign.[148] Far from being self-contained and independent units, counties and honors lay superimposed and intermingled on the ground, so that knights negotiating for county privileges might also be lesser crown tenants paying excessive commutation fines or tenants of escheats now burdened with new military obligations. John's Irish expedition of 1210, for example, included a little group of Yorkshire knights, Adam de Staveley and others, who either held single manors from the crown or else held of honors then in the king's hand, so making them liable to serve in person. Some had to borrow money in order to do so.[149] Here, as almost certainly elsewhere, county knights and harassed crown tenants were one and the same.

The origins of popular representation lie in this complex web of ties which bound locality to centre. The knights who represented their counties in bargaining with the crown might also be among the lesser tenants-in-chief whose presence at councils was envisaged by the Charter whenever taxation was under discussion. The offence which John's government had given to both groups, through pressures both fiscal and feudal, does much to explain the new role which, in the next two generations, they would begin to play at the centre of government.

5. Magnates and the Community of the Realm

The years which saw the knights emerge as the de facto representatives both of their local communities and of their particular social group also saw

---

[147] PR 6 Richard I, p. xxiv, 218.   [148] CR, 1242–47, 350; above, 130.
[149] Thomas, Vassals, Heiresses, 170–1 and n. 8.

the parallel emergence—or rather re-emergence—of the magnates as the representatives of a national community larger and more novel than that of the shire. Our *terminus ante quem* here must be the tax grant of 1225 already discussed. Conceded by the magnates of the great council, the grant could nevertheless be regarded by Henry as one made by all his subjects: the 'archbishops, bishops, abbots, priors, earls, barons, knights and everyone in our kingdom', to be identified a generation later as 'the community of the realm'.[150] If the knights spoke for their own small societies, the magnates had come to be seen as the spokesmen representatives of the whole kingdom, here set against the king as the negotiators of the tax which Henry needed. In terms of both institutional procedures and underlying concepts, we are within sight of parliament. The institutional development of the great council has already been discussed and its history will soon be taken forward; but what forces had created magnate representatives?

That a magnate council could represent the realm was not an entirely new perception. We have already seen that the pre-Conquest witan, whose composition was not very different from that of the great council of 1225, had been consistently regarded as a nationally representative body, 'the witan of the English people', for whom a king such as Cnut might consider it to speak.[151] Yet this perception failed to survive the Conquest, and the post-1066 feudal council could hardly be regarded in the same way. At a theoretical level the tenants-in-chief attending councils in the first century of English feudalism might perhaps be seen as standing not only for themselves but for their tenants, and those tenants fill the land. But no contemporary spoke in these terms, and it is difficult to see the councils which initiated the Domesday survey in 1085 or which tried Becket at Northampton in 1164 as being in any way representative. These were gatherings of feudal magnates summoned by their lord to provide the counsel which tenure obliged them to provide.

It was the advent of national taxation which changed this situation and which gave the magnate council a more representative role. At first that role was highly circumscribed. When a magnate assembly granted Henry II a levy on incomes for the Holy Land in 1166, those present, including the king, swore to compel 'all under our rule (*omnes sub potestate nostra*)' to pay. Only by the king's voluntary submission to the same oath as his magnates, so undertaking to bear down on his own tenants, could the obligation to

---

[150] Above, 107–8.   [151] Above, 51–5.

pay be extended beyond those making the grant. Even then, the tax would appear to have been limited in its application: less a levy on the realm than on the magnates and their own tenants.[152] If this was representation, it was both qualified (by tenure) and more implicit than overt. John's levy of a thirteenth in 1207 similarly acknowledged the bonds of tenure, but, by contrast, sweepingly overrode them. Conceded by a magnate council, the tax was to be paid, according to the king's writ for its assessment, 'by every layman of all England from the fee of whomsoever he may be'. As we have already argued, John was presumably concerned to ensure that it was not only the tenants of the immediate grantors who paid but also the tenants of all others holding from him in chief, and their tenants too. So a magnate council had been made to concede a tax which was universal in its application: by implication it stood for the whole body of taxpayers.[153] But one earlier levy had already taken the notion of representation more plainly for granted. When Richard I wrote home to ask for a ransom aid in 1193, his letters were addressed to his 'archbishops and bishops and abbots and earls and barons and clerks and free tenants': in effect, to all his free subjects. Yet the body intended to receive these letters can only have been the magnate council, regarded by the king as having sufficient authority to bind all those subjects to payment.[154]

In all these cases the initiative came from the crown. It was not the magnates who initially saw themselves as representing a larger body, whether their tenants or all the king's subjects, but the crown, in whose interests it was to link the consent to taxation of a few great men with the consequent obligation of all men to pay up. National taxation, the drive for access to the resources of all his subjects, created the need for the king to envisage and present the magnate council as a representative body, in which those present could speak for all. 'The witan of the English people' had gained its representative quality from its summoning by the king of that people, *rex Anglorum*, from the national business brought before it, and from its attendance by men from all parts of the kingdom. But the representative quality which the great council was beginning to acquire under Richard and John differed in its origins from the broader conceptions of pre-Conquest England. Its base and rationale was almost exclusively fiscal.

---

[152] *Gervase of Canterbury*, i. 198–9; Mitchell, *Taxation*, 168–9; above, 103–4.
[153] Stubbs, *Select Charters*, 278; above, 133–4.   [154] Howden, *Chronica*, iii. 208; above, 120.

At the same time both the represented and their representatives were beginning to be more closely defined—not only as an amorphous body of taxpayers but as a *communa*, a community. The language of realm as community had first appeared in Henry II's Assize of Arms of 1181, which had defined the arms to be held by 'the whole commune of free men (*tota communa liberorum hominum*)'. This was, however, a narrower term than it might seem, for this 'commune' was only a partial body, set alongside holders of knight' fees and wealthier freemen, who were to bear additional arms.[155] More inclusive was the phrase used in John's plans to counter a French invasion in 1205, laying down as they did that the whole realm should become a commune (*per totum regnum fieret communa*) for its defence and that it should incorporate the lesser communes of shire, hundred, and vill.[156] As this suggests, the concept of realm as commune ultimately came up from below, from the smaller communities of the localities which had a real existence prior to and more concrete than that of the more nebulous 'community of the realm'.[157] But, like the association of representation with taxation, the emergence of this larger grouping rested in part on the needs of the king. If the realm was to be regarded as a defensible social and political unit under its ruler, it could most conveniently be spoken of as a 'commune'.

Even before Magna Carta the royal principle that the magnates could represent the realm had begun to be turned against the king. Formerly the homage which they owed to the king had encouraged the concept that they were his barons, and only in the most exceptional circumstances, when there was no crowned king, such as the few days before Henry I's coronation, do we hear of 'barons of the realm', *barones regni Angliae*.[158] Now, however, their relationship with the realm began to move from one of occasional association to another of active spokesmanship. If they could stand for the king's subjects in matters of taxation, they could do the same on grounds of their own choosing. According to Gervase of Canterbury, it was at a council meeting at Oxford during the invasion scare of 1205 that the assembled magnates forced John to swear that he would preserve intact 'the rights of the kingdom of England (*iura regni Angliae*)' with their

---

[155] Stubbs, *Select Charters*, 183.

[156] *Gervase of Canterbury*, ii. 96–7; Stubbs, *Select Charters*, 276–7; Holt, *Magna Carta*, 57; below, 145 Note that Gervase appears here to be paraphrasing, not transcribing, an official document which does not survive.

[157] Holt, *Magna Carta*, 50–74, *passim*; Reynolds, *Kingdoms and Communities*, esp. chs. 5 and 6.

[158] Garnett, 'Origins of the Crown', 197–8.

counsel.[159] These 'rights' were left undefined, but it is clear that they were the subjects' rather than the king's and equally clear that the magnates saw themselves as their defenders. This was a significant turning point (though there may have been others like it). Not only is magnate counsel being invoked to threaten rather than to promote the king's interests, but for the first time so far as we know magnate counsellors have taken up a position which was often to be adopted by those in Henry III's parliaments: as representatives of the realm, they stand against the king. On this occasion at least the dual principle that a council of magnates is the king's council, and magnate counsel his to draw on, has been appropriated by the council's members.

It was in Magna Carta that this position was first fully worked out. The Charter took the form of a grant to 'all the free men of our realm'. It promised relief to others besides magnates—knights, baronial tenants, merchants, even freemen and villeins—and the 'commune of the whole land' (*communa tocius terre*) could be called on to enforce it.[160] The liberties which the Charter embodied were never spoken of as a concession to the whole community or *regnum*, for, as Holt has pointed out, this would have been to concede that the opposition could act for that community.[161] Yet a grant to the whole community, represented by the Charter's baronial makers, it effectively was: a community incorporating diverse social groups but nevertheless capable of possessing corporate liberties. The 'rights of the kingdom', vaguely referred to in 1205, had now been identified and defined in an assembly of king and barons which a later chancery clerk would describe, not entirely anachronistically, as 'the *parleamentum* of Runnymede'.[162] No longer an abstraction, the community of the realm represented by its barons had acquired a novel solidity. It perhaps owed something, too, to ecclesiastical and theological reinforcement, for behind the emergence of the *communitas regni*, there may also have lain Stephen Langton's parallel conception of the church as a congregation of the faithful, a *congregatio fidelium* of both clergy and laity, and not merely a prelate-ruled hierarchy.[163] The effect of scholastic ideas on the growth of institutions is harder to measure than the impact of events, but it is unlikely to have been negligible.

[159] *Gervase of Canterbury*, ii. 97–8; Holt, 'Rights and Liberties', 208–9; above, 119.
[160] Caps. 1, 2, 20, 29, 41, 61: Holt, *Magna Carta*, 450–1, 458–9, 460–3, 469–73.
[161] Holt, 'Rights and Liberties', 210.   [162] *CR, 1242–47*, 242.
[163] Baldwin, 'Master Stephen Langton', 822, 834.

There was one other side to this evolution, more cultural and ideological than political, constitutional, or theological. By 1215 the 'community of the realm' was coming to be seen as an English community, partly defined by being set against alien intruders. In the long term this development grew from an extended period of cultural appropriation by a once-Norman elite. Probably by about 1150 English had become the first language of the aristocracy, leaving French as an acquired language which had to be learnt.[164] By the 1170s and 1180s all those living in England could be spoken of simply as 'English', whatever their origins, so that Jordan Fantosme could speak of the losses inflicted by the Scots on 'the English of England', meaning Henry II's supporters, in the revolt of 1173–4, and Gerald of Wales could refer to the conquerors of Ireland as 'the English'. Fantosme in particular shows an already well-developed sense of English national identity.[165] More immediately, from about this time what had been an almost insensible transformation began to take on a more self-conscious, aggressive, and nationalistic edge. Its first victim was a Norman, William Longchamp, Richard I's unloveable chancellor. When Richard left on crusade, says William of Newburgh, he committed the kingdom to a foreigner without the consent of the nobility. Longchamp's foreign retinue, says Gerald of Wales, was used to oppress 'the native-born magnates of the kingdom (*naturales regni proceres*)'. His inability to speak English, says Howden, gave him away when he tried to flee England in disguise.[166] Forces are emerging here which would gain strength during the next reign: the opposition of native magnates to foreign ministers; baronial claims to be consulted on ministerial appointments; the English language as a touchstone of identity.

The same animosities broke surface again, though with a wider range of targets, in the opposition to John's alien supporters, men such as Philip Mark and Engelard de Cigogné, whose dismissal was demanded in the Charter.[167] John's promotion of these men, his reliance on them for counsel, and his

---

[164] Cf. J. C. Holt, *Colonial England* (London, 1997), 14 n. 71, and H. M. Thomas, *The English and the Normans: Ethnic Hostility, Assimilation and Identity, 1066–c.1220* (Oxford, 2003), 381, and sources there cited.

[165] *Jordan Fantosme's Chronicle*, ed. Johnston, 48–9; Giraldus Cambrensis, *Expugnatio Hibernica: The Conquest of Ireland*, ed. A. B. Scott and F. X. Martin (Dublin, 1978), 80–1, 230–3; I. Short, 'Patrons and Polyglots: French Literature in Twelfth-Century England', *ANS* 14 (1992), 246 and n. 85; Ashe, *Fiction and History*, 81–120, esp. 81–93 (a good survey of the whole subject).

[166] William of Newburgh, 306–7; Giraldus Cambrensis, *Opera*, iv. 425; Howden, *Chronica*, iii. 146. For other criticisms of Longchamp as a foreigner, see Thomas, *The English and the Normans*, 327–32.

[167] Cap. 50: Holt, *Magna Carta*, 464–5.

appointing them to office in the shires brought into the open a hostility towards foreigners which had usually been no more than latent. His undertaking in 1213 to remove the aliens from his 'familiarity' and to rely on the counsels of the magnates publicized a growing division between the king's friends from overseas and magnates who were by implication native born.[168] The London recension of the Laws of Edward the Confessor, dating from John's reign and already cited in another context,[169] shines a still brighter and more discriminating light on contemporary opinion. In his account of the mythical good deeds of King Arthur, its author recalled that his hero had ordained annual assemblies at which the whole people (*populi omnes et gentes universe*) had sworn to defend the realm 'against aliens (*alienigenas*) and against enemies'. Following this up, King Ine had laid down that Bretons, Saxons, and Jutes might remain in the kingdom because of their ancestral blood ties with the natives.[170] The retrospective division here was one between native friend and alien foe; but in writing of annual assemblies to administer oaths for the defence of the realm the author also moved forward towards the national *communa* proposed in John's defence scheme of 1205 (which he possibly had in mind). If he was a Londoner with some clerical training, as is usually supposed,[171] then we can deduce that anti-alien feeling was not confined to the magnates and to those who had suffered under the lash of Philip Mark and his like in the shires. Socially widespread, it persuaded others besides magnates to envisage a realm-wide community reified and reinforced by opposition to foreigners.

The London author's view of the realm as a closed ethnic unit suggests that opposition to particular figures might lead to more general conclusions, and that hostility to Longchamp, to John's alien friends, and to overseas invaders might promote the broader and more positive ideal of a national community bound together by common descent. Behind the prickly nationalism which underlay this progression lay not only the slow and subterranean rebirth of English identity after the trauma of 1066 and the more patent dislike of alien ministers, but also the emergence of a kingdom which could be regarded as more self-contained. Some reasons for this development are obvious. The web of cross-Channel connections binding England to the Continent a century earlier had weakened. The number of English magnates who also held land in Normandy at John's accession,

[168] Above, 114.   [169] Above, 118–19.
[170] *Gesetze*, ed. Liebermann, i. 655, 658.   [171] O'Brien, *God's Peace and King's Peace*, 118.

though still quite substantial, was smaller than in the days of the king's grand-father, and smaller still after Normandy's loss in 1204. Aristocratic families had often divided their English from their Norman lands; and the territorial interests of their sub-tenants and knights had become more exclusively English at a still earlier stage.[172] Neither group had any interest in the lands beyond Normandy, in Poitou, Anjou, and Aquitaine, which had come to the crown with Henry II's accession in 1154. The periodic expression of opposition to military service overseas which punctuated both Richard's reign and John's, culminating in the northerners' refusal to serve in Poitou in 1213, was the most obvious sign of this more forceful insularity.[173]

Other less obvious changes similarly pointed towards the growth of English self-sufficiency: for example, in the matter of tournaments. Popular under Stephen, tournaments in England had been prohibited by Henry II, leaving knights and nobles such as William Marshal to cross to northern France for their sport. Once there, the division of English and Normans into separate fighting teams was a further sign that the Channel now marked a boundary. But under Richard I tournaments were re-introduced into England and regulated by the crown, making foreign ventures less necessary.[174] Higher education provides a second example. It was in the 1190s, when the Anglo-French wars made travel to the pre-eminent schools of Paris more difficult, that those of Oxford began to expand. Distinguished scholars such as Alexander Neckham are found lecturing there, the syllabus broadened to take in theology and arts, and those who would one day become English bishops began to appear in Oxford, either as teachers or taught: notably Edmund of Abingdon, later archbishop of Canterbury, and Walter de Gray, later archbishop of York.[175] Paris retained its overwhelming intellectual superiority, but an English rival, later to train many of the leaders of the thirteenth-century English church, was on the horizon. The insular location of both tournament and university (an improbable pair of twins) was indicative of a cultural shift sharing in some

---

[172] D. Crouch, 'Normans and Anglo-Normans: A Divided Aristocracy?', in D. Bates and A. Curry (eds.), *England and Normandy in the Middle Ages* (London, 1994), esp. 62, 67; Carpenter, *Struggle for Mastery*, 269; Ashe, *Fiction and History*, 95–7.

[173] Holt, *The Northerners*, 90–1, 98–102, 115–16; id., 'The End of the Anglo-Norman Realm', in his *Magna Carta and Medieval Government*, 48–9.

[174] D. Crouch, *Tournament* (London, 2005), 9, 53–4; id., 'Normans and Anglo-Normans', 66 and n. 42; J. Gillingham, *Richard I* (London, 1999), 278–9.

[175] R. W. Southern, 'From Schools to University', in J. Catto (ed.), *The History of the University of Oxford*, i: *The Early Oxford Schools* (Oxford, 1984), 21–6; C. H. Lawrence, *St Edmund of Abingdon* (Oxford, 1960), 110–16.

of the same characteristics as the concurrent shift in political affiliations and outlook.

'It was not social equality which made the barons of Magna Carta sympathize with the lower ranks of society but similarity of oppression.'[176] This was indeed one of the forces which had brought the community of the realm into being. But in the first place it was the need for money which had led the crown to regard the magnates as able to speak for the whole body of taxpayers. Only consequentially, and at a secondary stage, did the initiative pass to the magnates themselves. By 1215 they were no longer merely conceding the king a share in the country's wealth but presenting him with the country's grievances, not merely reacting to the king's demands for money but proactively demanding redress on behalf of all. If the concept of the magnates as national spokesmen was the king's invention, devised for his fiscal advantage, it became the magnates' own instrument, and one all the more powerful because representatives and represented were increasingly seen as a single English entity. When Magna Carta was translated into French in 1215, the body charged with a share in its enforcement was no longer the *communa tocius terre*, 'the commune of the whole land' of the Latin text, but instead 'la commune de tote Engleterre', 'the commune of all England'.[177] The community of the realm had acquired an identity defined not in terms of social groups but of a country. That the Charter's twenty-five baronial guarantors who might call on the *commune* for support included a Clare, a Bigod, a Mandeville, a Vere, and a fitz Walter, all of them descended from major Domesday tenants-in-chief,[178] showed how thoroughly Norman origins and descent had been subsumed into a common Englishness.

6. The Minority of Henry III

Magna Carta led to a civil war, in the midst of which King John died and his son Henry came to the throne as a minor. By historical convention

---

[176] Reynolds, *Kingdoms and Communities*, 268.

[177] J. C. Holt, 'A Vernacular French Text of Magna Carta, 1215', in his *Magna Carta and Medieval Government*, 243, 256.

[178] Holt, *Magna Carta*, 478–80; id., 'Feudal Society and the Family in Early Medieval England. I: The Revolution of 1066', in his *Colonial England*, 174.

Henry III's minority lasted from John's death in October 1216 until January
1227, when Henry began to issue charters.[179] But in terms of politics and
the constitution its most formative phase had ended with the tax grant of
February 1225 and the king's reciprocal reissue of the Charters. By that time
the dangers which had earlier threatened the survival of the monarchy had
been overcome. The civil war had effectively ended at the battle of Lincoln
in 1217; the crown's revenues had been restored; the routine operations
of the exchequer and the royal courts had been re-established; the royal
demesne, alienated and occupied during the war, had been resumed; and
the dissident magnates and military captains whose hold on royal lands
and castles had threatened to turn England into a collection of feuding
principalities had been brought to heel. The granting of tax and Charters in
1225 showed that attempts at the violent subversion and appropriation of
royal power had been successfully countered and that what was to become
a more normal process of political bargaining and negotiation between
crown and magnates had been initiated.

For the historian of parliament John's death and the accession of his
nine-year-old son are important for one main reason: they brought in a
ten-year period when magnate assemblies were especially prominent and
when political claims were made on their behalf which were to surface
again in Henry's majority. It was in effect a period of proto-parliamentary
government, opening the way for the emergence of parliament *eo nomine*
in the 1230s and for what became the first age of parliamentary politics.[180]
Behind this development lay a simple necessity. During the minority
the realm was governed by small and shifting combinations of magnates,
ministers, and churchmen: until 1219, by the regency of William Marshal,
successively in alliance with the papal legates Guala and Pandulf; from 1219
to 1221 by the triumvirate of Hubert de Burgh, the justiciar, Peter des
Roches, bishop of Winchester, and Pandulf; and from 1221 increasingly
by de Burgh and a group of important but subordinate allies, Stephen
Langton, the archbishop of Canterbury, the earls of Salisbury and Pembroke,
and the bishops of Salisbury and Bath. Whether established formally, as
with the rule of the Marshal and the triumvirate, or informally, as with
that of de Burgh, all these parties suffered from a common disadvantage:
they could not claim to embody or deploy royal authority. By comparison

---

[179] Carpenter, *Minority of Henry III*, 389. As the footnotes show, this section draws almost exclusively
on Professor Carpenter's great work both for its information and for its interpretations.
[180] Below, 157, 166–84.

with a king who was crowned and of age, even a properly constituted regency had only a slippery foothold on legitimacy. For this reason those governing for the young king had to look for support as widely as possible: to consult the magnates, to seek general consent for their actions, and to use the customary machinery of great councils for both purposes. Only in this way could the rulers' deficit in authority be made good.[181]

From this abnormal situation came a form of conciliar government—or rather of government which relied heavily on councils and counsel. The councils which characterized the minority are not easy to define, largely because the word 'concilium' could cover both small meetings of ministers and other much larger assemblies in which ministers were joined by magnates. But it is clear that the latter, known conventionally, if not always by contemporaries, as 'great councils', were convened frequently and for a wide variety of business.[182] During the ten years from 1216 to 1225 some twenty-five great councils were summoned.[183] In 1218 and 1220 as many as four met in a single year. Though they sometimes coincided in a traditional way with Christmas courts, as in 1220 and 1223,[184] in general there was no temporal or locational pattern to their meetings. Only a minority, about twelve, met at London or Westminster, and they were often summoned to a place appropriate for some particular and immediate purpose. Thus a great council met at Worcester, not far from the Welsh marches, to negotiate a treaty with Llywelyn, prince of North Wales, in March 1218, and another at Rochester, near the Kent coast, to negotiate with French envoys in March 1219.[185] Much else besides foreign affairs came within their purview, including some of the most important political acts of the minority. The resumption of the king's demesnes, a crucial step in the recovery of royal power, for example, was sanctioned by a great council in 1222, and the decision to lay siege to the rebel Falkes de Breauté in Bedford castle by another in 1224.[186] Even the more routine business which came before the councils of the minority, such as the settlement of magnate disputes,[187] gained a special significance in this period from the need to enforce the peace in a country where peace was still fragile.

---

[181] Carpenter, *Minority of Henry III*, 3–4, 14, 84, 407–9. [182] Cf. ibid. 54.

[183] These are listed in the index to Carpenter, *Minority of Henry III*, 449–50.

[184] Ibid. 231, 325–6. [185] Ibid. 74–7, 104. [186] Ibid. 281, 359–62.

[187] e.g. between Maurice de Gant and the earl of Chester in May 1218 (ibid. 82) and between the earl of Pembroke and Falkes de Breauté in August 1220 (ibid. 203).

Two sorts of conciliar business were to be particularly significant for the future development of parliament: taxation and appointments. Prior to the grant of the fifteenth in 1225, the minority saw two general taxes, a levy on knights' fees in 1217, and a carucage on ploughs and ploughlands in 1220. Both were sanctioned at meetings of the great council.[188] In the case of the carucage, the grant was conceded, according to a royal letter, 'in common by all the magnates and *fideles* of our kingdom',[189] thus perpetuating the theory developed over the previous thirty years that the council stood for the whole realm and so could bind the king's subjects to the payment of taxes.[190] But in 1220 this proposition, developed as it had been to suit the crown's fiscal convenience, was resisted. In a famous episode the stewards of the Yorkshire magnates, meeting at York, claimed that their lords had not been consulted and so refused to pay.[191] Their protest may have been rooted in Magna Carta's demand for 'common counsel' in the granting of general aids,[192] but it is perhaps equally likely that it rested on the perceived need for individual consent to taxation and not the consent of nominal representatives. This view gains some force from the earlier but comparable action of the bishop of Winchester who had been excused payment of the 1217 tax on knights' fees on the grounds that he had never consented to it.[193] Both these incidents suggest that the government's notion of the great council as a representative body was not yet generally accepted.

If the linkage of general taxation to conciliar consent perpetuated earlier practices, confirmed and defined in the Charter, the council's initiative in ministerial appointments was almost wholly new. The only precedents dated from the period of Richard I's departure and subsequent absence on crusade in the early 1190s.[194] All the major appointments of the minority were made at meetings of the great council and seemingly with conciliar consent. This was true, for example, of the initial appointment of the Marshal as regent in 1216, of the appointment of Ralph de Neville as keeper of the seal, of Geoffrey de Neville as seneschal of Poitou, and

[188] Carpenter, *Minority of Henry III*, 67, 206–7.

[189] *Rot. Litt. Claus.* i. 437; Mitchell, *Studies in Taxation*, 129–30; Carpenter, *Minority of Henry III*, 206.

[190] Above, 133–4, 141.

[191] *Royal and Other Historical Letters Illustrative of the Reign of Henry III*, ed. W. W. Shirley, 2 vols., RS (1862–6), i. 151.

[192] Carpenter, *Minority of Henry III*, 210–11. But cf. Mitchell, *Studies in Taxation*, 131–2 and n. 54, who takes a slightly different view.

[193] *PR 5 Henry III*, 21; Mitchell, *Studies in Taxation*, 127–8; Carpenter, *Minority of Henry III*, 67.

[194] Above, 110.

of the appointment of the justices of the Jews, all in 1218, and of the elevation of the justiciar, the bishop of Winchester, and the papal legate as a governing triumvirate in 1219.[195] Conciliar sanction thus covered both extraordinary appointments, the results of the peculiar circumstances of the minority, and others that were more routine. Though inevitable in a period when personal kingship was in abeyance, this would in normal times have been regarded as a huge intrusion on the king's prerogative; for after all the ministers were *his* ministers. Conciliar initiatives here had important consequences for the future. They established precedents, promoting the claims made by the magnates in parliament during the 1240s and 1250s to share in royal appointments, and so contributing to the parliamentary politics and debates of Henry's maturity which helped to transform the consensual councils of the twelfth century into the more confrontational parliaments of the thirteenth.[196]

One result of the authority which the great council was now seen to possess, and of the need for general consent to the government's major *acta*, was a growing self-consciousness among the magnates about the role of both councils and consent. Occasionally it found a voice. In 1220 an order was issued by the justiciar and the council (*per eundem* [Hubert de Burgh] *et consilium domini Regis*) for the dismantling of the rebel Richard de Umfraville's castle at Harbottle in Northumberland.[197] But this decision was challenged by Robert de Vieuxpont and the earl of Salisbury, Umfraville's kinsmen and allies. In a letter to the legate, Vieuxpont alleged that the order had 'emanated from a certain part of the king's council, without the common counsel and assent of the magnates of England who are held to be and are of the chief council (*de capitali consilio*) of the king'. Salisbury wrote in terms so similar as to suggest collusion between the two men: 'such an order is not held to be done rightfully (*tale preceptum fieri de iure non tenetur*) without our assent and counsel, who are and are held to be of the chief council of the king, with other chief men'.[198] Both these letters use the phrase 'capitalis consilium' almost as a term of art, the equivalent of the 'magnum concilium' so frequently referred to in the chronicles of Henry's majority.[199] Both see it as defined by the presence of the magnates and distinguish it from lesser sorts of council; and both see

[195] Carpenter, *Minority of Henry III*, 14, 82–3, 94–5, 128. For general discussion, see ibid. 407–8.
[196] Below, 178–9, 229–30.   [197] *Rot. Litt. Claus.* i. 436–7; Carpenter, *Minority of Henry III*, 202.
[198] Carpenter, *Minority of Henry III*, 88, 209 and nn. 7, 8. I have followed Carpenter's translations.
[199] Below, 457, 459, 461, 463.

the consent of the 'chief council' as essential to the making of important political decisions. Salisbury's letter goes beyond this, to deny the legality of decisions made without conciliar consent. Here was a claim which went much further than that staked out in Magna Carta for conciliar consent to taxation. In the eyes of at least some magnates, the effect of the minority was to put the great council at the heart of political decision-making, not by long-standing custom and royal volition, but de iure, by legal right.

The minority saw one other development which contributed greatly to the hardening claims for magnate and conciliar consent, and to the restraints on royal power which those claims would later promote. That was the establishment of Magna Carta, along with the 1217 Charter of the Forest, as something like fundamental law. During the minority the Charter was reissued three times, always with a specific purpose in view. In 1216 its reissue was a concession made by the royalists to the rebels in an attempt to get them to negotiate; while in 1217 it was implicitly conceded in return for the tax on knights' fees, and in 1225, more explicitly, for the fifteenth on moveables.[200] On a fourth occasion, in 1223, Henry verbally confirmed both Charters in order to secure an unpopular enquiry into royal rights and customs.[201] Thus on all four occasions the Charter was used as a bargaining counter, twice given in return for a tax and twice for other measures designed to restore royal authority. It was equally significant that on all four occasions the deal was struck at a meeting of the great council.[202] The linkage between confirmation of the Charters and political bargaining between magnates and government, which was to be a prominent feature of Henry's middle years, begins here, in circumstances where the depression of royal power and the need to restore it made the regular reissue of the Charter possible and negotiation inevitable. Had King John lived, none of this would have been likely.

But it was not just at the level of high politics that the Charter put down roots. Together with the Charter of the Forest, it was in process of becoming a shibboleth for litigants in the courts, for magnates, gentry, and churchmen seeking individual and corporate rights under its terms, and for provincial society in general. Appeals were made to the Charter's ruling against unjust disseisins; amercements were reduced or pardoned in accordance with the Charter's demand that they should not exceed an

---

[200] Carpenter, *Minority of Henry III*, 22–4, 60–3, 67, 382–8, 403.
[201] Ibid. 295–7, 337.   [202] Ibid. 22–3, 60–1, 379.

individual's ability to pay; baronial reliefs were charged at the £100 rate which the Charter stipulated and not at the excessive and arbitrary rates prevailing under John.[203] The proclamation in the county courts of all three of the Charter's reissues and, in the case of the 1217 and 1225 versions, the subsequent laying up of copies in local monastic houses, publicized its terms and facilitated future reference to them.[204] It was both the local publicity given to the Charter and its everyday citation in the courts, as much as its successive reissues and confirmations at the centre, which ensured its permanence; while the social range of those looking to the Charter for justice and redress, from earls to freemen, reinforced its original standing as a national text, the property, not of any particular group, but of the community of the realm. Its reissues prompted by the great council, its particular clauses appealed to by a much wider constituency, the Charter had come to exemplify another way in which central assemblies could be seen to represent the realm.

The effect of the minority was thus to make the great council an indispensable part of the country's government, to give it a degree of independent initiative and authority which central assemblies had never previously possessed, and to establish Magna Carta as a conciliar cynosure, national bargaining counter, and practical code of redress. The Charter linked the principle of legal restraints on kingship both with the council's place at the centre of government and with the aspirations of political society in the provinces. These developments must now be placed in a broader context and their contribution to the larger development of parliament assessed.

7. Conclusion

The years between 1189 and 1225 saw the great council transformed into a body which closely resembled the parliamentary assemblies of Henry III's middle years. From a feudal gathering of tenants-in-chief summoned to give obligatory counsel to the king, it became one which claimed the right to advise, to consent to taxation, to have a say in such prerogative matters as ministerial appointments, and to represent the whole realm. It was still recognizably the descendant of the council of the Anglo-Norman kings,

[203] Ibid. 63, 191, 204, 237, 334–5, 403–4; Turner, *The King and his Courts*, 154–6.
[204] Maddicott, 'Magna Carta and the Local Community', 30–1; Carpenter, *Minority of Henry III*, 402–3; R. V. Turner, *Magna Carta* (Harlow, 2003), 83.

comprising magnates, churchmen, and occasionally lesser landholders whose attendance was determined by tenure, but it now possessed greater independence, larger functions, and, in the case of taxation, some legal basis for its powers (even though the 1215 linkage of general aids to conciliar consent was omitted in the Charter's reissues). It was a parliament in all but name.

The primary—but not the only—forces which governed this development were financial in origin: the costs of war. They were the essential cause of the general taxes, feudal levies, and provincial extortions which created the grievances articulated in Magna Carta. These pressures contributed powerfully to the breakdown of the more harmonious relationship between king and magnates which had existed for much of the twelfth century and to the impairment of the conciliar consensus through which that relationship had often been expressed. More positively, they induced the king to consult, for prudential reasons, before raising general taxes and, in an equally self-interested way, to regard the council as able to speak for all and conciliar grants as binding on all. But if the idea of representation grew from the crown's needs, it was soon extended to the subject's needs. If the magnates could represent the realm to the crown's fiscal advantage, they could also represent the realm against the crown, as they did most notably in Magna Carta: a Charter negotiated by the magnates but conceded by the king 'to all the free men of our realm'.

Fiscal pressures meant that the community of the realm whose interests the Charter embodied was in the first place a community of taxpayers. Though much money came in from the feudal incidents and the scutages which targeted only particular individuals and groups, and direct taxes were less frequent and less ferocious than they were to be a century later in the 1290s, the levy of a quarter for Richard's ransom, the thirteenth in 1207, and the fifteenth in 1225 nevertheless fell heavily on all, creating a 'similarity of oppression' which bound the magnates to their social inferiors and stimulated common grievances.[205] We can see this most clearly in the history of the thirteenth: opposed almost certainly by the magnates of the council, resisted and evaded in the localities.[206]

Within this larger whole some groups became particularly prominent. The period saw the increased politicization of the knightly class, the main producers of the county revenues which Richard and more especially

[205] Reynolds, *Kingdoms and Communities*, 268; above, 147.   [206] Above, 125–6.

John exacted on so large a scale and with such brutal efficiency.[207] Its members shared generally in the complaints of the magnates against royal government, if from a different perspective (more likely to be concerned about extortionate sheriffs, for example, than about familiar counsel), and often acted as the representatives of their shires in voicing those complaints. In so doing they made the middling ranks of the community into an active political force, capable of negotiating with the crown for fiscal privileges, concerting and promoting their grievances in Magna Carta, and appealing to both the Great Charter and the Forest Charter in defence of their rights during the minority and beyond.

The actions of the knightly class were one factor which helped to give form and substance to a community of the realm which might otherwise have remained no more than a vague and amorphous concept. Another, less closely connected with the fiscal agenda of government, was the emergent political outlook shaped by a hardening sense of English national identity and the increasingly close identification of the magnates with England. If this was in part a long-term evolutionary development, the product of the slow transformation of militant Norman colonizers into an English landed class, it also marked a more immediate response to contemporary circumstance: to the appointment as chancellor of the detested foreigner William Longchamp, to the loss of Normandy, to John's favour for aliens, and to the presence of the French invader Prince Louis and of John's surviving alien captains in the early years of the minority.[208] Aliens in particular, often local sheriffs and castellans as well as royal *familiares*, were as unpopular with the gentry of the shires as with the magnates of the council.[209] Hostility towards them was another bond which helped to unite socially disparate groups and to create a community which was both self-consciously national as well as nationalistic—the 'commune of all England', in the evocative words of the French translation of Magna Carta.

Yet all these changes might have proved ephemeral and of no permanent consequence had it not been for John's early death and his son's long minority. This was the point at which the adventitious and the unexpected cut across the rapid but steadier course of political and institutional change.

[207] Barratt, 'English Revenues of Richard I', 638, 642, 650; id., 'Revenue of King John', 845.
[208] For aliens in the minority, see Carpenter, *Minority of Henry III*, 20–1, 139–40, 262, 272–3.
[209] See, e.g., the charges made against Engelard de Cigogné arising from his time as sheriff of Gloucestershire: *Pleas of the Crown of the County of Gloucester, 1221*, ed. F. W. Maitland (London, 1884), pp. xv–xvii.

As mentioned at the start of this chapter, many of the developments occurring in England were common to other European countries in the years around the turn of the twelfth century: the rising costs of warfare, baronial discontents, and baronial demands for consultative government, and the rulers' issuing of national charters of redress and privilege, comprised a by no means uniquely English combination. But England differed from other countries in experiencing a minority which allowed the political outcomes of the previous two reigns to set firm. Chance intervened to perpetuate change. Had John survived and triumphed in the civil war, or had he even left a widow with the will and the political weight to fight for the undiminished rights of her son's monarchy, the situation might have been different. But Isabella of Angoulême was no Margaret of Anjou and was never a major player in the politics of the minority, returning to her homeland in 1218.[210] As it was, in the absence of a queen regent, the course of the minority was governed by the delicate balancing act of a regency government which had to seek the restoration of royal power by deploying not only force but also sufficient concessions to make that power acceptable. This entailed the need to satisfy some of the central claims and aspirations raised by the opposition before 1215. Hence Magna Carta became in effect an established code of law, taxation by consent, thrice repeated, became customary, and the magnates of the great council came to be regularly and widely consulted. What emerged from the minority was thus a restored but limited monarchy whose authority rested on the need to recognize the subordinate authority of magnate councils and of the traditions of consultation and consent that councils had come to embody. These were the circumstances which would soon give rise to a recognizable parliament.

[210] Carpenter, *Minority of Henry III*, 153.

4

Establishment

The First Age of Parliamentary Politics, 1227–1258

1. The Emergence of an Institution

Henry III's minority had established the great council as a leading force in politics and confirmed its alignment with the liberties now guaranteed by the Charters. In the middle years of his reign the English parliament emerged from this conciliar matrix to take on the shape which, with some variations, it was to maintain for the rest of the middle ages. In doing so it acquired much of the stability of form characteristic of an institution: a core membership which in type remained the same from one parliament to another; fairly regular summoning at times and places tending to become fixed; and the consolidation of generally recognized if loosely defined functions. By the time of the reform movement of 1258–9, and within a relatively short space of some twenty to thirty years, it had become an essential component of English government.

One mark of these changes may be the arrival of the word. From the mid 1230s 'parliament' begins to move into common use as a term for large assemblies. Its first official appearance comes in the course of a legal case of November 1236, when an action was deferred until the following *parliamentum* of January 1237.[1] Literary usage re-emerges, after its precocious appearance under Henry II, about the same time. It was probably also in 1236 that Matthew Paris began his Life of Edward the

---

[1] *CRR*, xv: 1233–37, no. 2047; H. G. Richardson and G. O. Sayles, 'The Earliest Known Official Use of the Term "Parliament"', in *EPMA* ii. 747–50.

Confessor, *La Estoire de Seint Aedward le Rei*, in which he spoke of Edward's granting a charter to his barons 'in this common parliament (*cest parlement commun*)'.[2] He first used the word in his more strictly historical *Chronica Maiora* in relation to the *parlamentum* of April 1239;[3] and it first occurs on the chancery rolls in June 1242.[4] By the mid 1240s other chroniclers besides Paris have also adopted it: the Dunstable annalist employs it for the first time in 1244, then—seemingly almost in concert—the annalists of Worcester, Burton, and Winchester, as well as Paris, for the parliament of March 1246.[5] By this time it was also spreading beyond official and monastic circles, making several appearances in the Winchester pipe roll for 1247 to denote the April *parlamentum* of that year.[6] When, a little later in the early 1250s, the leading Franciscan Adam Marsh wished to refer to central assemblies this was the word which he too invariably used.[7]

What lay behind this innovation is not easy to say. As we have seen, the word 'parlement' and its variants had, since the mid twelfth century, been applied informally and in literature to various sorts of meetings, and it is even possible that it was used in spoken French to describe the meetings of the great council from as early as Henry II's reign.[8] Its novel entry into records, chronicles, letters, and private accounts between 1236 and 1250 is unlikely to mark a mere semantic shift, of the kind which in our own day has turned international statesmen's conferences into 'summits'; and it is more likely that the word began to be employed in a more specific sense to denote exceptionally large assemblies, marked out from lesser and more ad hoc gatherings not only by their size but by the importance and generality of their business. It may be no coincidence that at just this time, in the mid 1230s, the king's ordinary council of ministers and magnates was

[2] *Lives of Edward the Confessor*, ed. H. R. Luard, RS (London, 1858), 78, 232, l. 1889. For the date, see D. A. Carpenter, 'King Henry III and Saint Edward the Confessor: The Origins of the Cult', *EHR* 122 (2007), 885–6.

[3] *Paris*, iii. 526. This early instance has been unaccountably overlooked by all who have written about parliament, and Paris's first use of the word is normally ascribed to 1246.

[4] *CR, 1237–42*, 447.

[5] *Ann. Dunstable*, 164–5; *Ann. Worcester*, 437; *Ann. Burton*, 278; *Ann. Winchester*, 90; *Paris*, iv. 518, 526. The use of the word by so many chroniclers for this particular assembly makes one wonder if it was perhaps used in the writs of summons issued to the heads of their houses.

[6] N. Vincent, 'The Politics of Church and State as Reflected in the Winchester Pipe Rolls, 1208–1280', in R. Britnell (ed.), *The Winchester Pipe Rolls in Medieval English Society* (Woodbridge, 2003), 165 and n. 62.

[7] *The Letters of Adam Marsh*, ed. and trans. C. H. Lawrence, OMT, 2 vols. (Oxford, 2006–10), i. 32–3, 46–7, 176 7.

[8] Above, 75–6.

taking shape as a defined body, perhaps making it necessary to distinguish between the two sorts of council through the use of a new word.[9] But if parliaments were different from this and other assemblies, the difference was not yet reflected in any exclusivity of title. The close roll's 'parleamentum' of August 1244 is Paris's 'concilium', while Paris's 'magnum parlamentum' of July 1248 is the 'colloquium' of the close roll.[10] Nevertheless the change was marked. That the reformers of 1258–9 consistently used the French 'parlement' for the assembly which was central to their schemes signified the word's full absorption into the language of politics.[11]

One indicator of the rising public prominence of parliament was the attention given to it by the chroniclers. Most attentive was Matthew Paris: our main source for most of what we know about parliamentary affairs, and a writer whose reports are often detailed enough to suggest that he was actually present in parliament. Certainly in attendance at the famous assembly of October 1247 which saw Henry's reception of the Holy Blood at Westminster, he may perhaps also have served from time to time as proctor for his superior, the abbot of St Albans.[12] No other chronicler at any point in the middle ages tells us so much about parliament and its workings. But if Paris was the most interested and best informed of parliament's chroniclers, he was not the only one. The Dunstable annalist records six assemblies between 1244 and 1257, two of which he calls parliaments; the Tewkesbury annalist, seven between 1250 and 1254, four of them termed parliaments; while the Burton annalist, besides mentioning one *parliamentum* in 1246 and two *parliamenta* in 1255, transcribed both the writ of summons to his abbot for the parliament of March 1257 and the magnates' written statement of the case against the king's involvement in Sicily drawn up in the same assembly.[13] The growing awareness of parliament as an occasion, demonstrable here among the handful of monasteries that maintained chronicles, is likely to have been equally widespread in lay society.

The interest of monastic historians in parliament may partly reflect the amount of important ecclesiastical business coming before the assemblies of

---

[9] For the development of the council, see below, 188–90, 391.

[10] *Paris*, iv. 380, v. 20; *CR, 1247–51*, 31; ibid. *1242–47*, 221.

[11] *DBM* 104–5, 110–11 (Provisions of Oxford), 150–1, 154–5, 156–7 (Provisions of Westminster).

[12] Cf. Maddicott, ' "An Infinite Multitude of Nobles" ', 18–19. For other pointers to Paris's attendance at parliament, see below, 192, 202.

[13] *Ann. Dunstable*, 164, 167, 186, 189, 195, 202; *Ann. Tewkesbury*, 142, 143, 146, 147, 148, 156; *Ann. Burton*, 278, 336, 360 384, 387–8.

the 1240s and 1250s, much of it centred on relations with the papacy. But
equally important in raising parliament's profile, and part of the same set of
developments, was the increasing frequency of its meetings, inadequately
recorded by such standard but lacunose lists of parliaments as that given
in the *Handbook of British Chronology*. The evidence suggests that the
23 years between 1235 and 1257 saw some 46 assemblies which could
be regarded with reasonable certainty as parliaments, with an additional
8 'possibles'.[14] Of this total of 54, 31 are mentioned by Paris; 12 of
these 31 are also mentioned in other chronicles; 5 are mentioned in
other chronicles but not by Paris; and 16 are mentioned in chancery
sources, most of which are confirmed by the chronicles. Eleven of the
54 are deducible primarily from the exceptional numbers of high-ranking
witnesses to royal charters on particular occasions. While the especially
large gatherings of bishops, earls, and barons sometimes recorded by the
charter witness lists are usually reliable pointers to special assemblies, there
must be a shade of doubt about these unchronicled gatherings. Some
may have been no more than afforced meetings of the king's ordinary
council, always difficult to distinguish in the sources from larger gatherings
of prelates and magnates. On the other hand, some parliaments have
almost certainly left no trace. For example, the disappearance of the charter
roll for 1256 may help to explain the apparent but surprising absence of
meetings in a year when the political furore over the Sicilian Business was
at its height. Taking one thing with another, the average of two to three
parliaments a year which the figures suggest is likely to be about right.
In some years this average was greatly exceeded. In both 1247 and 1252
the sources point to four parliaments, two of which in each year are so
termed. In general, meetings of parliament were at least as frequent as they
were to be under Edward I and certainly more frequent than those of
Edward III.[15]

What made these changes possible, and accelerated the growth of parliament as an institution, was a twofold development: first, the loss of
most of the crown's continental possessions and the consequent decline of
peripatetic kingship; and, second, the emergence of Westminster as both

---

[14] See the appended list of parliaments, 1235–57, below, 454–72. All the following figures derive
from this list.
[15] G. L. Harriss, 'The Formation of Parliament, 1272–1377', in Davies and Denton (eds.), *English
Parl.* 37; W. M. Ormrod, *The Reign of Edward III: Crown and Political Society in England, 1327–77* (New
Haven, 1990), 65.

the permanent seat of government and the focus for Henry III's religious interests. These two developments are connected.

For much of the second half of the twelfth century the need to defend the crown's lands in northern and western France had kept Henry II and his sons on the Continent and on the move. In a reign of 34 years and 11 months, Henry was abroad for approximately 21 years and 8 months, or 63 per cent of his time.[16] As long as the king remained itinerant over a wide empire, his movements often unknown and unforeseen, major assemblies might be numerous, as they sometimes were when the king was in England, yet they could not be regular or predictable.[17] But this situation was dramatically changed by the loss of Normandy and Anjou in 1204 and of Poitou in 1224. Henry III, the inheritor of these losses, spent only 4 years and 5 months abroad in a fifty-seven-year reign: about 8 per cent of his time. These statistics were the measure of the transformation of an Anglo-continental monarchy into an English one. The change which they marked did not contribute directly to the growth of parliament, but it was an essential precondition. With the king in England, assemblies could be convened with a new regularity and predictability. When he was abroad in 1260 Henry could take the line—admittedly for reasons of political expediency—that parliament was prohibited from meeting without him.[18] Its sessions were now seen to demand a royal presence in England which could normally be taken for granted.

Within England the focus of Henry's presence was on Westminster, for reasons partly to do with government. In the late eleventh and early twelfth centuries Winchester had carried equal weight as the chief place of Anglo-Norman kingship, its importance as the old Anglo-Saxon 'capital' of Wessex perpetuated beyond the Conquest by its convenience as a staging post and storehouse for men and money en route, via Portsmouth, to the crown's new possessions in Normandy. But in the second half of the twelfth century the situation changed as the institutions of government gravitated towards Westminster.[19] By Henry II's reign Westminster had superseded Winchester as the usual place for sessions of the exchequer, and under John it became the location for one of the crown's main treasuries, after

---

[16] Royal absences and their dates are noted in *HBC* 36-8.   [17] Above, 73.
[18] *DBM* 172-3; below, 249. For the context, see J. R. Maddicott, *Simon de Montfort* (Cambridge, 1994), 192-3.
[19] D. Keene, *Survey of Medieval Winchester*, Winchester Studies 2, 2 vols. (Oxford, 1985), i. 101; Le Patourel, *Norman Empire*, 149-50, 167, 175-6.

a probable move of the central treasury from Winchester to the Tower a generation earlier.[20] On the judicial side 'ordinary civil litigation was being heard at Westminster on a regular basis', almost certainly at the exchequer, from the late 1170s, and by the late 1190s such litigation had been hived off to a separate Westminster-based court, the bench. Though this was intermittently closed down under John, it reopened for business, with an enlarged jurisdiction, in 1217.[21] Westminster's growth as an administrative capital, enhanced by the loss of the northern French lands which robbed the old Winchester–Portsmouth axis of much of its one-time importance, had a social side to it too; for by the late twelfth century administrators and royal officials were beginning to reside there.[22] Government had moved away from a more exclusive identification with the person and court of the king and had come to be mainly concentrated in a fixed place.

Under Henry III, however, the king's own predilection for Westminster as a residence and a religious centre meant that the dichotomy between person and place hardly existed. This factor, as well as its establishment at the heart of government, ensured that from the 1230s onwards Westminster became parliament's normal meeting place. It had long been associated with royalty and religion, the abbey's role as the coronation place for English kings complemented by William Rufus' great hall and the social and curial functions which it symbolized. But in Henry's reign these roles were vastly expanded. Henry's inclinations were rooted in his early devotion to the memory of Edward the Confessor, which became evident from the mid 1230s. From 1238 Henry was almost invariably present at Westminster for the Confessor's two feast days, the Deposition on 5 January and the Translation on 13 October; from 1241 he began to reconstruct the saint's shrine; and in 1245 he put in hand the greatest of his lifetime's ambitions, the rebuilding of the abbey itself.[23] At the same time Henry was also

[20] Richard fitz Nigel, *Dialogus de Scaccario*, ed. and trans. E. Amt, OMT (Oxford, 2007), p. xxvii; R. A. Brown, ' "The Treasury" of the Later Twelfth Century', in J. C. Davies (ed.), *Studies Presented to Sir Hilary Jenkinson* (Oxford, 1957), 40–4.

[21] P. A. Brand, ' "Multis Vigiliis Excogitatam et Inventam": Henry II and the Creation of the English Common Law', *Haskins Soc. Jnl.* 2 (1990), 207–9; B. Kemp, 'Exchequer and Bench in the Later Twelfth Century: Separate or Identical Tribunals?', *EHR* 88 (1973), 570–3; Carpenter, *Minority of Henry III*, 64–5.

[22] G. Rosser, *Medieval Westminster, 1200–1540* (Oxford, 1989), 16–21; Keene, *Survey of Medieval Winchester*, i. 102.

[23] Carpenter, 'King Henry III and Saint Edward the Confessor', 868–71; id., 'King Henry III and the Tower of London', in his *Reign of Henry III*, 208; Brown, Colvin, and Taylor, *History of the King's Works*, i. 130, 147.

converting the palace into a grand residence, remodelling and decorating the 'great chamber' later known as the Painted Chamber. In his middle years he thus recreated at Westminster, though more solidly and on a much more magnificent scale, what Winchester had been less completely for the Old English monarchy: a dynastic shrine, cult centre, palatial residence, and seat of government.

These developments contributed powerfully if indirectly to the growth of parliament. In the second half of the twelfth century the great councils which were parliament's predecessors had had no fixed meeting-place. Though they had often met in London, as we have seen, they had as frequently convened at the king's rural manors and hunting lodges: places such as Clarendon, Woodstock, and Geddington. Even in the minority, when great councils had become a much more regular feature of the country's government, the exigencies of campaigning, the suppression of provincial disorder, and the needs of diplomacy in relation to Wales and France had all made it necessary for them often to meet outside the capital.[24] Of the 25 recorded great councils of the period, only about 12 met at Westminster or (what was almost always the same thing) in London. But during the years of Henry's maturity these proportions changed radically. Of our 54 parliaments meeting between 1235 and 1257, 39 convened at Westminster/London. When the assembly met elsewhere it was usually for some special reason: at Merton in 1236 because of the flooding of Westminster by the Thames, at York in 1237 and at Newcastle in 1244 for peace-making with the Scots, at Gloucester in 1240 for peace-making with the Welsh.[25] What facilitated frequent meetings at Westminster was not just Henry's frequent presence there but his lack of reason for being anywhere else: that is to say, in contrast to the conditions of the minority, the general prevalence of peace and the relative infrequency of war. Even though parliament might sometimes meet elsewhere, and rural venues were not entirely abandoned (there were three assemblies at Woodstock[26]), the most serious and regular business was always conducted at Westminster. All the king's many requests for taxes, for instance, were made at Westminster

---

[24] Above, 71–2, 149.

[25] Paris, iii. 339, 413, iv. 380; *Ann. Tewkesbury*, 115; *CR, 1237–42*, 240–1; *CPR, 1232–47*, 434; *CRR*, xv: *1233–37*, p. li n. 3. For a full list of meeting places, see the appended list of parliaments, below, 454–72.

[26] *Ann. Tewkesbury*, 107; *CRR*, xvi: *1237–42*, p. xix and no. 1493; *The Royal Charter Witness Lists of Henry III (1226–1272) from the Charter Rolls in the Public Record Office*, ed. M. Morris, List and Index Soc. 291–2, 2 vols. (2001), ii. 49.

parliaments. Precisely where the assembly met is rarely made clear by the sources. But in 1236 and 1237 its members came together in the royal palace (perhaps in the newly refurbished Painted Chamber), in November 1244 and May 1252 (for the trial of Simon de Montfort) in the abbey's refectory, and in March 1257 and January 1265 in the chapter house. Since these were all regular locations for meetings in the fourteenth century, it is probably safe to assume that they were already so by 1258.[27] The chapter house in particular, newly completed in the mid 1250s, was very probably intended by Henry to provide a fitting site for his own presence in parliament and for his occasional speeches to the assembled bishops and magnates. A building of exceptional beauty, and splendidly embellished to reflect Henry's regal and religious interests, it may well have been seen by him as an imposing part of the aesthetic armoury of his kingship.[28]

Within the calendar year a semi-regular pattern of parliamentary meetings began to emerge from the 1230s. Parliaments met most often in either January or (less frequently) February, the dates of their summoning being fixed in relation to the feast of Hilary (13 January) or the Purification (2 February); in April or (less frequently) May, in relation to Easter or Pentecost; in July; and again in October, in relation to Michaelmas (29 September). Between 1235 and 1257, for example, there were 14 January–February assemblies, 8 in April, 7 in July, and 8 in October. No parliament ever met in December,[29] and only the 'Scottish peace' meeting of 1244 in August; while September parliaments were highly unusual. In a general way the chief force behind this periodicity seems to have been the dates of three of the four law terms, Michaelmas, Hilary, and Easter. When parliament met the courts would normally be in session, and the judges who were an important part of the ministerial side of parliament would be on hand. Moreover, parliaments soon began to coincide, especially from the 1250s, with sessions of the exchequer fixed for the quindenes of these

[27] Paris, iii. 363, 380, iv. 362; C. Bémont, Simon de Montfort, comte de Leicester (Paris, 1884), 342; Ann. Burton, 386; De Antiquis Legibus Liber: Cronica Maiorum et Vicecomitum Londoniarum, ed. T. Stapelton, Camden Soc. (London, 1846), 71; J. G. Edwards, The Second Century of the English Parliament (Oxford, 1979), 4–7.
[28] D. Carpenter, 'King Henry III and the Chapter House of Westminster Abbey' (forthcoming). I am very grateful to David Carpenter for allowing me to see this important article in advance of publication.
[29] The Tewkesbury annals place a London magnum colloquium in December 1250, but Henry was not in London during that month and the annals may refer to the meeting of February 1251: Ann. Tewkesbury, 142–3; Paris, v. 233–4.

law terms (i.e. for the fourteenth day after the feast). To these sessions legal pleas, often involving franchises, were respited with increasing frequency.[30] The courts and the exchequer followed an unvarying timetable, alien to the more episodic summoning of parliament; but nevertheless magnate assemblies and curial sessions bringing together justices, officials, and litigants were often and increasingly synchronous. Two kinds of court were converging to give a periodic quality to the official year.

But Henry's own concerns were also important in determining the times of parliaments. The two great feasts of the saint whom he venerated, St Edward's Deposition in January and his Translation in October, were often made the occasion for magnate assemblies at Westminster. The October occasion was particularly important, for the Translation on 13 October coincided with the quindenes of Michaelmas. To some extent this was a revival of the equally loose practices of the eleventh century, when particular feasts had often but not invariably brought king and magnates together at particular places for the three annual crown-wearings and for counsel-taking.[31] The resemblances were heightened by Henry's enthusiasm, similar to that of William I, for the singing of the *laudes regiae*, the great liturgical hymn to kingship, not only at the three great feasts of Christmas, Easter, and Whitsun, but increasingly on other festal days, including those of Edward's Deposition and Translation.[32] The ancient conciliar rhythms of time, place, and function, impaired and vitiated in the twelfth century by the king's frequent absences overseas, were in part re-established.

By 1258 parliament had gone some way towards becoming an institution. Tending to meet frequently, with some regularity, and at the same place, it was coming to acquire more definition than that possessed by the former great councils of the twelfth century and of the minority. The transition from that earlier phase to the later was only partly evolutionary. It owed more to the unpredictable, the contingent, and the personal—to the loss of empire, the accident of the king's minority, the growth of Westminster as both capital and shrine, and to the religious sensibilities and passion

---

[30] J. E. A. Jolliffe, 'Some Factors in the Beginnings of Parliament', in *Historical Studies*, esp. 40–66.

[31] Above, 58–60; Carpenter, 'King Henry III and Saint Edward the Confessor', 868–9.

[32] E. H. Kantorowicz, *Laudes Regiae: A Study in Liturgical Acclamations and Mediaeval Ruler Worship*, 2nd printing (Berkeley and Los Angeles, 1958), 174–7; B. Weiler, 'Symbolism and Politics in the Reign of Henry III', *TCE* 9 (2003), 22–3; Carpenter, 'King Henry III and Saint Edward the Confessor', 870–2.

for ceremony of King Henry III. These things made possible the rise of parliament as a platform for politics: the setting not only for collaborative discussion, but for complaint, argument, confrontation, and the pressing of group interests. It is to politics and its part in the emergence of parliament that we now turn.

2. Parliament and Politics

In broad terms the agenda for Henry III's parliaments was no different from that of the great councils of Anglo-Norman England. Its chief component was still the 'vital business affecting the realm', as it had been in the days of William of Malmesbury.[33] Yet the context for such business had changed greatly, and for this there was one main reason. Discussions on tax were in process of becoming a central feature of parliament's work, augmenting the range of its activities in a way which was not only quantitative but which was to prove qualitative. Magna Carta had limited the king's fiscal powers, while the minority had consolidated and enlarged the achievement of 1215 by allowing the Charter's provisions to take root and by making consent both to tax grants and to government policies in general a matter of common practice. These three interlocking changes did much to determine the evolution of parliament between 1227 and 1258, and to ensure that it would not simply be a matter of accretion and of steady institutional growth. During the years of Henry's maturity a wilful king, governing first under the influence of powerful ministers and then from the mid 1230s more independently, was pressing his claims in what was a more restrictive and resistant environment. More often than not, parliament provided the setting both for these claims and for the counterclaims of Henry's opponents. In its earliest phase, as much as in any later, the trajectory of parliament's development was resolutely political.

These fruitful tensions did not appear immediately. In the period following Henry's full coming of age in 1227 the constitutional practices which had solidified during the minority were confirmed. There were local disputes over the sheriff's tourn and the extent of the royal forest,[34] but in general Henry showed little inclination to return to his father's autocratic

---

[33] William of Malmesbury, *Saints' Lives*, 82–3; above, 58.
[34] Maddicott, 'Magna Carta and the Local Community', 30–4, 38–40.

methods of government, now in any case barred by Magna Carta. On the central matters of taxation and foreign policy he continued to seek the consent of the magnates, just as those who governed for him had done during the previous decade. This was best shown in his preparations for his first foreign expedition of 1230, aimed at the reconquest of his lost continental lands. The expedition had first been proposed in 1226, but had then been deferred on the advice of prelates and magnates. It was eventually sanctioned, together with a scutage to pay for it, at a meeting of the earls and barons at Northampton in July 1229; and this was followed by a separate assembly of archbishops and bishops, who agreed to an equivalent aid on their knights' fees.[35] The expedition's failure, and the resulting unpopularity of Hubert de Burgh, Henry's justiciar and chief minister, had an important outcome. In March 1232 magnates and prelates, meeting as a great council, rejected Henry's request for an aid to pay the debts arising from this debacle.[36] Although the council gave Henry his grant later in the year, in September, this mark of conciliar independence was one unprecedented during the minority. Latent in Magna Carta's demand for 'common counsel' before the granting of aids was the assumption, borne out here, that the consent which 'counsel' implied could not be taken for granted.

During the next two years some of the main political conventions established since Magna Carta were to be impugned, but the challenge was one which in the end served only to strengthen them. The fall of Hubert de Burgh in July 1232 inaugurated the rule of Peter des Roches, bishop of Winchester, and his nephew Peter de Rivallis, and brought a return to the malpractices of King John, with whom des Roches had been closely associated as justiciar. They were most flagrantly revived in matters of law and justice. During the ministry of des Roches, Henry's government carried through arbitrary disseisins 'by the king's will' and without just judgements; revoked royal charters granting rights in perpetuity; attempted to exclude heirs from their inheritances; and disparaged heiresses by granting their marriages to aliens.[37] Both in letter and in spirit, Magna Carta was

[35] Wendover, *Chronica*, iv. 126; *CR, 1227–31*, 248; T. Madox, *The History and Antiquities of the Exchequer of England*, 2nd edn., 2 vols. (London 1769), i. 607, note z; Mitchell, *Studies in Taxation*, 181–9.

[36] Wendover, *Chronica*, iv. 233–4; Mitchell, *Studies in Taxation*, 199.

[37] Vincent, *Peter des Roches*, 310–428, but esp. 328, 334–5, 357–8, 378–9, 413–14; Carpenter, 'Justice and Jurisdiction under John and Henry III', in his *Reign of Henry III*, 38–9. My debt to Professor Vincent's book will be obvious throughout this paragraph.

ignored. Although des Roches was almost certainly the mastermind behind Henry's policies, he had no formal position in the king's government. But de Rivallis held an extraordinary concentration of offices—keeper of the wardrobe, keeper of the privy seal, and many more—none of which appears to have received the magnate consent judged indispensable for important appointments during the minority.[38] For Henry the inducement to transgress was perhaps the promise of solvency and financial salvation which for a time the administration of de Rivallis may have seemed likely to provide.[39] But the price paid by the king was a political reaction which defined still more precisely the limits of royal power. Not only did Henry have to face a magnate rebellion, led by Richard Marshal, son of the great William Marshal who had helped to save Henry's kingdom; he also had to acknowledge the value placed by his opponents on the liberties conferred by the Charter and, in the face of autocracy, on the necessity for consent. The need to proceed legally, via judgement of peers or the law of the land and in accordance with Magna Carta, clause 39, was, for example, invoked by the bishops assembled with the magnates in a great council at Westminster in October 1233.[40] Opposition to the regime was expressed, largely by the same group, through a number of such great councils in 1233 and 1234; while after the fall of des Roches in June 1234 action against the leaders of the disgraced was initiated in the court *coram rege*: a procedure which in itself vindicated the due process emphasized in the Charter.[41]

This aborted revival of Angevin-style rule showed that kingship resting on *vis et voluntas*, 'force and will', was no longer possible in England.[42] In so doing it reaffirmed the Charter's central place in the country's political life, identified it once again with good government, and brought to the forefront of public consciousness the political ideals of lawful, just, and consensual rule which the Charter had promoted. Henry never again attacked the Charter head on. Indeed for nearly two years after the fall of des Roches he ruled in an ostentatiously model way, in August 1234 ordering the Charter to be proclaimed and maintained in the counties, for the first time since 1225.[43] With the Charter safe, the great council returned to its former prominence. It became once more the forum for counsel and

---

[38] Vincent, *Peter des Roches*, 295–9.   [39] Ibid. 343–57.
[40] Wendover, *Chronica*, iv. 276–7; Vincent, *Peter des Roches*, 408–9.
[41] Wendover, *Chronica*, iv. 268–9, 294–7, 298–9, 309–11; *CRR*, xv: *1233–37*, p. xxxii; Vincent, *Peter des Roches*, 384, 429–30, 435–7, 441–51.
[42] Cf. Carpenter, 'Justice and Jurisdiction', 40–3.
[43] *CR, 1231–34*, 587–9; Vincent, *Peter des Roches*, 442–3.

consent, though now with its authority fortified through the participation of an active king. In January 1235 a great council considered the truce with France and, later, an important judicial case concerning the Jews of Norwich; in February consent was given in another council meeting, and after a long debate, to the marriage of the king's sister Isabella to the Emperor Frederick II; and in the summer a further council granted an aid for the marriage.[44] In January 1236 another council sanctioned the Provisions of Merton; the earls and barons refused to change the law on bastardy; and the emperor's request for military assistance from Richard of Cornwall was discussed and turned down.[45] In April a *colloquium* in London, though marked by rising tensions over Henry's friends at court, nevertheless did some ordinary work in receiving envoys from Alexander II of Scotland, sent to demand his rights, and seemingly approved of Henry's earlier change of sheriffs. Alexander's claims were settled, with the magnates' advice, at another *colloquium* at York in September 1237.[46] Foreign policy and taxation, major items on the council's agenda during the minority, were thus joined by justice, legislation, and administration as part of a broad range of conciliar business. Since the word 'parliament' first appears in the records for 1236, we may now call it parliamentary business.[47]

During the twenty years following this short period of harmonious government parliament gained a new weight, lacking even from the great councils of the minority. For the first time it emerged as a political force, with a collective will which was often voiced in opposition to that of the king. Its emergence owed most to two related factors, both closely bound up with the institutional developments already discussed and both more or less constant but gathering strength in the years immediately preceding the climacteric of 1258. Those factors were the unpopularity of Henry's policies and his lack of money to support them. From 1234 onwards he increasingly became his own master, free from the tutelage of the great ministers—first de Burgh, then des Roches—who had managed his affairs since the minority, and determined to avoid further ministerial restraints.[48]

---

[44] *CR, 1234–37*, 160–1, 186; *CRR*, xv: *1233–37*, pp. xlvi–xlvii and no. 1320; *Paris*, iii. 318–19.

[45] *Paris*, iii. 340–3; *Bracton's Note Book*, ed. F. W. Maitland, 3 vols. (London, 1887), i, no. 117; *CRR*, xv: *1233–37*, p. li n. 3.

[46] *Paris*, iii. 362–3, 372; R. Stacey, *Politics, Policy and Finance under Henry III, 1216–45* (Oxford, 1987), 99–100.

[47] Above, 157–8.

[48] Cf. Carpenter, 'The Fall of Hubert de Burgh', and 'King, Magnates and Society: The Personal Rule of Henry III, 1234–1258', in his *Reign of Henry III*, 58–60, 75.

His failure to revive the justiciarship after the fall of Stephen of Seagrave, the last holder of the office and des Roches's ally, may have been one mark of that determination; the removal of the seal from Chancellor Ralph de Neville in 1238 and its custody henceforth by a series of minor officials was more certainly another.[49] Henry now appeared to possess the autonomy and political elbow-room which he had previously lacked.

He used his new freedom to forward his own ambitions. Henry was not devoid of a genuine and religious concern for the welfare of his subjects: wards, orphans, widows, those mistreated by sheriffs and magnates.[50] But his interests here were rarely effective or more than sporadic, and much less important for politics than his secular projects. The chief of these was to recover his continental lands. Alongside the defence of his remaining territory in Gascony, this was the overriding object of all Henry's plans until it was formally abandoned by the Treaty of Paris in 1259. Just subsidiary to this was his wish to live like a king. The first ambition led him to subsidize continental allies, to attempt the reconquest of Poitou in 1242, at a total cost of at least £80,000, and to spend some £36,000 on a further expedition to Gascony in 1253–4.[51] The second meant essentially the promotion of what Henry saw as his own family and dynastic interests: the freedom to bestow patronage on his friends and relations, notably the Savoyard relatives of his queen, Eleanor of Provence, and, from 1247, his own Lusignan half-brothers, sons of his mother, Isabella of Angoulême, by her second marriage to Hugh of Lusignan; to seek the crown of Sicily for his second son Edmund from 1254, which entailed the underwriting of papal debts amounting to some £90,000;[52] and, from 1245, to rebuild Westminster Abbey on the grandest scale. Intended as a vast offering to secure the Confessor's intercession for Henry's earthly success and eternal salvation, as well as to provide a patronal shrine and dynastic mausoleum, the rebuilding of the abbey cost some £45,000 over the reign.[53] Continental and dynastic ambitions were not clearly separable. The lavish patronage of the Lusignans, for example, was supposed to provide Henry with a

---

[49] *CRR*, xv: *1233–37*, pp. xxvii–xxviii; Carpenter, 'Chancellor Ralph de Neville and Plans of Political Reform, 1215–58', in his *Reign of Henry III*, 61–3, 71.

[50] See his speech at the exchequer, October 1250: M. T. Clanchy, 'Did Henry III have a Policy?', *History*, 53 (1968), 215–16. Cf. Maddicott, 'Magna Carta and the Local Community', 54; Carpenter, 'King, Magnates and Society', 80–1.

[51] Stacey, *Politics, Policy and Finance*, 199; Maddicott, *Simon de Montfort*, 125.

[52] Maddicott, *Simon de Montfort*, 128.

[53] Colvin, Brown, and Taylor, *History of the King's Works*, i. 155–7.

possible bridgehead in Poitou, the acquisition of Sicily to elevate English power against that of France.[54] But what both had in common was expense.

These policies opened up clear lines of division between Henry and his magnates. None of them had any interest in the southern lands of the old Angevin Empire, and after the failure of the 1230 expedition even the continental interests of the surviving Anglo-Norman families with claims in Normandy—the expedition's supposed target—withered away.[55] Henry might try to persuade the magnates that his rights on the Continent were their concern, as he did in the parliament of July 1248,[56] but the point was not taken, and the need to make it showed its weakness. To some extent differences over foreign policy also underlay opposition to Henry's foreign favourites, for the Savoyards as well as the Lusignans had their part to play in Henry's continental schemes.[57] But the main grievances here concerned patronage: its cost to a debilitated monarchy in land, cash, wardships, and marriages; its exercise at the expense of aristocratic families, for example, through the disparagement of their widows and daughters by marriage to aliens; and, in the case of the Lusignans, its manifestation in legal and judicial partiality which seemed to place Henry's friends above the law.[58] The earlier opposition to John's alien *familiares* was thus perpetuated into the reign of his son. Insular already by territorial holdings, the magnates had their insularity confirmed by Henry's policies and preferences. Political differences had some of their deepest roots in the widening gap between an increasingly English aristocracy and a king whose hereditary and family interests remained continental.

This was not the whole story, nor were Henry's relations with his magnates invariably hostile. Henry was no tyrant and seems to have wished to live in peace with his great men. He often treated them indulgently, allowing their claims to local liberties to remain unchallenged, their debts to the crown to remain uncollected, and their abuses of power in their own localities to remain unpunished. As we shall see, magnates were represented on the king's council, and some, such as Richard de Clare,

---

[54] H. W. Ridgeway, 'King Henry III and the "Aliens"', 1236–72', *TCE* 2 (1988), 81–3; *Paris*, v. 516.

[55] Cf. Stacey, *Politics, Policy and Finance*, 172–3.   [56] *Paris*, v. 20–1.

[57] For the Savoyards, see Ridgeway, 'King Henry III and the "Aliens"', 82–3; M. Howell, *Eleanor of Provence: Queenship in Thirteenth-Century England* (Oxford, 1998), 11–12.

[58] *DBM* 80–1; Ridgeway, 'King Henry III and the "Aliens"', 85, 88; Maddicott, 'Magna Carta and the Local Community', 56–7; id., *Simon de Montfort*, 143.

earl of Gloucester, stood consistently high in royal favour.[59] Yet this group, mainly consisting of the earls and a few major barons such as Richard de Grey and John fitz Geoffrey,[60] the 'top ten' as it were, was hardly typical of the baronage as a whole. The majority stood outside the charmed circle. However well placed were Henry's supporters, and however eirenic his intentions, they failed to prevent political conflict which was often intense.

More often than not it came to turn on taxation and to be located in parliament. The sapping of the crown's landed revenues through demesne alienations had already greatly weakened its position by the time of John's accession, but that position took a sharp turn for the worse after Magna Carta. The Charter had made it much more difficult for the crown to fund its policies without magnate consent.[61] In defining reliefs, barring the payment of a relief when an estate had already been in royal wardship, and prohibiting the extra-legal processes which had facilitated the levying of excessive fines and amercements, the Charter had struck away some of the main fiscal props of Angevin government.[62] Most important of all for the future was its stipulation that no general aid should be levied 'without common counsel', which came to be interpreted as the consent of the great council. By the mid 1230s all these provisions had become entrenched in political practice through their everyday enforcement, through the Charter's repeated reissues, and, in the case of taxation, through the conciliar consent given to the two tax grants of 1225 and 1232.[63] To meet his needs Henry could not hope, therefore, to revive John's fiscal methods; but, given consent, he could hope for a direct tax. Since the fifteenth of 1225 and the fortieth of 1232 had raised some £40,000 and £16,000 respectively, this was a supremely tempting prospect.[64] For Henry, direct taxation was the great honeypot. But between the king and his subjects' wealth there now stood parliament, the firm controller of the honeypot's lid.

[59] This is the theme of Carpenter, 'King, Magnates and Society'. It does no injustice to Carpenter's fine article to say that it is largely concerned with the highest ranks of the nobility and that it fails to explain why, if Henry was apparently so willing to indulge his magnates, he faced such consistent opposition in parliament from 1237 to 1258.

[60] Carpenter, 'King, Magnates and Society', 94–5.

[61] Holt, *Magna Carta*, 45–7; Stacey, *Politics, Policy and Finance*, 43–4; Carpenter, *Struggle for Mastery*, 468–9; id., 'Beginnings of Parliament', in his *Reign of Henry III*, 385–6.

[62] Caps. 2, 3, 20, 21, 39, 40: Holt, *Magna Carta*, 450–1, 456–7, 460–1.

[63] Ibid. 394–7; Stacey, *Politics, Policy and Finance*, 217. For consent to the grant of 1232, see *CR, 1231–34*, 311, Mitchell, *Studies in Taxation*, 200.

[64] Carpenter, *Minority of Henry III*, 376, 380–1; Mitchell, *Studies in Taxation*, 205.

The need for parliamentary consent to taxation was the central influence on the evolution of parliament and parliamentary politics during Henry's middle years. It elevated parliament's political prominence, opened up the king's policies to debate, and made it possible for Henry's magnates to place redress of grievances against supply. After the concession of the fifteenth in the great council of 1225, a parliamentary grant in all but name, these developments first came together in the granting of what proved to be the only direct tax of these middle years, the thirtieth of 1237. The need for such a levy followed from Henry's inability to find the money for the enormous dowry due to the Emperor Frederick for his marriage to Henry's sister Isabella. In itself the match sprang from Henry's foreign ambitions, promising him an important continental ally in any campaign to recover his lands.[65] But when Henry's request for a tax was put to the parliament which met in January 1237 it was not well received. The king was criticized for his previous demands for taxes, for his failures abroad (an allusion to the expedition of 1230), and for acting without magnate consent; in part unfairly, for Isabella's marriage had been discussed and approved by the great council, as we have seen. In the end the king got his way—but only in return for reconfirming the Charters (Magna Carta and the Forest Charter), solemnly swearing personally to observe them, adding three magnates to his ordinary council (*consilium quod in praesentiarum habuit*), restricting his rights of purveyance, and taking new measures to protect the security of land tenure.[66] For the first time a request for taxation had been met in parliament by demands which went beyond the now customary demand for the confirmation of the Charter.

Variations on this theme were to be played out many times during the next twenty years. Between the grant made in the parliament of January 1237 and the start of the reform movement in 1258 Henry asked for a direct tax on at least ten occasions and was refused every time, though he secured consolation prizes in the form of the less valuable feudal aids in 1245, for the marriage of his daughter, and in 1253, for the knighting of his eldest son.[67] Most of these requests were intended to raise money for projected campaigns (as in 1242, 1248, and 1254) or to meet the

---

[65] Stacey, *Politics, Policy and Finance*, 98–9, 180; B. K. U. Weiler, *Henry III of England and the Staufen Empire, 1216–1272* (Woodbridge, 2006), 62–4.

[66] *Paris*, iii. 381–4, iv. 186; Stacey, *Politics, Policy and Finance*, 109, 112–15. For the development of the council, see below, 188–90.

[67] For a list, with references, see Maddicott, ' "An Infinite Multitude of Nobles" ', 25–6 and n. 45. This list cites eleven refusals rather than ten; but the non-grant in the parliament of January 1254

debts arising from such campaigns (as in 1244 and 1255).[68] There may well have been others which our sources pass over. The parliament of April 1252, for example, was followed immediately by orders for the collection of a tallage, a prerogative levy of limited value but needing no consent;[69] and it is a reasonable guess that this second-best option followed after yet another request for Henry's preferred tax had been turned down.

The exchanges between king and magnates occasioned by such requests provided the stuff of parliamentary politics during these years. Appeals for taxes were generally made by the king in person, either to the whole assembly or to prelates and magnates meeting separately. In the parliament of November 1244 Henry addressed them *ore proprio*, 'with his own mouth', and in February 1245 both *in propria persona*, 'in his own person', and through intermediaries.[70] His manner often combined hectoring and pleading. 'I am your prince and your king', he told the assembled bishops in November 1244. 'Without you I cannot live, nor you without me. Your being depends on me and mine on you, for if I am rich you also are rich, if I am poor you are also poor.'[71] The hostile reception given to such appeals not only showed the magnates' lack of interest in Henry's foreign ventures but often embodied a withering critique of the king's policies, just as it had done in 1237. In 1242 they told Henry that he had committed himself to campaigning in Poitou—the cause of his request—without consulting them; that he had squandered previous grants, and the profits from wardships, escheats, and vacant sees, to no advantage; that he was about to break dishonourably the current truce with France; and that in

---

ignores an offer of military service by bishops and magnates and the mere deferment of a further request to the laity (see below, 211–13). It cannot strictly be counted as a refusal.

    [68] *Paris*, iv. 181–2, 362, v. 20–1, 440, 493–4.

    [69] *Ann. Tewkesbury*, 147; *Paris*, v. 279–80, 283. The exceptionally large number of earls and barons witnessing royal charters between 21 and 29 April testifies to the holding of this parliament: *Charter Witness Lists*, ii. 62–3. Orders for the tallage were issued on 24 and 28 April: *CR, 1251–53*, 212–13. The tallage appears to have been overlooked by Mitchell, *Studies in Taxation*, and Jurkowski, Smith, and Crook, *Lay Taxes*.

    [70] *Paris*, iv. 362, 372–3.

    [71] Aberystwyth, National Library of Wales, MS Peniarth 390 (Burton formulary), fo. 40^r; Oxford, Bodleian Library MS Digby 11, fo. 96^v. I am very grateful to Professor Nicholas Vincent for making available to me his transcript and collation of these manuscripts. Paris's account of the king's speech (*Paris*, iv. 365–6) corresponds closely to this account: a pointer to his general reliability as a reporter of Henry's speeches and other parliamentary business. Cf. Carpenter, 'Matthew Paris and Henry III's Speech at the Exchequer in October 1256', in his *Reign of Henry III*, 141. For another and stronger example of Henry's hectoring manner of speaking in parliament, see *Paris*, v. 20.

any case he stood no chance of regaining his lost lands.[72] A similar request in 1248 met a similar broadside: Henry had bestowed his patronage on aliens, married off his noble wards to them, illegally seized supplies for the support of his household, kept bishoprics and abbacies vacant, failed to fill the two great offices of the chancellorship and the justiciarship, and appointed a treasurer without common counsel.[73] So it was again in 1255, when Henry's usual request was met with complaints that Magna Carta had not been observed and with demands for the appointment of the great officials 'by common counsel'.[74]

The need for consent to taxation, the legacy of Magna Carta, had thus made parliament into a platform from which the king's actions could be publicly examined and opposed, in ways quite unknown, so far as we can see, in the twelfth century. The refusal of Henry's magnates to grant him taxes—a parliamentary veto exercised more consistently and successfully in these years than at any other time in the middle ages—forced Henry to look elsewhere for money. The extra-parliamentary revenues which he was able to draw on, and the opposition which this produced, made their own contribution to parliament's development. Henry's needs drove him mainly to look to the counties, to provincial England, for it was there that he could find sources of revenue which needed no corporate consent, which remained unregulated by Magna Carta, and which therefore continued to be open to exploitation. Two of these sources were especially prominent and resented: the sheriff's farm, the sum rendered by the sheriff for his county, which was steadily increased between 1241 and 1257, at the cost of extortionately heavy pressure on the sheriffs' constituents; and the profits of the eyre, the provincial visitation of the king's justices, which rose rapidly in the 1240s and 1250s.[75] A third resource, affecting local society more indirectly, was royal taxation of the Jews, which reached unprecedented levels between 1241 and 1254. In order to meet the king's demands, the Jews were driven to bear down heavily on their debtors, often provincial knights and freeholders. Debts secured on the debtors' lands were often sold on for cash by Jewish creditors to the courtiers and relatives of the king, who made a profitable practice out of buying up these discounted debts and

---

[72] *Paris*, iv. 181–4.   [73] Ibid. v. 5–7.

[74] Ibid. 493–4. For other parliamentary criticisms of royal policies, see ibid. iv. 362–3 (1244), v. 327, 335 (1252), v. 520–1 (1255); *Ann. Burton*, 386–91; *Ann. Dunstable*, 200 (1257).

[75] Carpenter, 'Decline of the Curial Sheriff', in his *Reign of Henry III*, 171–4; Maddicott, 'Magna Carta and the Local Community', 43–8.

foreclosing on the land.[76] The collective result of all these measures was the rapid growth of local discontent among minor barons and gentry. It was often voiced in parliament, quite probably (as we shall see) by members of these same groups, men well below the level of the higher nobility. The burdens imposed by the eyre, for example, were raised in response to royal requests for taxation in the parliaments of January 1242, October 1252, and March 1257.[77] In this way the blocking of direct taxation in parliament served to widen the scope and ferocity of Henry's government and helped to give parliament a new representative quality, its discussions ranging beyond such matters of high politics as expeditions abroad and aliens at court.

Were there then no legal or ideological underpinnings to parliamentary refusals of taxation, beyond the discontents provoked by Henry's policies and the sanctions of the Charter which allowed parliament to block them? An answer to this question has been framed in the same terms as those invoked to explain the earlier origins of national taxation in the late twelfth century. For Henry III's reign, as for the preceding period, it has been argued that the ruler could claim the right to taxation in cases of necessity, but that necessity had to be defined in terms of the common good of the realm rather than the ruler's own private good. Once the necessity had been recognized, his subjects had no right to reject the ruler's plea; the only escape from their obligations lay in a denial of the necessity for which their resources were demanded. All this had a firm basis in Roman law, which embodied the notions of necessity, of the common good, and of the ruler's right of access to his subjects' resources in order to defend that good.[78]

Much here is open to dispute. It is true that Henry's requests for taxes were often cast as pleas of necessity, sometimes explicitly so. But parliamentary refusals owed more to everyday experience and the pragmatic grievances which it produced than to any rejection of the necessities by which Henry justified his requests. In March 1232, for example, it was Henry's debts arising from his recent campaign which, says Wendover, 'compelled him by necessity to ask for a general aid'. He was turned down,

[76] R. C. Stacey, '1240–60: A Watershed in Anglo-Jewish Relations', *Historical Research*, 61 (1988), 137–46.
[77] *Paris*, iv. 186–7, v. 327; *Ann. Burton*, 387; Maddicott, 'Magna Carta and the Local Community', 48.
[78] Harriss, *King, Parliament and Public Finance*, 20–6, 32–9; above, 122–3.

however, not through any denial of his necessity, but on the explicit grounds that those at the council had already given their military service on the campaign and so owed him no further aid. More implicitly, the unpopularity of his policies, including the failure of the recent French expedition, brought about this result.[79] When parliament rejected Henry's request for a subsidy to finance his Poitou campaign in 1242 his plea failed because it met the stone wall of hostile criticism already described. Disregarding the king's supposed needs, and ranging well beyond his campaigning plans, criticism ranged widely over his spendthrift and oppressive regime. In a famous episode from 1254, discussed in more detail below, Henry ordered that the necessity constituted by his supposedly parlous position in Gascony should be expounded to the shire courts in order to induce the shires' elected representatives to grant a tax at the forthcoming parliament. Yet his regents thought his appeal likely to fail, not because the representatives would decline to recognize his necessity, but because his local officials had not observed the Charter.[80] Here, once again, the unpopularity of Henry's administration seemed likely to trump any theoretical considerations in accounting for the denial of taxation. Those who rejected Henry's pleas were less well versed in the ideas of civilians and canonists than in the lessons learnt from the asperities of everyday life.

If taxation was one *point d'appui* for the growth of parliament, the wider issues of consultation and consent provided another. In defining the need for consent, the Charter had linked it only with taxation. At all points in the middle ages the range of possible royal initiatives in policy-making was so broad, and the king's prerogatives so relatively unfettered, that definition could hardly go further. Yet, as we have seen, both in the minority and again in the mid 1230s much of that policy-making *had* been subject to magnate consent, given in great councils and applied particularly to appointments, foreign policy, and legislation. To some extent Henry continued to accept this limitation during the period of his personal rule: he needed the support of his great men, just as his twelfth-century predecessors had done in their dealings with their magnates, and on many matters he did not have to give up anything of substance in order to secure it. The seeking of consent bought more than it cost. So, for example, he took counsel

---

[79] Wendover, *Chronica*, iv. 233; below, 422, 425–7.
[80] Stubbs, *Select Charters*, 365–6; *Royal Letters*, ii. 102; below, 211–12.

with his magnates in parliament in making peace with the Scots in 1237, in coming to terms with David of Wales in 1240, in planning his Welsh campaign in 1245, and in preparing his dossier against papal demands in 1246.[81] Consensus sometimes prevailed over confrontation.

But this was by no means the rule. Already under John the magnates were beginning to claim the right to advise the king,[82] and the subsequent precedents drawn from the events of the minority and the few years which followed its ending created a much stronger assumption that royal policy-making should be circumscribed by consultation and consent. Just how widespread such an assumption had become was shown in Matthew Paris's Life of Edward the Confessor, written about 1236, where he speaks of Edward's supposed need to accept the counsels and judgements of his magnates and to undertake no great enterprise without the permission of *la commune*.[83] These principles Henry was not always prepared to accept. In three related areas he particularly sought to retain the initiative: in matters affecting his family and inheritance, in matters of patronage, and in appointments. All fell within what he regarded as the domain of his prerogative and private control, fenced off from outside interference. Some of the most important political decisions of his middle years were taken without baronial consent: the marriage of his sister Eleanor to the French adventurer Simon de Montfort in 1238, the undertaking to campaign in Poitou in 1242, and, most egregiously of all, the acceptance of the throne of Sicily for his son Edmund in 1254.[84] In each case he offended baronial notions of what was proper, developed over the previous few decades, by treating matters of public and national interest simply as private business.

With regard to appointments Henry was more consistently high-handed (as his magnates saw it). In 1238, early on in his personal rule, he had disregarded the precedents of consent established in the minority by taking the great seal from Ralph de Neville, appointed chancellor by the great council in 1218. The minor household officials who kept the seal for most of the next fifteen years were essentially Henry's men, too insignificant to check his policies.[85] During this period the magnates repeatedly tried

---

[81] *Paris*, iii. 413, iv. 526–36; *Ann. Tewkesbury*, 115; *CR, 1237–42*, 240–1; ibid. *1242–47*, 357; *Ann. Burton*, 278.

[82] Above, 117, 142–4.   [83] *Lives of Edward the Confessor*, ed. Luard, 69–70, 223–4, ll. 1575–90.

[84] *Paris*, iii. 475, iv. 181, 183; *Ann. Burton*, 387–8; *Ann. Tewkesbury*, 170.

[85] Carpenter, *Minority of Henry III*, 94–5; id., 'Chancellor Ralph de Neville', 62–3.

to secure the appointment of a chancellor, justiciar, and treasurer to their liking by pressing for the filling of the chancellorship and the justiciarship, vacant since 1234, and for the right of consent to the appointment of all three great officials. They saw these three ministers as potential checks on Henry's power to misgovern: the chancellor and the justiciar as weighty and independent figures who could take a stand against royal autocracy, the justiciar additionally as the provider of justice for Henry's over-governed subjects, and the treasurer as a control on royal extravagance.[86] But they had no success. Henry viewed appointments as part of the *arcana imperii*, matters which were intimately related to the management of the kingdom and so belonged to him alone.[87] In terms of Anglo-Norman and Angevin practice there was much to be said for this line. But it ignored the political conventions established in the twenty years after 1215.

The arguments which resulted from Henry's challenge to these conventions both enhanced the growing authority of parliament and showed its weaknesses. It was in parliament, invariably in the course of the sharp exchanges which followed Henry's request for taxation, that the need for consent was raised: part of that broadening critique of royal policy which the need for consent itself—but to taxation alone—had made possible. It was parliament too which the magnates saw as the natural forum for securing consent. In the parliament of April 1249, for example, they gathered in expectation of the king's appointing the three great officials 'by their counsel'.[88] But Henry's ability to escape compliance demonstrated that, here as in other matters, parliament could not effectively limit his kingship. Though it met increasingly frequently it remained what it would be to the end of the middle ages and beyond—an occasional assembly with no means of influencing the daily operations of the king's government. Nor did parliament's essentially negative power to deny taxation necessarily secure its objectives, for the king's access to funds needing no consent freed him from ultimate dependence on parliamentary grants. These resources were not only the local ones already noticed. Denied a direct tax for his Poitou campaign in 1242, Henry fell back on scutage and fines, drew on money from Jewish tallages, appropriated vacancy revenues from Canterbury and Winchester, plunged into debt, and departed.[89] Parliament's refusal to fund

---

[86] *Paris*, iv. 362–3, 366–8, v. 6–8, 20–12, 73, 493–4; Carpenter, 'Chancellor Ralph de Neville', 69–71.
[87] Cf. esp. *Paris*, v. 20 for Henry's attitude.   [88] Ibid. 73.
[89] Stacey, *Politics, Policy and Finance*, 187–90.

his foreign policy had done nothing to alter its course. It was perhaps no wonder that the long parliamentary experience of Walter de Gray, archbishop of York, led him to regard these assemblies as ineffectual (*vana*). Rather than attend, he preferred to stay at home.[90]

For these reasons we find parliament beginning to devise other means of imposing controls on Henry's kingship. We have already seen that in the parliament of January 1237 the king was forced to add three barons to his council as part of the price for a tax grant; though their influence on policy-making was short-lived and ineffective.[91] In the parliament of November 1244 the famous Paper Constitution proposed more drastic controls: the election both of the great officials and, more radically, of four councillors, some of whom were always to be in attendance on the king; and magnate consent to the selection of a wide range of other officials.[92] The continuing demands through the 1240s and early 1250s for a magnate voice in the appointment of the great officials were part of the same drive to limit royal government, not only on the exceptional occasions when taxation was called for, but in its everyday work. For these attempts at limitation parliament had become the springboard, in a process which culminated in the baronial appropriation of the king's government at the Oxford parliament of April 1258.

Parliament's new standing as the locus for tax requests, the consequent presentation of grievances, and political debate in general helped to establish its institutional structures. Not all its characteristics were novel, though some were more in evidence. Procedure in tax debates is a case in point. If the king himself did not present his own case for a tax at parliament's opening, which (as we have seen) he often did, the job might be left to a royal minister, such as William Raleigh, chief justice *coram rege*, who spoke for the king in the parliament of January 1237: a practice which had precedents in Hubert de Burgh's speech to the great council of 1225 and, more distantly, in Lanfranc's to the autumn council of 1085, and which was normal in fourteenth-century parliaments.[93] But many of parliament's other features and attributes lacked such precedents, and originated in Henry's middle years. Of these, a form of prorogation was perhaps the most striking. On

---

[90] *Paris*, v. 373.   [91] Ibid. iii. 383: Stacey, *Politics, Policy and Finance*, 114–15; above, 173.

[92] *Paris*, iv. 366–8; C. R. Cheney, 'The "Paper Constitution" Preserved by Matthew Paris', in his *Medieval Texts and Studies* (Oxford, 1973), 231–41; Carpenter, 'Chancellor Ralph de Neville', 70–2.

[93] *Paris*, iii. 380–1; Wendover, *Chronica*, iv. 99–100; above, 62, 89, 107.

at least four occasions—in 1244–45, 1248, 1254, and 1255—consideration of Henry's request for a tax was postponed to a later session, some months off, usually to test the king's promises of the redress and reform offered in exchange for the tax.[94] Prorogation, like the ministerial speech, was thus closely linked to parliamentary control of direct taxation, the one novelty largely a consequence of the other. In the twelfth century, when great councils had chiefly met for such concentrated acts of state as the recognition of Matilda as Henry I's successor or the promulgation of Henry II's assizes, a divided session would have had little point. The effect, though it can hardly be measured, is likely to have been to help to bridge the inevitable discontinuities between assemblies and to enhance the public sense of parliament's centrality in politics.

Equally novel were the occasional semi-official records of parliamentary proceedings which now began to appear. Though twelfth-century chroniclers such as Howden had often noted great councils, occasionally incorporating into their narratives the legislative *acta* to which they might give rise, the councils themselves seem to have generated no records; and we have to wait until the 1290s for the first 'official' parliament rolls.[95] But the earliest precedents for the rolls, admittedly different in form and origin, date from the 1240s and 1250s. Though these texts were set down by chroniclers, they were apparently produced by those in parliament who wished to put on record their activities, usually in opposition to the king. The first originated in the parliament of January 1242, when prelates and magnates drafted a written account, transcribed by Paris after his own account, of their reasons for refusing a tax.[96] Next, from the parliament of November 1244, came the Paper Constitution—probably a draft representing the views of an individual or group rather than a proposal from the whole magnate body.[97] Finally, in the parliament of March 1257 a written statement was drawn up of the case against English involvement in Sicily ('Rationes magnatum contra regem'). Almost certainly resulting

[94] *Paris*, iv. 362–3, 372–4, v. 7–8, 20–1, 423–4, 493–5, 520–1; *Royal Letters*, ii. 101–2.

[95] J. C. Holt, 'The Assizes of Henry II: The Texts', in D. A. Bullough and R. L. Storey (eds.), *The Study of Medieval Records: Essays in Honour of Kathleen Major* (Oxford, 1971), 85–101; *PROME* i. 3, 35, 37, 52, 54, 57, 67, 77. There are isolated records of business in parliament from 1279 and 1280.

[96] *Paris*, iv. 181–4 (Paris's own account), 185–8 (the written account he transcribes). Stacey, *Politics, Policy and Finance*, 185 n. 113, believes Paris's contribution to be found on pages 182–4 and 186–7, and the written account on pages 181–2, 185, and 187–8; but this division seems to be partly erroneous and the reasons for it are unclear.

[97] *Paris*, iv. 366–8. Cf. Cheney, 'The "Paper Constitution" ', 234–5, and Stacey, *Politics, Policy and Finance*, 249.

from collaboration between clergy and magnates, it constituted a well-informed survey of Italian affairs and English weaknesses, and it was clearly circulated outside parliament since it appears in two monastic chronicles:[98] another testimony to a degree of external interest in parliamentary discussions.

In one other area, the appropriation of tax grants, those in parliament began to move towards a new extension and definition of their authority. Behind appropriation lay the view that taxes should be spent on the purposes for which they had been granted, broadly defined as the needs of the whole realm. As in so much else, the great council's grant of 1225 provided a precedent, for it had been intended that the money from that levy should be kept apart and spent under supervision, presumably on the French war whose financing was the grant's rationale and whose costs did indeed absorb the bulk of the tax.[99] This was followed up in 1237, when the king undertook to spend the proceeds of the thirtieth under the supervision of a committee of magnates and 'for the necessary uses of the realm'.[100] Similar action was taken in 1244, when a committee of twelve, carefully selected to include representatives of the archbishops, bishops, earl, barons, and abbots, was appointed to consider the king's request for a tax and to see that any tax granted was spent 'for the profit of the realm'. In the event none was.[101] On a last occasion, in 1253, Henry was granted a clerical tax for his supposedly forthcoming crusade to the Holy Land, to be spent under the supervision of the magnates when he should set out. This virtually repeated a similar stipulation of the previous year.[102] As two of these last three cases suggest, the inability of the whole body of prelates and magnates to supervise the spending of taxes pointed towards a further development originating in this period: the appearance of parliamentary committees.

All these innovations—the prorogation of parliaments, the writing down of procedures and grievances, and the attempts to use committees to control the spending of taxes—were not stages in some slow and evolutionary process of change. They were, like the whole development of parliament in this period, rooted in a set of particular political circumstances, defined

[98] *Ann. Burton*, 387–8; *Ann. Dunstable*, 200 (which is clearly a summary of the Burton document).
[99] Mitchell, *Studies in Taxation*, 167–8 and n. 240; above, 108.
[100] *Paris*, iii. 380–1, 410–11; G. L. Harris, 'Parliamentary Taxation and the Origins of Appropriation of Supply in England, 1207–1340', in *Gouvernés et gouvernants: recueils de la société Jean Bodin*, 14 (1965), 168; Stacey, *Politics, Policy and Finance*, 112, 121–3.
[101] *Paris*, iv. 362–3; Stacey, *Politics, Policy and Finance*, 247–8.   [102] *Paris*, v. 327–8, 374–5.

(though not exclusively) by Henry's need for taxes and by the magnates' distrust of the king and disapproval of his policies. Yet it would be wrong to assume that parliament was always and invariably an arena for confrontation, for it owed at least some of its growing political weight to its usefulness to the king. It could, for example, provide an appropriate setting for that love of ceremony and display also seen in Henry's fondness for the great liturgical celebrations of the *laudes regiae*.[103] His ends, though they were not always achieved, were political as much as aesthetic or religious, and the means to them might be consciously theatrical. Perhaps the best example of parliament as theatre came in March 1257 when Henry's second son Edmund was presented in Apulian dress to the assembled magnates and prelates in order to win support for his claim to Sicily.[104] The Westminster assembly of October 1247 was comparably theatrical, with the magnates summoned to attend in order to venerate the Confessor and to witness both Henry's reception of his precious new relic, the Holy Blood, and the knighting of the king's half-brother William de Valence.[105] In the arguments which they put up against royal policies, magnate assemblies might tend to subvert rather than glorify Henry's kingship. But Henry had seen how parliament might also be used as an occasion for grandeur, one which fused display, sociability, and religious sentiment to promote the figure of a transcendent impresario monarch whose deep and genuine piety meshed seamlessly with his secular needs. If there remained a sharp contrast between aspiration and achievement, this was nevertheless part of his personal contribution to the making of parliament.

In a more practical and effective way parliament could also be invoked in opposition to external powers and in defence of interests which the king shared with his subjects. This was shown most clearly in the joint objections of king, barons, and clergy to papal taxation in 1245–6, when resistance to the pope's demands was concerted at a number of councils and parliaments. When the bishops, under pressure from the pope, attempted to collect a subsidy in the spring of 1246, Henry was able to cite against them what had

[103] Above, 165.
[104] *Paris*, v. 623. But it may well be that this episode took place in the parliament of October 1255, when Edmund was invested with the kingdom of Sicily (ibid. 515; below, 471–2). For other examples of parliament as theatre, mainly drawn from Henry's later years, see Howell, *Eleanor of Provence*, 38–9, and Weiler, 'Symbolism and Politics', 19–25.
[105] *Paris*, iv. 640–4; N. Vincent, *The Holy Blood: King Henry III and the Westminster Blood Relic* (Cambridge, 2001), 7–19. No source calls this assembly a 'parliament' but it clearly had many of the characteristics of one.

been 'commonly provided' in a recent *convocatio*—the parliament of March 1246—by prelates and magnates.[106] J. O. Prestwich's dictum is as true for the first age of parliaments as it had been for an earlier age of councils: 'kings of England were never more "constitutional" than when confronted with demands from the Church as unwelcome to their leading lay subjects as to themselves.'[107] Here, as well as in his not infrequent consultations with the magnates on matters of foreign policy, Henry's relations with his assembled nobles revived the spirit of consensus which had characterized assembly relations for much of the twelfth century.

But it was as an occasion for the dispensing of justice that parliament could best prove its worth. 'The dispensing of justice' has sometimes been elevated into parliament's chief function and distinguishing characteristic, as much under Henry III as under Edward I. Regarding the assembly primarily as a judicial occasion has allowed its involvement in politics to be relegated to a very inferior position.[108] About such an extreme viewpoint three observations may be made. First, it is one which derives almost entirely from the records of government and which largely ignores the contrary evidence of the chronicles, especially Paris. Second, it makes an implicit distinction between justice and politics which is not always sustainable. And, third, it elides another more proper distinction between justice done at parliament time and justice done in parliament. If acknowledged, this distinction greatly circumscribes the true judicial work of parliament.

On the last two of these three points it is worth pausing. Of the relatively few judicial cases which were heard in parliament, as opposed to those

---

[106] *Paris*, iv. 554. For the background, see Lunt, *Financial Relations*, 206–19, esp. 216, and *C. and S.* II. i. 388.

[107] J. O. Prestwich, 'Anglo-Norman Feudalism and the Problem of Continuity', *Past and Present*, 26 (1963), 50; above, 89.

[108] Impressed by the number of petitions presented in the parliament of 1305, Maitland was the first to draw out the judicial functions of early parliaments, though in a measured way: see his introduction to *Memoranda de Parliamento*, ed. F. W. Maitland, RS (London, 1893), pp. lv–lxxxv. His views were built on by Richardson and Sayles, who gave a much greater and more exclusive weight to justice as the 'essence' of parliament: see the passages from their work cited by J. G. Edwards, ' "Justice" in Early English Parliaments', in *Historical Studies*, 280, and Edwards's own counter-arguments; and for the application of their views to Henry III's reign, Richardson and Sayles, 'Parliaments and Great Councils in Medieval England', in *EPMA* xxvi, esp. 8–12, 49. Though recognizing the importance of politics in parliament's work, A. Harding, *Medieval Law and the Foundations of the State* (Oxford, 2002), 170–7, broadly agrees with Richardson and Sayles. In one of his last works, *The King's Parliament of England* (London, 1975), ch. 3, Sayles was apparently inclined to give less weight to justice. The advent of petitioning under Edward I (below, 294–7) gave much greater emphasis to parliament's role as a court, and the tendency has been to read back the Edwardian situation into the Henrician. Cf. Carpenter, 'Beginnings of Parliament', 383–5.

heard at parliament time, almost all involved great men and had a marked political content. They fell into two broad categories: state trials, and disputes between magnates about land or other rights. Both had been staple fare for earlier councils. For state trials the great council had long provided venue and judges, and its role was now taken over by parliament, after a hiatus under John, when judgement at the exchequer and by the king's will had largely superseded conciliar justice.[109] The trial of Henry of Bath, senior justice of the court *coram rege*, for alleged corruption in 1251, and that of Simon de Montfort in 1252 on charges arising from his government of Gascony, both took place before the magnates in parliament, with the king as chief prosecutor.[110] Magnate disputes, on the other hand, were often called into parliament from inferior courts. When the archbishop of Canterbury and the bishop of Rochester were at odds in 1255 over the archbishop's temporal rights in the bishop's diocese, Henry told the eyre justices in Kent, before whom the case had initially come, that the plea should be respited until the Translation of St Edward, when he would be able to take counsel with Richard of Cornwall and the other magnates who would then be present.[111] Sometimes such cases might be heard at afforced meetings of the king's council, when the additional presence of many bishops and magnates created what were in effect parliaments in little. So, for example, the final partition of the county palatine of Chester was made before a large gathering of prelates and magnates at Westminster, probably in October 1239;[112] while in 1241 a comparable gathering heard a similar case which turned on whether a Welsh castle and district were held from the king or the earl of Pembroke.[113] Such assemblies did not invariably reflect the king's viewpoint: at Montfort's trial most of the leading magnates were among the earl's supporters. But they allowed the king to make the magnates participants in royal justice, to resolve disputes peacefully and in public, and to offer something approaching the trial by peers demanded in Magna Carta. In these ways, as much as in their

[109] Turner, *The King and his Courts*, 166–79, 278; above, 115–17.
[110] Henry of Bath: *Paris*, v. 213–14, 223–4; C. A. F. Meekings, 'Robert of Nottingham, Justice of the Bench, 1244–6', in his *Studies in 13th Century Justice and Administration* (London, 1981), x. 137–8; D. Crook, 'Henry of Bath', *ODNB*. Montfort: *Paris*, v. 287–96; *Letters of Adam Marsh*, ed. Lawrence, i. 79–91; Maddicott, *Simon de Montfort*, 115–17.
[111] *CR, 1254–56*, 223–4.
[112] *Bracton's Note Book*, ed. Maitland, iii, no. 1273, pp. 282–3; *CRR*, xvi: *1237–42*, p. xix; R. Eales, 'Henry III and the End of the Norman Earldom of Chester', *TCE* 1 (1986), 110.
[113] *CRR*, xvi: *1237–42*, p. xix and no. 1493.

content, cases heard in parliament were as much political as judicial. But the parliamentary politics of justice, unlike that of taxation, could work to the king's advantage.

Much of the judicial work associated with parliament, however, was not of this kind. It consisted rather of cases deferred until parliament met, so that they could be dealt with by the appropriate judges and officials or by courts then in session. The first known official use of the term 'parliament' occurs in just such a context. The advowson of the Wiltshire church of Stapleford was in dispute between the lay lord of the manor and the bishop of Salisbury. But after being set down for hearing in the court *coram rege* on 28 November 1236, the case was adjourned to the forthcoming Westminster parliament fixed for 20 January 1237: the assembly which was to see hard bargaining over taxation and the eventual grant of a thirtieth to the king.[114] It is inconceivable that such a comparatively trivial case would have been heard before the 'infinite multitude of nobles' (Paris's words) gathered at that parliament, and much more likely that the case had been removed there because it was known that the judges and at least one of the parties to the case, the bishop, would then be present—as indeed the bishop was.[115] Much parliamentary justice was of this sort: permission granted to John de Neville to hold his bailiwick of Shotover and Stow until the next parliament (when presumably his right to it would be under discussion); orders to respite a distraint against the archdeacon of Lincoln until the king could take counsel (*habere tractatus*) about the case in parliament; the quashing of an outlawry in parliament.[116] Parliament had a similar function as an occasion in those cases involving claims to franchises to which Jolliffe drew attention and which, from the late 1230s, were frequently respited to exchequer sessions held at the quindenes of the three great feasts—when, increasingly, parliament would be in session too.[117] Of course, such cases often involved great men, both lay and clerical, and magnates present at parliament might be wanted to advise and bear witness, in these as in other pleas. But in all these judicial matters parliament was essentially not a court but a convenience: a fixed point in the calendar when the presence of king, litigants, judges, magnates, and ministers could safely be reckoned on.

[114] *CRR*, xv: *1233–37*, no. 2047; Richardson and Sayles, 'The Earliest Known Official Use of the Term "Parliament" ', 747–50; above, 158.

[115] *Paris*, iii. 380; *Ann. Tewkesbury*, 102–3.

[116] *CR, 1237–42*, 447; *CR, 1247–51*, 104, 106–7; R. F. Treharne, 'The Nature of Parliament in the Reign of Henry III', in *Historical Studies*, 74.

[117] Jolliffe, 'Some Factors in the Beginnings of Parliament', 56–69; above, 164–5.

We should not, therefore, regard parliament as solely a political assembly. To it came a small number of political pleas involving important magnates and a much larger number of lesser cases, to whose resolution those attending parliament might contribute their expertise. Both sorts of case strengthened Henry's kingship by emphasizing the king's role as the fount of justice, by promoting the efficiency of his government, and by allowing his subjects to participate in its working. In all this there was some compensation for the opposition which those in parliament frequently offered to his political ambitions.

3. Parliamentarians: Ministers, Magnates, and Churchmen

An account of the issues of parliamentary politics does not necessarily tell us much about the forces which were at work within parliament: the various parties whom the king might trust, consult, or ignore, and who might support or oppose his policies. Behind the simplification of 'the magnates' there may lie a more complex social and political stratification. Here we need to look more closely at parliament's composition, at relationships within parliament, and at the wider relationship between parliament and those in the country who also formed part of 'the community of the realm'. This is the subject of the next several sections.

The men present in the parliaments of Henry III's middle years fell into several well-defined groups: the king's ministers and councillors; the ecclesiastical and lay magnates, comprising archbishops, bishops, abbots and priors, earls and barons; and on occasion members of what would later be called 'the commons'—knights from the counties, burgesses from the towns, and lower clergy from the dioceses. Largely overlooked for this period by historians, the knights at least, and perhaps the other groups in this last division, were occasional but by no means negligible participants in parliament.[118] There was some overlap between these categories—magnates might be among the king's councillors, minor barons and provincial knights might have a social background and political interests in common—but, formally at least, the composition of parliament was characterized by a clear-cut and distinct taxonomy.

[118] Below, 198–204, 221–4.

At the centre of any parliament were the king's ministers: the great officials, the justices, the barons of the exchequer, the men responsible for taking forward the judicial and administrative business which was concentrated in parliament and which we have just examined. We should probably view them too as a political steering group, as dedicated to promoting the king's policies as were their later counterparts under Edward III.[119] The sort of service which such men could provide is well illustrated by the role of William Raleigh, '*familiaris* of the lord king' as well as chief justice *coram rege*, in arguing the case for a tax at the parliament of January 1237.[120] Though normally their work was more routine, and though Henry directed much of his own business,[121] there may have been a good deal of invisible activity behind the scenes, of a wheeling and dealing kind, which lay in their hands.

From the mid 1230s the leading men in this group formed the core of the king's council. About this time the council first comes into view as a formal body, defined by its known and limited membership (there were twelve councillors in 1237) and by the oath taken by each councillor to give faithful counsel to the king.[122] Its emergence matched the emergence of parliament itself and may have been due to some of the same factors, notably the new opportunities for well-attended and regular meetings offered by a more stationary monarchy based in England.[123] The civil servants who dominated it were afforced by other men, often magnates, whose primary qualification for membership was royal favour rather than office or ability. So we find William of Savoy, bishop-elect of Valence and the queen's uncle, named as the king's *consiliarius principalis* within months of his arrival in England in 1237, and Simon de Montfort denounced as one of Henry's 'infamous' councillors in the same year.[124] In cases involving great men or large issues, council and parliament sometimes worked in tandem, their cooperation made easier by their overlapping membership.

---

[119] Cf. H. G. Richardson and G. O. Sayles, 'The King's Ministers in Parliament, 1327–77', in *EPMA* xxii, esp. 389–92.

[120] *Paris*, iii. 380–1; above, 180.   [121] Above, 171, 174.

[122] *Ann. Dunstable*, 145–6; Carpenter, 'Beginnings of Parliament', 388. The oath may date from a little earlier. It is first mentioned in 1233, which Richard Marshal accused the king's councillors of perjury in breaking their oath 'to furnish the king faithful counsel': Wendover, *Chronica*, iii. 286; J. F. Baldwin, *The King's Council during the Middle Ages* (Oxford, 1913), 23–7.

[123] Cf. Sayles, *The King's Parliament*, 35–6.

[124] *Ann. Dunstable*, 145–6; *Paris*, iii. 412. On the composition of the council see B. Wilkinson, 'The Development of the Council', in his *Studies in the Constitutional History of the Thirteenth and Fourteenth Centuries*, 2nd edn. (Manchester, 1952), 141–6.

When the king's eyre justices infringed the liberties of St Albans in 1253, for example, the resulting case was finally settled before 'the archbishop of Canterbury and almost all the bishops and magnates of the kingdom and all the king's council' at the parliament of April 1254.[125]

Despite instances such as these, there was a more constant tension between the two bodies. The formal council may have partly owed its origins to the king's wish for a smaller, more supple, and more supportive body than a parliament which had outstripped the ancient counselling functions of the great council, risen in power, and begun to challenge his authority in the name of the Charter. The council's close identification with the interests and policies of the king, whose *curiales* and household men were well represented among its members, might set it at odds with parliament. It was the council which applied pressure to the lower clergy in the parliament of April 1254 to induce them to grant Henry a tax, and which, in the following year, decided on the levying of a tallage to pay Henry's debts on his return from Gascony.[126] We have already seen that on at least two occasions those in parliament tried to exert some influence over this sectional grouping: in 1237, when Henry was forced to add three magnates to his council as part of the price of a tax grant, and again in 1244, when the Paper Constitution, drafted at parliament time, had sought the magnates' right to elect four of their number to the council, two of whom were always to be with the king.[127] These schemes may have been the products of particular crises; but the more frequent demands in the parliaments of the 1240s and early 1250s for a say in the election of the chancellor, treasurer, and justiciar had a similar intention and suggest more consistent aspirations; for the treasurer would have been ex officio a member of the council, as would the chancellor and the justiciar had their offices been revived.[128] The devising of a new oath in 1257 binding councillors to impartiality and just dealing in their work, though there is nothing to associate it specifically with parliament, may have been part of the same campaign to limit the council's independence.[129] Throughout the period those in parliament clearly realized that the everyday power to influence the king's policies lay with the council, a political as much as an administrative body and one which had a continuity and permanence

[125] *Gesta Abbatum Monasterii Sancti Albani*, ed. H. T. Riley, 3 vols., RS (London, 1867–9), i. 338–41.
[126] *C. and S.* II. i. 482–3; *CR, 1254–56*, 159–60. For the markedly royalist constitution of the council, 1239–45, see Stacey, *Politics, Policy and Finance*, 139–43, 252–3.
[127] Above, 173, 180.   [128] Above, 178–9.   [129] *Ann. Burton*, 395–7.

denied even to frequent and regular parliaments. Given that the council might also provide a sort of power-base for royal favourites, it is easy to appreciate that the relationship between parliament and council might vary between cooperation, ambivalence, and hostility. When parliament was in session, the council might stand at its centre, but parliament might also stand over against it.

The council was loosely descended from the more amorphous and less well-defined groups of *familiares* whom twelfth-century kings had gathered around them. Yet in its formal title and constitution, and its prominence in central assemblies, it represented a novel development. The position of the lay magnates, on the other hand, was more deeply rooted in custom and past practice, for these men owed their place in parliament to their standing as tenants-in-chief, just as their Anglo-Norman and Angevin ancestors had owed their place at great councils to the same tenurial obligation. Tenure determined the presence, for example, of William de Ferrers, earl of Derby, at the great council at Clarendon in January 1164 which saw the drafting of the Constitutions of Clarendon, just as it did the presence of his son and namesake at the parliament at Westminster in January 1237 which saw the confirmation of Magna Carta.[130] The rule laid down in the Constitutions of Clarendon that those 'who hold of the king in chief . . . ought to be present at judgements of the king's court' still held good,[131] and tenure as the qualification for attendance provided an essential point of continuity between early *concilia* and later parliaments.

It is difficult to know how large a body of parliamentary magnates this rule would normally produce, for there is no surviving list of those summoned to any of Henry III's pre-1258 parliaments. The lists presumably drawn up in the chancery prior to every meeting must have been to a degree ad hoc. Though containing a constant core of important men, they cannot but have varied according to the business of the forthcoming parliament, the known availability of those liable to be summoned, and the king's wishes. Under Edward I, when the records are more plentiful, numbers summoned varied between about forty and about ninety, though there was not always a full turnout.[132] The two longest lists of witnesses to parliamentary *acta* in Henry's reign may suggest lower numbers: the confirmation of the Charters in the great council of 1225 was witnessed

---

[130] *C. and S.* I. ii. 878; *Ann. Tewkesbury*, 103.   [131] *C. and S.* I. ii. 881–2; above, 78.
[132] M. Prestwich, *Edward I* (London, 1988), 446–8.

by thirty-two named magnates and the reissue of Magna Carta in the parliament of 1237 by twenty-six such men 'et aliis'.[133]

Better evidence comes from the occasional lists of military summonses to the tenants-in-chief. Later lists of parliamentary summonses were taken over from these military lists, since the obligation of the magnates to attend both musters and parliaments had the same tenurial basis. Though the rough correspondence of the two lists is provable only from Edward I's reign, it had probably obtained since the great councils of the post-Conquest period or even earlier.[134] To some extent councils and parliaments were always armies in another guise. The two surviving military lists for Henry III's reign are particularly enlightening. For Henry's projected Scottish campaign of 1244 summonses went out to 9 earls and 72 named barons; while for the projected Welsh campaign of 1258 5 earls and 87 barons were summoned. The first of these ended in a great peace-making assembly at Newcastle which official records termed a 'parleamentum', suggesting the close parallel in the minds of contemporaries between councils and armies.[135] In Henry's reign as later, some of those summoned for parliaments may have failed to appear; yet Paris often comments on the great numbers of magnates who *were* present,[136] and in a general way we should certainly see these assemblies as large or very large rather than small. If we envisage a gathering of perhaps fifty to eighty magnates at most parliaments we shall probably not be far out.

'Magnates', however, is a term of convenience rather than one of art, for it comprehended men with a very wide range of wealth and wealth's concomitants, power and status. Primacy lay with the eight or nine earls who towered over their contemporaries among the middling and minor barons. Few earls had incomes of less than £1,500 a year; few barons had more than £400 a year and many had less than £100.[137] The tariff for a poll tax taken in aid of the Holy Land in 1222 had assessed earls at three marks

---

[133] *Stat. Realm*, i. 25; *Ann. Tewkesbury*, 103–4. Cf. Maddicott, ' "An Infinite Multitude of Nobles" ', 19–20.

[134] Cf. Bisson, 'Military Origins of Medieval Representation', 1199–1218, and, for pre- and post-Conquest assemblies, above, 13–14, 66, 83.

[135] *Close Rolls (Supplementary) of the Reign of Henry III, 1244–66*, HMSO (London, 1975), 1–3; *CR, 1242–47*, 221; *CPR, 1232–47*, 434; *CR, 1256–59*, 294–6; Maddicott, ' "An Infinite Multitude of Nobles" ', 20–1.

[136] e.g. *Paris*, iii. 380 (1237), iv. 518 (1246), v. 493 (1255).

[137] For comital incomes, see the figures brought together in Maddicott, *Simon de Montfort*, 55, and M. Morris, *The Bigod Earls of Norfolk in the Thirteenth Century* (Woodbridge, 2005), 40–1. For baronial incomes, see Painter, *Studies in the English Feudal Barony*, 170–1.

and barons at one, eliding the enormous differences in wealth—probably nearer ten to one than three to one—between the two groups.[138] But if they were tenants-in-chief all could expect a personal summons to councils and parliaments. John de Ballon, a minor baron possessing some three or four manors in the west country and the west midlands, witnessed the confirmation of the Charters in the great council of 1225 alongside Ranulf, earl of Chester, the doyen and probably the richest of the lay aristocracy;[139] yet men such as Ballon probably had more in common, economically, socially, and politically, with the knights of the counties than with the likes of the earl of Chester. The point may be important when we come to consider the social location of parliamentary opposition to the crown.[140] Tenure had made some ill-proportioned bedfellows and they may not always have cohabited in harmony.

In terms of wealth the archbishops and bishops summoned to parliament spanned a similar range, with incomes varying from nearly £3,000 a year for the bishop of Winchester to just under £150 a year for Rochester.[141] These figures date from 1291, but probably differed little earlier in the century. Yet the small size of this group, its members' inclusion within a common order, and their common interest in the welfare of the church, gave the bishops a cohesion and a homogeneity which, though never total, contrasted sharply with the diversity of the magnates. To every parliament there would have been summoned the two archbishops and their nineteen suffragans, including the four Welsh bishops. Such a full turnout for parliament was, however, probably rare. Paris again illuminates the subject, giving for eight parliaments between 1245 and 1254 the precise details of episcopal attendance which provide part of the case for his own presence. For the parliament of February 1245, for example, he tells us that proctors were sent on behalf of those absent—the two archbishops and the chapters of the three vacant sees of Coventry, Chichester, and Bath and Wells. For that of February 1248 he tells us that the archbishop of York and eight named bishops were present, together with ten earls, also named. Absent were the archbishop of Canterbury, who was abroad, the bishop of Durham, who was ill and far away, and the bishop of Bath and Wells

---

[138] *Rot. Litt. Claus.* i. 516b, 567a; Mitchell, *Studies in Taxation*, 141.

[139] C. Bémont, *Chartes des libertés anglaises (1100–1305)* (Paris, 1892), 59; Maddicott, ' "An Infinite Multitude of Nobles" ', 20.

[140] Below, 218–24.

[141] Stubbs, *Constit. Hist.* ii, table facing p. 580. Cf. J. R. H. Moorman, *Church Life in England in the Thirteenth Century* (Cambridge, 1946), 169, whose figures differ slightly.

(who was dead). And for that of May 1253 he tells us that the archbishop of Canterbury and almost all the bishops were present, except for York, who had excused himself because he was old and distant, and Coventry, who was ill; while the see of Chichester was vacant.[142] The record here has some implications for the attendance of the magnates. Paris has less to say about their presence or absence,[143] but among those who should have been present there must also have been the old, the ill, the distant, and the dead.

The parliamentary churchmen comprised not only the archbishops and bishops but also the heads of religious houses: a numerically rather larger but politically much less significant body of men. By no means all heads received a summons, and in general the crown seems to have played variations upon those twenty-four houses owing knight service, emphasizing once again the importance of tenure. Of the twenty monastic witnesses to the confirmation of the Charters at the great council of 1225, for example, fifteen came from houses owing knight service; and it is hard to think what lay behind the summoning to that assembly of the abbots of such obscure houses as Cerne and Abbotsbury unless it was the military service due from them.[144] That there was no consistency of principle, however, is shown by the summoning of the prior of Durham, a 'non-service' cathedral priory, to the parliaments of March 1246, February 1248, and April 1255—raising the possibility, even probability, that not only the superiors of other cathedral priories but of an altogether wider range of monastic houses may have been summoned, as they certainly were to be under Edward I.[145] An earlier royal order to the bishop of Salisbury to attend a meeting of the great council in 1205, and to summon all the abbots and priors in his diocese to do likewise (reminiscent of the 'two-tier' system for secular summonses), suggests that on occasion large numbers of the religious may have been present at councils and parliaments.[146] Yet, whatever their numbers, none of these men appears to have played more

[142] Paris, iv. 372, v. 5-6, 373, 375.
[143] Though note ibid. v. 440 (late arrival of Richard of Cornwall and other magnates at the parliament of April 1254) and ibid. 520-1 (magnate absences from the parliament of October 1255).
[144] Compare the list of houses owing knight service in H. M. Chew, The English Ecclesiastical Tenants-in-Chief and Knight Service (Oxford, 1932), 5, with the list of witnesses in Stat. Realm, i. 25.
[145] A. J. Piper, 'Writs of Summons of 1246, 1247 and 1255', BIHR 49 (1976), 284-6; Chew, English Ecclesiastical Tenants-in-Chief, 171. The very large number of religious superiors, 102, summoned to Montfort's parliament of January 1265 cannot be taken as typical, since most are likely to have been summoned as Montfortian partisans: Maddicott, Simon de Montfort, 317.
[146] Stubbs, Select Charters, 279; id., Constit. Hist. i. 668-9.

than a nominal role in parliamentary business. In contrast to bishops, abbots and priors almost never witnessed royal charters made at parliament time;[147] they were almost never mentioned in Paris's parliamentary commentaries, again in contrast to bishops; and the only abbot to find a place on the numerous committees set up at the start of the reform movement was the abbot of Westminster, the king's friend.[148] When Henry addressed those present in the assembly of March 1246 he spoke separately, first, to the bishops, then to the earls and barons, and finally—showing a proper appreciation of their inferior place in the parliamentary hierarchy—to the abbots and priors.[149] We should be cautious about writing off the religious completely as a force in politics, for the abbots of Bury St Edmunds and Ramsey (both military tenants) were appointed to the committee set up in the parliament of November 1244 to consider the king's request for a tax.[150] But for the most part these often minor and local figures lacked the experience of government, the intellectual range, and the social standing which gave weight, in one combination or another, to their episcopal counterparts.

Within parliament the relationship between magnates and prelates was one of growing cooperation in the face of external threats. Although the two groups sometimes, and perhaps generally, met separately, with an occasional further separation between the meetings of the bishops and of the abbots and priors,[151] they regularly came together to bargain over the king's requests for taxes, occasionally by formal arrangements. In January 1242 Henry's demands were countered by an oath to resist them, taken by those present in parliament; in November 1244 by the establishment of a joint committee comprising four bishops, four earls, two barons, and two abbots, to consider them; in October 1252 by the refusal of the lay magnates to give an answer without hearing the prelates' response; and in May 1253, when a feudal aid was granted for the forthcoming expedition to Gascony, by both groups coming together to impose on the king a

---

[147] Between 1237 and 1257 the only instances of abbatial witnessings were: Richard, abbot of Evesham, three charters in 1241; Richard, abbot of Westminster, three charters in 1247–8; and Elerius, abbot of Pershore, five charters in 1252: *Charter Witness Lists*, i. 180–1, ii. 22, 29, 58–9, 64, 69. But these abbots were hardly typical. The abbot of Evesham was keeper of the great seal when he witnessed, the abbot of Westminster was head of Henry's most cherished house, and the abbot of Pershore was a civil servant and high in royal favour: D. M. Smith and V. C. M. London, *The Heads of Religious Houses in England and Wales*, ii: *1216–1377* (Cambridge, 2001), 41, 56, 78.

[148] *DBM* 100–1.   [149] *Paris*, iv. 526.   [150] Ibid. 362.

[151] Ibid.; ibid. 526; *C. and S.* II. i. 389, 397. That there could be a separate meeting for abbots and priors cautions us against too low an estimate of their numbers.

solemn reconfirmation of the Charters.[152] This was a conscious policy of strength through unity, and a response not only to Henry's importunings but to his attempts to break down resistance by negotiating separately with individuals or small groups, as he did in the parliaments of January 1242 and October 1252. The words of Robert Grosseteste, bishop of Lincoln, made in the face of the tax demand of 1244, summed up both motives and trends: 'Let us not separate ourselves from common counsel (*a consilio communi*). For it is written: "If we are divided we shall immediately die." '[153]

   Cooperation, however, rested on a broader basis of common interests than that provided by the immediate problems of royal taxation. That basis was partly social. Some bishops came from important magnate families: Ralph de Neville, bishop of Chichester (1224–44), Walter de Cantilupe, bishop of Worcester (1237–66), and Fulk Basset, bishop of London (1244–59), are the most obvious examples. Even Robert Grosseteste, from a much humbler background, had sympathies, manners, and practical skills which made him quite at home among the nobility.[154] In the great assemblies of the kingdom these men and their colleagues could mix on equal terms with the lay magnates. But much more significant was the respect of both parties for Magna Carta, their common inheritance. The bishops, led by Archbishop Edmund of Abingdon, had been instrumental in securing the Charter's reinstatement in public life in 1233–4, after its principles had been challenged by the rule of Peter des Roches.[155] They and their successors saw it not only as a guarantee of good government and the rule of law, as did the whole political community, but as offering specific liberties to the church. Its famous first clause, laying down that 'the English church shall be free', could be and was invoked against many of Henry's abusive interventions in church affairs, notably his denial of free elections and his wasting of church property during vacancies. Grosseteste appealed to the Charter during Henry's long campaign to bar William Raleigh, the duly elected bishop, from the see of Winchester, and the bishops as a body called upon Henry to restore free elections, according to the Charter's terms, during the parliament

---

[152] *Paris*, iv. 181, 362, v. 335, 373–6. For the oath of 1242, see Stacey, *Politics, Policy and Finance*, 185.

[153] *Paris*, iv. 182, 366, v. 330, 332.

[154] M. Gibbs and J. Lang, *Bishops and Reform, 1215–1272* (Oxford, 1934), 12–13, 188–9; R. W. Southern, *Robert Grosseteste: The Growth of an English Mind in Medieval Europe*, 2nd edn. (Oxford, 1992), 19–20, 63 and n., 192, 318–19.

[155] Vincent, *Peter des Roches*, 408–10, 429–30, 434–6, 463–4.

of May 1253.[156] In defending the Charter churchmen had a special role to play, for the spiritual sanction of excommunication, employed against infringers of the Charter in 1225, 1232, 1237, 1239, and 1253, was one way to its enforcement.[157] That on three of these occasions excommunication was linked with royal confirmation of the Charter in return for tax grants (that of 1253 a feudal aid) shows how closely bishops and magnates had drawn together in defence of what they saw as their common liberties.

They could also unite behind grievances which at first sight may seem more exclusively ecclesiastical. Foremost among these was the issue of papal provisions: the right of the pope, exercised with increasing frequency from the 1230s onwards, to appoint his own candidates, usually Italians, to benefices in the English church. To reforming bishops such as Grosseteste the abuse here lay in the appointment of men who were either absentee pastors or else immigrants ill equipped to preach and to administer the sacraments: duties which were essential for the effective pastoral care whose provision was now seen by the bishops as one of the clergy's chief obligations. More would have objected to the drain of money away from their dioceses and indeed from the kingdom.[158] The magnates' concern was more self-interested, though not entirely so. Papal provisions were an infringement of the rights of monasteries founded by their ancestors (since it was often monastic patronage which was the target of papal intrusions), and therefore an attack on their own rights as patrons. In addition, provisions cut into the supply of benefices customarily reserved for magnate kinsmen.[159] On a more overtly political plane, the Sicilian Business provoked common objections of the same kind. Insupportably expensive, it necessitated fiscal measures which fell mainly on the clergy but which the laity did not entirely escape. But its character as a crusade against the Christian subjects of the Emperor also constituted a moral outrage which, in 1264, both bishops and barons were to condemn.[160]

---

[156] *Roberti Grosseteste Epistolae*, ed. H. R. Luard, RS (London, 1861), 271–2; *Paris*, v. 373. For other appeals to the Charter in defence of ecclesiastical liberties, see *C. and S.* II. i. 280 (1239), 468–9 (1253), 483 (1254), 543, 547–8 (1257); *DBM* 268–71.

[157] J. W. Gray, 'The Church and Magna Charta [*sic*] in the Century after Runnymede', *Historical Studies*, vi (London, 1968), 24–5.

[158] For provisions see esp. F. M. Powicke, *King Henry III and the Lord Edward*, 2 vols. (Oxford, 1947), 274–89; W. A. Pantin, 'Grosseteste's Relations with the Papacy and the Crown', in D. Callus (ed.), *Robert Grosseteste: Scholar and Bishop* (Oxford, 1955), 193–6; Southern, *Robert Grosseteste*, 273–5.

[159] See esp. the magnates' complaints presented at the Council of Lyons, 1245: *C. and S.* ii. i. 391–5.

[160] *DBM* 278–9.

These grievances might have arisen and been voiced separately; it was parliament which made their coordination possible. By bringing together, on a common stage and at regular intervals, bishops and barons normally resident in scattered dioceses and on dispersed demesnes, it created possibilities for cooperation which would otherwise have been largely lacking. Opposition to papal exactions, resulting in letters of grievances from both the prelates and the magnates to the pope, was orchestrated at a series of parliaments and ecclesiastical councils in 1245–6; while the magnates' written objections to the Sicilian Business seem to have been drafted in the presence of, and probably in cooperation with, the clergy at the parliament of March–April 1257.[161] The effective working together of bishops and barons, more usually against the demands of the king than the pope but sometimes (as with the Sicilian Business) against those of both, was a feature of the political scene hardly present before 1215. Then, the defence of the particular liberties of the church by an Anselm or a Becket had been of no interest to—and indeed often opposed by—the lay magnates. Now, those sectional liberties had been largely subsumed by the national liberties embodied in the Charter, while a common front could be turned against aliens, whether Italian provisors or Lusignan relatives of the king. Parliament reflected both these powerful interests, lay and ecclesiastical, and it did so all the more weightily for their merger on some of the central issues of the day.

One final point is easily overlooked. In an age when the size of a man's following was one measure of his rank, neither bishops nor magnates are likely to have gone to parliament unaccompanied. So we find William Raleigh, bishop of Winchester, present at the parliament of April 1247 with his *familiares*; Aymer de Valence, bishop-elect of the same see, summoning his knight, Sir William de Lisle, to attend him at the Oxford parliament of 1258; and Richard de Clare, earl of Gloucester, bringing some forty young men to be knighted by the king at the parliament of June 1245.[162] Others might be called up to advise. Adam Marsh, leader of the Oxford Franciscans and seemingly a fairly frequent (though reluctant) attender at parliaments, was summoned by Grosseteste to one parliament and at another addressed the bishops and magnates on Simon de Montfort's behalf during the earl's

---

[161] C. and S. II. i. 388–95, 524–8; Ann. Burton, 386–8.
[162] Vincent, 'Politics of Church and State', 165 n. 62; Sayles, Functions, 64; N. Denholm-Young, 'Robert Carpenter and the Provisions of Westminster', in his Collected Papers (Oxford, 1969), 176; Paris, iv. 418–19.

trial in 1252.[163] Neither these men nor others like them played any formal part in the parliament which was taking shape behind the closed doors of the Painted Chamber or the other domestic buildings of palace and abbey. But as a conduit for the transmission of opinion from the country to the court, and of news from court to country, those on parliament's periphery may have been more important than the records reveal.

4. Parliamentarians: Lesser Landholders, Burgesses, and Lower Clergy

In Henry III's middle years parliaments began to incorporate an increasingly wide range of men who would have been absent from the great councils of the twelfth century, or at most only intermittent visitors. Chief among these, though generally unrecognized by historians, were the smaller landholders of the knightly class, most frequently present in their role as lesser tenants-in-chief but on one occasion as elected knights of the shire.[164] We have already seen that the lesser tenants had sometimes been summoned to the councils of the Anglo-Norman and Angevin kings and that clause 14 of Magna Carta had extended this practice by assuming that they would be present whenever taxation was on the concilar agenda. If fiscal business affecting the whole community was to be brought forward, their attendance was no longer to be left to the king's discretion.[165]

Given the disappearance of clause 14 from the later reissues of the Charter, it would be easy to assume that its prescription was from the start a dead letter. But this assumption would be wrong. The complementary clause 12, demanding 'common counsel' for the granting of direct taxes, also disappeared from the reissues. Yet in practice it was rigorously observed, providing the unspoken principle which governed the submission of the king's tax requests for parliamentary approval or rejection. That clause 14 was similarly kept in mind, despite its formal abandonment, is indicated by

[163] *Letters of Adam Marsh*, ed. Lawrence, i. 46–8, 78–81. Cf. ibid. 176–7, and *Monumenta Franciscana*, ed. J. S. Brewer, 2 vols., RS (London, 1858), i. 344, 387, for other possible instances of Marsh's attendance at parliament.

[164] This section supersedes Maddicott, ' "An Infinite Multitude of Nobles" ', 33–40, some of whose arguments it amends. The earlier article, however, is cited when it provides additional detail or corroborates what is said here.

[165] Above, 79–84, 124, 132–4.

exchanges at the parliament of October 1255. There, when Henry asked for a tax, his plea was parried by the magnates' assertion that they had not all been summoned according to the terms of the Charter and that without their absent peers they were unwilling to answer him or make a grant.[166] They can only have been alluding to clause 14 of the 1215 Charter, the sole clause in any version of the Charter which regulated attendance at assemblies. In this case it looks as though Henry had either failed to give sufficient notice of the meeting or to convene a full assembly of tenants-in-chief, as the Charter, at least by implication, demanded—and had been countered by the magnates' tenacious recollections of what the original Charter had contained and perhaps by their advantageous confusion of the Charter's various versions.[167]

Prima facie, therefore, we might also suppose that the lesser tenants-in-chief continued to be summoned to Henry III's 'tax parliaments' (as we shall call those assemblies at which a tax was requested), in accordance with this same clause. A catena of evidence suggests that this was indeed so and that the lesser tenants, often described as 'knights', were present or were expected to be present in such parliaments from the 1220s onward. Our earliest information comes from a supposed great council convened at Westminster in April 1229 to consider Pope Gregory IX's demand for a tenth from the laity and the clergy to support his war against Frederick II. According to Wendover, our only source, those summoned included, besides leading churchmen, 'earls, barons, rectors of churches and those who held from [the king] in chief', and the demand was rejected by 'earls and barons and all the laity'. Wendover's story of this phantom tax is implausible. But it nevertheless serves to show how one contemporary saw the constitution of a tax parliament, albeit one concerned with papal rather than royal taxation: as including other tenants-in-chief and laymen besides earls and barons.[168] The same author's account of the better evidenced tax parliament of March 1232 takes us a little further. The king asked this assembly for a grant to pay the debts incurred on his recent Brittany campaign. But the earl of Chester, speaking for the magnates, refused the

---

[166] *Paris*, v. 520–1; Holt, *Magna Carta*, 400; J. E. Powell and K. Wallis, *The House of Lords in the Middle Ages* (London, 1968), 181.

[167] For the confusion over the different versions of the Charter, especially at St Albans, see Holt, *Magna Carta*, 402–5.

[168] Wendover, *Chronica*, iv. 200–1; *C. and S.* II. i. 167–9; Maddicott, ' "An Infinite Multitude of Nobles" ', 26.

grant on the grounds that 'the earls, barons and knights who held from him in chief' had already provided the king with personal military service on the expedition and for this reason owed him no further aid.[169] Not only are the sub-baronial lesser tenants here clearly equated with the knights—a valuable confirmation of an equation which had certainly obtained in the twelfth century—but it seems to be implied that these men were present in the assembly along with the other groups for whom the earl spoke.

As we move forward into the 1230s and 1240s, the evidence for the attendance of the lesser tenants-in-chief becomes more substantial. The next tax after that of 1232 was the aid given for the marriage of the king's sister in the assembly of July 1235. The writ for its collection spoke of its having been granted by 'archbishops, bishops, abbots, priors, earls, barons and all others of our kingdom of England who hold from us in chief': a procedure glossed in a related writ as *per commune consilium regni*, 'by the common counsel of the kingdom', the words of Magna Carta's tax clauses. 'All others . . . who hold from us in chief' suggests again that the prelates, earls, and barons did not comprise the full tally of the attendant tenants-in-chief. The identity of these 'others', left vague here, is glossed with rather more precision in a letter contained in a contemporary formulary which spoke of the king calling on 'knights and barons' to grant the aid, and of the prelates setting out the case against it in another letter addressed to 'earls and barons and knights'.[170] Clearly the knights were seen as crucial parties to the grant. Since the tax took the form of a levy on knights' fees, akin to a scutage, it would not have been surprising if the lesser tenants had been summoned in accordance with the Charter's demand for 'common counsel' in the case of scutages as well as general aids.

A comparable conclusion emerges from the procedures governing the next tax, the thirtieth granted in the parliament of January 1237. In the writ for its collection the king states that it has been granted by the 'archbishops, bishops, abbots, priors and clerks holding lands which do not pertain to their churches, earls, barons, knights and freemen, on behalf of themselves and their villeins (*pro se et suis villanis*)'. If these named groups speak not

---

[169] Wendover, *Chronica*, iv. 233; Stubbs, *Select Charters*, 323–4. The above account of the 1232 assembly corrects that in Maddicott, ' "An Infinite Multitude of Nobles" ', 26, which was based on a mistranslation.

[170] *CR, 1234–7*, 186; Madox, *History and Antiquities of the Exchequer*, i. 593 note d; BL Add. MS 8167, fos. 105–105ᵛ; Sayles, *Functions*, 19–20; Mitchell, *Studies in Taxation*, 208–9; Maddicott, ' "An Infinite Multitude of Nobles" ', 26–7.

only for themselves but for their villeins, who, as the writ implies, are
certainly not present, the further implication must be that all the other
groups in the list *are* present, including 'knights and freemen'. Had this
been solely an assembly of the greater tenants-in-chief, then presumably
the prelates and magnates would have been left on their own to speak for
all others, knights, freemen, and villeins. To this widening of the concept
of representation we shall return.[171]

The thirtieth of 1237 was the last direct tax to be granted until 1270. But
its granting by no means marked the last appearance of the knights. They
played a part too in the levying of the scutage used to finance Henry's
Poitou campaign, after the denial of a direct tax in the parliament of
January 1242. At least three royal writs state that the scutage was granted *per
commune consilium regni*, while the pipe roll states that it had been 'willingly
conceded' by the knights.[172] Given the role of 'common counsel' in the
grant it is more likely that it had been made at the January parliament than
at the only possible alternative assembly, the muster immediately prior to
the king's departure.[173] In a similar way the parliament of February 1245
would deny Henry a general tax but grant him the lesser prize of an aid on
knights' fees.[174]

After 1242 the evidence for the knights' presence in parliament diversifies
and derives less exclusively from tax matters. In the mid 1240s it associates
the knights with those contemporary protests at the abuses of papal power
which we have already noted. According to an exchequer document, which
Paris edits, it was 'the barons, knights and the *universitas* of the baronage
of the kingdom of England' who in 1245 sent a letter to the Council of
Lyons protesting at papal exactions. Almost certainly drafted in the June
parliament of that year, it shows how the activities of the knights might
now extend beyond their share in the concession and denial of taxes.[175]
At the subsequent parliament of March 1246, significantly termed by Paris
a 'parlamentum generalissimum' (that is, one especially well attended),
further letters of protest were drafted by a seemingly identical group, 'the

---

[171] *CR, 1234–37*, 545; Stubbs, *Select Charters*, 358; Maddicott, ' "An Infinite Multitude of Nobles" ',
27 (where the list of those granting the tax is incomplete); below, 206–7.
[172] Mitchell, *Studies in Taxation*, 228, 232 n. 37, 235–6; Madox, *History and Antiquities of the
Exchequer*, i. 681 note p, 682 note r.
[173] For the muster, see Mitchell, *Studies in Taxation*, 224–5.   [174] *Paris*, iv. 372–3.
[175] *C. and S.* II. i. 388–9, 392–5; *Paris*, iv. 372–4, 441–4; Lunt, *Financial Relations*, 212–13. For
more detail on the sequence of events set out in this paragraph, see Maddicott, ' "An Infinite Multitude
of Nobles" ', 34–7.

barons, knights and *universitas* of the baronage of England'.[176] Paris goes on to mention the presence of knights at the tax parliament of February 1248, one which he describes with such particularity as to suggest that he was there.[177] We find them again at the next but one tax parliament of May 1253. Here the Dunstable annalist tells us that the king sought an aid from 'bishops, earls, barons, knights, abbots, priors' for his forthcoming Gascon campaign. Though this was refused, it was agreed, says Paris, that the king should receive a scutage 'from the knights (*a militibus*)'. This was actually an aid on knights' fees rather than a scutage proper. In return for a parallel grant from the clergy the Charters were confirmed and sentences of excommunication passed against their infringers. Clarificatory letters patent issued by the king and the lay magnates stated that, should any changes be subsequently introduced into the written sentences, 'the lord king and all the aforesaid magnates and the community of the people (*communitas populi*)' had declared that they had in no way consented to such changes, nor did they. The letters closed with the further statement that the king and three named earls had set their seals to the document 'at the instance of the other magnates and of the people present (*ad instantiam aliorum magnatum et populi presenti*)'. Both the 'community of the people' and the starker 'people' are here set apart from the body of the magnates and can be more plausibly identified with the knights whom our other sources show to have been present in this parliament than with any other body.[178]

The next parliament which almost certainly saw the lesser landholders in attendance was the famous assembly of April 1254, to which elected knights were summoned from the shires. Considered in more detail below,[179] it provides a natural terminus for a long story whose general message is difficult to doubt. From the 1220s until at least the mid 1250s the knights were fairly regular attenders at Westminster, their presence almost certainly determined by their status as lesser tenants-in-chief and by the Charter's ruling that their tenure should give them a place at tax parliaments. Seven of the eight assemblies which supply evidence for their presence come under this heading (the only exception is that of March 1246), and it is reassuring that we are not dependent on Paris alone for that evidence, but on chancery and exchequer records and on other chronicles as well.

---

[176] *C. and S.* II. i. 395–7; *Paris*, iv. 526–9.   [177] *Paris*, v. 5.
[178] *Ann. Dunstable*, iii. 186; *Paris*, v. 373–5; *C. and S.* II. i. 478–9.   [179] Below, 210–17.

Yet it may still seem implausible to envisage the amorphous mass of lesser tenants-in-chief turning out for parliaments, nor need we quite do so. There were probably about 450 of these men, their names largely unknown to the government and even to the sheriffs, who were driven to using proclamations in order to summon them to musters and perhaps to parliaments too.[180] But there seems to have been an informal division, utilized by the government for the projected muster of 1254 and perhaps on other occasions, between the lesser tenants with lands worth at least £20 a year, who were reckoned to be knights, and the inferior remainder.[181] It was probably the superior group of twenty-librate men, perhaps about 300 strong,[182] who formed the majority of the lesser tenantry at Westminster; though the reference to 'knights and freemen' among the grantors of the 1237 tax should remind us that there may have been a subordinate minority as well. When taxation was on the parliamentary agenda these men had an interest in attending. Under the terms of a Charter which was regarded as a palladium for local liberties they came to assemblies where the king's demands for money could be regularly blocked and their own grievances presented, as we shall see.[183] Their numbers may well have helped to inform Paris's comments on the great crowds of men whom he saw as especially characteristic of tax parliaments. On only three occasions does he remark on the special magnitude of the assembly and each of the three was a tax parliament. At the parliament of April 1255, for example, when a tax was refused, there were so many laity and clergy 'that such a multitude was never before seen gathered together there'.[184] Part of the special quality of

---

[180] See the summons for the 1244 army for Scotland, which ended in a *parleamentum* at Newcastle: *Close Rolls (Supplementary), 1244–66*, 1–3. The magnates were summoned individually, the lesser tenants via the sheriffs, in the way prescribed in Magna Carta. The sheriffs were to proclaim the summons 'in full county court' and throughout their counties. Cf. Maddicott, ' "An Infinite Multitude of Nobles" ', 28–31, where a rather smaller estimate of the numbers of lesser tenants is given.

[181] In 1254 the lesser tenants-in-chief possessing twenty librates or more of land were called upon to provide military service in Gascony: *CR, 1253–54*, 112, 114; below, 212–15.

[182] This figure is deduced from the returns from twenty-nine counties to the orders sent to the sheriffs in February 1254 to return the names of all tenants-in-chief holding twenty librates of land who were due to serve in Gascony: *CR, 1253–4*, 112; BL MS Cotton Claudius C. II, fos. 23^v–31; below, 212. The returns survive only as sixteenth-century transcripts made by Robert Glover. They are difficult to use, since they include the names of earls, barons, women, heirs in wardship, and heads of religious houses, as well as those of the lesser tenants-in-chief. In arriving at the above figure, which allows for the missing counties, I have as far as possible discounted those falling into these categories; but the figure can be regarded as only very approximate.

[183] *CR, 1234–37*, 545; Stubbs, *Select Charters*, 358; Maddicott, ' "An Infinite Multitude of Nobles" ', 30–1; below, 222–4.

[184] Ibid. 28–9; *Paris*, v. 493.

such assemblies thus resided in their size, to which the summoning of the lesser tenants must have contributed.

Henry's repeated requests for taxes brought the lesser tenants-in-chief to parliament with a frequency that cannot have been foreseen by the Charter's makers. Yet theirs was not the only group whose presence was beginning to enlarge the social base of parliament. About the same time as the knights started to appear regularly at Westminster, two other groups, the burgesses and the lower clergy, made their parliamentary debut. The first appearance of borough representatives is usually dated to the parliament of January 1265, to which Simon de Montfort summoned burgesses from York, Lincoln, and other towns.[185] But the practice had almost certainly begun before this, at first on a limited scale. Our earliest knowledge of the attendance of townsmen at a central assembly comes from 1225, when two were summoned from each of the Cinque Ports to attend the great council which saw the confirmation of the Charters. They were there, however, only to report on measures for coastal defence decided on at an earlier local meeting by the barons of the Cinque Ports, and they were too circumscribed in their brief and origins to create a true precedent for what came later.[186] Much more significant may be the statement in the Tewkesbury annals that at the tax parliament of January 1237 there were present 'archbishops, bishops, abbots and priors, earls and barons, citizens and burgesses, and many others'. Perhaps these 'citizens and burgesses' were among the 'free men' whom the writ for the collection of the thirtieth records as attending this parliament, alongside the knights. A piece of reforming legislation, discussed below, may corroborate this unique and near contemporary chronicle record.[187] A second piece of evidence also suggests their presence on another occasion; for among those groups writing to the pope from Paris's *parlamentum generalissimum* of March 1246 to complain of papal exactions were, so the letter itself tells us, 'the noble inhabitants of the sea ports'.[188] The evidence is too fragmentary to go far; but it does at least hint at the desultory attendance at parliament of representatives of the towns. If attendance was more regular than this, in an

[185] *DBM* 300–3; G. O. Sayles, 'Representation of Cities and Boroughs in 1268', in *EPMA* iv. 581.
[186] *PR, 1216–25*, 503; White, 'Some Early Instances of the Concentration of Representatives', 743; Holt, 'The Prehistory of Parliament', 21–2; Carpenter, *Minority of Henry III*, 379.
[187] *Ann. Tewkesbury*, 102; White, 'Some Early Instances of the Concentration of Representatives', 745–7; below, 224–5. The Tewkesbury annals for this period were probably written before the end of 1253 and incorporated earlier material: see Gransden, *Historical Writing in England*, 405 and n. 13.
[188] *Paris*, iv. 518, 533. For the context, see *C. and S.* II. i. 388–9.

age before the appearance of many town records and before the chancery's enrolment of writs of summons, we might well not know it.

The summoning of the lower clergy—the deans and priors of cathedral churches, the archdeacons, and the parish clergy[189]—was at this stage almost as sporadic, inchoate, and unsystematic as the summoning of the burgesses appears to have been. Since the start of Henry's reign these clerical groups or some of them (the parish clergy were generally excluded) had occasionally been convened in their dioceses by their bishops or in London by the archbishop, usually to discuss either royal or papal requests for taxes. Very occasionally one or other of the groups may have joined a meeting of the great council: twice in 1226, when papal taxation was under discussion, and then again possibly in April 1229, when, according to Wendover, rectors of churches joined the lay and ecclesiastical tenants-in-chief in order to consider a further papal request for a tax.[190] When papal demands were at their most exigent and unpopular between 1245 and 1247, representatives of the lower clergy appear to have attended at least three central assemblies, ecclesiastical and parliamentary, to present their grievances: archdeacons and deans were present at the parliament of March 1246; the proctors of the lower clergy at a purely clerical assembly at St Paul's in December 1246; and archdeacons, representatives of cathedral chapters, and possibly others at the parliament of February 1247.[191] But before the parliament of April 1254, which brought proctors of the clergy and knightly proctors from the counties together in parliament for the first time, the record is an exiguous one.

Though the burgesses and the lower clergy thus shared with the knights the distinction of attendance at central assemblies, their role seems to have been no more than occasional: an impression which may be partly illusory in the case of the burgesses, but is unlikely to be so in that of the clergy, who came from a milieu in which record-keeping was already well developed. Yet, despite these differences, a common factor lay behind the appearance of all three groups: the growth of taxation, national and

---

[189] Carpenter, 'The Beginnings of Parliament', 389.

[190] Wendover, *Chronica*, iv. 200–1; *C. and S.* ii. i. 167–9; W. E. Lunt, 'The Consent of the English Lower Clergy to Taxation during the Reign of Henry III', in *Persecution and Liberty: Essays in Honor of George Lincoln Burr* (repr. New York, 1968), 123–6; below, 209. For clerical assemblies in this period, see M. V. Clarke, *Medieval Representation and Consent* (London, 1936), 307–11, and J. H. Denton, 'The Clergy and Parliament in the Thirteenth and Fourteenth Centuries', in Davies and Denton (eds.), *Eng. Parl.* 96–7.

[191] *C. and S.* ii. i. 389–90, 398; *Paris*, iv. 590, 594.

papal, and the need to seek the widest possible authority for its granting. It remains to be seen how the demand for taxes, and the consequent social enlargement of parliament, affected and was affected by old and new notions of representation.

5. Representation

By the 1240s the widening range of interests and social groups embodied in parliament was beginning to create an assembly which was more broadly representative of the realm than its conciliar predecessor. True, the development of parliament as a representative assembly had been foreshadowed in the reigns of Richard I and John, when the magnates of the great council had begun to see themselves as standing for a public beyond their own ranks. Magna Carta had made their role still more explicit. Forced on the king by a group of rebellious barons, the Charter had taken the form of a grant 'to all the free men of our realm', conceded at what could later be described as 'the parliament of Runnymede'.[192] But it was not until Henry III's early and middle years that the notion of virtual representation implicit in the Charter—the notion, that is, that the wishes and interests of the many could be represented by the few without the need for any form of election—was first enlarged and then transcended.

The three general taxes of the period (1225, 1232, 1237) made a vital contribution to this process. Though actually granted by assemblies tiny in relation to the numbers of the king's subjects, they had to be regarded as having been granted by all in order to be binding on all. So the king could note in 1225 that the fifteenth had been conceded by 'the archbishops, bishops, abbots, priors, earls, barons, knights, free tenants, and everyone in our kingdom'. Where the list of actual attenders at the great council should terminate is a moot point, but plainly the role of 'everyone of our kingdom' is a legal fiction.[193] The tally of those supposedly making the grant of 1232 is still larger and slightly more specific, but leads to the same conclusion: it names 'archbishops, bishops, abbots, priors and clerks holding lands which do not pertain to their churches, earls, barons, knights,

---

[192] Above, 143.
[193] *Stat. Realm*, i. 25; Stubbs, *Select Charters*, 350; above, 107. Cf. Maddicott, ' "An Infinite Multitude of Nobles" ', 27–8, for this and the following paragraph.

freemen, and villeins of our kingdom'. Wherever we draw the line, it is clear once again that it has to be drawn somewhere, and that the 'villeins of our kingdom' cannot possibly have been present to consent.[194] Again, those present were tacitly deemed to stand for those absent.

It is the third grant, however, that of 1237, which carries the most telling implications. We have already seen that 'knights and freemen' were placed alongside the prelates and barons in the list of those making the grant 'on behalf of themselves and their villeins'.[195] Here the knights, presumably the lesser tenants-in-chief, have taken on an explicitly representative role which is disguised in the two earlier lists. Present at the assembly, they and the other granting groups stand for the taxpaying, but no longer even notionally tax-granting, villeins of the kingdom. Even before the appearance of directly elected knights of the shire in 1254, the lesser tenants who doubled up as knights could thus be seen as representative figures. Representation remained virtual; but, embracing as it did a wider body of representatives, it was less so than it had been a decade or two earlier, when the lay and ecclesiastical magnates alone spoke for the realm. It was the provisions of the Charter, the close proximity of three grants of direct taxation, and the consequent presence of the knightly lesser tenants at parliament which had brought this about.

But we should also remember that behind these developments lay the interests of the king as well as those of the tenants-in-chief. With a clarity lacking in the Charter's clauses regulating the conciliar appearances of this group, mention of the villeins in the two tax grants of 1232 and 1237 had shown that those present at council and parliament represented the peasantry who constituted the bulk of the country's taxpaying population. Under the Charter's terms the consent of those present, to tax grants and presumably to all else, could bind those absent; yet it clearly remained in the king's interest to secure as large a turnout as possible of his tenants great and small. Otherwise, and despite the Charter, he risked the noncompliance in taxation both of those absent and of their tenurial dependants. Only a full complement of tenants-in-chief could speak authoritatively for the multiple layers of tenants beneath them, down to the level of the villeins.

[194]   CR, 1231–34, 155; Stubbs, Select Charters, 356.
[195]   CR, 1234–37, 545; Stubbs, Select Charters, 358; above, 200–1.

Changes in the scope of representation were, however, more than a pragmatic response to the king's fiscal needs and to the forces set in motion by the Charter. Parallel to the process which we have traced ran another, rooted in the fertile soil of Roman and canon law, infiltrating at first the ideas of churchmen and the assemblies of the church, but eventually moving across to influence secular politics too. This second process rested on two principles, deriving from theory and already widely recognized in ecclesiastical circles during Henry III's minority: that taxation could not be imposed without the consent of the taxpayer, and that a body of taxpayers could mandate another to act for them in order to give that consent. Both these principles began to affect ecclesiastical politics from the late twelfth century onwards, and the stimulus in both cases was the introduction of clerical taxation.[196] To express the need for consent to taxation the Roman law maxim 'Quod omnes tangit ab omnibus approbetur', 'What touches all should be approved by all', began to migrate from its original place in private law, where it stated the need for all parties to a judicial case to be present at its hearing, into the public sphere.[197] The principle was known in England by 1213, though it was not yet applied to taxation.[198] Just prior to this, canon lawyers had begun to argue that cathedral chapters should be consulted when cathedral property was to be taxed and that such consultation could be achieved if the body concerned appointed proctors to represent it. Proctors already represented their chapters at Innocent III's Fourth Lateran Council in 1215, and the right of proctorial representation was statutorily established by the next pope, Honorius III, in 1217.[199]

But it was only from the mid 1220s that these changes in thought and practice began to make an impact on the politics of taxation. The catalyst was a proposal by Honorius III to fund the papal curia by imposing a tax on the prebendal income enjoyed by members of cathedral chapters. In November 1225 this proposal was discussed in France at the Council of

---

[196] R. Kay, The Council of Bourges, 1225: A Documentary History (Aldershot, 2002), 96–7.

[197] G. Post, Studies in Medieval Legal Thought: Public Law and the State, 1100–1322 (Princeton, 1964), 168–72; E. Hall, 'King Henry III and the English Reception of the Roman Law Maxim "Quod Omnes Tangit"', Studia Gratiana, 15 (1972), 131–2.

[198] A. Mercati, 'La prima relazione del Cardinale Nicolò de Romanis sulla sua legazione in Inghilterra', in H. W. C. Davis (ed.), Essays in History Presented to Reginald Lane Poole (Oxford, 1927), 280; Post, Studies, 227; Hall, 'King Henry III and the English Reception', 145. Cf. Carpenter, 'Beginnings of Parliament', 400–1, for this and what follows.

[199] Kay, Council of Bourges, 99.

Bourges, to which proctors from the cathedral chapters were summoned by the pope's legate: a tacit recognition of the principle of 'Quod omnes tangit'. The proposal was rejected.[200] In September 1225 a papal nuncio brought the same proposal to England and laid it before Henry III, but was told that the king could not settle the matter because it touched the laity and the clergy of the whole kingdom ('quod omnes clericos et laicos generaliter totius regni tangebat').[201] At a subsequent royal council in January 1226, where the deans of cathedral churches and their archdeacons acted as proctors for the lower clergy, final consideration of the proposal was deferred on the grounds that the king and many of the prelates were absent. Again, 'Quod omnes tangit' provided the guiding principle behind the deferral.[202] A second council, which met in May to consider the proposal, was attended by proctors from cathedral and other chapters. This time it was conclusively rejected in a formal decision made by the king. Both the January and the May assemblies appear to have been great councils, attended by magnates.[203] The model for both the summoning of proctors and the response was almost certainly the procedures followed at the council of Bourges, which were known in England;[204] and the presence of the proctors was intended to strengthen the authority of any decision.

The events of 1225–6 produced crucial precedents both for consent to taxation and for the related parliamentary procedures. The precedent was followed up in an irregular but consistent way at a number of ecclesiastical councils in Henry's middle years. In 1240 the bishops cited the principle of 'Quod omnes tangit' when they declined to grant a subsidy to the pope without consulting their archdeacons. It was cited again by the bishops in reference to a similar demand in 1245, and again by the clergy of the archdeaconry of Lincoln in their protests against taxation for the Sicilian Business in 1256. 'When it is a question of anyone being taxed', they said, 'his express consent is necessary.'[205] By the 1250s 'Quod omnes tangit' thus enjoyed a wide currency both among the higher and the lower clergy. Used from the start to deflect papal claims to tax the clergy without their consent, it is likely to have been silently absorbed into a wider political discourse,

---

[200] Ibid. 94–5, 175–9, 205–14.
[201] Ibid. 215, 217, 500–1; Hall, 'King Henry III and the English Reception', 130–1.
[202] Kay, *Council of Bourges*, 217–24.   [203] Ibid. 221, 228, 501, 503, 509.   [204] Ibid. 231.
[205] *C. and S.* ii. i. 287, 391, 506. Cf. Carpenter, 'Beginnings of Parliament', 400, whose translation is followed here.

secular as well as ecclesiastical, via the bishops who were co-attenders with the magnates at parliaments and who shared their opposition to taxation. If Magna Carta had established an unbreakable connection between taxation and consent, that connection was reinforced by a principle ultimately founded on Roman law and put into circulation by papal demands for taxation which ran parallel to those of the king.

The need for consent to taxation also explains why the use of proctors came to converge with the regular citation of 'Quod omnes tangit'. Following the model provided by the summoning of clerical proctors to the councils of 1226, capitular proctors were summoned to other clerical assemblies in 1237, 1240, and 1246, as well as to the parliament of February 1247.[206] Personal proctors, representing individuals rather than groups, began to be employed about the same time. The written record of proceedings in the tax parliament of January 1242, transcribed by Paris, states that the assembly was attended by the archbishop of York, all the bishops, and abbots and priors, either in person or by proctors (*per se vel per procuratores suos*); while in the parliament of February 1245 proctors represented the two archbishops and the chapters of the three sees then vacant, Coventry, Bath and Wells, and Chichester.[207] Paris's record here shows that bishops were normally seen as representing their chapters. That both these assemblies were tax parliaments points to the particular importance of securing not only the presence of the lesser tenants-in-chief but also that of the higher clergy, if necessary through representation, when taxation was on the agenda.

In the parliament of April 1254 these clerical practices were adopted as a model for the representation of the laity. The outcome marked the faltering start of a system of local representation by two knights from each shire which in essentials was to last until 1918.[208] Although this innovation resulted from exceptional circumstances and had no immediate effects, it was taken up again by Simon de Montfort in the 1260s and remained portentous in its later consequences. For these reasons it is worth exploring in a little detail.[209]

---

[206] Kay, *Council of Bourges*, 99; C. and S. II. i. 390.   [207] *Paris*, iv. 185, 372.

[208] It was ended only by the Representation of the People Act 1918, which abolished the division between county and borough seats.

[209] The account that follows replaces that in Maddicott, ' "An Infinite Multitude of Nobles" ', 33–4. Contrary to the views expressed there, I now believe that the elections of 1254 were a unique

In August 1253 Henry had departed for Gascony, leaving his kingdom in the hands of his queen, Eleanor of Provence, and his brother, Richard of Cornwall. By the end of the year, heavily in debt, he was preparing to defend his duchy from external attack by Alfonso X, king of Castile. Though he was at the same time negotiating for peace with Alfonso, and though the supposed emergency was to be viewed sceptically at home, Henry's fears were real enough.[210] His urgent need was for men and money, and on 27 December 1253 the regents, acting on his behalf, convened a parliament to consider that need.[211] It met on 27 January and its proceedings were reported to Henry in a letter from the regents dated 14 February.[212] At parliament's opening the assembled prelates and magnates had responded rapidly to an exposition of the king's plight. The prelates promised monetary aid if the king of Castile should invade Gascony, but said that they could make no offer on behalf of the lower clergy without their assent (*sed de auxilio clericorum suorum vobis faciendo nihil facere potuerunt sine assensu eorundem clericorum*). They did not believe that an aid would be forthcoming unless the terms for the current crusading tax owing to the pope were alleviated; but they would try to induce the clergy to make a grant if the king of Castile invaded. As for the laity, the earls and barons were willing to cross to Gascony with all their forces if the king of Castile should invade. But the regents did not believe that Henry would get any aid from 'the other laity', who were not to go overseas, unless he ordered the firm observance of the Charter, via royal letters to the sheriffs, and its public proclamation throughout the counties; for many complained that the Charter was not kept by sheriffs and other bailiffs. Another parliament was to meet on 26 April for further discussion with clergy and laity about the aid.

Matthew Paris corroborates and expands on much of this in his usual racy style. Henry, he says, sent special envoys to England, who elaborated in

event in Henry's middle years, that they were not part of a sequence, and that the attendance of the lesser tenants-in-chief at tax parliaments continued, with this exception, up to 1258.

[210] For the background, see J. P. Trabut-Cussac, *L'Administration anglaise en Gascogne sous Henri III et Édouard I de 1254 à 1307* (Geneva, 1972), pp. xxx–xxxix; Maddicott, *Simon de Montfort*, 119–24; and Howell, *Eleanor of Provence*, 109–12.

[211] *CR, 1253–54*, 107.

[212] *Royal Letters*, ii. 101–2. For the date of opening, see *Paris*, v. 423. There is another version of this letter in Paris's *Additamenta*, vi. 282–4. It makes no mention of 'the other laity' or of the Charter. Since it also fails to mention the coming of the king's envoys to parliament, dated to 4 February in the regents' letter, it was probably an early draft, discarded when the arrival of the envoys made it necessary to report afresh to Henry.

parliament on his supposedly desperate situation. According to the regents' letter, they arrived on 4 February, after the initial discussion and almost certainly after the offer of conditional grants. Responding to their pleas, and to set an example, Richard of Cornwall offered 300 knights to serve at his own cost for a year. The earl of Gloucester also promised service, but only if there should be an invasion from Castile, prompting Richard to add the same condition. The other magnates, however, poured scorn on the envoys' report and on the reality of any danger from Castile, and the assembly broke up with nothing accomplished.[213]

Here Paris was wrong. In letters written on 5 February to two minor barons, presumably both absent from the assembly, the regents said that the prelates, earls, and barons had agreed to provide aid for the king, some prelates in service and some in money, and the magnates in service. They had promised to assemble in arms on 3 May, ready to cross to Gascony, and the two addressees were to join them. In further letters the regents ordered the sheriffs to take security from all tenants-in-chief holding twenty librates of land from the king in order to ensure their joining the muster on that day. The names of these men were to be sent up to the king's council by 22 March.[214]

By negotiation and injunction the regents were thus on their way to providing the king with an army comprising the magnates, their forces, and the more substantial of the lesser tenants-in-chief. It remained to tap the financial resources of the rest of the country through 'the other laity' mentioned in the regents' letter. This was put in hand by another set of letters, sent to the sheriffs on 11 February. Not only were they now to increase the pressure on the £20 tenants by distraining them to appear at the muster, but they were also to ensure the appearance before the council at Westminster on 26 April of two knights from each county, chosen by the counties 'in place of each and all in their counties (*vice omnium et singulorum eorundem comitatuum*)'. The county representatives were jointly to decide in parliament on what aid they wished to give to the king in his necessity. The sheriffs were to expound that necessity to the knights and other men of the counties, so that when the knights came to Westminster they would be able to give a definite answer concerning the aid on behalf of everyone in their counties. Paris must have regarded this letter as especially novel and significant, since he included the copy sent to the sheriff of Hertfordshire

---

[213] *Paris*, v. 423–5.   [214] *CR, 1253–54*, 111–12.

among his *Additamenta*.[215] At the same time parallel letters were sent out to the archbishops and bishops directing them to assemble the lower clergy of their dioceses—cathedral chapters, archdeacons, the religious, and other clergy—and to induce them to make a generous grant. Representatives of every diocese were to certify the council on 26 April as to how much they were prepared to give and in what form.[216]

When parliament broke up, probably about 11 February, arrangements were thus in hand not only for the raising of troops but also for the raising of money through the elected knights and clergy who were expected to make tax grants at the forthcoming parliament on behalf of their constituents. We know that elections took place in the counties and in the dioceses, for we have a record of the names of those elected for Middlesex and Northumberland, a further close roll reference to one of the knights elected for Essex, and a memorandum of the actions of the clerical proctors in the subsequent parliament.[217] On 24 March, probably about the same time as the county elections were going forward, the king wrote home to the whole political community, prelates, magnates, knights, clerks, and others, in order to induce a favourable response. He emphasized the continuing threat from Castile, urged rapid acquiescence in his request for aid, asked those who could not serve personally to give money, and stated that he had commanded the regents to order the proclamation of Magna Carta in the counties, and its firm observance by sheriffs and magnates. This last provision, following as it did the earlier advice from the regents that the laity would probably not grant an aid unless the Charter was firmly maintained, must have been aimed especially at the knights. Indeed, the whole letter may have been intended as a kind of long-distance parliamentary 'speech', comparable to Henry's usual speeches requesting taxation in parliament, and intended to be read out to the assembled representatives at their forthcoming meeting in order to induce compliance with the king's wishes.[218]

Our knowledge of proceedings in the April parliament is limited. Paris tells us that it started late because of the tardy arrival of Richard of Cornwall and other magnates. While it was in session, new requests were received

---

[215] Ibid. 114–15; *Paris*, vi. 286–7.   [216] *CR, 1253–54*, 115–16.

[217] J. R. Maddicott, 'The Earliest Known Knights of the Shire: New Light on the Parliament of April 1254', *Parliamentary History*, 18 (1999), 109–30; *CR, 1253–54*, 42; *C. and S.* II. i. 482–3; below, 214, 216–7.

[218] *CPR, 1247–58*, 279–80; Maddicott, 'Earliest Known Knights of the Shire', 111.

from Henry for men and money to repel the expected invasion: quite possibly a reference to the king's letters of 24 March. These were met by fierce complaints at royal exactions, but also by a promise of military service should the invasion materialize. Before the session had ended, however, Simon de Montfort had appeared, hotfoot from Gascony, and 'announced the truth', meaning presumably the absence of any danger from Castile and the falsity of the king's assertions. The assembly then broke up in indignation.[219] That no grant was made is partly confirmed by what we know of the clergy's activities in the same parliament. Asked by the archbishop of Canterbury, the bishops, and the council to provide a subsidy, the clergy agreed to do so only under conditions so restrictive as to nullify any prospect of a grant.[220] We know nothing about the appearance of the knights, though the certainty of county elections and of the clergy's presence makes it very unlikely that they were absent.

Abortive in its outcome, this famous episode nevertheless reveals much both about representation and about the more general role of parliament by the 1250s. At the root of any analysis must lie the distinction between those called on for service (the magnates and the twenty-librate tenants-in-chief) and those called on for a tax (all those remaining at home, including the lower clergy).[221] The summoning of the £20 men established a further division which we have already noted in speculating that it may have been this group among the lesser tenants who came to parliament most frequently: a division, that is, between these 'greater' lesser tenants and their poorer and inferior colleagues perhaps numbered among the freemen present at the parliament of January 1237.[222] If the lesser tenants had previously been summoned to tax parliaments in accordance with Magna Carta, on this occasion their upper ranks must have been excluded by reason of their military contribution. What was wanted from them

---

[219] *Paris*, v. 440.

[220] *C. and S.* II. i. 481–3; Lunt, 'Consent of the English Lower Clergy to Taxation', 142–3; Clarke, *Medieval Representation and Consent*, 308–9.

[221] Holt, 'The Prehistory of Parliament', 27, comments on this distinction and notes that the regents 'planned to seek aid' from those not serving. But he sees this as 'a bid to develop and amalgamate the fine *pro non transfretando* and the payment of scutage by rear-vassals . . . It was not a general tax at all'. This seems unlikely to be right, since fines and scutage could be claimed only from those owing service but failing to serve: that is, in this case, the lower ranks of the lesser tenants-in-chief, worth less than £20, whose service was not required. But it is clear from the proposed consultations in the county courts which the regents envisaged and from the election of knights that the aid was intended to be raised from the whole taxpaying nation. A levy on moveables of the customary sort was probably hoped for.

[222] Above, 203.

was service, not the taxation from which service would have exempted them. Since a landed income of £20 was becoming established as the tariff rendering a man liable for distraint of knighthood, these men were or should have been knights; and indeed the sheriff of Norfolk and Suffolk's return of their names to the council is headed 'Names of the knights who hold in chief from the king'.[223] These are fresh pointers to what has already been argued, that those described as 'knights' who appear so frequently as attenders at parliament are the lesser tenants-in-chief in another guise.

The government's difficulty lay not with these men, whose obligation to serve was undoubted, but with the bulk of the population, the lay majority and the clerical minority, who owed no service but whose money the king wanted as a substitute. It is clear that neither the bishops nor the magnates felt able to answer for them. The bishops had specifically said that they could make no grant for the lower clergy without their assent, and the decision of the regents to seek access to the wealth of the laity via elected knights was an admission that the magnates thought likewise. Taken in the January parliament, this decision can hardly have been reached without magnate participation. According to the Dunstable annalist, who provides a brief independent account of this parliament, the magnates and prelates took the initiative in raising the question of the Charter, whose rigorous maintenance was to be seen by the regents as the key to the appeasement of the lay taxpayers and their representatives.[224] Temporarily at lease the virtual representation of the community by the magnates and lesser tenants-in-chief had been tacitly abandoned.

The consequent election of the knights in the counties was an expedient, a makeshift intended to facilitate taxation. It was almost certainly one derived from clerical precedents, as Professor David Carpenter has noted.[225] The proctors of the lower clergy had on several occasions been summoned to central councils of the church to discuss taxation; in 1247 they had been summoned to parliament; and the undertaking of the bishops in the January parliament to do what they could to ensure that the lower clergy granted a tax was matched and followed by the regents' instructions to

[223] M. R. Powicke, *Military Obligation in Medieval England* (Oxford, 1962), 73–5; BL, MS Cotton Claudius C. II, fo. 24.
[224] *Ann. Dunstable*, 189; *Royal Letters*, ii. 102. But the Dunstable annalist's account suggests that he may have conflated the proceedings of the January parliament with those of the later April assembly.
[225] Carpenter, 'Beginnings of Parliament', 401.

the sheriffs to apply the same pressure to the men of the counties.[226] The two clerical principles of 'Quod omnes tangit' and proctorial representation had merged to bring the knights of the shire to parliament for the first time.

These procedures show the extent to which the fulfilment of the government's aims had come to depend on the consent of those, both clerical and lay, below the nobility. The magnates, having offered service, lacked their usual voice in the granting or denial of taxation. To secure the consent of their inferiors the government had to bargain. The exposition of the king's plight and the king's needs in both clerical synods and in county courts was a central part of that process. But still more central to it was Magna Carta. It was predicted that the knights would grant no aid unless the Charter was enforced; while at the April parliament the clerical proctors demanded the reform of the church according to the Charter as one of their conditions for a grant.[227] We have already seen that the Charter provided common ground for bishops and magnates; but so it did too for knights and lower clergy.

Emerging here was a dialogue between government and locality, hard to detect in earlier assemblies but subsequently to become a characteristic feature of English parliamentary life. Similar exchanges can be seen earlier, under Richard I and John, in the counties' negotiations for privileges and liberties; but the contacts which these negotiations fostered were informal and had no particular focus save perhaps the exchequer and the person of the king. In 1254 parliament provided that focus, for it was there that discussions in shire and synod could be transmuted through elected representatives into decisions about tax. The unelected lesser tenants-in-chief may earlier have had a similar parliamentary role in voicing grievances, as we shall see,[228] but this too can only have been an informal one, lacking something of the force and legitimacy which came from election.

The sort of men whom we know to have been elected were well qualified to speak for their constituents. The few surviving returns and other sources for the elections show that in Northumberland and Essex, if not in Middlesex, they were prominent local landholders, experienced

---

[226] Above, 210; *Paris*, iv. 590, 594. The regents' letter suggests that the prelates' decision to refer the tax question to assemblies of the lower clergy preceded, and provided a model for, its reference back by the regents to comparable assemblies in the shires: *Royal Letters*, ii. 101–2.

[227] *C. and S.* II. i. 483; Lunt, 'Consent of the English Lower Clergy to Taxation', 143.

[228] Below, 222–4.

in local government, and with some experience too of soldiering overseas. The two shire knights for Northumberland, John of Eslington and John of Letwell, were typical of their class. Both had served on local commissions, including the important body set up in 1245 to determine the line of the Anglo-Scottish boundary, and on grand assize juries, and Eslington in particular, with an income of perhaps £40 a year, must have been among the wealthiest of the Northumberland gentry. Military service had taken him to Brittany on Henry III's expedition of 1230. Walter of Bibbesworth, elected for Essex, and lord of four manors in Essex and Hertfordshire, had also acted as a grand assize juror and had served abroad in Gascony in 1250. More unusually, he was the author of a guide to learning French for the purposes of estate management, written in the 1240s for the children of a baronial family but subsequently finding a much wider readership. Bibbesworth's choice of vocabulary for this work, with its descriptions of the practicalities of farming—threshing, turning corn into flour, the cultivation of flax—and of the flowers, birds, and beasts of the countryside, throws a vivid light on his everyday life and interests. In the event his activities as the keeper of the king's forest in Essex prevented his serving in parliament. But his other activities, including his authorship of a number of further works in poetry and prose, should remind us that the parliamentary knights, in 1254 as no doubt later, were not mere peas in a pod but distinctive individuals possessing talent, intelligence, and, in some cases, literary skills.[229]

The peculiar circumstances which led to the election of such men in 1254 makes it almost certain that county representation in parliament marked a new departure. There had been no earlier instances of the tenants-in-chief offering service while leaving their inferiors to provide cash. On the only comparable occasion, in the great council of March 1232, the service already performed by both the greater and the lesser tenants-in-chief was cited in order to rule out any tax grant.[230] Both the appearance of the writ for the election among Paris's *Additamenta* and the unique returns for Northumberland and Middlesex suggest that county elections were a novelty. For the moment they were also an isolated one, with no immediate follow-up. We know of three further tax parliaments before

[229] Maddicott, 'Earliest Known Knights of the Shire', 114–25; T. Hunt, 'Walter of Bibbesworth', *ODNB*. Cf. T. F. Tout on Edward II's earls, 'as like each other as a series of peas': *The Place of the Reign of Edward II in English History*, 2nd edn. (Manchester, 1936), 16.
[230] Wendover, *Chronica*, iv. 233; above, 176–7.

the start of the reform movement in 1258. That of April 1255 was one of Paris's 'multitudinous' assemblies, whose excessive size we have assumed to imply attendance by many of the lesser tenants-in-chief. Complaints in the same parliament about the continuing failure to observe the Charter and about local disorders could easily have come from the same group. In October of the same year and in March 1257 we hear only of prelates and magnates at parliament.[231] After 1254, as before, the dense trail of chancery and chronicle evidence surrounding the elections of that year is entirely lacking.

Between the 1220s and the 1250s the nature of representation had thus undergone a noticeable shift. Behind it lay the dual influence of frequent requests for taxation, chiefly royal but also papal, and of clerical insistence on the inability of great men to bind their inferiors to taxation's payment without some extended form of consent. The magnates were no longer seen as fully representative of the realm. They had been joined in their representative role, first by the lesser tenants-in-chief, and then, in the unique circumstances of 1254, by directly elected representatives of the shires and of the clergy. Since there was no social divide between the upper ranks of the lesser tenants and the elected knights, this was in one way a smooth progression. Yet in another way it marked a radical transformation. The counties had now been given—as yet only for the moment and on this one occasion—a direct say in those who were to speak for them, a direct voice in parliament, and through parliament an entrée into the processes of central government. We need now to try to identify the forces at work in parliament and the constituencies for which these men acted.

6. Groups and Grievances: The Dynamics of Parliamentary Politics

The relationship between the various groups in parliament, and the part which each played in parliament's activities, are not easy to plot with any precision. As we would expect, the magnates are generally seen to take the lead in debates and confrontations, their leadership resulting from consistency of attendance as well as rank. But their spokesmen almost

---

[231] *Paris*, v. 493–4, 520, 530–1, 621; *Ann. Dunstable*, 202; *Ann. Burton*, 384.

always remain anonymous. Paris usually refers to the king's parliamentary opponents simply as 'magnates', *magnates*.[232] When we do have a name, it belongs, again predictably, to one of the very great. It was Ranulf, earl of Chester, the elder statesman of the aristocracy, 'speaking for the magnates', who turned down the king's request for a tax in 1232. A speaker *avant la lettre*, he anticipated the role of the Commons' speaker from the late fourteenth century onwards.[233] In the 1240s and 1250s Richard of Cornwall sometimes played a similar part. Richard was named first among the four earls appointed to the committee set up to consider the grant of a tax in the parliament of November 1244, and his later absence from the parliament of April 1249 meant that the business could not go forward and the assembly dispersed. He was 'the chief of them all (*eorum omnium summus*)'.[234] But Richard was often absent from parliament and who then took his place is unclear.

We have already seen that within parliament the magnates and bishops shared a common agenda, defined by opposition to taxation, demands for the enforcement of the Charter, and hostility towards papal provisions.[235] On many matters a similar community of interest, again founded on the Charter, united the magnates with the knightly class of lesser tenants-in-chief. Under the headings of the Charter could be brought the desire of the lesser landholders for equitable and just local government, upright and incorruptible officials, and a light fiscal touch: a distinct programme which subsisted throughout the thirteenth century. In 1227, at the start of our first age of parliamentary politics, knights from the counties had been summoned to Westminster to present their complaints against the sheriffs on matters arising from the Charter, and its continuing centrality to knightly concerns was seen again in 1254, when the regents opined that the king would get no grant from those below the magnates unless he saw to the Charter's firm observance.[236] Objections to the financial burdens imposed by the eyre, and a desire for some say in the appointment of the three great officials, chancellor, treasurer, and justiciar, both of them issues frequently raised in parliament, were subsidiary facets of this mutual approach to Henry's government.

---

[232] *Paris*, iv. 181, 366.
[233] Wendover, *Chronica*, iv. 233; J. S. Roskell, *The Commons and their Speakers in English Parliaments, 1376–1523* (Manchester, 1965), 81–2.
[234] *Paris*, iv. 362, v. 73.   [235] Above, 194–7.
[236] Maddicott, 'Magna Carta and the Local Community', 30; above, 177, 211.

In the underlying motives for their criticisms of Henry's government magnates and knights may have differed in their emphases. To the magnates the Charter represented a code of liberties signifying the principle of restraint on royal power; to the knights, a set of safeguards, sometimes more imaginary than practical, against predatory local officials.[237] To the magnates, the eyre was a fiscal engine whose extortionate provision of funds for the king helped to justify refusals of taxation; to the knights, a resented force for the impoverishment of their localities.[238] To the magnates, the chancellor and the treasurer, whose appointment they sought to influence, were well placed to supervise two matters of vital concern, royal patronage and royal expenditure; to the knights, the chancellor's control of judicial writs and the justiciar's duty to do justice to all held out to the lesser men of the counties the prospect of legal protection against oppressive government.[239] Yet although both parties in parliament might view their common desiderata from rather different angles, there can have been little difference of opinion on what was wanted. Nor did they combine only against royal abuses. In 1245, for example, 'the barons, knights and whole baronage of the kingdom of England' came together in parliament to protest at the papal provisors whose intrusion into English livings affected all patrons of local churches, knights as well as magnates.[240] Much of parliament's emerging political weight was founded on the common ground shared by the whole landholding class.

Should we therefore regard the knights simply as the inferior branch of the parliamentary magnates, not only summoned on the same tenurial basis (save for the special parliament of April 1254) but possessing identical aims? The answer is almost certainly not. Differences there were, resting in the first place on the huge disparities in wealth which separated the top and bottom ranks of those attending parliament. We have already seen that the distance between the great earls and the lesser barons stretched downwards from an income of £1,500 or more to one of £100 or less; and that, further down still, even the more important of the knightly lesser tenants-in-chief might be worth no more than £20 and upwards. Differences in wealth were reflected in politics. The earls often stood high in royal favour, and in Henry's middle years the king's government gave free rein to their ambitions and acquisitiveness. They and their

---

[237] Maddicott, 'Magna Carta and the Local Community', 46–8.

[238] Cf. *Paris*, iv. 34, 186–7, v. 327; *Ann. Burton*, 387.

[239] Cf. Carpenter, 'Chancellor Ralph de Neville', 70–3.   [240] *C. and S.* II. i. 392–3.

confrères among the leading barons were allowed to build up their local power, often at the crown's expense, to enjoy their liberties without being subject to the same legal challenges as faced monastic houses, to benefit from favourable treatment in the courts, and to defer payment of their debts to the crown. The oppressive sway which they and their officials exercised in the localities, if less ubiquitous than that of the king and his officials, was certainly comparable. For this reason they probably had an ambivalent attitude towards the Charter. It may have represented a code of constitutional liberties, but its full enforcement threatened their provincial interests by protecting the rights of their tenants and neighbours; for the principle contained in the Charter that the 'customs and liberties' granted by the king to his men should be observed by the grantees towards their own men was one which Henry was vigorously able to exploit.[241]

Within parliament this upper group may have been less hostile towards the king's requests for taxation than were their inferiors. In 1254 it was Richard of Cornwall and the earl of Gloucester, men close to the king and gainers from his partisan justice, who took the lead in offering Henry the *auxilium*, in the form of military service, which the knights were thought likely to refuse, in the form of tax; and Richard again who, as one of the king's councillors, later put pressure on the clergy to concede a tax.[242] At a less exalted social level, the middling and lesser baronage, who lacked both the resources of the very great and their access to royal patronage, may have had more in common with the knights than with the earls, over taxation as over the government of the shires. If we cannot number and name those responsible for denying taxation to the king, we can be reasonably sure that the lesser landholders, often the victims rather than the beneficiaries of royal government, would have had more reason to do so than the greater. In parliamentary debates over taxation they are unlikely to have been mere ciphers. There would have been little point in the Charter's insistence on the presence of the lesser tenants-in-chief at tax parliaments had they not been expected to participate. The proceedings in the parliament of July 1235, when the king apparently called on 'knights

[241] Maddicott, 'Magna Carta and the Local Community', 49–54; Carpenter, 'King, Magnates and Society', 81–93, 98–106.
[242] Above, 212, 214; C. and S. II. i. 482–4; Lunt, 'Consent of the English Lower Clergy to Taxation', 143. For Henry's prohibition of legal action against these two earls and other members of his inner circle, see Paris, v. 594, and Maddicott, 'Magna Carta and the Local Community', 56–7.

and barons' to grant an aid, while the prelates stated the contrary case in a letter to 'earls and barons and knights', and the presence of 'knights and freemen' among those granting the tax of 1237, all suggest that in matters of taxation they were not a negligible quantity. If on this last occasion they did 'some real assenting', as A. B. White believed, they may on others have done some real refusing too.[243] It was a paradox, though presumably one that went unrecognized, that the money-making activities of the king via the eyre and the sheriffs, which provoked so much parliamentary complaint, were largely rooted in the parliamentary denial of direct taxation for which the complainants themselves are likely to have been partly responsible.

The knights may therefore have already begun to constitute an independent presence in parliament, with grievances of their own and interests which did not invariably coincide with those of the magnates. One or two scraps of evidence point more firmly in this direction. The first arises from the pressures brought to bear by Henry's government on potential knights to take up knighthood itself. Following a Whitsun parliament at Westminster on 4 June 1245, where some forty men had been knighted, Henry wrote on 8 June to the sheriffs of eight widely scattered counties to say that he had heard 'from the complaints of many (*ex multorum querela*)' that the sheriffs had distrained men to knighthood contrary to his orders. He was referring to earlier instructions to the sheriffs to distrain all those with twenty librates of land and all who held a knight's fee. Now, on 8 June, he said that no one was to be distrained who did not hold either twenty librates of land or a knight's fee worth £20.[244] This was a marked retreat from his earlier position, since his previous orders had said nothing about the value of the knight's fee, so leaving impoverished holders of very small fees liable to distraint. It is difficult to see how the complaints which apparently triggered this retreat, broadly distributed across the regions as they were, can have reached the king except through their voicing at the immediately preceding parliament, either by the lesser tenants or by those assembled to receive knighthood. Here was an issue which was of no interest to the magnates but of real concern to the lesser landholders,

---

[243] Above, 200; White, 'Some Early Instances of the Concentration of Representatives', 747.

[244] *CR, 1242–7*, 350, 354, 356–7; *Paris*, iv. 418–19. I am very grateful to David Carpenter for his advice on this sequence of events. That the complaints were apparently submitted on a county basis provides the one fact which might give one pause in arguing that no elected shire knights appeared in parliament before 1254; see Maddicott, ' "An Infinite Multitude of Nobles" ', 42.

and one on which they had managed to secure some redress, apparently through parliamentary action.

A second piece of evidence tentatively suggests that knightly grievances might be directed against the magnates as well as the king. In the tax parliament of April 1255 there were complaints, now almost customary, about the failure to observe the Charter, and demands, almost equally customary, for a say in the appointment of the three great officials and for their removal only 'by common counsel'—'for', continues Paris, 'there were so many petty kings (reguli) in England that the old times seemed to be renewed there' (perhaps an allusion to the civil wars of Stephen's reign or even to the much more distant days of the heptarchy). Paris had used similar words in commenting elsewhere on the misdeeds of William of Tarrant, Queen Eleanor's notoriously oppressive estate steward, and his bailiffs—'and thus', he concluded, 'as in the old days many kings tyrannized in England'.[245] The comparison may be significant, for in the first passage, as more certainly in the second, he probably had in mind not royal officials but magnates and their agents. More aptly described than royal officials as 'petty kings', they were a regular target for local complaint.[246] Much later, in the Merciless Parliament of 1388, the Commons spoke in similar terms when they complained about the destruction of 'poor people' in the counties by seigneurial officials 'and especially by the three or four within each county who are known as second kings'.[247] In writing of the 1255 parliament Paris suggests that the complainants coupled both the observance of the Charter and the appointment of an acceptable chancellor, treasurer, and justiciar, with objections to the 'petty kings' of magnate officialdom, in what all our other evidence would suggest to be an entirely plausible linkage. Its plausibility receives some slight confirmation from another source. When Henry wrote home in March 1254 in order to induce the elected knights to comply with his request for a tax, he ordered the Charter to be observed not only by sheriffs, as the regents had advised, but also by the magnates' officials, about whom the regents had said nothing.[248] If this was an attempt to turn the tables on the magnates by invoking their vaunted Charter against their own malpractices, it also marked a shrewd appeal to the interests and susceptibilities of the knights.

[245] Paris, v. 494, 621, 716; Howell, Eleanor of Provence, 140.
[246] Maddicott, 'Magna Carta and the Local Community', 54–9.
[247] Knighton's Chronicle, 1337–1396, ed. G. H. Martin, OMT (Oxford, 1995), 442–5.
[248] CPR, 1247–58, 279–80; above, 213.

We can thus perceive, if only dimly, something of the aspirations of the knights in these parliaments, of the interests which they shared with the magnates, and of the degree to which they stood apart from, or even against, their superiors. Our perceptions of how and how far their actions were coordinated are similarly dim; but not entirely obscure. That members of the knightly class held views in common, even before they reached parliament, is suggested by the regents' belief in 1254 that only the maintenance of Magna Carta would persuade these men to grant a tax. Respect for the Charter spanned counties as well as social groups. Within parliament views could be concerted, grievances pooled, and a common line devised: a process implied in the multiple presentation of complaints about unjust distraint. But the best example of concerted action by the non-magnates comes from the tactics of the lower clergy in the parliament of April 1254. The conditions which their representatives then imposed on their provisional grant to the king, including a demand for the reform of the Church according to the terms of the Charter, can only have been worked out at Westminster. They imply a meeting, discussion, and debate. It is inconceivable that the synodal electing bodies in each diocese could have decided on identical conditions for the granting of a tax and mandated their proctors accordingly.[249] If parliament offered a common platform for magnates and bishops, as has already been argued, so from time to time it did too for the lower clergy and more frequently for the knights. In each case men were removed from their provincial backgrounds, brought together in one place with like-minded others, and given a forum for the presentation of their views. Public opinion, so often a will-o'-the-wisp for the middle ages, was here taking shape on a parliamentary stage.

There is some evidence that the burgesses too, assuming that they sometimes attended parliament, shared in the same process and might be equally vocal in their grievances. An episode from 1237 is particularly suggestive. Immediately after that year's January parliament, where the Tewkesbury annals tell us that 'citizens and burgesses' had been present, and a thirtieth had been granted to the king, a new statute was issued by king and council. It regulated the king's right to prise (that is, the

---

[249] Lunt, 'Consent of the English Lower Clergy to Taxation', 143–4. But see *C. and S.* II. i. 481, where it is suggested, implausibly to my mind, that 'the bishops pointed the way to this "common decision" in their separate synods'.

forcible levying of goods), forbidding Henry's agents to appropriate more than was needed or warranted, enjoining them to take immediately what they wanted at markets and not to dally there, to the loss of merchants, and ordering them to pay a reasonable price, fixed by four merchants in each market, for what they took. These reforms would hardly have been of much interest to magnates or knights, and it is more likely that they were a response to the urban and mercantile grievances of townsmen voiced in the preceding parliament: perhaps a response which was part of the price paid for a tax grant.[250] That there were undoubtedly complaints about prises in other parliaments makes this seem all the more plausible. In the assembly of February 1248 there was fierce criticism of the royal purveyors' seizure of victuals, cloth, and wax, and also of herring and other fish, which drove English fishermen overseas to land their catches in safety.[251] Again, this does not sound like a landholders' grievance; and when we remember the 'noble inhabitants of the sea ports' who joined magnates and others in writing to the pope from the parliament of March 1246 we may wonder whether it is not their voice which we hear again in 1248.[252] Other more general grievances may have had a particular urban component. Complaints about the eyre in the parliament of January 1242, for example, were directed at its impositions not only on counties, hundreds, and vills but also on cities and towns.[253] Had burgess representatives here added their own reinforcement to parliamentary criticisms of royal government?

On most of these matters we can see only through a glass darkly. Almost wholly dependent as we are on Paris, and lacking the official records which later distinguish the contributions of the commons from those of the lords, we cannot be at all exact in determining, as it were, who said what in parliament. Yet we can be reasonably sure that the knights spoke up, and fairly sure that sometimes the burgesses did too. Though the knights had much in common with the magnates, they also had their own distinctive 'take' on the grievances of the day and to a lesser extent an altogether distinct agenda which may have made them critics of the magnates as well as the king. If we find it surprising that this can be said of a group so plainly inferior in rank to the higher nobility and, we might suppose, so deferential

---

[250] CR, 1234–37, 522; Stacey, Politics, Policy and Finance, 108–9. Stacey sees this statute as a concession made in the January parliament, but thinks that it was one made to the magnates. This seems unlikely.
[251] Paris, v. 5–7.   [252] Ibid. iv. 533; above, 204.   [253] Ibid. 186–7.

towards them in this hierarchical society, we ought to remember that in 1254 the regents feared that the knights would deny the king a grant and that the clergy effectively did so, though they were under pressure from the queen, the bishops, the king's brother, and the king's council to give way.[254] Not to be overawed, these local representatives possessed a degree of stubborn independence which sprang from the leading role which they played in their own communities, from their administrative experience, and probably from the bonding and cohesion imparted by parliamentary service itself. These qualities made them an essential component of the community of the realm which we must now finally assess.

7. Conclusion: Parliament and the Realm

By 1258 parliament had emerged as a genuinely representative body. Even though representation remained virtual, and nothing remotely like a popular franchise existed, those who, with a fair degree of regularity, assembled at Westminster could be thought to represent the realm in more than a notional sense.

In the first place, this was true of those attending. They covered a wide social range. Though ministers, magnates, and prelates, and of course the king, stood at the centre of parliament, this chapter has sought to show that many others beyond this core group attended from time to time. Even those magnates receiving a personal summons extended downwards from the great earls to minor barons such as John de Ballon, lord of a handful of manors.[255] For tax parliaments this already wide band of local landholders was expanded still further. To it were added the lesser tenants-in-chief, often described as 'knights' but sometimes no more than freemen; in 1254, elected knights; on at least some occasions burgesses from the towns; and very infrequently the representatives of the lower clergy. The attendance of the lesser tenants owed something to the obligations of feudal tenure transmitted by the conciliar practices of the twelfth century, but much more to Magna Carta, which had provided for their presence when taxes were under consideration. That Henry's financial needs made his requests for taxation a more commonplace occurrence than can ever have been envisaged in 1215 served gradually to embed the lesser landholders in

---

[254] *C. and S.* II. i. 482–3; above, 211, 214.   [255] Above, 192.

the structure of parliament. If they were hardly invariable attenders, they were nonetheless quite frequent ones. The origins of urban representation lacked such clearly discernible roots in custom and law. But we may guess that the wealth of the towns, their subjection to taxation along with the countryside, and perhaps the pervasive influence of 'Quod omnes tangit', all made it expedient to summon them when taxes were to be discussed. At any rate two of the three parliaments which show strong signs of their presence, those of January 1237 and February 1248, saw requests for taxes.[256]

If parliament was not quite a microcosm of the nation, it was thus already more than the gathering of an elite, at least on the more salient occasions for its summoning. Its social breadth helps to explain a second aspect of its emergence as a truly national assembly: that is, the comprehensive range of grievances voiced there. The failure of the king and his officials to observe the Charters formed their most continuous strand, and a provocation which united different social groups, but particular grievances arising from oppression in the counties, the depredations of the king's purveyors, and the king's disregard for the liberties of the church also drew on wide constituencies. Often these grievances were genuinely national because the incidences of the abuses which provoked them were also national. The fiscal exploitation increasingly associated with the eyre, for example, affected town and country, knights, freeholders, and villeins, and was the subject of loud and frequent complaints in parliament.[257] Henry's alien friends and relatives were likewise widely resented: by the magnates, for their greedy depletion of Henry's patronage resources and the royal poverty which this was thought to cause; by those in the countryside, for what one chronicler called 'the tyranny which they exercised in their lordships'. The extortions of their bailiffs, and the difficulties which even knights found in getting justice against them, helped to fuel the general undercurrent of local resentments which surfaced repeatedly in parliamentary complaints;[258] while the opposition to aliens on broader fiscal and political grounds was voiced there more explicitly and openly. Though the nature of their particular grievances might differ from one social group to another, the abuses reflected in those grievances were

---

[256] *Ann. Tewkesbury*, 102; *Paris*, v. 6–7.

[257] Maddicott, 'Magna Carta and the Local Community', 47–8.

[258] Ibid. 56; Carpenter, 'English Peasants in Politics, 1258–67', in his *Reign of Henry III*, 327–8; id., 'King, Magnates and Society', 101–2 and n. 132.

the common experience of many of the king's subjects, from barons to peasants. In voicing them those in parliament spoke for a larger public in the country.

The underlying cause of these developments was Henry's government: spendthrift, exacting, often oppressive, bearing down heavily on all except a few favoured groups of magnates and aliens, and the source of ill-judged decisions in foreign and domestic policy. One response from Henry's critics was a repeated emphasis on the need for consent in royal policy-making, again often expressed in parliament. Yet the political elevation of consent was only in part a reaction to contemporary discontents. It also owed much to the linkage of taxation and consent embodied in Magna Carta and to the widening categories of political decision-making subjected to conciliar consent during the minority. The later claims voiced in parliament to consent to the appointment of the great officials and to English intervention in Poitou and Sicily showed the extensive range of matters, beyond taxation, which parliament was now claiming to be able, if not to adjudicate, then at least to have a say in. The doctrine of 'Quod omnes tangit', though it was ostensibly applied only to taxation, is likely to have reinforced the view that national affairs were not the king's alone to decide; for after all many of the decisions which Henry took for himself *inconsulte*, especially those which committed his country to intervention overseas, had fiscal consequences. The broadening claims made in parliament for the right of consent to decisions which affected all the king's subjects was another significant mark of parliament's coming of age as a national assembly.

The varieties of men who attended parliament, the general and national nature of many of the grievances voiced there, and the expanding range of matters for which the right of consent was now claimed, all contributed to what is perhaps the most momentous development of the period: the emergence of a parliament which consciously stood for the whole realm. When the reformers who appeared before Louis IX in 1264 spoke of the tax conceded to Henry at the great council of 1225 as one granted in that year by the *communitas regni*, they were guilty only of a mild anachronism;[259] for certainly by the 1240s parliament could reasonably be seen as the embodiment of the community of the realm. The identification

---

[259] *DBM* 268–9; above, 107.

of the two could be seen most clearly in parliament's defence of the 'common good' of the realm against its adversaries. Parliamentary attacks on aliens, men such as William de Valence, the leader of the Lusignans, for example, frequently portrayed them as enemies of the whole kingdom. In the parliament of February 1248 the king was accused of bestowing on them 'all the goods of the kingdom (*omnia bona regni*)', and at the later July parliament of that year they were spoken of as 'enemies of the king and kingdom'.[260] The appointment of the three great officials was similarly seen as an issue which involved the interests of the kingdom. The right men, chosen by magnate consent, would strengthen 'the standing of the kingdom (*status regni*)', the king was told in the parliament of November 1244.[261] Those appointed, he was told again in the parliament of February 1248, were men who did not seek the advancement of the common weal but their own private interest (*nec qui rei publicae sed singularem quaerunt promotionem*), collecting money and obtaining wardships and revenues from themselves.[262] The magnates returned to the same theme in the parliament of April 1255, asking for an elected justiciar, chancellor, and treasurer 'for the common utility of the kingdom (*propter communem regni utilitatem*)'.[263] Henry's oppressive fiscal measures could similarly be seen as having implications for the whole kingdom, whose interests and resources they harmed. The written record of proceedings in the 1242 parliament stated that the amercements imposed in the eyre, along with other taxes, had oppressed and impoverished everyone in the kingdom (*omnes de regno ita gravantur et depauperantur*); while the further written record drawn up in the parliament of March 1257 gave as one of the magnates' reasons for declining to support Henry's Sicilian venture 'the destruction and impoverishment of the kingdom of England by divers and frequent judicial eyres and by extortions and many sorts of prises and oppressions'.[264] Prises had already been spoken of in the parliament of February 1248 as 'a scandal to the king and kingdom'.[265]

In all these cases those in parliament could be seen as the defenders of the kingdom's interests. In their outlook they were perhaps not so very distant from Professor Patrick Collinson's Elizabethan MPs, members of the *Republica Anglorum*, and, in their opposition to scandals such as monopolies, 'not only servants and subjects of a monarch but patriots and

---

[260] *Paris*, v. 6, 21.   [261] Ibid. iv. 363.   [262] Ibid. v. 7.
[263] *Ann. Burton*, 336; cf. *Paris*, v. 494.   [264] *Paris*, iv. 187; *Ann. Burton*, 387.   [265] *Paris*, v. 6.

citizens of a national commonwealth'.[266] Henry's 'patriots and citizens'
were the persecutors of the aliens who wasted the kingdom's resources,
the hostile critics of the eyres and taxes which impoverished its inhabitants,
and the proponents of the elected ministers intended to promote its
common welfare. Traditionally the promotion of the 'common good' and
the 'common utility' had been seen as primarily the duty of the ruler, in
association with his subjects.[267] Now, however, the roles of ruler and subject
were reversed. Henry's misgovernment, as his subjects saw it, had come
to be regarded as subverting the interests of the realm. Here was a ruler
who put his private interests above those of the state; while his subjects, as
represented in parliament, had come to stand for the advancement of the
common good, often against the king.

This situation both reflected and helped to make explicit two competing
ideologies. Henry took his stand on the prerogative. It was the prerogative
which he emphasized in the parliament of July 1248, when he made a
speech intended to parry the magnates' claims to share in the appointment
of the great officials. The magnates wished to bind him to their will, said
Henry. Every lord of a household had the right to appoint and dismiss his
officials, but this right the magnates presumed to deny him. They were
his servants, with no authority to impose on him conditions which would
make him their slave. No doubt his words gained force from his own
subjection to magnate control during his long minority, in appointments
as in much else, and his determination to avoid any repetition of what he
must have seen as humiliating circumstances. They were words echoed in
the arguments put into his mouth in the *Song of Lewes*, written in 1264,
and the consistency of the two accounts suggests that they reflected his
actual views. Just as an earl had the right to distribute castles, lands, and
revenues to whom he would, so too did the king. His unfettered power
protected the rights of the realm (*ius regni tuetur*), and to reduce it was to
make him a servant.[268] Henry's speech to the bishops in the parliament
of 1244, already cited in another context, had said something similar. 'I
am your prince and king', he had stated. 'Without you I cannot live, nor
you without me. Your being depends on me and mine on you, for if I

---

[266] P. Collinson, 'Servants and Citizens: Robert Beale and Other Elizabethans', *Historical Research*,
79 (2006), 491.
[267] Cf. Post, *Studies*, 372–8; Harriss, *King, Parliament and Public Finance*, 3–4, 22–3.
[268] *Paris*, v. 20; *The Song of Lewes*, ed. C. L. Kingsford (Oxford, 1896), 16–17, 43–4.

am rich you also are rich, if I am poor you also are poor.'[269] In Henry's uncompromising stance there was no concept of a public interest which was separable from that of the crown, of a realm whose interest might differ from that of its ruler. He saw the defence of his rights and liberties as a means to secure and protect those of others.[270] Yet it was just this concept of separate interests which was evolving through regular parliamentary criticism of Henry's policies and which parliament itself was coming to represent. 'Bracton' had already spoken of the barons' right to restrain an unjust king, and the *Song of Lewes*, speaking this time for the barons (and after the reforms of 1258–9), took the argument a stage further: Henry's great men had a duty to reform the realm when it was under threat, and in so doing they would restore the king's standing (*status regium*).[271] Radical though such a view was, it was no more than a logical extension of those advanced in the parliaments of the 1240s and 1250s. The realm was not an estate, a mere private interest, run for the benefit of its lord. It incorporated the notion of a public interest now recognized, defended, and represented by a parliament which acted in lieu of a king who had failed in his duty.

These parliaments did not forge an entirely new identity between their members and the common interests of the realm. The Charter itself, made by the sort of men who dominated later parliaments, had been a grant to 'all the free men of our realm', and in 1253 both magnates and prelates, meeting in parliament, could speak of it as 'the charter of the common liberties of the realm (*carta communium libertatum regni*)'.[272] The early notion that the realm could possess liberties was not far from the later notion that the realm could possess interests. Nor, it might be argued, was it parliament itself which was coming to be identified with those interests, but rather those who attended it, among whom the lay magnates were pre-eminent. Yet this is a distinction without a difference. Parliament provided the occasion which allowed grievances to be concerted, the platform from which they could be voiced, and the physical embodiment, through its varied membership, of a wide section

---

[269] Aberystwyth, National Library of Wales, MS Peniarth 390; Oxford, Bodleian Library, MS Digby, fo. 96ᵛ; above, 174.

[270] See his letters to the sheriffs, April 1244: *CR, 1242–7*, 242.

[271] Bracton, *De Legibus*, ed. Woodbine and Thorne, ii. 110; *Song of Lewes*, 17–23, 44–8. Cf. Carpenter, 'Justice and Jurisdiction', 40–2.

[272] Holt, *Magna Carta*, 450–1; *C. and S.* II. i. 477.

of the realm for whom its members spoke. Even before 1258 it was an institution which was more than the sum of those attending and which could be convincingly identified with the community of the realm. This was the most important political legacy of Henry's middle years to the baronial reform movement.

5

Consolidation
Parliament and Baronial Reform, 1258–1272

1. Parliament and the Reform Movement, 1258–1261

In 1258 the periodic conflicts which had marked Henry III's relations with his parliaments since the 1230s culminated in what was both a final crisis and a new beginning. For more than twenty years, complaint and protest, the tentative attempts to influence royal government, and even the denial of taxation, had all proved ineffectual in rectifying the grievances of the political community. The discontents caused by the king's failure to consult, his exploitation of the church, his thriftlessness, his fiscal harassment of the localities, his unwillingness or inability to discipline his local officials according to the supposed terms of Magna Carta, and, more immediately and pressingly, by his excessive favour to the Lusignans and his ill-judged pursuit of the Sicilian throne, had continued to accumulate. The only solution, as his baronial opponents now came to believe, lay in a thorough reform of the kingdom in which theirs would be the guiding hand. That some of their leaders, including Simon de Montfort himself, had formerly been attached to his court and members of his regime showed the depths of their disaffection. It was the division of the court against the king that finally brought the regime to heel.[1]

---

[1] Carpenter, 'What Happened in 1258?', 190–1.

The resulting reform movement of 1258–9 gave parliament a formal place in the country's government for the first time.[2] It played a central part in the novel realization of the political aspirations voiced in the assemblies of the previous twenty years. From being mere petitioners, pressing for a greater say in appointments, in the conduct of foreign affairs, and in royal policy in general, Henry's critics moved towards the only position which promised a satisfactory answer to their petitions: the appropriation of the king's authority. The Provisions of Oxford, drawn up in June 1258, saw the establishment of a baronial council and the institution of wholesale reforms in local and central government and, more surprisingly, in the administration of the barons' own estates. From these initiatives sprang the three main themes of the reform movement, the supervision of policy-making, the provision of justice, and the reform of the law, all three of them prosecuted in a series of administrative schemes and legislative *acta* which culminated in the Provisions of Westminster of October 1259. This was the high-water mark of reform and, as it turned out, the fulcrum of its decline. It was followed by widening divisions among the reformers themselves that prepared the way for Henry's resumption of power in 1261. The reaction came with Simon de Montfort's emergence as the leader of the opposition, his abortive attempts to organize that opposition in the summer of 1261, and his return to England, after more than a year's exile in France, in 1263. Montfort's reappearance precipitated disorder and civil war, marked by Henry's capture at the battle of Lewes in June 1264 and Montfort's own defeat in battle at Evesham in August 1265. With his death and the king's restoration both the whole reforming programme and the hopes vested in it seemed to have received their final quietus.

It is usual to see the last rather than the first part of the 'reform and rebellion' period as the more significant for the development of parliament. Simon de Montfort's summoning of the knights to parliament in June 1264 and of knights and burgesses in January 1265 is often thought to have marked the beginnings of local representation or even, and more vulgarly, of the foundation of parliament by Montfort himself: a popular myth which is astonishingly difficult to dispel. But we have already noted the presence in parliament before 1258 both of knights (though usually in the guise of lesser tenants-in-chief) and, more occasionally and less certainly,

---

[2] For the general history of the reform movement, see R. F. Treharne, *The Baronial Plan of Reform, 1258–63* (Manchester, 1932), 64–212, and Maddicott, *Simon de Montfort*, 151–91.

of burgesses; and important though Montfort's parliaments were, they should not be allowed to eclipse those of the early and more productive time of reform in 1258–9. The long-term significance of the reforming period for parliament's evolution lies in its opening phase as much as in its closing Montfortian coda. Though the battle of Evesham appeared to have discredited and vanquished both Montfort and reform, much of what had been established both in 1258–9 and 1264–5 survived. From these few years parliament emerged with its role enhanced rather than diminished. Yet it was no longer what it had been for much of the pre-1258 period, the embodiment of a national community set against the crown, but instead a reinvigorated part of the consensual apparatus of the state.

In the early stages of reform parliament was central to its processes in two ways: it provided a platform both for reform's launching and for its subsequent progress, and it was allocated a leading role in the reformers' schemes for the government of the country. It was at the Westminster parliament of 1258 that the baronial demands for general reforms were first made and then answered by Henry's agreeing to the establishment of a reforming committee of twenty-four.[3] Conventionally seen as the first act of the reforming period, this parliament also saw the last of the series of parliamentary confrontations which had perturbed Henry's relations with his magnates since the 1230s. In 1258, as so often before, confrontation was triggered by the king's request for a tax, arising, like the previous such requests of 1255 and 1257, from his Sicilian commitments. In March 1258 the papal legate had arrived in England bearing with him Pope Alexander IV's demand that Henry should meet his huge financial obligations for Sicily, including an immediate payment of 30,000 marks.[4] The April parliament was summoned to consider both this proposal and the consequent plea by Henry for a general tax to meet it. The tax which Henry had in mind was entirely unprecedented, both in its weight and its form: a levy of one-third, not only on moveables but also in 'immoveables'.[5] The earlier levies of 1225, 1232, and 1237 had been taken at the rates of a fifteenth, a fortieth, and a thirtieth, and the great tax for Richard's ransom had run to no more than a quarter. None of these levies had been combined

---

[3] For the April parliament, see esp. Carpenter, 'What Happened in 1258?', in his *Reign of Henry III*, 182–97.

[4] *Paris*, v. 493–4, 520–1, 530–1, 621–4; Lunt, *Financial Relations*, 278–81.

[5] *Paris*, v. 676; *Ann. Tewkesbury*, 163. The magnitude of the proposed tax has attracted surprisingly little comment from historians.

with the tax on immoveable land that was now apparently proposed. That Alexander had suggested Henry's turning to his subjects for this 'common subsidy', to support a project which, as the magnates later told the pope, he had undertaken in the teeth of their opposition, is likely to have deepened the parliamentarians' sense of outrage.[6]

In the armed demonstration in favour of reform which followed three days after Henry's request was made known, detestation of the Lusignans was a leading motive; but the linkage between tax and demonstration was equally direct.[7] The outcome of this stand-off was different from that of any of the parliamentary conflicts of the previous twenty years. In return for the king's enforced agreement to allow the reform of the realm by the committee of twenty-four, the magnates undertook, not to grant a tax, but to do what they could to ensure that one was granted by, in the king's words, 'the community of our realm'.[8] By comparison with previous confrontations prior to 1258, what now put the king's critics within sight of what they wanted was both their own coercive stand and Henry's complete inability to raise the money he needed without the community's cooperation. A parliamentary linkage was thus established between a general reform of abuses, going beyond the usual demand for the confirmation of Magna Carta, and the granting of taxation.[9] Yet in this case redress of grievances was in the way of being met with only the most tentative assurance of supply.

The parliament of April 1258 thus both epitomized and diverged from the parliamentary developments of the previous two decades. Conflicts in parliament over Henry's foreign ambitions, whether in Poitou, Normandy, or Sicily, and over the taxation needed to support them, had been commonplace since the 1240s. Nor were schemes of reform, hatched in parliament and often a response to those conflicts, a novelty in 1258. It was in the context of parliamentary bargaining over taxation that three barons had been added to the king's council in the parliament of January 1237 and that the Paper Constitution, with its visionary scheme for imposing controls

---

[6] Paris, vi. 400; Close Rolls (Supplementary), 1244–1266, 29–30; Carpenter, 'What Happened in 1258?', 184 n. 9.

[7] Carpenter, 'What Happened in 1258?', 187–8, does not give quite sufficient weight to the king's exorbitant tax demand as a cause of '1258'. The Tewkesbury annals make clear that the baronial demonstration was one consequence of that demand.

[8] DBM 74–7.

[9] P. Brand, Kings, Barons and Justices: The Making and Enforcement of Legislation in Thirteenth-Century England (Cambridge, 2003), 18.

on royal government, had been drafted in that of November 1244.[10] The agreement to set up the new reforming committee, taken in the April parliament, was therefore not unprecedented, either in its intention or its context. But Henry's now having to yield to the barons' demands, as he had never previously done except in the most temporary way, ended this whole long sequence of events. After April 1258 the issues of foreign policy, taxation, and consent, the stuff of parliamentary politics since the 1230s, largely disappeared from the political agenda. The Sicilian Business had effectively been wound up by the end of 1258;[11] the Treaty of Paris had settled Anglo-French relations by the end of 1259, putting a stop to Henry's plans for regaining lost territories which had often underlain his earlier tax demands;[12] and those demands were in any case not likely to be revived, for neither the baronial reformers nor Henry, in his intermittent periods of restored power, could justify attempts to impose taxation on a public whose support both sides needed. At the Oxford parliament of June 1258 a committee was set up to negotiate an aid for the king,[13] but nothing came of this initiative. It must in any case have evaporated with the Sicilian Business which had given rise to it. With the reformers in control, parliament now ceased to be the forum for confrontation between king and barons which it had so often been in the years before 1258 and became instead a positive instrument of government.

Its new role fully emerged in the Oxford parliament. The reforms enacted there—the appointment of a justiciar, the establishment of a new baronial council of fifteen, and all else recorded in the series of minuted decisions which became known as the Provisions of Oxford—were the work of the twenty-four, or more probably of the committee's baronial members. A further decision to allow the council to appoint the great officials emphasized the degree to which the new constitution had put the king's powers into commission.[14] In none of this was parliament the reformers' primary instrument. Under the terms of the Provisions that instrument was the baronial council, which was effectively given power to manage the kingdom. The council's role was in part an answer to parliament's main weakness in the years before 1258: its inability to influence the day-to-day workings of government.[15] Unlike parliament,

---

[10] Above, 180, 189.

[11] Lunt, *Financial Relations*, 280–2; Carpenter, 'What Happened in 1258?', 185–7.

[12] Maddicott, *Simon de Montfort*, 187–8.   [13] *DBM* 104–5.

[14] Ibid. 96–113, 222–3; Maddicott, *Simon de Montfort*, 57–9.   [15] Above, 179–80.

which was occasional, the council was to function all the year round. But the relationship between the two was complementary rather than hierarchical. The Provisions gave parliament a clearly defined place in the new scheme of things. It was to meet three times a year, on stated dates: on the octave of Michaelmas (6 October), the morrow of Candlemas (3 February), and 1 June. To these parliaments the king's elected councillors (that is, the fifteen) were to come 'to review the state of the realm and to deal with the common business of the realm and the king together'. 'The community' (*le commune*)—meaning the barons normally summoned to parliament—were also to choose twelve men to attend on the same occasions and to join the council in dealing with the same business; and the wider *commune* was to accept what these twelve should decide. The object of such representation, it was explained, was to avoid unnecessary expense to the community. A further clause named the chosen twelve 'to treat . . . of the common business': two bishops, an earl, and nine barons.[16]

These new rules reshaped existing practice towards an ideal end, and in doing so they regulated the role of parliament for the first time. Precision, system, and practicality were the keynotes of that regulation. The dates set for parliament's meetings were very roughly derived from the pattern obtaining before 1258, though the usual early summer parliament, previously summoned in most years with reference to the moveable feasts of Easter and Whitsun, was now given a fixed point in the calendar. More important, the intervals between the three meetings were almost exactly equal in length, at 17 weeks, 17 weeks, and 18 weeks, so partitioning the year into three divisions, each one terminated and initiated by a parliament.[17] The king had lost all initiative in deciding when to summon parliament and was now compelled to follow rules which epitomized the elements of foresight and order in the reformers' plans. The most transparent purpose of this new arrangement was to bring 'the common business of the realm' before regular assemblies containing both the new council, as the kingdom's effective governing body, and the representatives of baronage, and to prevent any imbalance in the accumulation of that business. The convening of the twelve representatives was not meant to

---

[16] *DBM* 110–11, 104–5.

[17] The only historian to have noticed this appears to be J. G. Edwards, *Historians and the Medieval English Parliament*, David Murray Lecture, University of Glasgow (repr. Glasgow, 1970), 17.

rule out participation by the wider baronage,[18] nor in fact did it do so;[19] it was a minimum requirement, intended not to exclude but merely to limit the inconvenience which attendance at parliament entailed. In some ways the council's role was a continuation of the work which the king's council had always undertaken at parliament time, at least since the mid 1230s.[20] But the close cooperation now envisaged between council and parliament, no more than a baronial ideal before 1258, put it on a different footing. Like the regular times for parliament's meetings, the operation of the council within parliament was an old practice to which reform gave new definition and a new direction.

Behind these mechanisms lay a much broader aim: to secure parliamentary consent to all major acts of policy-making, beyond the tax grants and legislation for which such consent had long been regarded as essential. The role which the Provisions gave to parliament was a riposte to Henry's disregard for consent which had been one of the main grievances of the previous twenty years. With parliament now meeting regularly and frequently, and established formally (and no longer merely by custom) as the voice of the community, the reformers might hope to prevent future follies of the 'Sicilian Business' sort, resulting from decisions taken behind closed doors by the king and his friends. As a regulated forum for public policy-making, parliament was one answer to what in the eighteenth century would have been called the politics of the closet. Now formally defined as the necessary arena for political discussion, it was seen as a means to embed consent within the constitution.

In the fifteen months following the Provisions, from July 1258 to October 1259, parliament continued to be the focus for reforming interests, just as it had been at Oxford. It provided the setting for two sorts of reform in particular: for administrative changes intended to secure equitable and just government, especially in the localities, and for legal reforms whose purposes were more miscellaneous but at least partly similar.

The two main administrative reforms of the period were both closely associated with parliament. The Ordinance of Sheriffs, which took the form of royal letters patent limiting the sheriff's powers by forbidding him to

---

[18] Cf. H. G. Richardson and G. O. Sayles, 'The Provisions of Oxford: A Forgotten Document and Some Comments', in *EPMA* iii. 8; Sayles, *The King's Parliament*, 56.

[19] For proof, see *DBM* 156–7, which suggests that the twelve dealt with the actual business of parliament, but in the presence of the wider baronage.

[20] For the earlier work of the council, see above, 185–6, 188–9.

take bribes or otherwise abuse his position, was issued on 2 October 1258, during the Michaelmas parliament, and is likely to have been discussed there.[21] Still more specifically 'parliamentary' was the Ordinance of the Magnates: an agreement between the council of fifteen and the twelve representatives of the community drawn up in the Candlemas parliament of February 1259. Its signatories promised to allow the wrongs done by their bailiffs to be corrected by the justiciar, to observe both Magna Carta and the reforming legislation already enacted and to be enacted, and to bind their own officials by oaths similar to those taken by the king's sheriffs.[22] The coming together of the fifteen and the twelve in parliament in order to limit their own powers (and presumably the powers of all those other magnates whom the twelve represented) followed precisely the lines laid down in the Provisions of Oxford for the conduct in parliament of 'the common business of the realm'.

But more consequential in the long term were the reforms of the law which were pursued throughout the period and which eventually bore fruit in the Provisions of Westminster, issued in the Michaelmas parliament of 1259. The significance of the Provisions lay partly in their bringing together a wide range of topics within a single legislative *actum* and so reviving a legislative tradition that had been dormant for many years. Their obvious precursors, and recognized as such by later lawyers, were the definitive 1225 text of Magna Carta and the Provisions of Merton of 1236.[23] Both were the products of conciliar assemblies and combined a variety of discrete legal rulings within a single text. The Provisions of Merton, for example, covered such diverse matters as dower, rights of common, and suit of court.[24] Both in the consent which they embodied and in their mixed contents they unconsciously reverted to the law-making principles of Anglo-Saxon England.

But for the most part legislation in Henry III's early and middle years had not been like this. Largely piecemeal and ad hoc, it had taken two other

---

[21] *DBM* 118–23. The Ordinance was issued on 20 October and writs *de expensis* for the knights attending parliament on 4 November: *CR, 1256–59,* 332–3. For the role of these knights, see below, 246.

[22] *DBM* 130–7; P. Brand, 'The Drafting of Legislation in Mid-Thirteenth-Century England', *Parliamentary History,* 9 (1990), 259; id., *Kings, Barons and Justices,* 31–2.

[23] Cf. Brand, *Kings, Barons and Justices,* 1–2, and id., 'English Thirteenth Century Legislation', in A. Romano (ed.), . . . *colendo iustitiam et iura colendo* . . . *Federico II legislatore del Regno de Sicilia nell'Europa del duecento* (Rome, 1997), 331–2. The latter is the best general survey of its subject.

[24] *CR, 1234–37,* 337–9; Powicke, *King Henry III,* 769–71.

forms. First, legislative *acta*, often indistinguishable from administrative orders, were sometimes drafted by the king's council (and not by the great council or by parliament), and then issued as letters patent or close. Usually addressing a narrow and precisely defined topic, some twenty to thirty acts of this sort are on record between 1219 and 1258. Typical was a conciliar ordinance of 1242 laying down that no chapters should henceforth be held by the Jews in England.[25] Different in origin and purpose but generically similar were the original writs drafted by the chancery, and occasioned by particular cases before the courts, in order to remedy new wrongs (to paraphrase 'Bracton'). The accumulation of legal change here was marked by the rapid expansion of the register of writs rather than by the emergence of anything like the later statute book. Under Edward I, wrote Maitland, 'to invent new remedies was to make new laws',[26] and this had been equally true of Henry III's reign. But the need for conciliar consent applied as much to law-making by writ as to other forms of legislation: Bishop Grosseteste reiterated an ancient principle when he stated in 1236 that 'laws cannot be made or changed without the counsel of the magnates and of the prince'.[27] Yet it is clear from complaints in parliament and others from church councils that in the decades before 1258 many new writs had lacked any such conciliar sanction. As Henry's opponents noted, the absence of a chancellor had made it easier for Henry to ignore the need for consent in yet another aspect of his governance.[28]

Before 1258 legislation, much of it reactive and extempore, had thus played no large part in the business of Henry III's parliaments. The reform movement changed this, putting a planned programme of legal reform on the agenda almost from the start. Its course has been meticulously traced by Dr Paul Brand.[29] One of the opening texts of reform, the Petition of the Barons—a medley of grievances coming from a variety of social groups, brought forward at the Oxford parliament and probably endorsed

---

[25] *CR, 1237–42*, 464. For a list of Henry's legislative acts, see Adams, *Councils and Courts*, 325–32.

[26] F. Pollock and F. W. Maitland, *The History of English Law before the Time of Edward I*, 2nd edn., 2 vols. (Cambridge, 1898), i. 196.

[27] *Early Registers of Writs*, ed. E. de Haas and G. D. G. Hall, Selden Soc. 89 (1970), pp. xi–xxii; Grosseteste, *Epistolae*, ed. Luard, 96. Cf. *Select Cases of Procedure without Writ under Henry III*, ed. H. G. Richardson and G. O. Sayles, Selden Soc. 60 (1941), pp. xxiii–xxv; Brand, 'English Thirteenth Century Legislation', 337–8.

[28] *C. and S.* II. i. 420, 535 and n. 1, 547; *Paris*, iv. 363, 367; B. Wilkinson, 'The Invention of Original Writs in the Thirteenth Century', in his *Studies in the Constitutional History of the Thirteenth and Fourteenth Centuries*, esp. 219–20.

[29] Brand, 'Drafting of Legislation', 243–71; id., *King, Barons and Justices*, 15–41.

there by the magnates—already contained some six to twelve clauses seeking changes in the law.[30] It was probably at the following Michaelmas parliament of 1258 that it was agreed that the judges should meet to decide what legal changes were needed, with one meeting to be held eight days in advance of the next parliament.[31] The implied intention to bring forward proposals for change in parliament was given substance at the following Candlemas parliament of 1259. Here a preliminary French text known as the Provisions of the Barons, setting out draft reforms mainly concerning suit of court and the sheriff's tourn, was probably discussed in parliament, amended there, and subsequently published in Latin, still as a draft, after parliament's conclusion. The unusual step of publishing a draft may have been taken in order to show that progress in reform was being made.[32] Much of the content of the Provisions of the Barons received definitive legal form in nine of the twenty-four clauses of the Provisions of Westminster, published in the Westminster parliament of October 1259.[33]

The protracted course of reform, spanning the sixteen months which separated the Petition of the Barons from the Provisions of Westminster, gave parliament a novel prominence. It had been associated throughout with all the preliminary moves towards legal reform as well as with the complementary reform of the administrative malpractices of sheriffs and others. What social forces were at work here, and how they were brought to bear on the process of change in parliament, are questions easier to ask than to answer. As far as can be seen, the parliaments of the period were baronial, ecclesiastical, and ministerial assemblies of the traditional sort; the actual drafting of reform was the work of magnates, judges, and legal experts;[34] and there is no certain evidence that any parliament included either the minor tenants-in-chief or still less the elected knights of the shire who had made their first appearance in 1254. Nothing in the work of the reformers suggests that they envisaged the formal summoning of the knights to parliament. Yet the influence of the social groups of whom these latter were the leaders was clearly omnipresent. One distinctive mark of the whole reforming programme was its responsiveness to the needs of the

---

[30] *DBM* 76–91; Brand, 'Drafting of Legislation', 247–8; id., *King, Barons and Justices*, 20–2.

[31] Richardson and Sayles, 'Provisions of Oxford', 33; Brand, *King, Barons and Justices*, 26–7 (modifying id., 'Drafting of Legislation', 252).

[32] *DBM* 122–31; Brand, 'Drafting of Legislation', 253–62; id., *King, Barons and Justices*, 27–33.

[33] Brand, 'Drafting of Legislation', 265–6; id., *King, Barons and Justices*, 33–7.

[34] Brand, *King, Barons and Justices*, 25–7, 31 n. 57, 394.

local societies from which the knights came, and its attempts to reform both local government and seigneurial administration in their interests. The initial Petition of the Barons included several grievances coming explicitly from the small and middling men of the localities. Knights and free tenants (*milites et libere tenentes*), for example, were singled out as the victims of arbitrary amercements by the sheriffs for non-attendance at sessions of the assize justices; and it was surely the lesser landholders whom the petitioners had in mind when they complained that magnates unscrupulously dispossessed *minores* whose lands and debts had been transferred to them by Jews to whom the *minores* owed money.[35] The subsequent Provisions of Oxford set up knightly panels in each county to collect complaints, and Hugh Bigod, the new justiciar, was sent on eyre into the provinces to begin delivering the justice which was the reformers' watchword.[36] From the start local voices were to make themselves heard.

But it was only with the Provisions of Westminster, the centrepiece of the reform movement and its most enduring achievement, that popular complaint was definitively addressed. The Provisions were particularly important in providing remedies for some of the main abuses associated with Henry's misgovernment of the localities in the years leading up to 1258. Under their terms, the exploitative levying of the murdrum fine in cases of accidental death, the amercement of villages for failing to turn out in full for coroners' inquests, and other practices introduced in the eyres of the 1240s and 1250s for purely fiscal reasons were now prohibited.[37] Further clauses curtailed the sheriff's power to demand attendance at his tourn and to amerce those absent, prohibited the imposition of beaupleder fines, levied on a county's suitors in advances of any mistakes which they might make in their judgements, and—perhaps most important of all—limited the lord's right to exact suit of court, a major cause of local discontent prior to 1258.[38] To more general advantage, mesne procedure

---

[35] Provs. Westminster, cls. 19, 25: *DBM* 84–7. Cf. Brand, 'Drafting of Legislation', 250; P. R. Coss, 'Sir Geoffrey de Langley and the Crisis of the Knightly Class in Thirteenth-Century England', *Past and Present*, 68 (1975), 29 and n. 124.

[36] Treharne, *Baronial Plan*, 108–17, 145–56; A. H. Hershey, 'Success or Failure? Hugh Bigod and Judicial Reform during the Baronial Movement, June 1258–February 1259', *TCE* 5 (1995), 66–82. For justice and reform, see Maddicott, *Simon de Montfort*, 353–4.

[37] Provs. Westminster, cls. 22 (murdrum), 21 (inquests): Brand, *King, Barons and Justices*, 424–7. For comment, see Maddicott, 'Magna Carta and the Local Community', 47, and Brand, *King, Barons and Justices*, 77–90.

[38] Provs. Westminster, cls. 1–3 (suit of court), 4 (tourn), 5 (beaupleder): Brand, *King, Barons and Justices*, 414–19. Comment: ibid. 43–53, 81–90.

in civil litigation was speeded up and other measures were put in hand to improve the efficiency of the royal courts.[39] If these new rulings lacked the manifest radicalism of the constitutional changes brought in by the earlier Provisions of Oxford which had made them possible, they were nevertheless of the greatest interest and prospective advantage to provincial communities. They favoured tenants against lords,[40] they backed the small man against the justices and sheriffs who were the king's agents, and they extended the benefits of reform to freeholders in the counties who were well below the social level of the knights. Even the villeins, still further down the social scale, stood to gain from the restrictions on the levying of the murdrum fine and on the holding of inquests. In all this the Provisions provided the reformers with a potentially broad and solid basis of local support, and they were accordingly given the widest publicity. After their making in 'a great and long parliament' the London chronicler reports that they were read out in Westminster Hall in the presence of 'many earls and barons and innumerable people'. The excommunication of those who broke them, by the archbishop of Canterbury and the other bishops dressed in full pontificals, added to the solemnity of the occasion.[41] Still more so than at the Oxford assembly of 1258, parliament and reform were now ineluctably associated in the public mind, brought together in this final scene with a degree of ceremonial theatricality previously exploited only by the king.[42]

Despite the lack of evidence for the summoning of the knights to these parliaments, it remains likely that the local opinion which lay behind the reforming programme was made known at the centre by local men and that parliament was its reception point. This was another way in which the reform movement served to enlarge the function of parliament. Of course, the necessity of reform may in part have been common knowledge, transmitted as if by osmosis and without any need for its formal expression. Anyone attending the parliaments of the previous twenty years would have been aware of the feelings against local officials, of the insufficiency of Magna Carta to restrain them, and of public hostility towards the eyre. But at most of these reforming parliaments there were very probably knights on hand to provide more direct information. Given the customary attendance of the lesser tenants-in-chief at tax parliaments, under the

---

[39] Provs. Westminster, cls. 6, 7, 8, 23: Brand: *King, Barons and Justices*, 418–21. Comment: ibid. 69–76.

[40] Ibid. 43, 390–1.   [41] *De Antiquis Legibus Liber*, 42.   [42] Above, 183.

terms of the Charter, it is unlikely that Henry would have asked for his huge tax of a third at the opening Westminster parliament of April 1258 without summoning them. Perhaps they were among the *milites* whom the Tewkesbury annals place alongside the earls and barons in forcing Henry to accept reform.[43] When, at the same parliament, the magnates responded to Henry's request by undertaking to do what they could to ensure that an aid was granted by 'the community of [the] realm', they recognized their inability to grant a tax by themselves and perhaps the need for the presence of a wider group at the next, Oxford, parliament.[44] There must certainly have been very large numbers of knights in Oxford during that parliament, for the assembly coincided with a feudal muster, the preliminary to a Welsh campaign, to which 137 tenants-in-chief had been summoned. The chroniclers point to a huge gathering of both *majores* and *minores*, including many baronial followers. They probably included William de Lisle, a leading knightly landholder from the Isle of Wight, summoned to attend on him at Oxford by Aymer de Valence, bishop of Winchester.[45] Whether present as lesser tenants-in-chief, owing both military service and parliamentary service as a consequence of their tenure, or as baronial tenants and retainers, the knights will have been out in force. They were perhaps among the bearers of the local grievances which went to the making of the Petition of the Barons and the Provisions of Oxford. It may have been intended to involve some directly in the business of taxation, via the committee of twenty-four established at Oxford to negotiate the king's tax. Although the committee's members were almost exclusively episcopal and baronial, they included at least one non-baronial figure, Sir Fulk de Kerdiston, a member of the knightly panel appointed to collect complaints in Norfolk; while two alternative versions of the committee listing include another knight, Sir John de Oare, a former sheriff of Somerset and Dorset, and a member of the panel for Somerset.[46] Neither was among the tenants-in-chief summoned for military service.

---

[43] *Ann. Tewkesbury*, 163–4.

[44] *DBM* 74–7; Brand, *King, Barons and Justices*, 17.

[45] *CR, 1256–59*, 294–6, 299; *Ann. Burton*, 438; *Paris*, v. 695–6; *The Chronicle of William de Rishanger of the Barons' Wars*, ed. J. O. Halliwell, Camden Soc. (London, 1840), 8; *Flores Historiarum*, ed. H. R. Luard, 3 vols., RS (London, 1870), iii. 253; Maddicott, *Simon de Montfort*, 156–7. For William de Lisle, see Sayles, *Functions*, 64, and Denholm-Young, 'Robert Carpenter and the Provisions of Westminster', 175–6.

[46] *DBM* 104–7; Richardson and Sayles, 'Provisions of Oxford', 6, 31; *CPR, 1247–58*, 648; *List of Sheriffs of England and Wales*, Public Record Office, Lists and Indexes, ix (London, 1898), 122.

Even among the higher ranks of the reformers, one or two knights thus had a place.

At the Michaelmas parliament of 1258 which followed that at Oxford the knights had a more formal presence. Those from at least fifteen shires were in attendance, not as elected representatives, but as bearers of the written complaints of their localities, collected under the terms of the Provisions of Oxford for delivery before the council at Westminster on 6 October. The information which they provided about local abuses probably contributed both to the Ordinance of Sheriffs, issued on 20 October, and to the ongoing process of law reform about to be taken up by the justices.[47] Nothing is then known of the presence of knights at the centre until we reach the Westminster parliament of October 1259. There 'the community of the bachelors of England' made their famous protest that, although the king had submitted to reforms, the barons had as yet done nothing for the common good (*ad utilitatem reipublicae*): a protest which, according to the annals of Burton, helped to expedite the issuing of the Provisions of Westminster.[48] Whether retainers of the parliamentary magnates (as seems most likely) or as men sent by their counties, the bachelors represented a collective knightly voice, favouring reform, using the language of the common good which had emerged in the parliaments of the 1240s and 1250s,[49] and speaking in parliament. In some of these ways their protest linked back to the grievances presented earlier in the Petition of the Barons.

The evidence thus points to the presence of knights in most of the parliaments of the early reform period, though they were brought there by means which, so far as we can see, were generally informal or ad hoc rather than as a result of direct summons or election. Whether they came as feudal tenants, baronial retainers, or as bearers of complaints from their counties, however, their attendance in parliament created another link between the reformers and their provincial supporters and strengthened parliament's role as a point of contact between government and provinces. It must also have provided a means of transmitting information not only from localities to centre but in the reverse direction too. The Provisions of Oxford,

---

[47] *DBM* 98–9, 112–15; Treharne, *Baronial Plan*, 115; Brand, *King, Barons and Justices*, 27.

[48] *Ann. Burton*, 471; Maddicott, *Simon de Montfort*, 184–5.

[49] Above, 228–31. To judge by the presence of the Provisions in the Burton annals and the copy once held at St Albans, the parliamentary abbots may have been among the main distributors of the text: *Ann. Burton*, 446–53; *Flores Historiarum*, ed. Luard, ii. 473–4; *DBM* 96.

for example, were essentially conciliar memoranda and never formally published, but the survival of at least three copies into the seventeenth century suggests that some of those attending at Oxford may have returned home with this foundation text for the new order in their saddlebags.[50] And among the audience who heard the Provisions of Westminster read aloud in Westminster Hall are likely to have been some of those 'bachelors' who had earlier complained about the slow progress of reform and who could now depart satisfied for their counties.

Parliament was thus central to the reforming programme of 1258–9. More than ever before, it was an occasion which brought together, in a newly prescriptive way, the leading groups in the political community: the council of fifteen, the baronage, the judges and lawyers probably most responsible for the drafting of legislation, and, by looser and more informal routes, the knights of the localities. For the first time it provided a matrix for planned legislation on a large scale, setting an important precedent for the great Edwardian statutes of the 1270s and 1280s. But perhaps still more significant was parliament's emergence as a popular institution, the occasion for beneficial changes in law and government which worked to the advantage not only of the gentry but of the ordinary freeholders, and to a lesser extent even the villeins, who formed the bulk of the rural population. Equally striking was the degree to which the new legislation ran contrary to the interests of the magnates who dominated the council: interests now voluntarily subordinated to the 'common good' for which the community of the bachelors had spoken out at the Westminster parliament of October 1259.[51] If the peasantry had direct contact with the mechanism of reform, through the complaints which they brought before Hugh Bigod's eyre,[52] it remains more likely that the knights were the chief mediators of popular complaint, as they certainly were in the reports which they delivered from their counties at the Michaelmas parliament of 1258. Here they took on a representative role more visibly and explicitly than at any time in the past. But that role also belonged to parliament itself. In responding to

[50] Richardson and Sayles, 'Provisions of Oxford', 3–4. But for a more positive view of the Provisions, which sees them not as mere memoranda but as formal and binding legislation, see C. Valente, 'The Provisions of Oxford: Assessing/Assigning Authority in Time of Unrest', in R. F. Berkhofer III, A. Cooper, and A. J. Kosto (eds.), *The Experience of Power in Medieval Europe, 950–1350* (Aldershot, 2005), 25–41.

[51] Brand, *King, Justices and Barons*, 43, 390–1. For some possible reasons for the magnates' willingness to limit their own powers, see Maddicott, *Simon de Montfort*, 166–70.

[52] For examples, see Hershey, 'Success or Failure? Hugh Bigod and Judicial Reform', 75–7.

popular grievances, and as the forge and workshop of the whole reforming enterprise, it had become the political embodiment of a community of the realm more concrete and more socially extensive than any previously imagined.

For the first eighteen months of the reform movement parliament had played the role assigned to it in the Provisions of Oxford. It met regularly at or near the appointed times, and in it the conciliar fifteen and the baronial twelve worked together.[53] If its functions remained in part traditional and routine—for example, it continued to provide an occasion for the settlement of deferred judicial pleas[54]—they had also widened to take in much of the realm's 'common business' from which parliament had been largely excluded before 1258. In the long term, legislation proved to be the most important item on the business agenda. But foreign affairs were also prominent, notably the negotiating of a peace settlement with France, the final stages of which were worked out over the three parliaments of 1259.[55] At the last of these assemblies, in October 1259, parliament reached the apogee of its reforming prominence. Its standing in the new order was reinforced not only by the proclamation of the Provisions of Westminster, but also by a number of administrative decisions taken in this parliament. Councillors were to be appointed to attend on the king from one parliament to another. They were to be changed at parliament and their actions reviewed there. Any important matters arising between parliaments were, if possible, to be dealt with by these councillors or else deferred to the next parliament. If neither of these alternatives proved possible, then the whole council was to be summoned. The three great officials, justiciar, chancellor, and treasurer, were to remain in office until the next parliament. Reforms needed at the exchequer and at the exchequer of the Jews were to be decided on before the next parliament (implying that they would later be discussed there).[56] Ad hoc though these decisions were, and in their textual form memoranda rather than legislation, they emphasized the role of parliament as the proper occasion for making—and by implication securing consent to—major appointments and, more generally, for dealing with all other important business. But they were also a vote of confidence in parliament's reforming credentials. Had it not been effective at doing

---

[53] See e.g. *DBM* 132–3, 156–7.   [54] See e.g. Sayles, *Functions*, 81–2.
[55] Maddicott, *Simon de Montfort*, 178–9, 181–2, 185–6.
[56] *DBM* 150–1, 154–5. For this text, see Brand, 'Drafting of Legislation', 264 n. 108.

the work assigned to it in the Provisions of Oxford, it is hardly likely that these new responsibilities would have come its way.

The parliament which should have followed that for October 1259, at Candlemas 1260, proved to be a turning point in the closely connected destinies of parliament and reform, and one which marked the king's recognition of the centrality of parliament to the whole reform movement. In a well-known episode, Henry, writing from France, ordered the justiciar, Hugh Bigod, to postpone the meeting of parliament until his return. He used the pretext of a Welsh attack on the castle of Builth in the marches, which was presumably thought to necessitate the presence of the magnates there rather than in London.[57] In prohibiting the Candlemas parliament Henry deliberately challenged the Provisions of Oxford, which had provided for such a parliament; though, to be fair to Henry, they had said nothing about what was to happen if the king was absent, a circumstance probably not even envisaged by their makers. Henry's aims, however, were aggressive. He sought to disrupt the regular relationship between the council and the body of the magnates which parliament was intended to facilitate, and to remove the platform from which further reforms might be launched.[58] In a telling and carefully calculated afterthought he ordered that common justice should continue to be done to all by the justiciar; thus indicating that no failure in the sequence of parliaments was to disrupt the dispensation of justice, one of the traditional functions of parliament and, in the hands of the justiciar, one of the most popular aspects of reform.[59] While undermining the institutions of reform, Henry was making a bid for the support of reform's beneficiaries. In defiance of the king's orders, and in an equally calculated and public defence of the Provisions, Simon de Montfort came to London to hold the parliament, but was countered by the justiciar's adjournment of the assembly.[60] Henry's intervention had had the incidental effect of setting two of the leading reformers at odds with each other. But his intention, and achievement, was to subvert the large place which parliament had come to occupy in the reformers' plans.

The later history of parliament was to show that the developments of 1258–9 had made a significant mark on parliament's evolution. This was not immediately obvious, however, and could not have been foreseen. After 1259, and in the short term, parliament ceased to be of much importance,

[57] *DBM* 168–9; cf. 172–3.
[58] For discussion, see Treharne, *Baronial Plan*, 219–23; Maddicott, *Simon de Montfort*, 192–3.
[59] *DBM* 172–3.   [60] Ibid. 206–7.

as the king gradually regained the initiative which he had lost in 1258. The reformers divided, the council's activity declined, and the stream of reforming legislation dried up. Although parliaments continued to meet, they had little in common with those of 1258–9. That of May 1260 brought Henry's reconciliation with his son Edward after Edward's dalliance with the reformers, and that of July 1260 saw Montfort's inconclusive 'trial' for his various acts of contumacy.[61] Parliament was now once again an instrument more to the king's purpose than to that of the reformers, and Henry was careful to avoid any step likely to provoke a confrontation there. His levying a tallage in June, probably to pay for the defence of the marches, showed that he had no intention of seeking the general aid for which parliamentary consent, and with it presumably the summoning of the lesser landholders, would have been necessary.[62]

Only the assembly of October 1260 stood outside this sequence as an isolated 'reform parliament'. It saw Montfort's return to prominence, the replacement of the three great officials, and the modification in the magnates' interests of earlier legislation against their abusive practices. Both these last measures were acts of the baronial council, prominent once again at parliament time.[63] This parliament was the last of its kind. The next assembly, the Candlemas parliament of February 1261, met at the season stipulated by the Provisions of Oxford. But to it Henry summoned his supporters in arms and its venue was the Tower, not Westminster, provoking the barons to refuse to attend on the grounds that parliaments had customarily been held at Westminster and nowhere else.[64] Their action showed how closely parliaments were now associated with the realm's headquarters. Taking the longer view, we may say that the whole sequence of events since the Provisions of Westminster—Henry's prohibition of the 1260 Candlemas parliament, his unwillingness to voice any request for a subsidy, and his final summoning of parliament to the security of the Tower—demonstrated his anxiety to undermine and circumvent parliament. It also demonstrated, at least by implication, parliament's key role in the whole process of reform and the restraints on royal authority which reform entailed.

---

[61] Treharne, *Baronial Plan*, 233, 238–41; Maddicott, *Simon de Montfort*, 195, 197–8.

[62] Mitchell, *Studies in Taxation*, 289.

[63] *Flores Historiarum*, ed. Luard, ii. 456–7; DBM 212–15, 222–3; Maddicott, *Simon de Montfort*, 200–3.

[64] *Flores Historiarum*, ed. Luard, ii. 463–4; *Ann. Dunstable*, 217; Treharne, *Baronial Plan*, 252; Maddicott, *Simon de Montfort*, 207.

During the summer of 1261, as Henry moved towards the resumption of full power, no parliament met. This disruption of the pattern of meetings established by the Provisions, which had subsisted long after reforming legislation had ceased, marked the end of a period.

2. The Montfortian Parliaments, 1261–1265

Henry's resumption of power in the summer of 1261 was underpinned by his securing papal absolution from his oath to the Provisions and by his dismissal of the baronial sheriffs appointed during the early period of reform.[65] It gave rise, first, to a period of confrontation between the king and the remaining baronial reformers, led by Simon de Montfort and backed by whatever local or foreign support Montfort could muster; and then, from 1263, to a more disturbed time of civil disorder, from which Montfort emerged as the leader of a new but short-lived regime. In these years conditions were too unfavourable to the rump of the reformers, or simply too chaotic and uncertain, for the promotion of new reforms. It is true that the Provisions of Westminster were reissued, with some amendments, both in January and in June 1263. But this was done on the king's initiative. The preamble to the new text had a distinctively royalist slant, and the reissue was a bid for support, unconnected with parliament, rather than a further stage in the reforming programme.[66] Competition between king and barons for support, especially that of the middling and minor provincial landholders who were the chief beneficiaries of the Provisions, was indeed the keynote of the period. In this struggle the role designated for parliament in 1258–9, as a forum for coordinating reformist initiatives, securing consent, bringing together council and magnates, and promulgating legislation, was at best secondary. Instead, it came to be seen in an alternative way: as a device for drawing in and winning over the uncommitted by appealing to their interests, most notably the interests of the knights of the localities and those whom they represented. Their role in these later parliaments of the reforming period was part of the period's permanent legacy.

Competition via parliament for the allegiances of the knights first became evident in 1261, when Simon de Montfort, the earl of Gloucester, and

---

[65] Treharne, *Baronial Plan*, 250–79; Maddicott, *Simon de Montfort*, 203–15.
[66] Brand, *King, Barons and Justices*, 140–8, 430–49 (text of the reissues); Maddicott, *Simon de Montfort*, 221, 226, 228.

the bishop of Worcester summoned three knights from each county to meet them at St Albans on 21 September: an incidental testimony to the baronial sympathies of the monks of St Albans, whose house can have been the only meeting place envisaged for so large a gathering. The episode is known, not from any surviving Montfortian summons, but from the mention of such a summons in the king's counter-orders to the sheriffs to direct the knights to an alternative venue at Windsor. In addition, we have a letter to the chancellor from Philip Basset, Henry's justiciar, telling him to ask the king to dispatch letters to Roger de Somery, a prominent baron. Somery was to be directed to come to the king's parliament—a word not used in Henry's own letter—rather than to St Albans, where he proposed to go.[67] This phantom parliament at St Albans was an incident in Montfort's comprehensive attempts to rally assistance at home and abroad in opposition to Henry's growing authority.[68] It showed not only the importance which both sides attached to the support of the knights, and to assemblies as a way of concentrating and rallying knightly allegiances, but also something of the knights' intended role. They had been summoned to St Albans, said Henry, 'to consider with [their Montfortian summoners] the common business of our realm (*super communibus negociis regni nostri*)'. This was a clear echo of the words used in the Provisions of Oxford to define parliament's work; and the principle which it embodied was taken up by the king, who called the knights to Windsor to share in discussions concerning peace with the barons. That he also intended, according to his letters to the sheriffs, to show them that he intended to do nothing 'save what is for the honour and common utility of our realm' was a further indication of the importance of knightly opinion and goodwill. These assets Henry was plainly seeking to cultivate. If his prohibition borrowed its wording from Montfort's summons, as seems probable, both sides clearly envisaged the knights as active participants in parliament. Going beyond their main pre-1258 function of sharing in discussions over taxation, and apparently not regarded merely as witnesses to or ratifiers of what their superiors decided, they were potentially given their head as a political force in parliament. Even more sharply than in the years before 1258, partisan politics provided an important stimulus to parliament's development.

One further point of significance, not always recognized, attached to Montfort's projected parliament at St Albans. This was the first time

---

[67] *DBM* 246–9; Sayles, *Functions*, 97–8.   [68] Maddicott, *Simon de Montfort*, 212–13.

since 1254 when we can be sure that the knights were summoned to parliament, not as lesser tenants-in-chief, but on a county basis. Whether this entailed election in the county court, as in 1254, or nomination by the sheriff, or a combination of the two, we do not know; though the king's countermanding letters to the sheriffs suggest that the latter had a role in the knights' dispatch. This shadowy occasion, rather than the better-known summoning of the knights to the parliaments of June 1264 and January 1265, was perhaps the real turning point in the history of county representation, inaugurating as it did an enduring connection between knights, counties, and parliament. An immediate precedent of a rather inexact sort was provided by the coming of the knights to the Michaelmas parliament of 1258, bearing the complaints of their counties. But it is much more likely that Montfort had in mind the parliament of April 1254, to which elected knights had been summoned, which they almost certainly attended—and at which Montfort himself had been present.[69] He had already seen, if sight were needed, how the knights could be used to represent, enlist, and direct the local opinion on which the reforming cause was so reliant.

The outcome neither of Montfort's summons nor of Henry's counter-summons is known. But the king's prompt action at least showed the danger which he saw from an independent parliament, convened by his opponents and drawing on a wide membership. The danger was not quite that anticipated by Henry when he had forbidden the Candlemas parliament of 1260: that parliament, meeting in the king's absence and under the terms of the Provisions, would continue to provide a focus for reform and for new restraints on royal authority. In 1261, when reform was all but dead, Henry's fears must have been rather that parliament would serve as a rallying point for opposition—and possibly armed opposition—to the crown. Those same fears probably underlay Henry's actions in relation to parliament when he was again abroad in the autumn of 1262. In his absence a parliament was held by the royalist justiciar Philip Basset. To it came Simon de Montfort, on a lightning visit from France, apparently bearing a letter from the pope ordering the observance of the Provisions of Oxford, which Montfort showed to 'the barons of the land' who were present. He clearly judged that it was at a meeting of parliament that such a momentous announcement would make its greatest impact. Nearly a fortnight later, and perhaps in response to this incident, Henry wrote to

---

[69] *Paris*, v. 440; above, 212–14.

Basset and the other great officials, ordering them to prevent the holding of any parliaments before his return to England.[70] It is likely that he too had identified parliament as a means by which his magnates might be brought together, their opinions swayed, and their opposition concerted.

But by April 1263, when Montfort returned to England again, Henry had once more lost the initiative and was in no position to dominate parliament through his ministers, to prohibit its meetings, or to otherwise impose his will. In the spring and summer of 1263 there were countrywide attacks on the royalists, on others opposed to the Provisions, and on their property. Montfort used parliament in September to ratify an eventual settlement which had the restoration of the Provisions of Oxford as its centrepiece: prelates and barons were convened 'so that the assent of the community might be sought' to his measures. By this stage the 'Provisions of Oxford' had come to embrace the whole reforming programme of 1258–9, subsuming the Provisions of Westminster within a broader framework.[71] Both at this parliament, however, and at another which followed in October, there was dissension between the despoilers and the despoiled. Montfort's attempts to utilize parliament to consider 'the common business of the realm', and at the same time to appeal for support to a broad political constituency, had backfired.[72] After this, as disorder expanded into civil war, there were to be no more parliaments for many months. The interval between that of October 1263 and the next, in June 1264, was the longest without a parliament since the reform movement had begun.

This period was ended by Montfort's victory at Lewes in May 1264. The two parliaments which met in June 1264 and January 1265, during his subsequent period of power, are among the best known of the thirteenth century. They owe their fame to Montfort's summoning of the knights from the counties and, in the case of the second parliament, of burgesses from the towns: expedients which, though largely forced on him by dangerous circumstances, were to set important precedents for the future. The first parliament met against a background of immediate triumph but lurking disaster. The great battle which Montfort had won a few weeks earlier had exalted his leadership and given him control of the king, his brother, and his eldest son. But the royalist barons of the Welsh

---

[70] Sayles, *Functions*, 99; *CR, 1261–64*, 162; Maddicott, *Simon de Montfort*, 219.

[71] *Ann. Dunstable*, 224; *Ann. Tewkesbury*, 176; *Flores Historiarum*, ed. Luard, ii. 484; Maddicott, *Simon de Montfort*, 185.

[72] Maddicott, *Simon de Montfort*, 242–3.

marches were still at large, royalist castles in the north and west remained unsubdued, an invasion force was gathering in France, and in France too was the papal legate, armed with a battery of sanctions, including excommunication and interdict, which could be launched against the rebels.[73]

In these circumstances the purposes of the June parliament were more instant than long term: to consolidate Montfort's position in power, rally support for him, provide for the government of the kingdom, and work out a common approach to the gathering dangers. In moving towards these objectives, parliament's work was chiefly a matter of giving public authority to the country's new leaders, whose existing authority rested on little more than victory in battle and the divine approval which it was thought to demonstrate. To this end parliament endorsed a new constitution setting up a new council of nine headed by a triumvirate, among whom Montfort was the chief, and effectively transferring the king's powers, including the vital power to appoint ministers, to the new council.[74] It marked a crucial assertion of parliamentary sovereignty that 'the community of prelates and barons' was authorized if necessary to remove and replace the three leaders.[75] In the restraints on the crown which its controlling circle reinstated, the parliament of June 1264 was thus in direct descent from the Oxford assembly of June 1258. But it went further than the Provisions of Oxford by confirming power to a narrow group, without regard for the regular and wider consultation envisaged in 1258. In this respect it was more radical than any of its predecessors. That it also discussed the coming of the legate, deciding to bar his entry into England, may have seemed to contemporaries a complementary and no less necessary part of its work.[76]

In these arrangements, and in the structure of parliament, the knights had an essential place denied to them in 1258. They came in response to orders issued on 4 June to Montfort's local keepers of the peace: they were to provide for the election in each county of four knights who were to discuss 'our business and the business of our realm' (the voice was Henry's but the hand was Montfort's) with the king, prelates, and magnates at the forthcoming parliament due to meet in London on 22 June.[77] The numbers

---

[73] Ibid. 282–5.   [74] DBM 294–9; Maddicott, *Simon de Montfort*, 285–7.
[75] DBM 296–7.
[76] J. Heidemann, *Papst Clemens IV: Das Vorleben des Papstes und sein Legationregister* (Münster, 1903), 200.
[77] DBM 290–3; Maddicott, *Simon de Montfort*, 285.

summoned were remarkable—only two per county had been summoned in 1254 and only three in 1261—and testified to Montfort's concern to draw into his enterprise as many as possible of the counties' leading men. We do not know how many appeared at a meeting called at less than three weeks' notice, but, had they all done so, some 140 would have been present—a group much larger than that of the prelates and magnates combined.[78]

Like the writs for the phantom parliaments of 1261, those issued for the June parliament imply that 'the business of our realm' was as much for the knights as for the magnates, and what we know of the knights' activity in parliament shows that this prescription was followed. Most important of all was their share in the sanctioning, and probably in the making, of the new constitutional arrangements for the government of the three and the nine. These were said to have been made 'with the consent, will and precept of the lord king, and of the prelates, barons and also of the community (*ac etiam communitatis*) at that time present'; and it is difficult to know who can have comprised 'the community', which was additional to the prelates and barons, if not the knights.[79] More specifically, the letter sent to the legate which recorded the discussion of his mission in parliament and rejected his claim for entry was sent in the names of 'the earls, barons, knights and communities of the kingdom of England'.[80] Not only had the knights apparently shared in that discussion, but they were associated with the 'communities', presumably those of their shires, which had chosen them and whose representatives they were. Notionally at least, the whole realm had come together in parliament to reject the legate's demands. In one important respect too the interests both of the knights and of those they represented were carefully protected. In late June new sheriffs were appointed in almost all counties on financial terms which favoured the counties, and seemingly after local elections. The enrolment of some of these appointments on 27 June, while parliament was still in session, suggests that the names of the new sheriffs may have been notified to the government by the shire representatives.[81] It looks as if part of the price which Montfort was prepared to pay for knightly support, in and out of parliament, was a measure of local self-government.

---

[78] For the numbers normally present in parliament, see above, 190–2, 203–4. For the shortness of the summons, Holt, 'The Prehistory of Parliament', 10–11.

[79] *DBM* 298–9; Maddicott, *Simon de Montfort*, 288–9.   [80] Heidemann, *Papst Clemens IV*, 200.

[81] *CPR, 1258–66*, 327–8; Maddicott, *Simon de Montfort*, 288–9.

The second Montfortian parliament, which lasted from late January to early March 1265, was probably the longest of the entire reign. Though it met in easier circumstances than its predecessor—for by the start of 1265 Montfort had faced down his enemies and seen off both the French and the legate[82]—it was a still more overtly partisan body and so less well equipped to confer on Montfort's illegitimate regime the authority and broad recognition which it still needed. To it were summoned a small group of some twenty-three anti-royalist magnates, a much larger body of prelates, heads of religious houses, and other churchmen, two knights from each county, two citizens from York, Lincoln, and other unnamed towns, and four men from Sandwich and each of the Cinque Ports.[83] The bias of the magnates summoned, and the disproportionate numbers of churchmen and Cinque Port representatives, two groups generally sympathetic to Montfort, all show how Montfortian an assembly this was; and it must be assumed that the knights and burgesses were reckoned to be in the same camp.

Still more was done than in the previous parliament to promote the interests of the knights and of the localities they represented, chiefly through the prominence given to the Provisions of Westminster. By this time the Provisions had come to be regarded not only as a practical code of reforms, introducing necessary changes in the law and providing safeguards against abuses of royal and baronial power, but almost as a talisman or shibboleth. Standing as they did for the principles of restraint and redress, their whole was greater than the sum of their parts. In this they had come to resemble Magna Carta itself. They had been intermittently enforced in the courts since their publication in 1259 and had brought benefits both to individual litigants and to local communities.[84] On at least two occasions county juries appealing to the Provisions before the eyre justices had noted their making in parliament (though incorrectly naming the parliament as that of Oxford rather than Westminster), thus showing the linkage between reform and parliament now established in the public mind.[85] The high value set upon them by local society explains Montfort's concern for their defence and enforcement. Throughout his negotiations with the legate in the autumn of 1264 he had insisted on their inviolability and on the need for their firm observance.[86] They were reissued in December 1264, at the time of the January parliament's summoning, accompanied by orders

[82] Maddicott, *Simon de Montfort*, 306–9.   [83] *CR, 1264–68*, 84–7; *DBM* 300–5.
[84] Brand, *King, Barons and Justices*, 106–39, 165–84.   [85] Ibid. 130–2.
[86] *DBM* 298–9; Maddicott, *Simon de Montfort*, 294, 297, 314.

providing for their future local publication with unprecedented frequency and ubiquity,[87] and they were kept in view throughout the course of the subsequent parliament. During the parliament measures were taken to enforce particular clauses of the Provisions dealing with the sheriff's tourn and with beaupleder fines,[88] and they were conspicuous in the terms for the Lord Edward's release from captivity, whose working out was one of the January parliament's main tasks. As part of those terms the Provisions were confirmed and an oath to observe them imposed upon the king, Edward himself, and all officials, royal and baronial. At parliament's conclusion in March 1265 the terms were read out in Westminster Hall before 'all the people', and excommunication was pronounced by nine bishops against future contraveners of Magna Carta, the Forest Charter, and the Provisions: a self-conscious reiteration of the original ceremony of public reading and excommunication which had been part of the first publication of the Provisions in October 1259, again in Westminster Hall and again at the end of a parliament.[89] Though the repeated emphasis on the Provisions had a larger context than that of knightly interests alone, for they represented a continuing Montfortian commitment to reform as much as anything else, their maintenance was an important way of keeping the knights on board a ship that by parliament's end was looking increasingly storm-bound.[90] The publicity given to them, and the role of 'the people' in their reception, made acclamation one of the new props of reforming government.

The contention that local pressures were largely at work here is strengthened by other evidence for their exertion. On 15 February royal letters were sent to the sheriff of Yorkshire (and presumably to other sheriffs) for the payment of the knights' expense in attending parliament. In justification of this measure the letters cited not only the costs of attendance but also the earlier expenses incurred by the counties in the previous year for defence against the threatened French invasion, 'by which [the communities of the counties] feel themselves somewhat excessively burdened'.[91] Behind the government's awareness of this evidently widespread local grievance it is

---

[87] Maddicott, *Simon de Montfort*, 314; Brand, *King, Barons and Justices*, 161–4, 451. The Provisions were to be published each month in county, hundred, wapentake, and baronial courts. For no other piece of medieval legislation, including the various reissues of Magna Carta, was such wide and frequent publication envisaged. The order for publication of legislation in baronial courts appears to be unique.

[88] Maddicott, *Simon de Montfort*, 315; Brand, *King, Barons and Justices*, 171, 173.

[89] *Foedera*, I. i. 451–2; *De Antiquis Legibus Liber*, 42, 71; above, 244

[90] Cf. Maddicott, *Simon de Montfort*, 327–30.   [91] *DBM* 304–7.

difficult not to hear the collective voice of the localities' representatives in parliament. They may have brought forward something like a petition and found private compensation in the payment of their expenses.

There is thus a reasonable presumption that the knights appeared in parliament both as defenders of the local interests which the Provisions of Westminster represented and as petitioners, to whom the government was prepared to lend a sympathetic ear. Did they also contribute to debate? It is fairly clear that they did. When, on 23 February, the king (or rather Montfort) wrote to the sheriff of Shropshire and Staffordshire to ask him to comply with the earlier order to send up knights from his counties, as he had not yet done, his writ spoke explicitly of parliament's purpose and of the knights' projected contribution to it. They were to come 'to treat with us and the magnates on behalf of the communities of those counties concerning. . . the liberation of our firstborn son Edward, and for providing security for this, and also for other things touching the community of our realm'.[92] The insertion into the conditions for Edward's release of a clause concerning the observance of the Provisions suggests that there was indeed some knightly contribution to the discussion of these conditions, and the terms themselves invoked at every stage the participation of 'les hauz homes et le commune de la tere', meaning presumably the magnates and knights (and possibly the burgesses), in order to provide for the settlement's enforcement.[93] Though we cannot recover the debates which must have preceded the drafting of the terms for Edward's release, it seems reasonable to suppose that the knights made their mark on them.

It would be easy to depreciate the importance of these Montfortian parliaments, for reasons both new and old. The summoning of the knights, and possibly of the burgesses too, was no innovation. As we have seen, the knights had long attended parliaments where taxes were to be negotiated, usually in the guise of lesser tenants-in-chief but in 1254 as the elected representatives of their counties. Their renewed attendance in the two parliaments of 1264–5 may easily be written off as a largely tactical move owing nothing to Montfort's constitutional sensibilities or notions of equity and everything to his need for support. We may agree with both these points while still believing that their presence marked an important moment in parliament's early history. Before 1258 their coming to parliament had, so far as we can see, almost always resulted from the Charter's prescriptive

---

[92] Ibid. 306–9. I have changed the word order in this letter.   [93] *Foedera*, I. i. 451–2.

linkage of their presence with tax grants. Although royal requests for taxation may have given them an opportunity to add to political debate through the presentation of their grievances, this had been incidental to their main role.[94] But between 1258 and 1265 taxation was never an issue in parliament, and the knights' attendance was independent of this earlier necessity for their presence. They were now called on to make their voices heard on the broader issues of the day: the new constitution of 1264, the legate's mission to England, the terms for Edward's release. Their earlier summoning to St Albans in 1261 had similarly been intended to draw them into general business. Montfort's achievement was not to summon the knights and burgesses to parliament for the first time, but, at least in the case of the knights, to extend their parliamentary role beyond taxation and to encourage their participation in the larger world of politics and government.

Participation allowed them to forward the interests of their communities. Over such issues as the appointment of sheriffs in 1264 and defence costs in 1265 they seem to have acted as the true representatives of local opinion. Their promotion of these local interests links their activities back to the Petition of the Barons of 1258, in which the concerns of the smaller landholders had been prominent, and forward to the common petitions of fourteenth-century parliaments. It was part of a continuum, a series of mechanisms hinging upon parliament, by which local grievances could be made known and redressed at the centre. In 1264–5 it also helped to revive the association forged in 1258–9 between parliament and reform. The new constitution devised in the parliament of 1264 and the efforts made to keep the Provisions in the foreground of parliamentary politics showed that the reform of central and local government remained a leading part of parliament's work, even if one now driven by the urgent pressure of events rather than by the slow accumulation of grievances which had initiated the more considered and leisurely reforms of 1258–9. The plausible contrast between the baronial parliaments of 1258–9 and those of 1264–5 in terms of reforming principles versus political pragmatism is at best a half truth. In both periods parliament and reform, what was just and what was expedient, went together.

We do not know how parliament would have developed further under Montfort's direction, for within a few months he was a dead man. That he

[94] Above, 222–3.

had certainly intended to hold another parliament was shown by a royal writ of 19 March summoning four dissident royalist magnates to appear before king and council in the next parliament, which was to meet in London on 1 June. The intention to subject them to what looks like a state trial suggests that the Montfortians were preparing to exploit one of the traditional judicial functions of parliament to their own advantage. Since the writ was issued shortly after the conclusion of the January parliament, it had almost certainly been decided in that parliament to hold a further summer meeting, on one of the three dates laid down in the Provisions of Oxford. In thus adhering to the letter of reform Montfort also showed that he cannot have been disappointed by what the recently terminated assembly had achieved. The subsequent summoning to the June parliament of two canons from the cathedral church of York (and perhaps from other cathedral churches?), as well as of the abbot of Ramsey, suggests that in the forthcoming assembly, as in the previous one, churchmen were to be well represented, this time apparently at the level of the lower clergy as well as that of the prelates.[95] But the whole scheme was aborted by the final crisis of Montfort's career, and the argument can be carried no further.

3. Parliament and the Royalist Reaction, 1265–1268

The two years following Montfort's defeat and death at the battle of Evesham in August 1265 were a time a disorder, confusion, and continuing resistance by the Montfortians. The disinheritance of the rebels at the Winchester parliament of September 1265, immediately after the battle, robbed them of any incentive to submit; there were disturbances in the north midlands, led by the earl of Derby, in the spring of 1266; the rebel stronghold at Kenilworth was under siege from June to December 1266; even when better terms had been conceded to the Disinherited by the Dictum of Kenilworth in October and the siege ended, resistance continued in the Isle of Ely; and the earl of Gloucester occupied London on behalf of the rebels in the spring of 1267. Only when Gloucester came to terms in June, and Ely surrendered in July, was peace restored. Until then, in the aftermath of Evesham, the barons' war continued by other means.[96]

---

[95] Sayles, *Functions*, 107–9.   [96] Powicke, *Henry III*, 503–50, for the best account.

These circumstances, combined with Henry's own probable misgivings about assemblies which had been exploited so effectively by his enemies, made parliament of little apparent importance in this period. The trend can be charted, if only crudely, by tallying the number of uses of the word in the printed chancery rolls. Between the early summer of 1258 and the middle of 1262 'parliament' was used thirty-one times on twenty-five occasions; in the Montfortian period from 1264 to August 1265 it was used twelve times on eight occasions; but from August 1265 to the end of 1267 it was not used at all. It returned on only five occasions between 1267 and 1269.[97] Since the word usually occurred in the context of pleas deferred and justice to be done, it was probably this routine side of parliament's business that fell away so sharply. Parliaments, usually recorded by the chronicles, there certainly were: at Winchester in September 1265, possibly at Northampton in May 1266, at Kenilworth in August 1266, and at Bury St Edmunds in February 1267.[98] But, as their dates and locations suggest, they were irregular and infrequent, meeting outside London and with their business dictated by the progress of war and peace. In all but their infrequency, they resembled the great councils of the minority, summoned in the aftermath of another civil war.[99] That at Kenilworth, for example, established the commission which went on to draw up the Dictum of Kenilworth; and its convening in August, the only parliament of the entire reign to meet in that month, showed how unusual conditions were. That at Bury was convened to deal with the nearby rebels at Ely.[100] None, so far as we know, contained knights or burgesses. The whole tradition of large and regular assemblies, summoned to consider taxation and the other 'common business of the realm', appeared to be on the point of being lost. It may have seemed that the Montfortian years had left only a negative parliamentary legacy, and that parliament's subversive association with reform and rebellion would drive it to the margins of a reviving regal constitution.

Yet even in these years, before the war had properly ended, there were strong signs that Henry had learnt some lessons from the events of 1258–65: the need to conciliate and to justify; to do so through and in parliament; and to avoid parliamentary conflicts. The misguided policy of disinheritance decided on at the Winchester parliament immediately after Evesham received an elaborate justification in terms of consent: 'by our

---

[97] Treharne, 'Nature of Parliament in the Reign of Henry III', 73.
[98] See *HBC* 543, and references there cited.
[99] Above, 149.   [100] *CPR, 1258–66,* 671–2; *Ann. Waverley,* 371–2; *Wykes,* 196.

common counsel', said the king, 'and with the assent of the magnates and *proceres* of our kingdom meeting at Winchester, it was provided and commonly agreed . . .'[101] If nothing else, 'reform and rebellion' had evidently taught Henry the importance of not going it alone, as he had done over Sicily. In the following year Magna Carta was confirmed in the Kenilworth parliament and orders given for its publication in the counties, with a surprising instruction to use for that purpose the copies dispatched to the counties at the conclusion of the last Montfortian parliament in March 1265.[102] An equally evident gesture towards conciliation was marked by Henry's unwillingness to call on the laity for a general tax. Although his financial situation was desperate, he preferred instead to seek help from the pope, given in June 1266 in the form of an ecclesiastical tenth payable by the clergy for three years.[103] Since its eventual yield was probably some £47,000, considerably more than that of any of the three earlier lay subsidies, this proved to be a well-judged decision.[104] Henry's looking to Rome was partly dictated by the disturbed and impoverished state of his kingdom, but it may also have reflected his wish to avoid the bout of parliamentary bargaining, with the knights among the bargainers, which lay taxation would have entailed. The king's early inheritance from the reform movement was thus an awareness of the constraints on his own position.

This was much more fully shown at the Marlborough parliament of November 1267: the first great parliamentary occasion since Montfort's defeat. That year had already seen the surrender of Ely in July and the sealing of the Treaty of Montgomery with Llywelyn of Wales in September, and this parliament's famous enactment, the Statute of Marlborough, was a contribution to the same process of general peace-making. In effect the Statute confirmed the Provisions of Westminster of October 1259, though in the revised version issued by the king in January 1263 and last reissued by Montfort in December 1264. This may have been recommended by the committee which drafted the Dictum of Kenilworth in 1265,[105] but it was

---

[101] *CR, 1264–68*, 295; cf. *CPR, 1258–66*, 490.

[102] *DBM* 320–1; *Ann. Waverley*, 371; *CR, 1264–68*, 259. For the dispatch and publication of Magna Carta in March 1265, see *DBM* 312–15, and Maddicott, *Simon de Montfort*, 319–20.

[103] Lunt, *Financial Relations*, 292–3. For Henry's financial position, see Powicke, *King Henry III*, 558–9.

[104] Lunt, *Financial Relations*, 309, estimates a yield of £44,000–49,000. For the yields of the earlier lay subsidies, see Carpenter, 'Beginnings of Parliament', 386.

[105] *DBM* 320–1; Brand, *King, Barons and Justices*, 186.

not until two years later, in the more settled conditions then obtaining, that any such recommendation could be acted on. All but the Statute's first eight clauses derived directly from the Provisions: restraints on the lord's right to exact suit of court, limitations on the sheriff's tourn, the abolition of beaupleder fines and of the murdrum fine in cases of accidental death, and all the other earlier rulings which mattered so greatly to local society, from knights to peasants, were now fully sanctioned by royal will and legislative fiat. One amendment to the original text extended an additional favour to tenants by further limiting their obligation to perform suit of court or other services.[106] At no point did the Statute acknowledge its paternity: it was presented as though it was an immediate response to the disorders of the recent past.[107] But its silence here was no more than a face-saving device on Henry's part, designed to avoid any public linkage between his actions and those of his former enemies. Even unstated, however, that linkage must have been obvious enough. Although no textual provision seems to have been made for the Statute's publication, it would have been wholly anomalous for this not to have been done, and we can assume that publication took place in the counties in the normal way.[108] There, at least one provincial observer recognized the apparently novel legislation for what it was, for the chronicler Bartholomew Cotton, writing from Norwich, noted that in 1267 'the king conceded that the statutes of Oxford [i.e. Westminster] should be observed, except in a few things'.[109]

The Statute was indeed a concession, chiefly to those local forces of knights and freeholders to whose interests and for whose support Simon de Montfort had appealed in 1264–5. It marked the belated recognition by the king, following in Montfort's footsteps, of their political weight and of what was needed to conciliate them. But it was also a recognition of reforming methods as well as principles. By enacting a diversified reforming code in parliament, Henry maintained the connection between parliament and legislation firmly established in 1258–9, creating a stepping-stone between that earlier legislation and the comparable Edwardian parliamentary statutes of the 1270s and 1280s.

---

[106] Brand, *King, Barons and Justices*, 189–90, 282. For the text of the statute, see ibid. 454–83.

[107] Ibid. 188.

[108] See *Cal. Liberate Rolls, 1267–72*, no. 228, for evidence of local distribution. Cf. Richardson and Sayles, 'The Early Statutes', in *EPMA* xxv. 23–4, and Brand, *King, Barons and Justices*, 188.

[109] *Bartholomaei de Cotton, Historia Anglicana*, ed. H. R. Luard, RS (London, 1859), 143. Cotton was copying an earlier Norwich chronicle for this period: see Gransden, *Historical Writing in England*, i. 444.

Given the momentous nature of what was done at Marlborough, it is particularly unfortunate that we know so little about *how* it was done. We have only the Statute itself to go on. But the reference in its preamble to the king having called together 'the wiser men of the . . . kingdom from both the greater and the lesser men (*tam ex majoribus quam minoribus*)' suggests that the knights may have been present among the *minores*, as Stubbs thought 'not improbable'.[110] The existence of two sets of letters patent issued about this time in favour of the citizens of Lincoln and Norwich, apparently after the king had received their complaints, makes it possible that the burgesses too were summoned.[111] Since the interests of these *minores* were very much bound up with the Statute, since Henry was emulating Montfort in other ways, and since he aimed at a broad social peace, there would have been nothing surprising in the Statute's promulgation in a particularly comprehensive assembly. The conjunction of parliament, representation, and reform so evident between 1258 and 1265 may not after all have been superseded.

One further assembly in the following year may have provided the Marlborough parliament with a kind of coda, if only in a minor key. According to a conciliar memorandum drafted in March 1268, writs of summons were to be issued to twenty-seven cities and boroughs ordering them to send their bailiffs and six of their greater, more discreet, and richer men, to an assembly which was to meet at Westminster on 22 April. Those sent were to be empowered to act for their communities. They were to meet at the same time as a church council convened by the legate Ottobuono, to which other 'faithful men' had also been summoned.[112] We do not know the purpose of this urban assembly or even if it met. But it is likely that it did and that its work was connected with the tallaging of the cities, boroughs, and royal demesnes put in hand in early May;[113] hence the summoning of townsmen, the stress laid on their wealth, and the need for them to be empowered to act as attorneys for their communities. If this was so, then it was remarkable, for tallage was a prerogative levy which the king could simply impose and which needed no consent. If the king now thought it prudent to seek that consent, he was going beyond what was

---

[110] Brand, *King, Barons and Justices*, 187, 454–5; Stubbs, *Constit. Hist.* ii. 101.
[111] *CPR, 1266–72*, 270, 272.
[112] Sayles, 'Representation of Cities and Boroughs in 1268', 580–6.
[113] *CPR, 1268–72*, 226; *CR, 1264–68*, 508–10; Mitchell, *Studies in Taxation*, 294; Powicke, *King Henry III*, 563. Powicke is wrong to say that assessors had been appointed for the tallage north of Trent by the end of 1267. They were not appointed until May 1268.

necessary, in deference probably (as at Marlborough in the previous year) to the social forces which had emerged, and the constitutional principles which had been strengthened, during the reforming period.

In the three years after Evesham Henry's government thus responded to what it had been taught. The reissuing of Magna Carta, the tacit acknowledgement and public re-enactment of a major part of the baronial programme, and the invocation of consent as the justification for the government's actions, all suggested that the political rupture brought by Montfort's defeat was neither so deep nor so final as it may at first have appeared to have been. This conclusion was to be reinforced in the coming years by the negotiating of the last tax of the reign.

4. Representation and Resistance: The Crusade Taxation of 1268–1270

In June 1268 the Lord Edward took the cross at Northampton: his first step towards a crusade which would eventually get under way more than two years later in August 1270.[114] The long interval was the product not only of the time needed to raise a crusading force, but also of the difficulties which stood in the way of raising money to pay for it. This could be achieved only by the levying of direct taxation, a process that was bound to be fraught with uncertainties. No such tax had been granted since 1237. In the 1240s and early 1250s Henry's frequent requests for taxes had been as frequently refused, and none had been asked for since 1257, though, as we have seen, taxation had been under discussion at the start of the reform movement.[115] After Evesham, and despite the desperate state of his finances, Henry seems to have been anxious to avoid asking for a tax, probably because of the negotiations which such a request would entail and the resistance which it would almost certainly encounter: hence his reliance on papal taxation of the clergy from 1266, on the eyre put in hand from 1267, which must have had a partly fiscal purpose,[116] and the tallage of 1268. None of these needed any form of consent, though Henry may have gone beyond what

---

[114] This episode is considered in more detail in my 'The Crusade Taxation of 1268–70 and the Development of Parliament', *TCE* 2 (1988), 93–117. Support for any unreferenced statements will be found there.

[115] Above, 235–6, 244–5.

[116] For the eyre, see D. Crook, *Records of the General Eyre*, HMSO (London, 1982), 133–4.

was necessary in asking for it in the case of the tallage. But to meet the very heavy costs of the crusade there was no alternative to direct taxation, an expedient likely to revive the parliamentary bargaining, presentation of grievances, and criticism of royal policies which had characterized the two decades before 1258. And so it did, but with this difference: that the knightly representatives of the counties were now the most prominent group among the bargainers.

The question of taxation for the crusade was almost certainly first raised at a parliament which met at York in September 1268. The one chronicle which records the assembly, the Furness continuator of William of Newburgh, seems to suggest that the king asked for a tax, but that his request was deferred until a later meeting in London because not all the 'maiores' were then present. 'Maiores' would normally mean 'nobles', but in this case the Furness continuator tells us that all the 'nobiliores' *were* present; and it is a reasonable assumption that in this case the chronicler meant by 'maiores', not the nobles, but the knights.[117] After all, the pre-1258 precedents suggest that the presence of knights, whether as lesser tenants-in-chief or as elected representatives, would have been normal in any tax parliament.

At the next parliament, meeting on 13 October in London, as previously arranged, the same chronicle tells us specifically that the knights and lower clergy (if that is how 'ecclesiarum rectores' is to be interpreted) were present, along with the prelates and magnates. Taxation was discussed, but what exactly those present had in mind or decided remains obscure. The close rolls show that at least two groups of counties came together in parliament to elect for each group a baronial committee whose members were to make arrangements for the levying of a tax, possibly a land tax rather than the customary levy on moveables. But the whole scheme proved abortive and nothing came of it. Its interest lies in what it suggests about representation, for what the close roll lists as county groups ('the counties of Hereford, Salop, Stafford and Warwick elect . . .', etc.) can only refer to their knightly representatives meeting in parliament.[118] The knights present were evidently there as the elected spokesmen for their counties, following the Montfortian precedents of 1261 and 1264-5, and

---

[117] *Continuation of William of Newburgh*, in *Chrons. Stephen . . . Richard I*, ii. 554; Maddicott, 'Crusade Taxation', 95-8.

[118] *Continuation of William of Newburgh*, ii. 554-5; *CR, 1264-8*, 557-9; Powicke, *King Henry III*, 564; Maddicott, 'Crusade Taxation', 99-101.

not as the lesser tenants-in-chief generally summoned to tax parliaments before 1258. Their election of baronial committees points to cooperation between these county knights and to a pooling of opinion which can only have occurred within parliament.

Even at this early stage in the negotiations, several points were clear. Henry considered that the granting of a tax necessitated a very large meeting—a parliament 'general, full, and solemn (*generale, plenum et sollempne*)', as he described the projected October meeting in a letter to Louis IX. The apparent attendance of the lower clergy as well as the knights is particularly noteworthy; so far as we know, this is the first time that they or their representatives had attended parliament since April 1254.[119] The nobility present seem to have been largely royalist, as they were throughout these parliamentary negotiations, conducted at a time when the crown's Montfortian opponents had been defeated and many of the remaining nobles, men often close to the Lord Edward, had taken the cross and had an interest in raising the money needed for the crusade. But despite these favourable circumstances, which contrasted strongly with the more hostile parliamentary climate of the 1240s and1250s, Henry had not secured his tax.

That his failure had much to do with the resistance of the knights is a view supported by the measures taken to placate them and those they represented in the parliaments which followed. At the Hilary parliament of January 1269 an ordinance was drafted promising restraints on Jewish money-lending and in particular on the creation of rent charges on the lands of the Jews' debtors—a means of repayment which had often caused the debtors to lose the land itself. The relief offered was particularly advantageous for the smaller landowners who formed the most prominent of the social groups caught up in debts to the Jews. Since the same group had already benefited from the comparable relief made available to Jewish debtors by Simon de Montfort in 1264–5, Henry was once again following Montfortian precedent.[120] The ordinance was published at a further parliament in April 1269 and must have been intended to win support for the king's still pending request for a tax. At the next parliament, in July, that tax was apparently granted 'by the magnates and other faithful men of our kingdom'. But the assembly, held in the harvest season and

---

[119] *CR, 1264–68*, 552; above, 211–14. Lunt, 'Consent of the Lower Clergy to Taxation', overlooks the probable presence of the lower clergy at this parliament..

[120] *CPR, 1266–72*, 376; Maddicott, *Simon de Montfort*, 315–16; id., 'Crusade Taxation', 101–2.

following close on that of April, seems to have been a small and badly attended affair, and subsequent events demonstrated that the grant made by this feeble body carried no authority.[121]

That authority was much more fully embodied in the next parliament, the fourth of the year, which met at Westminster in October, following the festivities to celebrate the translation of the relics of Edward the Confessor to the king's new church at Westminster. As in the assembly of the previous October, those summoned included both knights and lower clergy, and very probably too the burgesses who had been present at the preceding ceremonies.[122] Yet despite his conciliatory measure earlier in the year, the king did not fully obtain what he wanted. Consent was given to the assessment of a twentieth on moveables—that is, to the valuation of the taxpayers' moveable goods—but not to its collection, which was presumably intended to follow after the meeting of some (unknown) condition. The account given by the chronicler Wykes, though not entirely unambiguous, suggests that, once again, the nobles were more willing than the knights to sanction the granting of the tax. There was similar resistance from the heads of religious houses and from the clergy to the comparable willingness of the bishops to comply with the king's request. According to Henry himself, writing in December 1269, the tax was conceded 'as much by the magnates and knights as by other laymen'; but if this provides unequivocal evidence for the participation of the knights and possibly the burgesses ('other laymen') in whatever was done in the October parliament, it goes too far in assuming that a tax was actually granted.[123]

It was only at the next parliament, in April 1270, that the twentieth was finally and fully conceded, though in fact Henry had anticipated parliament's decision by ordering its collection to begin in some counties a few weeks in advance of its meeting. Once parliament had assembled, with both magnates and knights present, it was probably the king's willingness to confirm the Charters, the Forest Charter as well as Magna Carta, which broke the deadlock. The Charters were published by the bishops in London; those contravening them were excommunicated according to the solemn sentences first proclaimed in 1253; and the sentences were subsequently

[121] *Wykes*, 221; *Ann. Worcester*, 458; Maddicott, 'Crusade Taxation', 102–5.

[122] *Wykes*, 226–7; *Ann. Oseney*, 227–9; Maddicott, 'Crusade Taxation', 105.

[123] *Wykes*, 226–7; *CR, 1268–72*, 245; Maddicott, 'Crusade Taxation', 105–8. Cf. M. Prestwich, *English Politics in the Thirteenth Century* (Basingstoke, 1990), 141.

sent out for publication in parish churches. Clearly the full observance of the Charters had been central to whatever demands had been made of the king in parliament (and how much we miss at this point the insider's view of parliamentary happenings once provided by Matthew Paris). Shortly afterwards, in May, Henry ordered the enforcement of the earlier legislation directed at Jewish rent charges, evidently not yet implemented, and the cancellation of certain categories of rent charge. Like the confirmation of the Charters, it looks as if this too was a concession, intended to ensure that those in parliament would allow the tax to move forward from assessment to collection. This indeed is what now happened. By early July the money had begun to come in and the crusade at last to be feasible.[124]

This sequence of events was second only in importance to the reform movement itself for the development of parliament. At the most obvious level it re-established parliament as one of the state's central political institutions, after several years of largely irregular and ad hoc assemblies. The seven parliaments which met between September 1268 and April 1270 made this the most intensive period of parliamentary activity since 1258–9.[125] They began to revive the annual rhythm of parliaments noticeable before 1258, linking parliament once again, in October 1268 and October 1269, to the great feast of the Translation of St Edward. Such activity was prompted almost exclusively by Henry's (and Edward's) fiscal needs, which initiated the most protracted tax negotiations of the reign. Lasting more than eighteen months, they constituted a firm acknowledgement that, despite his defeat of his opponents' attempts to limit his prerogative, the king remained as dependent on parliamentary consent for taxation as he had been before 1258.

The most visible difference between pre-1258 and post-1265 practice lay in the role of the knights, whose collective voice and interests seem to have been crucial in delaying the progress of Henry's plans. Their absence had apparently made it impossible to proceed towards a tax grant at the York parliament of September 1268; cooperating together across the boundaries of their county constituencies, they were drawn into abortive arrangements for taxation at the October parliament; the anti-Jewish legislation associated with the parliaments of January and April 1269 was a concession to them and others like them in the counties; and

---

[124] Maddicott, 'Crusade Taxation', 108–11. [125] For a list of these parliaments, see ibid. 117.

they were among the leading prospective beneficiaries of the confirmation of the Charters in the parliament of April 1270 and of the implementation of the anti-Jewish legislation which followed. The restraints on Jewish money-lending were particularly significant, and not only because of the immediate relief which they promised to those former Montfortians forced to borrow from the Jews in order to redeem their lands under the terms of the Dictum of Kenilworth. They were part of a gathering wave of measures against the Jews, beginning with Montfort's cancellation of Jewish debts in 1264–5 and culminating in the Jews' expulsion by Edward I in 1290, by which successive governments sought to buy what they now needed: the support of the gentry, both inside and outside parliament.[126]

That theirs was the initiative behind this whole parliamentary campaign seems clear. The royalist character of the nobility at this point makes it highly unlikely that the delays and obstructions which Henry encountered owed much to the magnates; and what evidence we have suggests a division of interest between knights and magnates over the question of taxation. The ability of the nascent commons to impede the king's schemes, and the concessions which he was obliged to offer in order to appease them, were a testimony to their emerging strengths. Those concessions did not, of course, include any of the subtractions from the prerogative, such as parliamentary consent to the appointment of the king's ministers, which had been asked for in the 1240s and 1250s. That part of the former baronial programme was dead, along with the shackles on royal power imposed by the Provisions of Oxford. What was conceded was either traditional (the confirmation of the Charters) or largely immaterial to royal interests (restraints on the Jews). Though the Charters were particularly sacrosanct to the knights, who had been thought likely to demand their observance in advance of any tax grant in the 1254 parliament, it was the bishops who were instrumental in securing their confirmation in 1270:[127] an indication of the degree to which they continued to provide common ground for different political groups. Yet it was the commons who remained at the core of the whole process. There was a degree of independent self-assertiveness on their side, and a willingness to conciliate on the king's, which grew directly from the period of reform and rebellion. That parliament should have provided the stage on which both sides met owed much to the by now customary need

---

[126] Maddicott, *Simon de Montfort*, 315–16; id., 'Crusade Taxation', 101–2; R. C. Stacey, 'Parliamentary Negotiation and the Expulsion of the Jews from England', *TCE* 6 (1997), esp. 93–101.

[127] Above, 211; Maddicott, 'Crusade Taxation', 109.

for parliamentary consent to taxation, but something also to parliament's elevation during the same troubles.

5. Parliament Re-established, 1270–1272

In the relative political calm which marked Henry's final years, and following on from the re-ascent of parliament via the long and recent process of tax negotiation, the parliamentary routines of the pre-1258 period were fully re-established. This was true in two particular ways. First, parliament met regularly, on at least six occasions between October 1270 and Henry's death in November 1272, and at what had become—excluding the hiatus of the early and mid 1260s—the traditional times of Hilary, Easter, and Michaelmas.[128] The demands of 1258 for parliaments at Candlemas and on 1 June were, like the rest of the Provisions of Oxford, forgotten. There was nothing ad hoc about these latter-day assemblies, and their meetings clearly followed a preordained pattern, assumed and known about long in advance. Writing to Llywelyn of Wales on 24 August 1270, Henry was able to inform him that he would arrange 'in our next Michaelmas parliament' to send a deputation of councillors to meet him;[129] while Archbishop Walter Giffard of York, writing to Robert Burnell on 27 December 1270, asked Burnell to excuse his absence from the forthcoming feast of St Edward (the Deposition on 5 January) and the parliament which would follow it, but said that he would make up for his absence after Easter.[130] That there would be three great annual parliaments, fixed for midwinter, spring, and autumn, was a fact taken for granted.

Secondly, all six of the known parliaments met at Westminster, and two of them, those of midwinter and autumn, seem to have been as clearly linked to the two great feasts of the Deposition and Translation of St Edward as they had been prior to 1258. Both negative and positive considerations, the absence of the military activity in the provinces which had sometimes taken parliament into the front line between 1265

---

[128] To the four parliaments listed in the *HBC*, 545 (Oct. 1270, Oct. 1271, Jan. 1272, Oct. 1272) may be added those projected for Jan. and Apr. 1271, mentioned in the sources cited in n. 130 below.

[129] *CR, 1268–72*, 290–1; Sayles, *Functions*, 131.

[130] *The Register of Walter Giffard, Archbishop of York, 1266–79*, ed. W. Brown, Surtees Soc. 109 (1904), 211; Sayles, *Functions*, 131. Sayles is wrong in thinking that the 'Feast of St Edward' in Giffard's letter is the Feast of the Translation, 13 October; it is clearly that of the Deposition, 5 January. This error leads him to query unnecessarily the date of the letter, 27 December (1270).

and 1267, the completion of the Confessor's new shrine in the abbey, and the splendid ceremonies accompanying the translation of the saint's relics in October 1269,[131] served to rebase the king's government in the location which, during the first part of the reign, had become its normal home.

Parliament was now an integral part of that government, though not in any dramatic or particularly prominent way. As far as we know, the knights and burgesses were never summoned, nor were there any parliamentary confrontations or striking of political bargains. Taxation, which might have led to both, was not an issue, and the virtual absence of parliament from the chronicles is a testimony to the placidity of these occasions. Much important business, regarding, for example, the king's finances, the organization of his household, and the suppression of disorder, was dealt with by the council,[132] which, of course, included prelates and magnates; and there may have been some tendency to take such business there rather than to a full parliament. Yet other important matters, especially perhaps those concerning foreign affairs, continued to be discussed in parliament: in the parliament of Michaelmas 1270, the appointment of men to handle Llywelyn's complaints about the infringement of his rights by the men of Montgomery;[133] in those of Michaelmas 1270, Michaelmas 1271, and Hilary 1272, the measures to be taken against the Flemings in the current trade war.[134] Foreign policy had been a traditional part of parliament's business; but the treatment of these particular issues in Henry III's last parliaments may also have owed something to the lessons learnt from the misguided and extra-parliamentary launching of the Sicilian Business in the 1250s. In the case of the Flemish affair, it also showed how parliament could be made to embrace a wide range of economic and social interests—not just those of the landed but of merchants as well.

In these last years, therefore, the king acknowledged the necessity to consult his subjects regularly through parliament. So he had done in the years before 1258. But then the stimulus for parliament's summoning

---

[131] For the ceremonies, see *Wykes*, 226–7; *De Antiquis Legibus Liber*, 116–17; and Powicke, *King Henry III*, 575–6.

[132] e.g. *CPR, 1266–72*, 531, 574, 579, 583, 622.

[133] *CR, 1268–72*, 290–1; Sayles, *Functions*, 131.

[134] *De Antiquis Legibus Liber*, 127, 142; Sayles, *Functions*, 133. For the Anglo-Flemish war, see R. H. Bowers, 'English Merchants and the Anglo-Flemish Economic War of 1270–1274', in R. H. Bowers (ed.), *Seven Studies in Medieval English History and Other Historical Essays Presented to Harold S. Snellgrove* (Jackson, Miss., 1983), 21–54.

had frequently been financial, deriving from Henry's hopes for taxation. That there was no such stimulus in the early 1270s showed Henry's recognition that the conventions of politics, and the constraints which they imposed on royal power, rested on more than just the imperatives of fiscal need.

What difference, then, did baronial reform make to the evolution of parliament? In some ways reform merely accelerated and accentuated developments that were well in train before 1258. In Henry III's middle years, before the reformers gave parliament an almost statutory role, it had already become established as the central institution of the political nation and the point of contact—often the point of collision—between the policies of the crown and the wishes of the community. From the 1230s onwards parliamentary experiments had been made in controlling the king's daily government which were to culminate in the conciliar and parliamentary restraints devised in 1258. Most important of all in the long term, the knights, and perhaps the burgesses too, were already playing a part in parliamentary politics before Simon de Montfort and the reformers put in a bid for their loyalties. Their early attendance in parliament almost certainly linked back to that of the lesser crown tenants; their grievances had figured in parliamentary confrontations with the king; and their collective weight is likely to have been thrown behind the refusals of taxation which Henry encountered in parliament. In all these ways reform drew on past experience and on the past activities of an already experienced parliamentary group.

But the reform movement was more than a medium for parliamentary continuity and an accelerant of parliamentary evolution. It established parliament on a new and formal footing as a consultative body, to be summoned three times a year to deal with 'the common business of the realm'. The comparably regular meetings in Henry's last years, though not quite tied to fixed dates, showed that the principle had survived the overthrow of the Provisions of Oxford which embodied it. With the Provisions of Westminster, large-scale and diversified legislation became a part of that 'common business', to be transmitted to the future via the Statute of Marlborough. In several other ways parliament came through the reform period with its position confirmed and reinforced. As an occasion for seeking consent, for negotiating taxes, and for decisions on matters of state, parliament between 1268 and 1272 lost none of its importance as a central organ of the realm. It could play this role partly because it was no longer a threat to the monarchy. Even during the confrontations over the crusading tax, those in parliament were essentially satisfied with no more than measures against the Jews and the confirmation of the Charters, neither of them inimical to the crown's interests. The public defeat of reform had killed off the unwarrantable demands of the 1240s and 1250s. Henry's new ability to make concessions to parliament without compromising on the essentials of his authority partly explains why a parliament which had been the instrument of the reformers found a firm place in a revived monarchical constitution.

Within that constitution the knights now played a large part. So far as we can see, what political weight they had at the centre before 1258 came solely from their role in tax parliaments, where royal requests for taxation had required consultation with the lesser tenants-in-chief who were the knights' parliamentary predecessors. In the parliaments of 1264–5, however, Montfort had expanded that role, making the knights a party to general political discussions of great moment. His innovation was less to bring about their appearance in parliament than to give them more to do once they were there. But at the same time he also set their attendance on a new footing. Prior to 1258 knights had been elected by their county communities only for the parliament of April 1254; nor had they been regarded as integral to the parliaments and parliamentary arrangements of 1258. Yet Montfort summoned them from their counties in 1261, 1264, and 1265—in 1264, very probably in 1265, and possibly in 1261, after local elections.[135] In all likelihood it was his actions that put paid for ever to the summoning of the lesser tenants and substituted instead the county elections which were to become the norm under Edward I. The evidence for knights summoned by counties to the parliament of October 1268 suggests that the precedent which he had set was followed in at least one of Henry's post-Evesham parliaments: an occasion which helped to bridge the gap between the Montfortian parliaments and that of April 1275, when knights are next known to have been returned by their counties.[136] Montfort's actions were, as so often, dictated by political calculation. A limited number of leading knights chosen by their counties was more use to him than a mass of lesser tenants, some of them knights but many of them of no great social weight, whose summoning could in any case only

---

[135] *DBM* 246–9, 292–3, 302–3; above, 251–2, 255–8.   [136] Below, 287, 289.

be carried through as an adjunct to that of the greater magnates. But as with the involvement of the knights in general political business, so also with their summoning, measures determined by expediency and immediate need proved to have established guidelines for the future.

These developments of the 1260s explain why the texts deriving from the Montfortian parliaments set the knights apart. The knights alone (though possibly alongside the burgesses in the 1265 parliament) could be described in 1264–5 as 'the community' or 'the community of the realm', who came to speak on behalf of 'the communities of [the] counties'.[137] They had as yet no exclusive claim to these terms, which were more frequently used of the magnates or of the whole parliamentary body. Nevertheless they were beginning to be seen as a discrete group, a *communitas*, and a collectivity with interests separate from those of the magnates.[138] After 1265 their interests were again recognized and courted in the Statute of Marlborough and in the anti-Jewish legislation, both of which followed on from reforming and Montfortian measures. If the knights were summoned to the Marlborough parliament, which seems quite likely, they would again have been associated, in a Montfortian way, with a meeting which had nothing to do with taxation. In the parliaments which *were* concerned with taxation, between 1268 and 1270, the knights seem to have fought successfully to impose conditions on any grant, even in circumstances which 'Evesham' had made superficially favourable to authoritarian kingship. If the knights were a presence in parliament before 1258, they were on occasion a force after 1265. This was one of the two most important consequences of the reform movement. The other was the re-emergence of parliament, purged of its previously attempted intrusions on the prerogative, as a bulwark of consultative and consensual royal government, and one all the more bulwark-like because of the range of interests which it now embodied. Before Henry III's death the reform movement had, in a manner of speaking, already helped to create the parliaments of Edward I which are part of the subject of the next chapter.

---

[137] *DBM* 298–9, 308–9, 312–13; Heidemann, *Papst Clemens IV*, 200; *Foedera*, I. i. 451–2; above, 256, 259.
[138] Cf. W. A. Morris, 'Magnates and Community of the Realm in Parliament, 1264–1327', *Medievalia et Humanistica*, I (1943), 58–71, esp. 70–1.

6

Expansion

Parliament and Nation, 1272–1327

1. Edward I: Consensus, 1272–1294

The author of the *Modus Tenendi Parliamentum*, the tract on the supposed working of parliament probably written about 1320, began his text with a striking statement. He will describe, he says, how parliament was held in the time of Edward the Confessor. On one level this declaration is a further mark of the expansive but imaginary statesmanship of a king whom the mythmakers of the medieval English polity had always regarded as the author and giver of all good things: not only the Solon of English law, Edward also presided over a fully functioning English parliament.[1] Yet at another level the preface to the *Modus* tells us something real and important about parliament. By Edward II's later years it could be regarded as an organ of state both beneficent and venerable, existing almost time out of mind. That there was also thought to be a way of holding parliaments, a *modus*, suggests too that parliament was now seen as both institutionally well defined and a proper subject for description and conscious reflection. For all that we can say about the parliaments of Henry III, it is doubtful if such elevated views would have been possible fifty years earlier, at the time of Edward I's accession. Between the 1270s

---

[1] N. Pronay and J. Taylor, *Parliamentary Texts of the Later Middle Ages* (Oxford, 1980), 67, 80. For Edward as mythical law-maker, see O'Brien, *God's Peace and King's Peace*, esp. 17–18, 27–30; Wormald, *Making*, 128–9.

This chapter does not set out to provide a comprehensive account of the parliaments of Edward I and Edward II, but chiefly to pursue the theme set out in its title. For a more wide-ranging survey of Edward I's parliaments, see Prestwich, *Edward I*, 436–68.

and the 1320s parliament had acquired a new sort of prominence in English government and politics.

This development was defined by an expansion and deepening of parliament's national role: the theme of this chapter. The predecessors of the Edwardian parliaments shared, of course, many of their national characteristics. Focused on the king and drawing in large numbers of his subjects, dealing with the affairs of the realm, and involved with justice, legislation, and, latterly at least, with taxation, the pre-Conquest witan and (perhaps more questionably) the feudal councils of the twelfth century, as well as Henry III's parliaments, were in almost all respects national assemblies.[2] Yet under the first two Edwards there proved to be much room for a general enhancement of parliament's centrality to the nation's business. It took on a larger agenda, becoming more regularly associated with the granting of taxes, and of more sorts of tax, than ever before, and through the more frequent attendance of elected representatives, and the reception of written grievances from a wide social range of men and women, it broadened and deepened its contacts with provincial England. *Mutatis mutandis*, it was more than ever 'the witan of the English people'.

Parliament's evolutionary course owed most to the aspirations and policies of Edward I, especially in the years up to 1294.[3] Thereafter the crown's wars and the fiscal demands which accompanied them gave a very different but equally significant bias to parliamentary developments; though the following discussion of Edward's early dealings with parliament necessarily draws on some material from these later years. The first part of Edward's reign was a time of brilliantly successful kingship, during which Edward governed through a broadly based oligarchy of magnates and ministers, and in open reaction to the much narrower basis of his father's rule. The period was marked by successful expansion abroad and reform at home. In two relatively brief wars fought in 1277 and 1282—3 Wales was conquered. Yet this was one of those rare moments in English history when the reputation of a 'good' king owed less to successful foreign warfare than to effective domestic government. Edward's implicit abandonment of unrealistic claims in France, the reform of local government, the prosecution of delinquent officials, the new statutes of the 1270s and 1280s, and the chivalric interest in tournaments, warfare, and the crusade which the king shared with

---

[2] For a caveat regarding twelfth-century councils, see above, 140; below, 443—4.
[3] For an account which combines narrative and analysis, see Prestwich, *Edward I*, 89—108, 170—375.

his nobility, all helped to rebuild a harmonious political society after the
traumas of Henry III's reign. In much of what he did, Edward consciously
sought to distance himself from his father's regime by adopting the methods
of his father's opponents of 1258–9 and by attending to their programme,
notably in matters of local government.[4] Even his use of the Quo Warranto
proceedings to challenge magnate liberties, though it provoked a good
deal of baronial resentment, did little to disrupt the social peace.[5]

Edward's achievement during these years was to win the support of the
political nation, headed by the magnates and gentry, without compromising
on the essentials of royal authority. In this he displayed sensitivity and a
sharp political intelligence. Parliament was central to his mode of kingship,
for it provided a public stage for consensus politics and, via the council
which was most active at parliament time, a more enclosed setting for
much of the work of government. Its usefulness was emphasized by a
new degree of regulation, seen in the decision evidently taken soon after
Edward's return to England in 1274 to hold biannual sessions, at Easter and
Michaelmas. This scheme was disrupted by Edward's absence in Gascony
from 1286 to 1289 and by his visits to the north to settle the Scottish
succession in 1291–2, but in general it was followed until 1293.[6] Echoing
the demand in the Provisions of Oxford for regular parliaments at fixed
points in the calendar, it presumably had the same end in view: to provide
recognized occasions, known in advance, when king and magnates could
come together to discuss 'the common business of the realm and the king'.[7]
Neither the practices of the baronial reformers nor those of Henry III
were rigidly followed. The Provisions had called for three parliaments a
year rather than Edward's two, while the new king's abandonment of his
father's Hilary session was conspicuous. It may have owed something to
the difficulties of winter travel; but, like the abandonment of Westminster
Abbey's rebuilding after 1272,[8] it also marked Edward's indifference to his
father's pieties, for, as we have seen, Henry had timed the Hilary parliament
to follow the feast of Edward the Confessor's Deposition on 5 January.[9]
In a comparable divergence from the past there was a less exclusive
concentration on Westminster as parliament's meeting place. While it

[4] Cf. J. R. Maddicott, 'Edward I and the Lessons of Baronial Reform: Local Government, 1258–80',
TCE 1 (1986), 1–30.
[5] For Quo Warranto, see Prestwich, *Edward I*, 258–64.   [6] *PROME* i. 3, 47, 61.
[7] *DBM* 110–11; above, 237–8.
[8] Brown, Colvin, and Taylor, *History of the King's Works*, i. 150.   [9] Above, 162–5.

remained the usual venue, other sessions were also held at Gloucester in 1278, Shrewsbury and Acton Burnell in 1283, possibly at Winchester in 1285, at Clipston in 1290, Ashridge and Norham in 1291, and Berwick in 1292: deviations largely accounted for by Edward's wars, diplomatic needs, and personal interests.[10]

Probably more often than under Henry III, parliaments at Westminster might be social and 'patronage' as well as business occasions; though the distinction may be one that Edward would not have acknowledged. At the Easter parliament of 1285 which saw the publication of the Statute of Westminster II, many magnates' sons were knighted and many charters confirmed.[11] That of 1290 saw two great weddings, one between Edward's second daughter, Joan of Acre, and the earl of Gloucester, and the second between his third daughter, Margaret, and John, son of the duke of Brabant, which ended with a great ball in the royal palace.[12] Three aristocratic marriages, including those of two earls, were celebrated at the Whitsun parliament of 1306, which also saw the Feast of the Swans, the knighting of Prince Edward, and the mass knighting of some 300 others.[13] If mass knightings had sometimes been a feature of earlier assemblies, Edward's theatrical occasions, marked by ceremony and spectacle, stood in contrast to some of Henry III's superficially comparable parliamentary tableaux, such as the presentation of the king's second son Edmund in Sicilian dress to the watching magnates at the parliament of March 1257.[14] For Henry, parliamentary theatre might be no more than a misguided, even risible, attempt to drum up support for an unpopular policy. For Edward it was an instrument of kingship which brought magnates and gentry into the glamorous circle of the royal family and into alignment with the king's military needs and ambitions.

But royal marriages and mass knightings at parliament time were necessarily infrequent. More important for consensual politics were the opportunities which parliament provided for regular consultation and the securing of consent to royal policies. Here Edward in the first part of

---

[10] *PROME* i. 33, 41, 44, 52, 54, 56, 59.   [11] *Cotton*, 166; *PROME* i. 43.
[12] *Cotton*, 174, 176–7; Stacey, 'Parliamentary Negotiation and the Expulsion of the Jews', 86, 90–1; *PROME* i. 49.
[13] *The Chronicle of Pierre de Langtoft*, ed. T. Wright, 2 vols., RS (London, 1866–8), ii. 369; Coss, *The Knight in Medieval England*, 84–5.
[14] *Paris*, v. 623; above, 183. For earlier examples of mass knightings at councils and parliaments, see above, 94, 222, and, for Henry III, N. Denholm-Young, *History and Heraldry, 1254–1310: A Study of the Historical Value of the Rolls of Arms* (Oxford, 1965), 25–6.

his reign was a scrupulous observer of the constitutional conventions. The decision to go to war with Wales, for example, was taken with the 'common counsel' of the prelates and magnates in the Michaelmas parliament of 1276, and that for war with France similarly in the parliament of June 1294.[15] Edward's practices conformed much more closely to the reforming ideals of 1258–9 than to his father's more covert methods of decision-making, seen in Henry's private undertakings to campaign in Poitou in 1242 and to accept the throne of Sicily in 1254. It is true that citing magnate consent, or the need for it, could sometimes provide a constitutional pretext to allow the king to do what he wanted to do, as it had done in the past.[16] When in 1275 the pope called for the revival of the tribute due to him since John's reign for the English kingdom, Edward countered by saying that he had not yet been able to discuss the matter with his prelates and nobles, as he intended to do at the Michaelmas parliament, and that he could not answer without their 'imparted counsel'.[17] When the clergy pleaded for the repeal of the Statute of Mortmain in 1294, he was able to answer that the statute had been enacted by the counsel of the magnates and that it could not be repealed without that same counsel.[18] The need to consult might liberate a king as well as constrain him.

Edward's deference to those in parliament might sometimes be tactical, but it was not merely specious. He genuinely wanted advice and might on occasion speak exigently of his need for it. After papal proposals for an Anglo-French peace had been read out in the Easter parliament of 1299 Edward asked the assembled bishops, earls, and barons what he should do, and after debating apart for a while (an interesting sidelight on parliamentary procedure) they returned to advise 'with one voice' that he should accept the proposals.[19] Some years later, in 1305, at the conclusion of the parliamentary trial of Nicholas of Seagrave for treason, Edward asked 'the earls, barons, magnates and others of his council . . . on the homage, fealty and allegiance which they owed to him to advise him faithfully' on the appropriate penalty for Seagrave's crime.[20] Like his great-grandfather Henry II, whose counsel-seeking language his own sometimes resembled,[21] Edward demanded counsel in order to create a collective responsibility

---

[15] *Foedera*, I. ii. 536; *Cotton*, 154, 233–4. For other examples, see Prestwich, *Edward I*, 451–2.
[16] Above, 89, 98, 183–4.   [17] Sayles, *Functions*, 141–2.
[18] *The Chronicle of Walter of Guisborough*, ed. H. Rothwell, Camden Ser. 89 (1957), 250.
[19] *Willielmi Rishanger, Chronica et Annales*, ed. H. T. Riley, RS (London, 1865), 389–90.
[20] *PROME* ii. 182.   [21] Above, 87.

for difficult decisions, to enforce the feudal obligations of his great men, and, paradoxically perhaps, to win their support by engaging them in the work of government. That he also wanted the best advice from those most qualified to give it was shown by a more unusual feature of his rule: his calling in of specialists to afforce the less professional counsel available in parliament. Experts in Roman law were summoned from Oxford and Cambridge to the Norham parliament of 1291 in order to advise on the Scottish succession, and to the Lincoln parliament of 1301 to help Edward counter Pope Boniface VIII's legal challenge to his position in Scotland.[22] For similar ends burgesses from twenty-four towns, 'who best know how to plan and lay out a certain new town', were summoned to the Bury St Edmunds parliament of 1296 in order to advise on the rebuilding of Berwick.[23] Even during the years of confrontation with his subjects after 1294 Edward's moves towards a more autocratic style of kingship were thus tempered by a continuing awareness of the need for good counsel. That this was invariably to be given in parliament showed how parliament was still the focus for counsel-giving and for what remained of the consensus politics which had been more dominant in the first part of the reign.

A more consistently consensual activity, again with a parliamentary setting, was law-making. Almost all the great Edwardian statutes of the years up to 1290—Westminster I and II (1275 and 1285), Gloucester (1278), Mortmain (1279), Quia Emptores and Quo Warranto (1290)—were associated with sessions of parliament. The Statute of Winchester (1285) may have been the exception, but quite possibly was not.[24] In using parliament to carry through such a major legislative programme Edward once again followed the precedents set by the baronial reformers of 1258–9—here as in so much else the unwitting and unacknowledged architects of his early kingship.[25] Yet the precise role of parliament in

---

[22] E. L. G. Stones and G. G. Simpson, *Edward I and the Throne of Scotland, 1290–1296*, 2 vols. (Oxford, 1978), i. 154–5, ii. 5; Prestwich, *Edward I*, 490–2.

[23] *Parl. Writs*, I. 49; M. Beresford, *New Towns of the Middle Ages* (London, 1967), 3–5.

[24] The statute was published on 8 October 1285 at Winchester, and on the previous day an especially large number of magnates, including four earls (but no bishop save Robert Burnell, bishop of Bath and Wells, the chancellor), witnessed three royal charters there: *Stat. Realm*, i. 98; *The Royal Charter Witness Lists of Edward I*, ed. R. Huscroft, List and Index Soc. 279 (2000), 74. Whether or not we choose to call this assembly a parliament—and no source does so, though the season would have been an appropriate one—it seems highly likely that magnate consultation went to the statute's making. Cf. *PROME* i. 44, for a more negative view. The Statute of Acton Burnell, probably made by the council alone, provides a more certain instance of non-parliamentary legislation: Prestwich, *Edward I*, 453.

[25] Above, 239–44.

the making of the new statutes remains difficult to define. The effective instrument seems generally to have been the council and, within it, the judges, acting on the knowledge gained from long experience in the courts in order to propose and draft the reforms seen to be needed.[26] Parliament's role was probably one of ratification. This dualism is explicit in the preamble to Westminster I, made at the Easter parliament of 1275 by '[the king's] council and by the assent of the archbishops, bishops, abbots, priors, earls, barons and the community of the land summoned thither'. The reference to the role of 'the community of the land' provides the only direct evidence for the participation of the knights and burgesses in any part of the law-making process at any point in the reign.[27] For some statutes, such as Quia Emptores, 'made at the instance of the great men of the realm', where magnate interests were more narrowly at stake, there was a more definite (though still not precisely definable) magnate contribution.[28] But in general legislation moved downwards, from king and council to parliament. The reform of abuses which it embodied was more the product of the king's interest, the judges' expertise, the magnates' assent, and the common good as interpreted by king and council, than of popular complaint voiced by the commons, as it was to become in the fourteenth century.

The wide backing which Edward took care to secure for new statutes emphasized once again his willingness to use parliament as his main instrument of public government. For those with long memories the contrast with his father's resented pre-1258 habit of legislating by writ and without proper consultation would have been plain.[29] Even the one major piece of Edwardian legislation in writ form, the Statute of Mortmain, was made with 'the counsel of the prelates, earls and other faithful men of our realm on our council'.[30] Yet parliament was probably of more direct value to the crown in the promulgation of statutes than in their making. This could take several forms: publication to the assembled prelates, magnates, and commons, as presumably with Westminster I; publication to a wider audience in parliament's immediate environs, as with the reading aloud of

[26] Richardson and Sayles, 'The Early Statutes', in *EPMA* xxv. 22; Prestwich, *Edward I*, 269–70. For a general discussion of the origins of Edwardian legislation, often made in response to pressure from particular groups, see Brand, 'English Thirteenth Century Legislation', 335–7.

[27] *Stat. Realm*, i. 26; Brand, 'English Thirteenth Century Legislation', 338–9.

[28] *Stat. Realm*, i. 106; Prestwich, *Edward I*, 270; Brand, 'English Thirteenth Century Legislation', 335.

[29] Above, 241.   [30] *Stat. Realm*, i. 51.

Westminster II in Westminster Hall 'in the presence of the whole people' at the close of the Easter parliament of 1285;[31] and publication in the counties, sometimes by elaborately stipulated arrangements. The most elaborate were those laid down at parliament time for Westminster I, entailing publication of the statute in county and hundred courts, cities, boroughs, market towns, and wherever else seemed expedient, the distribution of copies to royal officials in the counties, and the preservation of the statute in the hands of committees of county knights.[32] But for all new laws some form of local publication had long been essential. More striking was the public recitation of Westminster II, for this may have been in deliberate emulation of the precisely similar reading of the Provisions of Westminster, also in Westminster Hall, some twenty-seven years earlier. On this earlier occasion Edward may well have been present as he certainly was at the later.[33]

The point of all these arrangements was not only to give publicity to new laws and so to facilitate their enforcement, but also, in Edward's case, to demonstrate the king's concern for the common good and thus to win support both in parliament and in the country. What was ordained in parliament, he told the pope in 1275, was intended, *inter alia*, 'to produce an increase in the general welfare of the people (*communis profectus populi*)'.[34] In winning support he was at least partly successful. The making of the statutes was widely reported in the chronicles, often without comment; but Westminster I received a unanimously favourable reception and Westminster II a largely favourable one.[35] If there was nothing especially new in the links which parliament thus provided between the king's government and the king's subjects in the localities, its traditional role was nevertheless enhanced by the volume of Edward's legislation, unparalleled in earlier reigns, and by the government's concern to see at least the major statutes publicized as widely as possible.

[31] *Ann. Oseney*, 304. For the publication of legislation, see Brand, 'English Thirteenth Century Legislation', 339–41.

[32] *Stat. Realm*, i. 39; Richardson and Sayles, 'Early Statutes', in *EPMA* xxv. 22–3; Maddicott, 'Edward I and the Lessons of Baronial Reform', 15–16.

[33] *De Antiquis Legibus Liber*, 42; above, 244. The Provisions of Westminster were proclaimed on 24 October 1259. Edward had been at Westminster or in London on 13 and 15 October and was at Bermondsey on 26 October: R. Studd, *An Itinerary of Lord Edward*, List and Index Soc. 284 (2000), 44–5. In 1285 Edward was at Westminster for the duration of the Easter parliament: *PROME* i. 43.

[34] *Parl. Writs*, I. 381; Sayles, *Functions*, 141.

[35] For Westminster I, see Maddicott, 'Edward I and the Lessons of Baronial Reform', 16 and n. 87, and sources there cited. For Westminster II, see *Ann. Oseney*, 304 (favourable), *Ann. Dunstable*, 317 (favourable), *Cotton*, 166 (neutral). Other statutes: see e.g. *Rishanger, Chronica*, 93, and *Guisborough*, 215–16, for the Statute of Gloucester.

Edward's law-making throws some light on the centrality of the council both to his government in general and to the workings of parliament in particular. As we have seen, the council as a defined group, consisting mainly of ministers but with some magnate members, all bound by oath, had emerged in Henry III's early years.[36] The extent to which its position changed under his son is difficult to gauge, but prima facie we might expect some enlargement of its role. To a king notable for his zeal in seeking counsel and for his readiness to consult widely, the council made available the practical intelligence and the technical and bureaucratic skills necessary for effective government. That it elicited a famous contemporary comment was perhaps a mark of its novel prominence and of a newly conscious recognition of its work. 'The king', said the author of *Fleta*, writing about 1290, 'has his court in his council in his parliaments, where prelates, earls, barons, magnates and others learned in the law are present. And doubts are determined there concerning judgements, new remedies are devised for wrongs newly brought to light, and there also justice is dispersed to everyone according to his desserts.'[37] With its probable reference to the statutes ('new remedies are devised . . .'), *Fleta* highlights one reason for a possible increase in conciliar activity at parliament time. But most of the council's work was more ordinary. At the Acton Burnell parliament of 1283, for instance, it dealt, among other matters, with the care and valuation of the goods of the deceased Patrick de Chaworth; the restoration of the Essex manor of Steeple to Emery Pecche; the payment by instalments of the fines owed to the king by two men imprisoned at Lincoln; the bishop of Worcester's request to be allowed to enfeoff the chapter of York with the manor of Burley; the request of the burgesses of Shrewsbury for a three-year grant of pavage; and the arrears of the fee of the constable of Dover. Some thirty items of this sort came before the council at this one session, in addition to twenty-two further petitions which Hugh of Kendale, a chancery clerk, was appointed to expedite.[38]

Much of this routine business was dealt with by the king and council alone. If the council was at its most active during a parliamentary session, it was because parliament brought together ministers and magnates, some of whom, particularly the justices, may normally have been dispersed around the country, and because difficult judicial cases were often reserved for these

[36] Above, 188-9.
[37] *Fleta*, vol. ii, ed. H. G. Richardson and G. O. Sayles, Selden Soc. 72 (1955), 109.
[38] *PROME* i. 147-61. For Hugh of Kendale, see *CCR, 1272-79*, 501.

special parliamentary sessions of the council. The interaction between the council and parliament itself was most visible at the highest level of national business. We have already seen this with regard to the statutes, drafted in council for parliamentary assent, and the same was true of taxation. A leading minister might put the king's request for a tax to magnates and commons, as did Roger of Seaton, chief justice of common pleas, at the Michaelmas parliament of 1275, and Roger Brabazon, chief justice of king's bench, at the Lincoln parliament of 1301.[39] Sometimes the whole council might act as the 'steering group' for a tax grant, expounding the king's needs to those assembled before it, as happened at the Trinity parliament of 1306.[40] But in essentials none of this was very new. The council had, for example, played a similar tax-inducing role, if unsuccessfully, at the April parliament of 1254.[41] Though magnate representation on the council may have increased,[42] and though the weight of business, given Edward's personal predilections and reforming programme, may have grown, any variations in the council's position between Henry's reign and Edward's are likely to have been quantitative rather than qualitative. The only major change in the relations of council and parliament was political. As far as can be seen, the tension sometimes evident in Henry's middle years between a distrusted council of king's friends and a baronial parliament had gone. Here, as generally in the early Edwardian polity, harmony reigned.

Both numerically and in terms of public standing, measured by wealth and land, the ecclesiastical and lay magnates summoned to Edward's parliaments greatly outweighed his councillors. The thirty-eight councillors summoned to the Lent parliament of 1300 may give an idea of the size of the council, usually unknown, in an average parliament. That they included thirteen *magistri*, some of them Oxford graduates, hints once again at the quality of the advice which Edward sought.[43] Magnate numbers were usually much

---

[39] *Gervase of Canterbury*, ii. 281; *Rishanger, Chronica*, 454.

[40] D. Pasquet, *An Essay on the Origins of the House of Commons*, trans. R. G. D. Laffan (Cambridge, 1925), 235, printing TNA, E.368/76, m. 43.

[41] Lunt, 'Consent of the English Lower Clergy to Taxation', 142–3; above, 214. For other and earlier examples of ministers presenting the case for taxation, see above, 62, 82, 107, 180, 188.

[42] Wilkinson, 'Development of the Council', 149. Wilkinson argues (ibid. 121–40) for major changes in the council under Edward I, notably in the growth of executive power. But cf. Prestwich, *Edward I*, 439–40.

[43] *Parl. Writs*, I. 83. The two Oxford graduates were Peter de Insula and (probably) Thomas de Luggore: see A. B. Emden, *A Biographical Register of the University of Oxford to A. D. 1500*, 3 vols. (Oxford, 1957–9), ii. 1003, 1174. The warden of Merton and two fellows of the College were also present at this parliament. J. H. Denton and J. P. Dooley, *Representatives of the Lower Clergy in Parliament, 1295–1340* (Woodbridge, 1987), 7.

larger. A hundred and ten lay magnates were summoned to the Shrewsbury parliament of 1283; 101 to the Lincoln parliament of 1301; 99 to the Carlisle parliament of 1307; and at least 78 to the parliament of May 1306.[44] But there was little consistency in the lists of those summoned, and numbers might sometimes be significantly smaller. Only 64 were summoned to the August parliament of 1295, for example, and only 41 to that of November 1296.[45] Nor did all those summoned necessarily attend.[46] The numbers of heads of religious houses varied in a similar way: some 73 were summoned to the parliament of March 1300 but only 44 for that of 1302.[47] Tenure was no longer the near exclusive determinant for a summons, either for the secular magnates or for the religious (though how and why it had ceased to be so remains to be discovered), and the lesser tenants-in-chief, summoned for most of Henry III's reign, have disappeared. It is not easy to see what alternative principle, if any, may have regulated the lists of those summoned, beyond the obvious need to call up the very great, such as the earls. It is no more than an impression that the numbers of lay magnates summoned may often have been higher than those called to Henry's less well-evidenced parliaments. That the highest number known to have been summoned was for the Shrewsbury parliament, which saw the trial of David of Wales, suggests one possible principle which may have been at work in some parliaments: the need to give maximum publicity to major acts of state.

In the first part of the reign the magnates in parliament were joined only relatively rarely by local representatives. Of the thirty parliaments between Edward's return to England in 1274 and the outbreak of war with France twenty years later, only two were attended by knights and burgesses (April 1275 and September 1283) and a further two by knights alone (October 1275 and July 1290).[48] In addition, there were two further assemblies, not generally called 'parliaments' but with parliamentary characteristics, to which both knights and burgesses were summoned: in January 1273, during the king's absence, and in

---

[44] *Parl. Writs*, I. 15–16, 90, 181–2; Powell and Wallis, *House of Lords*, 208, 249; M. Prestwich, 'Magnate Summonses in England in the Later Years of Edward I', *Parliaments, Estates and Representation*, 5 (1985), 98.
[45] *Parl. Writs*, I. 28–9, 48; Powell and Wallis, *House of Lords*, 220, 229; Prestwich, *Edward I*, 446 (whose figures differ slightly, partly because he omits the earls from those summoned in 1296).
[46] Prestwich, *Edward I*, 447–8.
[47] *Parl. Writs*, I. 83–4, 112; Powell and Wallis, *House of Lords*, 220–2; Prestwich, *Edward I*, 446.
[48] My statistics are derived from *PROME* i. 25–74, rather than *HBC* 545–8.

January 1283, when assemblies of the commons alone met at York and Northampton.[49]

The comparative infrequency of the commons' attendance signified the fiscal lighthandedness of Edward's early government. This does as much as anything to explain the domestic peace which generally prevailed throughout this time, marking it off from Henry III's pre-1258 regime and from Edward's own later years, both of which periods saw frequent and bitter confrontations over taxation. Low taxation did not create political consensus but it made it possible. Thanks largely to the customs duties on wool exports introduced in 1275, which produced an average annual income of nearly £10,000 before 1294,[50] to the loans from Edward's Italian bankers, the Riccardi, which could be repaid from the customs, to prudent housekeeping, and to military commitments in Wales which were light and temporary compared with those later incurred in France and Scotland, Edward was able to get by with only three levies of direct taxation in this twenty-year period: in 1275 (largely to pay for debts incurred on his crusade), in 1283 (for the Welsh war), and in 1290 (mainly for the payment of royal debts and other miscellaneous expenses). All three were granted in assemblies where the knights were present, and that of 1283 in the presence of the burgesses too.[51] One other tax assembly may also have been attended by the commons. At a gathering in London in 1288, held during Edward's absence in Gascony and so technically not a parliament, Wykes tells us that the treasurer, acting on the king's orders, sought a subsidy from the assembled earls and barons and 'also moreover from all the inhabitants of the kingdom'.[52] This sounds very like a request put to local representatives, and indeed it would be surprising if by this time such a request could be considered without their presence. Few though the occasions for taxation were in Edward's early and middle years, they showed that the link between taxes and local representation, forged during the negotiations for Edward's crusading levy in 1268–70 but with Magna Carta as its ultimate ancestor, was now unbreakable.

To demonstrate that the presence of the commons was necessary for grants of taxation is easier than to discover their actual role. Some have argued that they were merely summoned to ratify what the magnates had already agreed,[53] much as parliament itself seems to have ratified legislation

---

[49]   *Ann. Winchester*, 113; and for the assemblies of 1283, see below, 291.
[50]   R. W. Kaeuper, *Bankers to the Crown: The Riccardi of Lucca and Edward I* (Princeton, 1973), 164.
[51]   Prestwich, *Edward I*, 101–2, 238–9, 342–3.   [52]   *Wykes*, 316.
[53]   e.g. Harriss, *King, Parliament and Public Finance*, 42.

already agreed by king and council. It is certainly true that on those few occasions when we can see parliament at work, it is the magnates who take the lead in matters of taxation. It was the earl of Gloucester who turned down the treasurer's request for a subsidy in 1288, and Gloucester again who led the protests against the high rate of tax demanded in 1294 and secured its reduction.[54] As was shown earlier by Ranulf earl of Chester's comparable rejection of Henry III's request for a tax in the great council of March 1232,[55] the Speaker was a magnate before, in the late fourteenth century, he began to be drawn from the commons. The writs of summons for the knights seem to point in a similar direction, for while the early writs are vague about the reasons for their coming to parliament and their functions while there, they soon harden towards a subordinate view of their position. They are summoned to the Easter parliament of 1275 'to discuss (*ad tractandum*) together with the magnates . . . the business of [our] kingdom', while to the Michaelmas parliament of the same year they come 'on behalf of the community of the county . . . to discuss with us and with the . . . prelates and magnates . . . both the *status* of our kingdom and certain business of ours which we shall expound to them there'.[56] The writs for 1283 are more explicit, both as to the representatives' merely reactive role and to the power which they must have to bind their constituents. The knights (and burgesses) are to come 'having full power on behalf of their communities . . . to hear and do what on our part we shall cause to be explained to them'.[57] In 1290 their position as the inferiors of the magnates, whose decisions they were to endorse, seems to be established for the first time. They are to come 'with full power, for themselves and for the whole community of the county, to offer counsel and consent, for themselves and for that community, to those things which the earls, barons and magnates aforesaid shall be led to agree upon'.[58] 'Full power (*plena potestas*)' was demanded again in 1294, while for the assembly of the following year, Stubbs's famous 'Model Parliament', what was to be the essence of the definitive formula finally emerged. Both knights

---

[54] *Wykes*, 316; Prestwich, *Edward I*, 404, 457, citing the Hagnaby chronicle.

[55] Wendover, *Chronica*, iv. 233; above, 219; below, 422, 425, 427.

[56] Stubbs, *Select Charters*, 441–2; id., *Constit. Hist.* ii. 234 n. 5; J. G. Edwards, 'The *Plena Potestas* of English Parliamentary Representatives', in *Historical Studies*, 137. In translating the writ for the Michaelmas parliament I have changed the word order so as to simplify the convoluted Latin syntax while retaining its meaning.

[57] Stubbs, *Select Charters*, 457–8; Edwards, '*Plena Potestas*', 137, 145.

[58] Stubbs, *Select Charters*, 472–3; Edwards, '*Plena Potestas*', 137–8, 145.

and burgesses were to come 'with full and sufficient power' on behalf of themselves and their communities 'to do what shall be ordained by common counsel'.[59]

From the government's viewpoint, therefore, what mattered was the ability of the commons to bind their communities to the payments of taxes. That was the significance of the demand for *plena potestas*. But neither this consideration nor the forms of the writs themselves suggests that the representatives were invariably expected to be the mere endorsers of others' decisions. In both parliaments of 1275 they were called on 'to discuss (*ad tractandum*)' and in 1290 to offer counsel as well as consent. Given their role in Henry III's parliaments, which sometimes involved both discussing and consenting, no less would have been expected. In Henry's middle years the knights and perhaps the burgesses may already have been able to press their grievances on the crown, and in his later years they were able to delay the grant of a crusading tax, by a lengthy process of bargaining, until their grievances had been met.[60] The same process of bargaining, and over some of the same issues, accompanied at least two of the early taxes granted to Edward. The fifteenth of 1275 was granted in return for fresh restraints on Jewish money-lending, including the prohibition of all lending at interest. This was both a matter of continuing concern to the knights, the chief victims of Jewish usury, and an extension of their successful campaign for restraints on the Jews which had been central to the negotiating of the previous tax for the crusade.[61] Far more radical, but again a continuation of the same story, were the measures which accompanied the grant of the fifteenth in 1290; for there was widespread agreement among the chroniclers, backed in this instance by an official exchequer record, that the tax was granted in return for the expulsion of the Jews.[62] The knights were summoned to this parliament after it had been in session for nearly two months to 'offer counsel and to consent' to what the magnates were agreed upon.[63] Clearly the prelates and magnates did not feel able to make any

---

[59] Stubbs, *Select Charters*, 481–2; Edwards, '*Plena Potestas*', 138, 145–6.   [60] Above, 267–71.

[61] Maddicott, 'Edward I and the Lessons of Baronial Reform', 17; Stacey, 'Parliamentary Negotiation and the Expulsion of the Jews', 97.

[62] For the chronicle sources, see Stacey, 'Parliamentary Negotiation and the Expulsion of the Jews', 93 n. 105; for the official source, Pasquet, *Origins of the House of Commons*, 236, printing TNA E.368/76, m. 43 ('in taxacione quintedecime a communitate regni domino Regi anno regni sui xviii. concesse propter exilium Iudeorum').

[63] For the chronology of the parliament, see Richardson and Sayles, 'The Parliaments of Edward I', in *EPMA* v. 144, and *PROME* i. 49–50.

general grant—they had already conceded a feudal aid for the marriage of
the king's daughter—without the presence of the knights. Equally clearly,
the knights' counsel pointed towards the expulsion of the Jews as the price
paid by the crown for a grant. Among the social groups figuring in John of
London's later lamentation for Edward I's death, it was the knights alone
who praised him for this act.[64]

That these representatives were no mere ciphers is confirmed by the one
grant made by representative assemblies alone, without the presence of the
magnates: that of 1283, when knights and burgesses were summoned to
parallel assemblies at York (for the northern counties) and at Northampton
(for the southern) to consider taxation for the current Welsh war. No
source calls these assemblies 'parliaments', presumably because both the
king and the magnates were absent in Wales, and the meetings were
regional and divided. Yet the request for taxation put to the knights and
burgesses gave them a clear resemblance to more normal tax parliaments.
All the evidence suggests that in this instance the resulting grant of a
thirtieth was made directly by the representatives, that they did not take
their lead from the magnates, and indeed that any magnate grant followed
after that of the representatives. The writ for the collection of the tax was
addressed to 'the knights, free men and the whole county community' in
each county. It thanked them for their grant, noted that the grant had been
made on condition that the magnates should grant the same, and informed
the counties that they had in fact done so: they had ratified (*ratificaverunt*)
the common grant.[65] That two widely separated assemblies made identical
grants of a thirtieth suggests that the same demand was made of each of
them by the king's agents, whose role in putting to the local representatives
what they should 'hear and do' is referred to in the writs of summons.[66]
But on this occasion the knights and burgesses can have discussed the
demand only among themselves, without magnate guidance, and reached
their decision independently of, and prior to, that of the magnates.

There is thus a good case for saying that the knights, and sometimes
perhaps the burgesses too, played an active part in granting taxes. They

---

[64] *Commendatio Lamentabilis*, in *Chronicles of the Reigns of Edward I and Edward II*, ed. W. Stubbs, RS,
2 vols. (London, 1882–3), ii. 14; Stacey, 'Parliamentary Negotiation and the Expulsion of the Jews', 93
n. 105.

[65] *Parl. Writs*, I. 10–13. Harriss, *King, Parliament and Public Finance*, 41–2, argues incorrectly that the
magnates' grant preceded that of the representatives. Cf. Stubbs, *Constit. Hist.* ii. 119, and Mitchell,
Taxation, 226, who take the opposite view.

[66] *Parl. Writs*, I. 10.

could offer counsel, debate among themselves, press their grievances on the crown, and secure concessions as the price of their grant. If they had done 'some real assenting' as far back as 1237, as A. B. White thought, it is unlikely that their consent would have been any the less real fifty years later.[67] Implicit in their tax-granting role was a social and local weight which also does much to explain their presence at assemblies when taxation was not on the agenda. When the unusually large number of four knights from each county and four men from each city were summoned to the Westminster assembly of January 1273, held soon after Henry III's death and in Edward's absence, it was to take an oath of fealty to the new king and to make a firm undertaking to keep the peace.[68] At a time of potential danger the way to good order in the localities lay through the knights and senior townsmen who were their leaders. Rather more frequently, their attendance and subsequent return home was intended to give provincial publicity to important acts of government. This was most signally shown at Edward's first parliament in April 1275 which saw the publication of the first Statute of Westminster: in some senses Edward I's 'coronation charter' in the wide range of beneficial reforms which it introduced and in the support which it was intended to generate. To this parliament there were again summoned four knights from each county (rather than the usual two) and four or six burgesses from every city, borough, and market town. A summons on this scale could have produced as many as 700 to 800 representatives. Equally extraordinary was the number of heads of religious houses summoned: at least eleven from Warwickshire and Leicestershire alone.[69] To some extent the number of townsmen summoned may reflect the government's intention to secure a grant of customs duties from the urban merchants, successfully carried through. But a more compelling explanation lies in the need to publicize as widely as possible a new statute which was intended to bring general benefits and to secure Edward's throne. The elaborate arrangements for the statute's publication in the counties point in the same direction.[70]

[67] White, 'Some Early Instances of the Concentration of Representatives', 747; above, 222.

[68] *Ann. Winchester*, 113; *Ann. Waverley*, 379.

[69] C. H. Jenkinson, 'The First Parliament of Edward I', *EHR* 25 (1910), 240; Maddicott, 'Edward I and the Lessons of Baronial Reform', 14–17. Only the Warwickshire and Leicestershire return lists the religious houses summoned. It is clear that the chancery (or the king) decided which houses were to be summoned and that the sheriff forwarded to them the writs of summons which he had received from headquarters.

[70] Above, 284.

Publicity too was almost certainly what Edward wanted when he summoned two knights from every shire and two burgesses from London and twenty other specified towns to attend at Shrewsbury for the trial of David of Wales in September 1283. The writs for this parliament, worded in similar terms to magnates, knights, and burgesses, were themselves an exercise in propaganda, speaking of the treachery of the Welsh and their slaughter of old men, women, and children, and of David himself as 'the last survivor of the family of traitors'.[71] Save for the summoning of men from particular towns to advise on the planning of Berwick in 1296, this was the only occasion in the reign when the initiative in deciding which towns to summon is known to have been taken out of the hands of the sheriffs.[72] The towns were chosen with care to reflect size and regional importance. Besides London, they included the county towns of the marcher counties (Chester, Worcester, Hereford, and Shrewsbury itself), some other important county towns (Northampton and Nottingham), some great 'provincial capitals' (York, Lincoln, Exeter, and Norwich), and some major ports (Boston and Yarmouth). We have already noted that an exceptionally large number of magnates were summoned to this parliament.[73] Behind all this there was clearly a great deal of stage management, with parliament as the intended focus of a nationalist fervour which would radiate back to town and country. The return of the London representatives bearing David's head must have been an especially graphic way of presenting parliament's work, and the successful implementation of the king's wishes, to stay-at-homes whose support Edward judged worth cultivating.[74]

In providing publicity for such royal *acta* as new legislation and state trials, parliament could promote the outward and downward transmission of the crown's policies and intentions, from the centre to the regions and from the king and council to local audiences gathered in shire and hundred courts or in more domestic surroundings.[75] Representation was the best means of effecting this. Magnates (and prelates) represented no one but themselves, as the author of the *Modus Tenendi Parliamentum* noted in the

[71] *Parl. Writs*, I. 15–16; M. Prestwich, *War, Politics and Finance under Edward I* (London, 1972), 240.
[72] M. McKisack, *The Parliamentary Representation of the English Boroughs during the Middle Ages* (Oxford, 1932), 6–9.
[73] Above, 287.
[74] *Ann. London*, in *Chronicles of the Reign of Edward II*, ed. Stubbs, i. 92; McKisack, *Parliamentary Representation*, 7.
[75] For the local reception of parliamentary news in the fourteenth century, see Maddicott, 'Parliament and the Constituencies', 84–5, and below, 370.

next generation,[76] and they were in any case thin on the ground. Only the knights (and burgesses) were sufficiently numerous, sufficiently evenly distributed throughout the realm, and sufficiently in touch with local institutions, including the courts which elected them, to make possible, if not necessarily to ensure, a wide and friendly reception for the news which the government wished to broadcast. For the king, representation was a way of gaining access not only to his subjects' money but also to their goodwill.

But the contacts which parliament facilitated were by no means one way, and during Edward's reign the upward transmission of opinion and complaint came to complement what was sent down to the localities. In the long term this was one of the reign's most significant developments. To some extent it must have been carried through orally, in ways now impossible to assess. Knightly pressure for anti-Jewish measures, for example, so apparent in the parliaments of 1268–70, Michaelmas 1275, and 1290, is likely to have taken a primarily oral form, via discussion and the coordination and voicing of opinion in parliament. This last can be assumed more easily than it can be precisely identified. Much more evident is the sudden emergence of the written petition, requesting the king to provide a remedy for some grievance or injustice or to grant a particular favour, and from the 1270s presented in parliament in numbers which soon came to be overwhelming.[77] The written plaint, sometimes presented to the king's justices in eyre, was not in itself new, and its use had grown rapidly during the early years of the reform period, 1258–60, when barons and king had rivalled each other in providing justice for the discontented.[78] But such documents, now presented in parliament in a novel way, proliferated so rapidly after 1275, and from such barely visible parliamentary origins, that they are more likely to have been the product of some sudden act of creation than of any long course of development. It seems likely that they were initiated in the first parliament of the reign, that of Easter 1275,

[76] Pronay and Taylor, *Parliamentary Texts of the Later Middle Ages*, 90.

[77] For what follows, see Maddicott, 'Parliament and the Constituencies', 62–9, from which all unreferenced statements are taken. G. Dodd, *Justice and Grace: Private Petitioning and the English Parliament in the Late Middle Ages* (Oxford, 2007), is now the best general guide to its subject. For the content and purpose of early petitions, see also P. Brand, 'Understanding Early Petitions: An Analysis of the Content of Petitions to Parliament in the Reign of Edward I', in W. M. Ormrod, G. Dodd, and A. Musson (eds.), *Medieval Petitions: Grace and Grievance* (Woodbridge, 2009), 99–119.

[78] Dodd, *Justice and Grace*, 30–1.

probably by an invitation to submit petitions,[79] of the kind that we know Edward was to issue prior to the later parliament of 1305.[80] Edward's objects may well have been to provide an outlet for popular grievances, to enhance his general control of the localities, and in particular to keep a check on the royal officials whose misdeeds had been revealed by the Hundred Roll enquiries of 1274–5 and who had often been the subject of popular complaints. By providing justice, and so doing his royal duty, he also increased his own power and authority.[81]

Petitions submitted early in the reign were generally addressed to the king, later ones to the king and council.[82] Though 'landholders, churchmen, and merchants' may have predominated among the petitioners,[83] they were often sent in by men and women of no great social importance: by a group of London bakers and their wives reduced to beggary (so they said) by the failure of the government to settle debts owing from Henry III's reign, to take an example from 1278, or by the masons working on Norwich castle, whose wages had been in arrears for some years, to take another from 1290.[84] They were usually, but not invariably, delivered in parliament, often seemingly by the petitioners themselves,[85] because parliament's meetings now fell at more or less predictable times and because king, council, and the great departments of exchequer and chancery were all in session then. As early as 1278 the number of petitions coming forward had begun to promote institutional change: in that year we hear of two men 'assigned to receive petitions in parliament', and by this time too petitions were being retained on files.[86] By 1280 the problems posed for parliament by 'the multitude of petitions' had become so great that special arrangements had to be made for them. Petitions were to be directed to the appropriate department—chancery, exchequer, the justices, and the justices of the

[79] Maddicott, 'Edward I and the Lessons of Baronial Reform', 24–5; id., 'Parliament and the Constituencies', 62–4; P. Brand, 'Petitions and Parliament in the Reign of Edward I', in L. Clarke (ed.), *Parchment and People: Parliament in the Middle Ages* (Edinburgh, 2004), 14–16. Dodd, *Justice and Grace*, 23–5, generally accepts this view but raises some questions.

[80] *PROME* ii. 52.

[81] Maddicott, 'Parliament and the Constituencies', 64–8; Dodd, *Justice and Grace*, 25–6, 32–5.

[82] Brand, 'Petitions and Parliament', 25–7.   [83] Dodd, *Justice and Grace*, 206.

[84] *PROME* i. 338, ii. 570–1. For other examples, see Maddicott, 'Parliament and the Constituencies', 62, and Brand, 'Understanding Early Petitions', 109–10, 113–15.

[85] Brand, 'Petitions and Parliament', 37; Dodd, *Justice and Grace*, 205–6, 310–14.

[86] *PROME* ii. 590, 569; Richardson and Sayles, 'The Exchequer Parliament Rolls and Other Documents', in *EPMA* xix. 134; Dodd, *Justice and Grace*, 20.

Jews—and only those which could not be dealt with by the leading ministers were to be reserved for the king and his council, leaving them free to attend to 'the great business of his kingdom and of his foreign lands'.[87] By 1290 there were separate panels of auditors for petitions from England, Ireland, and Gascony, and in 1293 further efforts were made to see that petitions delivered in parliament were directed towards particular departments in the first instance.[88] By this time parliament's function as both a delivery point and a sorting house for petitions was well established, and so it was to remain until at least the reign of Edward III.[89]

The general importance of these developments was very great. They began to make parliament a more 'popular' institution: not an occasion only for the high state business of political decision-making, legislation, and taxation, but one which also extended parliament's complementary judicial function in a novel way. The opportunity to submit a petition freed those present from the trammels of legal process and allowed them to seek a remedy cheaply and informally. Of course, the petitioner did not necessarily 'get what he wanted, he was merely put in the way of getting it', in Maitland's words;[90] and the hearing of a petition by king and council, or more probably by a department of state, was no guarantee that it would receive a positive answer. Nevertheless, the very large inflow of petitions to parliament from the 1270s suggests a good deal of optimism about what might be gained. This was one way of creating a warmer climate of acceptance for Edward's monarchy and for a king who was placing a more expansive interpretation on his traditional and oath-bound obligation to do justice. The frequent issuing of judicial commissions from 1275 in the months following a parliament, in many cases to deal with complaints made by petition, shows how seriously and practically this duty was taken—even if the king might have an ulterior motive in calling to order the officials whose misdemeanours were frequently the subject of petitions.[91] Yet the

---

[87] Sayles, *Functions*, 172; Brand, 'Petitions and Parliament', 34; Dodd, *Justice and Grace*, 51.

[88] Sayles, *Functions*, 209; Richardson and Sayles, 'The King's Ministers in Parliament, 1272–1307', in *EPMA* vi. 542; Brand, 'Petitions and Parliament', 35; Dodd, *Justice and Grace*, 51–3.

[89] For the survival of private petitions in Edward III's reign, see G. Dodd, 'The Hidden Presence: Parliament and the Private Petition in the Fourteenth Century', in A. Musson (ed.), *Expectations of the Law in the Middle Ages* (Woodbridge, 2001), 135–49. Dodd, 'Parliamentary Petitions? The Origins and Provenance of the "Ancient Petitions" (SC 8) in the National Archives', in Ormrod, Dodd, and Musson (eds.), *Medieval Petitions*, makes a strong case for the presentation of the great majority of petitions in parliament.

[90] *Memoranda de Parliamento*, ed. Maitland, p. lxviii.

[91] Maddicott, 'Edward I and the Lessons of Baronial Reform', 24–5.

order of 1280 shows that petitionary justice had no priority in parliament and that for Edward himself 'the great business of the realm' came first.[92]

The degree to which petitioning was promoted by representation is difficult to assess. The connection cannot have been a strict one, for petitions were presented in many parliaments where neither knights nor burgesses were present. But when they did attend it is likely that they brought up with them the petitions of their constituents, as we know to have been the case by Edward II's early years.[93] That by the 1290s petitions were occasionally being presented in the names of shire and borough communities, as well as those of individuals, was one possible mark of the participation of representatives in the petitioning process. In the Easter parliament of 1290, for example, to whose concluding session the knights were summoned, the 'community of Hampshire' offered the king 200 marks by petition for the county's disafforestation, and 'the men of the county of Hertfordshire' asked to be allowed to build a prison in the county town.[94] The local drive for disafforestation, seen in the case of Hampshire, was by this time nearly a century old,[95] but the forum for its expression and the procedure were new. Though such county petitions were as yet uncommon and might, like individual petitions, be presented in parliaments where no representatives were present,[96] parliament was none the less coming to be the mouthpiece for corporate concerns at a level below that of the baronage. Through petitioning, through representation, and through the possible union of the two in parliament, the king's non-noble subjects were finding a voice.

In the first twenty years of Edward's reign the king's policies had situated parliament at the centre of his affairs and of the nation's. His awareness of the elevated place which parliament had assumed in the ideals and practices of the baronial reformers of 1258–9, his desire to rule with the counsel of his magnates, and his use of a parliamentary forum and

[92] Cf. Brand, 'Petitions and Parliament', 38.
[93] Maddicott, 'Parliament and the Constituencies', 65; below, 333, 340. For a more qualified view, see Dodd, *Justice and Grace*, 308–9.
[94] *PROME* i. 319, 337.   [95] Above, 137.
[96] Note the petition of 1278 in which 'the community of Cheshire' petitions against being made to travel outside their *pays* for the hearing of civil pleas: *PROME* ii. 518. Cheshire, as a palatinate, was never represented in parliament. G. L. Haskins, 'The Petitions of Representatives in the Parliaments of Edward I', *EHR* 53 (1938), 8–15, emphasizes the paucity of shire and borough petitions, and prints a list.

parliamentary ratification to carry through the most extensive programme
of legislation since the reign of Æthelred, all show how intrinsic parliament
was to his government. In an era of relative financial stability and moderate
taxation, its salience owed almost everything to consensus and nothing
to the confrontations which had placed parliament at the heart of politics
for much of the previous reign. If from the start of his reign Edward
invited his subjects to bring forward their petitions in parliament, as seems
likely, it was on his part another planned and deliberate enhancement
of parliament's role. At the same time the use made of the commons
not only to grant taxes but to influence local opinion, and the access to
parliament which petitioning made available to all comers, broadened its
national reach and its national appeal. Other groups now came within its
purview. It was the merchants, for example, who apparently conceded the
new customs duties of 1275 (the magnates merely giving their 'beneficent
assent') and whose interests were recognized and protected in the Statute
of Acton Burnell (1283) and the Statute of Merchants (1285), both made
in parliament.[97] Both the growth of petitioning and the recognition of
mercantile interests, as well as the occasional attendance of the burgesses,
extended the scope of parliament well beyond the landed classes who had
made up the great councils of a century earlier. In another direction, the
decision for war with Wales, taken in the Michaelmas parliament of 1276,
and the trial of David of Wales in the Shrewsbury parliament of 1283,
gave what was already a national institution a more sharply nationalistic
edge.[98] The king's foreign policy was not disputed in parliament, as so often
in his father's reign, but endorsed. The concurrent reception of petitions
from Gascony, Ireland, Wales, and (from 1292) Scotland, as well as from
England, and Edward's use of parliament to settle the Scottish succession
in 1291–2, conferred on parliament a still larger supranational role.[99] At
the same time the beginning of official parliamentary record-keeping,
with the first rolls of parliament surviving from 1279 and 1280, helped
to identify parliament's business as litigation, legislation, administrative
decisions, and, above all perhaps, the reception of petitions, visible through
their enrolment. If the less routine matters of political decision-making and

---

[97] Kaeuper, *Bankers to the Crown*, 145; Prestwich, *Edward I*, 277–8; Brand, 'English Thirteenth Century Legislation', 335.

[98] *Cotton*, 154; *Parl. Writs*, I. 5; above, 281, 293.

[99] Brand, 'Petitions and Parliament', 33–5; Dodd, *Justice and Grace*, 42–6; Stones and Simpson, *Edward I and the Throne of Scotland*, i. 102–4.

taxation were largely absent from the rolls, the new records nevertheless
clarified and strengthened parliament's institutional definition.[100] Though
Edward's parliaments necessarily descended from what had gone before, in
his own early and middle years their development was determined not so
much by insensible evolution as by conscious fashioning.

2. Edward I: Confrontation, 1294–1302

The development of parliament in Edward I's later years cannot easily be
separated from the general history of the period; the two are so intertwined
that in charting the one we cannot avoid some rehearsal of the other. The
years from 1294 to 1302 contrasted strongly with the preceding period, and
to a lesser extent that contrast was maintained until the end of the reign.
This was a time dominated by war and its demands. The war with France
which began in 1294, followed in 1295 by a Welsh revolt and war with
Scotland, placed the crown under greater financial strains than at any time
since Richard I's reign. Military expenditure from 1294 to 1298 totalled
some £750,000, and even though spending diminished after a truce was
made with France in 1297, the Scottish war continued to be a heavy drain
on Edward's resources. Between 1300 and 1304, the only years for which
accounts survive, it cost at least £60,000.[101] Expenditure on this scale could
be financed only by direct taxation. From 1294 to 1297 levies on moveables
were taken in four successive years, and others followed in 1301 and 1306.
The total yield for the fourteen years from 1294 to 1307, including the
further proceeds from a feudal aid in 1302 and a tallage in 1304, was some
£282,000.[102] In some ways more oppressive, since they were more arbitrary
and more difficult to anticipate, were the crown's indirect impositions: the
new customs duty on wool exports known as the maltolt, taken at £2
per sack from 1294 to 1297 and yielding, in conjunction with the old
customs, some £116,000; prises, that is, levies in kind, mainly in corn and
livestock, taken to feed the king's armies; seizures of wool in 1294 and more

[100] *PROME* i. 3–4.
[101] W. M. Ormrod, 'State-Building and State Finance under Edward I', in W. M. Ormrod (ed.),
England in the Thirteenth Century: Proceedings of the 1989 Harlaxton Symposium (Stamford, 1991), 16;
Prestwich, *War, Politics and Finance*, 175–6. I have assumed that Prestwich's figure of £75,000–80,000
for expenditure on the campaign of 1303–4 subsumes the figure of £64,026 which he gives for
spending in 1303.
[102] Ormrod, 'State Building and State Finance', 18.

damagingly in 1297; and demands for military service on novel terms, seen most notably in 1297 when the king attempted to secure unpaid service overseas in Flanders.[103]

These measures largely determined the history of the period. They broke up the harmonious relationship between the crown and the political nation which had obtained since 1274, brought local representatives to parliament with a frequency that was altogether new, formally confirmed the by now customary dependence of taxation on consent, created a powerful alliance between magnates and knights against oppressive royal government, and made parliament itself into a potential battleground, the political setting for confrontation and bargaining over taxation reminiscent of the years before 1258. In the long term royal demands made their most significant impact on parliamentary representation. Between 1294 and 1307 the knights, burgesses, and lower clergy were summoned to five out of twenty parliaments, the knights and burgesses to four, and the knights alone to two: so a majority of these parliaments, eleven, included representatives of the commons.[104] From 1294 to 1297 the knights attended in four successive years. We may contrast this with the thirty-two parliaments or parliament-type assemblies which met between 1273 and 1293, to only six of which knights and burgesses had been summoned. All six of the period's levies on moveables were granted in assemblies at which the commons in some combination were present. Of the five other parliaments which they attended, one, that of March 1300, saw the conditional grant of a tax, with the deferment of its collection, and two, those of 1298 and 1302, may have witnessed the rejection of the crown's demands for taxes.[105] The need for their consent to taxation had for the first time made the commons a regular and frequent presence in parliamentary politics.

Taxation was therefore the main force in shaping the evolution of parliament in Edward's later years. It gave parliament a still more prominent, but narrower, role within the polity than it had filled during the reign's

[103] For these levies, see Prestwich, *Edward I*, 401—2, 406—12, 418—19. For the yield of the maltolt, see id., *War, Politics and Finance*, 197.

[104] These statistics derive from the parliaments listed in *HBC* 549—52, and *PROME* i. 72—130. In arriving at twenty as the total number of parliaments I have discounted those for March 1298, given in both *HBC* and *PROME*, and for June—August 1294 given in *PROME* (both council meetings), but included the assembly of November 1294 given in *HBC* but omitted in *PROME*. Knights, burgesses, and clergy were all present at the parliaments of Nov. 1295, Nov. 1296, Mar. 1300, Feb. 1305, and Jan. 1307; knights and burgesses at those of May 1298, Jan. 1301, Oct. 1302, and May 1306; and knights at those of Nov. 1294 and Oct. 1297.

[105] Prestwich, *Edward I*, 522—5; *PROME* i. 90; Powell and Wallis, *House of Lords*, 245.

first decades. Until Edward's final two years, his wars pushed into the background, and in some cases brought to a halt, much that had characterized his early parliaments: legislation, the lengthy parliamentary sessions of king and council for judicial business, the cooperative discussion of foreign affairs. Petitioning too played a small part in most of these parliaments. In some, no provision seems to have been made for the reception of petitions and almost none were presented. This was particularly true of the crisis years 1297 and 1298, when private grievances were left largely unaddressed and unredressed.[106]

Yet the taxation which now dominated parliamentary proceedings was at first not especially contentious. The wartime subsidies taken in 1294, 1295, and 1296 provoked no conflicts, despite the lack of precedent for subsidies in three successive years. There were protests from Gloucester and other magnates at the rate initially set for the tax of 1294, and some delay before the king gained his subsidy in 1295,[107] but otherwise there was no discernible lay opposition to Edward's demands. For this there were probably two reasons. First, the war with France, the chief justification for taxes, had been approved in parliament, with magnate consent, and it could be and was consistently presented as a war for the defence of the realm.[108] 'Necessity', which had rarely pressed in Edward's early years, now urged his subjects to support him. Second, a disproportionate share of the burden of war taxation was borne by the clergy. Most notably, the enormous levy of a half which they were called on to pay in 1294 exceeded both in assessment and in yield the lay subsidy of that year, and from a far smaller tax base.[109] Lacking a leader until Archbishop Winchelsey arrived in England in January 1295, the clergy were exposed to Edward's bullying, and to the half at least they gave no free consent.[110] If Edward had lacked such relatively easy access to clerical wealth, the crisis with the laity might have come sooner.

As it was, that crisis came only in 1297.[111] The first open opposition from the laity to the king's demands was voiced at the Salisbury parliament

---

[106] Dodd, *Justice and Grace*, 65, 77.
[107] Prestwich, *Edward I*, 404, 457; *Cotton*, 299; *PROME* i. 81.
[108] *Cotton*, 233–4; Stubbs, *Select Charters*, 481; Harriss, *King, Parliament and Public Finance*, 49; J. H. Denton, *Robert Winchelsey and the Crown, 1294–1313* (Cambridge, 1980), 168; Prestwich, *Edward I*, 451.
[109] See the tables in Ormrod, 'State Building and State Finance', 18–19.
[110] Denton, *Robert Winchelsey*, 70, 74–5, 80.
[111] The next two paragraphs draw on and summarize *Documents Illustrating the Crisis of 1297–98 in England*, ed. M. Prestwich, Camden 4th ser. 24 (London, 1980), 3–32, supplemented by Denton, *Robert Winchelsey*, 136–71, and Prestwich, *Edward I*, 415–29.

of February 1297, when Roger Bigod, earl of Norfolk, refused to serve
overseas in Gascony, as Edward had ordered, unless the king was also
present. A broader conflict over military service emerged in May, when
writs were issued for a muster in London in July. Although the intended
expedition was to go to Flanders, the writs gave no indication of this,
and were issued not only to magnates but to all those holding £20 worth
of land. The vagueness of the writs, the summoning of the £20 knights
and gentry, and the absence of any mention of pay (though pay was later
offered) could all be regarded as breaches of custom. The expedition was
to be partly financed by a levy of an eighth from the counties and a fifth
from the towns and royal demesne. This was granted in July by an informal
assembly at Westminster to which no representatives had been summoned
and which had few claims to be regarded as a parliament. Probably later
in the month, about the same time as arrangements were put in hand for
the collection of a tax, the opposition stated its case for the first time in the
Remonstrances, a bill of grievances which circulated widely. It justified the
inability of the 'community of the land' to serve in Flanders, now rumoured
as Edward's destination, by reference both to the king's unprecedented and
uncustomary demand for service there and to the weight of taxation borne
by the community, especially the king's prises of foodstuffs and his maltolt
on wool exports. Unrelated to wartime levies were further complaints
about the harsh administration of the royal forests. All these abuses were
linked in a general way with the king's disregard for both Magna Carta and
the Forest Charter.

Direct action was, however, more effective in securing the opposition's
ends. In August the earls of Hereford and Norfolk came to the exchequer
and prevented the arrangements for the levy granted in the previous month
from going forward. The church meanwhile had aligned itself with the laity
against the crown's demands. The decision of the clergy, led by Winchelsey,
to refuse a tax in January 1297 had been followed first by their outlawry
and then by their gradual reception back into the king's grace in exchange
for fines equal in value to the tax. Winchelsey was reconciled to the king in
July, but the complaints made about taxation in the Remonstrances were as
much clerical as lay, and a further request from the king for a clerical grant
was refused by an ecclesiastical council in August. The crisis was resolved,
at least temporarily, at a parliament which met in October, during Edward's
absence in Flanders. A manifesto of baronial demands, the *De Tallagio Non
Concedendo*, set out the terms for a settlement: they included future consent,

from prelates, magnates, knights, burgesses, and freemen, to all subsidies, the ending of the maltolt, and the publication of these concessions in cathedral churches. Here the opposition did not get all that they wanted. Yet by the *Confirmatio Cartarum*, issued by the regency government in October, they did secure, not only the confirmation of the Charters, but, in additional articles, the promise of 'common assent' to all future 'aids, mises and prises', and the abolition of the maltolt. These were major concessions. In return the king was granted a new subsidy of a ninth, superseding the questionable grant of July and made this time in a parliament where the knights were present. This brought to an end the greatest crisis which the crown had faced since the days of Simon de Montfort.

After 1297 the pressures on Edward eased, as the truce with France plugged what had been the greatest drain on his revenues during the previous three years. The crisis nevertheless had a long aftermath, which lasted until 1302 and continued to colour the politics of Edward's remaining years. Its chief elements were those that had surfaced in 1297: distrust of the king, resentment at his impositions, and demand for the redress offered by the enforcement of the Charters. Parliament remained throughout at the centre of affairs. The assembly which followed the confirmation of the Charters, meeting at York in May 1298, was attended by knights and burgesses, summoned 'with full power', very probably in the hope that they would grant Edward a subsidy for his impending Scottish campaign. If so, he was to be disappointed: no grant was forthcoming.[112] The next parliament, that of March 1299, saw a renewal of disputes, with Hereford and Norfolk accusing the king of failing to confirm and maintain Magna Carta, as he had promised, and much dissatisfaction at his unwillingness to implement concessions on the forest, including a promised perambulation of the forest boundaries.[113] At the next parliament, in May 1299, Norfolk, speaking for *la commune*, pressed Edward to order the forest perambulations, over which the king had prevaricated.[114]

Edward's troubles moved to a climax in the two parliaments of 1300 and 1301. That of March 1300 presented him with his most uncomfortable experience since the assemblies of 1297. It opened with Edward agreeing to confirm Magna Carta at the request of Winchelsey and Norfolk; continued with the imposition on Edward of the *Articuli Super Cartas*,

---

[112] *Parl Writs*, I. 65; *PROME* i. 90.
[113] *Guisborough*, 329–30; Denton, *Robert Winchelsey*, 185; Prestwich, *Edward I*, 520.
[114] *Langtoft*, ii. 317–19; Denton, *Robert Winchelsey*, 185; Prestwich, *Edward I*, 520–1.

a new set of restraints calling for full enforcement of the Charters, the strict regulation of prises, and reforms in local government and legal administration; and concluded with the grant of a twentieth. The knights and burgesses had presumably been summoned to parliament for this latter purpose. But the grant was conditional on the implementation of certain concessions, including Edward's undertaking to maintain the Charters and to perambulate the forests, and probably to carry through disafforestations in accordance with the perambulators' verdicts; and since the tax was never put in hand it seems likely that Edward either refused to accept the conditions or to implement the concessions.[115] The need for taxation remained as unfinished business for the next parliament, which met at Lincoln in January 1301 and whose continuity with the previous parliament was marked by Edward's orders for the return of the same shire and borough representatives. Edward's request for a fifteenth was countered by a bill presented to the king by Henry of Keighley, one of the knights of the shire for Lancashire, in the name of the prelates and magnates speaking for 'the whole community'. Its central demands, once again, were for the full observance of the Charters and the completion of the perambulations, with the promise of the fifteenth on condition that these concessions had been carried through by Michaelmas. To these humiliating terms Edward had to agree.[116] To one further parliament, in October 1302, knights and burgesses were again summoned, probably in an attempt to secure another tax. That this failed may be deduced from the decision, taken while parliament was in session, to levy the feudal aid granted in 1290 for the marriage of the king's daughter but as yet uncollected. Unlike the lay subsidy, this needed no consent. The appointment in the same parliament of a committee of thirty-five, headed by Archbishop Winchelsey, to advise 'on the state of the church and the kingdom' was an additional pointer to a troublesome session.[117] But it was to be the last for some time, for no further parliaments were summoned until 1305.

Between 1297 and 1302 parliament was thus the cockpit of conflict. Not only was it what it had long been, a national occasion unique in providing

---

[115] Rishanger, Chronica, 405–6; Ann. Worcester, 544; Denton, Robert Winchelsey, 185–6; Prestwich, Edward I, 522–5.

[116] Parl. Writs, I. 90, 104–5; EHD iii: 1189–1327, ed. H. Rothwell (London, 1975), 510–12; Denton, Robert Winchelsey, 186–8; Prestwich, Edward I, 522–5.

[117] PROME i. 112; Powell and Wallis, House of Lords, 245; Denton, Robert Winchelsey, 207–8; Prestwich, Edward I, 525–7.

a political focus for the whole community; it was also a common stage on which the king confronted prelates, magnates, and, increasingly, elected local representatives. The frequent presence of the latter group was one of the features which distinguished these parliamentary contentions from the comparable collisions of Henry III's pre-1258 years. Contention moved towards resolution through the striking of political bargains between king and opposition and the setting of redress of grievances against supply. In October 1297, with the *De Tallagio* and the resulting *Confirmatio Cartarum*, in March 1300, with the *Articuli Super Cartas*, and in January 1301, with Keighley's bill, Edward was presented with written demands whose satisfaction was the price of a tax grant; and on the first and last of these occasions the king had to give way. The abortive attempts to secure further taxes in 1298 and 1302, assuming them to have been made, showed that parliamentary consent could not be counted on; while the terms laid down in 1300, when a tax was conditionally granted but never collected, marked a return to tactics used by Henry III's opponents in 1255 in order to ensure that the king kept his side of the bargain.[118] The progress of Edward's wars was almost wholly dependent on his receiving these grants. Unable to draw upon the resources of a Richard of Cornwall or to milk the Jews, and largely lacking access to the Italian credit which had underwritten his earlier Welsh wars,[119] his position was much weaker than his father's had usually been. Only in the period immediately before 1258 had Henry been comparably exposed. Those in parliament had rarely been more strongly placed to promote or obstruct the crown's ambitions.

The primary and initial cause of conflict was arbitrary taxation. The irregular grant of an eighth and a fifth, conceded to the king in July 1297 by 'the people standing around in his chamber', according to one chronicle,[120] had no justification in custom or recent precedent. No local representatives had been summoned to the July parliament, though in appointing assessors and collectors for the tax Edward mendaciously claimed both their consent and that of the magnates.[121] This, however, was only the most egregious of his authoritarian levies. The maltolt had almost certainly been conceded in 1294 by an assembly of merchants and not, like the original customs duties of 1275, by parliament; yet in causing wool

---

[118] *Paris*, v. 493–4; above, 180–1. Cf. the assessment of a tax, with collection to follow later, in 1269–70: above, 269–70.
[119] Prestwich, *Edward I*, 402–3.   [120] *Flores Historiarum*, iii. 296; Prestwich, *Edward I*, 422.
[121] *Docs. Illustrating*, ed. Prestwich, 110.

merchants to offer lower prices to home producers it became in effect a general tax on all who owned sheep.[122] Both prises and the seizure of wool in 1297 were forms of compulsory purchase, intended to allow Edward to anticipate his tax revenues;[123] yet to Edward's subjects they appeared, not unreasonably, as acts of outright appropriation. When Hereford came to the exchequer in August 1297 to complain about the seizure of wool and the illicit grant of the eighth, he said that the king's subjects were being tallaged like serfs—men subject to arbitrary taxation at their lord's will.[124] Edward was treating the realm as though it were a gigantic manor, the king its lord, and his subjects no more than villeins.

Against these excesses was raised the banner of Magna Carta. Edward's breaches of the Charter were complained against in the Remonstrances; the confirmation of both Charters was first promised in Edward's writ for the collection of the eighth in July and subsequently carried through in the October parliament; and their full observance was still being demanded as late as Keighley's bill of 1301.[125] The whole conflict, aptly termed 'the struggle for the Charters',[126] had these two texts as its single *point d'appui*. Edward's opponents saw Magna Carta as it had come to be regarded since Henry III's early years: as a fundamental law of the constitution embodying a general prescription for just and equitable government. But they also appealed to it as a specific set of restraints on that government. In particular, clause 12, demanding 'common counsel' for general taxes, had always provided the main parliamentary link between taxation and consent, and it was probably this clause that the opposition had in mind when they condemned the king's irregular tax of July 1297. Yet Edward's other levies, especially the maltolt and prises, were less well covered by the Charter's terms. It was true that clause 28 of the Charter, demanding cash payment or the seller's agreement to accept deferred payment when goods were taken by royal officials, sought to curtail the abuses of prise. But it was intended to

[122] *Calendar of Fine Rolls, 1272–1307*, 347; *Ann. Dunstable*, 389; Stubbs, *Constit. Hist.* ii. 131; T. H. Lloyd, *The English Wool Trade in the Middle Ages* (Cambridge, 1977), 76–7; Prestwich, *Edward I*, 402.

[123] J. R. Maddicott, *The English Peasantry and the Demands of the Crown, 1294–1341*, Past and Present Supplement 1 (Oxford, 1975), 16; Prestwich, *Edward I*, 407–10; *Docs. Illustrating*, ed. Prestwich, 10–12.

[124] *Docs. Illustrating*, ed. Prestwich, 157–8; J. R. Maddicott, ' "1258" and "1297": Some Comparisons and Contrasts', *TCE* 9 (2003), 12.

[125] *Docs. Illustrating*, ed. Prestwich, 116, 110, 158; *Parl. Writs*, I. 104; *EHD*, ed. Rothwell, 472, 485, 510–11.

[126] H. Rothwell, 'Edward I and the Struggle for the Charters, 1297–1305', in R. W. Hunt, W. A. Pantin, and R. W. Southern (eds.), *Studies in Medieval History Presented to F. M. Powicke* (Oxford, 1948), 319–32.

apply to limited provisioning for the royal household and not to the national provisioning of the king's armies which was becoming commonplace in the mid 1290s.[127] The insufficiency of the Charter for current circumstances explains the additions made to it in both the *Confirmatio* and the *Articuli*. Just as Henry III's adversaries, putting their case to Louis IX in 1264, had sought to present the Provisions of Oxford as an extension of the Charter,[128] so too did his son's opponents make their own additions to the Charter's terms. But with more credibility, since restraints on new taxes could be more easily seen as an extrapolation from the Charter, and in keeping with its spirit, than the institutional shackles on kingship devised in the Provisions of Oxford.

The central issue of the conflict was largely resolved by the settlement of 1297. In conceding the need for 'common assent' to 'aids, mises and prises', *Confirmatio Cartarum* acknowledged that direct taxes could not be levied by the king's will alone. Though this was a dilution of the more specific demand in the *De Tallagio* for the assent of 'archbishops, bishops, earls, barons, knights, burgesses and other free men of our realm', it must nevertheless have been assumed that the vaguer concession of the *Confirmatio* implied the assent of the parties listed in the baronial petition—and where could that assent be given but in parliament? Formal regulation had caught up with long-standing practice; and the 'common counsel' stipulated in 1215 as a necessity before the levying of a tax had been complemented so as to take account of the social forces which had since emerged in town and country and in parliament itself. After 1297 tax-granting representatives were present at all tax-granting parliaments. Given that the *Confirmatio* also abolished the maltolt, and that there were no further seizures of wool, it is fair to conclude that arbitrary taxation had been effectively checked.

This cannot be wholly presented as a victory for parliament. In the months preceding the *Confirmatio* extra-parliamentary pressures on Edward's government had been very evident. There had been a meeting of dissident magnates at Montgomery, in the march of Wales, during the spring of 1297, a further meeting at Stratford, outside London, in August, where Hereford had demanded the restoration of the kingdom's ancient and approved laws and customs,[129] and then Hereford's action at the exchequer

---

[127] Maddicott, ' "1258" and "1297" ', 4–5 (where other relevant clauses in the Charter are also discussed).

[128] Maddicott, *Simon de Montfort*, 260–2.

[129] J. H. Denton, 'The Crisis of 1297 from the Evesham Chronicle', *EHR* 93 (1978), 565, 576–7.

to disrupt the collection of the July tax. The threat of force had never been far away. Yet it was in parliament, and not by force, that a settlement was reached. The October assembly saw not only the confirmation of the Charters but also the supersession of the illicit eighth and fifth of July by a legitimately conceded ninth, and the issuing of orders for the perambulation of the forest;[130] while the 'common assent' laid down for future taxes entrenched parliament's future role as a tax-granting assembly. Much, however, still remained unsettled or else depended on royal cooperation which was not forthcoming. Prises, the local enforcement of the Charters, and above all the perambulation of the forests continued to be contentious issues until 1301 and, in the case of prises, until the end of the reign and beyond. Those who attended parliament lacked the means to oversee the implementation of their reforms once parliament was over (though the probable withholding of the tax granted in 1300 until the reforms promised in the complementary *Articuli* had been put into effect suggested one way forward). At the same time Edward's penury, in combination with the continuance of the Scottish wars, made it difficult for him to abandon such levies as prises. The weakness of parliament was as it had been in Henry III's middle years: its occasional nature and its inability to influence the executive. But in Edward's reign the remedy devised for that weakness by his father's opponents in 1258, the removal of the government from the king's hands, was never contemplated.[131]

Beneath the surface of these events powerful social forces were at work. These we must now examine. The opposition which Edward faced, both in and out of parliament, was headed by the magnates, naturally enough. The leading role of Hereford and Norfolk in 1297, from Norfolk's initial refusal of service at the Salisbury parliament in February to the pardons granted to both men, alone among the earls, as the crisis subsided, is plain from the sources.[132] In October 1298 the same two earls refused to move north on Edward's Scottish campaign until they had guarantees that the confirmation of the Charters would be observed and the forest perambulations carried through,[133] showing that redress and supply could be set against each other over military service as over taxes, and outside parliament as well as within. Norfolk again took the lead against the king

---

[130] *PROME* i. 87.
[131] For a more extensive discussion, see Maddicott, ' "1258" and "1297" ', 1-2.
[132] Above, 301-2; *Docs. Illustrating*, ed. Prestwich, 135-6.
[133] *Guisborough*, 324; Prestwich, *Edward I*, 518.

in the parliament of March 1299, this time in the company of his former
partner's son, Humphrey de Bohun, the new earl of Hereford;[134] while
Norfolk alone acted as spokesman in the following May parliament and
again in the assembly of March 1300 which saw the drafting of the *Articuli*.
In May 1299 he is said to have acted 'for the community (*pur la commune*)'
and in 1300 'in the name of the whole baronage'.[135] The first phrase is
probably a more accurate description of the earl's constituency than the
second. Throughout these years the magnates saw themselves as standing
for a larger public beyond their own ranks. The Remonstrances had been
presented as the grievances not only of prelates and magnates but of 'all
the community of the land'. Coming to the exchequer to prevent the
collection of the July tax, Hereford had spoken in similar terms, saying that
he was charged to speak not only for the magnates and knights present
but for 'the whole community of the realm, clerks as well as laymen'.[136]
Here was a return to the traditional notion of virtual representation which
had prevailed in the early thirteenth century, when the magnates could
plausibly see themselves as standing for the whole realm.[137]

   During his appearance at the exchequer Hereford had explicitly denied
the king's assertion, made in his writs for the collection of the July
levy, that the tax had been granted by 'earls and barons, knights and the
community of the realm'. 'The said eighth', he had apparently said, 'was
never granted by them or by the said community.'[138] It is striking that
the proper composition of a tax-granting parliament, and by implication
the need for the presence of local representatives, should have become
a cause championed by a great earl. Obvious economic discontents lay
behind these issues of custom and consent which allowed Hereford and his
allies to strike a representative pose. Edward's levies constituted a universal
burden. The maltolt's effect in reducing wool prices harmed all sheep
graziers, from monasteries and magnates to gentry and peasants, and if
prises and levies on moveables fell more heavily on the poor than on the
rich, the interests of magnates and gentry were also at risk, since the crown's
demands made it more difficult for peasant tenants to meet those of their
lords.[139] At their Montgomery meeting in the spring of 1297 the dissident

---

[134] *Guisborough*, 329–30.   [135] *Langtoft*, ii. 318–19; *Rishanger, Chronica*, 404.
[136] *Docs. Illustrating*, ed. Prestwich, 115, 137.   [137] Above, 142–3.
[138] *Docs. Illustrating*, ed. Prestwich, 137–8.
[139] Denton, *Robert Winchelsey*, 62, 142; Prestwich, *War, Finance and Politics*, 254–5; Maddicott, *The
English Peasantry*, 22–3; below, 427–8.

magnates had spoken out against the weight of direct taxation not only on themselves but on their villeins.[140] In a related way the king's attempts to launch campaigns overseas by expanding his claims to military service entailed what could reasonably be seen, both by the magnate constable and marshal, Hereford and Norfolk, and by the £20 landholders among the gentry, as breaches of custom with expensive consequences.[141] Even though burdens diminished after 1297, with the abolition of the maltolt and the less frequent levying of direct taxation, both prises and the harsh administration of the forest remained as subjects for general complaint. Not only in 1297 but throughout the period, constitutional and economic grievances were closely entwined.

If the magnates stood for the whole community it was with the knights that they had a particular affinity and with whom they shared a political programme. 'It is hardly possible in these years', writes Dr Harriss, 'to distinguish the different roles of magnates, parliamentary knights, and local gentry.'[142] Their cooperation, both outside parliament but more especially within it, was what gave the opposition to Edward's government much of its force. The evidence for that cooperation, in the formulation of complaint, in the exertion of pressure for redress through parliament, and in the granting of taxes, is limited but persuasive. Some of the key texts of the 1297 crisis, though emanating from the magnates, show signs of a likely input from the knights. The Remonstrances, presented as the grievances of prelates, magnates, and 'all the community of the land', embodied a complaint about Edward's demand for unpaid service in Flanders which would have burdened small landowners in particular; while the De Tallagio, which demanded the consent of the knights, among others, to direct taxes, sought a pardon for the same group, the £20 landholders who had refused to serve overseas.[143] The grant of a ninth which followed in the October parliament is said by the Evesham chronicle to have been made specifically by 'earls, barons, knights, and other lay persons' (and since the burgesses were not summoned to this parliament we can discount the latter group).[144] The cooperation suggested here is more fully revealed in a later parliament, one outside our immediate period but whose proceedings probably represent standard practice. At the parliament of May 1306 the king's request for a tax was put by the council to the whole assembly,

---

[140] Denton, 'The Crisis of 1297', 576.   [141] Prestwich, War, Finance and Politics, 77, 83–6.
[142] Harriss, King, Parliament and Public Finance, 106.
[143] Docs. Illustrating, ed. Prestwich, 115–16, 154.   [144] Denton, 'The Crisis of 1297', 579.

prelates, magnates, knights, and burgesses. The prelates, magnates, and knights then discussed the request and agreed on a grant of a tenth; while the burgesses held their own discussion, apart from the rest, and agreed on a twentieth.[145] Here the knights clearly stood alongside the magnates, meeting with them, and not with the burgesses, to consider taxation.

But more revealing still, and more directly within the framework of opposition politics, is a famous episode already alluded to. In the Lincoln parliament of 1301 a petition demanding redress of grievances before the levying of a tax was presented to the king by Henry of Keighley, knight of the shire for Lancashire, representing 'the prelates and leading men of the kingdom acting for the whole community'. Keighley's role in this affair, the first action that we can discern by a named MP in any parliament, is disclosed only by a later letter of 1306 from the king ordering his imprisonment for his offence.[146] It suggests the weight which an individual knight might now carry in parliament (and Edward's retribution implies that Keighley was more than just a messenger), and the probable cooperation of magnates and knights in drafting complaints and in setting conditions for taxes. But it also hints at what may be a multitude of similar joint activities behind the baronial face of the parliamentary record.

Underlying these activities were two obvious factors, both of them already discussed in a more general context: common grievances and a common belief that a remedy for those grievances lay in the full enforcement of the Charters and their various supplements. 'Similarity of oppression' brought together knights and magnates just as it had united their ancestors under King John;[147] but they now looked to parliament, rather than to ad hoc meetings and negotiations, for the discussion and often the rebuttal of the crown's demands. Nor was the knights' stand on the Charters any less determined than that of the magnates. They were summoned to the parliament of October 1297 specifically to receive the Charters which the king was to confirm; the *Articuli* of 1300 set up panels of knights in each county to hear complaints against the Charters' infringers; and Keighley's bill asked for the appointment of further panels of four knights in each county, chosen by 'the common assent of the counties' (and the element of local choice was a novelty), to collect the tax

---

[145] Pasquet, *Origins of the House of Commons*, 235–6; Richardson and Sayles, 'Parliaments and Great Councils', in *EPMA* xxvi. 29–30.

[146] *Parl. Writs*, I. 104; Stubbs, *Constit. Hist.* ii. 158 n.1; *EHD*, ed. Rothwell, 510, 522.

[147] Cf. Reynolds, *Kingdoms and Communities*, 268–9; above, 154.

which was to follow on from the full enforcement of the Charters and the implementation of the bill's other demands.[148] In Henry III's reign there had been a shade of ambiguity in the magnates' attitude to Magna Carta, which threatened to curtail their privileges and to protect the rights of their tenants.[149] No such ambiguity is visible in the changed circumstances of Edward's later years. Protecting the rights of magnates and knights and those of the whole political nation, the Charters were viewed as a common inheritance.

But magnates and knights were united by deeper and more long-standing affinities and interests than their present discontents alone. Both groups shared in a common chivalric culture and formed parts of an elite landed class, linked by a downward continuum of wealth and influence which elided the differences between parliamentary barons and parliamentary knights.[150] For this reason it was only to be expected that the knights would join with the magnates in granting taxes, to the exclusion of the burgesses. At this stage in parliament's development the main division within parliament was less between lords and commons than between the landed and all others, lower clergy as well as burgesses. Some men figured among the parliamentary baronage on one occasion and among the parliamentary knights on another. John of Wigton, summoned to the Salisbury parliament of 1297, sat as knight of the shire for Cumberland in 1301 and 1305; Ranulf de Frescheville, also summoned to the Salisbury parliament, sat for Derbyshire in 1301; Henry Tregoz, who sat for Sussex in 1301, received a personal summons to the parliaments of 1305 and 1307.[151] If parliamentary overlaps of this sort remained uncommon, there were many other points of contact between magnates and parliamentary knights. Two of the men listed among the knights in the *familia* of the earl of Norfolk in 1297, for example, would later represent their counties in parliament: Richard of Skoland sat for Kent in 1297, 1298, and 1300, and Ranulf de Munchensy for Hertfordshire in 1302, 1305, and 1306.[152]

But it would be wrong to think that the aspirations and activities of the knights were wholly subsumed within those of the magnates. They were evolving rapidly as a well-defined parliamentary group. Their frequent

---

[148] *Parl. Writs*, I. 56, 105; *Stat. Realm*, i. 136–7; *EHD*, ed. Rothwell, 496–7, 510.

[149] Maddicott, 'Magna Carta and the Local Community', 51–4; above, 220–1.

[150] Cf. above, 85, 219–20; and for the fifteenth century, K. B. McFarlane, *England in the Fifteenth Century* (London, 1981), 13–17.

[151] Prestwich, 'Magnate Summonses', 98; *Parl. Writs*, I. 52, 93, 101–2, 136, 181.

[152] *Docs. Illustrating*, ed. Prestwich, 157; *Parl. Writs*, I. 25, 26, 58, 70, 86, 143, 169.

summoning from 1294 onwards created new possibilities for the return of the same MPs to successive parliaments. The York parliament of May 1298, for example, contained at least 13 knights present in the immediately preceding parliament and at least 23 present for the same shire in some preceding parliament. The parliament of March 1300 was attended by at least 15 knights present in the previous parliament, by at least 23 present in some preceding parliament, and by 8 knights who were attending for the third time. At the Lincoln parliament of 1301, 31 county members were attending for the second time, 15 for the third time, 6 for the fourth time, and 2 for the fifth time.[153] These repeated appearances would have been impossible before the 1290s, when the attendance of the commons had been much more sporadic. But from then onwards a growing corps of old parliamentary hands were becoming habituated to parliamentary politics, and this must have contributed, in ways which cannot be precisely defined, to the corporate sense of those attending and to their general confidence and assertiveness. The intrepid Henry of Keighley was sitting for Lancashire for the third time when he was put up to challenge the crown in the 1301 parliament. That he had been summoned to serve in Scotland in 1297 and was appointed in his home county to enforce the Charters under the terms of the *Articuli* in 1300 shows the sort of subsidiary qualifications which such men might have to draw on when they came to parliament.[154] Since the magnates embodied still greater continuities of parliamentary service—for most were naturally summoned from one parliament to the next—it was an assembly partly formidable by reason of its members' political and parliamentary experience.

The growing strength of the knights in parliament, whether or not it was exercised in association with the magnates, derived in part from the vigorous engagement of the counties that they represented with the issues of the day. Feeding into the knights' parliamentary activities were local allegiances and a local political awareness which both sides sought to cultivate and win over. One stimulus to that awareness is likely to have been parliamentary elections in the county court, more frequent at this time than ever before. But more important were the efforts made by the king and by his opponents to influence opinion directly. Both the main baronial texts of 1297, the Remonstrances and the *De Tallagio*, seem to have

---

[153] J. G. Edwards, 'The Personnel of the Commons in Parliament under Edward I and Edward II', in *Historical Studies*, 152–3; id., *Historians and the Medieval English Parliament*, 31–3.
[154] *Parl. Writs*, I. 58, 71, 96, 300, 370.

circulated widely, while the *Confirmatio Cartarum*, which ended the first stage of the conflict, was sent out for publication to justices, sheriffs, and town mayors, in a slightly more elaborate version of earlier arrangements for the publication of statutes.[155] Edward had meanwhile circulated, again for publication by the sheriffs, a long justification for his taxes, pleading the need to defend the realm from his foreign enemies.[156] Few of those who were active in county courts—a group which extended well below the level of the gentry—or in the life of towns could have been ill informed about what was at issue.

In the struggle for local allegiances the crown had several advantages: an active corps of royal messengers,[157] tried and tested methods of publication for royal pronouncements, the services of sheriffs and other officials in the localities. But efficient machinery for propaganda was no guarantee of its success. This was vividly shown in an episode from Worcestershire which provides a rare glimpse of an independent public opinion and its consequences in the localities. It was given voice by the king's attempted levy of the eighth improperly granted to him in July 1297. Edward had taken great trouble in preparing for this tax, telling his exchequer officials on 4 August that writs for the collection of the tax were to be entrusted to men 'who know how to speak pleasingly (*beau*) to the people and how to manage the business well and wisely'. The collectors themselves were to tell the people, 'in the most civil and courteous way they know', that the king was aware of the great burdens he had imposed on them for the defence of the realm, that he had agreed at the request of the prelates and magnates to confirm the Charters in return for the tax grant, and that they owed it to him to do their duty as to their liege lord.[158] This message, with its mixture of promised concessions on the Charters, justification in terms of national needs, and appeals to obligation, offers a valuable guide to what might have been expected to sway local opinion. Yet it cut no ice in Worcestershire. When, on 26 September, the collectors tried to levy the tax they were obstructed by the united voice of the county, speaking presumably in the county court and as if in direct response to the

---

[155] *Docs. Illustrating*, ed. Prestwich, 26–7, 158; H. Rothwell, 'The Confirmation of the Charters, 1297', *EHR* 60 (1945), 300–3.

[156] *Docs. Illustrating*, ed. Prestwich, 125–9; *EHD*, ed. Rothwell, 477–80; J. R. Maddicott, 'The County Community and the Making of Public Opinion in Fourteenth-Century England', *TRHS* 5th ser. 28 (1978), 29–33; Denton, *Robert Winchelsey*, 147–9; Prestwich, *Edward I*, 424.

[157] M. C. Hill, *The King's Messengers, 1199–1377* (London, 1961), esp. ch. 1.

[158] *Docs. Illustrating*, ed. Prestwich, 120–2; *EHD*, ed. Rothwell, 476–7; Prestwich, *Edward I*, 424.

king's message. The collectors were reminded that Henry III had formerly promised the *communitas regni* that he would confirm the liberties conceded in the Charter in return for the grant of a fifteenth: an allusion to the definitive reissue of the Charters in 1225. But having taken the tax, the county said, he had surrendered their liberties to oblivion. Only when they possessed those liberties would they hand over the money.[159]

The county's riposte to Edward's tax shows clearly that parliamentary distrust of the king's good intentions was matched in the localities, and that county and parliament were united in seizing on the maintenance of the Charters as the central issue. In one way the Worcestershire men had a larger view of the matter than those in parliament, for they referred back to what had happened nearly three-quarters of a century earlier, and to a subversion of local liberties which had begun in the distant past: because they knew how worthless Henry's promises had been, they were not inclined to trust Edward's. In a precisely similar way Simon de Montfort's reforming barons, making their case to Louis IX for the maintenance of those liberties, had referred back to the tax grant of 1225 and the subsequent loss of those liberties confirmed in exchange for it.[160] The political activism which we can see in Worcestershire was rooted in a knowledge of history which was probably widespread.

Opposition to the crown in parliament could thus draw upon a public opinion in the counties which was both politically educated and sturdily resistant to central direction. Edward's realization that it could not be easily overridden was shown in the meticulous instructions for the levying of the 1297 tax which we have already looked at: his provincial subjects had to be coaxed rather than bullied. The symbiotic relationship between parliament and the counties deepened throughout the subsequent 'struggle for the Charters'. Both the *Articuli* of 1300 and Keighley's bill of 1301 shifted the focus of parliamentary opposition away from arbitrary taxation—which, with the partial exception of prises, had been brought to an end—and towards the inequities of local government. Demands for the enforcement of the Charters in the counties, their quarterly publication in the county courts, the punishment of their infringers by locally chosen panels of knights and others, and, more generally, the punishment of all delinquent local officials, and for the local election of sheriffs, brought before Edward

---

[159] *Ann. Worcester*, 534; Denton, *Robert Winchelsey*, 153; Maddicott, ' "1258" and "1297" ', 6–7.
[160] *DBM* 268–9; Maddicott, ' "1258" and "1297" ', 6–7.

and his ministers in parliament the grievances and aspirations of provincial England. In this respect both the written requests preceding the *Articuli*[161] and Keighley's bill, which incorporated some of the demands mentioned above, were not unlike the common petitions of the fourteenth century. If we knew more about the activities of Keighley and his fellow parliamentary knights, who may have played a larger part than the magnates in drafting these texts, the resemblance might appear still closer.

We can say, then, that both the magnates and the knights assembled in parliament were truly representative figures. Particularly on the question of the Charters, they brought forward grievances which were both their own and those of the counties; and if the magnates could claim to represent the whole community, by what was now a venerable but rather dated political concept, the knights possessed the representative legitimacy which came from direct election by their counties. Yet they were hardly equipollent. The magnates may have provided spokesmen and carried more parliamentary weight, but the knights are likely to have been more closely in touch with local opinion, via their local residence, their contacts with the fifty or so other gentry families in each county,[162] their standing in the county court, and their holding of local office. It was in an extension of this last role that the *Articuli* and Keighley's bill made them responsible for the local enforcement of the Charters and for the collection of the tax granted in exchange. In the creative dialogue between parliament and the localities which contributed to parliament's strengths, they were the main interlocutors.

But the knights were not, of course, the only local representatives, for the burgesses too represented an important interest, though one whose place in parliament is more difficult to gauge. When they were present, they greatly outnumbered the knights: by comparison with a notional 'full house' of 74 knights from 37 counties, 220 burgesses attended parliament in 1295, 156 in 1298, 187 in 1305, and 176 in 1307.[163] The need for their consent to taxation was increasingly acknowledged. From 1294, by an innovation of that year, the towns which they represented usually paid taxes at a higher

---

[161] The bill on which the *Articuli* were founded is Somerset Record Office, MS DD/AH, 186; cf. Prestwich, *Edward I*, 523.

[162] For the probable number of gentry families in the counties, see N. Saul, *Knights and Esquires: The Gloucestershire Gentry in the Fourteenth Century* (Oxford, 1981), 33–4 (about 50 in Gloucs., *c.*1340), and S. Walker, *The Lancastrian Affinity, 1361–1399* (Oxford, 1990), 250–1 (50 to 70 per county in the late fourteenth century).

[163] Pasquet, *Origins of the House of Commons*, 151.

rate than the counties, presumably in recognition of their greater wealth
and of the difficulty of taxing moveable property which was often in the
form of cash rather than goods.[164] In the case of the first such two-tier tax,
the counties' tenth was granted in the parliament of November 1294, when
knights but not burgesses were present, and the urban sixth was conceded
a little later, in separate negotiations with London which were then taken
to justify a similar levy on other towns.[165] The only subsequent tax to be
granted by the knights alone, and in a parliament from which the burgesses
were again absent, was that of October 1297. This was taken, notably, at
the undivided rate of a ninth as a replacement for the rural eighth and the
urban sixth which the king had tried to impose in July.[166] As in 1294, it
was presumably recognized that the knights were not competent to make
a separate grant for the towns and so to speak for the burgesses.

The institution of the two-tier tax grant may have served to mark
off the magnates and knights more sharply from the burgesses and to
define two interests which were rarely identical. If the proposal for two
separate tax rates came from the king, as it apparently did in 1294,[167] rather
than emerging from the deliberations of those assembled in parliament,
there would have been good reason for magnates and knights to meet
apart from the burgesses in order to discuss what were different, though
comparable, demands. The separate meetings which we have already seen
to have taken place in the parliament of 1306 may have been normal;
the chronicler Cotton hints at a similar procedure in the parliament of
1295.[168] Nor, probably, did the magnates and knights, conscious of their
social superiority, have any particular respect for the interests of the towns.
It is striking that when Hereford came to the exchequer to obstruct the
king's levy of July 1297, he inveighed repeatedly against the illicit nature
of the rural eighth without once referring to the urban (and heavier)
sixth which Edward had sought to impose in parallel.[169] His apparent

---

[164] J. F. Willard, *Parliamentary Taxes on Personal Property, 1290 to 1334* (Cambridge, Mass., 1934), 9.

[165] Ibid. 15; *Lancashire Lay Subsidies*, i: *Henry III to Edward I*, ed. J. A. C. Vincent, Lancashire and Cheshire Rec. Soc. 27 (1893), 180–3, 185–6.

[166] Willard, *Parliamentary Taxes*, 15; Prestwich, *Edward I*, 457. There were again separate negotiations with London, which granted a ninth subsequently applied to other towns.

[167] The Hagnaby chronicle says that in 1294 Edward demanded a tax of a third and a sixth, which was reduced to a tenth and a sixth after protests by Gloucester and the other magnates: Prestwich, *Edward I*, 404.

[168] *Cotton*, 299.

[169] *Docs. Illustrating*, ed. Prestwich, 137–8. Guisborough too, reporting Hereford's actions, speaks only of the eighth: *Guisborough*, 294.

disregard for the towns was symptomatic of an opposition programme which in many respects was more closely geared to the interests of the countryside. Prises, the boundaries of the forest, and the role of the sheriffs and other local officials were all rural rather than urban issues. Even the quarterly publication of the Charters laid down in the *Articuli* was to be made only in county courts, with no special provision for urban publication.[170]

It is in fact hard to detect any specifically urban contribution to 'the struggle for the Charters', and to judge by the petitions which townsmen frequently presented in parliaments the interests of the towns were local rather than national. In the parliament of 1305, for example, some twenty-five petitions were presented by thirteen towns, all but one of which were represented in that parliament. All raised local concerns. Norwich and Worcester asked for murage grants to finance the building or rebuilding of their walls; Appleby asked for a reduction in its farm because of migration from the town and the consequent fall in town revenues; Bristol asked that the Templars living within the town should contribute to tallage payments; and so on.[171] It is probably true to say that the larger national issues raised in parliament were mainly the business of the magnates and knights, while the burgesses, beyond their role in granting taxes, were chiefly concerned to forward the interests of their local communities.

Yet this argument cannot be pressed too far, for some matters were clearly of universal concern. Arbitrary taxation was one issue whose national importance transcended any differences between town and country, just as the appeal of Magna Carta, which offered protection against it, transcended social differences. The maltolt in particular may have weighed heavily on urban wool merchants, just as it did on rural wool growers. Even the apparently more limited issue of the forest could be seen to have similarly wide implications. Edward's prevarication over the confirmation of the Charters in the parliament of March 1299 threatened to provoke riots in London, only averted by the council's orders for the public reading of both charters in St Paul's churchyard. But various clauses of the Forest Charter were omitted from the reading, provoking the fury of the bystanders. The Charter's full maintenance was seen, in Professor Michael Prestwich's

---

[170] *Stat. Realm*, i. 136; *EHD*, ed. Rothwell, 496.

[171] *Return of the Names of Members of Parliament*, part I: *Parliaments of England, 1213–1702*, Parliamentary Papers (London, 1878), 18–20; *PROME* ii. 72, 77, 93, 110. Cf. Maddicott, 'Parliament and the Constituencies', 69–70.

words, as 'a test of the king's good faith', so affecting all, and not merely a set of specific remedies for specifically rural grievances.[172]

London may have been a special case, since its being in the king's hands and deprived of its mayor between 1285 and 1298 had induced much anti-royalist feeling.[173] But another episode suggests a more general urban awareness of the principles at stake in 'the struggle for the Charters', and one manifested this time through burgess representation. In June 1303 representatives from forty-two towns came to York at the king's summons to consider his proposal for an increase in the wool customs, to which some merchants had already agreed. They were told to come 'with full powers . . . to do and receive what shall be ordained by the advice and assent of the king and of the said merchants', and they appeared before the council. Yet despite these pressures they unanimously refused to sanction what they referred to, significantly, as a 'maltolt'.[174] In doing so they almost certainly had in mind the *Confirmatio Cartarum* of 1297, which had abolished the maltolt imposed in 1294, promised 'common assent' for any future levies on wool, and been sent out for publication in cities as well as counties and for the guidance of mayors as well as sheriffs.[175] Of the 84 burgesses present at York, at least 21 had represented their towns in some previous parliament, and one, John Lyghtfot of Hereford, in as many as five parliaments. Fourteen had been present in the 1298 parliament, the next representative assembly after the parliament of the *Confirmatio*, and eight in the parliaments of either 1300 or 1301, when the Charters had been in the forefront of political bargaining between king and opposition.[176] Here, then, was a group containing experienced parliamentarians, men not only alert to the constitutional issues of the day but also possessing some political courage and—since neither magnates or knights were present

[172] *Guisborough*, 329–30; Prestwich, *Edward I*, 518–20.

[173] G. Williams, *Medieval London from Commune to Capital* (London, 1963), 254–61; Prestwich, *Edward I*, 264–5, 520.

[174] *Parl. Writs*, I. 134–5; Prestwich, *War, Finance and Politics*, 268–9; Prestwich, *Edward I*, 530. Prestwich argues that the townsmen were under pressure from 'the opposition' to turn down the king's request, but this seems unlikely. The king's orders for election were issued on 7 May for an assembly to meet on 25 June, and it is not easy to see how such pressure could be brought to bear, at relatively short notice, on representatives from widely dispersed towns, including Bodmin and Launceston in Cornwall, Dunwich and Norwich in East Anglia, and Scarborough and Whitby in Yorkshire. In any case there was no visible 'opposition' at this time.

[175] *Docs. Illustrating*, ed. Prestwich, 158–9.

[176] These figures may be deduced by comparing the names of those present at York, given in *Parl. Writs*, I. 135, with the returns of borough members given in the same volume's 'Alphabetical Digest' or in the *Return of Members*, 8–15.

at York—some independence of will. Socially inferior though they may
have been, these burgesses had an *esprit de corps* and a degree of political
awareness which did not allow them simply to fall in with whatever
Edward's government proposed. They and their kind may have been a less
negligible parliamentary force than the usual silence of the records would
suggest.

More prominent than the burgesses in the parliaments of 1294 to 1302,
and manifestly more powerful, were the clergy. They fell into two main
divisions: the bishops and the heads of religious houses, and the lower
clergy, who from 1295 were summoned indirectly, via the bishops.[177] Of
these two divisions, the higher clergy were more closely integrated into
the structure and work of parliament. Not only were some of them on the
council, and many of them the recipients of personal summonses to every
parliament (though we have already seen that there were wide variations
in the lists of the religious summoned[178]), but in 1297 their leaders moved
into alignment with other parliamentary groups against Edward's wartime
impositions. If the lay taxes arising from the July assembly were rejected
as lacking in proper consent, so also, and on the same grounds, was a
comparable subsidy which Edward attempted to levy from the clergy in
August.[179] These common grievances produced a coalescence of forces.
The Remonstrances were drawn up in the name of the archbishops and
bishops, as well as of the earls and barons, and when Hereford appeared at
the exchequer a little later to prohibit the levy from the laity and, according
to one chronicle, the clerical subsidy, he claimed to speak for both laity and
clergy.[180] For both parties Magna Carta provided a partial remedy, as justly
invoked in defence of the freedom of the church, guaranteed in its first
clause, as in its prohibition of direct taxation 'without common counsel'.[181]
Confirmatio Cartarum, issued in the next parliament as a necessary updating
of the Charter's terms, was as much the victory of the clergy, led by
Archbishop Winchelsey, as of the laity;[182] and the *Confirmatio*'s provision
for the twice-yearly reading of the Charters in cathedral churches, and
for the excommunication of those who infringed them, made ecclesiastical
sanctions available to enforce that victory. Winchelsey had wanted to go

[177] Denton, 'The Clergy and Parliament', 89–92. My debt to Professor Denton's various works will
be obvious throughout what follows.
[178] Ibid. 90; Powell and Wallis, *House of Lords*, 220–1; above, 287.
[179] Denton, *Robert Winchelsey*, 144–53.
[180] *Docs. Illustrating*, ed. Prestwich, 115, 137; *Guisborough*, 294; Denton, *Robert Winchelsey*, 152.
[181] Cf. Denton, *Robert Winchelsey*, 142.   [182] Ibid. 160–2.

further and to secure the same sanctions for the *Confirmatio*'s additions to the Charter. In this he failed.[183] The Confirmation of the Charters was nevertheless the high-water mark both of successful opposition to the crown and of the collaboration between clergy and laity in parliament which had made that success possible.

There remained much in the subsequent political conflicts to concern the prelates as well as the magnates and knights, and to bring both groups together in parliament. The *Articuli* of 1300, with their provision for the local enforcement of the Charters and for restraints on prises, promised remedies for some long-standing grievances of both clergy and laity, just as the *Confirmatio* had done.[184] In the parliament of January 1301 the joint discussions which must have lain behind these formulations emerge briefly in the sources when the chronicler Langtoft tells us that a committee of twenty-five clergy and barons was set up at Edward's request to determine whether the king would be breaking his coronation oath if he agreed to the disafforestations wanted by the opposition. The result of the committee's deliberations was almost certainly the petition for reform which Keighley presented to the king and in which Edward subsequently saw the hand of Winchelsey.[185] The archbishop again was the leading figure on the further committee of thirty-five set up in the parliament of 1302, according to the Hagnaby chronicle, to advise on the state of the church and the kingdom.[186] It was probably through smaller bodies such as these, rather than through unwieldy assemblies of the 'whole house', that parliamentary cooperation between prelates, magnates, and knights went forward and common objectives were pursued.

There is much here to remind us of the parliamentary politics of the 1240s and 1250s. Then too prelates and magnates had come together in parliament and in opposition to royal government. On at least one occasion, in 1244, they had formed a joint committee. Magna Carta had been promoted as the touchstone for ecclesiastical and secular liberties, and new regulations had eventually been drafted, in 1258–9, to deal with abuses unforeseen by the Charter's makers.[187] In Edward's later years, however, the political bonding of the two groups was more fragile than it had been a

---

[183] *Docs. Illustrating*, ed. Prestwich, 158–9; Denton, *Robert Winchelsey*, 167.

[184] Denton, *Robert Winchelsey*, 186.

[185] *Langtoft*, ii. 330–1; Stubbs, *Constit. Hist.* ii. 158 n. 1; *EHD*, ed. Rothwell, 522; Denton, *Robert Winchelsey*, 187.

[186] Denton, *Robert Winchelsey*, 207–8; Prestwich, *Edward I*, 528; above, 304.

[187] Above, 194–7. For the committee of 1244, see *Paris*, iv. 362.

half century earlier. The grounds for their initial alliance in 1297 had been a common opposition to arbitrary taxation, against which both parties could appeal to the Charter.[188] But the clergy also acted here under a separate ecclesiastical sanction: Boniface VIII's bull *Clericis Laicos* of 1296, which had forbidden taxation of the clergy without papal licence.[189] This was a reminder that the clergy had allegiances which were not always those of the laity. Arbitrary taxation had in any case been effectively ended by *Confirmatio Cartarum*, weakening the *raison d'être* of the continuing alliance. A common veneration for the Charter still persisted. But the long lists of clerical grievances presented to the king in the parliaments of 1300 and 1301, mainly concerned as they were with the protection of ecclesiastical jurisdiction, showed that the 'freedom of the church' guaranteed by the Charter could cover much that was of no concern to magnates and knights.[190] Nor was parliament the only central forum for the political activity of the clergy, as it was for the laity, for church councils, summoned by Winchelsey and not by the king, met especially frequently in this period. There were four in 1297, excluding a fifth northern assembly, and that of November 1297 granted Edward a tax independent of any parliamentary grant.[191] In 1301 the clergy became vulnerable once again to external taxes, when Boniface VIII agreed to levy a tenth for three years on clerical incomes and to divide the proceeds with the king.[192] Since this tax was imposed on the pope's orders, the clergy had no grounds for resisting it; and since its effect must have been to reduce fiscal pressure on the laity, it is likely to have had the implicit approval of magnates and knights. When Edward secured Winchelsey's suspension by another friendly pope, Clement V, in 1306, there was, so far as we know, no whisper of protest from those surviving magnates who had stood with him in 1297.[193]

After 1297, therefore, the parliamentary front formed by prelates and magnates against the king's demands was in slow decline, though it subsisted until 1302 if we can believe the Hagnaby account of Winchelsey's parliamentary committee in that year. Did the weight of the lower clergy do anything to make up for the slackening bonds between their seniors and the laity? Certainly they came to parliament with increasing frequency. Never summoned in the first part of the reign, they attended five parliaments

---

[188] Denton, *Robert Winchelsey*, 141–2, 166, 183, 194, 204–5.   [189] Ibid. 89–90, 100–6.
[190] *C. and S.* II. ii. 1205–18; Denton, *Robert Winchelsey*, 194–9.
[191] Denton, *Robert Winchelsey*, 100–7, 119–21, 144–7, 153, 171–3.
[192] Ibid. 200–1.   [193] Ibid. 231–6; below, 327–8.

between 1295 and 1307, no doubt drawn in by the crown's wish for
the widest possible base for consent to taxation. In theory, they were a
substantial force, in numbers and status. Comprising deans and priors of
cathedral churches, one proctor representing each cathedral and two the
parish clergy of each diocese, they constituted at maximum a body of
148 men, many of them university-trained *magistri*.[194] In practice, numbers
were probably much smaller. Unlike the laity, the lower clergy were
not obliged to attend parliaments, and many proctors represented more
than one principal.[195] Within parliament they are unlikely to have been
politically inert. Taxation fell proportionately much more heavily on them
than on the prelates,[196] and in 1297 they cited Magna Carta in defence of
their liberties.[197] Yet they were hardly a force to be reckoned with. Unlike
the knights and burgesses, they had only a narrow representative role,
standing not for the large constituencies of town and county but merely for
their own kind.[198] In the Bury parliament of 1296, and probably in other
parliaments too, they met as two groups, archdeacons and deans, and parish
clergy, within the larger grouping of the whole clergy, and apart from
the laity.[199] When they wished to complain about taxation, as they did in
1297, they made their complaints to the bishops and not to the king.[200]
Neither records nor chronicles suggest that they produced a clerical Henry
of Keighley, able to participate in a direct challenge to royal power; and
probably there was none.

The five years between 1297 and 1301 were marked by the most intensive
and concentrated parliamentary conflicts that England had yet seen. Of the
eight parliaments which met during this period, six saw the king and his
subjects bitterly at odds, in almost all cases over the Charters;[201] and a seventh, that of 1298, about which we are badly informed, may have seen the
refusal of a tax.[202] Three successive sets of concessions were extracted from

[194] *HBC* 549–52; Denton, 'The Clergy and Parliament', 91–2; Denton and Dooley, *Representatives of the Lower Clergy*, 72–3.
[195] Denton and Dooley, *Representatives of the Lower Clergy*, 46, 49–50.   [196] Ibid. 62.
[197] *C. and S.* II. ii. 1156–7; Denton, 'The Clergy and Parliament', 102–3.
[198] Denton and Dooley, *Representatives of the Lower Clergy*, 77–8.
[199] *Cotton*, 314–15; Denton, 'The Clergy and Parliament', 93–4.
[200] *C. and S.* II. ii. 1156–7; Denton, 'The Clergy and Parliament', 102–3.
[201] I have discounted here those assemblies which seem to have been meetings of the council, with
or without a few extra magnates. My eight parliaments, with asterisks against those which saw conflicts,
are those of Feb. 1297*, July 1297, Oct. 1297*, May 1298, Mar. 1299*, May 1299*, Mar. 1300*, and
Jan. 1301*.
[202] Above, 303.

Edward: the *Confirmatio* of 1297, the *Articuli* of 1300, and the grudgingly positive responses which Edward was forced to give to Keighley's bill in 1301. All these texts were the products of negotiations in parliament, where the king's need for money could be traded against the opposition's need for redress. The concessions of 1301 were a final defeat for Edward. By his own later admission, his opponents had 'pressed him outrageously' at the Lincoln parliament,[203] forcing him to agree to extensive disafforestations and to abandon his claims to prises. We can hardly speak here of a struggle between 'king and parliament' or of 'parliament's' victory. But parliament was the stage which brought together the various forces in play; and since consent given in a properly constituted assembly was necessary for direct taxation—all the more so after *Confirmatio Cartarum*—parliament was the focus for politics and political bargaining to a novel degree.

How far was it 'the community of the realm' which stood together in parliament against Edward's impositions? Certainly the more frequent attendance of knights, burgesses, and lower clergy made parliament more socially comprehensive, and more regularly so, than it had been in the past. The frequent need for consent to taxation meant that what had formerly been merely intermittent and occasional was in process of becoming a feature of most parliaments. The close identification of the knights with the opinions and grievances of the counties extended the notion of such a community beyond the confines of parliament; while the magnates could continue to see themselves as speaking for the whole realm, as they did in 1297. The universal incidence of royal impositions, the universal resentments which they generated, and, above all, the protection which Magna Carta was seen to offer to every social group: all gave substance, weight, and a programme to a political community which, in more settled times, might have remained more nebulous.

Yet although all parties could unite against the king's demands, this was not an alliance of an incipient 'lords' and 'commons', though the elements of that future distinction were all in place. We have seen that magnates and knights stood together in a partnership of the landed. The burgesses, representing communities now taxed at a different rate from the counties, and apparently meeting apart to grant their taxes, can on no occasion be shown to have cooperated with the knights; though their opposition to the projected customs duties of 1303 suggests that they may have shared some

---

[203] Stubbs, *Constit. Hist.* ii. 158 n. 1; *EHD*, ed. Rothwell, 522.

of the same constitutional principles. As for the lower clergy, they appear to have identified to some extent with their episcopal and monastic superiors, and to a greater extent with their order, rather than with the knights and burgesses. Knights, burgesses, and lower clergy were all representatives, but the parliament which brought them together resembled a gathering of continental estates—the landed aristocracy, the clergy, and the third estate of the towns—more closely than has sometimes been recognized. It remains to be seen how this changed in the next reign.

3. Harmony Restored? 1302–1307

Following the parliament of October 1302, there was a long hiatus before another was called, some twenty-eight months later, in February 1305. This was largely a measure of Edward's political caution after his bruising experiences in the parliaments of the previous few years. The absence of parliaments in 1303 and 1304 is best explained by his wish to avoid further public opposition to his policies and to escape the sort of compromises, on what he regarded as the essentials of his sovereignty, forced on him in 1300 and 1301. Without parliament, of course, he could raise no subsidy, but he obviously regarded this handicap as a price worth paying for his freedom of action. In 1304 he even chose to raise money by a tallage rather than to face parliament in quest of the much more profitable levy on moveables. Although this tax yielded even less than the feudal aid which was all that he had been able to secure in 1302, and only about one-ninth as much as the last levy on moveables of 1301,[204] it needed no consent. But resort to parliament was in any case less necessary, thanks to the general easing of the king's financial position. He now possessed other sources of revenue which, like the tallage, were independent of parliamentary control, but which, unlike the tallage, provided regular money: income from clerical taxation imposed by the pope, as we have seen,[205] but also from the rising customs revenues generated by a booming export trade in wool, from additional customs duties imposed on foreign merchants in 1303, from the reform of the coinage, and from loans made by Edward's new Italian bankers, the Frescobaldi.[206] All helped to free him from the shackles of parliamentary negotiations.

[204] Ormrod, 'State-Building and State Finance', 18. [205] Above, 322.
[206] Prestwich, Edward I, 529–35.

The will to oppose was in any case dwindling after 1302, as financial pressures slackened and the war against Scotland moved towards a seemingly successful conclusion. The non-parliamentary revenues which Edward was able to raise allowed him to fund a Scottish campaign in 1303–4 which led to the fall of Stirling and the effective conquest of Scotland, capped by the seizure and execution of William Wallace in 1305.[207] The magnates had never been openly opposed to Edward's ambitions in the north, merely to the oppressive measures needed to pay for them, and the conquest could not have been achieved without their support. At the Lincoln parliament of 1301, in the thick of 'the struggle for the Charters', the earls and barons had backed Edward's claim to superior lordship over Scotland and had sealed a letter denying the rival claims of the pope. Service in war brought legal privileges, respite of debts, and, for some, grants of Scottish land.[208] For the king himself the victory of 1304 must have brought a welcome renewal of the military prestige of his youth. He was now *victoriosissimus*, a most victorious king, and the imposer of a 'triumphal peace'.[209]

These changed circumstances explain much about the last four parliaments of the reign, two in 1305, one in 1306, and one, at Carlisle, in 1307. They were assemblies at which consensus ruled. Their constructive work in government and legislation, and the harmonious cooperation of their participants with the king, made them more akin to the parliaments of the 1270s and 1280s than to those of 1297 and after. The first after the long caesura, that of February 1305, was called to discuss not only English business but also a settlement for newly conquered Scotland. 'The common business of the realm and the king together' was to be dealt with in its proper forum.[210] But the parliament also provided an outlet, on a probably unprecedented scale, for the pent-up grievances of the king's subjects. Attended by knights and burgesses, it saw the presentation of at least 540 petitions; and both the special invitation to deliver them, made by proclamation in London, and the arrangements for their reception, uniquely recorded together on the parliament roll, suggest that the need to attend to popular complaint, and the political advantages to be gained from this, played some part in Edward's parliamentary planning.[211] According

---

[207] Prestwich, *Edward I*, 498–503.   [208] Ibid. 492, 511–12; id., *War, Politics and Finance*, 236–7.
[209] *Flores Historiarum*, iii. 120.   [210] *Parl. Writs*, I. 136; *DBM* 110–11.
[211] *PROME* i. 119–20, ii. 52–367. The orders relating to the delivery of petitions are ibid. ii. 52. This was the first parliament in which triers of petitions were formally appointed to answer all incoming petitions except those needing the king's special attention: Dodd, *Justice and Grace*, 53.

to Langtoft, popular complaint also partly underlay the trailbaston ordinance, drafted in this parliament as a set of instructions to the justices, in order to deal with the growing problem of violence and disorder.[212] It represented a return to the practice of criminal legislation by administrative decree seen earlier in Henry II's assizes. One final *actum* was also very much in the parliamentary tradition. The parliament saw the state trial of the baron Nicholas of Seagrave for the treasonable offence of deserting the king's army. If the trial marked the resurrection of another ancient function of councils and parliaments, it also pointed to the king's new mood of conciliation, for Seagrave was treated with remarkable leniency, seemingly on the recommendation of the magnates. He escaped with his life and was later liberated from custody, restored to his property, and pardoned.[213]

The same spirit of collaborative enterprise characterized Edward's three remaining parliaments. The second parliament of 1305, to which no representatives were summoned, saw the drafting of a new ordinance for the government of conquered Scotland and of a full definition of conspiracy which, like the trailbaston legislation, took the form of an ordinance for delivery to the justices.[214] But it was the assembly of May 1306 which revealed most clearly the restoration of parliamentary harmony between the king and his subjects. This parliament followed shortly after Robert Bruce's rebellion of March 1306 which had reopened the Scottish war, and it was intended as a prelude to a new campaign to suppress the rising. Summonses for the parliament and for the campaign were issued on the same day, 5 April.[215] More significantly for Edward's domestic position, the parliament also followed soon after, and partly coincided with, Edward's successful reversal of his opponents' main political gains in 1297 and 1301. Parliament met on or a few days before 30 May and ended about 7 June.[216] On 29 December 1305 Pope Clement V had issued a bull freeing Edward from his oath to observe *Confirmatio Cartarum*, and (as the bull was interpreted) revoking the disafforestations which had been forced on him in 1301. This was published in England in Easter week, 5–11 April, about the

---

[212] *Langtoft*, ii. 358–61; *Rot. Parl.* i. 178; *PROME* i. 114.

[213] *PROME* ii. 180–5; *Flores Historiarum* iii. 122; F. M. Powicke, *The Thirteenth Century, 1216–1307* (Oxford, 1953), 331–3; Denton, *Robert Winchelsey*, 218 n. 161; Prestwich, *Edward I*, 461–2.

[214] *PROME* i. 121–2, ii. 442–3; *Anglo-Scottish Relations, 1174–1328: Some Selected Documents*, ed. and trans. E. L. G. Stones (London, 1965), 120–9.

[215] *Parl. Writs*, I. 164, 374.   [216] *PROME* i. 127–8.

same time as orders went out for the coming parliament and campaign.[217] Meanwhile, in February the obliging pope, acting on the king's request, had suspended Archbishop Winchelsey, Edward's chief clerical opponent in 1297, from office, and Winchelsey left England on 19 May.[218] On 27 May, at or shortly before parliament's opening, a new ordinance of the forest was used to announce the king's revocation of the earlier disafforestations following from the events of 1301, and the king's release from his oath regarding them;[219] on 5 June, about the time of parliament's close, Edward ordered the confinement in the Tower of Henry of Keighley, the barons' intermediary in the 1301 parliament;[220] and on the same day his release from his forest oath was publicly proclaimed at St Paul's.[221]

The king's *révanche* for the events of 1297 and 1301 thus fell almost wholly within the period between parliament's summoning and its dismissal. Its various elements were widely publicized. Yet we hear of no word of dissent from those in parliament but only of their cooperation. The agreement of the knights and magnates, meeting together, and of the burgesses, meeting separately, to an aid for the knighting of Edward's son—in effect a direct tax—was given *unanimiter* on the day of the representatives' arrival at Westminster, 30 May, suggesting wholehearted support for the king's policies. No doubt that support owed much to Bruce's rebellion, expounded to the assembled representatives by the king's councillors,[222] to the military situation in the north, and to the imminence of the forthcoming campaign, all of which made opposition unpatriotic. It cannot have been a coincidence that the public excommunication of Bruce took place on 5 June at St Paul's, on the same day and in the same place as the publication of Edward's absolution from his oath.[223] Edward could exploit the threat from his new foreign enemy to his own domestic advantage. No doubt too the mass knighting of about 300 young men at the Feast of the Swans, which took place on 22 May, a few days before parliament's opening, served to generate chivalric enthusiasm for Edward's cause and to ensure that it took precedence over all else.[224] All the same, it was remarkable that so much of what had been achieved by the king's opponents in 1297 and 1301 had been so easily and so compliantly undone.

[217] *Flores Historiarum*, iii. 130; Denton, *Robert Winchelsey*, 231–5.
[218] Denton, *Robert Winchelsey*, 231–5.
[219] *Stat. Realm*, i. 147–9; *Flores Historiarum*, iii. 130; Denton, *Robert Winchelsey*, 237–8.
[220] Stubbs, *Constit. Hist.* ii. 158 n. 1; *EHD*, ed. Rothwell, 522.   [221] *Ann. London*, 146.
[222] *PROME* i. 127; Pasquet, *Origins of the House of Commons*, 235–6.   [223] *Ann. London*, 146–7.
[224] C. Bullock-Davies, *Menestrellorum Multitudo: Minstrels at a Royal Feast* (Cardiff, 1978), pp. ix–xli.

This parliament had at least one feature in common with those of the earlier period of antagonism between king and subjects: the cooperation within it of magnates and knights, seen in their joint and prompt response to the king's request for a feudal aid. This same feature was carried forward to the last parliament of the reign, which met at Carlisle in January 1307. No further tax was contemplated at this parliament, yet knights and burgesses were summoned to it, presumably as potential contributors to the debates on the future governance of Scotland and other matters touching the king and the 'estate of the kingdom' which formed parliament's main business.[225] Their importance was recognized when parliament's opening was twice adjourned because 'all the prelates, knights and others of the community of the realm' had not fully arrived.[226] But since the burgesses seem to have been dismissed as soon as they appeared, while the knights remained for some two months, it was presumably the counsels of the latter group that were especially wanted.[227] Once again it had been shown that in parliament the knights counted for more than the burgesses.

In much of the ensuing work of parliament they partnered the magnates. A newsletter tells us that the prelates, earls, barons, king's councillors, and 'all the commune of the land' assented to the projected marriage between Edward, the king's son, and Isabella, daughter of Philip IV of France, which was a central part of the peace arrangements with France discussed in this parliament.[228] There are indications too that the knights aligned themselves with the magnates in the ecclesiastical and anti-papal legislation for which this parliament is best known. In 1305 a petition from 'the earls, barons and community of the realm of England' had resulted in a statute forbidding the export of monies by certain religious houses. But this was ratified and issued only at Carlisle in 1307, in part perhaps as a gesture towards those groups which had formerly asked for it.[229] More far-reaching was a comparable petition put forward by 'the community of the realm' and attacking papal provisions, various papal levies, and the papal tax collector, William Testa, who was responsible for them.[230] The petition was essentially a defence of the rights of lay patrons and

---

[225] *Parl. Writs*, I. 182–3; *PROME* i. 129.   [226] *PROME* ii. 468–9.
[227] Ibid. i. 129; Powell and Wallis, *House of Lords*, 260–1; Prestwich, *Edward I*, 458.
[228] Richardson and Sayles, 'The Parliament of Carlisle, 1307: Some New Documents', in *EPMA* xii. 436; Prestwich, *Edward I*, 458.
[229] *PROME* ii. 200–1, 459–62; *C. and S.* ii. ii. 1232–6.
[230] *PROME* ii. 528–36; *C. and S.* ii. ii. 1232–6; Richardson and Sayles, 'Parliament of Carlisle', 433–6.

benefactors;[231] and since knights as well as magnates possessed advowsons and had a potential interest in local churches and monasteries, we might expect the two groups to have come together in its drafting.

The cooperative and unconfrontational mode of these later parliaments was not just the product of light taxation (the rates of a thirteenth and a twentieth for the levy of 1306 were the lightest since 1283) and of the new Scottish emergency, which in any case broke surface only in 1306. The Scottish threat was certainly important in allowing Edward to reject the restraints imposed on him in 1297 and 1301 without provoking a public outcry. Like the parliamentary settlement of October 1297, negotiated under the shadow of the preceding English defeat at Stirling Bridge,[232] it showed how troubles abroad could impose peace at home. Yet the change of atmosphere also owed much to a quality for which Edward is not usually given much credit in his later years: his managerial skills. These were particularly well displayed in his relations with parliament. The petitioning arrangements of 1305, the summoning of local representatives in 1305 and 1307, when taxes were seemingly not contemplated, the willingness to seek consent for the feudal aid of 1306, which Edward could simply have taken by virtue of his lordship, the public discussion of law, order, foreign policy, and ecclesiastical affairs within parliament, and the king's responsiveness to the general petitions put forward by magnates and commons: all suggest, by comparison with the events of 1297 to 1301, a renewed willingness on Edward's part to engage with public opinion.

If in these various ways Edward's later parliaments resembled those of the 1270s and 1280s, there were perhaps two significant differences. First, circumstances were much more difficult, and the appearance of stability deceptive. The Scottish problem had shown itself to be unresolved, the crown's finances were in confusion and its debts huge, and some of the issues of the 1290s, such as prise, remained a latent source of grievance.[233] Second, the knights in parliament were more of a force to be reckoned with. Much that they did in these last parliaments is hidden from us; but what we can see them doing—voting taxes, petitioning with the magnates in defence of their common interests, concurring in foreign policy decisions, and simply being present when there was no constitutional need for their presence—suggests that the crown had recognized the elevation of their

---

[231] Denton, *Robert Winchelsey*, 242.   [232] Ibid. 160.
[233] Prestwich, *War, Politics and Finance*, 270–2, 288–90; id., *Edward I*, 509–11, 514, 554–5.

role resulting from their part in the 'tax politics' of 1294 to 1301 and the concomitant 'struggle for the Charters'. Here, in 1307, were two contrasting legacies from the old reign to the new.

4. Magnate Politics and the Growth of an Independent Commons, 1307–1322

The accession of Edward II did not immediately change the tenor of English political life. The renewal of the Scottish war in 1306 meant that the crown's oppressive exploitation of its subjects' resources to meet wartime needs resumed its place on the agenda of protest in the new king's early years. Prises in particular continued to be a major topic for complaint. They were as prominent in a general petition for reform presented to the king in the parliament of April 1309, in the subsequent statute of Stamford, and in the Ordinances of 1311, as in the earlier *Articuli Super Cartas* of 1300 which had set a precedent for these measures.[234] Yet over the reign as a whole, war and its demands did much less to determine the course of politics than had been the case in Edward I's later years. Its main determinant was now Edward II's personality, friends, and style of ruling. Favourites, first Piers Gaveston, then the courtiers of Edward's middle years, and finally the two Despensers, became the central point of contention between the king and his great men. Their influence over Edward and his government raised broader questions concerning the proper distribution of patronage and the right to counsel the king which had been in abeyance since the 1250s. If the king's leading opponent, his cousin Thomas of Lancaster, could plausibly be seen by contemporaries as a second Simon de Montfort,[235] Piers Gaveston was another William de Valence, redivivus and writ large.

These issues meant that for much of the reign politics were both predominantly baronial and virulently factious, as magnate groups formed and re-formed in different combinations, contended for power, and sought to exclude others from it. Naturally the wider problems raised by the wars could hardly be separated from these internal struggles, and the belief that taxes raised for the war were being wasted on favourites gave complaints

---

[234] J. R. Maddicott, *Thomas of Lancaster, 1307–22: A Study in the Reign of Edward II* (Oxford, 1970), 97–8, 103, 106–7.

[235] Ibid. 321–2; Maddicott, ' "1258" and "1297" ', 2.

against wartime levies an edge which they had lacked under the less partisan rule of Edward II's father.[236] So too did failure in the war for which taxes were granted but then misspent. It remained true, however, that the loom of political relationships produced a cloth woven by king and magnates, and had faction and feuding, court and country, royalists and rebels, for its warp and weft.

In this milieu it was not surprising that parliament itself took on a much more aristocratic complexion than it had displayed in the previous reign. This was particularly true of Edward's early years. Of the eight parliaments which met between 1307 and 1310, only two, those of October 1307 and April 1309, included local representatives, and in both they were present primarily to grant taxes.[237] No provision seems to have been made in any of these assemblies for the reception of petitions and very few were presented, draining parliament of much of its popular content. If this reflected Edward's own lack of interest in this sort of business (as indeed in most sorts), it was also a sign that, among parliament's priorities, justice had been trumped by politics; for these early parliaments were largely taken up with contentions over Gaveston.[238] The king and a party among the magnates were at loggerheads in the parliament of March 1308; Gaveston's exile was demanded by the magnates in that of April 1308; his recall may have been discussed in that of April 1309; and his renewed unpopularity overshadowed that of February 1310, at which the Ordainers were appointed with a brief to reform the kingdom and the king's household.[239] The Ordinances themselves, published in the parliament which convened in August 1311, took a resolutely baronial view of parliament and its functions. In future the consent of the baronage in parliament was to be necessary for some of the most important acts of kingship: for royal grants of castles, lands, offices, and feudal windfalls; for appointments to the great offices of state and to the main household offices; for making war; and for changes in the coinage. Complaints against royal officials were to be heard and determined in each parliament by a commission comprising one bishop, two earls, and two barons.[240] The role

---

[236] Maddicott, *Thomas of Lancaster*, 71–2, 110–11.

[237] *HBC* 552; Jurkowski, Smith, and Crook, *Lay Taxes*, 29–30. It is possible that knights (but not burgesses or clergy) were also present in the parliament of March 1308: see *HBC* 552, and *PROME* iii. 5.

[238] Dodd, *Justice and Grace*, 65–75.   [239] *PROME* iii. 5, 6–7, 11–12, 17–19.

[240] *Stat. Realm*, i. 158–60, 165, 167; *EHD*, ed. Rothwell, 528–30, 536; M. Prestwich, 'The Ordinances of 1311', in J. Taylor and W. Childs (eds.), *Politics and Crisis in Fourteenth-Century England* (Gloucester, 1990), 11–12.

envisaged here for parliament was a reversion to that set out by the baronial reformers of 1258, and for some of the same reasons. Parliament was seen as a public forum, where important matters of state, removed from the purview of an exclusive clique around the king, could be publicly debated and approved by the magnates.[241] The rise in the influence of the commons which had occurred in the meantime, and more especially in Edward I's later years, received no specific acknowledgement from the Ordainers.

This is not to say that the magnates in parliament promoted only their own concerns. One particular sequence of events suggests otherwise. The articles for reform presented in the parliament of April 1309, where knights and burgesses were present, embodied a number of popular grievances, notably those arising from prises, and were probably drafted by the local representatives in collaboration with the magnates.[242] The sixth clause, complaining that knights and burgesses found no one to receive their petitions when they came to parliament, can have originated only with the commons. Yet according to the chronicles they were put forward by earls and barons, and according to the official text they were presented to the king by 'the community of his realm'.[243] The tax of a twenty-fifth granted in this parliament was made conditional on the king's acceptance of the requested reforms, but it was only in the succeeding Stamford parliament of July 1309 that Edward made the required concessions in the Statute of Stamford. At this parliament the magnates alone were present.[244] Some of these reforming articles were later incorporated into the Ordinances, themselves made by an elite body of prelates, earls, and barons, whose reforming commission, drafted in February 1310, had said nothing about the participation of the commons. The Ordinances made provision, for example, for the holding of parliaments once or twice a year partly to ensure that petitions could be dealt with and determined.[245] In all this we can see another aspect of the aristocratic reaction which characterized Edward's early parliaments. Grievances might originate with the local representatives and with their constituents, but it was the magnates who brought them forward for redress and, in the Ordinances, proposed remedies. By a species of virtual representation which would have been

---

[241] Above, 239.   [242] *Rot. Parl.* i. 443–5; Maddicott, *Thomas of Lancaster*, 97–9.
[243] *Annales Paulini*, in *Chronicles of the Reign of Edward I and Edward II*, ed. Stubbs, 267; *Ann. London*, 157; *Rot. Parl.* i. 443; Maddicott, *Thomas of Lancaster*, 99; *PROME* iii. 12.
[244] Maddicott, *Thomas of Lancaster*, 103–4; *PROME* iii. 14.
[245] *Stat. Realm*, i. 165; *EHD*, ed. Rothwell, 237; Dodd, *Justice and Grace*, 73.

recognized by those attending Henry III's parliaments, or even the great councils of King John, they had reverted to their old position as spokesmen for the realm.[246]

After 1311 parliament remained the stage for the playing out of aristocratic conflicts, whether between king and barons or between opposing baronial factions.[247] The parliament of August 1312, the first following the parliamentary publication of the Ordinances in October 1311, was overshadowed by the negotiations between the king's party and Lancaster and his allies for the return of Gaveston's jewels and horses, seized at the time of the favourite's capture earlier in the year. Though these negotiations largely took place outside parliament, in parallel with its concurrent session, parliament provided the occasion for bringing the parties together.[248] The three parliaments of 1313 saw further peace negotiations, or projects for negotiations, culminating in the pardon for Gaveston's death issued to the dissenting barons during the course of the September parliament.[249] At the York parliament of 1314, after the king's crushing defeat at Bannockburn, Edward was forced to confirm the Ordinances and to yield to Lancaster's programme of reform;[250] while the Ordinances were confirmed again at the parliament of January 1315 and for a third time at the Lincoln parliament of January 1316, when Lancaster was appointed as head of the council.[251]

The two years which followed were marked by a growing conflict between Lancaster and the courtier magnates around the king, and no parliaments met. The five subsequent parliaments between 1318 and 1321 were dominated first by attempts to reach a settlement between Lancaster and the king, and then by the rising hatred of the two Hugh Despensers, father and son, now emerging as the leading influences at court. In the parliament of July 1321 formal judgement against them was given by the earls and barons, without the king's compliance, and they were exiled.[252] It was a less conspicuous mark of the magnates' parliamentary weight at this time that between 1316 and 1321 both the baronial and the episcopal element among the auditors of petitions grew at the expense of the

[246] Morris, 'Magnates and Community of the Realm', 68; Harriss, *King, Parliament and Public Finance*, 109–10, 119–20; above, 140–3, 206–7.
[247] Cf. G. Dodd, 'Parliament and Political Legitimacy in the Reign of Edward II', in G. Dodd and A. Musson (eds.), *The Reign of Edward II: New Perspectives* (Woodbridge, 2006), 170–1.
[248] Maddicott, *Thomas of Lancaster*, 133–7; *PROME* iii. 27–8.
[249] Maddicott, *Thomas of Lancaster*, 148–51; *PROME* iii. 37–42.
[250] Maddicott, *Thomas of Lancaster*, 164–7; *PROME* iii. 44–5.
[251] Maddicott, *Thomas of Lancaster*, 166–8, 180–2; *PROME* iii. 47, 162–3.
[252] Maddicott, *Thomas of Lancaster*, 278–89; *PROME* iii. 421–5.

king's officials. If there were practical reasons for this—those chosen were experienced administrators and crown servants—the change also worked to reinforce magnate authority within parliament.[253] Its manifestation through the hearing of petitions should perhaps remind us that all these assemblies also saw the transaction of much routine 'common business of the realm' and that they were not entirely enmeshed in conflict. In particular, the problems of Scotland and of relations with France, as well as taxation and petitions, were rarely off the agenda. But it remains true that baronial politics, disputes and peace-making, reform and resistance to it, provided the parliaments of 1311 to 1321 with their leitmotiv. Only with the defeat of Lancaster at Boroughbridge in 1322, the subsequent repeal of the Ordinances, and the establishment of the younger Despenser's supremacy in court and country did parliament, for the reign's concluding years, cease to be either the forum or the occasion for baronial opposition to the crown.

Yet it was within the unpromisingly aristocratic and factious environment of these parliaments that the position of the commons began to be transformed. There is fairly general agreement among historians that the middle years of Edward II's reign saw the emergence of the knights and burgesses as an independent force, increasingly detached from the magnates whom they had partnered during the previous reign's 'struggle for the Charters' and increasingly endowed with a collective voice.[254] A rising commons in a parliamentary milieu dominated by lords and their quarrels may seem to present an apparent paradox. The first step towards explaining it must rest on a fact which can be demonstrated statistically: that is, the increasingly frequent summoning of the commons.[255] Of the reign's 27 parliaments, the knights, burgesses, and lower clergy were summoned to 17, the knights and burgesses to 2, and the knights alone to 2—so the commons in some form were present in 21 out of 27 parliaments. This compares with their summoning to 11 out of 20 between 1294 and 1307: an attendance ratio of 1 in 1.8 parliaments under Edward I compared with 1 in 1.3 under his son. Moreover, those of Edward II's parliaments to which magnates alone were summoned almost all fell within the reign's early years.

---

[253] Richardson and Sayles, 'The King's Ministers in Parliament, 1307–27', in *EPMA* xvii. 197–9; Dodd, *Justice and Grace*, 55–6, 75.
[254] See, e.g. Harriss, *King, Parliament and Public Finance*, 118–21; W. M. Ormrod, 'Agenda for Legislation, 1322–c.1340', *EHR* 105 (1990), 2; Dodd, *Justice and Grace*, 132–3.
[255] The point was first made by T. F. Tout, *The Place of the Reign of Edward II in English History*, 2nd edn. (Manchester, 1936), 30, though his statistics differ slightly from those given below, which are derived from *HBC* 552–5, and *PROME* iii. Cf. Dodd, *Justice and Grace*, 131.

Up to 1310 there were five, possibly six, exclusively magnate assemblies, and after 1310 only two, those of January 1320 and June 1325. From the parliament of August 1311 to that of May 1322, knights, burgesses, and lower clergy were summoned to every parliament but one. They were therefore present at each of the parliaments mentioned in the preceding two paragraphs which saw political conflict. Nor was their attendance almost invariably the result of the need for their consent to taxation, since only seven of the twenty parliaments to which they were summoned made tax grants.[256] The trend towards attendance by the commons for what must be reasons unconnected with taxation, already becoming visible in Edward I's last years, has now become much more pronounced.

How should we account for this shift towards a more regular and less narrowly fiscal role for the commons? The answer almost certainly lies in the attempts of king and magnates to invoke their support for partisan measures, in order to give those measures weight and to make them carry weight in the localities. Dr Gwilym Dodd has argued that it was the need for legitimacy which drove the opposition magnates to work so frequently through parliament. They could thus counter (though with a certain speciousness) any charge that they were acting factiously and for their own interests alone.[257] If legitimacy was their concern, it could only be enhanced by an appeal to the commons, which might also promise additional publicity for their cause and hence a wider legitimization in the country at large. In this regard the parliament which began in August 1311 marked a turning point, as Maud Clarke was the first to recognize.[258] The only one to be attended by the knights and burgesses since that of April 1309, more than two years earlier, it was convened under the influence of the Ordainers, probably against the king's wishes,[259] in order that the Ordinances should be 'completed and affirmed'.[260] When the Ordinances were published in September, the Pipewell chronicle tells us that men from each city and town were publicly sworn to maintain them. So also were 'all

---

[256] Taxes were granted in the parliaments of Oct. 1307, Apr. 1309, Sept. 1313, Jan. 1315, Feb. 1316, May 1319, and Nov. 1322: Jurkowski, Smith, and Crook, *Lay Taxes*, 29–36.

[257] Dodd, 'Parliament and Political Legitimacy', 176–7.

[258] Clarke, *Medieval Representation and Consent*, 160–1.

[259] See the anonymous letter written from Alnwick on 4 April 1311: 'The king is in no mood yet for a parliament, but when the earl of Gloucester and the council meet in London he will have to do what they order': *Calendar of Documents Relating to Scotland*, ed. J. Bain, 4 vols. (Edinburgh, 1881–8), iii, no. 202. Cf. *PROME* iii. 22; M. Prestwich, *Plantagenet England, 1225–1360* (Oxford, 2005), 184.

[260] *Parl. Writs*, II. ii, appendix, 41; Tout, *Edward II*, 80–1.

the great men of the land', who must have included the knights. This was done in London. Copies were then sent to every county and cathedral, and the resulting local publicity can only have been reinforced by the personal witness of the local representatives.[261]

The same motives may explain why the commons were drawn into the essentially baronial quarrel with the Despensers at the time of the favourites' forfeiture and exile in the parliament of July 1321. Although judgement on the Despensers was passed by the earls and barons alone, the initial accusations against them were presented additionally by the prelates and the 'community of the realm', meaning the commons. In this way their indictment could be presented as a national act and not as a mere coup by a baronial faction.[262] That the king could play the same game was shown in the parliament of May 1322, which, following after Boroughbridge, undid both the programme of the Ordainers and the earlier baronial actions against the Despensers. Here the local representatives were made parties to the king's *révanche* and the re-establishment of royal power. The previous judgement against the Despensers was reversed with the counsel and assent of 'prelates, earls, barons, knights of the shire, and the community of the realm';[263] while the Ordinances were revoked with the assent of the 'prelates, earls and barons, and the whole community of the realm'.[264] Since the statute revoking the Ordinances was sent to the counties for publication on the same day, 19 May, as the knights received their writs *de expensis* signalling their departure and directed, like the statute, to the sheriffs, it is reasonable to suppose that the knights were expected to take the statute home with them.[265] Through the sanction of the commons and the informing of the shires, Edward's counter-revolution was given a broader social base.

We should thus see the regular summoning of the commons from 1311 onwards primarily as a means by which the actions of king and magnates might be validated and publicized. The principle was not so very different

---

[261] Clarke, *Medieval Representation and Consent*, 160 and n. 6. Cf. Harriss, *King, Parliament and Public Finance*, 77.

[262] *Stat. Realm*, i. 181–4; Morris, 'Magnates and Community of the Realm', 81–2; M. Prestwich, 'Parliament and the Community of the Realm in Fourteenth-Century England', in A. Cosgrove and J. I. McGuire (eds.), *Parliament and Community*, Historical Studies, 14 (Belfast, 1983), 11.

[263] *Stat. Realm*, i. 187; L. W. V. Harcourt, *His Grace the Steward and Trial of Peers* (London, 1907), 326; Prestwich, 'Parliament and the Community', 7.

[264] *Stat. Realm*, i. 189; Morris, 'Magnates and Community of the Realm', 82.

[265] *Stat. Realm*, i. 190; *Parl. Writs*, II. ii. 258.

from Edward I's occasional use of the commons for similar ends against his external enemies, seen, for example, in their summoning to the Shrewsbury parliament of 1283 to witness the trial of David of Wales.[266] Now, when enemies lay within rather than without, they became adjuncts to the manoeuvres of parties.

Largely as a result, however, they emerged as much more than that. The novel attendance of the commons in parliament after parliament had some momentous if unintended consequences. In the first place it increased the probability of members being re-elected, so creating broader bonds of continuity between the commons in successive parliaments. Already marked under Edward I, as we have seen, the carry-over of knights from one parliament to another became still more evident under his son. About eleven of Edward's twenty-seven parliaments had a majority of shire representatives who had attended before. Multiple re-election was also much commoner. Of the 75 knights known to have been present at the parliament of September 1313, for example, 26 had attended the immediately preceding parliament and 59 had attended for the same shire in some preceding parliament. Eighteen of these were attending for the second time, 21 for the third, 8 for the fourth, 3 for the fifth, 2 for the sixth, and 5 for the seventh time. In the parliament of July 1321, when judgement was passed on the Despensers, 9 of the 71 known county knights had attended the immediately preceding parliament and 43 had attended for the same shire in some preceding parliament. Of these, 17 were attending for the second time, 7 for the third, 7 for the fourth, and 4 for the fifth.[267] The re-election of borough members was similarly common. Some seven parliaments had a majority of burgesses who had sat in some preceding parliament—but of none of the parliaments of Edward I for which figures are available was this true.[268]

The increasingly frequent attendance of the commons, and the frequent re-election of individual MPs, must have strengthened the *esprit* of the entire *corps*, helping to create a continuing and corporate persona largely absent in the days of the commons' more intermittent summoning. This development is likely to have been enhanced by another which is frequently overlooked: the abnormal length of time for which Edward II's parliaments

---

[266] Above, 293.
[267] Edwards, 'Personnel of the Commons', 152; id., *Historians and the Medieval English Parliament*, 31–3.
[268] Edwards, 'Personnel of the Commons', 154, 156.

often sat. The 15 parliaments attended by the commons between 1311 and 1321 lasted on average for some 33 days and occupied altogether about 12 per cent of this eleven-year period.[269] By contrast, the 10 comparable parliaments which met in Edward I's later years, between 1295 and 1307, and for which we have comparable figures, lasted on average for some 17 days and occupied about 4 per cent of this twelve-year period. If we look ahead, we find that the average length of Edward III's parliaments, at 22 days (excluding the Good Parliament), was much closer to that for Edward I's parliaments than to that for Edward II's.[270] Some of the latter's parliaments were quite exceptionally protracted. The second session of the parliament which began in August 1312, lasting from 30 September to 16 December, saw the commons present for some 77 days, and the first session of the 1311 parliament, at 63 days, was not much shorter.[271] Five parliaments within the period lasted for seven weeks or more. By any medieval standard these were extraordinarily lengthy sessions. The Oxford parliament of 1258, which produced the Provisions of Oxford, lasted for only about 19 days; the 49-day duration of the Easter parliament of 1285, which saw the making of the Statute of Westminster II, was unusual enough to be remarked on by a chronicler; and even the Good Parliament of 1376, perhaps the most famous and eventful of the middle ages, lasted only for 73 days, rather fewer than the session of 1312.[272]

Political tensions again do much to explain the length of Edward II's parliaments: the use of parliament as a party platform, the irreconcilability of different sides, the slow progress of negotiations. The long session of 1311 began on 8 August but saw the publication of the Ordinances only on 27 September, reflecting Edward's initial refusal to accept the reforms and his long rearguard defence of his position.[273] The longest session of all, that of 1312, came after Gaveston's death and was deliberately drawn out by the king (so the Lanercost chronicle says) in order to wear down his baronial opponents.[274] The fifty-four-day session which began in September 1313 was largely taken up with the negotiating of pardons for those involved in

---

[269] These and the following statistics are deduced from *HBC* 552–5, and from *PROME* iii.

[270] S. L. Waugh, *England in the Reign of Edward III* (Cambridge, 1991), 196–7.

[271] Dodd, *Justice and Grace*, 65, gives to each of these two parliaments a considerably longer duration by amalgamating separate sessions of the same parliament.

[272] Treharne, *Baronial Plan*, 72, 77; Cotton, 166; *PROME* v. 289–91.

[273] Maddicott, *Thomas of Lancaster*, 116–17; *PROME* iii. 22.

[274] *Chronicon de Lanercost*, ed. J. Stevenson, Maitland Club (Edinburgh, 1839), 219; Maddicott, *Thomas of Lancaster*, 133–7; *PROME* iii. 27–8.

Gaveston's death.[275] On all these occasions the commons were present. The consequences for their development can hardly be measured. But it is a fair assumption that these protracted meetings contributed powerfully to their sense of identity and their collective outlook. They brought together large numbers of men from the shires and boroughs, many of them parliamentary veterans, and most of them presumably with time on their hands and a good deal to talk about.

One result may be seen in a seminal feature of the reign's parliamentary history: the emergence of the common petition. Presented by the commons and concerning matters of wide interest, the common petition testified not only to the evolution of the commons as a single 'house' but also to the growing perception that they alone represented the broader commons of the realm. It had its immediate roots in the general efflorescence of petitioning which marked Edward II's middle years. As we have seen, the articles presented in the parliament of 1309 had complained that the knights and burgesses coming to parliament could find no one to receive their petitions: our first proof of what may have been true for some time, that on at least some occasions the local representatives took up to Westminster the petitions of their constituents and that they saw the presentation of petitions as one of their functions. The very few petitions presented in Edward's early parliaments give support to the substance of this complaint, and their dearth was equally evident for some years beyond 1309.[276] But, as Dr Dodd has shown, in the parliament of January 1315 petitioning began again on a substantial scale with the presentation of some 229 petitions, more than in any other single parliament since 1305. This trend continued for the rest of the reign, though in a smaller way and only in those parliaments not dominated by other business, political, military, or fiscal.[277] It is hard not to see the revival of petitioning in these middle years as related in part to the political needs of contending factions. The parliaments of January 1315 and of January 1316, when petitions were also brought forward in large numbers, saw Thomas of Lancaster at the height

---

[275] Maddicott, *Thomas of Lancaster*, 150–1; *PROME* iii. 41–2.

[276] *Rot. Parl.* i. 444; Dodd, *Justice ad Grace*, 65, 72–4; Maddicott, 'Parliament and the Constituencies', 64–5; above, 333. Dodd, *Justice and Grace*, 77–8, 308–9, is inclined to depreciate the value of the 1309 complaint and the role of MPs as intercessors between the king and his subjects; and it is certainly the case that petitions were often presented in parliaments unattended by representatives. But the complaint would hardly have carried the weight which it was clearly meant to carry had its substance been altogether untrue.

[277] *PROME* iii. 46–7; Dodd, *Justice and Grace*, 65, 74–6.

of his power and popularity; while in subsequent parliaments the king himself seems to have taken an active interest in hearing and expediting petitions.[278] Both may have sought to cultivate the sympathies of the commons, whose expectations of redress for their constituents' grievances had been demonstrated in the complaint of 1309 and whose standing at home may have partly depended on the degree to which that redress was available in the parliaments which they attended.

An important link between the general revival of petitioning and the emergence of the common petition lay in the more frequent formulation of petitions from local communities. They came not only from towns, which were already regular petitioners for favour and privilege,[279] but more especially from counties. In the parliament of February 1305 some 5 out of 288 petitions (1.7 per cent) were presented in the name of county communities, but this increased to 10 out of 229 (4.4 per cent) in that of January 1315 and to 9 out of 123 (7.3 per cent) in October 1320.[280] Small though the numbers are, they seem to indicate a trend. That county petitions were backed and probably presented by the county knights, presumably after discussion and perhaps drafting in the shire court, is made plain by an exception which proves the rule. In the parliament of 1315 a petition said to have been 'made at the request of the community of Devon' was judged to be no such thing, 'as can be ascertained from the knights sent to parliament for the said shire'.[281] The knights were clearly expected to be able to recognize, and if necessary to disavow, the petitions put forward in the name of their county community.

Still more interesting is the surviving evidence, as yet slight, of cooperation between knights from different counties in the making of local petitions. It takes the form of an occasional petition presented jointly by adjacent counties. In the parliament of 1315, for example, the communities of Kent and Sussex asked for the removal of two named men from a local

---

[278] Maddicott, *Thomas of Lancaster*, 166–8, 180–1; Dodd, *Justice and Grace*, 74–6. For Lancaster's popularity in 1315–16 see *Vita Edwardi Secundi*, ed. and trans. W. R. Childs, OMT (Oxford, 2005), 168–9: 'O, what paeans of praise you had while you were constantly upholding the Ordinances! The goodwill of the people . . .'

[279] Above, 318.

[280] Petitions of 1305: *PROME* i. 119–20, ii. 53–201. In this calculation I have ignored petitions from Scotland and Ireland and counted the three successive and related petitions from Cumberland (ibid. ii. 87–8) as one. Petitions of 1315: *PROME* iii. 53–160. Petitions of 1320: ibid. iii. 380–419. Cf. Dodd, *Justice and Grace*, 254–60.

[281] Sayles, *Functions*, 319; D. Rayner, 'The Forms and Machinery of the "Commune Petition" in the Fourteenth Century', *EHR* 56 (1941), 207.

oyer and terminer commission; in 1318 Oxfordshire and Berkshire asked for a remedy for 'various trespasses' committed against 'divers men' in the two counties; and in 1320 Devon and Cornwall complained about profiteering by local wine merchants.[282] If we can assume that these petitions are genuinely from the knights of the counties named and not from particular interest groups, as with our earlier Devon example, they point towards cooperation within parliament between MPs from different counties. This had last been conspicuously visible when tax was under discussion in the parliament of October 1268[283] and no doubt it also underlay much of the united parliamentary opposition to Edward I in his later years. But petitioning was a different sort of activity from resisting taxation, and one more proactive than reactive. The alternative to parliamentary cooperation, prior collaboration between different county courts in formulating petitions, is hardly plausible. And if this be granted it suggests that, in cooperating, the knights exercised their initiative. They were not mandated to act by their counties but used their judgement in their counties' interests—true representatives rather than delegates.

Other forms of cooperation within parliament begin to appear about the same time, most notably perhaps between knights and burgesses. The division between the two groups which had prevailed under Edward I seems to be breaking down. That they now associate is suggested by their joint complaint in 1309 about the absence of parliamentary receivers for their petitions.[284] At a more particular level we find the city of Lincoln joining together with the county community, by a process which is likely to have involved collaboration between their MPs in parliament, to petition in 1315 for an enquiry into local crimes and disorders.[285] Nor was the hierarchical order which separated knights and burgesses quite so rigid. There is at least one case (and probably more) of a knight sitting indifferently for city and county on different occasions. Sir Matthew Crowthorne, a Devon knight, was returned for his county in 1318, but then displaced in the same year and returned for Exeter, which he represented again in 1319, 1320, and 1321, before being returned again for the county in 1322.[286] A burgess might similarly take a county seat, as did Andrew Pendock, a

---

[282] *PROME* iii. 141, 298, 389. Cf. Dodd, *Justice and Grace*, 257–8.   [283] Above, 267–8.
[284] Above, 333, 340.   [285] *PROME* iii. 154.
[286] *Parl. Writs*, ii. ii. 187, 211, 222, 238, 249; appendix, 138. H. G. Richardson, 'John of Gaunt and the Parliamentary Representation of Lancashire', *Bull. John Rylands Library*, 22 (1938), offprint, 18; Maddicott, 'Parliament and the Constituencies', 73.

burgess representative of Gloucester on at least eight occasions between 1307 and 1326, but a representative of the shire in 1327.[287] These are all straws in the wind. But they suggest that town and country could come together within parliament to discuss matters of common interest, that a knight might not regard a borough seat as beneath his dignity, and that a burgess might be looked on favourably by a county electorate. It is difficult not to believe that these developments owed something to the commons' regular attendance at the lengthy parliaments of Edward II's middle years, which, for weeks on end, made compulsory bedfellows of men from diverse backgrounds.

We should be wary then of accepting a recent verdict that 'the lower house was still a collection of disparate and politically uncoordinated men from the localities'.[288] The frequent re-election of these men, their lengthy parliamentary sojourns, and their ability to collaborate, all point tentatively in another direction. But perhaps the best riposte to this view comes from the initial subject of our investigation: the formulation of the petitions which are beginning to be presented in the name of 'the community of the realm' and 'the community of England' and which appear to embody the corporate complaints of the knights and burgesses. If not entirely new, these begin to proliferate only from 1315. They almost invariably concern matters of large and general interest, and, unlike most of the eleven or so supposedly 'common' petitions surviving from Edward I's reign,[289] they can more easily be ascribed to the commons in parliament than to particular interest groups or to groups with a magnate component. In 1315, for example, 'the community of the people of [the] realm' complain about the use of oyer and terminer commissions by 'great lords' to persecute their enemies and about their pillaging of the countryside; the 'community of England', about conspirators who confederated to maintain cases in the courts; and the 'community of England' again, about the use of protections by criminals to escape due punishment in cases of felony.[290] Some seven such petitions were presented in particular parliaments between 1315 and 1320.[291]

---

[287] Saul, *Knights and Esquires*, 126–7.
[288] Dodd, 'Parliament and Political Legitimacy', 173.
[289] G. L. Haskins, 'Three Early Petitions of the Commonalty', *Speculum*, 12 (1937), 314–18, surveys these petitions.
[290] *PROME* iii. 56, 58, 76–7.
[291] For the remainder, see ibid. 356, 381, 389, 410, and below, 347–8 Cf. Dodd, *Justice and Grace*, 130–1.

It would be easy to assume that the magnates had a major role, if no longer an exclusive one, in drafting these community petitions.[292] Yet the evidence goes against this. The petition of 1315 directed at the abuses practised by 'great lords' is unlikely to have been backed by the magnates; nor is a further petition of 1319, which again complains about the too liberal granting of oyer and terminer commissions, from which the magnates were the main beneficiaries, to the impoverishment of the people.[293] The petition against conspirators remarked that the offenders existed 'in every city, borough, hundred and wapentake', suggesting a problem which would have been recognized by both town and county representatives. More conclusive still is a petition of 1320 complaining about widespread breaches of the peace. Said in its enrolled heading to come from 'the entire community of the realm', the petition itself glosses this as 'the knights, citizens and burgesses present there on behalf of the counties, cities and boroughs of [the] realm'.[294] This both confirms the collaboration of knights and burgesses already discussed and implies that they could now be equated with 'the community of the realm'. Of course, other narrower groups, with more particular grievances, might ride behind the banner of 'the community', as did, for example, 'the community of [the king's] land' who in 1315 complained about the extortionate ferry charges levied for crossing the Humber.[295] But these petitions are easily recognized by their specific subject matter; and it is striking that in this particular case, and in another similar local petition,[296] the petitioners describe themselves not as 'the community of the realm' but 'of the land (terre)', meaning perhaps the locality. They may not have intended to present themselves as what they were not. Was there recognition here of 'the community of the realm' as a larger and more national community, represented, so our other evidence would suggest, by the parliamentary knights and burgesses?

In their petitions the commons were coming to possess an institutional device which expressed, if only from time to time, their own peculiar and separate identity.[297] If the emergence of that identity owed much to their frequent attendance, the long duration of their sessions, and the long service of many of their members, it also rested on another factor, often remarked

---

[292] Cf. Prestwich, 'Parliament and the Community', 8–9.
[293] PROME iii. 356; Prestwich, 'Parliament and the Community', 8.
[294] PROME iii. 76–7, 381.
[295] Ibid. 58; Prestwich, 'Parliament and the Community', 8; Dodd, Justice and Grace, 130.
[296] PROME iii. 101.   [297] Cf. Dodd, Justice and Grace, 132.

on, yet perhaps not fully explained: that is, their growing detachment from the magnates.[298] We have seen that in Edward I's later years both had shared a common political programme. Its main components had been opposition to arbitrary taxation, pressure for the alleviation of taxes and the curtailment of the boundaries of the royal forest, and insistence on the full enforcement of the Charters, both as a practical remedy for oppressive government and as a gauge of the king's trustworthiness.[299] What was now happening to dissolve the alliance which this programme had created?

One answer lies in shifting priorities. After 1307, and more especially after 1311, both taxation and the Charters lost much of their former political prominence. This was in some ways surprising. Because of the Scottish war taxation remained heavy. Between 1307 and 1322 there were seven levies of direct taxes, four of them falling in the six years between 1313 and 1319. Only between 1294 and 1297 had there been a more concentrated tax burden, as Dr Harriss has pointed out.[300] The acute famine which dominated much of this period made the burden all the more oppressive.[301] The imposition of a tallage at the conclusion of the very lengthy parliament of 1312 indicates resistance to taxation, at least on this one occasion; for then, as in some earlier parliaments, the raising of this prerogative levy, needing no consent, was almost certainly a *pis aller*, and a sign that the more lucrative levy on moveables had been refused.[302] The king's acceptance of the forest perambulations of 1300 as part of the price which he had to pay for a tax in 1316 showed that neither bargaining over taxation nor a major cause of contention in the previous reign had disappeared.[303] Yet taxation lacked the centrality which it had previously held in the agenda of protest. The constitutional issues were settled, and, unlike his father, Edward II never attempted to raise a direct tax without the consent of the commons. When the magnates told Edward in 1312 that they would do all they could to secure him a tax 'when they will have their peers more fully [with them], and the community',[304] they too recognized the necessity

---

[298] Harriss, *King, Parliament and Public Finance*, 113–19; Ormrod, 'Agenda for Legislation', 2.
[299] Above, 310–12.   [300] Harriss, *King, Parliament and Public Finance*, 113.
[301] Maddicott, *Thomas of Lancaster*, 163–4.
[302] Jurkowski, Smith, and Crook, *Lay Taxes*, 30–1. Stubbs, *Constit. Hist.* ii. 349, was the first to make an implicit connection between the probable refusal of a subsidy and the levying of a tallage. For earlier occasions when the king may have been forced to settle for a tallage rather than a subsidy (1252, 1288), see *Ann. Oseney*, 316; above, 174, 288; below, 467–8.
[303] *PROME* iii. 204; Harriss, *King, Parliament and Public Finance*, 115–17.
[304] *Ann. London*, 211; Maddicott, *Thomas of Lancaster*, 135; Prestwich, 'Parliament and the Community', 7.

of the commons for taxation and their own inability to represent them. Despite taxation's weight, the commons' position as its gate-keepers went unchallenged. This perhaps partly explains why the question of taxation was never raised in the petitions presented by the community of the realm. There was no Remonstrances or *De Tallagio* in Edward II's reign.

The political salience of the Charters was similarly rather less marked. The full maintenance of Magna Carta was laid down in the Ordinances; a tax was granted in the parliament of January 1315 only on condition that both the Charters and the Ordinances were observed; and in the York parliament of October 1318 orders were issued for the public recitation of both Magna Carta and the Ordinances.[305] As this history suggests, the Ordinances were now formally almost on a par with the Charters; and as a living text whose application would apply a salve to current political wounds, the new programme had largely superseded the old. Yet although the Ordinances were popular in the country, and viewed by some as 'a remedy for the poor and oppressed',[306] they lacked the universal and almost atavistic appeal formerly enjoyed by the more venerable Charters. Only for a few years after 1311 did they have anything like the united support of the baronage, some of whom, in the reign's middle period, stood to lose heavily from the restraints which the new reforms imposed on royal patronage and royal expenditure.[307] They failed signally to provide the kind of unifying totem which the Charters had supplied between 1297 and 1301. There was no 'struggle for the Charters' under Edward II; and if there was a struggle for the Ordinances, it was often that of Thomas of Lancaster alone, their sole defender for much of their brief life.[308]

Neither taxation nor the Charters, therefore, provided the same platform for a unified opposition as they had done under Edward I. Their place was taken by other causes which had a more partial and sectarian appeal. For the magnates, 'favourites' was perhaps the chief of these. Their initial pursuit of Gaveston was of little consequence for the knights and burgesses, and, as we have seen, local representatives were absent from most of the early parliaments which saw his prosecution. Gaveston's power was primarily exercised at and through the court, and to the disadvantage of those magnates whose customary right to advise the king and to benefit from

---

[305] *Stat. Realm*, i. 158; *Parl. Writs*, ii. ii, appendix, 89, 92; *PROME* iii. 264; Harriss, *King, Parliament and Public Finance*, 115.

[306] Maddicott, *Thomas of Lancaster*, 328.   [307] Ibid. 190–239.

[308] Ibid. 106–334 *passim*, but esp. 192, 221–3, 227, 253–4, 277, 297–8, 322–30.

royal patronage he had usurped.[309] Unlike the power of the Despensers (and unlike that of the Lusignans under Henry III), who built themselves a territorial empire which impinged oppressively on a multitude of local interests,[310] it made little impact on the countryside, and there are few signs that Gaveston was widely disliked outside the court circle and the ranks of the higher nobility. Even after his death in 1312 the great issues of politics remained the magnates' relationship with the king, and the concomitant questions of counsel, patronage, and the territorial aggrandizement of those close to him which it raised. These lay at the heart of Lancaster's disputes with the courtiers between 1316 and 1318, when the near absence of parliaments in any case denied the commons a voice, and of the baronial opposition to the Despensers in 1320–1. Though the commons might sometimes be purposely drawn into these rivalries, as potential supporters in parliament and in the country, they had a limited stake in the bitter and factious rivalries of king, court, and barons. The whole tenor of politics, aristocratic rather than communal, worked against the likelihood of any genuine alliance between knights, burgesses, and magnates, of the sort which had prevailed in the previous reign.

At the same time the interests of the commons were moving in a different direction. Both the general petitions presented in the name of the community of the realm as well as those from individual counties suggest that the commons had one overriding set of priorities: the enforcement of the law, the maintenance of order, and the delivery of impartial justice and equitable government in the localities. Edward I's trailbaston ordinance of 1305, resulting as it did partly from popular complaint, suggests that in the last years of the previous reign the problem of disorder was already beginning to cause concern to others than the king.[311] Whether the problem worsened after 1307 is impossible to say; though Edward's lax control of government, the surge in magnate power and violent feuding, and the continuance of the Scottish war, all make it seem likely. Certainly the commons' petitions give that impression. Of the seven presented in parliament between 1315 and 1320, all but one relate to the poor maintenance of the peace and to the abuse of the criminal justice system: to

---

[309] Ibid. 71–2, 74, 78–9.

[310] N. Fryde, *The Tyranny and Fall of Edward II, 1321–26* (Oxford, 1979), 106–18; N. Saul, 'The Despensers and the Downfall of Edward II', *EHR* 99 (1984), 22–8; A. Musson, 'Edward II: The Public and Private Faces of the Law', in Dodd and Musson (eds.), *Reign of Edward II*, 158–60.

[311] Above, 326–7.

the exploitation of oyer and terminer commissions for personal vengeance and gain; to conspirators who maintain cases and intimidate their opponents in the courts; to 'illegal leagues and confederacies' formed in the counties, against the peace and to the terror of the locals; to the wrongful release of dangerous prisoners on bail, endangering those who had indicted them; and so on.[312] The county petitions often provide a more local counterpoint to this general theme. In 1315, for example, the community of Lincolnshire complains about false indictments by sheriffs and others, and that of Suffolk about false presentments in the sheriff's tourn, to the people's financial loss. Quite frequently a remedy is sought through the dismissal of named officials and the appointment of others. So in 1320 Buckinghamshire asks for the appointment of two named keepers of the peace, and Norfolk for the replacement of Thomas of Ingoldsthorpe as justice of the peace 'because he does not conduct himself properly in the aforesaid office'.[313]

These are mostly the complaints of men who lacked the power and influence to protect themselves from misgovernment and injustice. They are emphatically not those of the magnates, who possessed both. With the exception of those petitions relating to the replacement of local justices, it seems probable too that most originated at a social level below that of the knights, who are unlikely to have been much troubled by intimidation in the courts or by the vengeance of released prisoners. In sponsoring these petitions in parliament, and so giving them their imprimatur, the commons showed that they represented more than just the class from whom they were chosen.

But still more distinctive of the growing independence of the commons and of their developing emancipation from the baronage is the blame laid on the magnates for some of these abuses. Particularly significant here is the anti-magnatial petition of 1315 already twice mentioned. It describes precisely how 'law goes as lordship biddeth him':[314] how 'great lords' used the machinery of justice to destroy their less powerful victims, bringing false accusations of trespass against them, purchasing commissions of oyer and terminer for partisan justices, arranging matters with sheriffs and bailiffs so that the other party was given little or no notice of the impending plea, forcing him to buy off the plea, or maintaining jurors to secure his conviction; how in all pleas maintenance by great lords deprived

---

[312] *PROME* iii. 56–7, 58, 76–7, 356, 381, 410.   [313] Ibid. 59–60, 64, 397, 414.
[314] The words of a late fourteenth-century preacher: *Middle English Sermons*, ed. W. O. Ross, Early English Text Soc. 209 (1940), 238–9.

their inferiors of their rights; and how such men took what they wanted from others' manors as they travelled the country, offering no payment or compensation. None dared to complain because of their power.[315] This last charge is particularly symptomatic of a new and more fissiparous political scene. The prises to which it refers had until recently been a form of royal exploitation against which both magnates and commons had joined forces, as, for example, in the reforming articles of 1309.[316] Now 'great lords' had joined the exploiters, and the issue was one which divided them from, rather than united them with, the commons. For the justice of these accusations there is plenty of supplementary evidence.[317]

In some such fashion the interests of commons and magnates began to diverge in Edward's middle years. Of course, this divergence was never total—more a separation than a divorce—and even on matters of local government a common line could prevail in parliament. The appointment of sheriffs, for example, was comprehensively regulated in the Statute of Sheriffs, passed in the Lincoln parliament of January 1316 'through the representations of the prelates, earls, barons, and other magnates of the realm summoned to this parliament, and through the grievous complaints of the people'. The dismissal of all the sheriffs in the York parliament of 1318 was similarly backed by the prelates, magnates, and 'the whole community of the realm'.[318] Yet in general the clamour for impartial local justice and the maintenance of the peace was indicative of an emerging commons' programme in which the lords had little say and which might even jeopardize their interests. Like the middle years of Henry III, this was a time when the indulgence or weakness of the crown gave the magnates free play in the localities, provoking a backlash from their subordinates. It was also perhaps the first period when we can begin to hear the commons' demand for 'good governance', to be voiced again in later periods of feeble and partial rule under Henry IV and Henry VI. For the knights and burgesses the good order of the localities mattered more than the struggle for power and favour which, between 1311 and 1322, was the central theme of magnate politics.

---

[315] *PROME* iii. 56–7.   [316] *Rot. Parl.* i. 444; above, 333.

[317] See e.g. R. W. Kaeuper, 'Law and Order in Fourteenth-Century England: The Evidence of Special Commissions of Oyer and Terminer', *Speculum*, 54 (1979), esp. p. 740 (which shows special oyer and terminer commissions to have reached a peak between 1310 and 1320); Maddicott, *Thomas of Lancaster*, 173–4 (for magnate prises); *Parl. Writs*, II. ii, appendix, 110–11 (non-royal prises). Cf. Dodd, *Justice and Grace*, 70–1.

[318] *PROME* iii. 187, 257.

If the petitions and grievances of the commons contributed to their more distinctive identity, a parallel change was sharpening the corporate identity of the baronage. Both changes promoted the separation of the two groups. Between the publication of the Ordinances in 1311 and their revocation in 1322 the magnates began to refer to themselves, and to be referred to by others, as 'peers'. The first known use of this term in this sense has already been mentioned. It occurred in 1312, when the magnates undertook to try to secure a tax for the king 'when they will have their peers more fully [with them], and the community'.[319] Within the next few years a clutch of similar instance is thrown up by the sources. In 1317 Lancaster accused the king of intending to discuss in a council matters which should be treated 'in full parliament and in the presence of the peers of the land'.[320] In 1318 the committee set up by the Treaty of Leake was to assent to all that could be done 'without parliament', while other matters were to be 'corrected in parliament by judgement of the peers'.[321] In the 1321 parliament, at the time of the Despensers' exile, the barons claimed to have the power, since they were peers of the realm, to make new laws 'in full parliament'; and the exile itself was promulgated in parliament by 'us, the peers of the land, earls and barons'.[322]

The consistency of context here suggests a change which is more than semantic, the mere transformation of an old word for 'equals' into a new synonym for 'magnates'. In every case of the word's use, the peers are associated with parliament: they are a parliamentary peerage in embryo. The point is made most explicitly in the statement of the *Modus Tenendi Parliamentum* that 'no single one of the peers of parliament (*de paribus parliamenti*) can or ought to leave parliament unless he has obtained permission from the king and from all his peers'.[323] It is hard not to link this change with the Ordainers' stress on the need for 'the assent of the baronage in parliament' to so much royal business[324] and with the magnates' general view of parliament as an aristocratic forum, where royal policies might be discussed and judged. Change was perhaps promoted by the stabilization

---

[319] *Ann. London*, 211; Prestwich, 'Parliament and the Community', 7; above, 345–6.

[320] *Adae Murimuth Continuatio Chronicarum*, ed. E. M. Thompson, RS (London, 1889), 273; Maddicott, *Thomas of Lancaster*, 192.

[321] *Parl. Writs*, II. ii. 184; Powell and Wallis, *House of Lords*, 287.

[322] Pronay and Taylor, *Parliamentary Texts of the Later Middle Ages*, 164, 168; *Stat. Realm*, i. 184; Powell and Wallis, *House of Lords*, 292; Prestwich, 'Parliament and the Community', 11.

[323] Pronay and Taylor, *Parliamentary Texts of the Later Middle Ages*, 90, 114.

[324] Cf. Dodd, 'Parliament and Political Legitimacy', 175–6.

in names and numbers of those magnates summoned to parliament, who stood at a steady eighty-eight from 1314 to 1321 (an incidental pointer to the existence of a chancery list of those to be summoned).[325] Always a more continuous and regular parliamentary force than the commons by reason of their largely unchanging composition, the magnates may have gained from consistency of summoning something of what the commons gained from re-election and the consequent increased consistency of attendance: an enhanced sense of their own group identity.

This development may mark an important turning point. It seems to suggest an emerging view of magnate peers as a distinct *ordo*, and not merely the upper echelon of a broad landed class which extended downwards into the ranks of the knights. The situation of the 1290s, when the magnates and knights had stood together not only politically but as a single landed group,[326] was beginning to dissolve. The author of the *Modus* did not reflect reality (nor use 'peers' in any but its old sense) when he wrote that a parliamentary summons ought to go to 'everyone of the earls and barons and their peers' with lands and revenues worth £400 or more, for there was no such wealth census.[327] But in implying that the parliamentary magnates were clearly marked off from those below them by more than their receipt of personal summonses, he was in line with contemporary doctrine.

One further change may possibly be related to this evolutionary course. From about 1314 the term 'great council' begins to appear in the records to stand, not for the large general assembly which it had denoted a hundred years earlier, but instead for a body of magnates sitting within parliament, often to deal with petitions (for the first time in 1315) but sometimes with more general matters of state, such as foreign relations.[328] In 1314, for example, we hear of a report on proceedings in the *parlement* of Paris which many of the king's councillors thought should be discussed 'in parliament and before the great council and by the greater and more prudent men'.[329] The distinction between this body and the generality of the magnates in

---

[325] Powell and Wallis, *House of Lords*, 310; Prestwich, *Plantagenet England*, 193.

[326] Above, 310-12, 324.

[327] Pronay and Taylor, *Parliamentary Texts of the Later Middle Ages*, 81; Powell and Wallis, *House of Lords*, 285-6.

[328] The best discussion is Richardson and Sayles, 'King's Ministers', in *EPMA* xvii. 199-201. See also Sayles, *King's Parliament*, 99-101; Dodd, 'Parliament and Political Legitimacy', 176; id., *Justice and Grace*, 75.

[329] Richardson and Sayles, 'King's Ministers', in *EPMA* xvii. 201 n. 2.

parliament is hard to detect, and it may be, as Richardson and Sayles suggest, that 'the difference is no more than that between transacting business *in camera* and in public'.[330] Whether or not this is the case, the appearance of the great council, at just the time when the vocabulary of peerage is beginning to appear, seems to give an institutional shape to the other developments which were transforming the parliamentary magnates into a more closely defined group.

5. The Making of the Late Medieval Parliament, 1322–1327

There are clear indications, then, that between 1311 and 1321 the commons and magnates were moving apart and that each body was acquiring a sharper sense of its own interests and identity. But the events of 1321–2 marked a real caesura. The brief and unsuccessful war waged by Thomas of Lancaster and his baronial allies against the king and the Despensers cut across these developments and brought a dramatic reordering of the political scene. Its effects on parliament were to intensify some earlier trends and to throw others into reverse. Broadly speaking, the lords declined as a political force, while the commons grew increasingly assertive. By the time of Edward's deposition they were regarded as indispensable not only for the traditional business of granting taxes and the rather more novel presentation of petitions but also for the unprecedented work of unmaking one king and making another.

It may seem surprising that there should have been any parliamentary developments in Edward's last years, for this was in general a period of parliamentary regression.[331] The king's victory over Lancaster at Borough-bridge in March 1322 inaugurated the change. Freeing him as it did from baronial restraint, it subsequently allowed him, in partnership with the avaricious Despensers, to accumulate a fortune. This did not altogether obviate the need for parliamentary taxation, particularly when impending trouble with France in 1323 turned to open war in 1324–5, but it made it less necessary. Though parliament continued to deal with the state's business, especially the increasingly fraught question of Anglo-French relations,

[330] Richardson and Sayles, 'King's Ministers', in *EPMA* xvii. 201.
[331] Fryde, *Tyranny of Edward II*, 66–8; Ormrod, 'Agenda for Legislation', 8, 16.

the assembly's political centrality diminished. Although six parliaments met in the four years after Boroughbridge, their sessions were quite short, averaging 19 days compared with the 28-day average from 1311 to 1322. None approached the two- to three-month sessions of 1311 and 1312. No parliament met in 1323 or 1326; that of October 1324 included knights but not burgesses; that of June 1325, neither.[332] Edward could apparently afford to treat parliament with a measure of indifference.

It was, however, an indifference deserved more by the lords than the commons. Deaths in the civil war of 1321–2, the proscription or flight of surviving rebels, and service abroad in the war for Gascony which began in 1324, all reduced drastically the number of magnates summoned to parliament: from 88 before 1321, to 72 in 1322, 48 in October 1324, and then to 38 in November 1325.[333] Those attending offered no resistance to the oppressive rule of Edward and the Despensers, leading the author of the *Vita Edwardi Secundi* to condemn them for their supine lack of spirit: 'The king's harshness has indeed increased so much today that no one, however great and wise, dares to cross the king's will. Thus parliaments, consultations, and councils decide nothing these days. For the nobles of the realm, terrified by threats and the penalties inflicted on others, let the king's will have free rein.'[334]

'The nobles of the realm . . .': it is worth emphasizing that these remarks, sometimes quoted as a general verdict on Edward's later parliaments, apply solely to the lords and not to the commons, in whom their author had no interest.[335] The commons, though hardly more effective than the lords in influencing the king's policies, were more forceful and innovative in their response to events. Their role beyond the granting of taxes was given some early if theoretical acknowledgement in the Statute of York, passed in the York parliament of May 1322 which repealed the Ordinances. In stating that future 'things' affecting the king's estate, realm, and people should be 'treated, agreed and established in parliament by our lord the king and by the assent of the prelates, earls and barons and the community of the realm, as has been the custom heretofore', the statute apparently admitted the need for the assent of the commons—for the 'community of the realm'

---

[332] HBC 555.

[333] Powell and Wallis, *House of Lords*, 297; Ormrod, 'Agenda for Legislation', 16.

[334] *Vita Edwardi Secundi*, 230–1.

[335] Fryde, *Tyranny of Edward II*, 67; *Vita Edwardi Secundi*, pp. lv–lvi; Prestwich, 'Parliament and the Community', 17.

can hardly refer to any other body—to a wide if undefined range of
political business.[336] If this had no immediate practical consequences, it may
nevertheless have been a recognition of the part which the commons had
come to play in parliament since 1311 ('as has been the custom heretofore')
and of their likely value to the king's side in any future political struggle.

Of much more practical importance as a signifier of the commons'
changing role were their petitions. Here, the years after 1322 accentuated
developments which had become evident in the previous decade: more
petitions from the commons as spokesmen for the realm, a deeper concern
with law, order, and magnate abuses, a closer identification between the
petitioning commons and the oppressed for whom they spoke, and a consequent magnification of their standing as their constituents' representatives.

Some of these trends became apparent soon after Boroughbridge, when
there were already bitter complaints from the commons against magnate
practices. Petitions probably put forward in the parliament of May 1322
enumerated them. Earls, barons, and other 'great men of the land' took
goods from the poor and from churches without paying for them or else
paid less than their true value; but if a 'man of the people' came to a great
lord's house and took his goods he would be charged with larceny and
robbery, and punished in life and limb. If a 'man of the people' impleaded
a great lord he would be so threatened that he dared not pursue his case.
If he did so, the jurors would also be threatened so that they dared not
come to court. If he impleaded a lord's retainer he would be punished
with outrageous damages.[337] Another petition on a related theme was
presented in the parliament of February 1324. Poor people, complained the
commons, could get no justice in the counties because of the fees and robes
which sheriffs and undersheriffs received from great lords.[338] In addition,
the poor were not able to seek justice in chancery without speaking to the
king or giving him money; and the commons asked for a remedy, so that
the poor could have access to the law as well as the rich.[339] In the second,

---

[336] *Stat. Realm*, i. 189; *EHD*, ed. Rothwell, 544. I have here broadly followed the interpretation of
Prestwich, 'Parliament and the Community', 11–13, and *Plantagenet England*, 205–6. For a different
opinion, identifying the 'community of the realm' with all those in parliament, see Sayles, *The
King's Parliament of England*, 103–5; and for a useful discussion of older views, Morris, 'Magnates and
Community of the Realm', 83–5, esp. n. 32.

[337] Text: Ormrod, 'Agenda for Legislation', 30. Date: ibid. 7, 20. My great debt to Professor
Ormrod's article will be obvious throughout what follows.

[338] Ormrod, 'Agenda for Legislation', 6 and n. 3.

[339] Text: ibid. 20 n. 1. Date: ibid. 9 and nn. 2 and 9. Cf. M. Buck, *Politics, Finance and the Church in
the Reign of Edward II: Walter Stapeldon, Treasurer of England* (Cambridge, 1983), 145.

October, parliament of 1324 sheriffs were again the main target of the commons, whose petitions embodied seven references to their abuses and those of their underlings.[340] Nor was it only on matters of injustice and on the misdeeds of magnates and sheriffs that the commons increasingly spoke for the community. Other common petitions submitted in the parliaments of 1324 and 1325 covered such grievances as the aggressive levying of ancient debts supposedly due to the crown, though often either pardoned or paid,[341] the illicit taking of land into the royal forest by the king's ministers, contrary to the Forest Charter and 'to the great destruction of the people',[342] the lack of uniformity in weights and measures in different parts of the realm,[343] and the failure of both the king and the chancellor to answer petitions adjourned before them.[344]

The common factor which gave consistency to all these petitions was Edward's misgovernment, more distinctly alluded to in an earlier petition of 1322 appealing to the king's oath to maintain the law, which should be the same for both rich and poor.[345] Within that broad area, the unnamed focus for the grievances of the commons is likely to have been the Despensers, and particularly the younger Despenser, whose influence in the central courts, and rapacious and often brutal control of local government, gave them the means to intimidate juries, suborn sheriffs, and engage in other malpractices mentioned in the petitions.[346] The elder Despenser, for example, in his capacity as justice of the forest south of Trent, is likely to have been at least a collaborator in the destructive extension of the forest referred to in the common petitions of 1325.[347] On all these matters it was now the knights rather than the magnates, themselves often the target of the commons' censure, who provided a voice for the community.[348] It was not mere rhetoric which led them to present themselves as speaking not only for 'the people of England', but more especially for 'the poor' and 'the poor people of the

---

[340] Ormrod, 'Agenda for Legislation', 6, 31–2.
[341] Buck, *Politics, Finance and the Church*, 176; Ormrod, 'Agenda for Legislation', 32–3.
[342] *Rot. Parl.* i. 430.
[343] Rayner, 'Forms and Machinery', 554–5; Ormrod, 'Agenda for Legislation', 31.
[344] *Rot. Parl.* i. 430; Ormrod, 'Agenda for Legislation', 9.
[345] Ormrod, 'Agenda for Legislation', 30.
[346] Kaeuper, 'Law and Order in Fourteenth-Century England', 778–80; Saul, 'The Despensers and the Downfall of Edward II', 16–27. For the guilt of the younger Despenser, and for criticism of the notion of a 'Despenser regime', see S. J. Harris, 'Petitioning in the Last Years of Edward II and the First Years of Edward III', in Ormrod, Dodd, and Musson (eds.), *Medieval Petitions*, 185–6.
[347] *Rot. Parl.* i. 430; *PROME* iv. 19; Saul, 'Despensers and the Downfall of Edward II', 25–6.
[348] Cf. Ormrod, 'Agenda for Legislation', 20.

realm';[349] for the abuses which they often described were more likely to
damage those lacking well-wishers and influence in the localities than to
hurt the gentry of county society who were now their true representatives
in parliament. It was, however, a sign of the Despensers' political dominance
that few private petitions, as opposed to those from the commons as a body,
complained about their subversion of the law on which that dominance
partly rested; though the flood of petitions on this theme in 1327, after
the regime had fallen, showed that the earlier paucity of complaint had
not implied any paucity of grievances.[350] In denouncing such abuses the
commons could rely on numbers and anonymity to protect themselves
from retribution. Lacking such safeguards, individuals are likely to have
kept silent out of fear and despondency, and not from complacence.[351]

Rather than marking any new departure, the activities of the commons
signified a rapid intensification and consolidation of trends which had
become apparent a decade earlier. As we have seen, their presentation of
petitions, their concern with law, order, and magnate delinquencies, and
their view of themselves as representatives of the community, had all been
features of the years between 1315 and 1321. More innovatory was one
further development, in this case to do with the form of petitions rather
than their content. Before the mid 1320s the petitions emanating from the
commons as a body had generally each put forward a single grievance or
very occasionally a cluster of related and interwoven grievances, as with the
anti-magnatial petition of 1315. But each of the parliaments of February
1324, October 1324, and November 1325 produced a set of petitions strung
together as a single document.[352] That for November 1325, for example,
covers not only the grievances already mentioned concerning the royal
forests and the failure of king and chancellor to deal with petitions, but
also such matters as the liberties of the city of London and the release
of those falsely accused of joining the rebels in the war of 1321–2.[353] In
two of the three sets of petitions the response from king and council,

[349] Cf. Ormrod, 'Agenda for Legislation', 20 and n. 1, 31.
[350] For the petitions of 1327 against the Despensers, see, e.g. *PROME* iv. 62 (no. 15), 64 (no. 24),
65 (no. 29), 66 (no. 31), 70 (no. 45); and for comment, Harris, 'Petitioning in the Last Years of Edward
II', 180–3, 192, and S. A. Sneddon, 'Words and Realities: The Language and Dating of Petitions,
1326–7', in Ormrod, Dodd, and Musson (eds.), *Medieval Petitions*, 197–8.
[351] Dodd, *Justice and Grace*, 138–9, 228–9.
[352] Rayner, 'Forms and Machinery', 552–6; Ormrod, 'Agenda for Legislation', 9; Dodd, *Justice and Grace*, 133–4.
[353] *Rot. Parl.* i. 430.

inserted in a different hand, follows each petition.[354] Common petitions of this sort were the precursors of those from Edward III's reign, which were often to provide the basis for legislation, and they themselves may have had precedents both in the lists of clerical grievances frequently presented in secular assemblies, and in the baronial and knightly grievances put forward as additions to the Charters in Edward I's later years.[355] But they must also represent a new form of activity within an increasingly cohesive commons. Behind each assemblage of petitions lay discussion, the concerting of grievances, and sometimes the drafting of a heading to the set of petitions which showed the commons in a corporate and self-consciously representative mode. 'Let it be remembered that the people of England are often oppressed and afflicted among other things by these undermentioned', ran the preface to their petitions in the parliament of October 1324.[356]

The commons' petitions were more significant for their content and the manner of their presentation than for their consequences. Edward's supremacy meant that he had no need to appease or mollify his government's critics, and the grievances of the commons went unremedied.[357] In another area, however, they were more successful. As Dr Mark Buck was the first to point out, they were once and probably twice able to deny the king a tax, and this was perhaps a truer measure of their growing weight and independence than their petitioning. In the parliament of February 1324 the king asked for subsidies both to ransom the earl of Richmond, captured by the Scots in 1322, and to meet future dangers.[358] Edward's willingness to entertain and then respond, often favourably, to the very large number of private petitions presented in this parliament may have been intended to induce an equally favourable response to his plea for taxes.[359] The dangers which he foresaw were left unspecified, but he may well have had in mind the gathering crisis over Gascony and the growing possibility of war with France. Yet according to the Westminster chronicler (who should have known), requests for both these purposes were turned down

---

[354] Rayner, 'Forms and Machinery', 555–6; Ormrod, 'Agenda for Legislation', 31–3.
[355] Harriss, *King, Parliament and Public Finance*, 119.
[356] Ormrod, 'Agenda for Legislation', 31. Cf. Dodd, *Justice and Grace*, 134–6.
[357] Ormrod, 'Agenda for Legislation', 8–10; Dodd, 'Parliament and Political Legitimacy', 172–3.
[358] M. C. Buck, 'The Reform of the Exchequer, 1316–1326', *EHR* 98 (1983), 252–4; id., *Politics, Finance and the Church*, 145–6. Cf. Ormrod, 'Agenda for Legislation', 8–10.
[359] At least 191 private petitions were presented in this parliament. For an analysis, see Dodd, *Justice and Grace*, 78–86, 222–9.

by the whole assembly, speaking as one man ('omnes et singuli quasi vir unus . . . constanter petita negarunt'). Edward then ordered the parliament to be extended, hoping to exhaust those present (and its twenty-four-day session was the longest of the post-Boroughbridge period). He had used the same tactic in the parliament of August 1312: on this later occasion as vainly as on that.[360]

The united response was almost certainly that of the commons, and the victory theirs; for while only 59 lay lords were summoned to parliament, not all of whom are likely to have been present, the names of 74 knights and 136 burgesses were returned.[361] If the rejection of a subsidy for Richmond's ransom was predictable, since there was no customary obligation to grant a tax for such a purpose, the further rejection of Edward's second request to meet future needs, probably those likely to be occasioned by war, was both more surprising and more courageous.[362] The next parliament to which both knights and burgesses were summoned, that of November 1325, was still more ominously overshadowed by the danger from France, and it saw the assembly being asked to provide for the king's expenses on a projected expedition to Gascony. Both the initial summoning of parliament to the Tower and a threatening speech addressed to the assembly by the younger Despenser must have been intended to ensure compliance. But again nothing resulted.[363]

The refusal of taxation in the parliament of February 1324, and the petitions critical of Edward's government presented at the same time, accusing the king among other things of obstructing the issue of chancery writs for personal gain,[364] may explain why the knights alone were summoned to the

---

[360] *Flores Historiarum*, iii. 219–20; *Chron. Lanercost*, 219; above, 339. *Murimuth*, 43, confirms the request of a subsidy for Richmond's ransoming.

[361] *Parl. Writs*, II. ii. 289, 299–314; *Return of Members*, 69–71.

[362] *Johannis de Trokelowe et Henrici de Blaneforde Chronica et Annales*, ed. H. T. Riley, RS (London, 1866), 140; Buck, *Politics, Finance and the Church*, 145. Dodd, 'Parliament and Political Legitimacy', 171–2, depreciates the significance of the commons' refusal of a tax, expressing scepticism about its occurrence (though it is reported in three chronicles), and pointing out that the ransoming of Richmond was 'hardly a matter of national emergency'. But this is to ignore both Edward's second request for a tax to meet unspecified dangers, recorded in the *Flores*, and the evidence from the writs *de expensis* for the length of the parliament, which supports the comment of the *Flores* on its deliberate protraction.

[363] Buck, 'Reform of the Exchequer', 254; id., *Politics, Finance and the Church*, 157–8. Dodd, 'Politics and Political Legitimacy', 172, is again sceptical: 'the evidence for parliament considering (and rejecting) a grant of taxation is tenuous indeed'. But this is to ignore the evidence of the well-informed Rochester chronicle, cited by Buck, for the request to parliament to provide for Edward's forthcoming Gascon expedition.

[364] Ormrod, 'Agenda for Legislation', 20 n. 1.

next parliament, in October 1324, and neither knights nor burgesses to that which followed in June 1325.[365] These assemblies, anomalously restricted in their composition by comparison with most that had met since 1311, perhaps bear witness to the commons' intransigence. If, during years of royal autocracy, they lacked 'actual political power',[366] they could at least cause trouble.

Demonstrated by refusals of taxation and aggressive petitioning, the rise in the prominence of the commons, at a time when the lords were fewer than usual in number and more than usually cowed in temper, helps to explain the part which they were to play in what proved to be the last parliament of Edward II's reign and the first of Edward III's. It followed after a thirteen-month gap in the sequence of parliaments. More crucially, it met after Queen Isabella and Roger Mortimer had landed from the Low Countries in September 1326 in pursuit of power and vengeance, Edward had been captured and placed in custody, the Despensers executed, and their regime swept away. Lasting from 7 January to 9 March 1327, this parliament's seventy-one-day duration made it the second longest of the entire period, exceeded only by the marathon session of 1312.[367] This was a measure of the scale and moment of its business. The first part of the session saw the deposition of the old king, while the second, falling after his son's coronation on 1 February, witnessed the presentation to king and council of the lengthiest set of petitions so far submitted by the commons. If their petitions drew on and extended the precedents of 1324 and 1325, their role in Edward II's deposition transcended their involvement in any earlier political episode.

   Parliament thus provided both the setting and the mechanism for the transfer of power from the old to the new king. Within parliament, as was only to be expected, the initiators of Edward's deposition were not the commons but the lords, and in particular a small group of prelates and magnates who looked outside their own ranks for support, including the support of the knights and burgesses. This they needed in order to legitimize the change of king, to ground the new regime on a firm basis of general acceptance, to bring potential doubters and dissidents into line,

---

[365] Ibid. 16; *HBC* 555.   [366] Dodd, 'Parliament and Political Legitimacy', 172.
[367] The writs *de expensis* show that the knights and burgesses attended for periods varying between 52 and 73 days (though these figures presumably include travel times): *Parl. Writs*, II. ii. 364–5; Prestwich, 'Parliament and Community', 13.

and to protect themselves against any possible counter-revolution. Though their aims entailed careful stage management, both of parliament and of forces outside parliament, as has often been stressed,[368] they were not too difficult to achieve; for the general detestation of Edward II meant that a movement with many of the characteristics of a baronial coup could, through parliament, be elevated into something like a national plebiscite.

The public inaugurators of the revolution were two bishops and two barons, Adam of Orleton, bishop of Hereford, John Stratford, bishop of Winchester, Roger Mortimer, and Thomas Wake. Queen Isabella was probably a powerful if less visible influence in the background. With the possible exception of Stratford, all these were longtime enemies of the old order. It is likely that they were set on Edward's deposition before parliament met; but whatever their initial plans may have been they were perhaps hindered by two early setbacks. Orleton and another bishop, sent to Kenilworth, where the king was held captive, to request his attendance at parliament, were rebuffed by him; and when Orleton addressed parliament on 12 January, after his return, he seems to have been unable to get an immediate answer as to whether Edward II or his son should be king.[369] The choice was stark and we know that Edward still had friends.[370]

Probably that evening the magnates and prelates, apparently meeting in private outside the main parliamentary assembly, decided that Edward should be deposed, and 'articles of accusation' were drawn up to justify this radical step.[371] On the morning of the next day, 13 January, various groups of men came to an assembly at the Guildhall convened by the mayor of London and other city leaders. There they swore, *inter alia*, to maintain the queen and her son Edward, and to keep the ordinances made or to be made in parliament. Those taking the oath included 24 barons, 14 archbishops and bishops, 7 abbots and priors, 13 'knights of the shires', 12 of whom were elected representatives in the current parliament, and 30 men from

---

[368] e.g. Fryde, *Tyranny of Edward II*, 195; C. Valente, 'The Deposition and Abdication of Edward II', *EHR* 113 (1998), 859, 865.

[369] Valente, 'Deposition and Abdication', 854–5. I have followed Dr Valente's chronology of the parliament throughout.

[370] Clarke, *Medieval Representation and Consent*, 181–2; R. M. Haines, *King Edward II* (Montreal, 2003), 190, 345.

[371] See the *Forma Deposicionis*, printed from a Canterbury manuscript in Haines, *King Edward II*, 343–4; and Valente, 'Deposition and Abdication', 856–7, 864.

the Cinque Ports, 5 from Bury St Edmunds, and 13 from St Albans. Four earls took the oath two days afterwards.[372]

Later that day came the climax of the proceedings. At a crowded meeting in Westminster Hall, which included not only the lords and commons but also many Londoners and probably other outsiders,[373] the previous evening's decision to depose Edward was announced by Roger Mortimer. This was followed by the reading of the 'articles of accusation', by sermons from three of the bishops, and by a final inflammatory oration from Thomas Wake asking 'the people' if they would accept the decision of the prelates and magnates. His question was answered with a clamorous acclamation. Archbishop Reynolds then addressed the crowd, taking as his text 'Vox populi, vox dei', and concluding by proposing that the king's son Edward should be made king, to which the crowd answered 'Let it be done, let it be done (*Fiat, fiat*)'.[374] The last act in the drama came two days later, when a second embassy was sent to Kenilworth to inform Edward of parliament's decision, to secure his renunciation of the throne, and to withdraw homage. The precise composition of this embassy is unclear, but it certainly included bishops, earls, abbots, knights of the shire (probably four), and burgesses (probably four or six): perhaps thirty men in all.[375] When the envoys reported back to parliament about 25 January, the first phase of the parliament was brought to an end and the way cleared for the young Edward's coronation.[376]

Unique in its business, the deposition parliament was in some other ways typical of the assemblies of Edward II's reign. It was dominated by an aristocratic group (though one in which the bishops were unusually prominent) who looked to the commons for support. In this it resembled, for example, the parliament of 1311, which saw the publication of the Ordinances, and that of 1321, when the Despensers had been exiled.[377] But much less usual was the degree of popular participation in parliament's proceedings, notably by the Londoners, whose leaders had initiated the

[372] *Calendar of Plea and Memoranda Rolls of the City of London, 1323–64*, ed. A. H. Thomas (Cambridge, 1926), 11–14; Clarke, *Medieval Representation and Consent*, 181–2; Valente, 'Deposition and Abdication', 858–9.
[373] For the role of the Londoners, see the extract from the Rochester chronicle printed in Haines, *King Edward II*, 344–5.
[374] *Forma Deposicionis*: Haines, *King Edward II*, 344–5; Valente, 'Deposition and Abdication', 858–9.
[375] Valente, 'Deposition and Abdication', 859–61. For the composition of the embassy, see Clarke, *Medieval Representation and Consent*, 185–9, and Haines, *King Edward II*, 192.
[376] *Murimuth*, 51; Valente, 'Deposition and Abdication', 861–2.   [377] Above, 336–7.

Guildhall assembly and whose rank-and-file played a large part in the popular endorsement of Edward's deposition in Westminster Hall. The magnates' alliance with the Londoners was prudential. London had played a large part in the violent overthrow of the previous regime and its people remained a threatening presence; but their support, if it could be obtained, would help to build a broad social base for revolutionary change. Others besides the Londoners may have been drawn into the latter process. The eighteen burgesses from Bury St Edmunds and St Albans who took the Guildhall oath, for example, cannot all have been elected representatives, and their presence hints at wider urban participation in these events. Parliament's venue may have been particularly significant here, for the choice of Westminster Hall was probably dictated by the need for space to accommodate not only the lords and commons, who on this occasion met together, but also the expected crowd of general well-wishers. Effectively an arena open to all comers, Westminster Hall provided a traditional setting for parliamentary *acta* requiring the widest possible publicity. The Provisions of Westminster in 1259, the terms for the Lord Edward's release from Montfortian captivity in 1264, and the Statute of Westminster II in 1285, had all been proclaimed in parliaments assembled there.[378] Its use in 1327 for both sanctioning and publicizing Edward's deposition was another aspect of the careful management by the controlling party which characterized the whole parliament.

To some extent those who planned the deposition reached out in parliament to those who had no rightful place there. Perhaps for the first time in parliament's history, the crowd was literally given a voice in its proceedings. This was not representation but direct participation. Yet the role of the knights and burgesses was still more vital, for as elected representatives they possessed a legitimacy which the crowd lacked. Their support was seen as essential at every stage. When, at the start, Edward had refused to attend parliament, Henry of Eastry, prior of Christ Church, Canterbury, had written to his friend Archbishop Reynolds advocating the dispatch of a second embassy to persuade him to do so. It should comprise, he said, two earls, two barons, four burgesses, and four knights of the shire 'specially elected by the whole community of the realm. This ought to be done in order that not only the prelates, but the magnates, nobles and chief persons of every estate and condition in the realm may be involved

---

[378] *De Antiquis Legibus Liber*, 42, 71; *Ann. Oseney*, 304; above, 244, 258, 284.

in the business.'[379] Although his advice was initially ignored, it was tacitly followed in the later deputation sent to secure Edward's abdication, on which, as we have seen, prelates, magnates, knights, and burgesses were all represented. Similar principles, aiming to give all parliamentary estates a share in the responsibility for the deposition and so to bind them to it, underlay the participation of the same groups in the Guildhall oath-taking. The commons themselves wished to apply those principles still more widely, for later in the parliament they asked the king to order 'that the commons be caused to swear in every county to swear, as we have sworn, to maintain the undertaking now begun'. If this is an allusion to the Guildhall oaths (and it can hardly be anything else), it suggests not only that the relatively few knights and burgesses known to have been present at the Guildhall may have been considered to represent the entire parliamentary commons, but also that the commons saw the need to get the wider political community in the localities to underwrite what had been done in parliament.[380] Though this request was refused by the king,[381] it shows the degree to which the commons regarded the deposition as a national enterprise, managed through parliament but to be acknowledged by all. In this sense too parliament was a truly representative assembly.

The commons had thus been a party to a great act of state, though one managed by the magnates and endorsed by parliament as a whole. In such a solemn and unprecedented act as the dethroning of a king, the authority conferred by their presence and assent was seen as essential to the act's validation. This was the culminative step in their rapid evolution under Edward II. But it was complemented and enhanced in a more mundane way by the enlargement of their role as petitioners. During the parliament's second phase, after Edward III's coronation on 1 February, forty-two petitions were presented to the new king and his council by 'the good men of the commune': by far the longest set of common petitions to date.[382] Many of them related to the abuses of the preceding years. Covering matters of general interest, and drawn up as a continuous series, they derived both in form and substance from the shorter sets presented in the parliaments of 1324 and 1325. Unlike those earlier petitions, however,

[379] *Literae Cantuarienses*, ed. J. B. Sheppard, 3 vols., RS (London, 1887–9), i. 204–5; Clarke, *Medieval Representation and Consent*, 177–8; Valente, 'Deposition and Abdication', 867.
[380] *PROME* iv. 21, 35; Harriss, *King, Parliament and Public Finance*, 122; Valente, 'Deposition and Abdication', 867 and n. 8.
[381] *PROME* iv. 21, 26.   [382] Ibid. 10–21, 27–35.

the petitions of 1327 received generally favourable answers, embodied in the seventeen articles of a new statute.[383] The commons' request that petitions and answers should be copied and delivered to the knights for proclamation in the counties (to which the king agreed) was an important affirmation of the links between MPs and their constituents, akin to their desire to see the Guildhall oath replicated locally. The whole sequence of common petitions, responsive legislation, and local publication provided precedents for procedures which would soon become normal.[384] And in addition to these 'public' petitions, numerous private petitions were also presented in the post-coronation parliament, many of them directed against the Despensers, especially the younger Despenser, and, like the common petitions, against the particular malpractices of the ousted regime.[385] The regime's individual victims, however, unlike the body of the commons, often failed to receive a favourable response to their requests and were frequently told to look to the courts for a remedy: a surprising contrast to earlier petitions presented between 1322 and 1326 by those involved in the civil war of 1321–2, which an autocratic government had generally answered much more positively.[386] None the less, the mere reception of this flood of private petitions, and the opportunity which parliament thus offered for the ventilation of grievances, together with the statutory redress made available to the commons, all helped to confirm the new mood of reconciliation which now existed between the crown and its subjects.

In the broad consensus which Edward's enemies were able to build up in favour of his deposition, the commons thus had a central place not only for the support which they could provide in parliament but also for the influence in favour of the new regime which they could bring to bear on their local communities. The intense involvement in the processes of politics which was theirs by 1327 should be assessed in conjunction with that mysterious text, the *Modus Tenendi Parliamentum*. The significance of the *Modus* as a staging post in parliamentary history was briefly noted at the start

---

[383] *Stat. Realm*, i. 255–7; *PROME* iv. 21–6; H. L. Gray, *The Influence of the Commons on Early Legislation* (Cambridge, Mass., 1932), 215–17; Prestwich, 'Parliament and the Community', 13–14.

[384] Prestwich, 'Parliament and the Community', 14; Maddicott, 'Parliament and the Constituencies', 81; Dodd, *Justice and Grace*, 137.

[385] *PROME* iv. 10, 57–81. There survive some 140 petitions presented between 1327 and 1330 that complain about extortions committed by the Despensers and their associates: Harris, 'Petitioning in the Last Years of Edward II', 192.

[386] Harris, 'Petitioning in the Last Years of Edward II', 175–92, esp. 184–5.

of this chapter. There is now a fair measure of agreement that it dates from the early fourteenth century, probably from around 1320; that it mixes practical description of parliament's workings with fantasy and perhaps with aspirations about the roles of the various groups in parliament; and that it was written by a clerk closely familiar with contemporary parliaments.[387] One unnoticed pointer to an early fourteenth-century date may lie in what the author has to say about petitions, for he is solely concerned with private petitions and ignores the common petitions beginning to appear by the early 1320s; though in his direction that two royal clerks should be assigned to assist the knights and burgesses respectively he may give us a clue as to how such petitions were drafted.[388]

Elsewhere, however, the author frequently stresses the functions and importance of the commons. If the king is ill, and so unable to attend parliament, two knights and four townsmen (but only two earls and two barons) are to serve on the deputation sent to verify his condition.[389] If difficult cases and disputes arise during parliament, five knights and ten townsmen (but only two earls and three barons) should serve on the committee of twenty-five set up to resolve them.[390] In the granting of aids, two knights serving for their shire 'have a greater say in granting and denying than the greatest earl', and the diocesan proctors for the clergy a greater voice than their bishop. If the bishops and magnates fail to appear for parliament, then a true parliament may be held without them. But it cannot be held without the knights, burgesses and lower clergy, who constitute the 'community of the realm (communitas regni)' and who may plead, for example, the king's misgovernment in order to justify their absence; for the commons represent 'the whole community of England', while the magnates represent no one but themselves.[391]

As a description of contemporary practice not much of this can be taken seriously. The committee of twenty-five is not known to have existed; the notion of a parliament without the magnates was an absurdity; and no

[387] For the text and translation, see Pronay and Taylor, *Parliamentary Texts of the Later Middle Ages*, 67–91. For the most recent commentary, ibid. 13–47; W. C. Weber, 'The Purpose of the English *Modus Tenendi Parliamentum*', *Parliamentary History*, 17 (1998), 149–77 (which puts the strongest case for a date around 1320); and Prestwich, *Plantagenet England*, 224–6.
[388] *Modus*, chs. xv, xvi, xxiv: Pronay and Taylor, *Parliamentary Texts of the Later Middle Ages*, 73–4, 78, 86–7, 90–1.
[389] *Modus*, ch. xiii: Pronay and Taylor, *Parliamentary Texts of the Later Middle Ages*, 72, 85.
[390] *Modus*, ch. xxvii: Pronay and Taylor, *Parliamentary Texts of the Later Middle Ages*, 74–5, 87.
[391] *Modus*, ch. xxxiii: Pronay and Taylor, *Parliamentary Texts of the Later Middle Ages*, 77, 89–90.

other contemporary would have given precedence to the commons over the magnates in parliament's general work. These seem to be the flights of fancy of a radical populist. Yet if we take a broader and less literal view of the characterization of the commons in the *Modus*, the author's descriptions and prescriptions may not seem entirely out of line with reality. By that time the commons were indeed recognized as constituting the *communitas regni*, a phrase which could no longer be applied to the whole parliamentary assembly and still less to the magnates alone.[392] Their assent was considered essential for taxation; and even if they could not be said to count for more than the magnates, the magnates themselves had acknowledged in 1312 that they could not grant taxes without them.[393] In saying that the king's misgovernment might provide a reason for the commons to absent themselves from parliament, the author hit upon a general grievance which was already implicit, and would soon be explicit, in some of the commons' petitions, even though it was put to no such extraordinary purpose.[394] Both this statement and the role assigned to the commons on the committee to settle disputes and difficult cases (which might cover such large matters as peace and war) conceived of the commons as the participants in the political work of parliament which they clearly were, justifiably taking them beyond their by now traditional role as grantors of taxes and presenters of petitions.

About the precise functions and powers of the commons the author of the *Modus* was, so far as we can see, often wrong. But about their general weight and position he was not so far out. Though he almost certainly wrote before the grand climacteric of 1327, it is not hard to envisage the sort of body which he had in mind playing its part in the deposition of a king.

6. The View from the Provinces

By 1327 there were probably few men in England who were unaware of parliament's existence and many who knew something of its work. The routes to that awareness and that knowledge were various. The more

---

[392] Morris, 'Magnates and the Community', 75–85; Prestwich, 'Parliament and the Community', 8–9, 11–13.

[393] Prestwich, 'Parliament and the Community', 7; above, 345–6.

[394] e.g. *PROME* iii. 56–7; Ormrod, 'Agenda for Legislation', 30.

frequent summoning of the commons, first from the mid 1290s and then with a marked rise in tempo from 1311, gave parliament a local prominence which it can hardly have had in its days as a largely magnate assembly. The personal written summons to a magnate to attend parliament bypassed the ordinary machinery of county administration and would have been known solely to the recipient who took it from the king's messenger.[395] The only summonses likely to have crossed the horizons of the provincial public were those issued through the sheriffs to the lesser tenants-in-chief, probably via proclamations, in Henry III's early and middle years.[396] But the summoning of the commons entailed elections in both shire courts and boroughs, and, under Edward II, more, and more frequent, elections than ever before. During the reign's most vigorous phase of parliamentary activity from March 1313 to January 1316, for example, knights, burgesses, and lower clergy were summoned to six successive parliaments. If we reckon that each parliament would have necessitated some 37 shire elections and about 70 borough elections, we have some 640 elections taking place in shire courts and borough assemblies in just under three years. For a full tally we would have to include the election of parliament's invisible men, the lower clergy, whose parliamentary proctors were elected by cathedral chapters and diocesan assemblies.[397] There was undoubtedly a very great deal of electing going on: seemingly much more so than, say, in the later England of Elizabeth I, when prorogation often extended the life of individual parliaments and so deferred elections for several years.[398] Election must have served to bring parliament into the foreground of provincial life and to have further stimulated a provincial consciousness of politics that was already well developed.

Within the shire court the management of elections was in the hands of the sheriff, often, it seems, in partnership with the great men of the county or their deputies. The sheriff of Oxfordshire and Berkshire, told by chancery in September 1322 of a forthcoming parliament, made a note to 'summon the magnates or their stewards for electing knights';[399] while in Devon in 1319 Sir Matthew Crowthorne was chosen for the county in the shire court 'by the bishop of Exeter and Sir William Martin, with

---

[395] Prestwich, 'Magnate Summonses', 97–9.   [396] Above, 203.
[397] Denton and Dooley, *Representatives of the Lower Clergy*, 18–39.
[398] The parliament which met in May 1572, for example, held three separate sessions and was dissolved only in April 1583: HBC 574.
[399] *Parl. Writs*, II. ii. 272; L. Reiss, *The History of the English Electoral Law in the Middle Ages*, trans. K. L. Wood-Legh (Cambridge, 1940), 52–3; Maddicott, 'County Community', 31.

the assent of the other good men of that county'. Magnate stewards were often prominent at elections, as they had always been in the affairs of shire courts.[400] But our Devon example suggests that they or their masters had also to carry with them the other suitors of the court. If the suitors' role was sometimes merely an assenting one, it was sometimes, and perhaps often, more than that. The statement by the sheriff of Westmorland in 1306 that short notice and the absence of all the knights and free tenants on the Scottish border prevented him from holding an election, and the comparable statement by the sheriff of Surrey and Sussex in 1297 that he had 'assembled before me at Southwark all the knights and freeholders of the county of Surrey, who elected . . .', both suggest that the gentry and those just below them in county society played a leading role in county elections. Freeholders as well as knights may have been a significant force. The returns contain enough references to elections made 'by the whole county court' or 'in the county court by the whole community of the same county' or 'in full county court by the assent of all the county' for us to think that a narrow oligarchy could not simply impose its men on the county.[401] In this respect county elections were more open and 'democratic' than those in boroughs, where the electorate was smaller and elections increasingly in the hands of ruling elites.[402]

From the county court, awareness of parliament was diffused downwards and outwards. Once elected, both knights and burgesses had to name mainpernors, usually two for each member, who were expected to guarantee the attendance of their principals in parliament. Their names were returned to the chancery by the sheriff below those of the elected men for whom they stood pledge. Though the mainpernors were occasionally drawn from the friends and relatives of the elected, they seem more often to have been their freehold or villein tenants, and quite frequently the reeves of their home manors, who would have been *ipso facto* villeins. In 1290, for example, the Yorkshire knight Sir Richard of Crepping had for his mainpernors William, reeve of Crepping, and Richard his son.[403] If such men were consulted

---

[400] *Parl. Writs*, II. ii, appendix, 138; Maddicott, 'County Community', 31–2; id., 'Parliament and the Constituencies', 73; above, 342.

[401] *Parl. Writs*, I. 60–1, 176; Pasquet, *Origins of the House of Commons*, 144; Maddicott, 'Parliament and the Constituencies', 72–3.

[402] For borough elections, see McKisack, *Parliamentary Representation of the English Boroughs*, 14–15, 30–43.

[403] Maddicott, 'County Community', 32–3; J. S. Illsley, 'Parliamentary Elections in the Reign of Edward I', *BIHR* 49 (1976), 28–30.

before they were nominated, as seems likely, they may be expected to have picked up from their principals some notion of what parliament was and of their own minor role in its working. It may even be the case that the occasional petitions from villeins and other peasants—when they were not directed against the malpractices of their lords—arrived in parliament via a friendly relationship between principal and mainpernor, master and man.

When parliament was over, and the knights and burgesses returned home, many more people, probably most of those in the county, would have been made forcibly aware of parliament's existence; for the cost of MPs' wages and travel expenses fell on their constituents. Before 1327 payment was enjoined by the crown, but the sums payable were usually fixed locally. Though the crown might occasionally set a rate—in 1318 as high as 5s. a day for the knights—it was only after Edward III's accession that wages were fixed, permanently and centrally, at 4s. a day for a knight and 2s. for a burgess.[404] This was another, minor, mark of the degree to which 1327 was a turning point in parliamentary history. But by whatever method wages were decided, the payment due to the knights was then normally divided among the shire's hundreds and villages, and collected by the reeve or other manorial official. The sums involved might be quite substantial. For the deposition parliament of 1327, for example, the sixty-seven-day service of the two Huntingdonshire knights cost the county £26. 8. 0, or just over 9 per cent of that year's lay subsidy of a twentieth.[405] The burden fell disproportionately heavily on the men of such small counties, whose knights were away for as long a period as those in larger shires but whose inhabitants were fewer. At a more parochial level we find the tenants of Merton College's manor of Cheddington paying 6d. towards the expenses of the Buckinghamshire knights at the 1318 parliament: the equivalent of about two days' wages for a contemporary building worker or five days' wages for a thatcher's mate. More significant than the sum raised, however, was the additional piece of information set down in this particular account by the bailiff or manorial clerk who compiled it and who recorded the payment. When he noted that the knights had been 'staying

---

[404] *Parl. Writs*, II. ii. 194; *Select Cases in the Court of King's Bench under Edward II*, ed. G. O. Sayles, Selden Soc. 74 (1957), 95–6. For a general account, see H. M. Cam, 'The Community of the Shire and the Payment of its Representatives in Parliament', in her *Liberties and Communities in Medieval England* (repr. London, 1963), 236–41.

[405] *Parl. Writs*, II. ii. 365; *Early Huntingdonshire Lay Subsidy Rolls*, ed. J. A. Raftis and M. P. Hogan (Toronto, 1976), 216; Cam, 'Community of the Shire', 358–9.

in parliament at York', his inclusion of parliament's meeting place showed some knowledge of a national horizon beyond the boundaries of his village and of a parliamentary scene larger than its local consequences.[406]

Besides such predictable consequences of parliament's every meeting as the payment of members' wages, there were other more haphazard and occasional ways in which awareness of its work might be extended. By a long-standing practice which we have often encountered already, statutes and other royal *acta* carried through in parliament, for example, were sent down to the counties for publication. The general pardon granted in the autumn parliament of 1313 for Gaveston's death, and the Statute of Sheriffs made in the Lincoln parliament of January 1316, were both dispatched for local proclamation—not only in the county courts, but very probably also in the many markets and small market towns which we know from later evidence to have been chosen for government proclamations.[407] It is inconceivable too that the returning representatives did not gossip to their friends and neighbours about what had gone on in parliament. The mention in the Leicester borough accounts for 1332 of wine bought for one of the town's members when he told the news (*narrand' rumores*) to the mayor and others is a rare record of what must have been a common scene.[408] Such oral reports and the talk they must have provoked have all gone with the wind, leaving their contents to the imagination. But in shaping local opinion they may have played a large part.

It is difficult to tell whether these exchanges between centre and locality produced anything like a common attitude to parliament. By the MPs themselves parliamentary service seems to have been welcomed. Their frequent re-election, which could presumably have been avoided, suggests no reluctance to serve, and a man such as Matthew Crowthorne would hardly have complained about his displacement by the sheriff's nominee as member for Devon in 1319 if he had not valued election; nor would the sheriff's man have wanted to take his place.[409] The attendance record of the knights, seemingly better than that of the magnates, confirms the impression of the desirability of a county seat.[410] The inducements to serve

---

[406] E. C. Lowry, 'Clerical Proctors in Parliament and Knights of the Shire, 1280–1374', *EHR* 48 (1933), 449; C. Dyer, *Standards of Living in the Later Middle Ages* (Cambridge, 1989), 215.

[407] *Stat. Realm*, i. 169, 174–5; Maddicott, 'County Community', 34–6.

[408] *Records of the Borough of Leicester*, ii: *1327–1509*, ed. M. Bateson (Cambridge, 1901), 11; Maddicott, 'Parliament and the Constituencies', 84.

[409] *Parl. Writs*, II. ii, appendix, 138; Maddicott, 'Parliament and the Constituencies', 73; above, 342.

[410] Prestwich, *Edward I*, 449–50; id., 'Parliament and the Community', 17–18.

are nowhere directly stated. But they must have included the prospect of a stay in London at the county's expense, the opportunity for representatives to present their own petitions and perhaps to suppress those of their enemies, and the gratification brought by being at the centre of events, all the more so under Edward II, when the commons were courted by both king and magnates. Nor are the wages likely to have been a trivial factor in persuading men to stand for parliament. They were more than could be earned by military service.[411]

The attitude of the MPs' constituents is likely to have been more ambivalent. For them parliament must have signified expense: not only the expense brought by the payment of their members' wages but also the far heavier, if under Edward II more occasional, expense of taxation. The use of the *plena potestas* formula, fully developed from the mid 1290s, ensured that there was no legal way in which those in town and country could deny the taxes to which their representatives might bind them. To judge by evidence from Edward III's reign, members of parliament were fully conscious of the local unpopularity which might come their way as a result of their tax grants.[412] Happy their constituents' contemporaries in the south of France, who were sometimes able to limit their proctors' powers in communal dealings with the royal government and to insist on reference back to the localities on matters of taxation.[413]

In the thirty-seven years between the outbreak of war with France in 1294 and Edward II's deposition in 1327 there were thirteen lay subsidies, compared with only eight levied in the previous ninety-five years since John's accession in 1199. What benefits did the men and women of provincial society gain in exchange for the taxes now conceded so much more frequently by their representatives? The ability to petition for redress was undoubtedly the chief, and it was one facilitated by representation, as we have seen. The development of petitioning created new channels of contact with the king's government which were open even to the poor and obscure, and by 1309 the delivery of petitions was seen as one of the main functions of local members.[414] These links between parliament, representation, and the relief of the commonalty were illuminated again

[411] Maddicott, 'Parliament and the Constituencies', 75–9.   [412] Ibid. 81–3; above, 289–90.
[413] E. A. R. Brown, *Customary Aids and Royal Finance in Capetian France* (Cambridge, Mass., 1992), 97–142; ead., 'Representation and Agency Law', in her *Politics and Institutions in Capetian France* (Aldershot, 1991), 343–64.
[414] Above, 294–7, 333, 340; Maddicott, 'Parliament and the Constituencies', 68.

in 1330, when some of those previously returned to parliament were accused by the king of preventing 'good men' from 'showing the grievances of the common people'.[415] The years between 1290 and 1330 marked the heyday of the private petitions alluded to here.[416] But they also saw the emergence of the common petition, through which grievances shared by many could be pooled, merged, and given the backing of the knights and burgesses: a new process which outstripped the presentation of individual petitions in force and authority and enlarged the possibilities of redress.

Yet mere possibilities they often remained, as two examples will show. The Statute of Sheriffs was enacted in the parliament of January 1316 in response to information from the magnates and to the 'grievous complaints of the people'. Behind it probably lay both written petitions and oral plaints. Of most interest to those oppressed by sheriffs was a clause which prohibited any steward or bailiff of a 'great lord' from serving as sheriff.[417] The government's case for this prohibition lay in the need for the sheriff to give all his time to the service of king and people; but it was more popularly viewed as a safeguard against bastard feudal ties between sheriff and magnate which fostered maintenance, corruption, and the denial of justice to the poor. Yet however loud the voice of complaint it achieved little here, for in 1324 a common petition which we have already noted complained that sheriffs continued to take fees and robes from magnates, contrary to the statute.[418] The problem of seigneurial power in the counties, and the perversion of the law which often resulted from it, was intractable. Edward II was no Henry V, fired with the energy, determination, and authority to impose order and good government on the localities,[419] and the waywardness of his kingship meant the stultification of reform. Parliamentary pressure for change was of no consequence.

A second instance leads to a similar conclusion. In September 1300 Edward I, through proclamations made in the counties, invited all those

---

[415] Rot. Parl. ii. 443; Maddicott, 'Parliament and the Constituencies', 77. For the identity of petitioners, see Dodd, Justice and Grace, 199–241, esp. 207–11 for 'peasants'.

[416] Dodd, Justice and Grace, 49–88.   [417] Stat. Realm, i. 174–5; PROME iii. 209.

[418] J. C. Davies, The Baronial Opposition to Edward II: Its Character and Policy (Cambridge, 1918), 295, 582; Ormrod, 'Agenda for Legislation', 6 n. 3; above, 354–5.

[419] Cf. E. Powell, 'The Restoration of Law and Order', in G. L. Harriss (ed.), Henry V: The Practice of Kingship (Oxford, 1985), 53–74; and id., Kingship, Law and Society: Crime and Justice in the Reign of Henry V (Oxford, 1989), esp. 117–41, 168–275.

who held lands within the forest boundaries, and who wished to challenge the findings of the recent forest perambulations, to appear before him in the next parliament to make their claims. Here was a potential point of contact between king, parliament, and people, one unusually direct and unmediated by local representatives. Yet in 1306 the resulting disafforestations were annulled without resistance, along with Edward's other earlier concessions to his opponents.[420] Failure here brought renewed demands in the next reign. Perambulations were made a condition of the parliamentary tax grant of 1315, but they were apparently not carried through, leading to the obstruction of the levy in some counties. Although the commons pressed for further perambulations in 1316, little seems to have resulted.[421] If the local resistance to the tax suggests local knowledge of the bargain struck in parliament (possibly disseminated by the returning knights), and indeed a local 'respect for parliamentary authority',[422] the ineffectiveness of the concessions made by the crown in 1300 and 1315 cannot have led many to take a favourable view of the possibilities of reform through parliament. The inability or unwillingness of the commons to impose any conditions on their tax grants after 1316 was another mark of their weakness.[423]

Parliament's inadequacy as a beneficial mediator between king and subjects is to be explained largely by its lack of control over the executive.[424] The same had been true in Henry III's middle years. Royal concessions granted in parliament might be easily made, as easily ignored by the crown, and impossible to enforce by the commons. Such relative impotence helps to explain the contemptuous attitude sometimes shown towards parliament by the chroniclers. Robert of Reading, for example, author of the *Flores Historiarum*, writing some twenty years later about the assemblies of 1308, took the view that wise men might depart from parliament without having found the justice which they sought.[425] It was to a degree paradoxical that

---

[420] *Parl. Writs*, I. 90; *Select Pleas of the Forest*, ed. G. J. Turner, Selden Soc. 13 (1899), p. cv; Denton, *Robert Winchelsey*, 237–8; above, 327.

[421] *Parl. Writs*, II. ii, appendix, 89, 92; Harriss, *King, Parliament and Public Finance*, 115–17; C. R. Young, *The Royal Forests of Medieval England* (Leicester, 1979), 143–5.

[422] Harriss, *King, Parliament and Public Finance*, 115.   [423] Ibid. 117.

[424] Ibid.; Maddicott, 'Parliament and the Constituencies', 85.

[425] *Flores Historiarum*, iii. 143; Prestwich, 'Parliament and the Community', 16–17. Cf. above, 373, for the similar comments of the author of the *Vita Edwardi Secundi* (though these apply specifically to the conditions of the mid 1320s), and Maddicott, 'Parliament and the Constituencies', 85, for later comments on the same theme. For the date and authorship of the *Flores Historiarum*, see A. Gransden, *Historical Writing in England*, ii: *c.1307 to the Early Sixteenth Century* (London, 1982), 17–22.

such practical remedies as were applied to misgovernment in Edward II's reign came from the Ordinances, in whose making the commons had no direct share and whose chief defender was Thomas of Lancaster, the greatest of the magnates.[426]

Yet the complicated dialogue between centre and locality cannot be wholly set down as a story of aspirations obstructed and representatives thwarted. The knights and burgesses would not have been summoned to parliament so frequently if they had not been substantial men whose support was worth having and whose influence counted. It was their position in their communities and their ability to sway those communities which made them carry weight. If they took to parliament the petitions and complaints of their constituents, including some of the humblest, they brought back the edicts of both the crown and its opponents (the Ordinances in 1311, the statute repealing them in 1322), the concessions which they themselves had sometimes been able to obtain, and a much less tangible burden of news and views. In both parts of the process they showed an awareness of their role as representatives and a sense of responsibility towards those they represented. The willingness of the knights in particular to put forward 'the grievances of the common people' on matters such as the crimes of great lords demonstrated sympathies which extended beyond their own class and which set them alongside the peasantry (for want of a better word) rather than the magnates who were their fellow landowners. In asking that the concessions which they had obtained from king and council in 1327 be made known through proclamations in the localities, they sought in return the local goodwill and approval on which their own standing partly depended.[427]

Those connections served to nurture and enlarge a politically active and well-informed public in the shires and boroughs. The opportunity to present petitions in parliament; elections in a variety of assemblies, lay and clerical; the choosing of mainpernors; and the raising of money for MPs' wages, as well as the homeward transmission of the gains and losses, reforms and taxes, coming from Westminster: by 1327 all these made parliament a more pervasive part of the background to provincial life than it had ever been before. Since unification in the tenth century England

[426] Maddicott, *Thomas of Lancaster*, 327–9.   [427] Above, 363–4.

had always been a state characterized by a degree of political participation and political awareness exceptional in Europe for its social breadth. The mature relationship between parliament and the provinces was both a confirmation and an enlargement of this most ancient feature of the English polity.

7

English Exceptionalism?

The Peculiarities of the English Parliament. Conclusion

1. Introduction: Gossip and Government

Sometime in 1227 a citizen of Caen known to us only as 'R. Gaudin' wrote to Henry III to report a conversation that he had recently overheard. The son of the castellan of Caen had been speaking to master Nicholas, clerk of Brother Guérin, one of the most trusted advisers of the former king of France, Philip Augustus, who had died in 1223. In the course of their talk the two men had compared the counsel-taking practices of the dead King Philip with those of contemporary English kings. Philip, they said, had thought it enough to take counsel with only two men, his household confidant, Brother Guérin himself, and Barthélemy de Roye, the grand chamberlain. But if the king of England wanted to make war he had to take counsel with many men, and as a consequence the council was known about even before counsel had been received.[1] Alongside this striking contrast between two conciliar styles of government we can place a much better-known passage from Sir John Fortescue's *Governance of England*, written about 1470. England, Fortescue famously remarked, was ruled by *dominium politicum et regale*, 'public and royal lordship', while France was governed only by *dominium regale*, 'royal lordship'. The practical

---

[1] *Diplomatic Documents*, i: *1101–1272*, ed. P. Chaplais, HMSO (London, 1964), 139. For comments, see J. C. Holt, 'The End of the Anglo-Norman Realm', in his *Magna Carta and Medieval Government*, 64–5, and J. W. Baldwin, *The Government of Philip Augustus* (Berkeley, Calif., 1986), 125. For Brother Guérin and Barthélemy de Roye, see ibid. 109–19.

significance of this distinction was that in England the king could not raise
taxes or make or change the laws without the consent of parliament, while
in France these powers were entirely in the hands of the prince.[2]

This pair of observations has two special points of interest. First, it suggests
that at least some contemporaries were aware of significant differences in
the conduct of royal government in England and France. These differences
were not merely the constructs of later historians. And, secondly, the
perceptions of difference, though separated by some 250 years, were
remarkably similar. In the 1220s, as in the 1470s, English government was
seen as being more open than that of France, with decision-making powers
vested in assemblies and not just in the ruler and his inner circle. The contrast
was one between a broadly 'constitutional' system and another in which
a later absolutism was already foreshadowed. Although Gaudin's letter was
written close to Henry III's minority, when large public councils had played
a particularly prominent part in English government, his comments were
hardly less applicable to more normal times. They also reveal an incidental
drawback to English practices, and one easily overlooked: wide and public
consultation meant that few secrets could be kept.

Historians attempting to place the rise of the English parliament in a
broader context need to bear these distinctions in mind. The tendency
among most has been to regard its emergence as a local variation on a
pan-European theme. As we have already noted, the evolution of central
assemblies in a number of European states followed a roughly similar
course to the years around 1200 and then took a roughly similar change
of direction.[3] The change has been characterized by the late Timothy
Reuter as 'the shift from assemblies to proto-parliaments' and by Professor
Thomas Bisson, with a slightly different emphasis, as 'the replacement
of celebratory consensus by politicized debate'.[4] Its essence lies in the

[2] Sir John Fortescue, *The Governance of England*, ed. C. Plummer (Oxford, 1885), 111–16; Sir John Fortescue, *On the Laws and Governance of England*, ed. S. Lockwood (Cambridge, 1997), 85–90. Note that the title of the work was given by Plummer: it was usually known, from the title of its first chapter, as *De Dominio Regale et Politico*. The distinction which Fortescue makes first appears, though with less clarity, in his *De Laudibus Legum Anglie* of c.1469: see Sir John Fortescue, *De Laudibus Legum Anglie*, ed. S. B. Chrimes (Cambridge, 1942), 79–89; for legislation and taxation, see ibid. 40–1, 86–7 (Fortescue, *On the Laws*, ed. Lockwood, 49–53, 27–8, 51–2). I have translated 'politicum' as 'public' rather than the usual 'political', since that word seems to convey a better sense of Fortescue's meaning. It has the sanction of the *Dictionary of Medieval Latin from British Sources*, fasc. xi: *Phi–Pos*, ed. D. R. Howlett (Oxford, 2007), 2332–3.
[3] Above, 107–8.
[4] Reuter, 'Assembly Politics', 194; T. N. Bisson, 'Medieval Parliamentarianism: Review of Work', *Parliaments, Estates and Representation*, 21 (2001), 12. The process outlined in this paragraph is well

transformation of magnate gatherings of the king's vassals into larger bodies which sometimes include lesser men, serving as representatives on a regional basis, most frequently from towns. The main lever of change is conflict between crown and subjects, usually resulting from royal demands for money and service, usually to support the king's wars. These pressures bring about, in the first place, a progression from a narrow notion of counsel-giving as a feudal duty to the broader notion of counsel-giving as a communal right; and, in the second place, a demand for chartered liberties and privileges—sometimes one purporting to emanate from the king's whole realm. But the same pressures also enlarge the social base of the assembly, so that the magnates' inferiors begin to appear alongside the magnates themselves. The result is a significant change in the concept of representation: a move away from the idea that the magnates represent the entire *regnum*, as feudal tenants of the crown, and towards a more direct if still virtual form of representation by local men. During the thirteenth century the word 'parliament' everywhere comes into use to describe these new assemblies, carrying with it the suggestion of discussion and debate, often Bisson's 'politicized debate'.[5] The ruler still takes counsel before expediting the affairs of the realm. But at least some of his actions, most obviously the raising of taxes, now require an additional element of consent, with all the room for argument that this provides.

Familiarity with the course of events in England may lead us to think that the English parliament provides the paradigm here. In fact almost all the transformative elements which its early history embodies can be paralleled elsewhere. The demand for chartered liberties was consummated in England with Magna Carta in 1215; but similar demands were addressed in Catalonia by a charter of Peter I, drafted in 1205; in Germany by Frederick II's *Privilegium in Favorem Principum Ecclesiasticum* of 1220; and in Hungary by Andrew II's Golden Bull of 1222.[6] 'Politicized debate' within

---

surveyed in two further articles by Bisson: 'Celebration and Persuasion: Reflections on the Cultural Evolution of Medieval Consultation', *Legislative Studies Quarterly*, 7 (1982), 181–204; and 'The Politicizing of West European Societies (*c.*1175–*c.*1225)', in C. Duhamel-Amado and G. Lobrichon (eds.), *Georges Duby: l'écriture de l'histoire* (Brussels, *c.*1996), 245–55. Cf. above, 107.

[5] Richardson, 'Origins of Parliament', 146–52; G. I. Langmuir, 'Politics and Parliaments in the Early Thirteenth Century', *Travaux et recherches de la Faculté de Droit et des Sciences Économiques de Paris*, série 'Sciènces Historiques' 8 (1966), 57–8, 60; T. N. Bisson, *The Crisis of the Twelfth Century: Power, Lordship, and the Origins of European Government* (Princeton, 2009), 544–5.

[6] T. N. Bisson, 'An "Unknown" Charter for Catalonia (A.D. 1205)', in his *Medieval France and her Pyrenean Neighbours: Studies in Early Institutional History* (London, 1989), 199–212; id., 'The Origins of the Corts of Catalonia', *Parliaments, Estates and Representation*, 16 (1996), 38–9; id., *The Medieval*

assemblies first becomes audible in England when Hubert Walter put Richard I's demand for additional military service, or money in its place, to a *colloquium* of magnates and bishops at Oxford in 1197; again, if more mutedly, with the conciliar resistance to John's exaction of the thirteenth in 1207; and then again with the granting of another tax in return for Henry III's reissue of the Charters in the great council of 1225.[7] But magnate assemblies had questioned and rejected the crown's policies in Catalonia in the late 1180s, and similar disputes erupted in the cortes of León in 1188.[8] Richard I, John, and Henry III were by no means the only rulers who were on the defensive. Bargaining over taxation, and the placing of redress of grievances against supply, was a feature of English councils and parliaments from 1225 onwards; but Alfonso IX of León in 1203, and James I of Aragon on four occasions between 1218 and 1236, had undertaken to maintain a stable currency in return for taxes.[9] Representatives from the shires were first summoned to the English parliament in 1254. But town representatives appear to have been first summoned to assemblies in León in 1188, and certainly in 1202 and 1208; in Castile in 1214 and 1217, and possibly earlier; in Catalonia and Aragon in 1214; and in Portugal in 1253.[10] In England the word 'parliament' is first used officially for a central assembly in 1236; but it was first used with a similar meaning in France during the 1220s, in Sweden from the mid thirteenth century, in Denmark in 1282, in Germany in 1294, and in Scotland too from the 1290s.[11] If the English magnates could impose

Crown of Aragon: A Short History (Oxford, 1986), 53–5; M. Toch, 'Germany and Flanders: (a) Welfs, Hohenstaufen and Habsburgs', in D. Abulafia (ed.), *The New Cambridge Medieval History*, v: *c.1198–1300* (Cambridge, 1999), 384; *The Laws of the Medieval Kingdom of Hungary*, i: *1000–1301*, trans. and ed. J. M. Bak, G. Bónis, and J. R. Sweeney (Bakersfield, Calif., 1989), 34, 39. For general surveys of charters of liberties, see E. Lousse, *La Société d'ancien régime*, 2nd edn. (Louvain, 1952), 270–342; Holt, *Magna Carta*, 24–7, 76–81; Bisson, *Crisis of the Twelfth Century*, 350–8.

[7] Bisson, *Crisis of the Twelfth Century*, 517; above, 107–8, 120–1, 125–6.

[8] Bisson, 'Origins of the Corts', 38; id., *Crisis of the Twelfth Century*, 507–8, 531, 537–8; E. S. Procter, *Curia and Cortes in León and Castile, 1072–1295* (Cambridge, 1980), 51, 57–9; J. F. O'Callaghan, *The Cortes of Castile-León, 1188–1350* (Philadelphia, 1989), 18–19.

[9] T. N. Bisson, *Conservation of Coinage: Monetary Exploitation and its Restraint in France, Catalonia and Aragon, (c. A.D. 1000–c.1225)* (Oxford, 1979), 93, 113–14; Procter, *Curia and Cortes*, 54, 82.

[10] Procter, *Curia and Cortes*, 105, 110, 255; Bisson, 'Origins of the Corts', 40–1; id., *Medieval Crown of Aragon*, 80. For a cautionary note about the presence of elected town representatives in León in 1188, see P. Linehan, *History and Historians of Medieval Spain* (Oxford, 1993), 306 and n. 161.

[11] Langmuir, 'Politics and Parliaments', 59–60; Bisson, *Crisis of the Twelfth Century*, 544–5; E. Lönnroth, 'Representative Assemblies of Mediaeval Sweden', *Études présentées à la Commission Internationale pour l'histoire des assemblées d'états, Xᵉ Congrès International des Sciences Historiques* (Rome, 1955), 126; P. Pulsiano (ed.), *Medieval Scandinavia: An Encyclopaedia* (New York, 1993), 544; Richardson, 'Origins of Parliament', 169 and n. 1; A. A. M. Duncan, 'The Early Parliaments of Scotland', *Scottish Historical Review*, 45 (1966), 37–9.

reform on an unwilling king in the parliament of 1258–9, the Catalan cortes acted hardly less aggressively at Barcelona in 1283, when Peter II was forced to agree to the calling of annual assemblies, general consent to legislation, and no more than customary taxes.[12] Surveying the whole scene, we can easily see how it might be concluded that 'there was no estate model from which England was a deviant. Rather, there were "many variations in the development of representative institutions in medieval Europe".'[13]

But is this right? Reversion to the remarks of our gossiping Normans suggests that the conciliar prototypes from which representative institutions were to spring took very different forms, at least in England and France. Fortescue later implies that in France these institutions had struck no deep roots. In what follows we shall first expand on the comparisons between English and French councils and counsel made in the Norman report to King Henry III. The intention, however, is not to make a fully comparative study but rather to use the French comparanda in order to give a sharper definition to the local circumstances which produced the English parliament. Some comparisons will next be made between methods of representation in England and in some other western states, mainly the Iberian kingdoms, again with the object of assessing the peculiarities of the English system. Finally, a topic so far largely unmentioned, the subjection of the English nobility to royal taxation (from which continental nobilities were often exempt), will be introduced and its contribution to the unitary and associative nature of the English parliament assessed. The approach throughout will aim to use comparative material in order to bring together some of the diverse themes of the preceding chapters, to place those themes in a longer perspective, and so lead towards a conclusion.

2. Councils and Counsel in England and France
to c.1200

At all times between, say, 930 and 1300 central assemblies made a much more important contribution to royal government in England than in

---

[12] Bisson, *Medieval Crown of Aragon*, 88.

[13] M. A. R. Graves, *The Parliaments of Early Modern Europe* (Harlow 2001), 27. The interior quotation is from H. G. Koenigsberger, 'Parliaments and Estates', in R. W. Davis (ed.), *The Origins of Modern Freedom in the West* (Stanford, Calif., 1995). For an expression of similar views, though mainly for the later middle ages, see Myers, *Parliaments and Estates in Europe to 1789*, 29–34.

France. From Æthelstan's day onward they were summoned frequently, not only at the great feasts of the church, but in some years on other additional occasions, in a succession which was hardly interrupted by the Norman Conquest. One mark of their political weight was their association with almost all the important political acts of the period: after 1066, for example, with the planning of the Domesday survey in 1085, the recognition of Matilda as Henry I's successor in 1126, the promulgation of the Constitutions of Clarendon in 1164, the trial of Becket in 1164, and the making of the Assize of Northampton in 1176.

The contrast with France, hardly demonstrable statistically, was by no means absolute. Under the early Capetians in the late tenth and eleventh centuries the witness lists to royal charters suggest that important men came to the royal court, in what were essentially conciliar gatherings, with some frequency. Yet the hinterland of these gatherings was circumscribed, and largely confined to the royal domain and the duchy of Francia, the region on either side of the Paris–Orléans axis and its northward projection. Bishops were more in evidence as attenders than secular nobles, and both groups were more prominent than the great territorial princes of central, southern, and western France, who were rare visitors. Particularly pronounced in the Frankish kingdom, the decline of assemblies since their Carolingian heyday was common to most western states at this time. England was the exception.[14] Nor did much change with the revival of the French monarchy under Louis VI between 1108 and 1137. Major assemblies barely feature in contemporary accounts, and the princes remained conspicuous by their absence, save on very exceptional occasions. The extraordinary assembly at Rheims in 1124, when Louis faced invasion from the Emperor Henry V, is the only one that we know of. Even festal gatherings of the nobility, fairly regular though they seem to have been, are presented in the sources primarily as religious and social occasions rather than as platforms for political counsel-taking.[15] Only in the reign of Louis VII, 1137–80, when the princes began to attend rather more regularly, did the conciliar landscape begin to shift. The crusading assemblies of 1146–7 set

[14] J.-F. Lemarignier, Le Gouvernement royal aux premiers temps capétiens (987–1108) (Paris, 1965), 41 and tables 3, a, b; J. Dunbabin, France in the Making, 843–1180, 2nd edn. (Oxford, 2000), 262–3; Wickham, Inheritance of Rome, 451–2, 522, 562.

[15] E. Bournazel, Le Gouvernement capétien au xiie siècle, 1108–1180 (Limoges, 1975), 134–43; Dunbabin, France in the Making, 263. But for some examples of counsel-taking at festal assemblies, see A. Luchaire, Louis VI le Gros: annales de sa vie et de son règne (Paris, 1890), nos. 73, 78. Cf. Bisson, Crisis of the Twelfth Century, 167.

a precedent for the more regular appearance at councils of men such as the
duke of Burgundy and the count of Blois; while the proclamation of the
Peace of God for the whole kingdom at a meeting at Soissons in 1155 was
a virtually unprecedented instance of 'national' legislation made through an
assembly.[16] But these great gatherings remained exceptional, and although
the magnates became more prominent at court in the second half of
the reign, the central role which councils had long played in England as
instruments of government and expressions of political consensus remained
peripheral to the management of Capetian France. We look in vain for
French parallels to the extended sequence of major conciliar occasions
which linked the Domesday council of 1085 to the legislative council at
Northampton nearly a century later. If they took place they have not been
recorded.

These contrasts reflect more fundamental differences between the
strength of the crown in the two countries and the ways in which the
two kingdoms were governed. From the tenth century onwards England
was ruled by a strong and wealthy monarchy exercising power through
a uniform structure of local institutions, and overseeing peoples united
by common obligations to the king and by a common language. These
royal assets, preserved through two conquests, made it both necessary and
relatively simple for the crown to convene assemblies. Exemplifying royal
power, they also contributed to it by drawing provincial magnates into
the king's orbit and into contact with his authority. The French kings,
exercising largely nominal rule over a much more fractured state, and
relatively strong only in the domain regions of their direct lordship and
regular travels, found it more difficult to convene councils, while their
development of other methods of government gave them less incentive to
do so, as we shall see.[17] The regionalization of France was incompatible
with national conciliar government.

Deriving from these contrasts, a more particular distinction bearing on
the development of councils in each country lay in the crown's relations
with the nobility. Both before and after 1066 the local powers of the

[16] F. Lot and R. Fawtier, *Histoire des institutions françaises au moyen âge*, ii: *Institutions royales* (Paris, 1958), 290; Bournazel, *Le Gouvernement capétien*, 157–61; Dunbabin, *France in the Making*, 263, 298; E. M. Hallam and J. Everard, *Capetian France, 987–1328*, 2nd edn. (Harlow, 2001), 220 (for a slightly different emphasis); C. W. Hollister and J. W. Baldwin, 'The Rise of Administrative Kingship: Henry I and Philip Augustus', *American Historical Review*, 83 (1978), 901.

[17] Below, 389–92.

greatest English magnates were limited. On either side of the Conquest their estates lay scattered through the shires, largely because, in the first instance, they had been built up piecemeal by royal grants from the tenth century onwards;[18] in the second, because the devisability of land before 1066 allowed holdings to be divided and dispersed by will on the holder's death;[19] and, in the third, because William I's predilection for antecessorial succession passed on these scattered estates to incoming Normans. If formerly compact estates were broken up after 1066, the result was to magnify this pattern of dispersal.[20] There were no provincial power blocs in England comparable to those which the later Carolingian rulers allowed the greatest nobles to accumulate in France and which were then transmitted to the kingdom of their Capetian successors.[21] The absence of castles in pre-Conquest England, the likelihood of noble itinerancy implied by the difficulty of discovering where nobles resided, and, most crucially, the lack of private courts of justice exercising anything like higher franchisal jurisdiction, were all subsidiary marks of private lordships less nucleated, more diffuse, and therefore weaker than those to be found in many parts of France.[22] Even within the French royal domain, outwith the frontiers of the great principalities, private jurisdiction could exclude royal officials; and there too private concentrations of power and resistance existed until a comparatively late date, as Louis VI found in his struggle to subdue such violent and obdurate castellans and neighbours as Hugh de Puiset and Thomas de Marle.[23]

After the Conquest the Anglo-Norman nobility came to possess more provincial power than the English nobility whom its members had displaced, but not so much as to diminish the crown's control in any very

[18] C. Wickham, *Problems in Doing Comparative History*, Reuter Lecture, 2004 (Southampton, 2005), 22–7; Baxter, *Earls of Mercia*, 62–71.
[19] Holt, 'Feudal Society and the Family: The Revolution of 1066', 163–5. But note Wormald's arguments against partible inheritance in the case of royal property descending as bookland: Wormald, 'Kingship and Royal Property', 264–77.
[20] Holt, *Magna Carta*, 27–9; G. Garnett, *Conquered England: Kingship, Succession and Tenure, 1066–1166* (Oxford, 2007), 24–33; Baxter, *Earls of Mercia*, 220–1.
[21] Wickham, *Problems*, 29–30.
[22] P. A. Clarke, *The English Nobility under Edward the Confessor* (Oxford, 1994), 150–2; P. Wormald, 'Lordship and Justice in the Early English Kingdom: Oswaldslaw Revisited', in his *Legal Culture*, 325–32; Baxter, *Earls of Mercia*, 62–3, 124; id., 'Lordship and Justice in Late Anglo-Saxon England', 383–8, 417–19.
[23] Hallam and Everard, *Capetian France*, 150–2; W. M. Newman, *Le Domaine royal sous les premiers Capétiens (987–1180)*, 38–51; Dunbabin, *France in the Making*, 296; Baxter, 'Lordship and Justice in Late Anglo-Saxon England', 385–6; Bisson, *Crisis of the Twelfth Century*, 229–43.

marked way. The anarchy of Stephen's reign, though it showed how greatly baronial castles might enhance local power, was an aberration without permanent consequences for the crown's hold on the shires. If in more peaceful times the new honorial courts brought new rights of jurisdiction to their holders, they hardly matched those available to many French nobles. From at least as early as Henry I's reign the honor court could entertain land pleas only when the two parties were both tenants of its lord;[24] and even at that early stage certain categories of case, in particular those involving 'default of justice' by the lord, may have been subject to withdrawal to the royal court. Lordly justice was rare by comparison with royal justice.[25] Nor did any Anglo-Norman lord exercise the high justice, giving the right to try such major offences as murder and rape, which the greater French nobles of the twelfth century were able to exercise, even in areas so exposed to royal power as the Île-de-France. The pre-Conquest emergence of the pleas of the crown had forestalled any such development in England.[26] Courts of another sort, permanent loci of sociability, patronage, and culture, centred on a seigneurial town or residence, such as those built up in the twelfth century by Henry the Liberal, count of Champagne, at Troyes, and by Geoffrey of Anjou at Angers and Tours,[27] seem to have been likewise unknown in England. All English nobles had households, more elaborately organized at this time than ever before, and a great noble such as Robert of Gloucester might be an important patron—in his case, of Geoffrey of Monmouth and William of Malmesbury.[28] But there is little sign that household and patronage coalesced to form courts resembling those of some of the princes of France.

[24] Stubbs, *Select Charters*, 122; R. Lennard, *Rural England, 1086–1135* (Oxford, 1959), 33–6; Green, *Government of England*, 110–11.

[25] J. Hudson, *Land, Law, and Lordship in Anglo-Norman England* (Oxford, 1994), 36–44, 133–41; id., *The Formation of the English Common Law* (Harlow, 1996), 112–15; P. Wormald, *Lawyers and the State: The Varieties of Legal History*, Selden Soc. (London, 2006), 13–16. For a cautionary note on the withdrawal of cases to the royal court under Henry I, see Brand, ' "Multis Vigiliis Excogitatam et Inventam": Henry II and the Creation of the English Common Law', 98.

[26] N. Civel, *La Fleur de France: les seigneurs d'Île-de-France au xiiᵉ siècle* (Turnhout, 2006), 224–7; N. D. Hurnard, 'The Anglo-Norman Franchises', *EHR* 64 (1949), 289–310; Wormald, 'Lordship and Justice', 317–18. For high justice, see further below, 433.

[27] J. F. Benton, 'The Court of Champagne as a Literary Center', in his *Culture, Power and Personality in Medieval France*, ed. T. N. Bisson (London, 1991), 3–43; Dunbabin, *France in the Making*, 312–18, 337.

[28] D. Crouch, *The Image of Aristocracy in Britain, 1000–1300* (London, 1992), 288–302; id., 'Robert, Earl of Gloucester', *ODNB*.

England therefore possessed neither semi-independent principalities nor local concentrations of baronial power which combined jurisdictional, political, military, and social command over a neighbourhood, to the exclusion of the crown's authority. If we disregard Anglo-Norman Northumbria, where lack of evidence inhibits any attempt to gauge the extent of private jurisdiction, the nearest approach to principalities were the liberties of Chester and Durham. But in the twelfth century the powers of earl and bishop here were still embryonic[29] and hardly resembled those of the counts of Champagne or the dukes of Burgundy. These provincial lacunae had two related consequences, both important for the evolution of council and parliament. They made it unlikely that there would be any strong centrifugal push, back to magnate centres in the provinces, to counter the centripetal pull exercised by the king's court and by the councils which marked the court's periodic enlargement; and they left the shire court in a position of undisputed provincial dominance. As the chief focus for community and neighbourhood, it was a forum both for their business and for that of the king in a way which no magnate court could rival, and, later, the natural venue for parliamentary elections.

To this second point we shall return.[30] The first is more immediately important. The radiation of power from the centre and the absence of competing provincial centres meant that 'English politics was court politics'.[31] Denied regional superiority, magnates found it in their interests to attend at courts and councils, whether to attempt to control the king, as under Edward the Confessor, or at all times to angle for his attention, favour, and patronage. So we find Earl Godwine witnessing all but one of the thirty-one charters issued by the Confessor before the earl's death in 1053.[32] Both under Henry I and Henry II, whose courts were much larger and grander than those of their Capetian contemporaries,[33] attendance at court, and more particularly at councils, gave magnates the chance to share in the making of policy, to consent to new legislation, to compete for place and honour, and, more occasionally, to participate in such momentous

[29] G. Barraclough, *The Earldom and County Palatine of Chester* (Oxford, 1953), 7–16; G. T. Lapsley, *The County Palatine of Durham* (New York, 1900), 26–8, 159–65. For the northern franchises, see Hurnard, 'Anglo-Norman Franchises', 314–16.

[30] Below, 411–13. [31] Bartlett, *England under the Norman and Angevin Kings*, 28.

[32] Keynes, *Atlas of Attestations*, table LXXIV; T. J. Oleson, *The Witenagemot in the Reign of Edward the Confessor* (London, 1955), 53–4; Baxter, *Earls of Mercia*, 70–1, 124; Wickham, *Problems*, 27.

[33] Green, *Henry I*; Vincent, 'Court of Henry II', 334; Dunbabin, *France in the Making*, 295.

decisions as the settlement of the succession to the throne.[34] Henry II may have maintained a less open court than his grandfather, and one to which at least some magnates may have been unwelcome.[35] But in general, and at most points in the twelfth century, voluntary absence would have been at best short-sighted and—as Robert de Mowbray found in 1095[36]—at worst contumacious.

Two further circumstances gave English councils a prominence denied to their French counterparts and embedded them more deeply into the structure of English government and decision-making. The first lay in the problems posed by relations with other powers. England's vulnerability to invasion and, after the Conquest, the planning of campaigns in Normandy, both created the need for public consultation if national resources were to be effectively deployed, either for defence or attack. During Æthelred's Danish wars the witan met frequently to take counsel on the country's defence.[37] The renewed Danish threat after the Conquest precipitated two emergency councils in the autumn and winter of 1085.[38] William's departure for Normandy late in the following year followed the great oath-taking assembly of magnates and undertenants at Salisbury in August 1086.[39] Rufus' plans for his first campaign in Normandy were put to a council meeting at Winchester, probably in 1089.[40] Another magnate assembly at Salisbury in March 1116, where homage was performed to William, Henry I's son and heir, came immediately before the king's crossing to Normandy. Similar pre-campaign councils were equally a feature of Henry II's reign.[41] The need to defend a rich but precariously held inheritance, whether in England alone or on the Continent, drew king and magnates together in a series of informal compacts grounded on common interests. The resulting councils played a central part in the consensus politics of the period. The French kings, who shared fewer interests with their great men, and whose kingdom was less vulnerable because less wealthy and less intrinsic to the calculations and ambitions of other powers, had no such frequent use for national assemblies.[42]

[34] Above, 68, 83, 92–5, 101–2. Cf. Vincent, 'Court of Henry II', 316.
[35] Vincent, 'Court of Henry II', 287–93.   [36] *ASC*, ed. Whitelock, 172; above, 78.
[37] William of Malmesbury, *Gesta Regum*, i. 278–9; *EHD*, ed. Whitelock, no. 127; *ASC*, ed. Whitelock, 82, 90; above, 27–8.
[38] Maddicott, 'Responses to the Threat of Invasion', 986–97; above, 62.
[39] *ASC*, ed. Whitelock, 162; *John of Worcester*, iii. 44–5; above, 66–7.
[40] *Orderic*, iv. 178–81; Barlow, *William Rufus*, 273; above, 78.
[41] *John of Worcester*, iii. 138–9; above, 73, 83, 88.   [42] Cf. Dunbabin, *France in the Making*, 263.

A second local circumstance lay in another sort of political crisis, recurrent in England but unknown in France: that arising from a disputed succession. Breaks in the succession to the throne, sometimes following from the violent displacement of the previous king and usually leading to disputes between rival claimants, occurred regularly in eleventh- and twelfth-century England, as in many other European kingdoms and principalities.[43] In England they produced a repetitive pattern of consequences: the need for the incoming king to legitimize his position, his claim to stand justly in his predecessor's place, his appeal for support through the promise of good government, given via the confirmation of old laws, the making of new ones, or the issuing of a national charter, and the voicing of that appeal in an assembly of the nobility. Elements of this sequence characterized Cnut's early stabilization of his throne in 1020–1,[44] and the elevation of Harold Harefoot in 1035,[45] Edward the Confessor in 1041,[46] William I in 1066,[47] Henry I in 1100,[48] Stephen in 1135–6,[49] and Henry II in 1154.[50] The results were twofold: the strengthening of the political role of assemblies, and their growing association, both as initiators and as witnesses, with restraints on kingship.

The concessions which helped new kings to secure their thrones were something like election programmes. They were ultimately the product of contingency, political accident, and structural defects in the English polity: of the failure of heirs, the absence of fixed rules for the succession in abnormal circumstances, conquest, usurpation, and disputes between relatives. As with the threat of invasion and the need to defend continental lands, so with interruptions to the succession, it was the instability of English conditions which reinforced the place of assemblies in the country's political

---

[43] Bisson, *Crisis of the Twelfth Century*, 186–91.

[44] *Laws of the Kings of England*, ed. and trans. Robertson, 154–5, 208–13; Wormald, *Making*, 349–50, 361–2; above, 37–8.

[45] *ASC*, ed. Whitelock, 102–3; above, 39.

[46] Maddicott, 'Edward the Confessor's Return', 650–66; above, 39–40.

[47] William I issued no coronation charter. But his writ to the Londoners granted them 'all those laws that yet were in the time of King Edward'; he was later associated with a broader undertaking to maintain King Edward's laws; and much of his policy, from his coronation to the making of Domesday Book, was designed to enforce his claim to be Edward's legitimate successor: *Laws of the Kings of England*, ed. and trans. Robertson, 230–1; Wormald, *Making*, 398–9, 408–9; Garnett, 'Coronation and Propaganda', 101–12.

[48] *EHD* ii: *1042–1189*, ed. D. C. Douglas (London, 1953), 400–2; Wormald, *Making*, 400–1; above, 99.

[49] *EHD*, ed. Douglas, 402–4; Crouch, *Reign of King Stephen*, 45–6; above, 99.

[50] *EHD*, ed. Douglas, 407; above, 99.

life. None of this applied to France. Because, astonishingly, every Capetian king from Hugh Capet (987–96) to Louis X (1314–16) produced a son, and because the dynasty was never overthrown by conquest but rather strengthened, until the reign of Philip Augustus, by associative kingship, with the filial successor being nominated and crowned in his father's lifetime, there were no French succession crises. Nor, in consequence were there any of the oral or written concessions, often in the form of charters, which in England sprang from such crises.[51] In terms of their feudal prerogatives and their inability to tax, French kings might be weak. But their very weakness, expressed through their lack of exploitative power, as well as the countervailing strengths provided by an uninterrupted line of male heirs, meant that they were never forced to bargain with their subjects. One mainstay of the French monarchy was dynastic continuity; of the English monarchy, institutional continuity, exemplified (but by no means wholly represented) by a long succession of assemblies.

The concessions so frequently offered by English kings at their accessions fed directly into the development of parliament in another way. Not only did they emphasize the political role of courts and assemblies, where magnates gathered to promote what was a tacit striking of bargains at a reign's inauguration, but they also helped to create an evolving narrative of restraints on kingship. In the years immediately before 1215 that narrative was embodied in and consolidated by the collection of all three of the twelfth-century coronation charters into a single text, now translated from Latin into more accessible French, and by the baronial demand for the confirmation of Edward the Confessor's laws and Henry I's coronation charter.[52] It found its culmination in Magna Carta, made in 'the parliament of Runnymede'. The Charter's authority thereafter meant a partial loss of identity for its contributory streams, so that, for example, we hear no more of Henry I's coronation charter. But it also brought their fertilizing waters, springing from distant sources, into association with parliament through the regular parliamentary demands for the Charter's confirmation and observance. The uncertainties of the English succession, in conjunction with the oppressive fiscal and feudal prerogatives which the English crown

---

[51] R. Fawtier, *The Capetian Kings of France*, trans. L. Butler and R. J. Adam (London, 1960), 48–50; A. W. Lewis, *Royal Succession in Capetian France* (Cambridge, Mass., 1981), 17, 19–20, 24–5, 37, 39–41, 44, 46, 51, 55–7, 59, 70, 74–7, 92, 103, 111; Holt, 'Origins of the Constitutional Tradition', 21.

[52] Holt, *Magna Carta*, 93–5, 113 16, 222–5; id., 'Origins of the Constitutional Tradition', 14–16; above, 99–100.

could deploy, had combined to create a 'constitutional tradition' to which the French crown was never subject.

There are two further ways of gauging the contribution made by councils to royal government in each kingdom: by comparing the relative importance, first, of royal itineration, and then of familiar counsel. In Capetian France, until at least the reign of Philip Augustus, itineration was the primary vehicle for the exercise of kingship. Kings travelled in order to assert their authority, to oversee their local servants, to keep in touch with the local nobility, and to distribute patronage. The presence with them of their great officials, such as the chancellor and the steward, emphasized the governmental aspects of these tours. In the kingdom's core area around Paris, which, even as late as Louis VII's reign, measured no more than about 160 miles from north to south and at most about 140 miles from east to west, such a method of government was entirely possible. Louis himself was intermittently to extend its reach by his other travels to Burgundy, Toulouse, and elsewhere.[53] One mark of the centrality of itineration to Capetian rule was the maintenance of the king's right to hospitality, *gîte*, from localities within the domain. Philip Augustus could draw on this right in at least a hundred places.[54] In such a small and easily traversable region there was less need for the central assemblies which duplicated many of the functions of the itinerant king.

Royal itineration was, of course, a standard practice in England too. But both before and after the Conquest the king's travels within England appear to have been largely confined to the south and the south midlands, except when campaigns or diplomatic negotiations took him northwards or westwards. From Æthelstan's reign onwards national councils took the stage as an alternative form of government, initially in response to the enlargement of the kingdom, the difficulties of devising other ways of controlling the areas of Scandinavian settlement in the north and east, and the need to maintain contact with nobles who might reside on the kingdom's periphery.[55] After the Conquest the crown's French possessions made it expedient for the king to remain within easy reach of the south

[53] Baldwin, *Government of Philip Augustus*, 31; Dunbabin, *France in the Making*, 260–1; ead., 'Henry II and Louis VII', in Harper-Bill and Vincent (eds.), *Henry II*, 50; Bournazel, *Le Gouvernement capétien*, 16. For a map showing the extent of the French domain and providing the basis for the above figures, see Hallam and Everard, *Capetian France*, 163.

[54] Hollister and Baldwin, 'Rise of Administrative Kingship', 892; Baldwin, *Government of Philip Augustus*, 47–8.

[55] Above, 3–4, 7–8. For the itineraries of the pre-Conquest kings, see Hill, *Atlas*, 87–91, 94.

coast and provided a further reason for the restricted range of his English travels.[56] It was John, the loser of Normandy, who was the first monarch to travel at all widely in midland and northern England.[57] One mark of this limited itinerary, and of the king's frequent absences overseas, was the early commutation for cash of the provincial food renders, or farms, which an itinerant king had once needed. The county farms rendered by the sheriffs had already been extensively if patchily commuted before 1066, and if the *Dialogus de Scaccario* can be believed, food renders at the exchequer were finally wound up under Henry I.[58] By contrast, it was not until the reign of Louis IX (1226–70) that there was any extensive commutation of *gîte* in France.[59] Here was an index of the relative usefulness of councils in each kingdom. English kings, using councils rather than itineration as a means to both control and consensus, valued money above victuals. Across the Channel the reverse was true.

The history of familiar counsel in each country presents a similar if less sharp contrast. Kings everywhere took public counsel from their magnates, and private counsel from their *familiares* and *curiales*, their trusted friends (who might of course be magnates), ministers, and household men, behind closed doors. But the balance between these two sorts of counsel varied from country to country and from period to period. Given the general prominence of the feudal counsel provided by magnate assemblies in England, and its lesser role in France, we might expect its relationship with familiar counsel to vary inversely in each country—and this is indeed what we seem to find. No conclusion on this point can be more than impressionistic; nor was either feudal counsel or familiar counsel ever a negligible feature of government in either country. But the latter clearly counted for more in France than in England. From Louis VI's accession in 1108 to Philip Augustus' death in 1223 French kings sought counsel

---

[56] For post-Conquest itineration in general, see Bartlett, *England under the Norman and Angevin Kings*, 133–43. For William I's itinerary, *RRAN*, ed. Bates, 75–84. For Henry I, Christelow, 'A Moveable Feast? Itineration and the Centralization of Government under Henry I', 187–228. For some cautionary thoughts on the difficulty of determining Henry II's itinerary, with implications for other reigns, see Vincent, 'Court of Henry II', 280–3.

[57] Holt, *The Northerners*, 195–8; Bartlett, *England under the Norman and Angevin Kings*, 135–7.

[58] *Dialogus de Scaccario*, ed. Amt, 62–5; J. H. Round, 'The Origin of the Exchequer', in his *The Commune of London and Other Studies* (Westminster, 1899), 65–74; J. Campbell, 'The Significance of the Anglo-Norman State in the Administrative History of Western Europe', in his *Essays in Anglo-Saxon History*, 175–6; Green, *Government of England*, 62–3.

[59] Hallam and Everard, *Capetian France*, 311; W. C. Jordan, *Louis IX and the Challenge of the Crusade* (Princeton, 1979), 148–52.

and service primarily from men in their own entourage: from the great officials (often themselves men of humble origins, such as Stephen de Garlande and Abbot Suger under Louis VI), from the royal knights, and from the king's chamberlains and chaplains.[60] The balance between these groups did not remain constant. The great officials, the chancellor and the seneschal, sank in prominence during Louis VI's last decade, 1127–37, and the chancellorship was vacant for long periods in the late twelfth century; while in Louis VII's later and in Philip Augustus' early years magnates played a greater role as private counsellors than at any other time in the twelfth century.[61] But the overriding trend towards familiar counsel was plain enough. It hardened under Louis VII, when the beginnings of a formal council, its members often named *consiliarii* and its role distinct from that of magnate *concilia*, can just be made out; and this despite Louis's revival of large-scale magnate assemblies, to which the *consiliarii* were perhaps a counter-balance.[62] It was not until the 1230s that royal government in England embraced similar moves towards the institutionalizing of familiar counsel.[63]

This last divergence was symptomatic of the different conciliar paths taken by the two countries. The *familiares* of English kings were always a force in politics and government, though hardly a measurable one. They might include such 'new men' (though not necessarily men from humble backgrounds) as Roger of Salisbury under Henry I or Thomas Becket under Henry II. But at all times they included magnates—Robert of Meulan in Henry I's early years, his son Waleran of Meulan in Stephen's early years, Robert de Beaumont, earl of Leicester, under Henry II—and in Henry I's reign in particular the king's *curiales* were often drawn from the nobility.[64] So those summoned to counsels might also be called upon to provide more private counsel.[65] This partial elision of magnates and *familiares* was much less consistently evident in France and helps to explain why, in England, private counsel could be held in balance with the more public counsel

[60] Hallam and Everard, *Capetian France*, 149–50, 203; Bournazel, *Le Gouvernement capétien*, 141–51; Bisson, *Crisis of the Twelfth Century*, 239–40.
[61] Hallam and Everard, *Capetian France*, 203–5; Bournazel, *Le Gouvernement capétien*, 161–3, 168–9; Baldwin, *Government of Philip Augustus*, 29–31, 104–5.
[62] Bournazel, *Le Gouvernement capétien*, 161–4; Baldwin, *Government of Philip Augustus*, 31, 124.
[63] Above, 188–90.
[64] Green, *Henry I*, 242–4; Hollister and Baldwin, 'Rise of Administrative Kingship', 888–90; D. Crouch, *The Beaumont Twins: The Roots and Branches of Power in the Twelfth Century* (Cambridge, 1986), 29–51, 89–96. For magnate *curiales* under Henry II, see Vincent, 'Court of Henry II', 289–93.
[65] Hudson, 'Henry I and Counsel', 112–13.

offered in assemblies. As far as can be seen, it was public counsel which did
more to shape important political decisions. Henry II might hear in open
council the case for Gerald of Wales's promotion to the see of St David's
in 1175, before dissolving the assembly in order to reveal his mind 'secretly
to those in whom he had greater trust'; but almost all his major legislation,
for example, was made by baronial counsel at assemblies.[66] The overlap
between the two groups perhaps does something to explain why the
king's *familiares* provoked so little public antagonism, at least until John
perturbed the balance by recruiting aliens to his *familia* and using them
against the magnates.[67] Excessive royal favour for a particular *familiaris*,
such as Stephen's for Waleran of Meulan, might on occasion provoke
factional conflict with a Robert of Gloucester.[68] But there are few signs
that the king's *familiares* were so exclusively influential as to be collectively
opposed. They do not feature, for example, on Diceto's list of the baronial
discontents underlying the 1173 rebellion, nor among the grievances of
the Lincolnshire knight Sir Roger of Asterby against Henry II's regime,
as recounted by Gerald of Wales.[69] Magnates were sufficiently drawn into
political decision-making, to a limited extent as counselling *familiares* but
much more conspicuously as attenders at councils, to give the familiar
counsel offered by lesser men a subordinate and acceptable place in the
processes of government.

The general contrast with France was illuminatingly drawn out in
one particular pair of royal responses to parallel issues of foreign policy.
Howden tells us that in July 1177 Henry II summoned a council to
meet at Winchester before his planned departure for Normandy. To it
came archbishops and bishops, earls, barons, and knights, prepared for the
forthcoming campaign, but on their advice Henry delayed his crossing
until his envoys had returned from the French court.[70] In 1213 Philip
Augustus faced a rather similar situation as he planned an invasion of
England. But instead of exposing his plans to a magnate assembly the
anonymous chronicler of Béthune relates that he called to advise him only

[66] Giraldus Cambrensis, *Opera*, i. 43; Jolliffe, *Angevin Kingship*, 175; P. Brand, 'Henry II and the Creation of the English Common Law', in Harper-Bill and Vincent (eds.), *Henry II*, 229–30; above, 69, 83. For other instances of Henry taking private counsel, see Vincent, 'Court of Henry II', 312–13.
[67] Above, 86, 113–16.
[68] Crouch, *Beaumont Twins*, 29–37; id., *Reign of King Stephen*, 68, 75.
[69] *Diceto*, i. 371; Giraldus Cambrensis, *Opera*, viii. 183–6; Warren, *Henry II*, 368, 382. But note also Ralph Niger's charge that Henry elevated his meanest servants above the nobility: ibid. 380.
[70] Howden, *Gesta Regis Henrici*, i. 177–8.

his three closest counsellors, Brother Guérin, Barthélemy de Roye, and Henri Clément, king's knight and marshal. They in turn summoned one of the king's chamberlains to join them.[71] Here we can see precisely the same contrast between 'open' counsel in England and 'closed' counsel in France referred to in the letter from the citizen of Caen cited at the start of this discussion—and the germ too of Fortescue's distinction between the 'royal lordship' of France and the 'public and royal lordship' more characteristic of England. Into this latter system parliament would soon be incorporated.

These comparisons have a central relevance to the early development of the English parliament. They suggest that the twelfth-century conciliar stock, out of which parliament would grow, was much stronger in England than in France. In England councils summoned by the king met frequently and were truly national assemblies. They drew in men from distant parts of the realm, discussed the realm's business, and saw the promulgation of laws for the whole realm. French assemblies, by contrast, were more intermittent in their summoning, more local in their complexion, and more limited in the range of their work. Hence the alternative reliance of the French kings on itineration and familiar counsel as pillars of their government; though cause and effect, whether itineration made councils less necessary or whether the difficulty of summoning councils necessitated itineration, are hard to disentangle. If we had to name one factor which explains the contrast between England and France it would be the continuity and rapid development of English assembly practice from the tenth century onwards. This was made possible in the first place by the preservation in England of a Carolingian-style model which had largely been lost in France. But equally important was the failure of the English nobility, unlike the French, to develop strong provincial power-bases, and the general weakness of regional sentiments and affiliations. Well before 1066 councils were essential to the workings of the English state. They were already established as law-making assemblies which, in their social, judicial, and political roles, faced no provincial or private rivals; and what was true under Æthelstan was equally true under Henry II. From their activities in the emergency circumstances of an impending invasion or a disputed succession a constitutional tradition had begun to take shape which would contribute to the making of Magna Carta and help to inform the later activities of parliament. By 1200 the

---

[71] Baldwin, *Government of Philip Augustus*, 113, 123.

conciliar preconditions from which parliament was to emerge were all in place. Not so in France.

3. Parliaments and Councils in England and France, *c.*1200–1300

The differences between English and French central assemblies in the thirteenth century were in part a projection of those already conspicuous in the twelfth. Broadly speaking, and whether measured by their regularity or by the extent of their business, English great councils and parliaments played a still larger part in politics and government, while that of their French equivalents hardly developed beyond its previous limits. But besides their traditional role in settling national affairs, promulgating new law, and judging state offenders, English assemblies took on new responsibilities in the granting or denial of taxation. This gave them a novel authority in bargaining with the crown, expressing popular grievances, and, on occasion, putting the weight of the king's subjects' money behind the king's policies. From Henry III's reign onwards most political calculations on the king's part had to take account of the likely reaction of councils and parliaments.

Little of this was true of French assemblies, whose peculiar features may serve to highlight those others located at Westminster. From the reign of Philip Augustus (1180–1223) to that of Philip IV (1285–1314) French assemblies maintained a previous pattern in being convened relatively infrequently. They were seemingly less politically engaged than their English counterparts and less vital to the government of the state. In the fifty-one years from 1180 to 1230 the sources yield evidence for only twenty-one consultative assemblies, and nine of these met during the brief reign of Louis VIII, 1223–6. These statistics bear out Philip's known reluctance to summon his magnates to court. With them we might compare the twenty-five or so English great councils which met between 1216 and 1225, during Henry III's minority, and the four which met in each of two years, 1218 and 1220.[72] No similar statistics are available for

[72] G. I. Langmuir, 'Concilia and Capetian Assemblies, 1179–1230', in *Album Helen Maud Cam: Studies Presented to the International Commission for the History of Representative and Parliamentary Institutions*, xxiv (Louvain, 1961), 34–47, 55–6; Baldwin, *Government of Philip Augustus*, 104–6; above, 149.

the period of Louis IX's majority. An irregular succession of assemblies met throughout the reign, in some years two or three, in some years more. But the assured and personal nature of Louis's power gave them a generally subordinate place in his policy-making and they remained inconspicuous in records and chronicles.[73] Under Philip III (1270–85) only six have been identified. Although there were almost certainly others, we have the word of Beaumanoir, writing in 1283, that the king rarely acts 'par tres grant conseil'.[74] Philip IV is known to have convened fifteen consultative assemblies in the nineteen years between 1296 and 1314—years which saw the meeting of some thirty English parliaments.[75] Throughout the period great assemblies met predominantly to consider foreign affairs, especially the crusades[76]—a more consistent concern of French monarchs than of English—and the range of their activities seems to have been altogether narrower than that of their English counterparts. Even allowing for the number of assemblies and the varieties of their business which the sources are likely to have overlooked, there is little doubt that French assemblies lacked the public prominence of English parliaments.

If this difference perpetuated the earlier distinction between the political weight of councils in Anglo-Norman and Angevin England and their relatively subordinate place in France, it rested in part on another inheritance from the past: the differing place of curial government, founded on familiar counsel, in each kingdom. In France the role of the king's intimate counsellors had been consolidated, and become a subject for comment, under Philip Augustus. The chronicler of Tours listed as one of Philip's chief characteristics his 'availing himself of the counsel of lesser men': men

[73] M. Parent, 'Les Assemblées royales en France au temps de Saint Louis', *Positions des Thèses*, Ecole Nationale des Chartes, 1939 (Nogent-le-Rotrou, 1939), 156–61; Hallam and Everard, *Capetian France*, 315; J. Richard, *Saint Louis: Crusader King of France*, ed. S. Lloyd, trans. J. Birrell (Cambridge, 1983), 173–4; A. Marongiu, *Medieval Parliaments: A Comparative Study* (London, 1968), 95; T. N. Bisson, 'Consultative Functions in the King's Parlements (1250–1314)', in his *Medieval France*, 94; J. Le Goff, *Saint Louis* (Paris, 1996), 689.
[74] C.-V. Langlois, *Le Règne de Philippe III le Hardi* (Paris, 1887), 289–90; S. J. T. Miller, 'The Position of the King in Bracton and Beaumanoir', *Speculum*, 31 (1956), 276–7 and n. 62a; Myres, *Parliaments and Estates in Europe to 1789*, 66.
[75] T. N. Bisson, 'The General Assemblies of Philip the Fair: Their Character Reconsidered', in his *Medieval France*, 103; HBC 550–3.
[76] For example, Louis VIII's councils of May 1224, May 1225, Nov. 1225, Jan. 1226, and Mar. 1226 were partly concerned with the Albigensians and the crusades against them (Langmuir, 'Concilia and Capetian Assemblies', 43–5); Louis IX's forthcoming crusades were discussed at assemblies in 1247 and 1269 (*Paris*, iv. 607–8; Marongiu, *Medieval Parliaments*, 96); and Philip III's impending crusade against Aragon was discussed at assemblies in 1283 and 1284 (Marongiu, *Medieval Parliaments*, 96). Cf. Parent, 'Les Assemblées', 156.

such as Brother Guérin and Barthélemy de Roye, whom the duo conversing
at Caen in 1223 had picked out as Philip's chief confidants and who went
on to serve his successor, Louis VIII.[77] By the 1230s, within ten years of
Philip's death, these *consiliarii*, mainly bishops, knights, and royal clerks,
were beginning to provide the core of what would soon become known as
the *parlement*: the king's council acting in its judicial capacity and drawing
especially on the expertise of laymen, many of whom had practical judicial
experience as royal *baillis*.[78] But although the *parlement* was primarily a court,
justice and politics might be hard to separate, and its activities sometimes
merged with, or even usurped, what might have been considered to
be the function of magnate assemblies. The meetings of *parlement* and
assembly might coincide when common business brought them together:
in December 1259, for instance, when the final promulgation of Louis IX's
Treaty of Paris with Henry III united prelates, barons, and counsellors in
what was effectively a joint session of *parlement* and great council.[79] The
trial of the great magnate Enguerrand de Coucy in another *parlement* of
1259, despite his claiming the right to trial by peers, represented a more
unilateral appropriation of what might normally have been the work of an
assembly (though some nobles were present at the trial).[80] In its timing too
the *parlement* was acquiring a periodicity that magnate assemblies had lost.
By the early thirteenth century, if not earlier, assembly meetings had ceased
to be linked to the great feasts of the church, while by about 1260 sittings
of the *parlement* were becoming tied to All Saints, Candlemas (or their
octaves), and Pentecost.[81] These mutations are suggestive of the relative
quantities of business coming before the two bodies: if magnate assemblies
could be ad hoc, sessions of the *parlement* needed to be regular.

Why were English developments so very different, with the rapid
establishment of parliament as a political body, the direct descendant of

---

[77] Baldwin, *Government of Philip Augustus*, 123–5, 356; Hallam and Everard, *Capetian France*, 268;
above, 376, 392–3.

[78] C.-V. Langlois, 'Les Origines du Parlement de Paris', *Revue historique*, 42 (1890), 89–92; Langmuir,
'Politics and Parliaments', 50–1, 60–1; J. H. Shennan, *The Parlement of Paris* (London, 1968), 14–15;
Bisson, 'Consultative Functions', 76–7; Jordan, *Louis IX*, 35; A. Harding, *Medieval Law and the
Foundations of the State* (Oxford, 2002), 162–3; Q. Griffiths, 'New Men among the Lay Counselors of
St Louis' Parlement', *Mediaeval Studies*, 32 (1970), 247–9.

[79] Bisson, 'Consultative Functions', 80–1.

[80] Hallam and Everard, *Capetian France*, 314; Bisson, 'Consultative Functions', 83; Richard, *Saint
Louis*, 212–14; Harding, *Medieval Law*, 162.

[81] Langmuir, 'Concilia and Capetian Assemblies'; 57; Parent, 'Les Assemblées', 158. But see Bisson,
'General Assemblies', 99–100, for the survival of ceremonial courts under Philip IV.

the English witan and the feudal great council, but with no comparable development of a judicial *parlement*?[82] A major part of the answer lies in the particular circumstances of Henry III's minority, when political decision-making, comprehending such royal prerogatives as the appointment of ministers, devolved on magnate councils in response to the absence of effective royal authority. Another part is supplied by the continuing imbalance, the reverse of that found in France, between magnate counsel and the counsel offered by *familiares*: officials, household men, the king's friends. Although the English crown could utilize a bureaucracy which, by the late twelfth century, was perhaps the most elaborate in western Europe after the papacy's, and although the king's *familiares* were as recognizable a feature of the English court as of the French, no English king came to rely so exclusively on an inner circle of counsellors as did Philip Augustus. Even under John, when familiar counsel was at a peak of political prominence, many of the big decisions on national affairs were taken with the counsel of the magnates.[83] In any case, John's early death gave his conciliar preferences no chance to take root. Here again the minority played a vital part in preserving 'open' government. Later, in the years of Henry III's maturity, the parliamentary magnates and the king's councillors may have had their differences, particularly when foreign favourites were among the councillors in the late 1230s and 1240s;[84] but there was no likelihood of England's developing a predominantly curial and familiar style of rulership. The limitations of conciliar power were sharply illuminated in the parliament of April 1254, when the council, acting for the absent king, failed to secure a tax from the local representatives of the clergy and probably from the knights of the shires as well.[85]

Within the English parliament the provision of justice occupied a much more subordinate place than it held in the *parlement*. The ostensible *raison d'être* of the *parlement* was judicial; though in matters such as a state trial or the descent of an apanage, justice and politics were hardly separable. In the English parliament, on the other hand, justice might be done in parliament or at parliament time, but little except state trials fell to the whole body of those comprising parliament. Even when petitions began to proliferate from the 1270s, parliament more often provided a point for their delivery and sorting than a court for their hearing.[86] The difference was rooted in the effective extra-parliamentary organization of English justice. It was

---

[82] For a questioning of this assumption, see Harding, *Medieval Law*, 170–5.
[83] Above, 112, 125–6.   [84] Above, 189–90.
[85] Above, 213–14, 225–6.   [86] Above, 295–6.

largely because England already had an efficient system of professionally staffed central courts—king's bench, common pleas, exchequer—and a means for delivering royal justice to the localities through the eyre, that parliament's judicial functions were so limited. Only the most intractable cases or those involving important magnates or the rights of the crown came to parliament, usually to be heard there by the king and council meeting in parliament rather than by parliament itself.[87] France lacked any comparable central courts, other than the *curia* of the king himself, until the *parlement* filled the gap. Much of the *parlement*'s business came by way of appeals from seigneurial courts, whose large numbers and wide jurisdiction had no parallel in England; while the dense entanglement of local custom, seigneurial rights and privileges, and royal claims were very productive of pleas and disputes that increasingly moved to the centre for resolution. The problem of local seigneurial coinages, for instance, frequently raised in the *parlement*, could never have been an issue in England, where a single royal coinage ran throughout the realm.[88] In these circumstances the judicial work of the *parlement* often had an implicitly political function. In intervening where there was a conflict of jurisdiction between inferior courts, in accepting appeals not only from the courts of lords but also from those of the royal *baillis*, and in creating and defining customary law, it helped to enhance royal authority and to impose a degree of uniformity on a kingdom which in some ways was still little more than an assemblage of jurisdictions.[89] It was the fragmentation of France which called the *parlement* into being, kept it in business, and made it 'the key institution in state-formation'.[90] But in England the state had been formed long since.

The limited role of French assemblies in law-making, and the limited nature of the law made, again suggested only a modest qualitative advance on what had been achieved by the predecessors of Philip Augustus. The quantitative increment may have been greater, for there were certainly more royal *ordonnances*. But national legislation, made by counsel and consent, and applicable outside the domain, rare in the twelfth century,[91] was almost as rare in the thirteenth. There was a convention, recorded by Beaumanoir, that legislation for the 'common profit' required the king to act by 'great

---

[87] Cf. Dodd, *Justice and Grace*, 40–6.

[88] Ibid. 38–9; Bisson, 'Consultative Functions', 82–3, 85; Le Goff, *Saint Louis*, 679.

[89] Griffiths, 'New Men', 264–72; Harding, *Medieval Law*, 162–7.

[90] Harding, *Medieval Law*, 167.   [91] Above, 382.

counsel'.[92] This bears a superficial resemblance to 'Bracton''s view, itself restating an assumption that went back to the pre-Conquest period, that changes in the law required general—that is, baronial—consent.[93] But in practice most French legislation before Philip IV's reign applied only to the domain and took the form of *ordonnances* often promulgated in the *parlement* but stemming from the king's initiative.[94] Even such a major piece of reforming legislation as Louis IX's great reforming *ordonnance* of 1254, comparable in form to Henry II's assizes and in content and effect to the Provisions of Westminster, went undiscussed in any magnate assembly and was the product only of the king's will and conscience and, at most, of the expertise of a few close counsellors.[95] On those few occasions when magnates participated in general legislative activity at assemblies, their participation might involve no more than individual consent, regarded as binding only on those who had given it. Such were the ordonnances of 1223, 1227, and, to a large extent, of 1230, issued in restraint of the Jews and of Jewish money-lending. Although this last measure contained one clause intended to bind non-consenters and to apply throughout the kingdom, legislation of this sort was unusual,[96] and France failed entirely to develop the sort of 'legal community'[97] that was represented, among much else, in the English parliament.

Following again from earlier practice, English legislation was both more closely associated with central assemblies and more widely enforced than any known in France. Louis VII's proclamation of the Peace of God was made in a great council at Soissons in 1155 and was intended to apply to the whole realm; but there is nothing to suggest that it was anything like so effective as the broadly comparable 'law and order' legislation marked by the introduction of the murdrum fine, very probably devised by William I in a baronial assembly and more certainly enforced by 1129

---

[92] Philippe de Beaumanoir, *Coutumes de Beauvaisis*, ed. A. Salmon, 2 vols. (Paris, 1899–1900), ii. 264, 257 (nos. 1515, 1499); Miller, 'Position of the King', 276–8; C. T. Wood, *The French Apanages and the Capetian Monarchy, 1224–1328* (Cambridge, Mass., 1966), 85–6.

[93] Miller, 'Position of the King', 276; above, 101–2, 241.

[94] Wood, *French Apanages*, 103; G. I. Langmuir, 'Community and Legal Change in Capetian France', *French Historical Studies*, 6 (1969–70), 284–5; Bisson, 'Consultative Functions', 86; Griffiths, 'New Men', 270–1.

[95] L. Carolus-Barré, 'La Grande Ordonnance de 1254 sur la réforme de l'administration et la police du royaume', in *Septième Centenaire de la mort de Saint Louis: actes du colloques de Royaumont et de Paris (21–27 mai 1970)* (Paris, 1976), 93–4.

[96] G. I. Langmuir, ' "Judei Nostri" and the Beginning of Capetian Legislation', *Traditio*, 16 (1960), 215–32.

[97] Langmuir's phrase: 'Community and Legal Change', 276, 286.

in at least twenty counties.[98] The same sequence of assembly promulgation and local application characterized the Assize of Northampton, issued in a great council in 1176 and enforced through the six judicial circuits, covering thirty-four counties, set up in the same council.[99] Later legislation took a similar course. The reforming laws of the second half of the thirteenth century, from the Provisions of Westminster and the Statute of Marlborough to the Edwardian statutes of the 1270s and 1280s, though their drafting may have been the work of professional lawyers and judges, had almost all required the endorsement of parliament.[100] The protests by bishops and barons at Henry III's resort to legislation by writ before 1258, bypassing the need for general consent, showed the value set upon what was by now an indivisible association of councils and parliaments with national law-making.[101] Such laws were worth making not only because they were needed but because they could be enforced: the result of the English state's possessing a uniform common law which overrode local custom (in any case insignificant), which could assimilate new legislation, and which could be administered through central and local courts.

In all this France was deficient. The slack hold of royal power on regions outside the domain, and the large degree of autonomy enjoyed by nobles within their lordships, provided little incentive for national legislation in central assemblies. These same factors worked to inhibit the enforcement of the law. Beaumanoir acknowledged the ability of the magnates to legislate within their own lands and their right to enforce any national *ordonnances* and to levy fines on those contravening them.[102] In provinces which had an earlier tradition of independence, such as Anjou and Touraine, local custom might even assert that royal commands could not be enforced without local baronial assent. A possible English parallel, the recognition by Henry II in 1166 that the enforcement of the Assize of Clarendon within the bishopric of Durham by the king's justices was merely a temporary measure which

---

[98] Dunbabin, *France in the Making*, 263; *PR 31 Henry I*, 8, 10, 14, 20, 39, 45, 56, 61, 65, 68, 74, 78, 93, 97, 105, 117, 123, 150, 155, 159; above, 61–2.

[99] Howden, *Gesta Regis Henrici*, i. 107–8; Brand, 'Henry II and the Creation of the English Common Law', 83–4.

[100] P. Brand, 'The Formation of the English Legal System, 1150–1400', in A. Padoa-Schioppa (ed.), *Legislation and Justice* (Oxford, 1997), 119–20; id., *Kings, Barons and Justices*, 37–41, 187–8; *Stat. Realm*, i. 19; Prestwich, *Edward I*, 452–3.

[101] Above, 241.

[102] Beaumanoir, *Coutumes de Beauvaisis*, ii. 257, 263 (nos. 1499, 1513); Miller, 'Position of the King', 277; Wood, *French Apanages*, 87–8.

would not become a custom, was very much the exception.[103] In both countries the role of council and parliaments in making the law was partly determined by the possibilities of its enforcement.

To a degree, therefore, the ways in which central assemblies developed in thirteenth-century England and France were predicated on past history. The contrasts in their general importance, their frequency and regularity, the extent to which their work was complemented or outweighed by that of curial and familiar counsel, and their judicial and legislative functions, were all the products of evolution rather than sudden change. More latent and uncertain were the elements of contingency which affected this evolution. In France a wholly improbable succession of male heirs kept the crown clear of succession disputes, while in England a series of such disputes contributed to the growth of a 'constitutional tradition' which came to be embodied in parliament. In England too the accident of John's early death and the consequentially long minority of the young Henry III promoted the central role of the great council in politics and government; and this in turn provided the immediate grounding for the growth of parliament. In France the building up of the judicial role of the *parlement* owed little to Louis IX's shorter minority, but much to the quiddities of his character, his conscience, his personal zeal for justice, and his desire to be involved in its doing.[104] None of this was predictable.

But there was one factor which sprang neither from past circumstance nor from chance, and which came to create a much sharper divergence between English and French assemblies. That was taxation. In the years around 1200 the English crown began to levy direct taxes from the whole country for the first time since the demise of geld in 1161–2. The Saladin Tithe, the levy for Richard's ransom, and the thirteenth of 1207, all showed the immense potential of these new taxes on revenues and moveables (after 1207 on moveables alone). From the start, however, they were linked with consent, imposed from the time of Magna Carta by formal regulation: no general aids were to be levied 'except by the common counsel of our realm'.[105] The need for consent created the conditions for the 'politicized debate' within parliament which is explicitly recorded,

---

[103] Langmuir, 'Community and Legal Change', 285; *English Lawsuits*, ed. van Caenegem, ii. 466; Hurnard, 'Anglo-Norman Franchises', 322–3.
[104] Richardson, 'Origins of Parliament', 162–3; Jordan, *Louis IX*, 142–4; Richard, *St Louis*, 170–2; Le Goff, *Saint Louis*, 323–4; Bisson, 'Consultative Functions', 83.
[105] Above, 124.

usually by Paris, for almost every parliament in which Henry III requested a tax—parliaments more numerous than those in which a tax was actually granted. The king's case, most frequently made in terms of the need to finance foreign campaigns or to repay debts, and the baronial response, which usually amounted to a critique of Henry's oppressive and spendthrift government, showed the substantial content of such debates.[106] Of course, the crown still had large resources available to it which were not subject to parliamentary consent: feudal profits, revenues from ecclesiastical vacancies, and the profits of justice accruing through the eyre were among the chief. But these too were often the target of baronial protests,[107] so making their own contribution to parliamentary contentions. Requests for taxation thus provided the occasion for broader criticisms of the crown's money-raising methods.

That this never happened in France owed much to the comparative inferiority of magnate assemblies, but more to a related factor: the financial stability of the French crown. During the period of just over a century between Philip Augustus's accession in 1180 and that of Philip IV in 1285, the kings of France were able to avoid revenue-raising methods likely to prove politically damaging. They owed this good fortune largely to the possession of a very substantial domain revenue which obviated the need for national taxes. The contrast with England was palpable. The English royal demesne, huge in the generation after the Conquest, had been steadily run down in the succeeding hundred years, leaving the crown perilously dependent on the profits of justice, of feudal lordship, and latterly of taxation.[108] The opposition provoked by these levies can be gauged by the fiscally restrictive chapters of Magna Carta, defining the crown's rights to reliefs, wardships, and marriages, forbidding the sale of justice, and setting out the conditions for the granting of taxes. Although domain revenues could be augmented in response to these restrictions, by improved methods of land management and by raising the shire farms, they could never rival the sums to be raised from the more occasional taxes. Demesne manors and county farms produced between them just over £7,000 in 1240-1.

---

[106] Above, 173-5.

[107] Criticism of feudal profits: parliament of Jan. 1242 (*Paris*, iv. 186-7). Vacancy revenues: parliaments of Jan. 1242 (ibid.), Feb. 1248 (ibid. v. 7). Profits of justice and eyre: parliaments of Jan. 1242 (ibid. iv. 186-7), Oct. 1252 (ibid. v. 327), Mar. 1257 (*Ann. Burton*, 387).

[108] J. Green, 'William Rufus, Henry I and the Royal Demesne', *History*, 64 (1979), 337-52; Holt, *Magna Carta*, 36-47; Carpenter, *Struggle for Mastery*, 468-9.

The yield of the nearest tax available for comparison, that of the thirtieth granted in the parliament of 1237, had been some £22,500.[109]

French royal finance went in a different direction. Already under Louis VII in the 1170s a large domain revenue was one of the crown's greatest assets. This was boosted mightily by Philip Augustus' territorial acquisitions, of which Normandy and Touraine, obtained by conquest in 1204–5, were the most valuable.[110] Their acquisition raised royal revenues by some 70 per cent. Philip's conquest of the former Angevin lands was crucial in elevating his revenues above those of his rival, King John, and in doing so without his having to call on his subjects in any substantial way. The English crown, on the other hand, could not finance such a limited operation as the defence of Gascony in 1225 without summoning a council and securing the grant of a fifteenth—and paying the price in the confirmation of the Charters.[111] Despite the subsequent alienation of many of Philip's gains, in the form of apanages for the sons of Louis VIII, domain revenues continued to grow under Louis IX, thanks to Philip's earlier reorganization of domainial administration and to a generally benevolent economic climate.[112]

In these circumstances direct taxation on anything like a national scale was neither so necessary nor so possible as in England. The history of the Saladin Tithe is particularly instructive here. In England the levy of 1188 provided a basis and a precedent for all future taxation of moveable goods, preparing the way for the thirteenth of 1207, the consequent restraints on direct taxes in Magna Carta, and ultimately for the parliamentary debates nurtured by those restraints. But in France the Saladin Tithe led nowhere. Philip Augustus was soon forced to abandon the levy, to renounce its future use, and to fall back on revenues from his expanding domain.[113] He lacked the political authority and perhaps the incentive to do more. The

---

[109] Stacey, *Politics, Policy and Finance*, 44–92, 208; Mitchell, *Studies in Taxation*, 218; W. M. Ormrod, 'England in the Middle Ages', in R. Bonney (ed.), *The Rise of the Fiscal State in Europe, c.1200–1815* (Oxford, 1999), 24.

[110] J. F. Benton, 'The Revenue of Louis VII', in his *Culture, Power and Personality in Medieval France*, 184–5, 190; R. W. Southern, 'England's First Entry into Europe', in his *Medieval Humanism and Other Studies* (Oxford, 1970), 152–4; Baldwin, *Government of Philip Augustus*, 247–8, 352. J. Dunbabin helpfully summarizes Philip's financial achievements in her review of Baldwin's book, *EHR* 103 (1988), 668.

[111] N. Barratt, 'The Revenues of John and Philip Augustus Revisited', in Church (ed.), *King John: New Interpretations*, 90–2.

[112] Baldwin, *Government of Philip Augustus*, 125–36, 155–8, 220–5, 239–48; J. Favier, 'Les Finances de Saint Louis', in *Septième Centenaire*, 133–4.

[113] Baldwin, *Government of Philip Augustus*, 53–4.

magnate assembly which had sanctioned the Tithe was the last to assent
to national taxation for more than a hundred years.[114] Philip's inability to
develop the Saladin Tithe into a national tax may in the long term have
been one among several 'serious blows to the unity of the realm' inflicted
by his policies.[115] But it may also have spared him and his successors from
the aggressive 'politicized debate' opened up by the tax requests of the
English kings. In the long reign of his grandson Louis IX, even the sizeable
revenues from the domain proved inadequate for the crown's needs, and
extraordinary expenses, notably for Louis's crusades, were met by a variety
of fiscal expedients. In particular, tenths from the church (taken with papal
support), levies from the Jews, and aids from the towns were all brought
into play.[116] Expeditions nearer home might be financed by the redemption
for cash of the military service owed by rear-vassals and by the inhabitants
of noble fiefs. All this constituted a heavy burden of taxation, for which
Louis was duly criticized. But the burden fell largely on particular groups
and on those non-nobles who lacked the power to resist.[117]

For these reasons the financing of the French state had none of the
constitutional consequences arising from the same process in England.
Taxation was hardly associated with magnate assemblies, which in any case
lacked the established place that they held in the English political system. It
is true that tax matters came before the *parlement* with some frequency. But
they usually concerned claims for local exemption or individual privilege,
and had nothing to do with general consent.[118] The nearest approach to
national taxes came with the aids levied for the knighting of the king's sons,
Philip, son of Louis IX, in 1267, and Philip, son of Philip III, in 1284. These
aids the crown claimed by customary and feudal right, without the need for
consent.[119] Strictly speaking, the same right could be claimed by the English
crown; yet aids for the knighting of Henry III's son Edward in 1253, and

[114] For the assembly of prelates and magnates which sanctioned the Saladin Tithe in France, see
Œuvres de Rigord et de Guillaume le Breton, ed. H. F. Delaborde, 2 vols. (Paris, 1882–5). i. 84–5, and
William of Newburgh, 273. For the role of assemblies (but often small and local ones) in sanctioning the
levies of the 1290s, see e.g. J. R. Strayer and C. H. Taylor, *Studies in Early French Taxation* (Cambridge,
Mass., 1939), 46, 48.

[115] Dunbabin, review of Baldwin, *Government of Philip Augustus*, EHR 103 (1988), 670.

[116] Jordan, *Louis IX*, 79–99; J. B. Henneman, 'France in the Middle Ages', in Bonney (ed.), *Rise
of the Fiscal State*, 104–5; E. A. R. Brown, *Customary Aids and Royal Finance in Capetian France: The
Marriage Aid of Philip the Fair* (Cambridge, Mass., 1992), 54.

[117] Favier, 'Les Finances', 137–40; Brown, *Customary Aids*, 54–5.

[118] Bisson, 'Consultative Functions', 85, 91; Brown, *Customary Aids*, 54–7.

[119] C. Stephenson, 'The Aids of the French Towns in the Twelfth and Thirteenth Centuries', in
his *Medieval Institutions: Selected Essays*, ed. B. D. Lyon (paperback edn., Ithaca, NY, 1967), 32–3;

Edward I's son Edward in 1306, were both conceded in parliament.[120] Even though both could be regarded, on the two occasions when they were granted, as substitutes for direct taxes, the necessity for consent could be seen to have spread its tentacles far more widely in England than in France. It was this above all else which reinforced the position of parliament as a political assembly. It was not merely what its conciliar predecessors had long been, an occasion for settling the affairs of the realm, but one where the fiscal demands of the king and the responses of his subjects now met in creative interplay, to establish parliament as a platform for public and political debate. Starting in any case from an inferior position, magnate assemblies in France, unnecessary for the crown's fiscal purposes, could not take on the same role or attain a comparable centrality to the working of the state.

In the 1290s these two system were juxtaposed in competition for the first time. War now subjected both France and England to intense fiscal pressures, similar to those which England had already sustained under Richard I and John, but which were largely new to France. Conflict on several fronts, with England, Flanders, and the papacy, meant that the French fiscal system, which had been adequate for most of the thirteenth century, would no longer suffice. In the absence of any standard national tax comparable to the English levy on moveables, Philip IV had to improvise, with results that can best be described as 'piecemeal'.[121] His new taxes were based on the principle, utilized on a more limited scale under Philip Augustus and Louis IX, that all men were liable for military service but that money could be taken in lieu.[122] These were supplemented by sales taxes, by the levying of an aid for the marriage of the king's daughter in 1308, and by a variety of other expedients.[123] The main and most unpopular taxes on property and income were usually imposed by the king's own authority, as (probably) in 1294 and (certainly) in 1300,[124] or, at most, by the counsel and consent of a small council which might include a few magnates, as in

J. R. Strayer, 'The Crusades of Louis IX', in his *Medieval Statecraft and the Perspectives of History* (Princeton, 1971); Langlois, *Le Règne de Philippe III*, 342; Brown, *Customary Aids*, 57.

[120] *CR, 1251–53*, 353; *Paris*, v. 374–5; *Parl. Writs*, i. 167, 178–9; Jurkowski, Smith, and Crook, *Lay Taxes*, 18, 28–9.

[121] Cf. E. B. Fryde, 'The Financial Policies of the Royal Governments and Popular Resistance to them in France and England, *c.*1270–*c.*1420', in his *Studies in Medieval Trade and Finance* (London, 1983), i. 837.

[122] Baldwin, *Government of Philip Augustus*, 166–73; Favier, 'Les Finances', 136–7; Stephenson, 'Aids of the French Towns', 26–8, 33.

[123] Strayer and Taylor, *Early French Taxation*, 8–21.   [124] Ibid. 44–5, 53–4, and n. 173.

1296 and 1303.[125] But no matter how taxes were sanctioned at the centre, they were liable to be questioned and disputed in the provinces, both by local assemblies and by nobles, with the result that the terms of the tax were often amended to the crown's disadvantage. The subsidy of 1303, for example, had to be negotiated in southern France with the nobles and townsmen of each *sénéchausée*, and substantial concessions made to the nobility, some of whom were allowed to pay in instalments and to submit their own estimates of their incomes.[126]

What the French state lacked was the means to legitimize and secure national taxes through consent at the centre and effective collection in the provinces. Most of the reasons for this deficiency should be obvious from what has already been said. Because of the semi-independence of many French nobles, the crown's relatively weak hold over them, and the general deficit of crown authority for much of the twelfth century, France had never developed the sort of central assemblies known in England from an early date. Because the crown's fiscal pressure on the French nobility had hitherto been generally light, and in consequence France had never experienced the type of reaction against oppressive royal government seen in Magna Carta, taxation had never become linked to consent given in a central assembly. Because the French nobility had no natural constituency beyond their own lordships, stood only (and then comparatively rarely) for their own regions, possessed compact rather than dispersed estates, and assembled together infrequently, they had never come to see themselves as representing the *regnum* of France. Because the *regnum* was itself fragmented, and divided by local custom and self-contained jurisdictions, there was—even allowing for the unifying authority of crown and *parlement*—little sense of common interest among the crown's subjects. Nor, given the absence of local representatives, such as the knights and burgesses summoned with increasing frequency to English parliaments, was there any means by which local interests could be expressed in a concerted way.[127]

The results of these contrasts became emphatically visible during the wars which began in the 1290s. In England as in France the crown's wars brought the crown's subjects under the hammer of taxation. The four lay subsidies levied between 1294 and 1297 equalled in number those raised during the

---

[125] Strayer and Taylor, *Early French Taxation*, 48–50, 59.   [126] Ibid. 67–8.
[127] For a more positive view of French 'regnal solidarity', see Reynolds, *Kingdoms and Communities*, 283–9.

whole of Henry III's reign. But the long establishment (if infrequent utiliza-
tion) of a system of direct taxation, granted in central assemblies and raised
by tried and tested procedures, meant that Edward I could secure consent in
parliament to levies which all had to pay. The price which the crown paid
was opposition at the centre and the placing of conditions on tax grants, seen
most clearly in the demand for the Charters in 1297 and for the *Articuli Super
Cartas* in 1300. The occasional acts of collective resistance in the counties,
notably the refusal of the Worcestershire county court to allow the collection of the illicit eighth in 1297, were closely aligned with resistance at the
centre. In the counties as in parliament, the defence of Magna Carta and of
the customary right to consent to taxation provided common ground for
magnates, knights, and freemen.[128] The French crown avoided any such bargaining at the centre, only to have its authority contested and curtailed in the
localities. It was not surprising that opposition to the subsidy demanded for a
Flemish campaign in 1314–15, the fiercest that the crown had to face during
this period, took the form of provincial leagues, headed by nobles and each
demanding particular local privileges, rather than centralized opposition of
the sort that had confronted Edward I between 1297 and 1301.[129]

The different roles played by central assemblies in England and France
were set on course well before the thirteenth century. But it was the
advent of national taxation, a century later in France than in England,
which separated those roles more widely than ever before. In England,
and in conjunction with Magna Carta, taxation transformed an advisory
great council into a much more powerful parliament, whose consent was
required for grants and whose members, whether magnates alone initially
or magnates, knights, and burgesses at a later stage, could reasonably be
seen as representing the *communitas* of taxpayers. The relative insignificance
of assemblies in France, the longtime solvency of the French crown,
and the divided nature of the French realm left France immune to these
developments. The central body of the French state was not a parliament
but the *parlement*, and by 1300 the crown's strength lay less in its access to
its subjects' resources via their consent to taxation than in the justice which
the *parlement* provided and the concomitant jurisdictional sway which was
a unifying substitute, if an inadequate one, for fiscal power.

---

[128] Above, 313–16; below, 436–7, 439–40.
[129] A large literature is usefully summarized in Hallam and Everard, *Capetian France*, 390–3.
Cf. below, 428, 433–4, 438.

4. Local Representation

In one respect French central assemblies differed not only from English
parliaments but from the assemblies of most western European countries
in the thirteenth and early fourteenth centuries: they failed to develop
and embody any system of local representation.[130] Here England, but not
France, shared in what was a widespread transmutation of feudal councils
into representative assemblies. Yet indigenous methods of representation,
their antecedents, and their political implications sharply separated the
English parliament from its continental counterparts. Representation took
different forms in different places, but so different in England as to make
its parliament entirely distinctive. The chief contrast lay in the nature of
the unit represented. In England the primary unit was the shire, joined
only later by the borough; but in the Spanish kingdoms, in Scotland, in
the few French central assemblies convened by Philip IV which were the
forerunners of the estates-general, and in the French provinces, the local
electing body was the town.

This was only natural. In many parts of western Europe towns had
a much larger administrative and political role than was the case in
England. Over much of France, especially in the south, they were the
main units of local organization, after the noble and ecclesiastical lordships of which they sometimes formed part. In both France and Spain
they often possessed a large territory and jurisdiction beyond their walls,
sometimes giving their name to the surrounding countryside with which
they were so closely enmeshed.[131] They frequently owed their rulers
military service, which in Castile and probably in the Agenais of south-
west France might include cavalry service: an important contribution to
peace-keeping as well as to warfare. These military arrangements were
closely bound up with the early development of assemblies.[132] For the
towns of the Agenais, court service and military service were sometimes

---

[130] But for the (irregular) appearance of local deputations at the *parlement*, see Bisson, 'Consultative
Functions', 87, and Brown, *Customary Aids*, 52, 112–42, 147–57.

[131] Procter, *Curia and Cortes*, 95–6; O'Callaghan, *Cortes of Castile-León*, 14, 193–4; T. N. Bisson,
Assemblies and Representation in Languedoc in the Thirteenth Century (Princeton, 1964), 36–8, 304–5.

[132] Procter, *Curia and Cortes*, 102; O'Callaghan, *Cortes of Castile-León*, 14, 193–4; Bisson, *Assemblies
and Representation*, 34 8, 84–90; id., 'The Organized Peace in Southern France and Catalonia
(c.1140–c.1233)', in his *Medieval France*, 231–2, 234–5.

twin obligations, demanding attendance at assemblies which might double up as the gatherings of armies.[133] Sometimes the representatives might themselves be knights, as they were (it is now thought) in the earliest Leónese assemblies and later in Castile, where knightly representation at the cortes might sometimes be demanded by the king.[134] More generally, towns and their hinterlands constituted fertile islands of taxable wealth, all the more valuable to their rulers because of the tax exemptions often enjoyed by the rural nobility, and because the standing of the towns as organized communities made it possible for them, by about 1300, to empower their representatives to act as their proctors.[135] It was not surprising that the Iberian kingdoms, where all these traits were most marked, should have been the first to draw town representatives into central assemblies.[136]

Some of the same factors explain the summoning of the French towns by Philip IV to his three great assemblies of 1302, 1308, and 1314: the first occasions on which townsmen had attended en masse at the centre. The first two of these gatherings, 'exercises in propaganda',[137] were intended to secure political consent to Philip's campaigns, against Pope Boniface VIII in 1302, and against the Templars in 1308—or rather to whip up feelings against these enemies of the state. Only the third was concerned with taxation. As Professor Bisson has pointed out, what was needed on the two earlier occasions was the support of 'prestigious persons and communities', whose political awareness set them above the less educated communities of the countryside;[138] unusually, their wealth was important only insofar as it contributed to their status. Yet here were further reasons for the peculiar prominence of the towns as represented communities. The French crown's administrative units, the *bailliages* and the *sénéchaussées*, could never provide effective substitutes, for their shifting configurations and uncertain

[133] Bisson, *Assemblies and Representation*, 86–8; id., 'An Early Provincial Assembly: The General Court of Agenais in the Thirteenth Century', in his *Medieval France*, 10–11.

[134] T. N. Bisson, review of O'Callaghan, *Cortes of Castile-León*, Speculum, 66 (1991), 672; id., *Crisis of the Twelfth Century*, 562–3; Procter, *Curia and Cortes*, 166. I am grateful to Professor Bisson for advice on the attendance of knight-townsmen at the cortes.

[135] C. H. McIlwain, 'Medieval Estates', in J. R. Tanner, C. W. Previté-Orton, and Z. N. Brooke (eds.), *Cambridge Medieval History*, vol. vii (Cambridge, 1932), 699–703; Post, *Studies*, 70–9; Procter, *Curia and Cortes*, 162–7.

[136] Procter, *Curia and Cortes*, 105, 108–10; Bisson, *Medieval Crown of Aragon*, 80.

[137] J. R. Strayer, *The Reign of Philip the Fair* (Princeton, 1980), 110. For general discussion of these assemblies, see ibid. 110–11; Hallam and Everard, *Capetian France*, 388–9; and Bisson, 'General Assemblies', 106–22.

[138] Bisson, 'General Assemblies', 110, 120.

boundaries,[139] as well as their artificial and relatively recent construction, all deprived them of the cohesiveness, the compactness, and the corporate sense which existed in at least the upper ranks—the only ones to be truly represented—of urban society.

The history of English local representation begins from an entirely different starting point: not with the towns, nor even with the shire, but with the early attendance of lesser landholders at central assemblies. This has been a main theme of the preceding chapters and was a constant throughout the period covered by this book, though one which has generally gone unrecognized. Even before the Conquest there is enough evidence to suggest that the minor nobility and local thegns were sometimes present at meetings of the witan.[140] Their attendance was a reflection of their importance in the shires, as suitors of the shire court, guarantors of the rights conveyed by the charters which they sometimes witnessed, and executors of royal decisions conveyed to the localities by writ.[141] It was also a reflection of a deeply politicized world, in which there were multiple links between centre and localities, political participation, with its communal duties enforced by royal command, stretched downwards to a degree inconceivable in France or Germany, and the witan could realistically be seen as representing 'the English people'.[142] After the Conquest the mechanisms and rationale of the lesser landholders' attendance changed more than the substance. As minor tenants-in-chief they were present at the council which settled the succession on Matilda in 1126, at the later assembly of 1176 where the Assize of Northampton was promulgated with their counsel, and no doubt at others too.[143] Their weight in the shires, and their probable importance as sources of opinion and information, provided reasons for their presence which would have been familiar to King Edgar or to Æthelred the Unready. But, beyond what was traditional, they now owed their summoning to the *consilium et auxilium* which, like all tenants-in-chief, they were duty-bound to provide.[144] No king would have been willing to forgo this, especially when some major act of state needed endorsement and publicity. Nor would he want to risk forfeiting his right to the reliefs, wardships, and marriages of these men, incidents

---

[139] J. B. Henneman, *Royal Taxation in Fourteenth-Century France: The Development of War Financing, 1322–1356* (Princeton, 1971), 10 n. 20; Reynolds, *Kingdoms and Communities*, 234–5.

[140] Above, 8–10. Cf. Gillingham, 'Thegns and Knights in Eleventh-Century England', 166–7.

[141] See e.g. *Anglo-Saxon Charters*, ed. Robertson, 150–3, for the role of thegns in the shire court.

[142] Above, 50–5.   [143] Above, 83–4.   [144] Above, 76–80.

of their tenure which might be fastened on them by their attendance and clear identification at councils.

If tenure defined these men as tenants-in-chief, their social standing and military role placed them in the large and as yet undifferentiated class of knights; and so they were known. The most crucial step towards their regular attendance in parliament was taken in 1215, when Magna Carta recognized the need for the presence of the lesser tenants, summoned via the sheriffs, when taxation was to be discussed at councils. What amounted to a prescription here was followed in at least some and probably all of those parliaments at which Henry III demanded taxes.[145] The further transition to the election of knights in the shires, and the consequent disappearance of the lesser tenants whom the elected knights replaced, came not so much with the false start of shire elections for the parliament of April 1254, important though that was as a precedent, but with the Montfortian parliaments of the 1260s, when specified numbers of knights were thrice summoned (1261, 1264, 1265) from the shires.[146] The sequence of these parliaments laid the basis for the shires' future representation; and at a time when taxation was not at issue, it showed the weight now attached to knightly opinion by drawing the knights into discussion of the more general business of the realm. Their renewed summoning to the parliaments of 1268–70 drew on the precedents of both 1254 and 1264–5 to establish what was to become the norm: the need for the consent of elected knights before taxation could be granted in parliament.[147]

The history of small landholders at central assemblies thus embodied both long continuities and significant changes. Knights were present at the Northampton council of 1176 and at the two Westminster parliaments of 1275,[148] but in different capacities. The lesser tenants-in-chief, summoned on a tenurial basis to offer the *consilium* which was originally their duty but later their right, and prominent after 1215 at tax parliaments, had given way to a more elite body of elected shire representatives. The early role of the sheriff in summoning the lesser tenants shows that the shire was in some senses the 'unit of attendance' even before the sheriff began to take responsibility for the conduct of shire elections and the return of shire representatives from the mid thirteenth century onwards. Here was another sort of continuity. No doubt the change to election, when it came,

[145] Above, 198–204.
[147] Above, 267–72.
[146] *DBM* 246–9, 292–3, 300–3; above, 251–60.
[148] Above, 83–4, 287, 289; *HBC* 545.

partly sprang from the inefficiencies of the old system, which gave the government little idea of the numbers and identity of those who might appear at parliament.[149] But it also marked an advantageous recognition by the crown that locally elected representatives could bind their constituents to the payment of taxes far more effectively than lesser tenants-in-thief who were merely the notional (and unauthorized) spokesmen for their own tenants and those below them.[150]

In this process a new notion of representation had emerged. The knights who sometimes attended the great councils of Norman and Angevin England were not in any formal sense representatives, except insofar as they could be regarded as standing for their own tenants. After 1215, when their presence in parliament was deemed necessary for the granting of taxes, this latter principle came more overtly to the fore. The *milites* who were among the other tenants-in-chief granting the king a thirtieth in the parliament of 1237 'on behalf of themselves and their villeins' were more directly representative, if only of their peasant tenants, than their twelfth-century predecessors had ever been.[151] The advent of national taxation had made the difference here. But the knights who were summoned in 1254 'in place of each and all in their counties', in 1264 'for the whole county', and in 1265 and 1275 'for the community of the county', were still more explicitly representative but in a very different sense.[152] They stood not for atomized and dispersed groups of rural tenants, but for geographical units which were also communities. We may stress the continuity of the small-landholder presence at central assemblies while still believing that the representation of counties by elected knights marked a turning point.

Two currents met here: the relatively new, post-1215, need for broad consent to taxation, and the more ancient and gradual evolution of the shire. If representation was to be geographical rather than tenurial, then the shire was its natural and obvious basis. Long a social as well as an administrative unit, and finding a focus in its court, the shire by the late twelfth century was already coming to be represented by its knights, though at first in a judicial rather than political context. As we have seen, if an action was removed from the shire to the royal court, it was a posse of

---

[149] Maddicott, ' "An Infinite Multitude of Nobles" ', 38–9.
[150] Cf. Carpenter, 'Beginnings of Parliament', 400–3.
[151] Stubbs, *Select Charters*, 358; above, 200–1, 207.
[152] Ibid., 365–6; *DBM* 292–3; Edwards, '*Plena Potestas*', 136–7; above, 212, 289.

shire knights who bore the record to Westminster,[153] while in 1194, a little after Glanvill had borne witness to this practice, three knights were to be elected in each shire to keep the pleas of the crown.[154] By this time the knights were beginning to bargain with the crown on behalf of their shires for relief from burdens, a process that was to continue into Henry III's reign; while on two occasions under John knights from the counties were summoned to appear before the king, on one of those occasions at a general assembly.[155] The election of shire knights for parliament may have been a turning point, but it also marked a natural progression, determined by precedent: by the local duties imposed on knights by Angevin legal reforms, by the strengthening identification of knights with counties, and by their prior role as their counties' occasional political representatives.

The primacy of the shire and its gentry, first thegns, then knights, was one of the factors which differentiated England most sharply from continental states. Neither in France nor Spain did the shire have any close equivalent. Representation of a sort there was in the *parlement*, even political representation expressing itself through the voicing of grievances. But the groups represented were ad hoc and invariably brought together by region or lordship for some particular purpose: the viscount and nobles of Narbonnais (1278), 'the count of Champagne's men' (1281), 'many men from the mountains of the Auvergne' (1281), the towns and villages of Quercy (1281), the barons and nobles of Gevaudan (1308).[156] Beyond these temporary groupings, and in the countryside at least, there were no constant and stable units that could be represented. A similar conclusion could be drawn from the provincial leagues which rose against Philip IV's projected tax in 1314–15 and which again were generally organized by ancient regions and lordships: the duchy of Burgundy, the county of Champagne, the counties of Auxerre and Tonnerre with their counts, and so on.[157] With the protests of these loose and transient associations we might contrast the rejection by the county of Worcestershire of Edward I's demand for a

---

[153] *Glanvill*, ed. Hall, 98–9, 102; Pollock and Maitland, *History of English Law*, i. 536; Poole, *Obligations of Society*, 54–5.

[154] Stubbs, *Select Charters*, 254; Bisson, *Crisis of the Twelfth Century*, 393; above, 136–7.

[155] Maddicott, 'Magna Carta and the Local Community', 25–40; above, 137–8.

[156] Bisson, 'Consultative Functions', 87, 89–90. Groups given in inverted commas appear in that form in the original record; groups lacking inverted commas are given in the forms used by Bisson.

[157] E. A. R. Brown, 'Reform and Resistance to Royal Authority in Fourteenth-Century France: The Leagues of 1314–1315', in her *Politics and Institutions in Capetian France* (Aldershot, 1991), v. 113–14, 117, 121, 128–9.

tax in 1297. This was almost certainly the work of a shire court that
had enjoyed a continuous existence since at least the reign of Cnut some
250 years earlier.[158] Nor was there any unit larger than the shire. Both
before and after 1066 earldoms and baronies crossed shire boundaries in the
distribution of their lands and in the allegiances they attracted, while the
courts of different shires might occasionally come together to do justice.[159]
But neither development resulted in the formation of supra-shires which
might stand comparison with Champagne or Burgundy. And there was a
further difference. Within the shire the gentry had an administrative role,
as sheriffs, jurors, assessors and collectors of taxes, and commissioners of
every kind, which made them part-time royal servants but also identified
them firmly with their local communities. Both France and the Iberian
kingdoms, as well as Germany and Scotland, had their lesser nobilities, but
they neither participated so actively in the government of the state nor
bonded so closely with a defined rural locality as did the English gentry; and
they were as likely to be found residing in the town as in the country.[160]
These differences were the marks of societies in which state power and the
administrative patterns which it created had made a much fainter imprint
on the countryside than was the case in England.

  Hence in these countries the most serviceable unit of representation was
the town. Like the shire, it was a demarcated community, organized in such
a way as to facilitate the dispatch of representatives and delegates to central
assemblies. English towns resembled this model in more ways than one. By
the early thirteenth century the leading towns had acquired a governing
structure of mayors, councils, and officials; many enjoyed chartered liberties;
and some were militarily formidable.[161] If their forces lacked the weight
of those of some of the Spanish towns, nurtured through the wars of
the Reconquista,[162] they might nevertheless be called out on the king's

[158] Above, 314–15. For what is probably the first appearance of the Worcestershire shire court in the surviving records, see Cnut's writ to 'Bishop Leofsige and Earl Hakon and Leofric the sheriff and all the thegns in Worcestershire': *Anglo-Saxon Writs*, ed. Harmer, 227.

[159] Baxter, *Earls of Mercia*, 62–71, 85–9, 266–9; D. Crouch, *William Marshal: Knighthood, War and Chivalry, 1147–1219*, 2nd edn. (London, 2002), 148–51. For the assembling together of separate shire courts, see e.g. *English Lawsuits*, ed. van Caenegem, i. 44–5.

[160] M. Jones (ed.), *Gentry and Lesser Nobility in Late Medieval Europe* (Gloucester, 1986), 11, 119–30, 169–73, 210–12; Gillingham, 'Thegns and Knights in Eleventh-Century England', 166.

[161] J. Campbell, 'Power and Authority, 600–1300', in D. M. Palliser (ed.), *The Cambridge Urban History of Britain*, i: *600–1540* (Cambridge, 2000), 64–5, 69–72. For the military role of towns, see also Powicke, *Military Obligation*, 45–6, 51–2, 84–6, 122–3.

[162] O'Callaghan, *Cortes of Castile-León*, 165, 193–4; S. Barton, *The Aristocracy in Twelfth-Century León and Castile* (Cambridge, 1997), 34–5, 106.

campaigns. But although they were far from being negligible quantities, large differences separated them from their continental counterparts and do much to explain why they failed to take a parallel course towards early representation in central assemblies. Unlike most Spanish and some French towns, they had no jurisdictional control over large hinterlands, but were instead, in Professor David Palliser's felicitous phrase, 'small islands set in the royal sea of the shires'.[163] Despite their internal organization and their charters, they lacked independence and most were firmly under the authority of the crown.[164] Like the structure of the shire, their subordinate status was an inheritance from the pre-Conquest past, in their case going back ultimately to the king's role in the founding and ordering of the late ninth- and tenth-century burhs. That for much of the twelfth and thirteenth centuries the towns could be tallaged at the king's will was a mark of their subjection, and one which for a time set them apart from the shires. Until the 1290s it was the landed classes, the magnates and shire knights, whose grants or refusals of taxation usually triggered the levying of tallage from the towns.[165] When, from the 1290s, the towns began regularly to elect their own representatives for parliament, it was the sheriff, the king's agent in the shire, who chose the towns to be so represented.[166] In terms of its political weight, the shire took precedence over the town at every point. Its antiquity, its fundamental role in English local government, and the existence of its court as the hub of an administrative and social community, all gave the shire a dominance among English local institutions which the town could not rival.

Despite what we might see as the inferiority of towns to shires, from the time of their regular summoning to parliament English towns contributed substantially to a web of local representation that was denser than that found in other European states. The election of men for both town and country

---

[163] D. M. Palliser, 'Towns and the English State, 1066–1500', in Maddicott and Palliser (eds.), *The Medieval State*, 134.

[164] Ibid. 136–8; Campbell, 'Power and Authority', 73.

[165] C. Stephenson, *Borough and Town: A Study of Urban Origins in England* (Cambridge, Mass., 1933), 160–6; Mitchell, *Taxation*, 321–32; Campbell, 'Power and Authority', 62–3. For the tallage of 1226–7, following the levy on moveables of 1225, see Mitchell, *Studies in Taxation*, 171–3; for that of 1238, following the levy on moveables of 1237, ibid. 319–20; for a tallage levied in 1252, after the possible refusal of a levy on moveables, see *CR, 1251–3*, 212–13, and below, 467–8. The taxation of towns in the thirteenth century is much in need of investigation.

[166] McKisack, *Parliamentary Representation*, 16–18; J. F. Willard, 'Taxation Boroughs and Parliamentary Boroughs, 1294–1336', in J. G. Edwards, V. H. Galbraith, and E. F. Jacob (eds.), *Historical Essays in Honour of James Tait* (Manchester, 1933), 426–8.

created in effect a double layer of representation unknown elsewhere. This was reflected in the numbers of those returned to parliament. Edward I's opening parliament in April 1275, attended by some 148 knights and perhaps by about 600 burgesses, may have been quite exceptional; but the number of towns represented at Edward's other parliaments remained high, to judge by the surviving returns. It averaged some eighty-six, dropping to about seventy in the next reign.[167] Even little Dorset, to descend to the micro level, returned two knights and ten burgesses from five towns to the York parliament of May 1322.[168] A full turnout of clerical representatives—cathedral dignitaries, archdeacons, and proctors of the cathedral and local clergy—when these were wanted, would have added another 148 to the tally of 'members of parliament'.[169] There is much room for error in these calculations, not least because we are better informed about numbers due or summoned than about numbers attending. But we may not be far out if we reckon the commons' attendance in a 'full' Edwardian parliament to have comprised about 70 shire knights, 160 burgesses, and perhaps 120 clergy, some 350 in all; and this, of course, excludes another hundred or so magnates and prelates.

Comparable figures for continental assemblies are hard to come by. But few can have been larger than Philip IV's great convocation in Tours in 1308 for the condemnation of the Templars, which Bisson reckons may have been attended by 'possibly a thousand persons'. The largest known assemblies of French towns in our period occurred in 1316, when some 227 were summoned to regional assemblies meeting in at least three places: more than double the number known to have been summoned to any other meeting before 1328.[170] Across the Pyrenees, in Castile-León, perhaps as many as 130 towns took part in the cortes of Valladolid of 1295, and one hundred towns sent 201 representatives to that of Burgos in 1315, probably the largest Castilian assembly of the period.[171] If these numbers seem quite large, we need to remember that they came together relatively infrequently. There were only three central assemblies involving towns in Philip IV's reign; and in the century between 1250 and 1350 there were

---

[167] Maddicott, 'Edward I and the Lessons of Baronial Reform', 14–15; McKisack, *Parliamentary Representation*, 11, 25.

[168] *Return of Members*, 64.   [169] Denton, 'The Clergy and Parliament', 91–2; above, 323.

[170] Bisson, 'General Assemblies', 97; C. H. Taylor, 'Assemblies of French Towns in 1316', *Speculum*, 14 (1939), 287.

[171] O'Callaghan, *Cortes of Castile-León*, 53–4. T. F. Ruiz, 'Oligarchy and Royal Power: The Castilian Cortes and the Castilian Crisis, 1248–1350', *Parliaments, Estates and Representation*, 2 (1982), 97.

only some fifty-seven meetings of the Castilian cortes, compared with about 140 meetings of the English parliament.[172]

If a little more than impressionistic, comparisons can hardly be rigidly statistical. But by whatever standards we may attempt to measure the depth of representation, whether by the ratio of representatives to population or to land area, or by the relative frequency of assemblies in different countries, it seems almost certain that England would score more highly than its closest comparators. Still more certainly, a greater variety of interests, greater and lesser landed, urban and clerical, were represented in English assemblies, The result was the enlargement and energizing of an already broad and vigorous channel of communications between king and subjects: up to Westminster went petitions, complaints, local opinion, and news (forces rarely revealed in the sources), and on occasion the *plena potestas* needed for local representatives to consent to taxation; down to town and county passed statutes, orders, other news, royal opinion, and royal propaganda. From parliamentary representation came a more closely integrated state.

5. Nobles as Taxpayers

One of the distinctive strengths of the English parliament thus lay in the part played by multiple local representatives as mediators between the crown and the localities. Another, equally distinctive, lay in the common interests which, for much of the time, allied those representatives with their parliamentary superiors, the prelates and the magnates: an alliance which bridged social and political divisions and which was much rarer in the estates and assemblies of continental Europe. Some of the general factors underlying this association will be suggested in the next section, but one particular reason is worth separate discussion. It lies in the subjection of the English nobility, like all the king's subjects, to royal taxes. Setting them apart from most continental nobles, who to some degree or other enjoyed exemption from taxes, the magnates' tax liabilities here helped to shape the whole development of parliament in the later middle ages and beyond. Their obligation to pay gave them an abiding

---

[172] Ruiz, 'Oligarchy and Royal Power', 96–7. The figures for England derive from *HBC* 538–61; Maddicott, 'Crusade Taxation', 117; and the list of parliaments, 1235–57, below, 455–72.

interest in the institution and processes through which taxation was granted and in the policies which it was intended to support, so linking the magnates to other 'parliamentarians'. Already apparent under Henry III, this community of interest was brought more fully into the limelight by the heavy taxation of Edward I's later years. But earlier still, from the turn of the twelfth century, taxation had begun to play a determining part in the evolution of parliament, and it was in this earlier period that the magnates' status as taxpayers, with no rights of exemption, first became clear.

How did this situation come about? It was in no way preordained, and for nearly a century it looked as if England would share in an emerging pan-European pattern of noble exemptions. Just as England was the first western state after the collapse of the Carolingian empire to impose general taxes, in the form of geld, so it was one of the first to offer partial exemption to the nobility. We have already noted the introduction of this privilege. In the thirty years or so after the Conquest, the demesne manors of the tenants-in-chief benefited from sweeping reductions in their geld liability. In some cases it was wiped out altogether.[173] Symptomatic of the crown's 'very lax attitude towards tenants-in-chief', these concessions far outdid any available in pre-Conquest England, where, for example, even the great earls had paid geld.[174] Henry I's undertaking in his coronation charter to free from geld the demesne lands of knights holding by military service, in order to allow them to equip themselves better for the king's service, seemed to hold out the prospect of similar concessions to an inferior social group.[175] Neither the demesne exemptions of the tenants-in-chief, however, nor the privileges of the fighting knights were to last (if indeed the latter were ever effective at all). But they were replaced by frequent and piecemeal individual exemptions from geld, granted to some nobles, some monastic houses, some officials, and some undertenants.[176] Important as a form of royal patronage, these continued during the final stages of the geld's levying in Henry II's early years. These latter-day exemptions were on a substantial scale. Dr Emilie Amt reckons that about 20 per cent of the 1156 levy was pardoned, and the beneficiaries included some great men, among them William, King Stephen's surviving son, and William, earl of

---

[173] Harvey, 'Taxation and the Economy', 259–63; J. A. Green, *The Aristocracy of Norman England* (Cambridge, 1997), 229–30.
[174] Harvey, 'Taxation and the Economy', 264; Baxter, *Earls of Mercia*, 106–9.
[175] Stubbs, *Select Charters*, 119; Green, 'Last Century', 246.   [176] Green, 'Last Century', 246–53.

Gloucester.[177] Except in the case of the concessions made to the military
knights by Henry I, these exemptions remained a personal privilege and
not one arising from rank. Here they differed, as we shall see, from later
exemptions conferred on continental nobilities. They had nevertheless a
far from negligible effect on the crown's fiscal resources.

Practice changed sharply when large-scale direct taxation began again,
with Henry II's Saladin Tithe of 1188 and the levies for Richard I's ransom
in 1193–4. No provision was then made for either collective or individual
exemption. The only exceptions were for those who themselves took the
cross in 1188; exempt from payment, they were also allowed to keep the
tithe from their lands.[178] The universality of these obligations is hardly
surprising. Onerous and bitterly resented though both were, each had a
defensible justification: the Saladin Tithe in moral and canonical terms as
a tax for the crusade, the ransom levy as one of the three gracious aids
to which any lord *in extremis* was entitled to expect from his men.[179] Less
predictable was the similarly inclusive nature of the subsequent general
taxes which lacked these justifications. For the carucage of 1198, a land tax
reminiscent of the earlier geld, specific arrangements were made for the
taxation of baronial lands, using information provided by the magnates'
stewards and by the lords and bailiffs of vills.[180] The thirteenth of 1207
was still more explicitly comprehensive. It was to be paid 'by every
layman of all England from the fee of whomsoever he may be', with
stewards and bailiffs testifying to the value of their masters' revenues and
moveables.[181] Nothing suggests that there were exemptions from either
of these levies. Indeed, had noble exemptions been at all widespread,
it is unlikely that controls on direct taxation would have featured so
prominently in Magna Carta.[182]

Once established, the same pattern of socially all-embracing levies, with
the absence of exemption remaining the general rule, persisted through

---

[177] Ibid. 251; E. Amt, *The Accession of Henry II in England* (Woodbridge, 1993), 60–1, 75–6, 136–7,
174–5. Amt finds more examples of late exemptions than does Green. Cf. S. M. Christelow, 'The
Fiscal Management of England under Henry I', in D. F. Fleming and J. Pope (eds.), *Henry I and the
Anglo-Norman World: Studies in Memory of C. Warren Hollister*, Haskins Soc. Jnl., Special Volume, 17
(Woodbridge, 2006), 166–70.
[178] Howden, *Gesta Regis Henrici*, ii. 31; Mitchell, *Taxation*, 119.
[179] Baldwin, *Masters, Princes and Merchants*, i. 219–20; Tyerman, *England and the Crusades*, 75–9;
Magna Carta, cap. 5: Holt, *Magna Carta*, 454–5; Stenton, *First Century*, 173–5.
[180] Howden, *Chronica*, iv. 46–7; Mitchell, *Taxation*, 129–31.
[181] Stubbs, *Select Charters*, 278; Carpenter, 'The Second Century of English Feudalism', 63.
[182] Above, 124–5.

the few direct taxes collected under Henry III and the more numerous levies taken by his son and grandson. One particular group among the nobility, those serving in royal armies, were very occasionally exempted, as we shall see; but the only class exempted with any regularity were the poor, who from 1237 often benefited from the establishment of a taxable minimum of goods.[183] If the magnates enjoyed certain tax advantages, none amounted to a group privilege. Perhaps most specifically helpful to them was the crown's abandonment of the direct taxation of revenues after 1207, and its restriction henceforward to moveables alone; for nobles were more likely than others to draw the income from rents which was now in effect exempted.[184] And if there was no personal exemption, there were at least exempt goods, listed in the schedules for most taxes. Yet these schedules usually distinguished only between the goods of freemen and villeins, and did no more than recognize the right of all men to their *contenementa* and *wainagia*, the goods essential for the maintenance of their status and livelihood.[185] Only from 1290 were the armour, horses, jewels, and robes of 'knights [presumably including magnates], gentlemen and their wives' singled out for special exemption.[186] There was not much here to qualify the basic principle of the subjection of the nobility to tax.

From the late twelfth century onwards this principle began to distinguish English practice quite sharply from that of other countries.[187] Already in the late eleventh and early twelfth centuries the *caballeros villanos* of Castile and León, the commoner knights of the frontier, were beginning to secure individual exemptions from taxation on the grounds of their military service. They were perhaps a group not unlike the fighting knights who received a similar privilege for similar services in Henry I's coronation charter. The *caballeros hidalgos*, the nobles, were already exempt. Able to claim a share of the taxes collected within their lordships, they appear to have been exempt too from the *servicios*, the direct taxes brought in

[183] Stubbs, *Select Charters*, 358–9, 422; Willard, *Parliamentary Taxes*, 87–92. There were other very minor exemptions: e.g. the moneyers of London and Canterbury and, under Edward II, a very few individuals, mainly London citizens: Willard, *Parliamentary Taxes*, 117–18, 120–2.

[184] Mitchell, *Taxation*, 115, 118–20, 124, 134.

[185] Stubbs, *Select Charters*, 352, 356, 358; Mitchell, *Taxation*, 139, 143, 145–6, 148; Jurkowski, Smith, and Crook, *Lay Taxes*, 12–13, 16, 20–1; Willard, *Parliamentary Taxes*, 77–81; *Lancashire Lay Subsidies*, ed. Vincent, 93; J. Tait, 'Studies in Magna Carta: 1, Waynagium and Contenementum', *EHR* 27 (1912), 720–8.

[186] *Lancashire Lay Subsidies*, ed. Vincent, 178; Willard, *Parliamentary Taxes*, 77.

[187] M. Bush, *Noble Privilege* (Manchester, 1983), 27–64, provides a general survey of fiscal privilege throughout Europe, but should be used cautiously.

by Alfonso X of Castile in the mid thirteenth century.[188] In Portugal, the commoner-knights received a similar exemption in return for their service, while the nobility were exempted from the tax granted in 1261 in exchange for the maintenance of an undebased coinage.[189] In Hungary, the upwardly mobile *servientes regis*, the king's direct dependents, who were soon to merge with the nobility, gained exemption by the Golden Bull of 1222. Although this privilege was soon overridden by the crown, it was reinstated in 1351, when the nobility secured a general exemption through their obligation to provide military service.[190] In Denmark and Sweden, service also exempted the lands of the nobility from tax, though in Norway only demesne lands were so privileged, while tenant land continued to be taxed.[191] In Brandenburg the same principle began to be applied from 1283: a proportion of a knight's demesne lands was exempt in return for service.[192]

France was the late developer here, largely because the introduction of general taxation came later than in other states, for reasons already discussed.[193] But from the time of its inception in the 1290s, to meet the costs of Philip IV's wars, the nobility began to claim the same privileges as their peers elsewhere. In return for agreeing to the levy of 1295, the duke of Burgundy was given half the proceeds from taxation on his lands. The southern French nobility objected to being taxed in 1297, partly on the grounds that they had already done military service against the English. In 1304 the nobility of Toulouse would agree to pay taxes only if they were exempted from service. These piecemeal negotiations and concessions continued into the early phases of the Hundred Years War, later to be swept up and superseded by the much more wholesale exemptions from the *taille* and the *aides* which followed at the end of the fourteenth century.[194] The consequent indifference of the French nobility towards tax-granting representative institutions has been seen as a main cause of the decline of the French estates, on which Fortescue's remarks, cited earlier, stand as a direct

[188] E. Lourie, 'A Society Organized for War: Medieval Spain', *Past and Present*, 35 (1966), 55–7; Procter, *Curia and Cortes*, 190–1; O'Callaghan, *Cortes of Castile-León*, 134–5, 149–50; Barton, *Aristocracy in Twelfth-Century León and Castile*, 34–5, 106.

[189] H. V. Livermore, *A New History of Portugal* (Cambridge, 1967), 68–9, 82.

[190] M. Rady, *Nobility, Land and Service in Medieval Hungary* (Basingstoke, 2000), 35–9, 144–6.

[191] B. and P. Sawyer, *Medieval Scandinavia* (Minneapolis, 1993), 92.

[192] F. L. Carsten, *The Origins of Prussia* (Oxford, 1954), 24–5, 77.   [193] Above, 402–5.

[194] Strayer and Taylor, *Studies in Early French Taxation*, 47, 52–3, 67–8; Henneman, *Royal Taxation*, 316–18; id., 'Nobility, Privilege and Fiscal Politics in Late Medieval France', *French Historical Studies*, 13 (1983), 1–17, esp. 14–17; id., 'France in the Middle Ages', 116–17.

comment. The similar privileges of the Castilian nobility have supplied a similar explanation for the weakness of the late medieval cortes.[195]

The common factor in these cases, often underlying exemptions even when not directly invoked, was the generally held belief that military service should leave its performers exempt from taxes. The vassal's duty to provide *auxilium* meant either service or money, but not both. It was here that English practice sometimes converged with that of other states. Yet the convergence was never very close, for in England the link between service and exemption was no more than haphazard and occasional. It was seemingly first demonstrated at the great council of March 1232, when the earl of Chester, speaking for the lay tenants-in-chief, refused Henry III a tax. They owed the king no *auxilium*, he said, because they had served on the earlier French campaign (in 1230) which had occasioned the debts for whose payment the tax was now demanded.[196] But his justification for refusing cannot be taken entirely at face value, for at a later council in September Henry was granted the tax. It was given for the same ends and assessed even on those who had served.[197] Early refusal and later grant had much more to do with the magnates' initial hostility towards Henry's policies, reversed by their subsequent approval for his dismissal in July of his unpopular justiciar Hubert de Burgh, than with the pretext of special claims for exemption.[198] Less equivocal in its implications was the famous episode of 1254, when the tenants-in-chief and twenty-librate holders called up for that year's projected Gascon campaign were exempted from the tax needed to support them. This was to be paid by those who stayed at home—the majority of the population. But in the event there was no campaign and no tax.[199] Equally clear was the principle employed for Edward I's Welsh campaign in 1283, when the magnates serving with the king as a consequence of their tenure were exempted from the thirtieth raised for the campaign's support, while those serving for pay were taxed.[200] But the principle never struck root in the more numerous campaigns of

---

[195] P. S. Lewis, 'The Failure of the French Medieval Estates', *Past and Present*, 23 (1962), 12–13; id., *Later Medieval France* (London, 1968), 366–7; A. Mackay, *Spain in the Middle Ages* (Basingstoke, 1977), 154.

[196] Wendover, *Chronica*, iv. 233; above, 176–7.

[197] e.g. the earl of Albemarle and Richard de Percy, both tenants-in-chief, had served in France but did not thereby escape taxation (despite, it must be said, their protestations and initial resistance): Sanders, *Feudal Military Service in England*, 122, 124; Mitchell, *Studies in Taxation*, 200–5, 387.

[198] Cf. Carpenter, 'Fall of Hubert de Burgh', 50, 58; Vincent, *Peter des Roches*, 287, 321–2.

[199] Above, 210–16.   [200] *Parl. Writs*, I. 12.

the 1290s. Between 1294 and 1296 a number of those serving in Gascony and Wales were exempted from the three subsidies levied during those years. The exemption was far from universal, however, and was abandoned after 1296, from which time service brought no exemption.[201] In any case not all thirteenth-century taxes could sustain such grounds for privilege, since not all were linked with campaigns. In 1237, 1275, and 1290 they were granted for the relief of the king's general financial needs: a purpose which allowed no obvious claims to exemption.[202] Though exemption in exchange for service might sporadically be permitted, neither this practice nor the military reasons for taxation were regular and consistent enough to create the steady set of precedents needed for the emergence of any general principle of exemption.

Why did the English nobility generally remain subject to the taxation which continental nobilities were often able to escape? Insofar as this question has been raised (surprisingly rarely), one answer in particular has usually been given: their subjection sprang from 'the overwhelming power of the English crown'.[203] Yet this will hardly do. At several points in the thirteenth century the power of the crown was far from overwhelming. In 1215, 1258, 1297, and 1300–1, opposition magnates, backed by knights, were able to impose reforming programmes on kings weakened by the strident discontents of their subjects. The power of the crown had brought about its limitation; yet nobles still paid taxes. A more covert and extended intrusion on the crown's authority was seen in the substantial reduction, between about 1190 and 1240, in the quotas of knight service owed by tenants-in-chief. Described by Professor Michael Prestwich as 'a major success for the magnates in their relationship with the crown', this was a kind of ad hoc class privilege, from which the greater barons were the main beneficiaries.[204] But despite these obvious demonstrations of magnate power, neither the victories of reform nor the winning of reduced military obligations was accompanied by any apparent pressure for tax exemption. In the Anglo-Norman period, on the other hand, before the age of the

---

[201] Willard, *Parliamentary Taxes*, 111–14.

[202] *Paris*, iii. 380–3; *Gervase of Canterbury*, ii. 281; *Rot. Parl.* i. 224; Prestwich, *Edward I*, 342–3.

[203] R. Stacey, 'Social Change in the Thirteenth Century. (a) Nobles and Knights', in D. Abulafia (ed.), *The New Cambridge Medieval History*, v. 18. Cf. Lewis, 'Failure of the French Medieval Estates', 12; Bush, *Noble Privilege*, 49. Ormrod, 'England in the Middle Ages', 45, notes the subjection of the nobility to direct taxation, but without comment.

[204] Prestwich, *Armies and Warfare*, 69–71; above, 128–30. Cf. Painter, *Studies in the English Feudal Barony*, 44: 'a magnificent baronial victory in a struggle the details of which have been lost to us'.

Charters and the restraints which it brought in, exemptions had been commonplace. The power of the crown will account for much in the early history of parliament; but not for the nobility's subjection to taxes.

A more plausible explanation lies, first, in the early imposition of direct taxes in circumstances where it could hardly be refused, and, secondly, in the simultaneous and later development of corporate consent. The first two major tax levies, after the hiatus which followed the last levy of geld in 1161–2, were taken in 1188 for Henry II's projected crusade and in 1193–4 for Richard I's ransom; and we have seen that they were, for different reasons, obligatory.[205] In the case of the ransom, the tenants of the king, that is, the baronial and knightly tenants-in-chief, would have had a more immediate obligation to pay than their own tenants. Direct taxes from which none were exempt created important precedents for the future. But more important still was the development of corporate consent. This began with the consent given to the Saladin Tithe and probably to the ransom tax, continued with the consent claimed by John (with whatever degree of speciousness) to the thirteenth of 1207,[206] and culminated in Magna Carta's demand for 'common counsel' before the taking of general aids, interpreted after 1215 as necessitating first conciliar and then parliamentary consent to direct taxation. Here was a new political principle. Thus established, the king's need for consent to taxation obviated the magnates' need for fiscal privilege, for which consent was in some ways a more valuable substitute. It opened up the possibility of a complete denial of taxation, from which all would benefit, and not merely the favoured few or those magnates performing military service. This possibility became a reality on at least ten occasions under Henry III, and probably on two occasions under Edward I and a further three under Edward II.[207]

Support for this thesis may be found both in the earlier history of geld and in the occasional claims for exemption from later direct taxes. Only very exceptionally, and then not certainly, had the levying of geld been subject to any form of consent. More usually, it was regarded as one of the crown's prerogatives, listed among the 'rights of the king' in the *Leges Henrici Primi*.[208] A specific exemption, whether of land in demesne or in favour of a particular beneficiary, was the only means to escape it. But with the levies on moveables, and initially on revenues, which superseded

---

[205] Above, 120, 419.   [206] Above, 125–6.

[207] Henry III: above, 173. Edward I, above, 288, 303, 323, 345. Edward II, above, 345, 357–8.

[208] *Leges Henrici Primi*, ed. Downer, 108–9; above, 103.

geld from the late twelfth century onwards, the principle of 'no consent, but exemption' gave way to that of 'consent, but no exemption'. The emergence of the latter principle is highlighted by the exceptions to it which prove the rule. In the best known of these cases, Peter des Roches, bishop of Winchester, refused to contribute to the scutage of 1217—which was in effect a general tax and one granted by the great council—on the grounds that he had not consented to it ('nunquam concessit nec assensum praebuit').[209] His claim was followed by a trickle of similar ones, mainly from the clergy, mainly before 1230, and mainly for exemption from types of tax other than the general aids for which the Charter had legislated.[210] To escape taxation the individual must therefore register his dissent from a corporate decision. Such dissent was, however, uncommon. Most prelates and magnates seem to have accepted from the start that corporate consent was binding on all—not only on the majority of the taxpaying population who had no claim to consent, but also on those of their own number who had the right to consent but for whatever reason had failed to give it. It had after all been stated in Magna Carta that the business of the great council should go forward even if not all those summoned were present. The implication was that decisions which bound those who had failed to appear might be taken in their absence and without their individual consent.[211]

One final episode is particularly significant in showing how the power of the great council to grant or deny national taxes might obviate the need for individuals to make their own claims. We have already referred several times to the earl of Chester's actions in bringing forward the prior military service of the tenants-in-chief as a reason for refusing Henry a tax at the council of March 1232. At one level his actions show that such service could provide at least the pretext for a claim to exemption, as has already been argued. But at another level the refusal of the tax indicates that the 'exemption' extended beyond the ranks of those who had served, to comprehend the whole body of taxpayers. Chester apparently did not consider claiming exemption merely for those serving personally: a claim which would have been in line with continental practice. Instead, he tacitly

---

[209] *PR 5 Henry III*, 21; Madox, *History and Antiquities of the Exchequer*, i. 675 and note q; Mitchell, *Studies in Taxation*, 127–8; Holt, *Magna Carta*, 399; Carpenter, 'Beginnings of Parliament', 400; Vincent, *Peter des Roches*, 150–1.

[210] Mitchell, *Studies in Taxation*, 386–8.

[211] Cap. 14: Holt, *Magna Carta*, 455. For discussion, see ibid. 322–3, 399–400, and Clarke, *Medieval Representation*, 256–9.

invoked the principle of conciliar consent to taxation, by now an established custom, in order to deny the king a tax altogether. He could do so because he spoke not only for the tenants-in-chief but, less directly, for the whole body of taxpayers who were bound to them in descending lines of tenurial relationships. With the weapon of the right to consent at his disposal he had no need to raise any narrower claim to individual exemption.

The early onset of consent to direct taxation, intermittently from 1188, consistently from 1207, thus does much to explain why the nobility did not press for the lesser privilege of tax exemption. But how far their personal obligation to pay taxes, once corporate consent had been given to them, affected their attitudes to the giving of that consent is a more difficult question. As our earlier chapters have shown, many different factors influenced the response of both magnates and knights to both Henry III's and Edward I's requests for taxation: from time to time, their recognition of the crown's financial needs, especially in wartime, but more often (and more particularly under Henry III) their disapproval of royal foreign policy, of the general oppressiveness of royal government, of royal extravagance, and of the wasting of previous taxes.[212] We might reasonably think that their private interests as taxpayers counted for much less. The restriction of direct taxes to moveable goods after 1207, exempting the revenues taxed earlier, limited the magnates' tax liabilities, and historians have generally agreed that they paid so little in taxation on their moveables as to leave their incomes barely affected.[213] Their social weight, and their ability to influence assessors and collectors, are likely to have meant that the yield from assessments already modest enough in relation to income was reduced still further at the collection stage. In any case direct taxes were very infrequent before the 1290s and unlikely to have had a serious effect on anyone's livelihood. The magnates' criticisms of royal policies and the tax demands often needed to support them, as recorded by Paris and other chroniclers, were naturally couched in terms of the public interest and the common good; and perhaps we should take their assertions largely at face value.

But we need not doubt the genuineness of these protestations and convictions to believe that financial self-interest also influenced their views.

---

[212] Above, 172–5, 211–14, 223, 288, 301, 304–7.

[213] e.g. Willard, *Parliamentary Taxes*, 162–4; Prestwich, *War, Politics and Finance*, 192; E. Miller, 'War, Taxation and the English Economy in the Late Thirteenth and Early Fourteenth Centuries', in J. M. Winter (ed.), *War and Economic Development: Essays in Memory of David Joslin* (Cambridge, 1975), 15–16; Ormrod, 'England in the Middle Ages', 45–6.

When Henry was refused a tax in March 1232, it was the poverty resulting from the magnates' service in France, as well as the service itself, that Chester invoked in order to justify their refusal.[214] Taxes may have been uncommon for much of the thirteenth century, but Henry III sought them more often than he received them. Regularly parried in parliament, the threat of taxation to magnate incomes was more frequent than its realization, and it may have played a part in shaping attitudes. Such grants as there were may not have had the negligible effect usually supposed. By this time most noble estates were managed directly, to produce an income from sales on the market rather than from the money rents left untaxed after 1207. In these circumstances a tax on moveables, falling as it did largely on the value of saleable corn and livestock, may have struck relatively hard. The twelfth of 1296 cost the earl of Cornwall as much as 10 per cent of net income on manors whose receipts came from agricultural sales, but only about 2 per cent or less on those contrasting manors whose income derived largely from rents and the profits of lordship.[215] The shift from direct management towards the leasing of the demesnes, which was occurring on many great estates in the years around 1300, may have had the lord's wish to avoid direct taxation as a contributory factor;[216] and it is undeniable that the general leasing of demesnes which marked the agrarian regime of the fourteenth century left magnate rentiers with a smaller tax bill and peasant lessees with a larger one.[217]

But probably much more important in determining baronial attitudes towards taxation were its effects on the resources of the peasantry and hence indirectly on those of the barons themselves. Since two-thirds to three-quarters of England's taxable wealth was in peasant hands, 'the interest that every lord possessed in preventing his peasants being exploited by anyone other than himself' must have been an unspoken element in baronial calculations whenever taxes were discussed in parliament.[218] Occasionally it came to the surface. It may have been extreme circumstances that led

---

[214] '. . . quod comites, barones ac milites, qui de eo tenebant in capite, cum ipso erant ibi corporaliter praesentes, et pecuniam suam ita inaniter effuderunt, quod inde pauperes recesserunt . . .': Wendover, *Chronica*, iv. 233.

[215] Miller, 'War, Taxation', 15–16.

[216] E. Miller and J. Hatcher, *Medieval England: Rural Society and Economic Change, 1086–1348* (London, 1978), 234–9, for a general survey. Cf. Maddicott, *The English Peasantry*, 7.

[217] Ormrod, 'England in the Middle Ages', 45–6.

[218] *Rolls of the Fifteenth and Rolls of the Fortieth*, ed. F. A. Cazel and A. P. Cazel (PRS, New Ser. XLV, 1983), p. x; Carpenter, 'English Peasants in Politics, 1258–67', 341 (the source of the quotation).

the abbot of Malmesbury to complain in 1340 that his tenants had been so impoverished by the extortions of those collecting the levies on moveables that they could no longer render their rents and services; for the complaint came during a period of excessively oppressive taxation.[219] But even in more normal times the same considerations can be detected. In 1283, when magnates performing feudal military service in Wales were exempted from that year's levy, the same exemption applied to their villeins. This was only a partial relief, however, intended to cover the lords' property which the villeins constituted; the free tenants, not part of that property, were to pay.[220] When taxes were levied lords may occasionally have been able to protect their tenants, both free and villein, in less formal ways. For the fortieth of 1232, for example, the sums due from tenants were to be assessed by local juries under the supervision of county knights. But the lords' stewards and bailiffs were authorized to collect the taxes, creating perhaps a little elbow-room for alleviation.[221] For the most part, however, it was impossible to shield peasant tenants from royal taxes.

It was here that the contrast with continental conditions was particularly marked. In most continental states the tax exemptions enjoyed by nobles left them better placed to safeguard the interests of their men. Nowhere was this more true than in France. From the time when regular taxation began in the 1290s the French nobility sought with some success to protect their peasants and vassals from taxes. In 1300, for example, those enjoying rights of high justice were allowed to supervise the collection of that year's levy on their lands, and in the provincial charters which the nobility won from the crown in 1314–15 they were able to insist that their rear-vassals should not be taxed. Similar concessions marked the early stages of the Hundred Years War, when the subjects of important lords in Languedoc in 1338 and in Champagne in 1339 were given exemption from the payment of taxes.[222] In thirteenth-century Castile too the vassals of nobles were exempt from taxation; it was an exception when, in 1269, the nobility in the cortes agreed to the payment of *servicios* on behalf of their men.[223] In Denmark and Sweden the tenanted lands of those performing military

[219] *CPR, 1338–40*, 435–6; Maddicott, *The English Peasantry*, 23, 45–50, 71.
[220] *Parl. Writs*, I. 12; above, 422. Cf. Willard, *Parliamentary Taxes*, 111–13, 165–7, for other examples from the 1290s.
[221] *CR, 1231–34*, 155–6; Mitchell, *Studies in Taxation*, 203–4; Carpenter, 'Beginnings of Parliament', 399–400.
[222] Strayer and Taylor, *Studies in Early French Taxation*, 54, 88; Henneman, 'Nobility, Privilege', 3–4.
[223] Procter, *Curia and Cortes*, 191.

service, as well as their own demesnes, were exempt; while, further south, the Hungarian nobility pressed consistently for the reduction or abolition of taxes falling on their peasant tenants.[224] The point made much later by one of the deputies to the French Estates General of 1484 'that it was from the peasantry that the clergy and nobility derived all their living and that it was in their own interest to resist the taxation of the people' would have been recognized throughout much of Europe from the thirteenth century onwards.[225] The absence of noble tax exemption in England meant that it was here that resistance was least possible. The seigneurial desideratum of a protected peasantry could be achieved only by the outright refusal of taxes in parliament.

Even though the nobility's attitude towards taxation may have been largely shaped by politics, there remains a case for saying that taxation was also a matter of personal concern to them. If much of that case has to be inferred for Henry III's reign, it becomes altogether better evidenced in the 1290s. The new levies then imposed to support Edward I's wars went beyond direct taxation in the severity and social breadth of their consequences. As we have seen, the maltolt imposed on wool exports between 1294 and1297 lowered the price of wool to all home producers, noble and peasant; while the crown's arbitrary prises of corn and livestock, though falling mainly on the peasantry, are likely to have had a secondary impact on their lords.[226] Since any losses which these levies brought were indirect, even privilege could not have saved the nobility from their effects. When the prelates, magnates, and gentry came together in the Remonstrances of 1297 to complain about the impoverishment resulting from the maltolt, prises, and taxes of all kinds, their case may have been exaggerated, but it cannot be dismissed as mere special pleading.[227] During these years the fall in wool prices alone, the sufferers from which included Roger Bigod, earl of Norfolk, amounted to some 24 per cent;[228] while the levies on moveables, taken in every year from 1294 to 1297, had never been more frequent or more sharply felt. It is an interesting reflection both of the burdens imposed on the magnates by these taxes and of their self-interested concern for their tenants' resources, that when they met at

---

[224] Sawyer and Sawyer, *Medieval Scandinavia*, 92; Rady, *Nobility, Land and Service*, 145.

[225] Lewis, 'Failure of the French Medieval Estates', 12 (Lewis's paraphrase of the original source); id., *Later Medieval France*, 282.

[226] Maddicott, *The English Peasantry*, 15–34, 60.

[227] Prestwich, *Docs. Illustrating*, 115–17; above, 302.   [228] Miller, 'War, Taxation', 14.

Montgomery in the spring of 1297 to concert their opposition to Edward's demand for service in Flanders, they went so far as to list the levies already imposed and to note that they fell on their villeins as well as themselves.[229] We should take seriously the more particular complaints of the earl of Warwick that his poverty prevented his serving in Flanders and of the earl of Arundel that he was unable to find the money to raise men for the same campaign.[230] That the nobility took the lead in the parliaments of the 1290s in opposing Edward's wartime measures was not only due to their position as the natural leaders of the political community and to their constitutional objections to the arbitrary nature of Edward's impositions. It also owed something, perhaps much, to their personal experience of the effects of excessive taxation on their own fortunes—and to their inability to claim exemption.

The payment of taxes by the nobility continued to be a peculiar feature of the English political system long after the close of our period. While continental nobilities assumed or were granted increasingly broad rights of exemption, the English nobility remained bound by the precedents established in the Saladin Tithe of 1188 and the ransom levy of 1193–4. The occasional later exemptions for military service hardly perturbed the general picture. This influenced the evolution of parliament in two particular ways. First, if we are right in thinking that corporate consent to taxation developed early enough to forestall any claims to tax privileges and to make them less necessary, then the absence of those privileges strengthened and underpinned one of the central features of the early English parliament. Had there been extensive individual exemptions from the Saladin Tithe and other early levies on moveables, following the pattern of geld exemptions established under the Anglo-Norman kings, the principle of corporate consent might never have developed.

Secondly, the obligation of the nobility to pay taxes gave them an interest which was more than purely political or constitutional in considering, questioning, and, under Henry III, often rejecting the crown's demands

---

[229] '. . . dixerunt omnes una voce se nullo modo facere aut posse . . . tum propter tricesimam, vicesimam, quintam decimam, duodecimam, decimam, necnon et sextam et quintam partem omnium bonorum suorum ac nativorum [quas] totiens ab eis extorserat': Denton, 'The Crisis of 1297', 576. The list presumably refers to the thirtieth of 1283, the fifteenth of 1290, the twelfth of 1296, the tenth and urban sixth of 1294, and the clerical fifth of 1296–7. The reference to the twentieth applies to no known levy. For a list of taxes for the period, see Ormrod, 'State-Building and State Finance', 18–19.
[230] Prestwich, Docs. Illustrating, 6, 141–2.

for taxes. In Henry's reign that interest may have been limited by the infrequency of royal taxes and by the relatively small direct burden which they imposed on wealthy payers. The impact of taxation on peasant tenants, however, may have had a larger if secondary effect on their lords; or so those lords, in debating royal requests for taxation, may have foreseen. We need to remember that other fiscal levies, such as rising shire farms and the penalties imposed by the eyre,[231] were also bearing down on peasant resources in the years before 1258, and presumably on their rent-paying capacities too. In what could be crudely seen as a competition between king and lords for the wealth of the peasantry, each side had certain advantages: the king's lay in the possession of some unassailable fiscal prerogatives, such as the right to profit from justice; the lords', in their control of the king's access to direct taxes. In the 1290s, during the period of Edward I's wars, these tensions grew, as the income of both lords and peasants came under more pressure from royal taxation than ever before. When taxation was debated, whether under Henry or under Edward, those with the power to grant or deny it often presented their arguments in familiar constitutional and political terms. This was no mere façade. But lurking behind the projection of a public case was the basic fact that lords and their tenants paid taxes. If throughout western Europe in the years around 1200 'celebratory consensus' gave way to 'politicized debate', the shift in England, reinforced by the peculiarities of local circumstance, was notably emphatic.

6. Bishops, Barons, and Knights: Association and the Rise of Parliament

A common subjection to direct taxes was thus a burden shared by all, so creating room for alliances in and out of parliament. So it was again in the 1370s and early 1380s, when the lords' payment of taxes contributed to the community of interest that existed between lords and commons and helped to shape their decisions on tax grants to the crown.[232] But this was by no means the only factor which, in the thirteenth century,

---

[231] Above, 175–6.
[232] G. Dodd, 'The Lords, Taxation and the Community of Parliament in the 1370s and Early 1380s', *Parliamentary History*, 20 (2001), 291–5, 300, 308–10.

impelled different social groups towards a common viewpoint and the common parliamentary activities which often followed from it. Initially the process was more evident in the localities than at the centre. The pipe roll for 1222 tells us that in that year the bishop of Exeter and the barons, knights, and all men of Cornwall gave the king 1,300 marks for the disafforestation of their county and for other liberties conceded to them by King John. A further 500 marks was offered for the appointment of a sheriff from among the men of the county and for quittance from the recent carucage.[233] Some years later, in 1229, the bishop of Worcester and the archbishops, bishops, abbots, priors, earls, barons, and other free men living within the liberties of the forest of Horewell and Ombersley in Worcestershire gave 400 marks for disafforestation alone.[234] Fairly numerous between 1190 and 1235,[235] proffers of this kind have in the past been used to illustrate some particular features of provincial society and its relations with the centre: the desire of the local community to acquire and retain local privileges, the larger appetites thus created for the larger liberties eventually conceded in Magna Carta, and the leading role in these movements often assumed by the knights.[236] But they also show something equally important and more relevant to our current theme: the strong associative impulse which brought together churchmen, magnates, and knights in pursuit of common objectives. Some of these supposedly comprehensive groupings may contain an element of fiction (how many archbishops lived in the forest of Ombersley?). Nevertheless, communal proffers must have entailed practical cooperation in deciding on tactics, raising money, and negotiating with the crown. So much is suggested, for example, by the individual payments made in Cornwall by the local bishop and by named barons towards one such proffer recorded on the pipe roll.[237]

These collaborative activities in the shires were a microcosmic anticipation of what would later happen in parliament. If local charters of liberties were the forerunners of the Great Charter,[238] local associations were the

---

[233] *PR 6 Henry III*, 129–30; Madox, *History and Antiquities of the Exchequer*, i. 414.

[234] *CR, 1227–31*, 220; Madox, *History and Antiquities of the Exchequer*, i. 418.

[235] For other examples, see Madox, *History and Antiquities of the Exchequer*, i. 408, 412, 420; Maddicott, 'Magna Carta and the Local Community', 27–9.

[236] Holt, *Magna Carta*, 50–74; Maddicott, 'Magna Carta and the Local Community', 26–30, 36–41; above, 135–6.

[237] Madox, *History and Antiquities of the Exchequer*, i. 414 note n; Maddicott, 'Magna Carta and the Local Community', 48.

[238] Holt, *Magna Carta*, 62.

forerunners of the larger associations, bringing together the same social groups, which from time to time joined forces in parliament and which then gave parliament much of its political weight. Among the more fissile and class-bound assemblies and political alliances of continental Europe it is much less easy to detect any similar principle at work.

In explaining this peculiarly English development, social considerations rather than politics *per se* must come first. One in particular stands out: the relatively unprivileged status of the English nobility, which was a precondition for the cohesion of different social groups, whether in the counties or at Westminster.[239] Their lack of exemption from royal taxes was far from being the only way in which they were inferior to continental nobilities. We have already noticed, for example, that they lacked the powers of high justice which many nobles, and even *petits seigneurs*, possessed in France and which, besides the pleasure of hanging the more felonious criminals, conferred ancillary privileges, such as the right to collect royal taxes within the holder's lordships. French lords with high justice were allowed to collect both the Saladin Tithe of 1188 and other taxes in the early fourteenth century.[240] The statement in the *Histoire des ducs de Normandie* that the barons negotiating with John in 1215 'wished to have all powers of *haute justice* in their lands' suggests that the English magnates knew what they were missing; but nothing was conceded.[241]

Still more debilitating to the authority of some continental rulers, and an impediment to any effective alliance between nobles and other landed or urban groups, was the right to private war. Unknown in England,[242] this was a privilege particularly cherished by the French nobility. Despite

---

[239] Cf. Stacey, 'Nobles and Knights', 18. The unprivileged status of the English nobility has elicited surprisingly little historical comment.

[240] R. W. Kaeuper, *War, Justice and Public Order: England and France in the Later Middle Ages* (Oxford, 1988), 162; Strayer, *Reign of Philip the Fair*, 194; Tyerman, *England and the Crusades*, 75; Strayer and Taylor, *Studies in Early French Taxation*, 54; Henneman, *Royal Taxation*, 74–5.

[241] Cited in Holt, *Magna Carta*, 271. Cf. Hudson, *Formation of the English Common Law*, 225.

[242] For the accusation laid against Ivo of Grandmesnil by Henry I that he had waged war in England and burnt the crops of his neighbours, and the comment of Orderic Vitalis that this was 'an unheard-of crime in that country', see *Orderic*, vi. 18–19. Glanvill apparently contradicts this in speaking of the allegiance due from a homager to his several lords when they are attacking one another, and of the aid which a lord might claim from his men to maintain his wars: *Glanvill*, ed. Hall, 104, 112; Pollock and Maitland, *History of English Law*, i. 301, 349. But his comments hardly point to a right of private war and may refer to special circumstances, such as the rising of 1173–4: see J. G. H. Hudson, 'Faide, vengeance et violence en Angleterre (ca 900–1200)', in D. Barthélemy, F. Bougard, and R. Le Jan (eds.), *La Vengeance, 400–1200* (Rome, 2006), 368–70.

its prohibition by Louis IX in 1258 and Philip IV's later campaign against it, the recognition of its legality remained a major aim of the nobles who joined the leagues of 1314–15.[243] Earlier, in Catalonia between 1173 and 1196, Alfonso II had attempted to limit the violent depredations and 'bad customs' of his barons, a form of private warfare as abhorrent to its peasant and clerical victims as to royal and ecclesiastical notions of public order. Alfonso's enlistment of churchmen and townsmen in his support showed the existence of an important social dividing line, but was largely in vain.[244] One mark of England's immunity from such noble-dominated *émeutes* was the failure of the peace movement, utilized by continental rulers and ecclesiastics to contain social violence, to cross the Channel. In England it was the king's peace that already did the job.[245]

Indeed at all points except in their subjection to taxes, the English nobility's lack of privilege reflected the early impress of royal power. Prior to the Conquest the strength of the Anglo-Saxon monarchy had already enabled the king to establish a royal monopoly of jurisdiction over major crimes.[246] After the Conquest the plantation of a new nobility holding from the crown greatly augmented the inherited potential of his position. Aided by a precociously well-organized administration, the crown was able to develop and enforce its tenurial rights, with consequences seen in the harsh exploitation of the feudal incidents and in the reaction which came in Magna Carta. That the Charter nonetheless made so few concessions to noble privilege—witness again its ignoring of any possible baronial aspirations towards high justice—owed most to a third development which had supervened between 1066 and 1215. Henry II's legal reforms not only strengthened and extended the crown's criminal jurisdiction and the machinery to enforce it, so building further barriers against noble violence,[247] but also ensured the equality of all free men in the king's

---

[243] Kaeuper, *War, Justice and Public Order*, 225–68, esp. 231–2, 247, 260; Hudson, *Formation of the Common Law*, 14–15, 145, 210–12. Cf. id., 'Faide, vengeance et violence', 375–6.

[244] T. N. Bisson, 'The Rise of Catalonia: Identity, Power and Ideology in a Twelfth-Century Society', in his *Medieval France*, 144–9; id., *Crisis of the Twelfth Century*, 499–514.

[245] Cf. O'Brien, *God's Peace and King's Peace*, 14, 73–7; Campbell, 'Was it Infancy in England?', 179–80, 194–5. But for English parallels to the peace movement in Æthelred's legislation and in the writings of Wulfstan, see Lawson, 'Archbishop Wulfstan and the Homiletic Element', 150, 152–6, 161, 163–4, and Wormald, *Making*, 453–4, 459–61.

[246] Wormald, 'Lordship and Justice', 316–18; id., *Making*, 155–6; Campbell, 'Was it Infancy in England?', 180; above, 383–4.

[247] Consider, for example, the directions to the eyre justices in the Assize of Northampton, given in the wake of the 1173 rebellion, to supervise the destruction of adulterine castles: Stubbs, *Select Charters*, 180.

court.[248] By barring the unfree from the possessory assizes and from the action of right, Henry set the legal dividing line in English society between free men and villeins, and not between noble and non-noble. Some of the implications of this development were revealed during the rebellion of Richard Marshal in 1233. When the bishops then complained that many barons had been exiled and despoiled without the judgement of their peers, only to be countered by the haughty response from Peter des Roches, the king's minister, that 'there were no peers in England as there were in France', both sides were right. England had no equivalent to the *pares* of contemporary France, the group of about a dozen great nobles who were beginning to claim the right of trial before their own number in a special court. But the bishops were correct in their assumption that the meaning of the Charter's terms which they had cited[249] was that a man should be judged by his social equals. There was no elite among the English magnates which commanded special privileges; but the magnates did enjoy the legal rights common to all free men.[250]

These social circumstances had a close bearing on the informal partnership between magnates and gentry which contributed to the underpinning of parliament's authority for much of the thirteenth century. Had a privileged nobility existed, its members claiming not only a degree of tax exemption but also such rights as those of high justice, private warfare, and special trial courts, it seems unlikely that their partnership would ever have formed. Unrestrained privilege would have riven political society. Yet its absence was only a necessary condition for this relationship and hardly a sufficient one. More directly important were questions of tenure and politics. Even before the emergence of parliament, the magnates had been fortuitously joined with that particular group among their inferiors who also held in chief from the king and whom the chronicler Howden calls 'knights'.[251] Magnates and minor knightly tenants-in-chief had been brought together in the twelfth century by common obligations of military service and,

---

[248] Hudson, *Formation of the Common Law*, 157–85, 218–19, esp. 175–80; M. T. Clanchy, *England and its Rulers, 1066–72* (Oxford, 1983), 220–1; Campbell, 'Late Anglo-Saxon State', 12.

[249] Cap. 39: 'No free man shall be taken or imprisoned or disseised or outlawed or exiled or in any way ruined, nor will we go or send against him, except by the lawful judgement of his peers or by the law of the land': Holt, *Magna Carta*, 460–1.

[250] Wendover, *Chronica*, iv. 276–7; Holt, *Magna Carta*, 327–9; Vincent, *Peter des Roches*, 408–9; Clanchy, *England and its Rulers*, 220–1. For the peers of France, see B. C. Keeney, *Judgement by Peers* (Cambridge, Mass., 1949), 15–23, and Bisson, *Crisis of the Twelfth Century*, 544. My interpretation of this episode runs contrary to that of Vincent and Clanchy.

[251] Howden, *Gesta Regis Henrici*, i. 107, 138; above, 83–4.

probably more occasionally, of attendance at councils. Subject as they all
were to the oppressive feudal lordship of the crown, they may from the
start have possessed some political interests in common. These became
more visible in Magna Carta. The Charter's setting of a knight's relief
at a £5 maximum, as against £100 for an earl or baron, was specifically
intended to help, not the knightly tenants of all lords, but those knights
who were themselves tenants-in-chief.[252] Their protection under the terms
of the Charter suggests both their prior exploitation by the crown and
the ties created by 'similarity of oppression'[253] which bound them to their
co-tenants among the nobility. The assumption in cap. 14 of the Charter
that the lesser tenants would be present with the *maiores* when taxes were
to be discussed was a further recognition of their claims. It was in line with
the shared interests evident here that when the earl of Chester denied the
king a tax at the great council of March 1232 he cited in justification the
burdens imposed upon all the tenants-in-chief, knights as well as earls and
barons, who had already provided the feudal *auxilium* of military service.[254]
Among the tenants-in-chief, ranging from earls to knights and even to
ordinary free men, there were obviously enormous differences of wealth;
but in their liabilities all stood together.

From about this time onwards the shared grievances and interests of
magnates and this one particular group of knights, rooted in the common
ground of tenure, were enlarged by the growth of a more generalized
hostility to the crown's demands and to some of its policies. The main
features of this development have been discussed in earlier chapters and
need only be summarized here. Both under Henry III in the years up to
1258, and still more markedly so under Edward I between 1297 and 1301,
magnates and knights joined forces in opposition to the crown. Though the
knights sometimes had their own agenda, they shared with their superiors
in a common opposition to royal misgovernment and, in the later period,
to excessively heavy taxation and to arbitrary rule. Like the knights, the
bishops too had their own programme, but in their objections to royal
misgovernment and royal taxation their leaders stood foursquare with the
magnates and gentry, in 1297 as in 1258. For all these groups Magna Carta
provided a unifying force and a rallying point, enjoying from the time of
its making not so much an afterlife as a process of continuous renewal and

---

[252] Above, 138.   [253] Reynolds, *Kingdoms and Communities*, 268.
[254] Wendover, *Chronica*, iv. 233; above, 176–7, 217, 425–6.

development. Central to this process were its repeated confirmations and the aspirations of the diverse parties who looked to it for remedies and liberties. On its foundations they built a superstructure of further restraints on the crown: the Provisions of Oxford in 1258, *Confirmatio Cartarum* in 1297, the *Articuli Super Cartas* in 1300. But if royal power and its misuse, and a common regard for common liberties, gave bishops, barons, and knights cause to associate, it was parliament which provided the occasion and the venue for their association. It fostered cooperation, whether in the assembly of November 1244, when a committee of prelates, earls, and barons was set up to consider the king's demand for a tax, in the Montfortian parliament of June 1264, which brought shire knights into the company of reforming bishops and barons to endorse a new scheme for the country's government, or in the three parliaments of 1258, 1297, and 1300 which provided the public stage for the making of those reforming texts just mentioned. The former regional associations of bishops, barons, and knights active at the start of the century had been transcended by, and subsumed into, a larger national association.

The associative impetus within parliament began to divide and re-form in a different pattern under Edward II, as the shire knights drew apart from the magnates and moved closer to the burgesses. This division had to some extent been anticipated earlier: in the projected parliament of April 1254 the knights had seemed more likely than the magnates to resist the king's demands, and their resistance materialized again in the face of their more pliant superiors during the parliamentary process leading to the crusade tax of 1270.[255] But these were temporary aberrations from a more consistent pattern. For most of the thirteenth century the association of different groups within parliament, often taking their stand on Magna Carta and in pursuit of common objectives, had contributed powerfully to parliament's emerging role as the voice of the *communitas regni*.

Continental contrasts shine a bright light on the local peculiarities of this situation. France, lacking any central institution comparable to a representative parliament, and possessing instead only its judicial *parlement* and its irregular magnate assemblies, was perhaps the country furthest removed from the English model. There was little cooperation at the centre between different social groups. The collaboration of bishops and barons, a main feature of the parliaments of Henry III's middle years,

---

[255] Maddicott, 'Crusade Taxation', 114–15.

is difficult to detect in the French assemblies of Henry's contemporary, Louis IX, probably because the bulk of Louis's taxes fell on the church and the towns, to whose fortunes the nobility were indifferent.[256] National taxation, in England one of the great political unifiers, was absent. When it was introduced, under Philip IV, the nobility's ties proved to be mainly vertical rather than horizontal, with their own tenants, particularly their knightly tenants, rather than with bishops and nobles from other lordships. It was primarily their rear-vassals whom the nobles sought to protect from the king's taxes.[257] There was in any case no platform, no venue or occasion, which could facilitate a wider cooperation. The contrast with the contemporary alliance of magnates and gentry in parliament under Edward I is obvious. It is true that regional alliances were not unknown. They were seen in the delegations which sometimes brought up petitions to the *parlement*—'the viscounts and nobles of Narbonnais' and so on[258]—and they appeared more conspicuously and forcefully in the regional and inter-regional leagues formed to oppose royal taxation in 1314–15. Headed by the nobles, these last brought together knights, ecclesiastics, and townsmen in defence of local liberties as well as the caste privileges of the nobility. Yet these were all temporary groupings, shaped by their particular ends, and the leagues in particular papered over deep divisions between the nobles and the commons of the towns.[259] If they had any English parallels it was with the provincial associations formed a century earlier to secure local sheriffs and local disafforestation. But in England these objectives were carried forward in later parliaments in ways prohibited in France by the country's institutional and class structure.

It might be thought that the cortes of the Spanish kingdoms would have promoted political association in ways more closely comparable to those found in the English parliament. These were, after all, central assemblies of estates: nobles, clergy, and—sometimes or usually, depending on time and place—townsmen. But association was often more nominal than real, more a matter of physical contiguity than of shared political programmes. In Castile, for example, the town leagues known as *hermandades* were a

[256] Bisson, 'Consultative Functions', 83; Favier, 'Les Finances', 138–40.
[257] Strayer and Taylor, *Studies in Early French Taxation*, 43, 77, 88.
[258] Bisson, 'Consultative Functions', 87; above, 413.
[259] Brown, 'Reform and Resistance to Royal Authority', 116–19, 121–2; P. Contamine, 'De la puissance aux privilèges: doléances de la noblesse française envers la monarchie aux xive et xve siècles', in P. Contamine (ed.), *La Noblesse au moyen âge: essais à la mémoire de Robert Boutruche* (Paris, 1976), 246–9.

source of independent power which tended to overshadow the cortes. The violence and rapacity of the great nobles, and the frequent encroachment of nobles and clergy on urban liberties, set the representatives of the towns against them when the cortes met. Those representatives were often *caballeros villanos*, non-noble knights whose exemption from taxation set them apart from their constituents but who were no friends of the magnates. The towns themselves were often divided by regional rivalries.[260] The main point of contrast with England is perhaps an obvious one. Until the regular summoning of the burgesses began in the 1290s, the English parliament was primarily a gathering of the landed. Magnates and knights, whether (to begin with) tenants-in-chief or (later) elected shire representatives, had much in common. But both groups had much in common too with the landed bishops and abbots. These were ecclesiastical tenants-in-chief with large estates which might fall to the crown during vacancies, just as those of the lay tenants-in-chief might suffer the same fate during the minorities of heirs. They were, too, men whose peasant tenants were as exposed as those of the lay magnates to the predatory attentions of sheriffs, eyre justices, and royal purveyors. This natural community of interests was hardly likely to characterize other political systems in which towns and town representatives had much greater prominence.

Nor did other European states possess the equivalent of Magna Carta to serve as a permanent pole of attraction for all the ruler's subjects: subjects who, in England, and partly through the instrumentation of the Charter, came to see themselves as constituting a *communitas* unknown elsewhere.[261] Although it has become a commonplace to note that other rulers conceded grants of national liberties in the period of the Charter, few if any were addressed to so socially comprehensive a list of grantees, from archbishops to 'everyone in our kingdom', as Magna Carta's 1225 reissue;[262] and few were of more than temporary importance. (Hungary's Golden Bull may be a possible exception.[263]) The reason for these differences lay in two characteristics of the English state. In no other country was the pressure of royal government, which produced the Charter and kept it in the forefront of political consciousness for the next century, so intense; and no other

[260] Procter, *Curia and Cortes*, 97, 103; O'Callaghan, *Cortes of Castile-León*, 58, 202; Ruiz, 'Oligarchy and Royal Power', 97–9; McIlwain, 'Medieval Estates', 697; Post, *Studies*, 153 n. 196.
[261] For the absence of a *communitas regni* in France, see, e.g. Bisson, 'Consultative Functions', 83, and Brown, 'Reform and Resistance to Royal Authority', 109.
[262] Holt, *Magna Carta*, 273; above, 107.
[263] For the afterlife of the Golden Bull, see Rady, *Nobility, Land and Service*, 39–40, 54, 57, 170.

country possessed so vigorous a conciliar tradition as to be able to match a national charter with the aspirations of those meeting regularly in a national assembly. The charters obtained by the leagues in France, though their common features reflected common aims, were granted to loose and temporary regional federations—not to established local communities like those of the English shires and still less to a single *communitas* reified in a national assembly, like that which received the 1225 reissue in England. In both social and political terms, in terms of interests which bridged classes and the institutions through which these interests were expressed, association remained a more potent force in England than in any other western monarchy.

7. Conclusion

Modern writing on the origins of the English parliament generally takes the thirteenth century as its starting point.[264] It was then that the word moved into common usage, while the thing itself acquired its later constitution of king, lords, and commons within a comparable pan-European context of rising representative institutions. This study has taken a different (and older) approach in attempting to show that parliament's ultimate origins lay much further back, with the great assemblies which first appeared under Æthelstan in the tenth century and which may in turn, like so many early English institutions, have had Carolingian antecedents. These portentous gatherings were the lineal ancestors of the more brightly illuminated councils and parliaments of the post-Magna Carta world. From this time onwards the line joining the witan to the *concilia* and *colloquia* of Anglo-Norman and Angevin England, and thence to the parliaments of the thirteenth and fourteenth centuries, remained essentially unbroken. There were occasional short periods of interrupted domestic kingship when assemblies may have been few or absent, in Stephen's reign after 1140 or in Richard I's last years abroad; and others when, conversely, conciliar activity was redoubled in kingship's deficit, as in the time of Richard I's absence on crusade or during Henry III's minority. But it would be hard to pinpoint any particular moment between Æthelstan's accession in 924 and

---

[264] e.g. E. Miller, 'Introduction', in *Historical Studies*, 1–6; P. Spufford, *Origins of the English Parliament* (London, 1967), 1–17; Richardson, 'Origins of Parliament', 146–78.

Edward II's deposition in 1327 when conciliar arrangements broke down completely, to restart later on a completely different basis.

Beyond the successional nature of assembly meetings, continuity was of two main kinds: of personnel in attendance and of function. To state that the prelates and magnates served as counsellors throughout this long period is to state the obvious. By virtue of their offices the two archbishops must have been the most regular of those summoned between the tenth century and the fourteenth; while at a secular level the ealdormen and king's thegns witnessing the assembly-made charters of Æthelstan or Edgar were the predecessors of the earls and barons who granted or denied taxes in the parliaments of Henry III. Less obvious perhaps are the long continuities in the attendance of two other groups: the king's ministers and the lesser landholders. Tenth-century charters were frequently witnessed by men whose appended titles showed that they had a place in the king's household, whether as stewards (*disciferi*), butlers (*pincernae*), or chamberlains (*camerarii*). The scribes who wrote those charters must also have been in attendance;[265] and given their expertise and their literacy it is not inconceivable that they contributed to discussion. If men of this sort look very different from the ministers present in thirteenth-century parliaments—chancellor, treasurer, judges, royal clerks—the difference marks the expansion of public offices in the meantime, beyond the boundaries of the royal household, rather than any break in the succession of skilled men whom the king trusted, at assemblies as elsewhere. As for the lesser landholders, titles again differ across the centuries, but local standing remains essentially similar, whether we focus on the local thegns who sometimes witnessed charters or the knightly tenants-in-chief who sometimes appear at the councils and parliaments of the twelfth and early thirteenth centuries, or their successors, the elected knights of the shire. At all points assemblies were rather more capacious than the prominence of their episcopal and magnate core might suggest.

More important still was continuity of function. Throughout the period the main work of central assemblies was resolutely political. Contemporary perceptions, as well as the historical record, show them to have been engaged above all in the management of the affairs of the realm. William of Malmesbury's remarks of *c.*1130 on the Conqueror's crown-wearing councils, where three times a year the great men came to court 'to deal with vital business affecting the realm (*de necessariis regni tractaturi*)', compare

---

[265] Keynes, *Diplomas*, 130–2, 158–60; above, 6, 9.

closely with the statement made in the Provisions of Oxford, more than a century later, that parliaments were to be held three times a year 'to review the state of the realm and to deal with the common business of the realm and of the king together (*pur treter les cummuns bosoingnes del reaume et del rei ensement*)'. When Edward I issued instructions in 1280 that the petitions then flooding in to parliament should not obstruct the work of king and council in attending to 'the great business of his realm (*grosses busoignes de sun reaume*) and of his foreign lands', he showed that he too was of the same mind.[266] The consistency of language here, over a period of about 150 years, is striking. A later source is rather more specific. The *Modus Tenendi Parliamentum* tells us that the first item on parliament's agenda is 'war, if there is a war, and other matters concerning the persons of the King, Queen, and their children', and, secondly, 'matters of common concern to the realm (*de negotiis communibus regni*)'. Only then comes 'private business according to the order of petitions filed', pointing to the clear priority which the *Modus*, like Edward I's directions, gives to politics over justice in parliament's work.[267] We have no similar contemporary appraisal of assembly business for the pre-Conquest period, but the role of the witan in planning the country's defence during Æthelred's Danish wars anticipates the prescriptions of the *Modus* by some 300 years.[268] And if parliament's part in deposing a king in 1327 was new (and as 'political' an act as one could imagine), earlier councils had taken a large share in determining the succession, whether in choosing Edward as successor to Edgar in 975 or in supporting Matilda as Henry I's successor in 1126.[269] Set besides these affairs of state, the assembly's work in law-making and passing judgement in state trials was much more intermittent; though hardly less political in its implications.

Yet much, of course, did change between Æthelstan's reign and Edward II's. The first important turning point came with the Norman Conquest. As we have seen, the assemblies that William I inherited from his English predecessors were occasions for charismatic display, social bonding, and the transaction of national business. Like so many Anglo-Norman institutions, the councils of the Conquest were those of

---

[266] William of Malmesbury, *Saints' Lives*, pp. xiv–xv, 82–3; *DBM* 110–11; *CCR, 1279–88*, 56–7; Sayles, *Functions*, 172; above, 238, 296. Cf. Edwards, ' "Justice" in Early English Parliaments', 282–5.

[267] Pronay and Taylor, *Parliamentary Texts of the Later Middle Ages*, 75–6, 88; Campbell, 'Stubbs and the English State', 265–6.

[268] Above, 27–8.   [269] Above, 33, 68, 80.

Anglo-Saxon England under new management.[270] It was the basis for the magnates' attendance that was innovatory. A new landed class holding from the king replaced the shattered nobility of pre-Conquest England, who had held their lands more freely, often by bookright.[271] 'By the conquest at Battle we were all enfeoffed,' as Richard de Lucy succinctly put it nearly a century later.[272] Dependent tenure carried with it defined obligations, and from some point after 1066 the obligation to provide the king with 'counsel and aid' began to determine attendance at assemblies. The men present were there as tenants-in-chief; and from a surprisingly early date, perhaps as early as William I's writ of summons to Æthelwig, abbot of Evesham, the system of summoning set out in Magna Carta, with personal summonses for the greater tenants-in-chief and summonses through the sheriff for the lesser, was already in operation.[273]

The change affected neither the social categories of those summoned to councils (bishops, magnates, some lesser landholders) nor the sort of business transacted. But it did radically alter the position of the assembly in relation to the wider realm. The Anglo-Saxon assembly had been 'the witan of the English people'. It was seen as a representative body which could speak and act for the whole country, so that Cnut, in his letter of c.1019, could regard the legislation confirmed at a meeting of the witan as having been accepted by 'all men' and could instruct 'all the nation' to observe it.[274] Stubbs noted, in tones almost of disappointment, that the witan failed to embody the principle of representation, which would have entailed its incorporation of lesser communities. This principle he found rather in the shire courts, whose representational continuity from the tenth century to the time of Edward I was more marked.[275] Yet the ideal of representation which the witan embodied was real enough. It rested, however, not on election, but on the implied notion, made explicit in Cnut's letter, that the country's assembled great men could act as spokesmen for the realm.[276]

[270] Above, 57–64.
[271] Garnett, *Conquered England*, 31, 45–6; Baxter, *Earls of Mercia*, 145–9, 230–6.
[272] *Chronicle of Battle*, ed. Searle, 310–11; Garnett, *Conquered England*, 4.
[273] Above, 76–84. It is just possible that the 'two-tier' summons was another inheritance from Carolingian practices, though before 1066 it could not have rested on tenure. F. L. Ganshof, *The Carolingians and the Frankish Monarchy* (London, 1971), 128, points out that Charlemagne's military summonses were normally delivered by the *missi*, but that important individuals might receive a personal summons. For a cautionary note, see J. L. Nelson, 'Literacy in Carolingian Government', in McKitterick (ed.), *Uses of Literacy in Early Medieval Europe*, 278–9.
[274] Above, 53–4.   [275] Stubbs, *Constit. Hist.* i. 130, 133; ii. 214–15.
[276] Cf. Reynolds, *Kingdoms and Communities*, 250–1.

For about 150 years after the Conquest this ceased to be true. None of the councils of the late eleventh and twelfth centuries can be seen, or were seen by contemporaries, as representative bodies, and no one wrote of 'the *concilium* of the English people'. The councils which initiated the Domesday survey or settled the succession on Matilda were feudal gatherings of a royal lord and his tenants. In this sense they were akin to the private honor courts of the magnates, and indeed Henry I, in his ordinance for the shire and hundred courts, could speak of a plea that might arise between vassals 'of any baron of my honor'.[277] This more confined role for the assembly was not only a consequence of the new tenurial structure introduced after 1066 which had turned England into a gigantic honor. The pre-Conquest witan had been organically rooted in English society, and its representative qualities rested in part on a common English identity shared with those it helped to govern. This in turn derived from a common body of customs and laws, and a common language which was both the language of government and the language of the people. But the post-Conquest councils, though indigenous by descent, stood for the conquerors against the conquered, and their members were largely separated by language, culture, and social outlook from their inferiors. They were the vassals of a foreign lord, not the representatives of a native people.

A second turning point in the evolution of assemblies sprang from this first one, though it greatly outstripped the introduction of feudal tenure in ultimate importance. It arose from the complex of changes attendant on the reintroduction of national taxation between 1188 and 1225. National taxation restored to great councils (as they can now be termed), for onward transmission to the parliaments of the thirteenth century, the representative qualities which assemblies had lacked since the Conquest. The taxes intermittently levied from 1188 on moveable goods, and initially on revenues, derived most of their legitimacy from the conciliar consent which had authorized them. The Saladin Tithe itself, the levy for Richard's ransom, the thirteenth of 1207, and the fifteenth of 1225, all fell into this category (though there is a shade of doubt about the authorization of the ransom tax[278]). In these cases the consent given by the relatively few tenants-in-chief was regarded as binding on the many, both their own tenants and all others holding by dependent tenure: effectively all rural

---

[277] Stubbs, *Select Charters*, 122; J. E. A. Jolliffe, *The Constitutional History of Medieval England* (4th edn., London, 1961), 173–4.
[278] Above, 120.

landholders of whatever status or condition who, for the first time since the demise of geld, were now drawn into the payment of taxes. This assumption was first explicitly made in the writ for the levying of the thirteenth in 1207. Granted 'by common counsel and the assent of our council', it was to be paid 'by every layman of all England from the fee of whomsoever he may be'.[279] In other words, a grant made by tenants-in-chief obliged all tenants to pay, no matter from whom they held. The same principle became still more clearly visible in two later grants, those of 1225 and 1237. The fifteenth of 1225 was granted by the great council but spoken of by the king as conceded by prelates, priors, earls, barons, knights, free tenants, and 'everyone in our kingdom'. The thirtieth of 1237 was said, in the writ for its collection, to have been granted by prelates, churchmen, earls, barons, knights, and free men 'on behalf of themselves and their villeins'.[280] In both cases those attending the assembly are viewed by the crown as explicitly representative figures, though not elected ones.

But at the same time as the universal embrace of tenure, unique in Europe, allowed the crown to develop the notion of representation in its own fiscal interest, this idea was also emerging from below, largely in response to the fiscal pressures applied by the crown. When the magnates, meeting in council at Oxford in 1205, forced John to swear to preserve intact 'the rights of the kingdom of England with their counsel', they took a tentative step towards identifying themselves with the realm and its interests.[281] A further move in that direction came with Magna Carta, negotiated by barons and churchmen but granted to 'all free men'. The process was capped and placed within a firmer institutional framework when Henry III reissued the Charters in 1225 in return for a tax grant. Just as the grant was actually made by the great council but notionally by 'everyone in our kingdom', so on the same occasion the Charters were conceded to 'archbishops, bishops, abbots, priors, earls, barons, and everyone in our kingdom'.[282] The great council thus acts on behalf of the realm, not only in granting taxes in the crown's interest, but in receiving liberties in the subjects' interests.

It was in this way that the kingdom's central assembly, soon to be its parliament, re-emerged as a representative body after the long hiatus initiated by the Conquest. The 'witan of the English people' had been

[279] Stubbs, *Select Charters*, 278; above, 133.
[280] Stubbs, *Select Charters*, 350, 358; above, 107, 200.
[281] *Gervase of Canterbury*, ii. 97–8; above, 142–3.　　[282] Stubbs, *Select Charters*, 350; above, 107.

reborn as the *communitas regni* represented by the great council: a rebirth made possible, perhaps paradoxically, by the system of tenurial dependence introduced by Norman rule and arising in the first place from the crown's fiscal needs. Yet although national taxation does much to explain the growth of notions of representation from *c.*1200 onwards, and nothing to explain their earlier embodiment within the witan, the two processes shared some common ground. By the late twelfth century the common English identity which allowed the pre-Conquest English to view the witan as a nationally representative body had begun to re-emerge. The growing use of the English language by the aristocracy, the decline of magnate holdings in Normandy, and the increasingly xenophobic temper suggested by opposition to foreigners, whether to William Longchamp under Richard I or to John's alien captains and counsellors,[283] all gave plausibility to the magnates' conciliar stand in 1205 for 'the rights of the kingdom of England'. Such a stand would have been inconceivable a hundred years earlier. The great council's almost insensible adoption of a corporate English persona left it well placed to revive, equally insensibly, the representative role once played by the witan.

A third turning point was intimately related to the same circumstances of fiscal necessity and taxative response which had recreated representative assemblies. From 1215 onwards taxation became dependent on the consent of an assembly to which all tenants-in-chief were summoned; statutorily dependent, one might say, since this principle was enshrined in clauses 12 and 14 of Magna Carta, observed henceforth even in their absence from the Charter's reissues. The linking of taxation to conciliar consent was perhaps the most momentous of all the interpositions which punctuated the development of assemblies over a period of some 400 years. It opened the way for 'politicized debate' between king and magnates, creating the conditions for bargaining over taxation, and allowing those in parliament to demand, if not always to secure, the redress of grievances before the supply of taxes. In so doing it confirmed and enlarged the primordial political function of assemblies, while overlaying the conciliar consensus which had sanctioned (for example) the Domesday survey with the confrontations which often marked Henry III's parliaments. Since 'redress' usually meant the Charter's confirmation, reissue, and observance, it helped to embed the Charter in the consciousness of the political nation and to associate this

---

[283] Above, 144–6.

code of liberties more closely with parliament. Finally, taxation by consent brought the minor tenants-in-chief to parliament with what was almost certainly a novel frequency, matching that of the crown's numerous tax requests; and in this way it broadened parliament's social base and allowed the complaints of those below baronial status to begin to be heard.[284] Most of these tendencies converged at the *parliamentum* of January 1237 (the first so called), where the king was criticized, *inter alia*, for his failures abroad and his reliance on aliens at home, and where he secured a tax grant, from knights as well as from churchmen and magnates, only on condition that he confirmed the Charter and added three barons to his regular council.[285] The Charter's terms had profoundly altered the content and conduct of conciliar business, in ways impossible to envisage for the generation or so after the Conquest.

If we now take a larger and more general view of the transition from the assemblies and councils of pre- and post-Conquest England to the parliaments of the thirteenth century, we can observe an overarching change. From being periodic extensions of the king's court these gatherings took on a more public character, acquired more public functions, and moved more fully into the public eye. The history of early assemblies may suggest that there is exaggeration here; and it is true that by comparison with the familiar counsel that often guided the policies of the Capetian kings, witan and *concilium* were already public bodies. The letter of 1227 from the citizen of Caen contrasting the closed and restricted counsel of a few confidants drawn on by the French king with the larger and more open councils of his English counterpart, their activities widely advertised, suggests the degree to which a meeting of the great council took place in an arena rather than a chamber.[286] Yet much that happened at these early assemblies was internally directed and concealed from any larger audience. Crown-wearings, for example, could impress only those present and were sometimes staged at such out-of-the-way places as Brampton in Huntingdonshire[287] which were not intended to facilitate participation by any besides those summoned. Even after the decline of crown-wearing in the middle years of Henry I, those attending councils had little or no direct and formal engagement with any wider public beyond their own membership. Though 'the vital business of the realm' that they discussed

---

[284] Above, 175–7, 198–202.
[285] *CRR*, xv: *1233–37*, no. 2047; *CR, 1234–37*, 545; *Paris*, iii. 380–4; above, 173.
[286] Above, 376–7.   [287] Above, 72.

might affect the population at large, as with the conciliar planning of the Domesday survey, there was no countervailing response at the centre from those affected.

Some episodes from the reign of Edward I emphasize an obvious contrast. In 1275 some hundreds of local representatives and heads of religious houses were summoned to the Easter parliament in order to hear the reforms proposed in the Statute of Westminster I. In 1283 elected knights and burgesses were summoned to the Shrewsbury parliament in order to witness (and no doubt report home on) the trial and execution of David of Wales. Two years later, in 1285, the Statute of Westminster II, the most comprehensive of all Edward's reforming measures, was read out in Westminster Hall after a seven-week-long parliament and 'in the presence of all the people'. Finally in 1305 proclamations were made throughout London and in the central courts inviting the delivery of petitions at the forthcoming February parliament.[288] On each of these occasions parliamentary activity extended outwards, to bring within the ambit of national politics many whose ancestors would have been left untouched by the activity of the great councils of the twelfth century.

In part this reflected no more than the sagacity of one particular king and his realization of parliament's value as a means of publicizing the beneficence of his rule. But Edward's use of parliament had its place in a more long-term evolutionary trend which had created a novel public awareness of parliament's role and of its centrality to national life. This was chiefly the result of an enlargement of functions which sprang from changes already discussed: the advent of national taxation and its quasi-legal dependence, after 1215, on corporate consent. Debates on taxation (with which twelfth-century councils had little or no concern), the questioning of royal policies which such debates often produced, and the supplementary presentation of grievances, all drew in more participants: first, the lesser tenants-in-chief, then increasingly from the late 1260s the elected knights and burgesses. Particularly in the case of this last development, the outcome was the expansion of ties between parliament and the provinces, as local communities began to play a part in parliamentary arrangements: MPs had to be elected in local courts, 'full power' given to them to act for their communities, pledges found for their appearance in parliament, and money

---

[288] Above, 283–4, 292–3, 326. For the proclamations of 1305, see also *PROME* ii. 52.

raised locally for the payment of their wages.[289] The activities of parliament, and especially its promotion of a Charter granted to 'all free men', now affected a multitude of interests, helping to lodge some parliamentary events in provincial memory. Thus the shire community of Worcestershire, faced in 1297 with royal demands for an illicit tax, could appeal to 'the liberties of the great charter and the charter of the forest' granted to the *communitas regni* in the great council of 1225.[290] But national taxation was not the only issue with wide public implications, though it was the most important. The question of papal provisions and papal taxation, recurrent items on the parliamentary agenda of the 1240s and 1250s (but never raised in the twelfth century), affected every individual and institution with rights of ecclesiastical patronage: bishops, magnates, knights, and monasteries. Here too those outside parliament as well as those within might have strong personal interests in parliament's business.

The effect of these developments was to raise the public profile of parliament and to make possible a wider degree of social participation in its work. The almost explosive growth in petitioning from the mid 1270s onwards was an extension of this latter process, springing not only, like taxation, from the king's needs but also from his subjects' grievances. It probably did more than any other single factor in our period to heighten public awareness of a parliament which now facilitated not only taxes but also remedies for complaint. But even before the advent of petitioning parliament had become associated with redress. The Provisions of Westminster, the most permanent legacy of the baronial reform movement of 1258–65, had promised general benefits to all, even to the villeins who stood outside Magna Carta's magic circle of 'all free men'. Made in parliament and read aloud by the king's order in Westminster Hall in October 1259 at parliament's conclusion and in the presence of earls, barons, and 'innumerable people', the Provisions had shown how parliament might work for the common good and how—the lesson learnt by Edward I—public dissemination of that fact might be exploited to the advantage of those in power. The value of such publicity was seized on again by Simon de Montfort when, in March 1265, after another lengthy parliament, the conditions for the Lord Edward's release were read aloud in Westminster Hall 'in the presence of all the people'. These two appeals for public support set a precedent

---

[289] Above, 364–70.   [290] Above, 314–15.

not only for the public recitation of Westminster II in 1283 but for the revolutionary process of Edward II's deposition in 1327, carried through as it was in Westminster Hall during a clamorous parliament and in the presence of earls, barons, 'and a great multitude of people, especially the Londoners'.[291]

The use of the kingdom's prime public space for what were in effect appeals to the crowd was one mark of the emergence of a more public politics and a larger political nation. More than distance in place and time separated Henry III's Westminster Hall from Henry I's hunting lodge at Brampton. The elements of charismatic display present in Anglo-Norman kingship, signalized by crown-wearing and the singing of the *laudes regiae* at festal courts and at the councils with which they had often coincided, had dwindled almost to vanishing point. Parliament now provided a platform which allowed the king to project himself and his policies to an audience much larger than any of his predecessors had addressed in the more circumscribed councils of the twelfth century; and on occasion it allowed his opponents to do something similar. There were long continuities in parliament's evolution; but there was also transformation.

Was the English parliament then—to return to our starting point—no more than a variation on a general European theme? Certainly the general trajectory of its development, from Germanic assembly to feudal council and thence to representative institution, was one common to most western states. Yet in some of its individual and most salient features it was qualitatively different from its continental analogues. Even those most inclined to question the notion of English exceptionalism would probably agree that the early English state, as it emerged in post-Carolingian Europe, was unique in two particular ways: in the strength of its monarchy and in the extent of popular participation in the processes of government and politics on which that strength partly rested.[292] In palpable contrast to France, the

---

[291] Above, 243–4, 257–8, 283–4, 361.

[292] Wickham, *Inheritance of Rome*, 460–71, provides an excellent survey of both themes; but see also Campbell, 'Late Anglo-Saxon State', 12–13; id., 'Stubbs and the English State', 257–8; id., 'Was it Infancy in England?', 180–4; P. Wormald, 'James Campbell as Historian', in Maddicott and Palliser (eds.), *Medieval State*, p. xx; Bates, 'England and the "Feudal Revolution"', 617, 644–5; id., 'Britain and France and the Year 1000', *Franco-British Studies*, 28 (1999), 14, 17.

strength of the tenth-century monarchy created large assemblies drawing in men from the whole realm. They rapidly became an essential part of the consensual apparatus of royal government, and by the twelfth century they were both more prominent and more firmly embedded in the country's political structure than their stunted French equivalents. At a secondary stage the crown's powers were further enhanced by the introduction of universal dependent tenure which followed from the Conquest and which again set England firmly apart from the rest of Europe, where no other ruler had the Conqueror's territorial *tabula rasa* on which to operate. The king's tenurial sovereignty allowed him to exploit new powers as feudal lord, in addition to the ancient regal powers inherited from the Anglo-Saxon past, to a degree which, by John's reign, proved intolerable to the crown's baronial subjects. The crown's strength impelled its restriction. When, as a consequence, both feudal rights and regal powers came to be limited in Magna Carta, and the Charter to be enforced during Henry III's minority, it was the tried and tested instrument of the great council, long central to the work of government, that was given quasi-statutory powers to consent to general taxation and a less regulated but still comprehensive role in political decision-making. Had the familiar counsel of royal colleagues and confidants gained the primacy in government that it possessed in France, at the expense of large magnate assemblies, such an outcome would not have been possible.

The exceptionally prominent role of assemblies and councils in the country's government prior to John's reign, and still more so during his son's minority, does much to explain the development of parliament thereafter. Tenure provided one of several connecting links, largely determining the attendance of the major tenants-in-chief at all councils and of the lesser tenants-in-chief at some, notably those called after 1215 to discuss taxation. The elected knights who from the mid thirteenth century began to replace the lesser tenants-in-chief exemplified the second aspect of the English state's distinctiveness: its dependence on the engagement in its work of many local men. The setting for that engagement was the shire. Though some were certainly older, the shire emerged fully as a social and administrative unit in the mid tenth century, about the same time as the first appearance of the large national assemblies which were the complement and counterpart of those in the localities. The many duties imposed on the men of both shires and hundreds, especially the judicial

duties associated with their courts, created a system of 'self-government at
the king's command' not found in any other European state. The knights
who, in the later twelfth century, come into view as their shires' leaders
were the lineal descendants of the local thegns who filled the same role
before the Conquest and who played a prominent part in the administration
of local justice.[293] But they were now elevated to greater prominence by
their standing as unprofessional and unpaid royal officials, as intermediaries
between the local and the central courts, and in some cases as their
communities' representatives in bargaining with the crown. That all these
activities continued to be set within the ancient framework of the shire
made the subsequent election of knights for parliament a natural extension
of the exchanges between crown and locality that had begun long before.
The knights might be mandated, at the crown's command, to come with
'full power' to grant taxes on their communities behalf, but they could also
speak for those communities.

There were many points of contrast between the English parliament
and other continental assemblies. In no other state was general taxation
so closely tied to assembly consent as in England, largely because no
other state possessed so sacrosanct and enduring a code of liberties as
the Charter which gave rise to that principle. In no other state was
the nobility so strictly subject to taxes, with all the scope thus provided
for political association with other taxpayers and for an abiding interest
in the parliaments and processes through which taxes were granted. In
no other state were assembly representatives drawn predominantly from
the rural gentry, creating the potential, realized more often than not,
for a landed alliance between magnates and gentry hard to detect in
continental societies. And in no other state did a national assembly come
to embody so close an enmeshment of central authority and local action.
If before the Conquest communications had been mainly downward,
from royal authority to local courts[294]—in itself a feature which set
England apart from other European polities—by 1327 transmission had
been replaced by exchange. Private petitions, common petitions, the
participation of the commons in tax grants, the public proclamation of
statutes and political decrees both in parliament and in the counties,

[293] For the thegns' role in local justice, see, e.g. III Æthelred, 3. 1, 4, 13. 2: *Laws of the Kings of England*, ed. and trans. Robertson, 64–9.
[294] Cf. J. Campbell, 'The United Kingdom of England: The Anglo-Saxon Achievement', in his *Anglo-Saxon State*, 38–40.

all testify to a degree of integration between local aspirations and royal government which is difficult to identify in any continental state. We may freely acknowledge the evolution of parliament to have been part of a general European pattern. All the same, we need not baulk at the notion of English exceptionalism.

A List of Great Councils and Parliaments, 1235–1257

This list comprehends all those meetings of the king, bishops, and magnates which could be considered as parliaments. It errs on the side of generosity by including meetings to which only limited numbers may have been summoned, some of them probably afforced meetings of the council rather than full magnate assemblies. These less certain parliaments are indicated by a question mark. I have assumed that a large gathering of magnates at an appropriate time (e.g. early January) marks a parliament, even though the meeting lacks any description. The list is arranged thus:

(1) Start date of meeting and any other dates recorded.
(2) How described.
(3) Those present.
(4) Place of meeting.
(5) Business.
(6) Comment.

The source is given under each heading. The omission of a bracketed number indicates that no information under this heading is available for that parliament. Tax parliaments at which a tax was either granted or refused have been noted after the year. Evidence from the royal charter witness lists, published as *The Royal Charter Witness Lists of Henry III (1226–1272) from the Charter Rolls in the Public Record Office*, ed. M. Morris, List and Index Soc. 291–2, 2 vols. (2001), has been noted where it provides the only evidence for an assembly, but has usually been ignored in cases where it merely corroborates the holding of a parliament known from chronicle or chancery sources. 'Business' includes the more important political business, important grants, and miscellaneous business dealt with during the parliament. It does not include most judicial cases remitted to parliament. Details are given in note form in order to save space.

1. 1235

(1) 20 Jan. (*CR, 1234–37*, 160).
(3) Archbish. Canterbury, certain bishops, earls, and others our faithful men (ibid.).
Archbish. Canterbury, greater part of bishops, earls, and barons (*CRR*, xv:
1233–37, 335).
(4) Westminster (*CR, 1234–37*, 160).
(5) Truce with France; Hugh of La Marche's demand for isle of Oléron debated
and refused (ibid.; Powicke, *King Henry III*, 185 n. 1). Case concerning forcible
circumcision of a Christian boy by Jews of Norwich (*CRR*, xv: *1233–37*, 335).

2. 1235

(1) *c*.19 Feb. (*Charter Witness Lists*, i. 142); month of February (Wendover,
Chronica, iv. 332; *Paris*, iii. 318–19).
(3) Bishops and magnates (Wendover, *Chronica*, iv. 332; *Paris*, iii. 318–19). Charter
witness lists include archbish. Canterbury, 3 bishops, 2 earls.
(4) Westminster (Wendover, *Chronica,* iv. 332; *Paris*, iii. 318–19).
(5) Three-day discussion of marriage of Isabella, king's sister, to Frederick II; king
and magnates consent to this (Wendover, *Chronica*, iv. 332; *Paris*, iii. 318–19).

3. 1235—TAX GRANTED (AID AT 2M. PER FEE)

(1) *c*.8 July (*Charter Witness Lists*, i. 149).
(3) Archbishs., bishops, abbots, priors, earls, barons, and all others holding in chief
from king (*CR, 1234–37*, 186). Charter witnesses, 8–10 July, include archbish.
Canterbury, 8 bishops, 5 earls (*Charter Witness Lists*, i. 149; *CRR*, xv: *1233–37*,
p. xlix n. 2). Knights (BL Add. MS 8167, fos. 105–105ᵛ).
(4) Westminster (*Charter Witness Lists*, i. 149).
(5) Grant of feudal aid for marriage of king's sister (*CR, 1234–37*, 186).

4. 1236

(1) *c*.20 Jan. Probably lasted until *c*.27 Jan. (*Charter Witness Lists*, i. 154).
(3) Magnates (*Paris*, iii. 340). Charter witness lists include archbish. Canterbury,
6 bishops, 8 earls.

(4) Merton (Paris, iii. 340; *Charter Witness Lists*, i. 154).

(5) Frederick II's request for help from Richard of Cornwall is discussed and refused; Provisions of Merton promulgated on 22 Jan. (*Paris*, iii. 340–3; *Stat. Realm*, i. 1).

(6) The meeting at Merton was probably occasioned by the flooding of Westminster (*Paris*, iii. 339; *CRR*, xv: *1233–37*, p. li n. 3).

5. 1236

(1) 28 Apr. (*Paris*, iii. 362).

(2) 'colloquium' (ibid.).

(3) Magnates of England (ibid.).

(4) London (ibid.); palace at Westminster (ibid. 363).

(5) King retreats to Tower before returning to palace to meet magnates. Criticism of William of Savoy; replacement of sheriffs; Alexander II of Scotland sends messengers to demand his rights (ibid. 362–3).

?6. 1236

(1) 8 June (*Paris*, iii. 368).

(3) Magnates of England (ibid.).

(4) Winchester (ibid.).

(5) King seeks to annul grants made before his marriage, causing much discontent (ibid.).

(6) Cf. Stacey, *Politics, Policy and Finance*, 101–2.

?7. 1236

(1) c.23–4 July (*Charter Witness Lists*, i. 157).

(3) Charter witness lists include archbish. Canterbury, 1 bishop, 2 earls (*CRR*, xv: *1233–37*, p. liii n. 3, errs in adding two further bishops).

(4) Worcester (*Charter Witness Lists*, i. 157).

(5) *Coram rege* proceedings in case involving abbot of Osney—judgement given in presence of king and magnates (*BNB*, no. 1189; *CRR*, xv: *1233–37*, p. liii n. 3).

8. 1237—TAX GRANTED (THIRTIETH ON MOVEABLES)

(1) 20 Jan. (*CRR*, xv: *1233–37*, no. 2047; *CR, 1234–37*, 399, 545); 13 Jan. (*Paris*, iii. 380).

(2) 'parliamentum' (*CRR*, xv: *1233–37*, no. 2047); 'magnum concilium' (*Paris*, iii. 380; *CRR*, xvi: *1237–42*, no. 924); 'magnum colloquium' (*Ann. Tewkesbury*, 102).

(3) Archbishs., bishops, abbots, priors, clerks holding lands which do not pertain to their churches, earls, barons, knights, and freemen (*CR, 1234–37*, 545); magnates (ibid. 399); 'an infinite multitude of nobles' (*Paris*, iii. 380); archbishs., bishops, abbots, priors, earls, barons, citizens, burgesses, and many others (*Ann. Tewkesbury*, 102).

(4) Westminster (sources as above).

(5) King, through William Raleigh, asks for aid. He is criticized by magnates for previous tax demands, foreign policy failures, and for taking political decisions without securing consent. Demand for king to set aside counsel of aliens and take only that of native-born men. After four-day discussion thirtieth granted in return for confirmation of Magna Carta and addition of three barons to king's council (*Paris*, iii. 380–4; *CR, 1234–37*, 545). In the infirmary chapel of St Katherine, king swears to observe the Charter and bishops publicly excommunicate its violators (*Paris*, v. 360–1, anomalously appearing in account of events in 1253). Demands of Roger of Essex, king's escheator, on tenants of honor of Peverel to be discussed (*CR, 1234–37*, 399).

(6) The first occasion on which 'parliamentum' is used for a central assembly. Knights, freemen, citizens, and burgesses apparently among those attending.

9. 1237

(1) 22–8 Sept. (*CRR*, xvi: *1237–42*, p. xliv); 14 Sept. (*Paris*, iii. 413).

(2) 'colloquium', 'concilium' (*Paris*, iii. 413–14).

(3) All magnates summoned (ibid. 413). Charter witnesses include archbish. York, 1 bishop, 3 earls (*Charter Witness Lists*, i. 164–5; *CRR*, xvi: *1237–42*, p. xxx n. 1).

(4) York (ibid.).

(5) Peace settlement with Alexander II.

?10. 1238

(1) *c.*4 Apr. (?) (*Ann. Tewkesbury*, 107).

(2) 'magnum colloquium' (ibid.).

(4) Woodstock (ibid.).

(5) Baldwin de Béthune present (ibid.).

(6) A doubtful assembly, though the king was at Woodstock 19–23 Apr. (*CRR*, xvi: *1237–42*, p. xiv). There are no charter witness lists for this period.

11. 1239

(1) 3 Apr. (*Paris*, iii. 526). Long charter witness lists 17–23 Apr. (*Charter Witness Lists*, i. 170–1).

(2) 'parlamentum' (*Paris*, iii. 526).

(3) Longest witness list includes archbish. Canterbury, 6 bishops, 4 earls.

(4) Westminster (*Charter Witness Lists*, i. 170–1).

(5) 19 Apr., Amaury de Montfort quitclaims his share of the honor of Leicester to his brother Simon (*CChR*, *1226–57*, 243).

(6) The first occasion on which Paris speaks of a 'parlamentum': the king fearfully anticipates that magnates will rise against him in this *parlamentum* on account of his frequent 'excesses' (*Paris*, iii. 526).

12. 1239

(1) *c*.20 Oct. (*Charter Witness Lists*, i. 173–5).

(3) Longest witness list includes 1 bishop, 6 earls.

(4) Westminster (ibid.).

(5) Settlement with Hubert de Burgh (*CRR*, xvi: *1237–42*, p. xxxvi). Probable that final partition of county palatine of Chester also took place at this meeting (*CRR*, xvi: *1237–42*, p. xix, and no. 136c; Eales, 'Henry III and the End of the Norman Earldom of Chester', 109–10).

13. 1240

(1) 15 May (*CR*, *1237–42*, 240–1).

(2) 'magnum colloquium' (*Ann. Tewkesbury*, 115).

(3) Agreement with David of Wales witnessed by archbish. York, 4 bishops, 1 earl, 3 barons, and various Welsh (*CR*, *1237–42*, 241).

(4) Gloucester (ibid.).

(5) Knighting of David of Wales and agreement with him (ibid.; *Ann. Tewkesbury*, 115).

14. 1240

(1) *c.*5 June (N. Denholm-Young, *Richard of Cornwall* (Oxford, 1947), 41).

(2) 'magnum concilium' (*Ann. Tewkesbury*, 115).

(4) London (ibid.).

(5) Richard of Cornwall sets off from council for his crusade (ibid.). Settlement between Gilbert Marshal, earl of Pembroke, and king probably made in this parliament (ibid.; *CChR, 1226–57*, 252–3; *Paris*, iv. 56).

?15. 1241

(1) *c.*1–3 March (*CRR*, xvi: *1237–42*, no. 1493, p. 289).

(3) Archbish. York, 3 bishops, 2 earls, *c.*16 barons, senior bench justice and another justice (ibid., no. 1493 (p. 289) and p. xix; *Charter Witness Lists*, i. 180).

(4) Woodstock.

(5) Judgement in dispute about whether a Welsh castle and lands were held from the king or Gilbert Marshal (*CRR*, xvi: *1237–42*, p. xix).

(6) This assembly may be an afforced meeting of the council, though Meekings (ibid.) thinks that it could be called a parliament.

16. 1241.

(1) *c.*1–16 Oct. (*Charter Witness Lists*, i. 182–3).

(3) Charter witnesses include archbish. York, 3 bishops, 5 earls (ibid.).

(4) Westminster (ibid.).

(5) William de Forz surrenders his claim to a share in the county of Chester (*CChR, 1226–57*, 263; Eales, 'Henry III and the End of the Norman Earldom of Chester', 110). Possible that king's orders to bishops to enquire into benefices held by Italians originated at this meeting (*CR, 1237–42*, 365).

17. 1242—TAX REFUSED

(1) Writs of summons issued on 14 Dec. 1241 for assembly on 28 Jan. 1242 (*CR, 1237–42*, 428); immediately before 2 Feb. (*Paris*, iv. 181).

(2) 'magnum concilium' (*Paris*, iv. 181); 'colloquium' (*CR, 1237–42*, 431).

(3) All the nobility of England, prelates, earls, and barons (*Paris*, iv. 181).

(4) London (*CR, 1237–42*, 428, 431; *Paris*, iv. 181).

(5) Henry seeks tax for campaign in Poitou, but is refused. Royal policy criticized by magnates: his undertaking to cross to Poitou given without their consent; king has had many taxes; has made money from escheats, wardships, vacancy revenues, and the eyre; would be breaking truce with France in going to war; has failed to observe Magna Carta. King summons them individually to persuade each of them to give money, but fails. Magnates' reply is put in writing (*Paris*, iv. 181–8).

18. 1242

(1) 22 July. Forthcoming assembly at this date is mentioned in writ of 30 June (*CR, 1237–42*, 447).
(2) 'parliamentum regis' (ibid.).
(4) London (ibid.).
(5) John de Neville to be permitted to hold a forest bailiwick until this parliament (ibid.)
(6) Sayles, *King's Parliament*, 41, doubts if this parliament met, since the king was overseas; but Walter de Gray, archbish. York, who was regent and who attested the writ concerning Neville, was at Westminster *c.*9–27 July (*CPR, 1232–47*, 298–300).

19. 1244

(1) *c.*15 Aug. (*Paris*, iv. 380). The king was at Newcastle from 1 to 15 Aug. (*CRR*, xviii: *1243–45*, p. xxii).
(2) 'concilium' (*Paris*, iv. 380); 'parleamentum' (*CR, 1242–47*, 221).
(3) 'the *universitas* of all the nobles of England' (*Paris*, iv. 380). Writs of summons issued to 9 bishops, 26 abbots and priors, 9 earls, and 72 barons. Lesser tenants summoned through sheriffs (*Close Rolls (Supplementary) of the Reign of Henry III, 1244–66*, 1–3).
(4) Newcastle-on-Tyne (*Close Rolls (Supplementary)*, 1–3; *CR, 1242–47*, 221).
(5) What had begun as a military expedition against the Scots ends with a peace settlement at Newcastle (*Paris*, iv. 380; *CPR, 1232–47*, 434).
(6) The assembly of an army is transformed into a parliament. Cf. Maddicott, ' "An Infinite Multitude of Nobles" ', 21, 29–30).

20. 1244

(1) 9 Sept. (*Ann. Dunstable*, 164; Powicke, *King Henry III*, 298 n. 2).
(2) 'parliamentum' (*Ann. Dunstable*, 164).
(3) Magnates.
(4) Windsor.
(5) Temporalities of his see restored to William Raleigh, bishop of Winchester (ibid.; *CR, 1242–47*, 227).

21. 1244—TAX REFUSED

(1) *c*.3 Nov. (*Paris*, iv. 395; Powicke, *King Henry III*, 298 n. 2). Lasts one week (*Paris*, iii. 365).
(2) 'magnum concilium' (*Paris*, iii. 362).
(3) Magnates of the whole kingdom, archbishs., bishops, abbots, priors, earls, and barons (ibid.).
(4) Westminster—abbey refectory (ibid.).
(5) King asks for tax to pay debts incurred in Gascony. Committee of prelates, earls, and barons set up to consider this. King criticized for failing to observe Magna Carta, and wasting money already granted. Magnates ask to be able to choose justiciar and chancellor. King refuses but promises amends. Further parliament to meet on 23 Feb. If magnates are content with his actions in the meantime, they will consider an aid, to be spent under the direction of the committee. King fails to secure grant from clergy. 'Paper Constitution' follows (*Paris*, iv. 362–8, 395).

22. 1245—TAX GRANTED (AID OF 20S. PER FEE FOR MARRIAGE OF KING'S DAUGHTER)

(1) 23 Feb. (*Paris*, iv. 372).
(2) 'concilium' (ibid.).
(3) Magnates and prelates. Proctors sent on behalf of two archbishs. and chapters of Bath and Wells, Coventry, Chichester, sees then vacant (ibid.).
(4) London (ibid.).
(5) Continuation of previous parliament. King renews request for tax. He promises to observe Magna Carta and is granted an aid at 20s. per fee from those holding from him in chief. He is reminded of how many previous taxes he has received (ibid. 372–4; *Ann. Dunstable*, 167).

23. 1245

(1) *c.*4 June (*CR*, 1242–47, 357).

(3) Magnates (ibid.). 7–12 June, charters witnessed by archbish. York, 1 bishop, 2 earls (*Charter Witness Lists*, ii. 5). Barons and knights (*C. and S.* ii. i. 392). *CPR, 1232–47*, 454, 463, indicates that the letter in the name of barons and knights was drafted at this June parliament and not at the preceding February meeting, as *C. and S.* ii. i. 388 suggests.

(4) Westminster.

(5) Richard de Clare, earl of Gloucester, brings *c.*40 young men to London to be knighted at Whitsun, 4 June (*Paris*, iv. 419). Consent of magnates secured for Welsh campaign (*CR, 1242–47*, 357). King orders enquiries to be made throughout counties as to revenues paid to papal and Italian appointees. Baronial letters of protest at papal exactions prepared for dispatch to curia (ibid.; *CR, 1242–47*, 356–7; *CPR, 1232–47*, 454; *C. and S.* ii. i. 391–5). Possible protest from knights at illicit distraints to knighthood (*CR, 1242–47*, 356).

24. 1246

(1) *c.*17 Jan. (*Charter Witness Lists*, ii. 9).

(3) Charter of 17 Jan. witnessed by 4 earls, 9 barons.

(4) Westminster (ibid.).

(5) Concessions to countess of Leicester, abbey of Chester, and burgesses of Chester possibly associated with this parliament (*CR, 1242–47*, 382–3).

25. 1246

(1) 18 Mar. (*Paris*, iv. 518). Writ of summons for prior of Durham issued on 25 Jan. for meeting on 18 Mar. (Piper, 'Writs of Summons of 1246, 1247 and 1255', 286).

(2) 'parlamentum generalissimum', 'magnum parlamentum' (*Paris*, iv. 518); 'convocatio' (ibid. iv. 554); 'magnum parliamentum' (*Ann. Worcester*, 437); 'parliamentum' (*Ann. Burton*, 278); 'parliamentum' (*Ann. Winchester*, 90).

(3) Abbots, priors, bishops, earls, and barons (*Paris*, iv. 518); magnates and clergy (*Ann. Burton*, 278); bishops, abbots, and priors (*Ann. Dunstable*, 169). That archdeacons and deans were also present is suggested by *C. and S.* ii. i. 398.

(4) London (Piper, 'Writs of Summons of 1246, 1247 and 1255', 286; *Paris*, iv. 518; *Ann. Winchester*, 90); Westminster (*Ann. Burton*, 278).

(5) King addresses first bishops, then earls and barons, then abbots and priors on matters concerning which envoys had been sent to council of Lyons. Further letters of protest at papal exactions sent to curia (*Paris*, iv. 526–36).

(6) King, magnates, and prelates unite against papal exactions.

26. 1246

(1) 7 July (*Paris*, iv. 560). 15 July (*Ann. Winchester*, 90).

(2) 'parlamentum', 'magnum concilium' (*Paris*, iv. 560); 'grande colloquium' (*Ann. Winchester*, 90).

(3) Magnates (*Paris*, iv. 560).

(4) Winchester (ibid.).

(5) Business of the whole kingdom and esp. 'desolation of the church'. Return of envoys from papal curia. They report pope's refusal to make concessions, provoking anger of king and magnates (ibid.). Countess of Warenne is given seisin of the Marshal's staff of office (*Ann. Winchester*, 90).

27. 1247

(1) 3 Feb. (*Paris*, iv. 594).

(2) 'magnum concilium', 'parlamentum' (ibid. 590, 594).

(3) Magnates, clergy, archdeacons; dean of Wells and representatives of chapter; bishops absent themselves (ibid. 590; *C. and S.* ii. i. 390).

(4) London (*Paris*, iv. 594).

(5) French threat to Gascony discussed by king and magnates. Further discussions about papal exactions. Decided *de communi consilio* to send further remonstrance to curia (ibid. 594–7).

28. 1247

(1) 7 Apr. (*Paris*, iv. 622).

(2) 'magnum parlamentum' (ibid.); 'parlomentum, parlamentum, parliamentum' (Winchester pipe roll: Vincent, 'Politics of Church and State', 165); 'generalis congregatio' (*Wykes*, 96).

(3) Magnates and prelates (*Paris*, iv. 622); magnates, bishops, earls, and barons (*Wykes*, 96).

(4) Oxford (ibid.).

(5) Bishops strictly summoned because king saw how much they were impoverished by papal exactions and how much money was leaving the country. But they agree to a levy of 11,000 marks, though they make further protests to curia (*Paris*, iv. 622–3, vi. 144–6; *C. and S.* II. i. 390). Recoinage agreed by counsel and assent of those present (*Wykes*, 96).

29.   1247

(1) *c.*15–21 May (*Charter Witness Lists*, ii. 22–3).
(3) Charters witnessed by 4 bishops, 6 earls (ibid.).
(4) Windsor (ibid.).
(5) Revocation of earlier grant of Winchelsea and Rye to abbey of Fécamp, in consideration of the safety of the realm, 'by the counsel of the great men of the realm', on 15 May (*CChR, 1226–57*, 321).

30.   1247

(1) 13 Oct. (*Paris*, iv. 640).
(3) Magnates and prelates (ibid.).
(4) Westminster (ibid.).
(5) Reception of the Holy Blood at the abbey. Knighting of William de Valence (ibid. 640–5).

31.   1248—TAX REFUSED

(1) 9 Feb. (*Paris*, v. 5). Writ of summons for prior of Durham issued on 20 Nov. 1247 for meeting on 9 Feb. (Piper, 'Writs of Summons of 1246, 1247 and 1255', 286).
(2) 'generalis parlamentum' (*Paris*, v. 5); 'parleamentum' (*CR, 1247–51*, 104, 109).
(3) Barons and knights, abbots, priors and clerks, archbish. York, 8 bishops, 10 earls. Archbish. Canterbury, bishops of Durham and Bath and Wells absent (*Paris*, v. 5).
(4) London (*Paris*, v. 5; Piper, 'Writs of Summons of 1245, 1247 and 1255', 286).
(5) King asks for a tax. He is criticized for going back on his undertaking to ask for no further taxes; for patronage of aliens; for forcible purveyance of goods; for keeping bishoprics and abbacies vacant; for having no justiciar or chancellor, nor a treasurer appointed by common counsel. He promises to make amends. Business deferred until 8 July in order to assess king's conduct in the meantime (*Paris*, v. 6–8). Annulment of illicit outlawries in four counties decided on

in parliament (*CR, 1247–51*, 106–7). King issues orders endorsing magnates' wishes, made known in parliament, that churches in lay gift should not give a year's revenues to church of Canterbury, as pope had granted, during vacancies (ibid. 109).

32. 1248—TAX REFUSED

(1) 8 July (*Paris*, v. 20; *CR, 1247–51*, 31).
(2) 'magnum parliamentum' (*Paris*, v. 20); 'colloquium' (*CR, 1247–51*, 31).
(3) All *primates*, magnates (*Paris*, v. 20).
(4) London (ibid.).
(5) Continuation of previous parliament. King addresses magnates, refusing to take account of their views on appointment of great officials, and asking for a tax to recover his rights overseas. All refuse this: he has wasted their money on aliens and the kingdom's enemies (ibid. 20–1).

33. 1249

(1) 5 Jan. (*Paris*, v. 47).
(3) 'A copious multitude of magnates', including the queen, 6 earls, and 6 bishops (ibid.).
(4) Westminster (ibid.).
(5) Magnates summoned to celebrate feast of St Edward. They also come to venerate the Holy Blood (ibid.).

34. 1249

(1) 11 Apr. (*Paris*, v. 73).
(3) Magnates (ibid.). Charter witness lists, 23–5 April, include 4 bishops, 4 earls (*Charter Witness Lists*, ii. 35).
(4) London (*Paris*, v. 73).
(5) Magnates gather expecting king to fulfil his promise to appoint great officials with their counsel. But nothing done because of absence of Richard of Cornwall (ibid.).

35. 1249

(1) 14–26 Oct. (*Charter Witness Lists*, ii. 38).

(3) Charter witness lists for the period include 5 bishops, 6 earls (ibid.).

(4) Westminster (ibid.).

(5) Appointment of bishop of Hereford and Peter Chaceporc as king's proctors to pope on 23 Oct. Protection for earl of Norfolk, going to Lyons (*CPR*, *1247–58*, 52). Grant to bishop of Lincoln on 17 October (*CR*, *1247–51*, 210). Grant of Agenais to Lord Edward on 24 Oct. (*CChR*, *1226–57*, 345).

36. 1250

(1) 5 Jan. (*Paris*, v. 94).

(3) Archbish. Canterbury, 7 bishops, very many magnates (ibid.).

(4) London (ibid.).

(5) Celebration of feast of St Edward (ibid.).

37. 1251

(1) 17 Feb. (*Paris*, v. 223); *c*.2 Feb. (*Ann. Tewkesbury*, 142); *c*.16 Feb. (*Wykes*, 101).

(2) 'parlamentum', 'magnum parlamentum' (*Paris*, v. 223); 'magnum colloquium' (*Ann. Tewkesbury*, 143); 'parliamentum' (*Wykes*, 101).

(3) Charter witness lists, 16–24 Feb., include 3 bishops, 5 earls (*Charter Witness Lists*, ii. 43–4).

(4) London (*Paris*, v. 223; *Ann. Tewkesbury*, 142); Windsor (*Wykes*, 101).

(5) Trial of Henry of Bath on corruption charges (ibid.).

(6) The king was at Windsor until 19 Feb. and at Westminster from 21 Feb. The trial may have begun at Windsor and then been transferred to Westminster.

38. 1251

(1) 6–16 May (*Charter Witness Lists*, ii. 47).

(3) Charter witnesses include 5 bishops, 4 earls (ibid.).

(4) Westminster (ibid.).

(5) Grants to bishop of Lincoln and earl of Gloucester on 5 and 18 May respectively (*CR*, *1247–51*, 438, 445).

?39. 1251

(1) 8–13 July (*Charter Witness Lists*, ii. 49).
(3) Charter witnesses include 3 bishops, 3 earls (ibid.).
(4) Woodstock (ibid.).
(5) Orders to sheriffs on 8 July that only king's new money shall circulate (*CR, 1247–51*, 549). King's orders to justiciar of Chester, on complaint from poor men, to desist from undue exactions, 15 July (ibid. 551).
(6) This assembly may be an afforced meeting of the council rather than a parliament.

40. 1251

(1) 14–18 Oct. (*Charter Witness Lists*, ii. 52); Oct.? (*Ann. Tewkesbury*, 146).
(2) 'magnum parliamentum' (*Ann. Tewkesbury*, 146).
(3) Charter witnesses include 6 bishops, 5 earls (*Charter Witness Lists*, ii. 52).
(4) Westminster (ibid.); London (*Ann. Tewkesbury*, 146).

?41. 1252

(1) 18–22 Feb. (*Charter Witness Lists*, ii. 59).
(3) Charter witnesses include 7 bishops, 1 earl.
(4) Westminster (ibid.).
(5) Town of Gannoc (Degannwy) set up as a free borough by grant of 21 Feb. (*CChR, 1226–57*, 378–9).

42. 1252—TAX REFUSED?

(1) After Easter, 31 Mar. (*Ann. Tewkesbury*, 147); c.14 Apr. (*Paris*, v. 279–80); 21–8 Apr. (*Charter Witness Lists*, ii. 62–3).
(2) 'magnum parliamentum' (*Ann. Tewkesbury*, 147); 'parlamentum' (*Paris*, v. 283—seems to refer to this assembly).
(3) Magnates (*Ann. Tewkesbury*, 147). Charters witnessed by 9 bishops, 8 earls, 21–8 Apr. Grant of Gascony to Lord Edward on 28 Apr. witnessed by 7 bishops, 8 earls, c.12 barons (*Charter Witness Lists*, ii. 63; *CChR, 1226–57*, 389).
(4) London (*Ann. Tewkesbury*, 147); Westminster (*Charter Witness Lists*, ii. 62–3).

(5) Magnates summoned to discuss crusade (*Paris*, v. 279–80); king had sworn, at a public ceremony in London on 14 April, to set out on crusade on 24 June 1256 (ibid. 281–2; W. E. Lunt, *The Valuation of Norwich* (Oxford, 1926), 58). Possible that this parliament saw refusal of prelates to agree to pope's grant of crusading tax without sanction of archbish. Canterbury (*C. and S.* II. i. 449–50). Orders for a national tallage issued on 24 and 28 April (*CR, 1251–3*, 212–13) suggest that king may have been refused the more valuable levy on moveables.

43. 1252

(1) *c.*9 May–11 June (*Letters of Adam Marsh*, ed. Lawrence, i. 79).

(2) 'magnum colloquium' (*Ann. Tewkesbury*, 148—probably refers to this meeting).

(3) King, prelates, magnates, Gascon petitioners against Montfort (*Letters of Adam Marsh*, ed. Lawrence, i. 79). Charter witnesses, 9 May–11 June, include 9 bishops, 6 earls (*Charter Witness Lists*, ii. 64–7).

(4) Westminster—abbey refectory (Bémont, *Simon de Montfort, comte de Leicester*, 342).

(5) Trial of Simon de Montfort. See *Paris*, v. 287–96, and *Letters of Adam Marsh*, ed. Lawrence, i. 79–91, for full accounts.

44. 1252—TAX REFUSED

(1) 13 Oct. (*Paris*, v. 324).

(2) 'magnum parliamentum' (ibid.); 'concilium' (ibid., 336).

(3) Bishops summoned—almost all came except two archbishs., Coventry and Lichfield, Hereford (ibid. v. 324). Charter witness lists, 12–20 Oct., include 6 bishops, 5 earls (*Charter Witness Lists*, ii. 72–3).

(4) London (*Paris*, v. 324); Westminster (*Charter Witness Lists*, ii. 72–3).

(5) King asks bishops to agree to crusading tenth; they object; king asks for voluntary aid; they agree if king will confirm Magna Carta and allow money to be spent under supervision for benefit of the Holy Land; king rejects these terms (*Paris*, v. 324–32; *C. and S.* II. i. 451). Discussions on Gascony with magnates. King asks for a tax for Gascon expedition. Magnates say that their answer depends on that of the prelates. No tax granted (*Paris*, v. 334–6).

45. 1253—(AID/SCUTAGE AT 3 M. PER FEE)

(1) 4 May (*Paris*, v. 373); immediately after Easter, 20 Apr. (*Ann. Dunstable*, 186).

(2) 'magnum parliamentum' (*Paris*, v. 373).

(3) Earls, barons, almost all bishops except York, Coventry and Lichfield, Chichester (*Paris*, v. 373). Bishops, earls, barons, knights, abbots, priors (*Ann. Dunstable*, 186).

(4) London (*Paris*, v. 373).

(5) Subsidy sought for recovery of Gascony (*Ann. Dunstable*, 186). Ecclesiastical deputation seeks liberties of the church from king. After more than fifteen days' debate bishops finally agree to crusading tenth, to be spent under supervision of magnates when king departs for Holy Land. Aid on knights' fees also conceded. Solemn confirmation of Charters, which king promises to observe, in exchange (*Paris*, v. 373–8).

(6) Two taxes sought: one, from bishops, for Henry's crusade; another, from magnates and knights, for king's expedition to Gascony.

?46. 1253

(1) 15–21 June (*Charter Witness Lists*, ii. 90–1).

(3) Charter witnesses include 6 bishops, 3 earls.

(4) Winchester (ibid.).

(5) Probably concerned with government of England in king's absence: e.g. arrangements for custody of great seal (*CPR*, *1247–58*, 200; *CR*, *1251–3*, 480–1).

(6) May be an afforced meeting of the council rather than a parliament.

47. 1254

(1) 27 Jan. (*Paris*, v. 423). Writs of summons issued on 27 Dec. for 27 Jan. (*CR*, *1253–54*, 107).

(2) 'parlamentum' (*Paris*, v. 423); 'consilium' (*CR*, *1253–54*, 107).

(3) Almost all magnates and bishops, except two archbishs., Durham, Bath and Wells (*Paris*, v. 423). Archbish Canterbury, many bishops, earls, barons, priors (*Ann. Dunstable*, 189).

(4) Westminster (*CR*, *1253–54*, 107).

(5) King, in Gascony, seeks aid. Request backed by two royal envoys, sent from Gascony. Bishops promise personal service and money conditionally, but are unwilling to promise anything on behalf of lower clergy. Magnates promise military service, also conditionally. Richard of Cornwall reports to king that he is unlikely to receive aid from the other laity unless he orders Charters to be firmly observed. King's statement as to emergency in Gascony disbelieved (*Paris*, v. 423–5; *Royal Letters*, ii. 101–2; *Ann. Dunstable*, 189).

48. 1254—TAX REFUSED

(1) 26 Apr. (*Paris*, v. 440; *C. and S.* ii. i. 482). On 11 Feb. orders were issued for the election of knights in the counties to attend at Westminster on 26 Apr. (*CR, 1253–54*, 114–15).

(2) 'parlamentum' (*C. and S.* ii. i. 482).

(3) Magnates (*Paris*, v. 440). Archbish. Canterbury, bishops, king's councillors, representatives of lower clergy (*C. and S.* ii. i. 482–3). Knights?

(4) Westminster (*C. and S.* ii. i. 482); London (*Paris*, v. 440).

(5) Lower clergy grant one year's worth of triennial tenth, but under such restrictive conditions as to make grant nugatory. Magnates offer service to king if Gascony invaded. Simon de Montfort appears and reveals king's deceitfulness. No grant made (*Paris*, v. 440; *C. and S.* ii. i. 482–3).

49. 1255—TAX REFUSED

(1) 11 Apr. (*Paris*, v. 493—editor's marginal date, 6 Apr., is wrong; *Ann. Dunstable*, 195; *Ann. Burton*, 336). Writ of summons issued to prior of Durham probably in late Jan. for meeting on 18 Apr. (Piper, 'Writs of Summons of 1246, 1247 and 1255', 286). Two other chancery writs issued in February also give 18 Apr. (*CR, 1254–56*, 162; *CPR, 1247–58*, 399).

(2) 'magnum parlamentum', 'concilium' (*Paris*, v. 493, 495); 'parliamentum' (*Ann. Burton*, 336); 'parliamentum solemne' (*Ann. Dunstable*, 195); 'parleamentum' (*CR, 1254–56*, 162).

(3) All the nobles, ecclesiastical and secular, 'so that never before was seen such a populous multitude gathered there' (*Paris*, v. 493); archbish. York, Richard of Cornwall, all bishops, abbots, earls, and barons of the kingdom (*Ann. Burton*, 336). Charter of 23 Apr. witnessed by archbish. York, 6 bishops, 3 earls (*Charter Witness Lists*, ii. 95).

(4) London (Piper, 'Writs of Summons of 1246, 1247 and 1255', 286; *Paris*, v. 493); Westminster (*Ann. Burton*, 336).

(5) King asks for aid to pay debts. Magnates demand observance of Charters; great officials to be appointed and removed by common counsel. Consideration of king's request deferred until Michaelmas to see if king observed Charters in the meantime. Reported that king did not accept these conditions (*Paris*, v. 493–4; *Ann. Dunstable*, 195; *Ann. Burton*, 336).

?50. 1255

(1) 19 July. Summons to archbish. York issued on 7 June for meeting on 19 July (*CR, 1253–54*, 140–1).

(2) 'consilium' (ibid.).
(3) Archbish. York, Richard of Cornwall, and other magnates (ibid.).
(4) Oxford (ibid.).
(5) Business affecting king's status and lands, including Gascony (ibid.). Also discussed amercements imposed on London citizens in respect of the exchange (Sayles, *King's Parliament*, 45).
(6) This assembly may be an afforced meeting of the council rather than a parliament.

51. 1255—TAX REFUSED

(1) 13 Oct. (*Paris*, v. 520; *CR*, 1254–56, 223–4).
(2) 'parlamentum' (*Paris*, v. 520); 'concilium' (ibid. 531); 'parliamentum' (*Ann. Burton*, 360).
(3) Almost all the magnates (*Paris*, v. 520).
(4) Westminster (ibid.).
(5) Conditions for Sicily announced [thus Lunt, *Financial Relations*, 269 and Powicke, *King Henry III*, 375 n. 1. This seems highly likely, although there is no firm statement in the chronicle sources to this effect. See account of next parliament]. 18 Oct., Edmund is invested with the kingdom of Sicily (*Paris*, v. 515). King asks magnates for aid, beginning with Richard of Cornwall. He refuses: Sicilian Business undertaken without his consent or that of baronage. Magnates say they have not been summoned according to Magna Carta, and decline to respond without their peers. Discussion prolonged for a month but no tax granted (*Paris*, v. 520–1, 529–31). In an undated letter king reports to cardinals that magnates judged conditions for Sicily excessively severe (*CR*, 1254–56, 406—this letter can be assigned to *c*. Mar. 1256). Conditions simultaneously revealed to ecclesiastical assembly by papal legate Rostand (*Paris*, v. 524–7). Tax sought from clergy (*Ann. Burton*, 360). Plea between archbishop of Canterbury and bishop of Rochester (*CR*, 1254–56, 223–4).

52. 1257—TAX REFUSED

(1) 18 Mar. (*Paris*, v. 621); writ of summons issued to abbot of Burton on 12 Feb. for meeting on 16 Mar. (*Ann. Burton*, 384).
(2) 'magnum parliamentum' (*Paris*, v. 621); 'tractatus' (*Ann. Burton*, 384).
(3) Bishops, earls, abbots, priors (*Ann. Dunstable*, 202; prelates and magnates (*Ann. Burton*, 384).
(4) London (*Ann. Burton*, 384); Westminster—abbey chapter house (ibid. 386).

(5) Discussion of Richard of Cornwall's departure and state of kingdom (*Ann. Burton*, 384; *Ann. Dunstable*, 202). Richard comes to say farewell (*Paris*, v. 622). King presents his son Edmund to parliament in Apulian costume and appeals for aid. He reveals to those assembled papal conditions for conferring Sicily on Edmund, to general consternation. [But it seems very probable that Paris's account of Edmund's presentation and of the revelation of the conditions for the Sicilian grant refers to the parliament of Oct. 1255. The royal letter to the cardinals, *CR, 1254–56*, 406, is proof that the conditions had already been made known to the magnates before Mar. 1257.] Clergy offer £52,000 on condition that Magna Carta is observed (*Paris*, v. 623; *C. and S.* II. i. 524—notes that this offer may date to May meeting). After Rostand's address to clergy and laity on Sicilian Business, the magnates put forward in writing their reasons for opposing the project (*Ann. Burton*, 386–8; *Ann. Dunstable*, 199–200). Possible that further discussion on Sicily took place at later session of parliament on 22 Apr. (*Ann. Burton*, 392) and that the church council briefly mentioned by Paris as taking place on 30 Apr. 1256 (*Paris*, v. 553; *C. and S.* II. i. 509–10) refers to the same meeting.

53. 1257

(1) 20 May–4 June (*Charter Witness Lists*, ii. 107–8).
(3) Charter witnesses include 2 bishops, 5 earls (ibid.). Representatives of lower clergy summoned to clerical meeting (*Ann. Burton*, 389).
(4) London (ibid.); Westminster (*Charter Witness Lists*).
(5) Clerical assembly, *c.*6 May. The clergy offer the king a lump sum for Sicily (*Ann. Burton*, 389; *C. and S.* II. i. 524).
(6) A clerical council in May may have followed or overlapped with the parliament recorded for 22 Apr. in *Ann. Burton*, 392 (*C. and S.* II. i. 524).

54. 1257

(1) 18–27 Oct. (*Charter Witness Lists*, ii. 114).
(2) Charter witnesses include 5 bishops, 3 earls (ibid.).
(6) Some corroboration of the holding of a major assembly at this time is offered by the king's orders for the provision of large quantities of supplies for the feast of St Edward (*CR, 1256–59*, 153).

Bibliography

MANUSCRIPT SOURCES

Aberystwyth, National Library of Wales, MS Peniarth 390.

London, British Library, Add. MS 8167.

London, British Library, Cotton MS Claudius C. II.

Oxford, Bodleian Library, MS Digby 11.

Taunton, Somerset Record Office, Acland Hood MSS, MS DD/AH, 186.

PRINTED SOURCES

Adae Murimuth Continuatio Chronicarum, ed. E. M. Thompson, RS (London, 1889).

Aelfrics Grammatik und Glossar, ed. J. Zupita (Berlin, 1880), repr. with preface by H. Gneuss (Hildesheim, 1996).

Anglo-Saxon Charters, ed. and trans. A. J. Robertson (Cambridge, 1939).

Anglo-Saxon Charters: An Annotated List and Bibliography, ed. P. H. Sawyer, Royal Historical Soc. Handbook (London, 1968).

The Anglo-Saxon Chronicle, ed. and trans. D. Whitelock (London, 1961).

Anglo-Saxon Prose, ed. and trans. M. Swanton (London, 1975).

Anglo-Saxon Writs, ed. F. Harmer (Manchester, 1952).

Anglo-Scottish Relations, 1174–1328: Some Selected Documents, ed. and trans. E. L. G. Stones (London, 1965).

Annales Londonienses, in *Chronicles of the Reigns of Edward I and Edward II*, ed. W. Stubbs, 2 vols., RS (London, 1882).

Annales Monasterii de Burton, 1004–1263, in *Ann. Mon.* i.

Annales Monasterii de Oseneia, 1016–1347, in *Ann. Mon.* iv.

Annales Monasterii de Theokesberia, in *Ann. Mon.* i.

Annales Monasterii de Waverleia, AD. *1–1291*, in *Ann. Mon.* ii.

Annales Monasterii de Wintonia, 519–1277, in *Ann. Mon.* ii.

Annales Monastici, ed. H. R. Luard, 5 vols. RS (London, 1864–9).

Annales Paulini, in *Chronicles of the Reigns of Edward I and Edward II*, ed. W. Stubbs, 2 vols., RS (London, 1882).

Annales Prioratus de Dunstaplia, AD. *1–1297*, in *Ann. Mon.* iii.

Annales Prioratus de Wigornia, AD. *1–1377*, in *Ann. Mon.* iv.

Asser's Life of King Alfred, ed. W. H. Stevenson, 2nd edn., with introd. by D. Whitelock (Oxford, 1959).

Bartholomaei de Cotton, Historia Anglicana, ed. H. R. Luard, RS (London, 1859).

Bede's Ecclesiastical History of the English People, ed. B. Colgrave and R. A. B. Mynors, OMT (Oxford, 1969).

Béroul, *Roman de Tristan*, ed. E. Muret, 4th edn., rev. L. M. Defourques (Paris, 1957).

—— *The Romance of Tristan*, trans. A. S. Fedrick (London, 1970).

The Book of Fees, Commonly Called Testa de Nevill, ed. H. C. Maxwell-Lyte, 3 vols., HMSO (London, 1920–31).

Bracton, *De Legibus et Consuetudinibus Anglie*, ed. G. E. Woodbine, trans. and rev. S. E. Thorne, 4 vols. (Cambridge, Mass., 1968–77).

Bracton's Note Book, ed. F. W. Maitland, 3 vols. (London, 1887).

Byrhtferth of Ramsey, *The Lives of St Oswald and St Ecgwine*, ed. and trans. M. Lapidge, OMT (Oxford, 2009).

Calendar of Charter Rolls, 1226–57, HMSO (London, 1903).

Calendar of Documents Relating to Scotland, ed. J. Bain, 4 vols. (Edinburgh, 1881–8).

Calendar of Fine Rolls, 1272–1307, HMSO (London, 1911).

Calendar of Liberate Rolls, 1267–72, HMSO (London, 1964).

Calendar of Patent Rolls, 1232–72, 4 vols., HMSO (London, 1906–13).

Calendar of Plea and Memoranda Rolls of the City of London, 1323–64, ed. A. H. Thomas (Cambridge, 1926).

The Carmen de Hastingae Proelio of Guy, Bishop of Amiens, ed. and trans. F. Barlow, OMT (Oxford, 1999).

Cartularium Monasterii de Ramseia, ed. W. H. Hart and P. A. Lyons, 3 vols., RS (London, 1884–94).

Cartularium Saxonicum, ed. W. de Gray Birch, 3 vols. (London, 1885–99).

Charters of Abingdon Abbey, part 2, ed. S. E. Kelly, ASCh. VIII (Oxford, 2001).

Charters of Burton Abbey, ed. P. H. Sawyer, ASCh. II (Oxford, 1979).

Charters of Peterborough Abbey, ed. S. E. Kelly, ASCh. 14 (Oxford, 2009).

Charters of St Paul's, London, ed. S. E. Kelly, ASCh. X (Oxford, 2004).

Charters of Sherborne, ed. M. A. O' Donovan, ASCh. III (Oxford, 1988).

Chrétien de Troyes, *Erec et Enide*, ed. M. Roques (Paris, 1952).

Chronica Rogeri de Houedene, ed. W. Stubbs, 4 vols., RS (London, 1868–71).

'The Chronicle attributed to John of Wallingford', ed. R. Vaughan, *Camden Miscellany* XXI (1958).

The Chronicle of Æthelweard, ed. and trans. A. Campbell (London, 1962).

The Chronicle of Battle Abbey, ed. E. Searle, OMT (Oxford, 1980).

The Chronicle of John of Worcester, ed. and trans. R. R. Darlington, P. McGurk, and J. Bray, 2 vols., OMT (Oxford, 1995–8).

The Chronicle of Pierre de Langtoft, ed. T. Wright, 2 vols., RS (London, 1866–8).

The Chronicle of Richard of Devizes, ed. J. T. Appleby (London, 1963).

The Chronicle of Richard, Prior of Hexham, in *Chrons. Stephen . . . Richard I*, iii.

The Chronicle of Robert of Torigni, in *Chrons. Stephen . . . Richard I*, iv.

The Chronicle of Walter of Guisborough, ed. H. Rothwell, Camden Ser. 89 (1957).

The Chronicle of William de Rishanger of the Barons' Wars, ed. J. O. Halliwell, Camden Soc. (London, 1840).

Chronicles of the Reigns of Edward I and Edward II, ed. W. Stubbs, 2 vols., RS (London, 1882–3).

Chronicles of the Reigns of Stephen, Henry II and Richard I, ed. R. Howlett, 4 vols., RS (1884–9).

Chronicon de Lanercost, ed. J. Stevenson, Maitland Club (Edinburgh, 1839).

Chronicon vulgo dictum Chronicon Thomae Wykes, 1066–1288, in *Ann. Mon.* iv.

Close Rolls, 1231–1272, 14 vols., HMSO (London, 1905–38).

Close Rolls (Supplementary) of the Reign of Henry III, 1244–66, HMSO (London, 1975).

Codex Diplomaticus Aevi Saxonici, ed. J. M. Kemble, 6 vols. (London, 1839–48).

Commendatio Lamentabilis, in *Chronicles of the Reigns of Edward I and Edward II*, ed. W. Stubbs, 2 vols., RS (London, 1882–3), ii.

Continuation of William of Newburgh, in *Chrons. Stephen . . . Richard I*, ii.

The Correspondence of Thomas Becket, Archbishop of Canterbury, 1162–70, ed. and trans. A. Duggan, 2 vols., OMT (Oxford, 2000).

Councils and Synods, I: A.D. *871–1204, with Other Documents Relating to the English Church*, ed. D. Whitelock, M. Brett, and C. N. L. Brooke, 2 vols. (Oxford, 1981).

Councils and Synods, II: A.D. *1205–1313, with Other Documents Relating to the English Church*, ed. F. M. Powicke and C. R. Cheney, 2 vols. (Oxford, 1964).

Crook, D., *Records of the General Eyre*, HMSO (London, 1982).

Curia Regis Rolls, vii: *1213–1215*; xv: *1233–37*; xvi: *1237–42*, HMSO (London, 1935–79).

De Antiquis Legibus Liber: Cronica Maiorum et Vicecomitum Londoniarum, ed. T. Stapleton, Camden Soc. (London, 1846).

Dialogus de Scaccario, ed. E. Amt, OMT (Oxford, 2007).

Diplomatarium Anglicum Aevi Saxonici, ed. B. Thorpe (London, 1865).

Diplomatic Documents, i: *1101–1272*, ed. P. Chaplais, HMSO (London, 1964).

Documents Illustrating the Crisis of 1297–98 in England, ed. M. Prestwich, Camden, 4th ser. 24 (1980).

Documents of the Baronial Movement of Reform and Rebellion, 1258–1267, ed. R. F. Treharne and I. J. Sanders, OMT (Oxford, 1973).

Eadmer, *Historia Novorum in Anglia*, ed. M. Rule, RS (London, 1884).

Early Huntingdonshire Lay Subsidy Rolls, ed. J. A. Raftis and M. P. Hogan (Toronto, 1976).

Early Registers of Writs, ed. E. de Haas and G. D. G. Hall, Selden Soc. 89 (1970).

The Ecclesiastical History of Orderic Vitalis, ed. and trans. M. Chibnall, 6 vols., OMT (Oxford, 1969–80).

English Historical Documents, i: *c.550–1042*, ed. and trans. D. Whitelock, 2nd edn. (London, 1979).

English Historical Documents, ii: *1042–1189*, ed. D. C. Douglas (London, 1953).

English Historical Documents, iii: *1189–1327*, ed. H. Rothwell (London, 1975).

English Lawsuits from William I to Richard I, ed. R. C. van Caenegem, 2 vols., Selden Soc. 106–7 (1990–1).

Eynsham Cartulary, ed. H. E. Salter, 2 vols., Oxford Historical Soc. (1907–8).

Fleta, vol. ii, ed. H. G. Richardson and G. O. Sayles, Selden Soc. 72 (1955).

Flores Historiarum, ed. H. R. Luard, 3 vols., RS (London, 1870).

Foedera, Conventiones, Litterae et Acta Publica, ed. T. Rymer, new edn., vol. I, part i, ed. A. Clark and F. Holbrooke, Record Comm. (London, 1816).

Fortescue, Sir John, *De Laudibus Legum Anglie*, ed. S. B. Chrimes (Cambridge, 1942).

—— *On the Laws and Governance of England*, ed. S. Lockwood (Cambridge, 1997).

—— *The Governance of England*, ed. C. Plummer (Oxford, 1885).

Geffrei Gaimar, *L'Estoire des Engleis*, ed. A. Bell, Anglo-Norman Text Soc. (1960).

Geoffrey of Monmouth, *The History of the Kings of Britain*, trans. L. Thorpe (London, 1966).

Die Gesetze der Angelsachsen, ed. F. Liebermann, 3 vols. (Halle, 1903–16).

Gesta Abbatum Monasterii Sancti Albani, ed. H. T. Riley, 3 vols., RS (London, 1867–9).

The Gesta Guillelmi of William of Poitiers, ed. and trans. R. H. C. Davis and M. Chibnall, OMT (Oxford, 1998).

The Gesta Normannorum Ducum of William of Jumièges, ed. and trans. E. M. C. van Houts, 2 vols., OMT (Oxford, 1992–5).

Gesta Regis Henrici Secundi Benedicti Abbatis [by Roger of Howden], ed. W. Stubbs, 2 vols., RS (London, 1867).

Gesta Stephani, ed. and trans. K. R. Potter, rev. R. H. C. Davis, OMT (Oxford, 1976).

Giraldus Cambrensis, *Expugnatio Hibernica: The Conquest of Ireland*, ed. A. B. Scott and F. X. Martin (Dublin, 1978).

—— *Opera*, ed. J. S. Brewer, J. F. Dimock, and G. F. Warner, 8 vols., RS (London, 1861–91).

Glanvill: The Treatise of the Laws and Customs of the Realm of England, ed. and trans. G. D. G. Hall (London, 1965).

Guernes de Pont-Sainte-Maxence, *La Vie de Saint Thomas Becket*, ed. E. Walberg (Paris, 1936).

Henry of Huntingdon, *Historia Anglorum*, ed. D. Greenway, OMT (Oxford, 1996).

Hincmar, *De Ordine Palatii*, ed. T. Gross and R. Schieffer, Monumenta Germaniae Historica (Hanover, 1980).

Historia Ecclesie Abbendonensis: The History of the Church of Abingdon, ed. and trans. J. Hudson, 2 vols., OMT (Oxford, 2002–7).

The Historia Regum Britanniae of Geoffrey of Monmouth, ed. N. Wright (Cambridge, 1985).

The Historical Collections of Walter of Coventry, ed. W. Stubbs, 2 vols., RS (London, 1872–3).

The Historical Works of Gervase of Canterbury, ed. W. Stubbs, 2 vols., RS (1879–80).

The History of Feudalism, ed. D. Herlihy (London, 1970).

History of William Marshal, ed. A. J. Holden, 3 vols., Anglo-Norman Text Soc. (2002–6).

The Homilies of Wulfstan, ed. D. Bethurum (Oxford, 1957).

Hugh the Chanter, *The History of the Church of York, 1066–1127*, ed. and trans. C. Johnson, rev. M. Brett, C. N. L. Brooke, and M. Winterbottom, OMT (Oxford, 1990).

Die *'Institutes of Polity, Civil and Ecclesiastical': Ein Werk Erzbischof Wulfstans von York*, ed. K. Jost (Bern, 1959).

Ioannis Saresberiensis Policratici, ed. C. C. J. Webb, 2 vols. (Oxford, 1909).

Johanni de Trokelowe et Henrici de Blaneforde, Chronica et Annales, ed. H. T. Riley, RS (London, 1866).

John of Salisbury, *Policraticus*, trans. C. J. Nederman (Cambridge, 1990).

Jordan Fantosme's Chronicle, ed. R. C. Jordan (Oxford, 1981).

Knighton's Chronicle, 1337–1396, ed. G. H. Martin, OMT (Oxford, 1995).

Lancashire Lay Subsidies, i: *Henry III to Edward I*, ed. J. A. C. Vincent, Lancashire and Cheshire Rec. Soc. 27 (1893).

The Laws of the Earliest English Kings, ed. and trans. F. L. Attenborough (Cambridge, 1922).

The Laws of the Kings of England from Edmund to Henry I, ed. and trans. A. J. Robertson (Cambridge, 1925).

The Laws of the Medieval Kingdom of Hungary, i: *1000–1301*, ed. and trans. J. M. Bak, G. Bónis, and J. R. Sweeney (Bakersfield, Calif., 1989).

The Letters and Charters of Gilbert Foliot, ed. A. Morey and C. N. L. Brooke (Cambridge, 1967).

The Letters and Poems of Fulbert of Chartres, ed. and trans. F. Behrends, OMT (Oxford, 1976).

The Letters of Adam Marsh, ed. and trans. C. H. Lawrence, 2 vols., OMT (Oxford, 2006–10).

The Life of King Edward the Confessor, ed. and trans. F. Barlow, 2nd edn., OMT (Oxford, 1992).

List of Sheriffs of England and Wales, PRO, Lists and Indexes, 60 (London, 1898).

Literae Cantuarienses, ed. J. B. Sheppard, 3 vols., RS (London, 1887–9).

Lives of Edward the Confessor, ed. H. R. Luard, RS (London, 1858).

Magna Vita Sancti Hugonis, ed. D. L. Douie and H. Farmer, 2 vols. (London, 1961).

Matthew Paris, *Chronica Majora*, ed. H. R. Luard, 7 vols., RS (London, 1872–83).

Memoranda de Parliamento, ed. F. W. Maitland, RS (London, 1893).

Memorials of St Dunstan, ed. W. Stubbs, RS (London, 1874).

Memorials of St Edmund's Abbey, ed. T. Arnold, 3 vols., RS (London, 1890–6).

Middle English Sermons, ed. W. O. Ross, EETS, 209 (1940).

Monumenta Franciscana, ed. J. S. Brewer, 2 vols., RS (London, 1858–82).

Norman London, by William FitzStephen, introd. F. D. Logan (New York, 1990).

Œuvres de Rigord et de Guillaume le Breton, ed. H. F. Delaborde, 2 vols. (Paris, 1882–5).

The Old English Orosius, ed. J. Bately, EETS, supplementary ser., 6 (1980).

The Old English Version of the Heptateuch, ed. S. J. Crawford, EETS 160 (1922).

Parliamentary Writs and Writs of Military Summons, ed. F. Palgrave, Record Comm., 2 vols. in 4 (London, 1827–34).

The Parliament Rolls of Medieval England, 1275–1504 (Woodbridge, 2005). Vols. i–ii: *Edward I, 1294–1307*, ed. P. Brand. Vol. iii: *1307–1327*, ed. S. Phillips. Vol. iv: *1327–1348*, ed. S. Phillips and M. Ormrod.

Patent Rolls of the Reign of Henry III, 2 vols., HMSO (London, 1901–3).

Philippe de Beaumanoir, *Coutumes de Beauvaisis*, ed. A. Salmon, 2 vols. (Paris, 1899–1900).

Pipe Rolls, 34 Henry II, 2 Richard I, 10 Richard I, 9 John, 13 John, PRS (London, 1925–53).

Pleas of the Crown of the County of Gloucester, 1221, ed. F. W. Maitland (London, 1884).

Pseudo-Cyprianus, De XII Abusivi Saeculi, ed. S. Hellmann (Leipzig, 1909).

Radulfi de Diceto Decani Londoniensis, Opera Historica, ed. W. Stubbs, 2 vols., RS (London, 1876).

Radulphi de Coggeshall, Chronicon Anglicanum, ed. J. Stevenson, RS (London, 1875).

Records of the Borough of Leicester, ii: *1327–1509*, ed. M. Bateson (Cambridge, 1901).

Recueil des actes des ducs de Normandie de 911 à 1066, ed. M. Fauroux (Caen, 1961).

The Red Book of the Exchequer, ed. H. Hall, 3 vols., RS (London, 1896).

Regesta Regum Anglo-Normannorum: The Acts of William I (1066–1087), ed. D. Bates (Oxford, 1998).

Regesta Regum Anglo-Normannorum, 1066–1154, ii: *Regesta Henrici Primi, 1100–1135*, ed. C. Johnson and H. A. Cronne (Oxford, 1956).

The Register of Walter Giffard, Archbishop of York, 1266–79, ed. W. Brown, Surtees Soc. 109 (1904).

Return of the Names of Members of Parliament, part I: *Parliaments of England, 1213–1702*, Parliamentary Papers (London, 1878).

Roberti Grosseteste Epistolae, ed. H. R. Luard, RS (London, 1861).

Roger of Wendover, *Chronica, sive Flores Historiarum*, ed. H. O. Coxe, 4 vols. (London, 1842).

Rolls of the Fifteenth and Rolls of the Fortieth, ed. F. A. Cazel and A. P. Cazel, PRS, NS 14 (1983).

Rotuli Chartarum, ed. T. D. Hardy, Record Comm. (London, 1837).

Rotuli de Oblatis et Finibus Tempore Regis Johannis, ed. T. D. Hardy, Record Comm. (London, 1835).

Rotuli Litterarum Clausarum, ed. T. D. Hardy, 2 vols., Record Comm. (London, 1833–44).

Rotuli Parliamentorum, vols. i–ii, n.p., n.d.

Royal and Other Historical Letters Illustrative of the Reign of Henry III, ed. W. W. Shirley, 2 vols., RS (1862–6).

The Royal Charter Witness Lists of Edward I (1272–1307), ed. R. Huscroft, List and Index Soc. 279 (2000).

The Royal Charter Witness Lists of Henry III (1226–1272) from the Charter Rolls in the Public Record Office, ed. M. Morris, List and Index Soc. 291–2, 2 vols. (2001).

Select Cases in the Court of King's Bench under Edward II, ed. G. O. Sayles, Selden Soc. 74 (1957).

Select Cases of Procedure without Writ under Henry III, ed. H. G. Richardson and G. O. Sayles, Selden Soc. 60 (1941).

Select Charters and Other Illustrations of English Constitutional History from the Earliest Times to the Reign of Edward the First, ed. W. Stubbs, 9th edn. (Oxford, 1913).

Select English Historical Documents of the Ninth and Tenth Centuries, ed. F. E. Harmer (Cambridge, 1914).

Select Pleas of the Forest, ed. G. J. Turner, Selden Soc. 13 (1899).

The Song of Lewes, ed. C. L. Kingsford (Oxford, 1896).

Statutes of the Realm, vol. i, Record Comm. (London, 1810).

Symeon of Durham, *Opera Omnia, Historia Regum*, ed. T. Arnold, 2 vols., RS (London, 1882–5).

Tacitus, *Germania*, trans. J. B. Rives (Oxford, 1999).

Thomas of Marlborough, *History of the Abbey of Evesham*, ed. and trans. J. Sayers and L. Watkiss, OMT (Oxford, 2003).

Two of the Saxon Chronicles Parallel, ed. C. Plummer, 2 vols. (Oxford, 1892).

The Valuation of Norwich, ed. W. E. Lunt (Oxford, 1926).

'La Vie de S. Édouard par Osbert de Clare', ed. M. Bloch, *Analecta Bollandiana*, 41 (1923).

Vita Edwardi Secundi, ed. and trans. W. R. Childs, OMT (Oxford, 2005).

'Vita Lanfranci', ed. M. Gibson, in G. Onofrio (ed.), *Lanfranco di Pavia e l'Europa del secolo XI, nel IX centenario della morte (1089–1989)* (Rome, 1993).

Wace, *The Roman de Rou*, trans. G. S. Burgess, with the text of A. J. Holden, Société Jersiaise (St Helier, 2002).

Walter Map, *De Nugis Curialium*, ed. and trans. M. R. James, C. N. L. Brooke, and R. A. B. Mynors, OMT (Oxford, 1983).

Willelmi Rishanger, Chronica et Annales, ed. H. T. Riley, RS (London, 1865).

William of Malmesbury, *Gesta Regum Anglorum*, ed. and trans. R. A. B. Mynors, R. M. Thomson, and M. Winterbottom, 2 vols., OMT (Oxford, 1998–9).

—— *Gesta Pontificum Anglorum*, ed. and trans. M. Winterbottom and R. M. Thomson, 2 vols., OMT (Oxford, 2007–8).

—— *Historia Novella*, ed. E. King, trans. K. Potter, OMT (Oxford, 1998).

—— *Saints' Lives*, ed. M. Winterbottom and R. M. Thomson, OMT (Oxford, 2002).

William of Newburgh, *Historia Rerum Anglicarum*, in *Chrons. Stephen . . . Richard I*, i–ii.

The Will of Æthelgifu, trans. D. Whitelock, Roxburghe Club (Oxford, 1968).

Wulfstan of Winchester, *Life of St Æthelwold*, ed. and trans. M. Lapidge and M. Winterbottom, OMT (Oxford, 1991).

SECONDARY SOURCES

Abels, R, *Alfred the Great* (Harlow, 1998).

Adams, G. B., *Councils and Courts in Anglo-Norman England* (New Haven, 1926).

Amt, E., *The Accession of Henry II in England* (Woodbridge, 1993).

Anderson, M. O., 'Lothian and the Early Scottish Kings', *Scottish Historical Review*, 39 (1960).

Ashe, L., *Fiction and History in England, 1066–1200* (Cambridge, 2007).

Aurell, M., *The Plantagenet Empire, 1154–1224* (Harlow, 2007).

Baker, N., and Holt, R., *Urban Growth and the Medieval Church: Gloucester and Worcester* (Aldershot, 2004).

Baldwin, J. F., *The King's Council during the Middle Ages* (Oxford, 1913).

Baldwin, J. W., *Masters, Princes and Merchants: The Social Views of Peter the Chanter and his Circle*, 2 vols. (Princeton, 1970).

—— *The Government of Philip Augustus* (Berkeley, Calif., 1986).

—— 'Master Stephen Langton, Future Archbishop of Canterbury: The Paris Schools and Magna Carta', *EHR* 123 (2008).

Banton, N., 'Monastic Reform and the Unification of Tenth-Century England', in S. Mews (ed.), *Religion and National Identity* (Oxford, 1982).

Barlow, F., *The English Church, 1000–1066* (London, 1963).

—— *William Rufus* (London, 1983).

—— *Thomas Becket* (London, 1986).

Barnwell, P. S., 'Political Assemblies: Introduction', in P. S. Barnwell and M. Mostert (eds.), *Political Assemblies in the Earlier Middle Ages* (Turnhout, 2003).

—— 'Kings, Nobles, and Assemblies in the Barbarian Kingdoms', ibid.

—— 'The Early Frankish *mallus*: Its Nature, Participants and Practices', in A. Pantos and S. Semple (eds.), *Assembly Places and Practices in Medieval Europe* (Dublin, 2004).

Barraclough, G., *The Earldom and County Palatine of Chester* (Oxford, 1953).

Barratt, N., 'The Revenue of King John', *EHR* 111 (1996).

—— 'The English Revenues of Richard I', *EHR* 116 (2001).

—— 'The Revenues of John and Philip Augustus Revisited', in S. Church (ed.), *King John: New Interpretations* (Woodbridge, 1999).

Bartlett, R., *England under the Norman and Angevin Kings, 1075–1225* (Oxford, 2000).

Barton, S., *The Aristocracy in Twelfth-Century León and Castile* (Cambridge, 1997).

Bates, D., *Normandy before 1066* (Harlow, 1982).

—— 'Britain and France and the Year 1000', *Franco-British Studies*, 28 (1999).

—— 'England and the "Feudal Revolution"', in *Il feudalesimo nell'alto medioevo*, Settimane di Studio, 2 vols. (Spoleto, 2000).

Baxter, S., *The Earls of Mercia: Lordship and Power in Late Anglo-Saxon England* (Oxford, 2007).

—— 'Lordship and Justice in Late Anglo-Saxon England: The Judicial Functions of Soke and Commendation Revisited', in S. Baxter, C. E. Karkov, J. L. Nelson, and D. Pelteret (eds.), *Early Medieval Studies in Memory of Patrick Wormald* (Farnham, 2009).

Bémont, C., *Simon de Montfort, comte de Leicester* (Paris, 1884).

—— *Chartes des libertés anglaises (1100–1305)* (Paris, 1892).

Benton, J. F., 'The Court of Champagne as a Literary Center', in his *Culture, Power and Personality in Medieval France* (London, 1991).

—— 'The Revenue of Louis VII', in his *Culture, Power and Personality*.

Beresford, M., *New Towns of the Middle Ages* (London, 1967).

Biddle, M., 'Seasonal Festivals and Residence: Winchester, Westminster and Gloucester in the Tenth to Twelfth Centuries', *ANS* 8 (1986).

Bisson, T. N., 'Celebration and Persuasion: Reflections on the Cultural Evolution of Medieval Consultation', *Legislative Studies Quarterly*, 7 (1962).

Bisson, T. N., *Assemblies and Representation in Languedoc in the Thirteenth Century* (Princeton, 1964).

—— 'The Military Origins of Medieval Representation', *American Historical Review*, 71 (1966).

—— *Conservation of Coinage: Monetary Exploitation and its Restraint in France, Catalonia and Aragon (c. A.D. 1000–c. A.D. 1225)* (Oxford, 1979).

—— *The Medieval Crown of Aragon: A Short History* (Oxford, 1986).

—— 'An "Unknown" Charter for Catalonia (A.D. 1205)', in his *Medieval France and her Pyrenean Neighbours: Studies in Early Institutional History* (London, 1989).

—— 'Consultative Functions in the King's Parlements (1250–1314)', in his *Medieval France*.

—— 'The General Assemblies of Philip the Fair: Their Character Reconsidered', in his *Medieval France*.

—— 'The Organized Peace in Southern France and Catalonia (c.1140–c.1233)', in his *Medieval France*.

—— 'An Early Provincial Assembly: The General Court of Agenais in the Thirteenth Century', in his *Medieval France*.

—— 'The Rise of Catalonia: Identity, Power and Ideology in a Twelfth-Century Society', in his *Medieval France*.

—— review of O'Callaghan, *Cortes of Castile-León*, *Speculum*, 66 (1991).

—— 'The Politicising of West European Societies (c.1175–c.1225)', in C. Duhamel-Amado and G. Lobrichon (eds.), *George Duby: l'écriture de l'histoire* (Brussels, c.1996).

—— 'The Origins of the Corts of Catalonia', *Parliaments, Estates and Representation*, 16 (1996).

—— 'Medieval Parliamentarianism: Review of Work', *Parliaments, Estates and Representation*, 21 (2001).

—— *The Crisis of the Twelfth Century: Power, Lordship and the Origin of European Government* (Princeton, 2009).

Blair, J., *Anglo-Saxon Oxfordshire* (Far Thrupp, 1994).

—— *The Church in Anglo-Saxon Society* (Oxford, 2004).

Blunt, C. E., 'The Coinage of Athelstan, King of England, 924–939', *British Numismatic Journal*, 42 (1974).

—— Stewart, B. H. I. H., and Lyons, C. S. S., *Coinage in Tenth-Century England* (Oxford, 1989).

Bournazel, E., *Le Gouvernement capétien au XIIᵉ siècle, 1108–1180* (Limoges, 1975).

Bowers, R. H., 'English Merchants and the Anglo-Flemish Economic War of 1270–1274', in R. H. Bowers (ed.), *Seven Studies in Medieval English History and Other Historical Essays Presented to Harold S. Snellgrove* (Jackson, Miss., 1983).

Brand, P., '"Multis Vigiliis Excogitatam et Inventam": Henry II and the Creation of the English Common Law', *Haskins Soc. Jnl.* 2 (1990).

—— 'The Drafting of Legislation in Mid-Thirteenth Century England', *Parliamentary History*, 9 (1990).

—— 'English Thirteenth Century Legislation', in A. Romano (ed.), . . . *colendo iustitiam et iura colendo . . . Federico II legislatore del Regno de Sicilia nell'Europa del duecento* (Rome, 1997).

—— 'The Formation of the English Legal System, 1150–1400', in A. Padoa-Schioppa (ed.), *Legislation and Justice* (Oxford, 1997).

—— *Kings, Barons and Justices: The Making and Enforcement of Legislation in Thirteenth-Century England* (Cambridge, 2003).

—— 'Petitions and Parliament in the Reign of Edward I', in L. Clarke (ed.), *Parchment and People: Parliament in the Middle Ages* (Edinburgh, 2004).

—— 'Henry II and the Creation of the English Common Law', in Harper-Bill and Vincent (eds.), *Henry II*.

—— 'Understanding Early Petitions: An Analysis of the Content of Petitions to Parliament in the Reign of Edward I', in Ormrod, Dodd, and Musson, *Medieval Petitions*.

Brooks, N., 'Arms, Status and Warfare in Late-Saxon England', in D. Hill (ed.), *Ethelred the Unready*, BAR, British ser. 59 (Oxford, 1978).

Brown, E. A. R., 'Representation and Agency Law', in her *Politics and Institutions in Capetian France* (Aldershot, 1991).

—— 'Reform and Resistance to Royal Authority in Fourteenth-Century France: The Leagues of 1314–15', in her *Politics and Institutions*.

—— *Customary Aids and Royal Finance in Capetian France: The Marriage Aid of Philip the Fair* (Cambridge, Mass., 1992).

Brown, R. A., '"The Treasury" of the Later Twelfth Century', in J. C. Davies (ed.), *Studies Presented to Sir Hilary Jenkinson* (Oxford, 1957).

—— Colvin, H. M., and Taylor, A. J., *The History of the King's Works*, vols. i–ii: *The Middle Ages*, HMSO (London, 1963).

Buck, M., 'The Reform of the Exchequer, 1316–1326', *EHR* 98 (1983).

—— *Politics, Finance and the Church in the Reign of Edward II: Walter Stapeldon, Treasurer of England* (Cambridge, 1983).

Bullock-Davies, C., *Menestrallorum Multitudo: Minstrels at a Royal Feast* (Cardiff, 1978).

Bullough, D. A., *Friends, Neighbours and Fellow-Drinkers: Aspects of Community and Conflict in the Early Medieval West*, H. M. Chadwick Memorial Lecture (Cambridge, 1991).

Bush, M., *Noble Privilege* (Manchester, 1983).

Cam, H. M., 'The Community of the Shire and the Payment of its Representatives in Parliament', in her *Liberties and Communities in Medieval England* (repr. London, 1963).

Campbell, J., 'Observations on English Government from the Tenth to the Twelfth Century', in his *Essays in Anglo-Saxon History* (London, 1986).

—— 'The Significance of the Anglo-Norman State in the Administrative History of Western Europe', in his *Essays in Anglo-Saxon History.*

—— 'England, c.991', in his *The Anglo-Saxon State* (London, 2000).

—— 'The Late Anglo-Saxon State: A Maximum View', in his *Anglo-Saxon State.*

—— 'Stubbs and the English State', in his *Anglo-Saxon State.*

—— 'The United Kingdom of England', in his *Anglo-Saxon State.*

—— 'Was it Infancy in England? Some Questions of Comparison', in his *Anglo-Saxon State.*

—— 'Some Agents and Agencies of the Late Anglo-Saxon State', in his *Anglo-Saxon State.*

—— 'Power and Authority, 600–1300', in D. M. Palliser (ed.), *The Cambridge Urban History of Britain*, i: *600–1540* (Cambridge, 2000).

Carpenter, D. A., *The Minority of Henry III* (London, 1990).

—— 'The Decline of the Curial Sheriff in England, 1194–1258', in his *The Reign of Henry III* (London, 1996).

—— 'Justice and Jurisdiction under John and Henry III', in his *Reign of Henry III.*

—— 'The Fall of Hubert de Burgh', in his *Reign of Henry III.*

—— 'King, Magnates and Society: The Personal Rule of King Henry III, 1234–1258', in his *Reign of Henry III.*

—— 'The Beginnings of Parliament', in his *Reign of Henry III.*

—— 'Chancellor Ralph de Neville and Plans of Political Reform, 1215–1258', in his *Reign of Henry III.*

—— 'English Peasants in Politics, 1258–67', in his *Reign of Henry III.*

—— 'Matthew Paris and Henry III's Speech at the Exchequer in October 1256', in his *Reign of Henry III.*

—— 'What Happened in 1258', in his *Reign of Henry III.*

—— 'Abbot Ralph of Coggeshall's Account of the Last Years of King Richard and the First Years of King John', *EHR* 113 (1998).

—— 'The Second Century of English Feudalism', *Past and Present*, 168 (2000).

—— *The Struggle for Mastery in Britain, 1066–1284* (Oxford, 2003).

—— 'King Henry III and Saint Edward the Confessor: The Origins of the Cult', *EHR* 122 (2007).

—— 'King Henry III and the Chapter House of Westminster Abbey' (forthcoming).

Carolus-Barré, L., 'La Grande Ordonnance de 1254 sur la réforme de l'administration et la police du royaume', in *Septième Centenaire de la mort de Saint-Louis: actes du colloque de Royaumont et de Paris (21–27 mai 1970)* (Paris, 1976).

Carsten, F. L., *The Origins of Prussia* (Oxford, 1954).

Chadwick, H. M., *Studies on Anglo-Saxon Institutions* (Cambridge, 1905).

Charles-Edwards, T., 'Early Medieval Kingships in the British Isles', in S. Bassett (ed.), *The Origins of Anglo-Saxon Kingdoms* (London, 1989).

Chauou, A., *L'Idéologie Plantagenêt: royauté arthurienne et monarchie politique dans l'espace Plantagenêt (XIIe–XIIIe siècles)* (Rennes, 2001).

Cheney, C. R., *Hubert Walter* (London, 1967).

—— 'The "Paper Constitution" Preserved by Matthew Paris', in his *Medieval Texts and Studies* (Oxford, 1973).

—— *Pope Innocent III and England* (Stuttgart, 1976).

Chew, H. M., *The English Ecclesiastical Tenants-in-Chief and Knight Service* (Oxford, 1932).

Christelow, S. M.., 'A Moveable Feast? Itineration and the Centralization of Government under Henry I', *Albion*, 28 (1996).

—— 'The Fiscal Management of England under Henry I', in D. F. Fleming and J. Pope (eds.), *Henry I and the Anglo-Norman World: Studies in Memory of C. Warren Hollister*, Haskins Soc. Jnl., Special Volume, 17 (Woodbridge, 2006).

Church, S. D., *The Household Knights of King John* (Cambridge, 1999).

—— (ed.), *King John: New Interpretations* (Woodbridge, 1999).

Civel, N., *La Fleur de France: les seigneurs d'Île-de-France au XIIe siècle* (Turnhout, 2006).

Clanchy, M. T., 'Did Henry III have a Policy?', *History*, 53 (1968).

—— *England and its Rulers, 1066–1272* (Oxford, 1983).

Clarke, M. V., *Medieval Representation and Consent* (London, 1936).

Clarke, P. A., *The English Nobility under Edward the Confessor* (Oxford, 1994).

Clayton, M., 'Ælfric and Æthelred', in J. Roberts and J. Nelson (eds.), *Essays on Anglo-Saxon and Related Themes in Memory of Lynne Grundy* (London, 2000).

Collinson, P., 'Servants and Citizens: Robert Beale and Other Elizabethans', *Historical Research*, 79 (2006).

Contamine, P., 'De la puissance aux privilèges: doléances de la noblesse française envers la monarchie aux xive et xve siècles', in P. Contamine (ed.), *La Noblesse au moyen âge: essais à la mémoire de Robert Boutruche* (Paris, 1976).

Coss, P., 'Sir Geoffrey de Langley and the Crisis of the Knightly Class in Thirteenth-Century England', *Past and Present*, 68 (1975).

—— *The Knight in Medieval England, 1000–1400* (Far Thrupp, 1993).

—— *The Origins of the English Gentry* (Cambridge, 2003).

Cowdrey, H. E. J., 'The Anglo-Norman *Laudes Regiae*', in his *Popes, Monks and Crusaders* (London, 1984).

—— *Lanfranc: Scholar, Monk and Archbishop* (Oxford, 2003).

—— 'Stigand', *ODNB*.

Crook, D., 'Henry of Bath', *ODNB*.

Crossley, A., *Victoria County History of Oxford*, vol. xiii (Oxford, 1996).

Crouch, D., *The Beaumont Twins: The Roots and Branches of Power in the Twelfth Century* (Cambridge, 1986).

—— *The Image of Aristocracy in Britain, 1000–1300* (London, 1992).

—— 'Normans and Anglo-Normans: A Divided Aristocracy?', in D. Bates and A. Curry (eds.), *England and Normandy in the Middle Ages* (London, 1994).

—— *The Reign of King Stephen, 1135–54* (Harlow, 2000).

—— *William Marshal: Knighthood, War and Chivalry, 1147–1219*, 2nd edn. (London, 2002).

—— *Tournament* (London, 2005).

—— *The Birth of Nobility: Constructing Aristocracy in England and France, 900–1300* (Harlow, 2005).

—— 'Robert of Gloucester', *ODNB*.

Cubitt, C., *Anglo-Saxon Church Councils, c.650–c.850* (London, 1995).

Darlington, R. R., 'Æthelwig, Abbot of Evesham', *EHR* 48 (1933).

Davidson, J. B., 'On Some Anglo-Saxon Charters at Exeter', *Jnl. of the British Archaeological Assoc.* 39 (1883).

Davies, J. C., *The Baronial Opposition to Edward II: Its Character and Policy* (Cambridge, 1918).

Davies, R. G., and Denton, J. H., *The English Parliament in the Middle Ages* (Manchester, 1981).

d'Avray, D. L., '"Magna Carta": Its Background in Stephen Langton's Academic Biblical Exegesis and its Episcopal Reception', *Studi Medievali*, 3rd ser. 38 (1997).

Davy, G., *Le Duc et la loi: héritages, images et expressions du pouvoir normatif dans le duché de Normandie, des origins à la mort du Conquérant (fin du IXe siècle–1087)* (Paris, 2004).

Denholm-Young, N., *Richard of Cornwall* (Oxford, 1947).

—— *History and Heraldry, 1254–1310: A Study of the Historical Value of the Rolls of Arms* (Oxford, 1965).

—— 'Robert Carpenter and the Provisions of Westminster', in his *Collected Papers* (Cardiff, 1969).

Denton, J. H., 'The Crisis of 1297 from the Evesham Chronicle', *EHR* 93 (1978).

—— *Robert Winchelsey and the Crown, 1294–1313* (Cambridge, 1980).

—— 'The Clergy and Parliament in the Thirteenth and Fourteenth Centuries', in Davies and Denton (eds.), *English Parl.*

—— and Dooley, J. P., *Representatives of the Lower Clergy in Parliament, 1295–1340* (Woodbridge, 1987).

Devisse, J., 'Essai sur l'histoire d'une expression qui a fait fortune: *consilium et auxilium* au IXe siècle', *Le Moyen Âge*, 74 (1968).

Dodd, G., 'The Hidden Presence: Parliament and the Private Petition in the Fourteenth Century', in A. Musson (ed.), *Expectations of the Law in the Middle Ages* (Woodbridge, 2001).

—— 'The Lords, Taxation and the Community of Parliament in the 1370s and Early 1380s', *Parliamentary History*, 20 (2001).

—— *Justice and Grace: Private Petitioning and the English Parliament in the Late Middle Ages* (Oxford, 2007).

—— 'Parliamentary Petitions? The Origins and Provenance of the "Ancient Petitions" (SC 8) in the National Archives', in Ormrod, Dodd, and Musson, *Medieval Petitions*.

Dodwell, C. R., *Anglo-Saxon Art: A New Perspective* (Manchester, 1982).

Douglas, D. C., *William the Conqueror* (London, 1964).

Duffy, S., 'Henry II and England's Insular Neighbours', in Harper-Bill and Vincent (eds.), *Henry II*.

Dumville, D., 'The Ætheling: A Study in Anglo-Saxon Constitutional History', *ASE* 8 (1979).

—— *Wessex and England from Alfred to Edgar* (Woodbridge, 1992).

Dunbabin, J., review of Baldwin, *Government of Philip Augustus*, *EHR* 103 (1988).

—— *France in the Making, 843–1180*, 2nd edn. (Oxford, 2000).

—— 'Henry II and Louis VII', in Harper-Bill and Vincent (eds.), *Henry II*.

Duncan, A. A. M., 'The Early Parliaments of Scotland', *Scottish Historical Review*, 45 (1966).

Dyer, C., *Standards of Living in the Later Middle Ages* (Cambridge, 1989).

Eales, R., 'Henry III and the End of the Norman Earldom of Chester', *TCE* 1 (1986).

Edwards, J. G., *Historians and the Medieval English Parliament*, David Murray Lecture, University of Glasgow (repr. Glasgow, 1970).

—— *The Second Century of the English Parliament* (Oxford, 1979).

—— 'The *Plena Potestas* of English Parliamentary Representatives', in *Historical Studies*.

—— 'The Personnel of the Commons in Parliament under Edward I and Edward II', in *Historical Studies*.

—— ' "Justice" in Early English Parliaments', in *Historical Studies*.

Emden, A. B., *A Biographical Register of the University of Oxford to* A.D. *1500*, 3 vols. (Oxford, 1957–9).

Eyton, R. W., *Court, Household and Itinerary of Henry II* (London, 1878).

Faulkner, K., 'The Knights in the Magna Carta Civil War', *TCE* 8 (2001).

Favier, J., 'Les Finances de Saint Louis', in *Septième Centenaire de la mort de Saint Louis: actes du colloque de Royaumont et de Paris (21–27 mai 1970)* (Paris, 1976).

Fawtier, R., *The Capetian Kings of France*, trans. L. Butler and R. J. Adams (London, 1960).

Feeney, B., 'The Effects of King John's Scutages on his East Anglian Subjects', *Reading Medieval Studies*, 11 (1985).

Fleming, R., *Kings and Lords in Conquest England* (Cambridge, 1991).

—— 'Rural Elites and Urban Communities in Late-Saxon England', *Past and Present*, 141 (1993).

—— *Domesday Book and the Law: Society and Legal Custom in Early Medieval England* (Cambridge, 1998).

Foot, S., 'The Making of *Angelcynn*: English Identity before the Norman Conquest', *TRHS* 6th ser. 6 (1996).

—— 'English People', in *Blackwell Enc.*

Foreville, R., 'The Synod of the Province of Rouen in the Eleventh and Twelfth Centuries', in C. N. L. Brooke, D. E. Luscombe, G. H. Martin, and D. Owen (eds.), *Church and Government in the Middle Ages: Essays Presented to C. R. Cheney* (Cambridge, 1976).

Fryde, E. B., 'The Financial Policies of the Royal Governments and Popular Resistance to them in England and France, *c*.1270–*c*.1470', in his *Studies in Medieval Trade and Finance* (London, 1983).

—— and Miller., E., *Historical Studies of the English Parliament, i: Origins to 1399* (Cambridge, 1970).

Fryde, N., *The Tyranny and Fall of Edward II, 1321–26* (Oxford, 1979).

Ganshof, F. L., *The Carolingians and the Frankish Monarchy* (London, 1971).

Garnett, G., '"Franci et Angli": The Legal Distinction between Peoples after the Norman Conquest', *ANS* 8 (1985).

—— 'Coronation and Propaganda: Some Implications of the Norman Claim to the Throne of England in 1066', *TRHS* 5th ser. 36 (1986).

—— '"Ducal" Succession in Early Normandy', in *Law and Government in Medieval England and Normandy: Essays in Honour of Sir James Holt* (Cambridge, 1994).

—— 'The Origins of the Crown', in J. Hudson (ed.), *The History of English Law: Centenary Essays on 'Pollock and Maitland'* (Oxford, 1996).

—— *Conquered England: Kingship, Succession and Tenure, 1066–1215* (Oxford, 2007).

—— 'Coronation', in *Blackwell Enc.*

Gibbs, M., and Lang, J., *Bishops and Reform, 1215–1272* (Oxford, 1934).

Gillingham, J., 'Historians without Hindsight: Coggeshall, Diceto and Howden on the Early Years of John's Reign', in S. D. Church (ed.), *King John: New Interpretations* (Woodbridge, 1999).

—— 'Thegns and Knights in Eleventh-Century England: Who was then the Gentleman?', in his *The English in the Twelfth Century* (Woodbridge, 2000).

Gransden, A., *Historical Writing in England, c.550–c.1307* (London, 1974).

—— *Historical Writing in England*, ii: *c.1307 to the Early Sixteenth Century* (London, 1982).

Graves, M. A. R., *The Parliaments of Early Modern Europe* (Harlow, 2001).

Gray, H. L., *The Influence of the Commons on Early Legislation* (Cambridge, Mass., 1932).

Gray, J. W. 'The Church and Magna Charta [*sic*] in the Century after Runnymede', *Historical Studies*, 6 (London, 1968).

Green, J. A., 'William Rufus, Henry I and the Royal Demesne', *History*, 64 (1979).

—— 'The Last Century of Danegeld', *EHR* 96 (1981).

—— '"Praeclarum et Magnificum Antiquitatis Monumentum": The Earliest Surviving Pipe Roll', *BIHR* 55 (1982).

—— *The Government of England under Henry I* (Cambridge, 1986).

—— *The Aristocracy of Norman England* (Cambridge, 1997).

—— '"A Lasting Memorial": The Charter of Liberties of Henry I', in M. T. Flanagan and J. A. Green (eds.), *Charters and Charter Scholarship in Britain and Ireland* (Basingstoke, 2005).

—— *Henry I: King of England and Duke of Normandy* (Cambridge, 2006).

Griffiths, Q., 'New Men among the Lay Counselors of St Louis' Parlement', *Mediaeval Studies*, 32 (1970).

Haines, R. M., *King Edward II* (Montreal, 2003).

Hall, E., 'King Henry III and the English Reception of the Roman Law Maxim "Quod Omnes Tangit"', *Studia Gratiana*, 15 (1972).

Hallam, E. M., and Everard, J., *Capetian France, 987–1328*, 2nd edn. (Harlow, 2001).

Harcourt, L. W. V., *His Grace the Steward and Trial of Peers* (London, 1907).

Harding, A., *Medieval Law and the Foundations of the State* (Oxford, 2002).

Hare, M., 'Kings, Crowns and Festivals: The Origins of Gloucester as a Royal Ceremonial Centre', *Trans. Bristol and Gloucestershire Archaeological Soc.* 115 (1997).

Harper-Bill, C., and Vincent, N., *Henry II: New Interpretations* (Woodbridge, 2007).

Harris, S. J., 'Petitioning in the Last Years of Edward I and the First Years of Edward II', in Ormrod, Dodd, and Musson (eds.), *Medieval Petitions*.

Harriss, G. L., 'Parliamentary Taxation and the Origins of Appropriation of Supply in England, 1207–1340', in *Gouvernés et gouvernants: recueils de la société Jean Bodin*, 14 (1965).

—— *King, Parliament and Public Finance in Medieval England to 1369* (Oxford, 1975).

Harriss, G. L., 'The Formation of Parliament, 1272–1377', in Davies and Denton (eds.), *English Parl.*

Hart, C., *The Early Charters of Northern England and the North Midlands* (Leicester, 1975).

—— *The Danelaw* (London, 1992).

Harvey, S. P. J., 'Domesday Book and Anglo-Norman Governance', *TRHS* 5th ser. 25 (1975).

—— 'Taxation and the Economy', in J. C. Holt (ed.), *Domesday Studies* (Woodbridge, 1987).

Haskins, G. H., *Norman Institutions* (New York, 1918).

Haskins, G. L., 'Three Early Petitions of the Commonalty', *Speculum*, 12 (1937).

—— 'The Petitions of Representatives in the Parliaments of Edward I', *EHR* 53 (1938).

Heidemann, J., *Papst Clemens IV: Das Vorleben des Papstes und sein Legationregister* (Münster, 1903).

Henneman, J. B., *Royal Taxation in Fourteenth-Century France: The Development of War Financing, 1322–1356* (Princeton, 1971).

—— 'Nobility, Privilege and Fiscal Politics in Late Medieval France', *French Historical Studies*, 13 (1983).

—— 'France in the Middle Ages', in R. Bonney (ed.), *The Rise of the Fiscal State in Europe, c.1200–1815* (Oxford, 1999).

Hershey, A. H., 'Success or Failure? Hugh Bigod and Judicial Reform during the Baronial Movement, June 1258–February 1259', *TCE* 5 (1995).

Hill, D., *An Atlas of Anglo-Saxon England* (Oxford, 1981).

Hill, M. C., *The King's Messengers, 1199–1377* (London, 1961).

Hill, T. D., '*Consilium et auxilium* and the Lament for Æschere: A Lordship Formula in *Beowulf*', *Haskins Soc. Jnl.* 12 (2002).

Hollister, C. W. 'The Anglo-Norman Succession Debate of 1126', in his *Monarchy, Magnates and Institutions in the Anglo-Norman World* (London, 1986).

—— *Henry I* (New Haven, 2001).

—— and Baldwin, J. W., 'The Rise of Administrative Kingship: Henry I and Philip Augustus', *American Historical Review*, 83 (1978).

Holt, J. C., *The Northerners: A Study in the Reign of King John* (Oxford, 1961).

—— 'The Prehistory of Parliament', in Davies and Denton (eds.), *English Parl.*

—— 'The Assizes of Henry II: The Texts', in D. A. Bullough and R. L. Storey (eds..), *The Study of Medieval Records: Essays in Honour of Kathleen Major* (Oxford, 1971).

—— 'The Origins of the Constitutional Tradition in England', in his *Magna Carta and Medieval Government* (London, 1985).

—— 'The End of the Anglo-Norman Realm', in his *Magna Carta and Medieval Government.*

—— 'A Vernacular French Text of Magna Carta', in his *Magna Carta and Medieval Government*.

—— 'Rights and Liberties in Magna Carta', in his *Magna Carta and Medieval Government*.

—— '1086', in J. C. Holt (ed.), *Domesday Studies* (Woodbridge, 1987).

—— *Magna Carta*, 2nd edn. (Cambridge, 1992).

—— 'The Introduction of Knight Service in England', in his *Colonial England, 1066–1215* (London, 1997).

—— 'Feudal Society and the Family in Early Medieval England. I: The Revolution of 1066', in his *Colonial England*.

Howell, M., *Eleanor of Provence: Queenship in Thirteenth-Century England* (Oxford, 1978).

Hudson, J., 'Administration, Family and Perceptions of the Past in Late Twelfth-Century England: Richard Fitz Nigel and the Dialogue of the Exchequer', in P. Magdalino (ed.), *The Perception of the Past in Twelfth-Century Europe* (London, 1992).

—— *Land, Law and Lordship in Anglo-Norman England* (Oxford, 1994).

—— *The Formation of the English Common Law* (Harlow, 1996).

—— 'Henry I and Counsel', in J. R. Maddicott and D. M. Palliser (eds.), *The Medieval State: Essays Presented to James Campbell* (London, 2000).

—— 'Faide, vengeance et violence en Angleterre (ca 900–1200)', in D. Barthélemy, F. Bougard, and R. Le Jan (eds.), *La Vengeance, 400–1200* (Rome, 2006).

Hunt, T., 'Walter of Bibbesworth', *ODNB*.

Hurnard, N. D., 'The Anglo-Norman Franchises', *EHR* 64 (1949).

Illsley, J. S., 'Parliamentary Elections in the Reign of Edward I', *BIHR* 49 (1976).

Insley, C., 'Assemblies and Charters in Late Anglo-Saxon England', in P. S. Barnwell and M. Mostert (eds.), *Political Assemblies in the Earlier Middle Ages* (Turnhout, 2003).

Jenkinson, C. H., 'The First Parliament of Edward I', *EHR* 25 (1910).

John, E., *Orbis Britanniae* (Leicester, 1966).

Jolliffe, J. E. A., *The Constitutional History of Medieval England*, 4th edn. (London, 1961).

—— *Angevin Kingship*, 2nd edn. (London, 1963).

—— 'Some Factors in the Beginnings of Parliament', in *Historical Studies*.

Jones, M. (ed.), *Gentry and Lesser Nobility in Late Medieval Europe* (Gloucester, 1986).

Jordan, W. C., *Louis IX and the Challenge of the Crusade* (Princeton, 1979).

Jurkowski, M., Smith, C. L., and Crook, D., *Lay Taxes in England and Wales, 1188–1688*, Public Record Office Handbooks 31 (Kew, 1998).

Kaeuper, R. W., *Bankers to the Crown: The Riccardi of Lucca and Edward I* (Princeton, 1973).

——— 'Law and Order in Fourteenth-Century England: The Evidence of Special Commissions of Oyer and Terminer', *Speculum*, 54 (1979).

——— *War, Justice and Public Order: England and France in the Later Middle Ages* (Oxford, 1988).

Kantorowicz, E., *Laudes Regiae: A Study in Liturgical Acclamations and Mediaeval Ruler Worship*, 2nd printing (Berkeley and Los Angeles, 1958).

Kapelle, W. E., *The Norman Conquest of the North* (London, 1979).

Kay, R., *The Council of Bourges, 1225: A Documentary History* (Aldershot, 2002).

Keefe, T. K., *Feudal Assessments and the Political Community under Henry II and his Sons* (Berkeley, Calif., 1983).

Keene, D., *Survey of Medieval Winchester*, Winchester Studies 2, 2 vols. (Oxford, 1985).

Keeney, B. C., *Judgement by Peers* (Cambridge, Mass., 1949).

Kemble, J. M., *The Saxons in England*, new edn., 2 vols. (London, 1976).

Kemp, B., 'Exchequer and Bench in the Later Twelfth Century: Separate or Identical Tribunals?', *EHR* 88 (1973).

Kennedy, A., 'Cnut's Law Code of 1018', *ASE* 11 (1983).

——— 'Law and Legislation in the Libellus Æthelwoldi episcopi', *ASE* 24 (1995).

Kerr, J., 'Food, Drink and Lodging: Hospitality in Twelfth-Century England', *Haskins Soc. Jnl.* 18 (2006).

Keynes, S., *The Diplomas of King Æthelred 'the Unready', 978–1016* (Cambridge, 1980).

——— 'The Additions in Old English', in *The York Gospels*, ed. N. Barker, Roxburghe Club (London, 1986).

——— 'Regenbald the Chancellor (*sic*)', *ANS* 10 (1987).

——— 'Royal Government and the Written Word in Late Anglo-Saxon England', in R. McKitterick (ed.), *The Uses of Literacy in Early Medieval Europe* (Cambridge, 1990).

——— 'A Charter of Edward the Elder for Islington', *Historical Research*, 66 (1993).

——— *An Atlas of Attestations in Anglo-Saxon Charters, c.670–1066* (Cambridge, 1998).

——— 'England, c.900–1016', in T. Reuter (ed.), *The New Cambridge Medieval History*, iii: *c. 900–c.1024* (Cambridge, 1999).

——— 'Ely Abbey, 672–1109', in P. Meadows and N. Ramsey (eds.), *A History of Ely Cathedral* (Woodbridge, 2003).

——— 'Edgar, *Rex Admirabilis*', in D. Scragg (ed.), *Edgar, King of the English, 959–975* (Woodbridge, 2008).

——— 'Thegns', in *Blackwell Enc.*

King, E., 'Stephen of Blois, Count of Mortain and Boulogne', *EHR* 115 (2000).

Knowles, D., *The Monastic Order in England*, 2nd edn. (Cambridge, 1963).

Koziol, G., 'England, France and the Problem of Sacrality in Twelfth-Century Ritual', in T. N. Bisson (ed.), *Cultures of Power: Lordship, Status and Process in Twelfth-Century Europe* (Philadelphia, 1995).

Langlois, C.-V., *Le Règne de Philippe III le Hardi* (Paris, 1887).

—— 'Les Origines du Parlement de Paris', *Revue historique*, 42 (1890).

Langmuir, G. L., '"Judei Nostri" and the Beginning of Capetian Legislation', *Traditio*, 16 (1960).

—— 'Concilia and Capetian Assemblies, 1179–1230', in *Album Helen Maud Cam: Studies Presented to the International Commission for the History of Representative and Parliamentary Institutions*, xxiv (Louvain, 1961).

—— '*Per Commune Consilium Regni* in Magna Carta', *Studia Gratiana*, 15 (1965).

—— 'Politics and Parliaments in the Early Thirteenth Century', *Travaux et recherches de la Faculté de Droit et des Sciences Économiques, série 'Sciences Historiques'*, 8 (1966).

—— 'Community and Legal Change in Capetian France', *French Historical Studies*, 6 (1969–70).

Lapidge, M., 'B. and the *Vita S. Dunstani*', in his *Anglo-Latin Literature, 900–1066* (London, 1993).

—— 'Byrhtferth and the Early Sections of the *Historia Regum* Attributed to Symeon of Durham', in his *Anglo-Latin Literature*.

—— 'Ealdred of York and MS Cotton Vitellius E. XII', in his *Anglo-Latin Literature*.

—— 'Byrhtferth and Oswald', in N. Brooks and C. Cubitt (eds.), *St Oswald of Worcester* (London, 1996).

—— (ed.), *The Blackwell Encyclopaedia of Anglo-Saxon England* (Oxford, 1999).

Lapsley, G. T., *The County Palatine of Durham* (New York, 1900).

Lawrence, C. H., *St Edmund of Abingdon* (Oxford, 1960).

Lawson, M. K., *Cnut: The Danes in England in the Early Eleventh Century* (London, 1993).

—— 'Archbishop Wulfstan and the Homiletic Element in the Laws of Æthelred II and Cnut', in A. R. Rumble (ed.), *The Reign of Cnut* (London, 1994).

Legge, M. D., *Anglo-Norman Literature and its Background* (Oxford, 1963).

Le Goff, J., *Saint Louis* (Paris, 1996).

Lemarignier, J.-F., *Le Gouvernement royal aux premiers temps capétiens (987–1108)* (Paris, 1965).

Lennard, R., *Rural England, 1086–1135* (Oxford, 1959).

Le Patourel, J., *The Norman Empire* (Oxford, 1976).

Lewis, A. W., *Royal Succession in Capetian France* (Cambridge, Mass., 1981).

Lewis, P.S., 'The Failure of the French Medieval Estates', *Past and Present*, 23 (1962).

—— *Later Medieval France* (London, 1968).

Leyser, K. J., *Rule and Conflict in Early Medieval Society: Ottonian Saxony* (London, 1979).

—— 'Ritual, Ceremony and Gesture: Ottonian Germany', in his *Communications and Power in Medieval Europe: The Carolingian and Ottonian Centuries*, ed. T. Reuter (London, 1994).

—— 'The Ottonians and Wessex', in his *Communications and Power*.

Liebermann, F., *The National Assembly in the Anglo-Saxon Period* (Halle, 1913).

Linehan, P., *History and Historians of Medieval Spain* (Oxford, 1993).

Livermore, H. V., *A New History of Portugal* (Cambridge, 1967).

Lloyd, T. H., *The English Wool Trade in the Middle Ages* (Cambridge, 1977).

Lönnroth, E., 'Representative Assemblies of Mediaeval Sweden', *Études présentées à la Commission Internationale pour l'histoire des assemblées d'états, Xe Congrès international des sciences historiques* (Rome, 1955).

Lot, F., and Fawtier, R., *Histoire des institutions françaises au moyen âge*, ii: *Institutions royales* (Paris, 1958).

Lourie, E., 'A Society Organized for War: Medieval Spain', *Past and Present*, 35 (1966).

Lousse, E., *La Société d'ancien régime*, 2nd edn. (Louvain, 1952).

Lowry, E. C., 'Curial Proctors in Parliament and Knights of the Shire, 1280–1374', *EHR* 48 (1935).

Loyn, H., *Societies and Peoples: Studies in the History of England and Wales, c.600–1200* (London, 1992).

Luchaire, A., *Louis VI le Gros: annales de sa vie et de son règne* (Paris, 1890).

Lunt, W. E., 'The Text of the Ordinance of 1184 Concerning an Aid for the Holy Land', *EHR* 37 (1922).

—— *Financial Relations of the Papacy with England to 1327* (Cambridge, Mass., 1939).

—— 'The Consent of the English Lower Clergy to Taxation during the Reign of Henry III', in *Persecution and Liberty: Essays in Honor of George Lincoln Burr* (repr. New York, 1968).

McFarlane, K. B., *England in the Fifteenth Century* (London, 1981).

McIlwain, C. H., 'Medieval Estates', in J. R. Tanner, C. W. Previté-Orton, and Z. N. Brooke (eds.), *Cambridge Medieval History*, vol. vii (Cambridge, 1932).

Mackay, A., *Spain in the Middle Ages* (Basingstoke, 1977).

McKisack, M., *The Parliamentary Representation of the English Boroughs during the Middle Ages* (Oxford, 1932).

McKitterick, R. (ed.), *The Uses of Literacy in Early Medieval Europe* (Cambridge, 1990).

Macquarrie, A., 'The Kings of Strathclyde, c.400–1018', in A. Grant and K. J. Stringer (eds.), *Medieval Scotland: Crown, Lordship and Community: Essays Presented to G. W. S. Barrow* (Edinburgh, 1993).

Maddicott, J. R., *Thomas of Lancaster, 1307–22: A Study in the Reign of Edward II* (Oxford, 1970).

—— *The English Peasantry and the Demands of the Crown, 1294–1341*, Past and Present Supplement 1 (Oxford, 1975).

—— 'The County Community and the Making of Public Opinion in Fourteenth-Century England', *TRHS* 5th ser. 28 (1978).

—— 'Magna Carta and the Local Community, 1215–1259', *Past and Present*, 102 (1984).

—— 'Edward I and the Lessons of Baronial Reform: Local Government, 1258–80', *TCE* 1 (1986).

—— 'The Crusade Taxation of 1268–70 and the Development of Parliament', *TCE* 2 (1988).

—— *Simon de Montfort* (Cambridge, 1994).

—— '"An Infinite Multitude of Nobles": Quality, Quantity and Politics in the Pre-Reform Parliaments of Henry III', *TCE* 7 (1999).

—— 'The Earliest Known Knights of the Shire: New Light on the Parliament of April 1254', *Parliamentary History*, 18 (1999).

—— '"1258" and "1297": Some Comparisons and Contrasts', *TCE* 9 (2003).

—— 'Edward the Confessor's Return to England in 1041', *EHR* 119 (2004).

—— 'Responses to the Threat of Invasion, 1085', *EHR* 122 (2007).

—— 'Parliament and the Constituencies, 1272–1377', in Davies and Denton (eds.), *Eng. Parl.*

—— and Palliser, D. M. (eds.), *The Medieval State: Essays Presented to James Campbell* (London, 2000).

Madox, T., *The History and Antiquities of the Exchequer of England*, 2nd edn., 2 vols. (London, 1769).

Marongiu, A., *Medieval Parliaments: A Comparative Study* (London, 1968).

Mason, J. F. A., *William the First and the Sussex Rapes*, Historical Assoc. (London, 1966).

Meekings, C. A. F., 'Robert of Nottingham, Justice of the Bench, 1244–6', in his *Studies in 13th Century Justice and Administration* (London, 1981).

Meens, R., 'Politics, Mirrors of Princes and the Bible: Sins, Kings, and the Well-Being of the Realm', *EME* 7 (1998).

Mercati, A., 'La prima relazione del Cardinale Nicolò de Romanis sulla sua legazione in Inghilterra', in H. W. C. Davis (ed.), *Essays in History Presented to Reginald Lane Poole* (Oxford, 1927).

Miller, E., 'War, Taxation and the English Economy in the Late Thirteenth and Early Fourteenth Centuries', in J. M. Winter (ed.), *War and Economic Development: Essays in Memory of David Joslin* (Cambridge, 1975).

Miller, E., 'Introduction', in *Historical Studies*.

Miller, E., and Hatcher, J., *Medieval England: Rural Society and Economic Change, 1086–1348* (London, 1978).

Miller, S. T., 'The Position of the King in Bracton and Beaumanoir', *Speculum*, 31 (1956).

Mitchell, S. K., *Studies in Taxation under John and Henry III* (New Haven, 1914).

—— *Taxation in Medieval England* (New Haven, 1951).

Moorman, J. R. H., *Church Life in England in the Thirteenth Century* (Cambridge, 1946).

Morris, M., *The Bigod Earls of Norfolk in the Thirteenth Century* (Woodbridge, 2005).

—— *Edward I: A Great and Terrible King* (London, 2008).

Morris, W. A., 'Magnates and Community of the Realm in Parliament, 1264–1327', *Medievalia et Humanistica*, 1 (1943).

Musset, L., 'Gouvernés et gouvernants dans le monde scandinave et dans le monde normand (XIe–XIIe siècles)', in *Gouvernés et gouvernants: recueils de la société Jean Bodin*, 17 (1968).

Musson, A., 'Edward II: The Public and Private Faces of the Law', in G. Dodd and A. Musson (eds.), *The Reign of Edward II: New Perspectives* (Woodbridge, 2006).

Myers, A. R., *Parliaments and Estates in Europe to 1789* (London, 1975).

Nelson, J. L., 'The Earliest Royal *Ordo*: Some Liturgical and Historical Aspects', in her *Politics and Ritual in Early Medieval Europe* (London, 1986).

—— 'The Second English *Ordo*', in her *Politics and Ritual*.

—— 'The Rites of the Conqueror', in her *Politics and Ritual*.

—— 'Legislation and Consensus in the Reign of Charles the Bald', in her *Politics and Ritual*.

—— 'Inauguration Rituals', in her *Politics and Ritual*.

—— 'Ritual and Reality in the Early Medieval *Ordines*', in her *Politics and Ritual*.

—— 'The Lord's Anointed and the People's Choice: Carolingian Royal Ritual', in D. Cannadine and S. Price (eds.), *Rituals of Royalty: Power and Ceremonial in Traditional Societies* (Cambridge, 1987).

—— 'Literacy in Carolingian Government', in R. McKitterick (ed.), *The Uses of Literacy in Early Medieval Europe* (Cambridge, 1990).

—— 'Kingship and Royal Government', in T. Reuter (ed.), *The New Cambridge Medieval History*, iii: *c.900–c.1024* (Cambridge, 1999).

—— 'Liturgy or Law: Misconceived Alternatives', in S. Baxter, C. E. Karkov, J. L. Nelson, and D. Pelteret, *Early Medieval Studies in Memory of Patrick Wormald* (Farnham, 2009).

Newman, W. M., *Le Domaine royal sous les premiers capétiens (987–1180)* (Paris, 1937).

Noble, F., *Offa's Dyke Reviewed*, ed. M. Gelling, BAR, British ser. 114 (Oxford, 1983).

O'Brien, B. R., *God's Peace and King's Peace: The Laws of Edward the Confessor* (Philadelphia, 1999).

O'Callaghan, F., *The Cortes of Castile-León, 1188–1350* (Philadelphia, 1989).

Oleson, T. J., *The Witenagemot in the Reign of Edward the Confessor* (London, 1955).

Ormrod, W. M., *The Reign of Edward III: Crown and Political Society in England, 1329–1377* (New Haven, 1990).

—— 'Agenda for Legislation, 1322–*c*.1340', *EHR* 105 (1990).

—— 'State Building and State Finance under Edward I', in W. M. Ormrod (ed.), *England in the Thirteenth Century: Proceedings of the 1989 Harlaxton Symposium* (Stamford, 1991).

—— 'England in the Middle Ages', in R. Bonney (ed.), *The Rise of the Fiscal State in Europe, c.1200–1815* (Oxford, 1999).

—— Dodd, G., and Musson, A., *Medieval Petitions: Grace and Grievance* (Woodbridge, 2009).

Painter, S., *William Marshal* (Baltimore, 1933).

—— *Studies in the History of the English Feudal Barony* (Baltimore, 1943).

—— *The Reign of King John* (Baltimore, 1949).

Palliser, D. M., 'Towns and the English State, 1066–1500', in J. R. Maddicott and D. M. Palliser (eds.), *The Medieval State: Essays Presented to James Campbell* (London, 2000).

Palmer, J. J. N., 'The Wealth of the Secular Aristocracy in 1086', *ANS* 22 (2000).

Pantin, W. A., 'Grosseteste's Relations with the Papacy and the Crown', in D. Callus (ed.), *Robert Grosseteste: Scholar and Bishop* (Oxford, 1955).

Parent, M., 'Les Assemblées royales en France au temps de Saint Louis', *Positions des thèses*, École Nationale des Chartes, 1939 (Nogent-le-Rotrou, 1939).

Parry, C. H., *The Parliaments and Councils of England* (London, 1839).

Pasquet, D., *An Essay on the Origins of the House of Commons*, trans. R. G. D. Laffan (Cambridge, 1925).

Piper, A. J., 'Writs of Summons of 1246, 1247 and 1255', *BIHR* 49 (1976).

Pollock, F., and Maitland, F. W., *The History of English Law before the Time of Edward I*, 2nd edn. (Cambridge, 1898).

Poole, A. L., *Obligations of Society in the XII and XIII Centuries* (Oxford, 1946).

Poole, R. L., 'The Publication of Great Charters by the English Kings', *EHR* 28 (1913).

Post, G., *Studies in Medieval Legal Thought: Public Law and the State, 1100–1322* (Princeton, 1964).

Powell, E., 'The Restoration of Law and Order', in G. L. Harriss (ed.), *Henry V: The Practice of Kingship* (Oxford,1985).

—— *Kingship, Law and Society: Crime and Justice in the Reign of Henry V* (Oxford, 1989).

Powell, J. E., and Wallis, K., *The House of Lords in the Middle Ages* (London, 1968).

Power, D., 'Henry, Duke of the Normans', in Harper-Bill and Vincent (eds.), *Henry II*.

Powicke, F. M., 'England: Richard I and John', in *The Cambridge Medieval History*, vol. vi, ed. J. R. Tanner, C. W. Previté-Orton, and Z. N. Brooke (Cambridge, 1929).

—— *King Henry III and the Lord Edward*, 2 vols. (Oxford, 1947).

—— *The Thirteenth Century, 1216–1307* (Oxford, 1953).

Powicke, M. R., *Military Obligation in Medieval England* (Oxford, 1962).

Prestwich, J. O., 'Anglo-Norman Feudalism and the Problem of Continuity', *Past and Present*, 26 (1963).

—— 'The Military Household of the Norman Kings', *EHR* 96 (1981).

—— 'Mistranslations and Misinterpretations in Medieval English History', *Peritia*, 10 (1996).

Prestwich, M., *War, Politics and Finance under Edward I* (London, 1972).

—— 'Parliament and the Community of the Realm in Fourteenth-Century England', in A. Cosgrove and J. I. McGuire (eds.), *Historical Studies*, 14 (Belfast,1983).

—— 'Magnate Summonses in England in the Later Years of Edward I', *Parliaments, Estates and Representation*, 5 (1985).

—— *Edward I* (London, 1988).

—— *English Politics in the Thirteenth Century* (Basingstoke, 1990).

—— 'The Ordinances of 1311', in J. Taylor and W. Childs (eds.), *Politics and Crisis in Fourteenth-Century England* (Gloucester, 1990).

—— *Armies and Warfare in the Middle Ages: The English Experience* (New Haven, 1996).

—— *Plantagenet England, 1226–1360* (Oxford, 2005).

Procter, E. S., *Curia and Cortes in León and Castile, 1072–1295* (Cambridge, 1980).

Pronay, N., and Taylor, J., *Parliamentary Texts of the Later Middle Ages* (Oxford, 1980).

Pulsiano, P. (ed.), *Medieval Scandinavia: An Encyclopaedia* (New York, 1993).

Rady, M., *Nobility, Land and Service in Medieval Hungary* (Basingstoke, 2000).

Ramsay, J. H., *A History of the Revenues of the Kings of England, 1066–1399*, 2 vols. (Oxford, 1925).

Rayner, D., 'The Forms and Machinery of the "Commune Petition" in the Fourteenth Century', *EHR* 56 (1941).

Reiss, L., *The History of the English Electoral Law in the Middle Ages*, trans. K. L. Wood-Legh (Cambridge, 1940).

Reuter, T., 'The Making of England and Germany, 850–1050: Points of Comparison and Difference', in T. Reuter, *Medieval Polities and Modern Mentalities*, ed. J. L. Nelson (Cambridge, 2006).

——'Assembly Politics in Western Europe from the Eighth Century to the Twelfth', in Reuter, *Medieval Polities*.

Reynolds, S., *Kingdoms and Communities in Western Europe, 900–1300*, 2nd edn. (Oxford, 1997).

Rezak, B. B., 'The King Enthroned: A New Theme in Anglo-Saxon Royal Iconography: The Seal of Edward the Confessor and its Political Implications', in J. Rosenthal (ed.), *Acta*, xi: *Kings and Kingship* (New York, 1986).

Richard, J., *Saint Louis: Crusader King of France*, ed. S. Lloyd, trans. J. Birrell (Cambridge, 1983).

Richardson, H. G., 'John of Gaunt and the Parliamentary Representation of Lancashire', *Bulletin of the John Rylands Library*, 22 (1938).

——'The Coronation in Medieval England', *Traditio*, 16 (1960).

——'The Origins of Parliament', in H. G. Richardson and G. O. Sayles, *The English Parliament in the Middle Ages* (London, 1981).

——'The Commons and Medieval Politics', in *The English Parliament*.

——and Sayles, G. O., *The Governance of Medieval England* (Edinburgh, 1963).

————'The Earliest Known Official Use of the Term "Parliament"', in Richardson and Sayles, *The English Parliament*.

————'Parliaments and Great Councils in Medieval England', in *The English Parliament*.

————'The King's Ministers in Parliament, 1272–1307', in *The English Parliament*.

————'The King's Ministers in Parliament, 1307–27', in *The English Parliament*.

————'The King's Ministers in Parliament, 1327–77', in *The English Parliament*.

————'The Provisions of Oxford: A Forgotten Document and Some Comments', in *The English Parliament*.

————'The Early Statutes', in *The English Parliament*.

————'The Parliaments of Edward I', in *The English Parliament*.

————'The Exchequer Parliament Rolls and Other Documents', in *The English Parliament*.

————'The Parliament of Carlisle, 1307: Some New Documents', in *The English Parliament*.

Ridgeway, H. W., 'King Henry III and the "Aliens", 1236–72', *TCE* 2 (1988).

Robinson, J. A., *Gilbert Crispin, Abbot of Westminster* (Cambridge, 1911).

Rollason, D. W., 'Goscelin of Canterbury's Account of the Translation and Miracles of St Mildrith (BHL 5961/4): An Edition with Notes', *Mediaeval Studies*, 48 (1986).

Roskell, J. S., *The Commons and their Speakers in English Parliaments, 1376–1523* (Manchester, 1965).

—— 'The Problem of the Attendance of the Lords in Medieval Parliaments', in his *Parliaments and Politics in Late Medieval England*, 3 vols. (London, 1981).

Rosser, G., *Medieval Westminster, 1200–1540* (Oxford, 1989).

Rothwell, H., 'The Confirmation of the Charters, 1297', *EHR* 60 (1945).

—— 'Edward I and the Struggle for the Charters, 1297–1305', in R. W. Hunt, W. A. Pantin, and R. W. Southern (eds.), *Studies in Medieval History Presented to F. M. Powicke* (Oxford, 1948).

Round, J. H., 'The Origin of the Exchequer', in his *The Commune of London and Other Studies* (Westminster, 1899).

—— *The King's Serjeants and Officers of State* (London, 1911).

Ruiz, T. F., 'Oligarchy and Royal Power: The Castilian Cortes and the Castilian Crisis, 1248–1350', *Parliaments, Estates and Representation*, 2 (1982).

Sanders, I. J., *Feudal Military Service in England* (Oxford, 1956).

Saul, N., *Knights and Esquires: The Gloucestershire Gentry in the Fourteenth Century* (Oxford, 1981).

—— 'The Despensers and the Downfall of Edward II', *EHR* 99 (1984).

Sawyer, B. and P., *Medieval Scandinavia* (Minneapolis, 1993).

Sawyer, P., 'The Royal *Tun* in Pre-Conquest England', in P. Wormald (ed.), *Ideal and Reality in Frankish and Anglo-Saxon Society: Studies Presented to J. M. Wallace-Hadrill* (Oxford, 1983).

Sayles, G. O., *The King's Parliament of England* (London, 1975).

—— 'Representation of Cities and Boroughs in 1268', in H. G. Richardson and G. O. Sayles, *The English Parliament in the Middle Ages* (London, 1981).

—— *The Functions of the Medieval Parliament of England* (London, 1988).

Sharpe, R., 'The Prefaces of "Quadripartitus"', in G. Garnett and J. Hudson (eds.), *Law and Government in Medieval England and Normandy: Essays in Honour of Sir James Holt* (Cambridge, 1994).

Shennan, J. H., *The Parlement of Paris* (London, 1968).

Short, I., 'Patrons and Polyglots: French Literature in Twelfth-Century England', *ANS* 14 (1992).

Smith, D. M., and London, V. C. M., *The Heads of Religious Houses in England and Wales*, ii: *1216–1377* (Cambridge, 2001).

Sneddon, S. A., 'Words and Realities: The Language and Dating of Petitions, 1326–7', in Ormrod, Dodd, and Musson (eds.), *Medieval Petitions*.

Southern, R. W., *St Anselm and his Biographer* (Cambridge, 1963).

—— 'England's First Entry into Europe', in his *Medieval Humanism and Other Studies* (Oxford, 1970).

—— 'From Schools to University', in J. Catto (ed.), *The History of the University of Oxford*, i: *The Early Oxford Schools* (Oxford, 1992).

—— *Robert Grosseteste: The Growth of an English Mind in Medieval Europe*, 2nd edn. (Oxford, 1992).

Spufford, P., *Origins of the English Parliament* (London, 1967).

Stacey, R. C., *Politics, Policy and Finance under Henry III, 1216–45* (Oxford, 1987).

—— '1240–60: A Watershed in Anglo-Jewish Relations', *Historical Research*, 61 (1988).

—— 'Parliamentary Negotiation and the Expulsion of the Jews from England', *TCE* 6 (1997).

—— 'Social Change in the Thirteenth Century: (a) Nobles and Knights', in D. Abulafia (ed.), *The New Cambridge Medieval History*, v: *c.1198–1300* (Cambridge, 1999).

Stafford, P. A., 'The Reign of Æthelred II: A Study in the Limitations of Royal Policy and Actions', in D. Hill (ed.), *Ethelred the Unready*, BAR, British ser. 59 (Oxford, 1978).

—— 'The "Farm of One Night" and the Organisation of King Edward's Estates in Domesday', *Economic History Review*, 33 (1980).

—— 'The Laws of Cnut and the History of Anglo-Saxon Royal Promises', *ASE* 10 (1982).

—— *The East Midlands in the Early Middle Ages* (Leicester, 1985).

—— *Unification and Conquest* (London, 1989).

—— 'Political Ideas in Late Tenth-Century England: Charters as Evidence', in P. Stafford, J. L. Nelson, and J. Martindale (eds.), *Law, Laity and Solidarities: Essays in Honour of Susan Reynolds* (Manchester, 2001).

Stenton, F. M., *The First Century of English Feudalism, 1066–1166*, 2nd edn. (Oxford, 1961).

—— *Anglo-Saxon England*, 3rd edn. (Oxford, 1971).

Stephenson, C., *Borough and Town: A Study of Urban Origins in England* (Cambridge, Mass., 1933).

—— 'The Aids of the French Towns in the Twelfth and Thirteenth Centuries', in his *Medieval Institutions: Selected Essays*, ed. B. D. Lyon (paperback edn., Ithaca, NY, 1967).

Stones, E. L. G., and Simpson, G. G., *Edward I and the Throne of Scotland, 1290–1296*, 2 vols. (Oxford, 1978).

Strayer, J. R., 'The Crusades of Louis IX', in his *Medieval Statecraft and the Perspectives of History* (Princeton, 1971).

—— *The Reign of Philip the Fair* (Princeton, 1980).

—— and Taylor, C. H., *Studies in Early French Taxation* (Cambridge, Mass., 1939).

Strickland, M., 'On the Instruction of a Prince: The Upbringing of Henry, the Young King', in Harper-Bill and Vincent (eds.), *Henry II*.

Stubbs, W., *The Constitutional History of England*, 5th edn., 3 vols. (Oxford, 1891).

Studd, R., *An Itinerary of Lord Edward*, List and Index Soc. 284 (2000).

Tabuteau, E. Z., *Transfers of Property in Eleventh-Century Norman Law* (Chapel Hill, NC, 1988).

Tait, J., 'Studies in Magna Carta: 1, Waynagium and Contenementum', *EHR* 27 (1912).

Taylor, C. H., 'Assemblies of French Towns in 1316', *Speculum*, 14 (1939).

Thomas, H. M., *Vassals, Heiresses, Crusaders and Thugs: The Gentry of Angevin Yorkshire* (Philadelphia, 1993).

—— *The English and the Normans: Ethnic Hostility, Assimilation and Identity, 1066–c.1220* (Oxford, 2003).

Thornton, D. E., 'Edgar and the Eight Kings, AD 973: *Textus and Dramatis Personae*', *EMU* 10 (2001).

Toch, M., 'Germany and Flanders: (a) Welfs, Hohenstaufen and Habsburgs', in D. Abulafia (ed.), *The New Cambridge Medieval History*, v: *c.1198–1300* (Cambridge, 1999).

Tout, T. F., *The Place of the Reign of Edward II in English History*, 2nd edn. (Manchester, 1936).

Trabut-Cussac, J. P., *L'Administration anglaise en Gascogne sous Henri III et Édouard I de 1254 à 1307* (Geneva, 1972).

Treharne, R. F., *The Baronial Plan of Reform, 1258–63* (Manchester, 1932).

—— 'The Nature of Parliament in the Reign of Henry III', in *Historical Studies*.

Turner, R. V., *The King and his Courts: The Role of John and Henry III in the Administration of Justice, 1199–1240* (Ithaca, NY, 1968).

—— 'Roman Law in England before the Time of Bracton', in his *Judges, Administrators and the Common Law in Angevin England* (London, 1994).

—— *King John* (Harlow, 1994).

—— *Magna Carta* (Harlow, 2003).

—— and Heiser, R. R., *The Reign of Richard Lionheart* (Harlow, 2000).

Tyerman, C, *England and the Crusades, 1095–1588* (Chicago, 1988).

Valente, C., 'The Deposition and Abdication of Edward II', *EHR* 113 (1998).

—— 'The Provisions of Oxford: Assessing/Assigning Authority in Time of Unrest', in R. F. Berkhofer III, A. Cooper, and A. J. Kosto (eds.), *The Experience of Power in Medieval Europe, 950–1350* (Aldershot, 2005).

van Caenegem, R. C., *Royal Writs in England from the Conquest to Glanvill*, Selden Soc. 77 (London, 1959).

Vincent, N., *Peter des Roches: An Alien in English Politics, 1205–1238* (Cambridge, 1996).

—— *The Holy Blood: King Henry III and the Westminster Blood Relic* (Cambridge, 2001).

—— 'The Politics of Church and State as Reflected in the Winchester Pipe Rolls, 1208–1280', in R. Britnell (ed.), *The Winchester Pipe Rolls in Medieval English Society* (Woodbridge, 2003).

—— 'The Court of Henry II', in Harper-Bill and Vincent (eds.), *Henry II*.

Walker, S., *The Lancastrian Affinity, 1361–1399* (Oxford, 1990).

Warren, W. L., *Henry II* (London, 1973).

Waugh, S. L., *England in the Reign of Edward III* (Cambridge, 1991).

Weber, M., *The Theory of Social and Economic Organization*, trans. A. M. Henderson and T. Parsons (London, 1947).

Weber, M. C., 'The Purpose of the English *Modus Tenendi Parliamentum*', *Parliamentary History*, 17 (1998).

Weiler, B., 'Symbolism and Politics in the Reign of Henry III', *TCE* 9 (2003).

—— *Henry III of England and the Staufen Empire, 1216–1272* (Woodbridge, 2006).

White, A. B., 'Some Early Instances of the Concentration of Representatives in England', *American Historical Review*, 19 (1914).

Whitelock, D., 'The Dealings of the Kings of England with Northumbria in the Tenth and Eleventh Centuries', in P. Clemoes (ed.), *The Anglo-Saxons: Studies in Some Aspects of their History and Culture Presented to Bruce Dickins* (London, 1959).

—— 'Some Charters in the Name of King Alfred', in M. H. King and W. M. Stevens (eds.), *Saints, Scholars and Heroes: Studies in Medieval Culture in Honor of Charles W. Jones* (Collegeville, Minn., 1979).

Wickham, C., *Problems in Doing Comparative History*, Reuter Lecture, 2004 (Southampton, 2005).

—— *The Inheritance of Rome: A History of Europe from 400 to 1100* (London, 2009).

Wilkinson, B., 'The Government of England during the Absence of Richard I on the Third Crusade', *Bulletin of the John Rylands Library*, 28 (1944).

—— 'The Development of the Council', in his *Studies in the Constitutional History of the Thirteenth and Fourteenth Centuries*, 2nd edn. (Manchester, 1952).

—— 'The Invention of Original Writs in the Thirteenth Century', in his *Studies*.

Willard, J. F., 'Taxation Boroughs and Parliamentary Boroughs, 1294–1336', in J. G. Edwards, V. H. Galbraith, and E. F. Jacob (eds.), *Historical Essays in Honour of James Tait* (Manchester, 1933).

—— *Parliamentary Taxes on Personal Property, 1290 to 1334* (Cambridge, Mass., 1934).

Williams, A., 'Some Notes and Considerations on Problems Connected with the English Royal Succession, 860–1066', *Proceedings of the Battle Conference, 1978/ANS*, i (1979).

—— '*Princeps Merciorum Gentis*: The Family, Career and Connections of Ælfhere, Ealdorman of Mercia, 956–83', *ASE* 10 (1982).

—— *Kingship and Government in Pre-Conquest England, c.500–1066* (Basingstoke, 1999).

Williams, G., *Medieval London from Commune to Capital* (London, 1963).

Wood, C. T., *The French Apanages and the Capetian Monarchy, 1244–1328* (Cambridge, Mass., 1966).

Wood, M., 'The Making of King Aethelstan's Empire: An English Charlemagne?', in P. Wormald (ed.), *Ideal and Reality in Frankish and Anglo-Saxon Society: Studies Presented to J. M. Wallace-Hadrill* (Oxford, 1983).

Wormald, P., *The Making of English Law*, i: *Legislation and its Limits* (Oxford, 1999).

—— '*Engla Lond*: The Making of an Allegiance', in his *Legal Culture in the Early Medieval West* (London, 1999).

—— 'A Handlist of Anglo-Saxon Lawsuits', in his *Legal Culture*.

—— 'Giving God and the King their Due: Conflict and its Resolution in the Early English State', in his *Legal Culture*.

—— 'Lordship and Justice in the Early English Kingdom: Oswaldslaw Revisited', in his *Legal Culture*.

—— 'James Campbell as Historian', in J. R. Maddicott and D. M. Palliser (eds.), *The Medieval State: Essays Presented to James Campbell* (London, 2000).

—— '*On þa wænedhealfe*: Kingship and Royal Property from Æthelwulf to Edward the Elder', in N. J. Higham and D. H. Hill (eds.), *Edward the Elder, 899–924* (London, 2001).

—— 'Germanic Power Structures: The Early English Experience', in L. Scales and O. Zimmer (eds.), *Power and the Nation in European History* (Cambridge, 2005).

—— *Lawyers and the State: The Varieties of Legal History*, Selden Soc. (London, 2006).

—— (ed.), *Ideal and Reality in Frankish and Anglo-Saxon Society: Studies Presented to J. M. Wallace-Hadrill* (Oxford, 1983).

Wright, C. E., *The Cultivation of Saga in Anglo-Saxon England* (Edinburgh, 1939).

Young, C. R., *The Royal Forests of Medieval England* (Leicester, 1979).

Index

The main discussions of some important topics are indicated in **bold**. Persons are listed by second name-elements, even when convention might seem to dictate otherwise (e.g. Cornwall, Richard of; Ramsey, Byrhtferth of). Place-names are identified by reference to pre-1974 counties. The following abbreviations are used: abp (archbishop), bp (bishop).

crown-wearing 22
laws 29, 53–4
Edith, half-sister of King Æthelstan 21
Edmund Ironside, king of England 38, 52
Edmund, king of England 33, 34, 77
Edmund, earl of Cornwall 427
Edmund, St 84
Edmund, second son of Henry III 170,
    178, 183, 280, 471–2
Edward I, king of England 28, 82, 193
    and the Charters 302–16 passim
    finances **288**, 299–301, 305–6, 325
    and France 278, 281, 287, 299, 329
    and Gascony 279, 288, 296, 298, 302,
        423
    general qualities of his kingship **278–9**,
        284, 292–3, 297–8, 306, 330
    as prince 173, 250, 258–60, 266, 268,
        284, 362, 404, 449, 466, 467
    and Scotland 279, 282, 288, 298, 299,
        303, 308, 326
    statutes of 247, 264, 278, 280, 281,
        282–5, 400
    and Wales 278, 281, 288, 291, 293, 298,
        305, 423, 428
    see also Forest Charter; forests, royal;
        Magna Carta; parliaments and great
        councils; taxation
Edward II, king of England:
    deposition 359–64
    and favourites 331, 346–7
    and France 335, 352–3, 357–8
    and Gascony 353, 357–8
    misgovernment 347–9, 354–6
    as prince 280, 328
    rising importance of commons in
        reign 335–45, 354–9
    and Scotland 331, 334, 335, 347, 357
    and taxation 345–6, 357–9
    see also parliaments and great councils;
        taxation
Edward III, king of England 108, 188, 339,
    359
Edward the Confessor, king of England 57,
    63, 99
    assemblies 39–49, 58
    court 55, 385
    crown-wearing 19, 43–5, 58
    cult of 162–3, 170, 183, 269, 272, 465
    laws 99–100, 101, 102, 118, 145, 287 n.
        47, 388
    and parliamentary myths 158, 178, 277

return to England (1041) 39–40, 46–7,
    51, 99, 387
Edward the Elder, king of Wessex 3, 6, 20
    n. 75, 28, 33, 51, 77
Edward the Martyr, king of England 33,
    442
Edwin, king of Northumbria 2
Edwin, Earl 60, 64
Elerius, abbot of Pershore 194 n. 147
Elizabeth I, queen of England 229, 367
Ely (Cambs.) 11, 261–2
Emma, queen, wife of Æthelred and
    Cnut 39
England:
    limited itineration of kings 11, 389–90
    popular participation in government
        9–10, 49, 374–5, 450–1
    royal revenues 401–2
    strength of crown 382, 397–8, 434–5,
        450–1
    succession disputes 387–8
English language 36, 52, 100, 144, 382,
    444, 446
Eric Bloodaxe, king of York 3
Eslington, John of, MP 217
Essex 213, 217
Essex, earl of, see Mandeville, William de
Essex, Roger of, escheator 457
Estoire de Seint Aedward le Rei, La 158, 178
Evesham (Worcs.):
    abbot of 80, 147, 194 n. 147, 443
    battle of (1265) 234, 261, 276
    chronicle of 310
exchequer 69, 113, **116–17**, 161, 164–5,
    170, 185, 186, 248, 295, 302, 306, 390,
    398
Exeter (Devon) 13, 293, 342
Exeter, bp of, see Apulia, Simon of; Leofric;
    Stapeldon, Walter de
Eynsham (Oxon.), abbey 5, 9
eyre 69, 134–5, 257, 434 n. 245
    fiscal value of and complaints against
        under Henry III 176, 219–20, 222,
        225, 227, 229–30, 243, 244, 266,
        402, 431, 439, 460
    reforming eyres (1258–60) 243, 247,
        257

Falaise (Normandy) 73
familiares **86–8**, 91, 95, **113–16**, 117, 119,
    144–5, 171, 190, **390–3**, 397
Fantosme, Jordan 75, 144